Public Personnel Administration

Fourth Edition

Public Personnel Administration

PROBLEMS AND PROSPECTS

Edited by

Steven W. Hays
University of South Carolina

Richard C. Kearney
East Carolina University

Prentice
Hall

Upper Saddle River, New Jersey 07458

Library of Congress Cataloging-in-Publication Data

Public personnel administration: problems and prospects/edited by Steven W. Hays,
Richard C. Kearney.—4th ed.
    p. cm.
  Includes bibliographical references and index.
  ISBN 0-13-041378-X (alk. paper)
    1. Civil service—United States—Personnel management. I. Hays, Steven W. II.
  Kearney, Richard C.

  JK765 .P797 2002
  352.6′0973–dc21

                                                              2001052358

Senior acquisitions editor: Heather Shelstad
Assistant editor: Brian Prybella
Production editor: Cheryl A. Keenan
Copy editor: Barbara Christenberry
Editorial assistant: Jessica Drew
Prepress and manufacturing buyer: Ben Smith
Director of marketing: Beth Mejia
Marketing assistant: Jennifer Bryant
Marketing manager: Claire Rehwinkel
Cover art director: Jayne Conte
Cover design: Bruce Kenselaar

This book was set in 10/11 Baskerville Book by ElectraGraphics, Inc.
The cover was printed by Phoenix Color Corp.

© 2003, 1995, 1990, 1983 by Pearson Education, Inc.
Upper Saddle River, New Jersey 07458

Printed in the United States of America
10   9   8   7

ISBN: 0-13-041378-X

Pearson Education LTD., London
Pearson Education Australia PTY, Limited, Sydney
Pearson Education Singapore, Pte. Ltd
Pearson Education North Asia Ltd, Hong Kong
Pearson Education Canada, Ltd., Toronto
Pearson Educación de Mexico, S. A. de C.V.
Pearson Education—Japan, Tokyo
Pearson Education Malaysia, Pte. Ltd
Pearson Education, Upper Saddle River, New Jersey

Contents

Preface

The third edition of this volume was published in 1995. In the preface to that book, we offered the opinion that the field of Public Personnel Administration (PPA) or Human Resource Management (HRM)—both terms will be used interchangeably—stood at the threshold of a new age. Specifically, we stated, "It is probably not an excessive burst of hyperbole to suggest that we have entered the third great stage of civil service reform in modern times." Although no acute forecasting talents were needed to generate that observation, succeeding events have reaffirmed and deepened our conviction that PPA (or HRM) is immersed in an epic attempt to alter its techniques, goals, and underlying value system. To opine that "lots has changed" since 1995 is to engage in gross understatement.

The previous edition was written and published just as the so-called *reinvention* movement was beginning to take hold in civil service systems. At that point, there was far more speculation than fact as to the ultimate impacts that *decentralization* and the emphasis on *accountability* would exert. Because reform of the civil service is almost a constant, few words carry sufficient power and scope to impart the true meaning of what is now occurring in state and local HRM systems. We are now far enough into the current reform craze to draw some weighty conclusions, most of which *do* elicit descriptions that should be saved for truly momentous times. An expression such as *paradigm shift* may be hackneyed and melodramatic, but it certainly comes to mind when one surveys the contemporary landscape of public personnel administration. The pace of change is so rapid that it is sometimes bewildering. Moreover, the enthusiasm for revolutionizing basic approaches to human resource management is so great that it represents an almost irresistible force. Seldom has there been a stronger conviction and a more widespread consensus about how the public personnel system of the future ought to look.

As has been our intent in the other three editions of this anthology, our purpose here is to provide readers with a concise overview of the *problems* and *prospects* of modern public personnel administration. The goal has not changed, but the challenge has certainly become more formidable. Whereas previous editions attempted to keep our audience up-to-date on such diverse issues as workplace diversity, the productivity challenge, unionization, ethics, and a plethora of related dilemmas, we must now contend with additional topics that transcend every other facet of the PPA system and permeate the fiber of both the theory and practice of this field. In a very real sense, HRM is being turned on its head before our eyes. One unmistakable example is the simple fact that the most basic element of public personnel operations—the merit system—is being abolished (or at least fundamentally altered) by reformers. Changes of this nature reverberate through the entire HRM system, affecting every technique and shifting the expectations that managers have of their offices of personnel management.

The chapters in this anthology represent another attempt to tap the exciting trends in PPA and to probe their implications. To this end, we have assembled original manuscripts that represent a cross-section of the timeliest and best-informed scholarship in the area of human resource management. The book contains a mix of thought pieces, descriptive analyses, overviews of occurrences in various settings, and theoretical essays. Consistent with our "problems and prospects" theme—one that has served us well for twenty years—the selections summarize the biggest problems confronting HRM practitioners and offer substantive suggestions for improving the practice of public personnel management. Obviously, then, the chapters focus more on the *future* of the field than on its past. We are more concerned with providing the reader with a firm sense of where the discipline may be headed, rather than where it has been.

Each chapter was prepared specifically for inclusion in this volume. The authors are all established figures in public personnel administration; many of them practice and consult in the field as well. They were selected on the basis of their recognized competence in, and past contributions to, the topical areas that are addressed in their essays. The present volume is almost completely different from its predecessor. Only seven (of 25) chapters constitute what one might consider to be updated versions of previous writings. Fifteen new authors are represented, evidence of the changing nature of human resource management and the expanding ranks of new and established scholars. We confess to being quite proud of the group that has been assembled to share their perspectives, and hope that you will agree that their insights are worthy of recognition.

The contributions are organized into four broad sections: The Setting, The Techniques, The Issues, and Reform and the Future. Although reform is expressly addressed only in the last section, you will quickly find that this is a topic that is woven throughout the entire volume. It is impossible to discuss modern HRM without examining the changes that dominate our field at any given moment. Insofar as the specific sections are concerned, Section One focuses primarily on the social, political, economic, and legal trends that have served as catalysts in the transformation of public personnel administration. Section Two summarizes developments in the practice of HRM, with special emphasis on emerging personnel techniques and the ways that traditional approaches to the staffing function are being revised. Section Three discusses, and suggests responses to, some of the most troublesome or pervasive issues in modern personnel management. The final section assesses probable trends in the field's future, and analyzes the efficacy of recent reform efforts.

As in the case of the earlier editions, a prime consideration in the design, preparation, and organization of the book was that it be sufficiently readable for both graduate and undergraduate students. For this reason, the authors were asked to provide enough background information so that both beginning and advanced students could understand and benefit from the content. Additionally, the authors were requested to furnish concrete examples and practical information to enhance the volume's applicability to practitioners wishing to broaden their perspectives in the field. We are satisfied that these objectives have been met in every respect.

Our principal debt in assembling this anthology is to our contributing authors. They richly deserve our sincere thanks, for their efforts are the heart and soul of what follows. Because there are so many luminaries and emerging scholars in the area of public sector HRM, it was very difficult to decide which ones to ask for contributions. One of our continuing objectives is to change the authorship assignments with some regularity so as to bring new perspectives to this work. In so doing, we sincerely hope that anyone not included in this particular volume is not offended. With luck, we'll both live long enough to generate a fifth edition within a few years, thereby enabling us to call upon the talents of other leading scholars.

The contributors to the fourth edition of *Public Personnel Administration: Problems and Prospects* produced quality manuscripts on short notice, and exhibited remarkable patience with our repeated requests for revisions, clarifications, and elaborations. Many endured hardships in meeting the deadlines we imposed, especially those whose chief professional responsibility is to *provide* HRM services, not write about them. We hope that all of the contributors are aware of the depth of our appreciation. We also thank the reviewers of this edition for their helpful comments: Rhonda Allen, California State University–Fullerton; Laurie N. DiPadova, University of Utah; Wendell C. Lawther, University Central Florida; Emmett N. Lombard, Oakland University; and Lloyd G. Nigro, Georgia State University.

Finally, we would like to thank those kind academic souls who have adopted the previous volumes for their courses in public personnel administration. This book has proven to have very "long legs" in the profession, a reality that could only be made possible by the thoughtfulness of our fellow HRM faculty colleagues. Should any of you wish to communicate with us about this volume, or to propose future amendments or clarifications, please do not hesitate to do so.

Steven W. Hays
Richard C. Kearney

Section One

THE SETTING

To a great extent, public personnel administration is a mirror of the society it serves. Public jobs are ultimately public resources, so everyone potentially has a claim (or at least an interest) in how civil service jobs are apportioned and managed. And, because of the critical role that public employees play in conducting the people's business, society has a direct and appropriate stake in ensuring that the personnel function operates according to its wishes. For these reasons, a proper understanding of the problems and prospects of contemporary HRM must begin with an appreciation for the environmental factors that influence the practice of public personnel administration.

Since its inception, the merit system has been enmeshed in the fiber of the American political and social fabric. To say that "politics" exerts a profound influence on the public personnel function is hardly revealing or surprising. Yet, as examined in the first six chapters here, the nature and purposes of political intrusions into the personnel process have undergone important changes. In the initial essay, Lana Stein provides an overview of the essential value conflicts that imbue the civil service system. Her brief analysis of the historical progression of patronage and merit provides a framework for understanding the later chapters in which this critical distinction is further dissected.

Donald Klinger picks up this theme in the second chapter, and provides additional perspective on the complex web of pressures and demands that our society places on the HRM function. He includes what has become a rallying cry of many reformers, that of *privatization*. An underlying current that runs through both of these essays is that the design and operation of any personnel system involves political and ideological choices, whether or not they are made explicit by the managers and politicians who are ultimately responsible for breathing life into personnel policy.

The remaining four chapters in the section examine specific elements of the contemporary HRM setting. Rosenbloom and Bailey provide a concise analysis of the legal context of public personnel administration. As one of the primary forces shaping personnel policy, judicial decisions affect every facet and technique in the field. In effect, PPA has been "constitutionalized" to such an extent that every personnel manager needs to have a basic familiarity with the law. Chapters Four and Five examine two different levels of the public personnel system, local and federal. Saltzstein's examination of personnel management in local government provides an interesting contrast in both scale and sophistication to the picture of the federal system that is painted by Patricia Ingraham. In addition to updating the reader on the status of HRM reform in the federal sector, Ingraham provides an overview of the reinvention phenomenon and its implications for personnel practices in the nation's capital. The final chapter in the section ties these discussions together by analyzing how the personnel function has been "deregulated." Basing his discussion on empirical studies of merit systems across the nation, Coggburn examines both the consequences and the potential risks associated with the decentralization and "de-bureaucratization" of civil service systems.

The Political Context of Public Personnel Administration

LANA STEIN

University of Missouri-St. Louis

The public personnel process in the United States is political. It is part and parcel of who gets what from government. Yet, traditionalists in the personnel field aver that the relationship between politics and personnel practice is an oxymoron. They see administration and politics as separate entities. For them, merit is the gauge by which personnel decisions are to be made and use of any other criteria corrupts the process.

This chapter will explore the historical roots of the separation of politics from personnel administration. It then assesses the interplay of politics in contemporary personnel practice by looking at hiring and firing, workforces representative by gender and race, and the role of collective bargaining in the public sector. Finally, attempts by recent presidents to use appointments to ensure ideological compatibility in the executive branch will represent a modern twist to politics and the personnel process.

The denial of the political in public personnel administration has institutional and cultural roots. In fact, the American distrust of government and politics goes back to revolutionary times. That distrust became more manifest in the last half of the nineteenth century. While the nation grew rapidly, its methods of governance remained remarkably unsophisticated at every level. Political ties and cash payments assured people of jobs in the public sector. Corruption in the form of kickbacks, benefitting from insider knowledge, and outright bribery were far from uncommon.

Reformers, gathered under the Progressive umbrella, sought to replace inefficient and, at times, unsavory practices of machine politics with a scientifically based system that would ensure a competent and efficient workforce. Progressives, for the most part, were urban reformers of the upper middle or upper class. They were native-born white Protestants who did not benefit from the machines and wanted to see men like themselves in government instead of recent immigrants. It is from Progressive thinkers that the concept of a dichotomy between politics and administration arose. After all, their bête noire was the political party and politics in general and some of their reforms purposefully weakened political parties in the United States. As Mosher (1982:68) noted, the Progressive movement was essentially negative. "It associated what we now refer to as personnel administration with morality, with a connotation of intrinsic 'goodness' versus 'badness.'"

Using the growing number of sizeable corporations as models, Progressive reformers sought to discover administrative principles that would assure good government. Ironically, however, the rules they devised to guard against any taint of political favoritism in the personnel sphere frequently had no counterpart in the world of business. To this day, those interested in governmental reform continue to look to the private sector for answers much as the Progressives did. Another part of the Progressive legacy is the continuing distrust of politics and politicians by the American public.

Today, public personnel administration remains identified with civil service—a merit-based system. However, the passage of time has revealed that the principles Progressives devised to govern employee selection are not immutable. In fact, they have been shown to disproportionately favor certain societal groups. Although some still believe in a personnel system untainted by political considerations, others recognize that different sets of rules lead to different outcomes. Mosher (1982:70) succinctly stated that,

> The concept of neutrality gave the early enthusiasts for civil service reform difficulties, even as it continues to pose difficulties today. How can a public service which is neutral in political matters and which is protected be responsive to a public which expresses its wishes through the machinery of elections, political parties, and interest groups?

Initially, reforms put into place by the Progressives from 1900 to 1915 resulted in the replacement of immigrants and their children on the public payroll by upper-middle class native-born white Protestants (Hays:1984). The Progressives were structural reformers who realized and desired that their institutional changes would result in different procedures and different players. Their schema of classification, testing, and rule of three had a dual purpose, eliminating the spoils system and changing workforce composition. Adoption of their new operating rules did not prevent discrimination against women, African Americans, and other non-elite groups.

Progressive reforms certainly diminished the hiring of political friends without any requisite qualifications. But, elaborate personnel structures based on merit did not prevent inefficiency or bureaucratic dysfunction. In fact, these structures may have contributed to these very problems. In recent years, new solutions for public personnel administration's shortcomings have again been sought in the private sphere. Some practitioners and critics continued to eschew the politics in administration. Yet, public personnel administration and public administration generally are part of the American political process. As such, they are bound to address the questions of equity and effectiveness and have to work with the numerous interests that have a stake in public programs in the United States.

Through a discussion of contemporary public hiring, representative bureaucracy, labor organizing, as well as reforms to and reinvention of the public sector, public personnel emerges as part of the wider area of governance and of the politics that permeate that governance. Finding the best person for the job is just one objective of public personnel practices that does not and cannot exist in isolation. Practices vary by department at all government levels and they also vary city by city and state by state. Political form and political culture combine to shape the nature of recruitment and selection and of the recognition of bargaining rights. Politics does not play the same hand in every jurisdiction but it is present in some form.

POLITICS AND HIRING

Blatant political hiring is no longer commonplace in the United States as it was a century ago. Most governmental jurisdictions hire according to the general precepts of a merit system. At the federal level and in most large cities there is a civil service. States and counties have come later to the merit fold and some patronage employment remains in scattered locations. In certain cities where machine politics has managed to endure, civil service rules and regulations frequently have operated in tandem with political influence on hiring. For example, in 1952 Philadelphia began operating under a new charter that provided for a civil service commission independent of operating departments. However, Philadelphia's rigid classification scheme actually subverted its merit intentions. According to Shafritz (1973:59) the rules were sidestepped and informal procedures were used at times "to reward personal favorites." Since Philadelphia came late to civil service—1952— it was easy for "organizational" politics to hold sway over civil service's rigid specifications. In keeping with the morality inherent in American personnel administration, Shafritz (1973:59) noted that "organizational politics tends to be beneficial when merit is rewarded, deleterious when favoritism is rewarded."

St. Louis also has strict civil service rules. These rules became part of the city charter when voters, somewhat surprisingly, adopted a strict merit system in 1941. Despite the addition of civil service, St. Louis has remained a bastion of factional ward politics. Although its charter prescribes testing for every position and the rule of three for selection, as well as prohibitions against any political influence in personnel decisions, a strange hybrid has emerged. In St. Louis, after job candidates have been tested and ranked, elected officials frequently supply letters of recommendation to the appointing party (usually a department head). If a recommendation is from the mayor or from the chair of the aldermanic committee overseeing that department, the hiring choice is an easy one. (In St. Louis, members of the city council are called aldermen.) As one elected official has said, "You take the candidate who has exhibited qualifications and also has well-placed friends" (Stein, 1991:36–38). Mayors also intrude into this process. Usually, it is for a more senior position but sometimes department heads are asked to appoint a mayoral friend or someone's brother-in-law. Many department heads are mayoral appointees; they "go along to get along" when asked to hire a particular individual. Politicized merit in St. Louis does not touch every municipal hiring—but it is not unusual either.

Surely in other cities, counties, states, and at the federal level, whom you know may affect your chances of being hired or promoted as well. Wholesale patronage, on the other hand, appears to have died out in the embers of the Richard J. Daley machine in Chicago. Daley had about 20,000 city jobs at his disposal and he personally authorized every political hire (Biles, 1995:188). Even before his death in 1976, however, his ability to dispense patronage was limited by court decree. In 1969, Michael Shakman "filed a lawsuit challenging the constitutionality of Chicago's patronage system" (Freedman, 1988:847). Shakman alleged that "public employees were required to work for the machine and to contribute a portion of their salaries to the machine war chest" (Freedman, 1988:847). With the suit before the U.S. Court of Appeals, Mayor Daley and other officials entered into a consent judgment in 1972 that banned terminations for political purposes. *Shakman v. Democratic Organization of Cook County* weakened Chicago's patronage system because it prohibited the wholesale replacement of workers when there is turnover among elected officials. In 1976, in *Elrod v. Burns,* the United States Supreme Court entered a very similar finding. The Supreme Court clarified its ruling further in *Branti v. Finkel* in 1980, stating that dismissals of patronage employees could occur only when party affiliation is an appropriate requirement of the job.

Harold Washington, Chicago's first African American mayor, ran for that office as a reformer. However, he had to confront a largely hostile municipal workforce when he assumed office. His hands were tied. Having campaigned against patronage, he could not try to defy the Shakman strictures. Mayor Washington, though, like many mayors and elected executives, found the letting of contracts to be another way of rewarding or encouraging political support (Freedman, 1988).

The courts later added more limitations to political hiring. In 1990, the U.S. Supreme Court ruled 5–4 in *Rutan et al. v. Republican Party of Illinois et al.* that political loyalty could not be the test for hiring or promotion unless a compelling governmental interest also was served. Court decisions could then be used to curtail patronage at both ends: by elimination of a political test for hiring and by prohibition of terminations for political reasons unless policy-making responsibility was involved.

Electoral politics plays a less significant role in governmental personnel processes than it did a century ago or even four decades ago. Merit-based selection generally dominates many public personnel systems. Yet, some form of politics affects numerous other aspects of personnel-related functions, even though hiring political friends does not enter into the picture. Other considerations emanating from the judicial, executive, or legislative branches have brought public personnel administration outside its originally narrow confines. The desire for a representative workforce and a demand for collective bargaining do not readily fit the traditional merit system model devised by the Progressives. In addition, the need of executives to ensure policy responsiveness from their bureaucracies also creates a new challenge for personnel professionals who have long espoused the need for a depoliticized civil service.

REPRESENTATIVE BUREAUCRACY

Traditional personnel methods of recruiting, hiring, classifying, and promoting individuals resulted in a largely white male workforce in the public sector. The standard operating procedures of the public personnel profession were not solely responsible for that result. Biases present in all spheres of American life also entered into personnel decision making. Greater societal norms helped to dictate the appropriateness of certain groups for certain occupations.

Title VII of the Civil Rights Act of 1964 prohibited employment discrimination based on race, religion, sex, or national origin. (Disability and age were added to the terms of the act in later legislation.) Subsequent presidential orders required recipients of federal funds—private or public—"to remove all barriers, however informal or subtle that prevent access by minorities or women" to employment (Benokraitis and Feagin, 1978:1). State and local governments were not covered by the 1964 Act or the presidential orders that created affirmative action until the enactment of the Equal Employment Opportunity Act of 1972.

The lack of representation of minority groups and women in public jobs was well documented in the 1960s and 1970s. Meier (1975:540) found that nonwhites and women were underrepresented in the federal workforce, especially in the higher grades. In the early 1970s, only 4.5 percent of employees at grade GS-14 and above were nonwhite and only 3 percent were female. Rodgers and Bullock (1972:123) also described striking evidence of minority underrepresentation in local government. They stated that "local governments practice many of the same discriminatory acts found in private industry. They . . . use methods of hiring and promotion which place minorities at a serious disadvantage." In 1969, a study by the U.S. Commission on Civil Rights also illustrated the paucity of minority representation in local government, particularly in the protective services.

Federal affirmative action orders meant that the vast majority of public employers had to take steps to see that their workforces reflected the distribution of minority group members and women in the area labor market. In order to attempt to increase such representation, changes in recruitment and selection were needed. These changes to longstanding personnel practice were not uniformly welcomed by personnel professionals or by some officials and members of the general public.

Recruitment was the easiest area to address. As Thompson (1975) demonstrated in his description of the Oakland Fire Department, hiring opportunities were advertised through a traditional good old boy network. The pool of candidates contained the friends, relatives, and neighbors of existing firefighters. By expanding the recruitment network—contacting more agencies and groups, advertising in minority newspapers, and taking recruiters to African American neighborhoods for example—the pool of candidates could increase to reflect the greater diversity in the population (Stein and Condrey, 1987).

Wider recruitment efforts were not all that was needed. Examination and selection instruments had to be reexamined and modified. Traditional personnel practitioners sometimes resisted such change as a political challenge to the civil service process. The author of a widely used public personnel text, O. Glenn Stahl (1983:74–83), spelled out a number of objections to affirmative action in his work.

Stahl (1983:78) felt that the goal of a public workforce representative of the racial and gender make-up of the labor force of a certain jurisdiction meant "to achieve such ratios, qualifications and merit would have to be overridden by group identification as the prime criterion for entry and retention in government employment. . . . It is a negation of both the constitution and the mores of a free society." For Stahl and his cohorts, the requirements of an affirmative action program were political tests imposed on a professional system that had functioned according to the strictures of merit. The methods designed to ensure meritorious selection had been developed early in the twentieth century.

In many bureaucratic organizations, Stahl's views held sway. Selection methods adopted long ago had become ends in themselves rather than the means to hire the best workforce. Whatever the pros and cons of affirmative action, it is clear that requirements to achieve a representative workforce challenged the long-standing modus operandi, and those objecting to the challenge often couched it in terms of the politics/administration dichotomy.

Since 1972, minorities and women have increased their presence in public workforces at all governmental levels. This greater diversity in workforce composition has brought symbolic as well as actual benefits to various communities. Nonetheless, politicians and citizens alike have continued to question both the methods and goals of affirmative action. Public jobs have always been a concrete manifestation of "who gets what" from government and who holds public jobs has been of concern from the earliest days of the Republic to the present. Krislov and Rosenbloom (1981:197) felt that "the emphasis upon affirmative action to obtain 'pieces of the pie' has exacerbated, rather than eased, group conflict and tensions." Those who have not benefitted from the policy have continued to question its fairness and its constitutionality. Many have said that they would have gotten the job except that the agency had to hire a woman or an African American. However, one might ask how public workforces would look if affirmative action had *not* existed. Details from the 1969 report from the U.S. Commission on Civil Rights, as well as the perusal of many EEO-4 forms collected by the federal government from cities and states, would lead us to believe that more representative public workforces would not have been realized without affirmative action.

In the late 1990s, California and Texas removed affirmative action considerations from student selection at their public universities. Conflict over the issue of workforce representation is certain to continue: A material good emanating from government is at stake. Hiring once again has become part of political agendas although partisan favoritism is not an issue in this instance.

Public personnel officials also have had to grapple with the issue of comparable worth. Jobs traditionally occupied by women often had been classified at lower rungs on the pay scale than jobs held predominantly by men, which sometimes required less formal training. The findings are not always clear-cut. Aaron and Lougy (1986:7) recognized that classification schemes could be "inherently arbitrary." For them, that is only part of the problem. "While wage adjustments based on evaluations of comparable worth can correct some forms of labor market discrimination, they are simply irrelevant to others—for example, where women are denied entry to particular jobs or promotions that they merit." In either case, the standard operating procedures developed by personnel professionals did not mitigate inequality based on gender; they contributed to it. Public personnel professionals will have to grapple with the question of equal access to jobs as well as equity in compensation and benefits. However, given the nation's federal system, affirmative action in public employment may become a moot question in some states.

LABOR ORGANIZING

Public employees who join an organization designed to lobby and negotiate for better pay and working conditions challenge the traditional public personnel emphasis on the individual and replace it with one on the collective. It also means that seniority becomes a criterion for career advancement—a nonmerit criterion.

President John F. Kennedy gave union organizing a heads-up in 1962 with his executive order that affected federal employees (Kearney, 2001:14). Prior to that time, unionization had occurred in certain locations, such as cities with highly organized private sectors—New York, San Francisco, and Detroit. Kennedy's order provided that federal employees could join unions which then could bargain on issues not related to compensation. Federal employee unions have been particularly active in the area of disciplinary actions and concerns about working conditions.

The interests of the state can come into conflict with the actions of organized workers. To the alarm of many, police officers and firefighters have gone on strike. For example, protective services' workers walked off the job simultaneously in San Francisco for several days in 1974. Perhaps the most memorable labor dispute involved federal air-traffic controllers who walked off the job in 1981. President Reagan responded by firing all the strikers and de-certifying their union (Kearney, 1984:234–36).

Public sector labor unions will continue to present challenges to public personnel administrators. Unions may intercede in the promotion process, stressing the importance of seniority as a deciding factor. Labor activity also may not be congruent with pressures for affirmative action. In any case, the presence of public unions expands the personnel playing field, drawing in higher ranking executives and possibly legislators. Union activity challenges traditional civil service authority and merit-system practices. Unions present a political, although not necessarily a partisan, intervention in administration. In many parts of the country, public employee unions are a force to be reckoned with because of their alliances with elected officials and other unions.

A RESPONSIVE WORKFORCE

Elected executives from president to mayor have wondered whether their bureaucracies are responsive to the policy direction they were trying to set. It was no accident that Franklin D. Roosevelt created many new "alphabet soup" agencies to administer New Deal programs. He avoided turning his programs over to existing bureaus that could smother his initiatives amidst their standard operating procedures. The bureaucratic desire for autonomy, along with adherence to the familiar means of operation, can weaken innovation emanating from the chief executive.

Conservative presidents such as Richard Nixon and Ronald Reagan feared the purported liberalism of federal employees, a liberalism that could damage their new conservative policies. Meier (1975:541) discovered that public employees had issue stands "which were more 'liberal' than the American people" although their voting decisions frequently mirrored national electoral outcomes.

President Nixon attempted "to expand the policy and administrative capacities of the White House through the creation of centralized White House councils and offices" that would oversee the bureaucracy (Knott and Miller, 1987:248). Fred Malek, an aide to Nixon, prepared a manual that warned that the federal bureaucracy could sabotage Nixon's programs. He argued for political control of the bureaucracy and offered advice on how to accomplish that. Malek's manual became a guide for the hiring and placement of personnel (Cole and Caputo, 1979:403).

President Reagan had a similar desire to ensure loyalty to his policies and his conservative vision. Reagan also placed considerable emphasis "on partisan loyalty and ideological compatibility in selection of personnel" (Knott and Miller, 1987:271). Following a strategy begun by Nixon, Reagan without question used the appointment powers of the president to ensure such loyalty, and he was able to place key people in important posts throughout the federal government (Cole and Caputo, 1979:401).

Many questioned Reagan's strategy. It certainly added a clear political dimension to hirings and promotions. Both Nixon and Reagan felt that public servants should demonstrate a fealty to their presidential program initiatives and political philosophy as well as competence in performing their tasks. These two presidents couched their desire for responsiveness in terms of the conservative initiatives they proffered—conservative thrusts in a sea of liberalism.

Yet, the question still lingers as to whether bureaucrats will subvert policy on ideological grounds. It is probably more useful to discuss certain other traits of bureaus. It is often the tendency of bureaucracies in the United States to carve out their own niche and develop their own carefully guarded modus operandi, without any ideological underpinning. At times, bureaus develop powerful allies among legislators and interest groups. American governmental institutions— namely separation of powers and checks and balances—create an adversarial political culture (Wilson, 1989). Public employees, hired through some variant of the civil service process, respond to the organizational culture in which they find themselves placed. Responsiveness generally depends on the incentives available to bureaucrats in their work milieu.

The question remains though for any top official, be it president, governor, or mayor, of how to ensure that the policy he or she supports is implemented as intended. For many involved in public personnel administration, the conundrum becomes attempting to foster responsiveness without subjecting civil servants to ideological litmus tests that would change every four or eight years. Even so, such tests probably would pale in importance to the institutional factors determining performance and outcomes.

The Civil Service Reform Act of 1978 tried to address the issue of responsiveness at the federal level. One device used was the creation of the Senior Executive Service (SES). Those in the highest ranks of federal service were to be ranked in-person instead of by position. It was hoped that those in the SES would be moved amongst the federal cabinet-level departments and agencies serving as managerial experts. Presidents were permitted to add their own appointees to join the careerists in the SES. Such political appointments were to be limited to only 10 percent of the total. SES members would be eligible to receive merit pay. The establishment of the SES also reflected "a wholesale transfer of private motivational techniques to the public sector" (Ingraham, 1982:26). Implementation of these features of the Civil Service Reform Act did not carry with them resources sufficient to bring about the anticipated result of greater responsiveness. The quest for a more responsive workforce will continue. The answer may not necessarily lie in personnel practices alone but also in the nature of American institutions and the political culture they enable.

GOVERNMENTAL REINVENTION

Turn of the century reformers designed public personnel practices with the goal of creating a nonpolitical means of choosing a qualified, professional, and competent workforce. The reforms set in place decades ago were at the core moral reforms (Mosher, 1982:68). These reforms were intended to eradicate the evils of machine politics and to place government on a sound managerial footing. In recent times, traditional personnel practices in recruitment, selection, and promotion have been subject to attack. Public workers organized to increase their pay, improve working conditions, and to gain a collective voice in determining personnel policy. Courts and legislatures and presidents also intruded into public personnel decision making to answer the overdue need for greater representation by minority groups and women on the public payroll. A pair of presidents also tried to exert greater authority over policy implementation because of their distrust of a purportedly liberal federal workforce. These various challenges, all arising after 1960, applied political tests that threatened the structure of merit the Progressives had assembled. Certain sacrosanct ways of operating had to be adapted to a different reality. The historic struggle between good and evil, between principles and politics, became far more complex and challenging.

In the 1990s, additional questions came to the fore. Practitioners and scholars alike questioned the efficacy of civil service systems to hire and maintain a competent workforce. These critics spoke of "reinventing government" by using strategies most often derived from the private sector and perhaps modified for a governmental context. Reinvention gurus Osborne and Gaebler (1992:124–25) took on public personnel management because, in their view, its historic emphasis on control prevented supportive, genuinely merit-based administration.

> A typical Progressive reform, civil service was a well-intended effort to control specific abuses: patronage hiring and political manipulation of public employees. In most places, it accomplished its goals. . . . Designed for a government of clerks, civil service became a straitjacket in an era of knowledge workers. . . . (M)ost of what civil service procedures were established to prevent has since been ruled illegal or made impossible by collective bargaining agreements. Yet, the control mentality lives on, creating a gridlock that turns public management into the art of the impossible.

Osborne and Gaebler (1992:125–26) go on to question a number of civil service standard operating procedures. These include hiring the highest scorer on a test without consideration of other factors, the slow pace of the hiring process which can allow the most able candidates to find other positions, classification schemes that do not allow for performance, pay structures based on longevity, and the difficulties involved with trying to terminate a nonperforming employee. To these, one may add losing a competent employee because a position cannot be reclassified or because of the length of time needed to fill vacancies. In St. Louis several years ago, temporary summer employees who worked in city parks and recreation programs were not available to work until weeks after the date of hire desired by parks superiors. Grass was not cut and sports fields were not maintained because of cumbersome hiring and testing procedures. The irony here is that such workers are needed every year at the same time and delays continued to occur despite the initial problems.

Osborne and Gaebler and their adherents advocate a complete redesign of public personnel systems to increase flexibility in hiring, promoting, and compensating employees. In fact the Civil Service Reform Act of 1978 did move toward those objectives (albeit haltingly and incompletely) by, for example, moving federal hiring decisions to individual departments and agencies.

The fear of possible politicization remains palpable for many in the personnel field and for some in the public at large. The evil of politics and the need for control because of that evil have been part of the lexicon for over 100 years. Yet, the need for change or at least a modification in standard practices has become evident to many. At a minimum, civil service structures are frequently cumbersome and can impede the work of managers. At the same time, reforms proposed by advocates of reinvention can boomerang if applied in wholesale fashion in every locale and especially in those with less reformed practices.

For example, St. Louis, mentioned earlier, is a classic example of fragmented ward-based machine politics. Its municipal hiring is a combination of merit and politics. However, if testing were limited and selection delegated to city department heads to a greater degree than at present (eliminating the rule of three), the broader field of candidates might well become a broader field of political favorites (Stein, 1994:61). In an unreformed jurisdiction such as St. Louis, "politicized personnel practices are not something from the distant past. . . . Before embarking on any changes, the pros and cons need to be evaluated within the context of a machine politics city. . . . The reformer has to assume that different political cultures affect institutions and rules differently" (Stein, 1994:62).

Little doubt remains in the minds of most key administrators and scholars that practices devised to hire the best employees in bygone times need to be reevaluated. When the seemingly most qualified job candidates may be lost to governmental service because of untimely delays and antiquated procedures, change becomes inevitable. However, traditionalists may resist such change because of their desire for continued autonomy and because of a dislike of disruption of established routine.

Reformers or reinventers advocate solutions to remedy government's personnel woes. However, in a manner reminiscent of their professional forebears, they tend to emphasize the "one best way" of doing things. Given the myriad number of governments in the United States, each with particular institutions and culture, such homogeneity in remedy can be a prescription for further disasters. This is not to say that there is no transferability in personnel reform. Rather, it is a caution to those who would prefer reinventing in like manner everywhere. Remedies need to fit the environment in which they are placed.

Vice President Al Gore led the charge to reinvent our national government during the presidency of Bill Clinton. The reinventions he spearheaded tended to achieve cost savings due to attrition and downsizing (Kettl, 1998). In regard to the federal civil service, Kettl (1998:53-54) finds the record a mixed one. The Clinton administration continued the devolution of personnel functions to the departments. The Office of Personnel Management was weakened and "lost most of its ability to train government employees—a function left increasingly to private contractors—and to engage in strategic work force planning—a function largely abandoned" (Kettl, 1998:54).

Sometimes, latter day reformers discard the baby with the bath water. In addition to reform being sensitive to individual institutional environments, reform should remain an exercise in trial and error. Change does not necessarily occur in the manner intended. Although Wildavsky (1972) found that government was not an ideal self-evaluating mechanism, there is a lesson here. The private sector is but an imperfect model. Further, reforms are suggested solutions, not icons whose utility is guaranteed without a shadow of a doubt. Yet, the nature of complex organizations makes experiment in personnel issues or otherwise unlikely. And, problem and solution fall into the political sphere.

IMPLICATIONS

There is politics in public personnel administration no matter the era, no matter the rules. Public jobs are part of "who gets what" from government and will be viewed that way by job seekers and elected officials alike. The various debates about personnel practices demonstrate that the dichotomy between politics and merit has truly not been bridged in over a century and is indicative of wider debates about American governance.

In the early part of the twentieth century, the adoption of the merit system at many governmental levels was viewed as a triumph of good over evil. As such, it was difficult to view it as a means that could be modified over time as government and society changed. The old fears instead became shibboleths and reinforced practice. Modifications to merit rules were seen by many as a means to restore the corruption of an earlier era. Civil rights, labor rights, and the need for accountability and responsiveness have forced certain changes in public personnel administration. These changes have not yet been accepted in all quarters. In some locations, means—traditional practices—have become ends.

In the United States, politics and government itself are frequently viewed as necessary evils. American institutions have given rise to governmental fragmentation and political parties have been weak, certainly by European standards. Yet, the debate over modernization of personnel structures can be obscured by old myths and the residue from battles fought long ago. Osborne and Gaebler (1992) are correct in decrying the ever-evident struggle for control rather than effectiveness in public personnel management. But, change comes only with difficulty and even then may not take into account the tremendous variability in governance beyond the federal level.

Politics and the public personnel process may well be viewed as opposing forces for years to come. The normative dimensions of institutional arrangements are not always acknowledged because of the history of public administration and personnel practice in the United States. If scholars, practitioners, or citizens continue to look at structures as *all or nothing,* or as *good or evil,* adaptation to changing needs and technology will remain problematic.

REFERENCES

AARON, HENRY J., and CAMERON M. LOUGY. 1986. *The Comparable Worth Controversy.* Washington, DC: The Brookings Instititution.

BENOKRAITIS, NIJOLE V., and JOE R. FEAGIN. 1978. *Affirmative Action and Equal Opportunity: Action, Inaction, Reaction.* Boulder, CO: Westivew.

BILES, ROGER. 1995. *Richard J. Daley: Politics, Race, and the Governing of Chicago.* DeKalb, IL: Northern Illinois University Press.

Branti v. Finkel. 1980. U.S. Supreme Court no. 78–1654 (March 31).

COLE, RICHARD L., and DAVID A. CAPUTO. 1979. Presidential Control of the Senior Civil Service: Assessing the Strategy of the Nixon Years. *American Political Science Review* 73:399–413.

Elrod v. Burns. 1976. 96 S.Ct. 2673.

FREEDMAN, ANNE. 1988. Doing Battle with the Patronage Army: Politics, Courts, and Personnel Administration in Chicago. *Public Administration Review* 48:847–59.

HAYS, SAMUEL P. 1984. The Politics of Reform in the Progressive Era. In *Readings in Urban Politics.* 2nd ed. Edited by Harlan Hahn and Charles H. Levine. New York: Longman.

INGRAHAM, PATRICIA W. 1984. Civil Service Reform and Public Policy: Do We Know How to Judge Success or Failure? In *Legislating Bureaucratic Change: The Civil Service Reform Act of 1978.* Albany: State University of New York Press.

KEARNEY, RICHARD C. 2001. *Labor Relations in the Public Sector,* 3rd ed. New York: Marcel Dekker, Inc.

KETTL, DONALD F. 1998. *Reinventing Government: A Fifth-Year Report Card.* Washington, DC: Center for Public Management, The Brookings Instituituion. CPM Report 98-1.

KNOTT, JACK H., and GARY J. MILLER. 1987. *Reforming Bureaucracy: The Politics of Institutional Choice.* Upper Saddle River, NJ: Prentice Hall.

KRISLOV, SAMUEL, and DAVID H. ROSENBLOOM. 1981. *Representative Bureaucracy and the American Political System.* New York: Praeger.

MEIER, KENNETH JOHN. 1975. Representative Bureaucracy: An Empirical Analysis. *American Political Science Review* 69:526–542.

MOSHER, FREDERICK C. 1982. *Democracy and the Public Service.* 2nd ed. New York: Oxford University Press.

OSBORNE, DAVID, and TED GAEBLER. 1992. *Reinventing Government: How the Entrepreneurial Spirit Is Transforming the Public Sector.* Reading, MA: Addison-Wesley.

RODGERS, HARRELL R., JR., and CHARLES S. BULLOCK III. 1972. *Law and Social Change: Civil Rights Laws and Their Consequences.* New York: McGraw-Hill.

Rutan et al. v. Republican Party of Illinois et al. 1990. 110S.Ct. 2729.

SHAFRITZ, JAY M. 1973. *Position Classification: A Behavioral Analysis for the Public Service.* New York: Praeger.

Shakman v. Democratic Organization of Cook County. 1972. 671 F2d 303.

STAHL, O. GLENN. 1983. *Public Personnel Administration.* 8th ed. New York: Harper & Row.

STEIN, LANA. 1991. *Holding Bureaucrats Accountable: Politicians and Professionals in St. Louis.* Tuscaloosa: University of Alabama Press.

——. 1994. Personnel Rules and Reform in an Unreformed Setting: St. Louis' Politicized Merit System. *Review of Public Personnel Administration* 14:55–63.

——, and STEPHEN E. CONDREY. 1987. Integrating Municipal Workforces: A Study of Six Southern Cities. *Publius* 17:93–104.

THOMPSON, FRANK J. 1975. *Personnel Policy in the City: The Politics of Jobs in Oakland.* Berkeley: University of California Press.

U.S. Commission on Civil Rights. 1969. *For All the People . . . By All the People: A Report on Equal Opportunity in State and Local Government.* Washington, DC.

WILDAVSKY, AARON. 1972. The Self-Evaluating Organization. *Public Administration Review* 32:509–520.

WILSON, JAMES Q. 1989. *Bureaucracy: What Government Agencies Do and Why They Do It.* New York: Basic Books.

2

Competing Perspectives on Public Personnel Administration
Patronage, Civil Service, and Privatization

DONALD E. KLINGNER

University of Colorado

INTRODUCTION

Public personnel management has been studied extensively from at least four perspectives. These are (1) the *functions* needed to manage human resources in public agencies, (2) the *process* by which public jobs are allocated, (3) the interaction among fundamental societal *values* that often conflict over who gets public jobs and how they are allocated, and (4) *systems*—the laws, rules, organizations, and procedures used to express these abstract values in fulfilling personnel functions. Public personnel management in the United States may be described as a dynamic equilibrium among these competing values, each championed by a particular personnel system, for allocating scarce public jobs in a complex and changing environment. As one might expect, this conflict exhibits a commingling of technical decisions (*how* to do a personnel function) with political ones (*what* value to favor or *what* system to use). This article will:

- Describe why public personnel management can be viewed as functions, a job allocation process, values, and systems.
- Discuss the four traditional values that have historically shaped public personnel management and the emergent market-based values that are currently competing with them.
- Describe the traditional and contemporary systems that represent these competing values.
- Develop a model of public personnel management based on conflict and compromise among these competing values and systems.

- Evaluate how the interaction among these competing values and systems affects current conflicts among patronage, civil service, and privatization.

PUBLIC PERSONNEL MANAGEMENT AS FUNCTIONS

Public personnel management consists of four fundamental functions needed to manage human resources in public organizations—planning, acquisition, development, and sanction. *Planning* includes budget preparation and human resource forecasting dividing tasks among employees (job analysis, classification, and evaluation), and deciding how much jobs are worth (pay and benefits). *Acquisition* is recruitment and selection of employees. *Development* is orienting, training, motivating, and evaluating employees to increase their knowledge, skills, and abilities. And *sanction* is establishing and maintaining the rights and responsibilities that the employer and employee have toward one another (discipline, grievances, and health and safety).

PUBLIC PERSONNEL MANAGEMENT AS A PROCESS
FOR ALLOCATING SCARCE JOBS

In our society, jobs are the most visible way we measure individuals' and groups' social and economic status. Public jobs are scarce because tax revenues limit them. Therefore, competition is intense among individuals and advocates of competing values and systems.

PUBLIC PERSONNEL MANAGEMENT AS TRADITIONAL VALUES:
POLITICAL RESPONSIVENESS, ORGANIZATIONAL
EFFECTIVENESS, INDIVIDUAL RIGHTS, AND SOCIAL EQUITY

Traditionally, conflict within public personnel management in developed countries is centered on four values: political responsiveness, organizational efficiency and effectiveness, individual rights, and social equity (Klingner and Nalbandian, 1998). *Political responsiveness* is the belief that government answers to the will of the people, as expressed through elected officials. Applicants' responsiveness is best ensured through an appointment process that considers political and personal loyalty (with education and experience) as indicators of merit. *Organizational efficiency and effectiveness* reflect the desire to maximize the ratio of inputs to outputs in any management process. This means that decisions about whom to hire, reassign, or promote should be based on applicants' and employees' competencies, rather than political responsiveness. *Individual rights* emphasizes that individual citizens are to be protected from unfair actions of government officials. As citizens, public employees' rights to job security and due process are maintained through merit system rules and regulations that protect them from inappropriate partisan political pressure. Due process essentially means that a regularized set of procedures be followed before any discipline or other negative sanctions are imposed. Procedures that are typically provided include a hearing of some type in which the employee can meet and try to rebut adverse evidence. Likewise, due process assumes that procedures will be applied consistently to everyone. In a parallel fashion, public employees who are union members will have recourse to work rules, contained in collective bargaining agreements, that protect them from arbitrary management decisions. *Social equity* emphasizes fairness to groups (like women, racial minorities, the disabled, and veterans) that would otherwise be disadvantaged by a market economy that accepts the legitimacy of discrimination in hiring and in pay. Like individual rights, social equity is concerned with fairness. But unlike individual rights, it is the social aspect of equity that provides its group orientation.

PUBLIC PERSONNEL MANAGEMENT AS EMERGENT VALUES: INDIVIDUAL ACCOUNTABILITY, LIMITED AND DECENTRALIZED GOVERNMENT, AND COMMUNITY RESPONSIBILITY

The four traditional values implicitly endorse collective action through government. However, contemporary political, social, and economic forces have shaped three emerging antigovernment values that together reflect disappointment and lack of faith in government. They are *personal accountability, limited and decentralized government, and community responsibility.* First, proponents of *individual accountability* expect that people will make individual choices consistent with their own goals and accept responsibility for the consequences of these choices, rather than passing responsibility for their actions on to the rest of society. Second, many proponents of *limited and decentralized government* fundamentally fear government for its power to arbitrarily or capriciously deprive individuals of their rights. Even if they do not fear government, proponents also believe it is easier to connect public policy, service delivery, and revenue generation in a smaller unit of government than in a larger one because decision makers are known, revenues are predictable, and services are directly visible. And for some, the reduction in size and scope of government is justified by the perceived ineffectiveness of government; by the high value accorded to individual freedom, responsibility, and accountability; and, finally, by a reluctance to devote a greater share of personal income to taxes. Third, proponents of *community responsibility* believe that governmental agencies' efforts to provide social services, recreation, and community development need to be supplemented by not-for-profit nongovernmental organizations. The most significant consequence of the emergence of this value has been the creation of thousands of nonprofit organizations that routinely provide local services funded by taxes, user fees, and charitable contributions.

PUBLIC PERSONNEL MANAGEMENT AS SYSTEMS: LAWS, POLICIES, AND PRACTICE

Values become more than philosophical or ideological statements when they are concretely reflected in laws and policies. In public personnel management, values are articulated through personnel systems—the laws, policies, rules, regulations, and practices through which personnel functions are fulfilled. There are four basic systems in traditional public personnel management: patronage, civil service, collective bargaining, and affirmative action. *Patronage* systems are characterized by legislative or executive approval of individual hiring decisions (particularly for policy-making or confidential positions). Appointees serve at the will of those who appoint them; successful job performance depends on political or personal loyalty.

Proponents of *civil service systems* favor a professional public service as the best way to achieve efficiency, individual rights, and a responsive bureaucracy (Freyss, 1995). They think that staffing public agencies rationally (based on jobs needed to carry out specific programs and the competencies needed to accomplish these goals) and treating employees fairly are the best ways to maintain an efficient and professional public service. This means pensions and health benefits, equal pay for equal work, hiring and promotion based on competencies, and protection from management favoritism and partisan political influences. Civil service is the dominant system and organizational culture underlying the practice of public personnel management. Overall policy objectives of civil service systems are controlled by elected officials, who often appoint agency heads responsible for managing the bureaucracy. The legislature maintains control over resources by limiting the total number of employees an agency can hire, staffing levels in particular agencies or programs, and the personnel budget. These help ensure political responsiveness. Civil service is supported by citizens and groups who want to keep "politics" out of personnel decisions and "run government like a business," by employees holding civil service jobs, and by job applicants seeking fair consideration for public jobs. But because advocates of privatization and "cutting the fat out of big government" also believe in efficiency and effectiveness, there are some conflicts among proponents of this objective.

Collective bargaining systems exist within civil service. They support individual rights for union members, based on seniority. Even though collective bargaining is viewed as negotiation over wages and benefits, its main goal is to ensure equitable treatment by management. Contracts may also provide additional protection against disciplinary action or discharge. Because some overlap exists in civil service and collective bargaining system grievance procedures, employees are usually required to select one procedure but not both. In all cases, contracts negotiated between managers and the union are subject to legislative approval.

Affirmative action systems also usually exist within civil service. For them to operate, the governmental jurisdiction must have acknowledged an imbalance in the percentage of minorities in its workforce and availability of qualified minorities in the labor market. Or, members of a group protected against discrimination may have sued the public employer, resulting in a court ruling requiring the agency to give special consideration to members of the "protected class" in various personnel decisions, especially hiring and promotion. Affirmative action is supported by members of underrepresented classes (such as female, minority, and disabled), and by advocates who contend that the effectiveness of democracy depends upon a representative bureaucracy (Mosher, 1982).

The rise of antigovernment values has led to new market-based personnel systems: reducing the role of government and the number of public employees by using *alternative organizations or mechanisms for providing public services* (ICMA, 1989) and (2) increasing the *flexibility of employment relationships* for the public employees that remain (USMSPB, 1994).

Alternative Mechanisms and Organizations

Purchase-of-service agreements with other governmental agencies and nongovernmental organizations (NGOs) enable cities and counties with excess capacity to offer services within a given geographic area, utilizing economies of scale. They offer smaller municipalities a way to reduce capital costs, personnel costs, political issues associated with collective bargaining, and legal liability risks. Also, hiring outside consultants and businesses "as needed" increases expertise *and* flexibility by reducing the number of technical and professional employees the agency must hire full-time. While service purchase agreements contract for delivery of a particular service to a public agency, *privatization* abolishes the entire agency and replaces it with an outside contractor. Privatization offers all the advantages of service purchase agreements, but holds down labor and construction costs on a larger scale. It is commonplace in areas like solid waste disposal, where there is an easily identifiable "benchmark" (standard cost and service comparison with the private sector), and where public agency costs are higher because of higher pay and benefits.

Franchise agreements allow businesses to monopolize a previously public function within a geographic area, charge competitive rates, and pay the government for the privilege. Examples are cable TV and jitneys as a public transit option. Municipalities often encourage franchising because it reduces costs, provides revenue, and provides a desirable public service.

Subsidy arrangements enable businesses to perform public services, funded by either user fees to clients or cost reimbursement from public agencies. Some examples are airport security provided by private contractors and paid for by both passengers and airlines, emergency medical services provided by private hospitals and reimbursed by public health systems, and subsidizing rent in private apartments for low-income residents as an alternative to public housing projects.

Vouchers enable individual recipients of public goods or services to purchase them from competing providers on the open market. Under proposed educational voucher systems, for example, parents would receive a voucher that could be applied to the cost of education for their child at competing institutions (public or private), as an alternative to public school monopolies.

Volunteers provide contributed services otherwise performed by paid employees. These include community crime watch programs (in cooperation with local police departments), teachers' aides who provide tutoring and individual assistance in many public schools, and community residents who volunteer as individuals or through churches and other NGOs. Frequently, such contributions are required to "leverage" a federal or state grant of appropriated funds. And though they would probably not consider themselves volunteers, prison inmates are often responsible for laundry, food service, and facilities maintenance.

Regulatory and tax incentives are typically used to encourage the private sector to perform functions that might otherwise be performed by public agencies. For example, zoning variances for roads, parking, and waste disposal are often granted to condominium associations. In return, the association provides services normally performed by local government (security, waste disposal, and maintenance of common areas). This explains the increasing popularity of condominiums. Their lower unit cost often makes them the only available low- or moderate-cost housing available; and they are popular among builders and local planning officials because they increase the local tax base, yet shift the cost of providing city services to con-dominium residents.

Flexible Public Employment Relationships

Increasingly, public employers reduce costs and enhance flexibility by meeting minimal staffing requirements through career employees, and by hiring exempt, temporary, part-time, or seasonal workers to meet peak workload demands. These low skill positions usually offer lower salaries and benefits than career positions. And employees can be hired and fired "at will" (without reference to due process entitlements of civil service employees, or collective bargaining agreements). Conversely, where commitment *and* high skills are required on a temporary basis, employers may seek to save money or maintain flexibility by using contract or leased employees in positions exempt from civil service protection. While contracts may be routinely renewed with the approval of both parties, employees may also be easily "let go" in the event of a personality conflict, a change in managerial objectives, or a budget shortfall. Professional and technical experts hired on these contracts may receive higher pay and benefits than even highly qualified civil service employees; and management retains the flexibility to trim personnel costs quickly should this be necessary, without having to resort to the bureaucratic chaos precipitated by the exercise of civil service "bumping rights" in a layoff situation.

Impact of Emergent Systems on Traditional Values

These two emergent public personnel systems (alternative organizations or mechanisms for providing public services and flexible employment relationships) have implications for the four values that underlie the traditional model of public personnel management.

They diminish employee rights. It is more likely that employees hired "at will" into temporary and part-time positions will receive lower pay and benefits and will not be protected by civil service regulations or collective bargaining agreements. It is presently unknown whether the political neutrality of public employees suffers in this environment, but it seems logical to assume that as the criteria for success become more arbitrary or capricious, civil service employees—particularly those in mid-management positions—will begin to behave more like the political appointees whose jobs depend on loyalty to elected officials.

The new systems diminish social equity. Comparisons of pay equity over the past twenty years have uniformly concluded that minorities and women in public agencies are closer to equal pay for equal work than are their counterparts in the private sector. Yet consultants are mainly white and male. And many part-time and temporary positions are exempt from laws prohibiting discrimination against persons with disabilities or family medical responsibilities.

Emergent systems have a mixed impact on public agency efficiency. On the plus side, the cultural change toward identifying customers and providing market-based services increases productivity. And the threat of privatization or layoffs can compel unions to agree to pay and benefit cuts and changes in work rules (Cohen and Eimicke, 1994). But use of market-based techniques may actually increase some personnel costs, particularly those connected with employment of independent contractors, reemployed retirees, and temporary employees (Peters and Savoie, 1994). Downsizing may eventually lead to higher recruitment, orientation and training costs, and loss of organizational memory and "core expertise" necessary to effectively manage service contracting or privatization initiatives. Maintaining minimum-staffing levels also results in increased payment of overtime, and higher rates of employee accidents and injuries. As the civil service workforce shrinks, it is also aging. This means unforeseen increases in several critical areas: pension payouts, disability retirements, workers' compensation claims, and health care costs.

These emergent values and systems place much less importance on government, and more on individuals. For example, if public problems are viewed as the results of individuals' personal choices rather than as indicators of the need for changes in public policy, then the responsibility for dealing with the consequences of these problems is individual rather than governmental. Second, downsizing and decentralization reduce the comparative importance of government in society, and refocus governmental activity from a national to a state and local level. Continual budget cuts and pressure to "do more with less" result in agencies that are budget driven rather than mission driven. And budget-driven agencies that address public problems with short-term solutions designed to meet short-term legislative objectives are not likely to be effective (Moe, 1987). Long-range planning, or indeed any planning beyond the current budget cycle, is likely to become less important. Agencies will not be able to do effective capital budgeting or to adequately maintain capital assets (human or infrastructure).

CONFLICT AND COMPROMISE AMONG ALTERNATIVE PUBLIC PERSONNEL SYSTEMS

Because jobs and resources are finite, jobs allocated through one system cannot be allocated through others. So conflict among values and systems may require resolution at a micro level with each specific selection decision. Conflict among values and systems is limited and regulated by the dynamics of the competition itself. That is, each value, carried to its extreme, creates distortions that limit the effectiveness of human resource management because other values are suppressed. So attempts at domination by one system or value inevitably lead to reactions that in practice increase the power of other values or systems. Responsiveness carried to extremes results in the hiring of employees solely on the basis of patronage, without regard for other qualifications; or in the awarding of contracts based solely on political considerations (graft and corruption). Efficiency, carried to extremes, results in overrationalized personnel procedures—for example, going to decimal points on test scores to make selection or promotion decisions, or making the selection process rigid in the belief that systematic procedures will produce the "best" candidate. Individual rights, carried to extremes, result in overemphasis on seniority or on due process and rigid disciplinary procedures. Social equity, carried to extremes, results in personnel decisions being made solely on the basis of group membership, disregarding individual merit or the need for efficient and responsive government. And antigovernment values, carried to extremes, eventually result in a society regulated by markets rather than the public policy-making process. And market models' weakness—primarily their inability to effectively address issues such as distributive equity or indivisible public goods—limits reliance on service contracting, privatization, user fees, and other "antigovernment" personnel systems.

Under ideal circumstances, public personnel management might reflect one dominant value and, hence, one dominant system. But in reality, it is often hard to distinguish between political appointments and those resulting from civil service or affirmative action systems. Nor is the boundary between politics and administration easy to determine. Over time, personnel systems will reflect the dominant values in a jurisdiction. The more stable the values, the more permanent the personnel system and practices will become, and the more that culture will dominate the organization.

Public personnel management in the United States is complex because there are multiple levels of government and thousands of governments, each with its own personnel system. But there is general agreement that the development of public personnel management has proceeded according to a temporal pattern summarized in the following table:

TABLE 2–1 Evolution of Public Personnel Systems and Values in the United States

Stage of Evolution	Dominant Value(s)	Dominant System(s)	Pressures for Change
One (1789–1828)	Responsiveness	"Government by elites"	Political parties + Patronage
Two (1828–1883)	Responsiveness	Patronage	Modernization + Democratization
Three (1883–1933)	Efficiency + Individual rights	Civil service	Responsiveness + Effective government
Four (1933–1964)	Responsiveness + Efficiency + Individual rights	Patronage + Civil service	Individual rights + Social equity
Five (1964–1980)	Responsiveness + Efficiency + Individual rights + Social equity	Patronage + Civil service + Collective bargaining + Affirmative action	Dynamic equilibrium among four competing values and systems
Six (1980–present)	Responsiveness + Efficiency + Individual accountability + Limited government + Community responsibility	Patronage + Civil service + Collective bargaining + Affirmative action + Alternative organizations and mechanisms + Flexible employment relationships	Dynamic equilibrium among four pro-governmental values and systems, and three antigovernmental values and systems

First, public jobs were allocated primarily among elites ("government by gentlemen"). Second, the development of political parties signaled the birth of the patronage system, which rewarded party members and campaign workers with jobs once their candidate was elected. While it did not result in the selection of highly qualified employees, the patronage system has many virtues. Elected officials achieve partisan political objectives by placing loyal supporters in key confidential and policy-making positions within administrative agencies. Officials get reelected by providing voters with access to bureaucrats who often don't seem to understand that rules must sometimes be bent, or broken, for voters to feel that justice has been done.

Third, civil service reformers forced a gradual transition from patronage to merit systems. They emphasized the civil service ideal that a competent, committed workforce of career civil servants is essential to the professional conduct of the public's business. Position classification is often cited as the cornerstone of civil service because it epitomizes this link between management efficiency and employee rights. It offers management a uniform basis for grouping jobs by occupational type and skill level, an equitable and logical pay plan based on the competencies needed to perform the job, a way to translate individual pay and benefit costs into agency budget projections, and it aids recruitment, selection, training, and assessment processes by specifying the duties and qualifications for each position. At the same time, it protects employee rights by minimizing political or administrative abuse. Pay rates are tied to positions, with duties specified in the position description, so individual favorites cannot be paid more than others. Thus, paying people a high salary and giving them few if any responsibilities—which occurs frequently in patronage positions—is minimized. Budgets are allocated based on positions, so ceilings can be established to limit hiring. Units may also be assigned an average allowable position grade, thereby limiting average salaries and ensuring that the agency will not become top heavy.

The relationship between politics and administration centers around the enduring question of how governments can bring expertise to bear on the development of public policy while retaining the supremacy of political values (Sayre, 1948). It results in a fourth-stage hybrid model that achieves efficiency and effectiveness by filling most positions through civil service, and responsiveness by filling a few confidential and policy-making positions through patronage. This combination results in programs consistent with elected officials' philosophy and vision of government, and with administrators' ability to make operational plans and manage resources efficiently (including human resources). Inevitably, the emergence of administrative effectiveness as a hybrid of politics and efficiency created strains in the civil service reform model, which had been based on the fundamental distinction between politics and administration. The civil service model viewed personnel management as a neutral administrative function; the effectiveness model viewed it as a management-oriented function under the direction of the executive branch (Lan and Rosenbloom, 1992; Nalbandian, 1981).

The fifth evolutionary stage was the development of public sector collective bargaining during the 1960s and 1970s. Under collective bargaining the terms and conditions of employment are set by direct contract negotiations between agency management and unions. This is in contrast to a patronage system, where they are set and operationally influenced by elected officials, or to the civil service system, where they are set by law and regulations issued by management and administered by management or an outside authority like a civil service board. Collective bargaining in the public sector has many of the same procedures as its private sector counterpart, such as contract negotiations and grievance procedures. But fundamental differences in law and power outweigh these similarities. Public sector unions never have the right to negotiate binding contracts with respect to wages, benefits, or other economic issues. The right to approve or disapprove negotiated contracts is reserved to the appropriate legislative body (such as the city council, school board, or state legislature) with the authority to appropriate money to fund contracts. So both labor and management realize that ratification of negotiated contracts is more critical than negotiation of them, and they set their political strategies accordingly.

During this same period, affirmative action emerged to represent social equity through voluntary or court-mandated recruitment and selection practices to correct underrepresentation of minorities and women in the workplace. Affirmative action arose as a result of the civil rights movement of the 1960s and the women's rights movement of the 1970s. It was supported by the beliefs that a representative bureaucracy was essential for our government to function as a democracy; and that other personnel systems had not been effective at ensuring proportional representation. In fact, all these systems had worked (albeit for different reasons) to perpetuate the dominance of white males. Since most elected officials are white males, as a rule they appoint white males to patronage jobs. Civil service systems favor education and experience, which traditionally have been a strength of white males who have access to higher education and managerial positions. And the seniority systems favored by collective bargaining tend to perpetuate the racist or sexist bias toward the selection of white males.

State and federal administrative agencies monitor compliance with affirmative action laws and control public agencies' or contractors' voluntary affirmative action programs; thus, state and federal courts are also responsible for implementation and enforcement. This system takes effect when a gross disparity exists between the percentage of minority or female employees in an agency and their percentage in a relevant labor pool (such as the community served by that agency or the percentage of applicants qualified for the position), and when the agency has resisted the voluntary adoption of recruitment, selection, training, or promotion techniques that would reduce this disparity. In such a case, members of the affected class may sue the agency to force it to intervene. If successful, these court efforts may result in considerable judicial control of the agency's personnel system. The court can require an agency to hire or promote specific numbers or percentages of qualified women or minorities until their representation in the agency workforce is more proportionate with their representation in the community. They can discourage avoidance of affirmative action compliance by requiring agencies to justify the transfer of positions to political patronage systems; they can order the abandonment of civil service rules or techniques that have a disparate effect on women and minorities; and they can abrogate collective bargaining agreements that use seniority rules to perpetuate previous patterns of racism or sexism. But courts cannot compel affirmative action compliance for legislative or judicial positions. They cannot require an agency to hire minority or female employees if agency managers elect not to fill any vacancies, or require an agency to retain minorities and women in civil service positions if funds are not available to do so.

The sixth and current stage in the evolution of public personnel systems in the United States clearly reflects the growing importance of market models, and the importance of the private sector in achieving public policy objectives in developed countries since the 1970s. Pressure to *do more* caused government to become more accountable through such techniques as program budgeting, management by objectives, program evaluation, and management information systems. Pressure to do more *with less* caused governments to lower expenditures through such methods as tax ceilings, expenditure ceilings, deficit reduction, deferred expenditures, accelerated tax collection, service fees, user charges, and a range of legislative and judicial efforts to shift program responsibilities and costs away from each affected government.

This gradual shift in emphasis from progovernment to antigovernment values leaves the fundamental issue of the appropriate role of government unresolved. Both the ways the debate is framed in the minds of partisans on both sides and the outcome of the conflict are still the subject of political and social controversy. Progovernment adherents see the declining quality of public life as equivalent to a declining quality of life; antigovernment value adherents view it as an enhanced opportunity for individuals to make personal choices about their own spending priorities, including community responsibilities. Adherents to the emergent model see their values as liberating, in the sense that they emphasize individual choice and community responsibility. Adherents to the traditional model see the emergent values as a hypocritical overlay atop greed and self-interest. But whatever the eventual outcome of this controversy, one thing is certain. Historically, it was taken for granted that public program innovations would be accomplished by a staff of career civil service employees, working within the structure of centralized public agencies budgeted with appropriated funds. Today, none of these is true–public programs are more than likely performed by alternative market mechanisms rather than directly by public agencies; and when public agencies are used, they are more likely to be staffed by temporary employees hired through flexible employment mechanisms rather than by permanent employees protected by civil service regulations and collective bargaining agreements.

SUMMARY

Public personnel management can be viewed from several perspectives. First, it is the functions (planning, acquisition, development, and sanction) needed to manage human resources in public agencies. Second, it is the process by which a scarce resource (public jobs) is allocated. Third, it reflects the influence of seven symbiotic and competing values (political responsiveness, efficiency, individual rights, and social equity under the traditional progovernment model; and individual accountability, downsizing and decentralization, and community responsibility under the emergent antigovernment model) over how public jobs should be allocated. Fourth, it is the laws, rules, and regulations used to express these abstract values–personnel systems (political appointments, civil service, collective bargaining, and affirmative action under the traditional model; and alternative mechanisms for providing public services and flexible employment relationships under the emergent antigovernment model). Because jobs and resources are finite, jobs allocated through one system cannot be allocated through others. Thus, the history of public personnel management in the United States tends to reflect the tension between competing and coexisting values, each supported by different values.

So what does the future look like? First, continued tension will exist among the four traditional values and the respective systems. Second, the conflict between market mechanisms and government policy as the primary decision-making mechanisms in the United States will continue. And in this respect, it should be noted that a considerable body of research in state and local governments over the past twenty years has established some conclusions about the comparative effectiveness of market mechanisms and government action. First, positive privatization or service contracting outcomes require public administrative competence, particularly a civil service that can rationally plan, manage, and evaluate privatization efforts. Privatization outcomes are most likely to be successful when governments: (1) pick a service with clear objectives that can be measured and monitored; (2) use in-house or external competition and avoid sole source contracting; (3) develop adequate cost accounting systems to compare service alternatives and monitor contractor performance; and (4) consider negative externalities such as impacts on an existing work force, on the local economy, on other governments or functions, on governmental policies, or on certain societal groups (Siegel, 1999). Thus, given the self-limiting nature of conflict among public personnel systems, it is likely that excessive efforts to privatize government will lead to reactions by proponents of employee rights, social equity, the transparent effectiveness of a neutral civil service, or the ultimate responsibility of elected and appointed officials to work toward the interests of the general public they represent. In this sense, it is important to remember that, while markets are responsive to customers who make choices among products, elected officials are responsive to voters who make choices among candidates who claim to represent their interests as citizens—citizens who vote them in and out of office.

REFERENCES

COHEN, S., and W. EIMICKE. 1994. The Overregulated Civil Service. *Review of Public Personnel Administration* 15:11–27.

FREYSS, S. F. Fall 1995. Municipal Government Personnel Systems. *Review of Public Personnel Management* 16:69–93.

ICMA (International City Management Association). 1989. *Service Delivery in the 90s: Alternative Approaches for Local Governments.* Washington, DC: ICMA.

KLINGNER, DONALD E., and JOHN NALBANDIAN. 1998. *Public Personnel Management: Contexts and Strategies.* 4th ed. Upper Saddle River: Prentice Hall.

LAN, Z., and D. H. ROSENBLOOM. 1992. Public Administration in Transition? *Public Administration Review* 52:535–538.

MOE, R. C. 1987. Exploring the Limits of Privatization. *Public Administration Review* 47:453–460.

MOSHER, F. 1982. *Democracy and the Public Service* 2nd ed. New York: Oxford University Press.

NALBANDIAN, J. 1981. From Compliance to Consultation: The Role of the Public Personnel Manager. *Review of Public Personnel Administration* 1:37–51.

PETERS, B. G., and D. J. SAVOIE. 1994. Civil Service Reform: Misdiagnosing the Patient. *Public Administration Review* 54:418–425.

SAYRE, W. 1948. The Triumph of Techniques Over Purpose. *Public Administration Review* 8:134–137.

SIEGEL, GILBERT B. March 1999. Where Are We on Local Government Service Contracting? *Public Productivity and Management Review* 365–388.

USMSPB (United States Merit Systems Protection Board). 1994. *Temporary Federal Employment: In Search of Flexibility and Fairness.* Washington, DC: U.S. Merit Systems Protection Board.

3

What Every Public Personnel Manager Should Know About the Constitution

DAVID H. ROSENBLOOM
MARGO BAILEY
School of Public Affairs, The American University

Since the 1970s, constitutional law has become central to public personnel management at all levels of government in the United States. Examinations, recruitment, selection, training, promotions, drug testing, and disciplinary procedures are all regulated in one way or another by constitutional considerations. Moreover, the decisions of the courts are not just another concern to be balanced among the many competing pressures that public personnelists often face. Individual administrators and agencies may be held liable for money damages if they violate the constitutional rights of applicants or employees. Consequently, knowledge of constitutional law is now part of the basic job competence public personnel administrators need. In fact, contemporary public sector strategic personnel management is risky and subject to failure through law suit in the absence of such knowledge.

This chapter explains how the current constitutional doctrine regarding public employees' constitutional rights is structured and reviews the leading cases in the areas of greatest concern to today's public personnel administration. Its purpose is to familiarize those interested in public personnel with constitutional concepts and to provide an up-to-date survey of the constitutional law that is relevant to their work. The chapter concludes with a discussion of how strategic personnel management can help protect public employees' constitutional rights.

CONSTITUTIONAL DOCTRINE

As shocking as it may seem to the modern public personnel manager, prior to the 1950s public employees at all levels of government in the United States had very few federally protected constitutional rights that could be effectively asserted within the framework of their employment. Their position was governed by constitutional reasoning which held that because public employment was a privilege, rather than a right, it could be offered on almost any terms the governmental employer saw fit. Not having a right to a public sector job, upon dismissal, one lost nothing to which he or she was entitled. As Justice Oliver Wendell Holmes expressed the core idea, "The petitioner may have a constitutional right to talk politics, but he has no constitutional right to be a policeman" (*McAuliffe v. New Bedford,* 1892:220). Therefore, it was perfectly constitutional to fire a police officer (or any other public employee) for his or her speech. Under this approach, known as the "doctrine of privilege," constitutional law failed to check a variety of interferences with the ordinary rights of public employees and applicants, including even the right to equal protection of the laws.

Although the doctrine of privilege had a certain logic, it also ignored the realities of citizens' interactions with government in the modern administrative state. If public employees and applicants could be fired or denied jobs for virtually any reason without violating their constitutional rights, would not the same principle apply to other kinds of privileges, such as welfare benefits, government contracts, passports, public housing, drivers' licenses, and so forth? Could those be denied, as public employment sometimes was, partly because the individual favored racial integration, read Tom Paine or *The New York Times,* failed to attend church services, or engaged in a host of nonconformist and unconventional activities (Rosenbloom, 1971:160–168)? To the extent that big government creates a dependency of the people on government services which were defined as privileges, strict adherence to the doctrine of privilege could easily lead to circumvention of the fundamental protections found in the Constitution's Bill of Rights.

The federal courts fully discarded the doctrine of privilege by the early 1970s. After a variety of shifting emphases, they developed the current "public service model" for assessing the constitutional rights of public employees (*Harvard Law Review,* 1984). This model balances three often competing concerns: 1) the public employee or applicant's interests as a member of the political community in exercising constitutional rights and enjoying constitutional protection from arbitrary or repressive treatment by the governmental employer; 2) the government's interest as an employer in having an efficient and effective workforce; and 3) the public's interest in the operation of public administration and government more generally. Importantly, the public's interest can coincide with either that of the employee or the government, depending on the specific circumstances. For instance, the public shares a strong interest with a public employee who engages in "whistle-blowing" by alerting the media to gross governmental mismanagement or dangers to the community's health or safety. However, when it comes to the quick dismissal of inefficient, dishonest, or unreliable civil servants, the public's interest would correspond with that of the government.

The key to the public service model is the tenet that "the government's interest in achieving its goals as effectively and efficiently as possible is elevated from a relatively subordinate interest when it acts as a sovereign [in dealing with ordinary citizens] to a significant one when it acts as employer" (*Waters v. Churchill,* 1994:675). This enables governments to place special requirements on their employees which would be unconstitutional if applied to ordinary citizens. For example, the constitutional law permits governments to prohibit their employees from taking an active part in partisan campaign management and electioneering (*Civil Service Commission v. National Association of Letter Carriers*, 1973). As an employer, the government's concern with workforce harmony and the appearance of partisan neutrality outweighs the employees' interests in exercising the same free speech and association rights as other citizens.

It is important to note that the public service model is not weighted either in favor of or against broad constitutional rights for public employees. The courts may side with either the government or the individual. Everything depends on how judges apply the model in varying contexts and circumstances. As Chief Justice William Rehnquist once noted, such jurisprudence places a heavy emphasis on "ad hoc weighing which depends to a great extent upon how the Court subjectively views the underlying interests at stake" (*Cleveland Board of Education v. Loudermill*, 1985:562). This quality of the public service model can be frustrating because it makes it difficult to apply general constitutional principles to specific personnel decisions. However, it is all the more reason why public personnelists should closely follow the case law.

FREEDOM OF SPEECH

Rankin v. McPherson (1987) outlines the current approach for analyzing public employees' constitutional rights to nonpartisan free speech. Ardith McPherson was a nineteen-year-old probationary clerical employee in the office of Constable Rankin in Texas. She had been talking with a coworker, whom the Supreme Court characterized as her "boyfriend" (322). Referring to an assassination attempt on President Ronald Reagan, she remarked, "Shoot, if they go for him again, I hope they get him" (322). Her comment was overheard by a third employee, who reported it to Rankin. After discussing the comment with McPherson, Rankin fired her. Believing that her right to free speech under the First and Fourteenth Amendments[1] was violated by the dismissal, McPherson brought suit for reinstatement, back pay, and other relief.

In analyzing the case, the Supreme Court's majority noted that "even though McPherson was merely a probationary employee, and even if she could have been discharged for any reason or for no reason at all, she may nonetheless be entitled

---

[1.] The first ten amendments to the Constitution, known as the Bill of Rights, apply directly to the federal government. The Fourteenth Amendment, which was ratified in 1868, prohibits the states (and their political subunits) from violating many of these rights as well. Its due process clause, protects individuals from the deprivation of life, liberty, or property by subnational governments. Over, the years the term "liberty" has been read by the Supreme Court to "incorporate" much of the Bill of Rights, including the First and Fourth Amendments, which are of particular importance to public personnel administration. This is why McPherson can argue that her First Amendment rights, which are incorporated into the Fourteenth Amendment, have been violated. Since the Fourteenth Amendment is what applies the First Amendment to state and local governments, she argues that it has been violated as well.

As is discussed later in the chapter, the Fourteenth Amendment also prohibits the states and their subunits from depriving any person within their jurisdiction "equal protection of the laws." Known as the equal protection clause, this provision is interpreted to apply to the federal government through the word "liberty" in the Fifth Amendment, a process called "reverse incorporation."

to reinstatement if she was discharged for exercising her constitutional right to freedom of expression" (324). The Court went on to explain the logical structure of public employees' right to free speech.

First, a key issue is whether the employee's remark is about a matter of public concern. This is how the public's interest is brought into the analysis. If a remark is on a matter of public concern, then it is of value to the public's informed discussion of government and public policy. Such comments are part of the free marketplace of ideas that is vital to the operation of constitutional democracy. By contrast, statements of purely private concern, such as what one employee thinks of another's personality, intelligence, or clothes, are afforded minimal (if any) protection when they interfere with the proper functioning of government offices.

In *Rankin*, a 5-4 majority of the Court concluded that the remark was on a matter of public concern. It had been made in the context of a discussion of Reagan's policies, and McPherson, an African American, apparently offered it as a way of punctuating her disdain for the administration's approach to minorities. This illustrates how context becomes a central consideration.

Second, once the Court determined that McPherson's comment was on a matter of public concern, it proceeded with the balancing required by the public service model . . . in weighing the State's interest in discharging an employee based on any claim that the content of a statement made by the employee somehow undermines the mission of the public employer, some attention must be paid to the responsibilities of the employee within the agency. The burden of caution employees bear with respect to the words they speak will vary with the extent of authority and public accountability the employee's role entails. Where, as here, an employee serves no confidential, policy-making, or public contact role, the danger to the agency's successful function from that employee's private speech is minimal (328).

> It is obvious that the Supreme Court has given public personnel administrators much to think about regarding the scope of public employees' constitutionally protected speech. The following must be considered: whether the remarks at issue were on a matter of public concern; the context in which they were uttered; the nature of the employee's position with reference to confidentiality, policymaking, and public contact; and the remarks' disruptive quality. To these factors must be added others from earlier case law, including, whether the speech involves prohibited political partisanship, suggests disloyalty to the United States, or is so without foundation that the employee's basic competence is called into question. Under the circumstances, it is not surprising the Supreme Court admits that "competent decisionmakers may reasonably disagree about the merits of [a public employee's] First Amendment claim" (*Bush v. Lucas*, 1983, note 7).

Public employees' free speech protections include a right to whistle-blow, which generally involves alerting the public to gross waste, fraud, mismanagement, or specific dangers to the health or safety of the community. The Supreme Court has reasoned that due to their positions inside government, public employees are sometimes uniquely able to contribute to the "free and open debate [which] is vital to informed decision-making by the electorate" and "accordingly it is essential that they be able to speak out freely . . . without fear of retaliatory dismissal" (*Pickering v. Board of Education*, 1968:571–572).

Public employees' right to engage in whistle-blowing is frequently bolstered by protective statutes, such as the federal Civil Service Reform Act of 1978. If a statement is covered by the terms of such a statute, it is automatically considered a matter of public concern and the government is prohibited from retaliating, regardless of how disruptive the comments may be. Even false statements are likely to be protected unless the government can show that the speaker knew they were false or acted with reckless disregard of their truth or falsity (*Pickering v. Board of Education*, 1968). However, when an adverse action follows an act of whistle-blowing, the employee involved may have to demonstrate that it was, in fact, retaliatory. Moreover, the government may have the opportunity to show that it would have taken the action at issue even in the absence of the protected whistle-blowing.

As noted earlier, public employees' constitutional right to free speech does not extend to partisan management and campaigning. In the Supreme Court's view, the damage that restrictions on political activity do to public employees' rights is outweighed by the governmental interests in efficiency and the appearance of partisan neutrality. Such measures also protect civil servants from being coerced by elected and politically appointed officials to support parties and candidates (*United Public Workers v. Mitchell*, 1947; *Civil Service Commission v. National Association of Letter Carriers*, 1973). The Court has given wide berth to governmental employers in this policy area by allowing considerable imprecision in the drafting of restrictions (*Broaderick v. Oklahoma*, 1973).

Of course, the fact that political neutrality regulations are apt to be constitutional does not mean that governments will choose to impose them. In recent years the trend has been away from comprehensive restrictions on public employees' participation in partisan activities. For example, the 1993 Federal Hatch Act Reform modified a variety of restrictions, some of which reached back to the early 1900s (Rosenbloom, 1971:94–110). It allowed most federal employees to distribute partisan campaign literature, solicit votes (though not funds), work for partisan campaigns, and hold office in political parties. It did not extend to the Senior Executive Service. Some agencies, including the Merit Systems Protection Board, and positions, such as Administrative Law Judge, were exempt on the grounds that overt partisanship would undermine their missions or functions.

Can whistle-blowing and related political speech always be distinguished from partisan expression? The answer is patently no, but the Supreme Court has yet to be confronted with the need to create a distinction between them. In terms of public personnel management, therefore, some uncertainty remains in this area, especially during electoral campaign periods.

Applying the public service model to employees' speech can sometimes be further complicated by disputes over the exact content of the remarks at issue. Reports from speakers and bystanders may differ. Here, the public employer is permitted to act on what it *reasonably believes* was said. The government is not required to be completely certain or have proof beyond a reasonable doubt. The Supreme Court has mandated merely that the employer take reasonable steps to find out what the employee may actually have said. However, its guidance in this area has been exceptionally vague: "only procedures outside the range of what a reasonable manager would use may be condemned as unreasonable" (*Waters v. Churchill*,

1994:678). Nevertheless the overall message is clear: an employee should never be disciplined for a remark he or she did not make.

FREEDOM OF ASSOCIATION

The contemporary constitutional law regarding public employees' freedom of association is also central to some aspects of public personnel management. In general, public employees' rights to join organizations voluntarily (including political parties, labor unions, and even highly distasteful extremist groups) is well established, as is their right to refrain from associating with or supporting organizations (*AFSCME v. Woodward*, 1969; *Elfbrandt v. Russell*, 1966; *Shelton v. Tucker*, 1960; *Elrod v. Burns*, 1976; *Abood v. Detroit Board of Education*, 1977). However, two areas of public personnel management that have been specifically "constitutionalized" in this context should be noted.

First, it is possible for union security agreements to violate public employees' constitutionally protected freedom not to associate. No public employee can be required to join a union as a condition of holding his or her job. However, an agency shop is permitted. This arrangement requires nonunion members to pay a "counterpart" or "fair share" fee to the union that represents their collective bargaining unit. In *Abood v. Detroit Board of Education* (1977) the Supreme Court "rejected the claim that it was unconstitutional for a public employer to designate a union as the exclusive collective-bargaining representative of its employees, and to require non-union employees . . . to pay a fair share of the union's cost of negotiating and administering a collective bargaining agreement" (*Chicago Teachers Union v. Hudson*, 1986:243–244). But the Court also held that "nonunion employees do have a constitutional right to 'prevent the Union's spending a part of their required service fees to contribute to political candidates and to express political views unrelated to its duties as an exclusive bargaining representative'" (*Chicago Teachers Union v. Hudson*, 1986:244).

The constitutional right not to be compelled to underwrite a union's political agenda is accompanied by procedural safeguards. In the Supreme Court's words, ". . . the constitutional requirements for the Union's collection of agency fees include an adequate explanation of the basis for the fee, a reasonably prompt opportunity to challenge the amount of the fee before an impartial decision maker, and an escrow for the amounts reasonably in dispute while such challenges are pending" (*Chicago Teachers Union v. Hudson*, 1986:249).

Second, in a series of decisions since 1976, the Supreme Court established substantial constitutional barriers to the use of political partisanship in public personnel decisions. In *Elrod v. Burns* (1976), the Court held for the first time in American history that patronage dismissals could violate public employees' freedom of association and belief. But the Court was divided and unable to form a majority opinion on the standard that the government must meet when dismissing someone based on partisan affiliation. Four years later, in *Branti v. Finkel* (1980), a majority agreed that in such cases, "the ultimate inquiry is not whether the label 'policymaker' or 'confidential' fits a particular position; rather, the question is whether the hiring authority can demonstrate that party affiliation is an appropriate requirement for the effective performance of the public office involved" (518). This standard places a heavy burden of persuasion on elected officials and political appointees who would dismiss employees based on their partisan affiliation. In *Rutan v. Republican Party of Illinois* (1990), the Court held that "the rule of *Elrod* and *Branti* extends to promotion, transfer, recall, and hiring decisions based on party affiliation and support" (79). Accordingly, for most intents and purposes, partisanship is an unconstitutional basis for taking public personnel actions.

In reaching these decisions regarding public employees' freedom of association, the Supreme Court considered the various claims that union security arrangements strengthen labor-management relations and that patronage promotes democracy, loyalty to elected officials, and governmental efficiency. However, using the public service model, it concluded that these interests could be secured by means that were less invasive of public employees' First Amendment rights. The patronage cases illustrate that the constitutional law is forever changing and that even "a practice as old as the Republic" may eventually succumb to new constitutional thinking (*Elrod v. Burns*, 1976:376). *Chicago Teachers Union*, in particular, illustrates why public personnel managers must stay abreast of the constitutional law. It introduced, on a constitutional basis, an additional adjudicatory function into public personnel administration.

PRIVACY

The Fourth Amendment affords protection against "unreasonable searches and seizures." During the 1980s, as drug testing became common, the scope of the amendment's application to public employees emerged as an important issue in public personnel management. In law enforcement cases, the amendment requires that searches and seizures be pursuant to warrants or, where these are impracticable, probable cause (that is, reasonable suspicion that an individual is engaged in criminal wrong doing). But under the public service model, the amendment is construed to require much less for non-law-enforcement, administrative searches by the governmental employer. Again, this is because governments have a significant interest in the performance of their employees.

In *O'Connor v. Ortega* (1987), a divided Supreme Court agreed that "individuals do not lose Fourth Amendment rights merely because they work for the government instead of a private employer" (723). The justices also agreed that the threshold question is whether the employee has a reasonable expectation of privacy in the workplace. Such an expectation is defined as one that, according to the courts, society is prepared to share. If there is no reasonable expectation of privacy, then the search will not violate the Fourth Amendment. If there is such an expectation, then the search must be reasonable in its inception and scope. In practice, this approach often requires that cases be analyzed individually on their own merits rather than according to broad principles.

O'Connor requires that workplace searches of offices, desks, files, and so forth be based on a reasonable suspicion that an employee may have engaged in behavior for which discipline would be appropriate. Many drug testing programs involve suspicionless searches. That is, they require random or universal testing regardless of whether there is a reasonable basis for believing that any particular employee uses illegal drugs. In *National Treasury Employees Union v. Von Raab* (1989), the Supreme Court ruled that suspicionless drug testing may be constitutional if the overall program is reasonable. However, it limited its holding to those employees who carry firearms and/or are engaged in drug interdiction. The Court noted that such employees have a reduced expectation of privacy "by virtue of the special, and obvious, physical and ethical demands of those positions" (*National Treasury Employees Union v. Von Raab,* 1989:711).

AIDS and other health testing present similar issues. Blood- and urine-testing regimes must be reasonable in terms of purpose and procedure. However, as such practices become more common it is increasingly difficult for employees and applicants to claim that they violate a reasonable expectation of privacy (see *Fowler v. New York,* 1989). A federal circuit court of appeals held that contact with an agency's clients, who were mentally retarded, was not enough to justify AIDS and hepatitis B testing (*Glover v. Eastern Nebraska Community Office of Retardation,* 1989). By contrast, anyone engaged in law enforcement, public safety, and national security positions can be subjected to a reasonably designed suspicionless drug testing program. It should be remembered that such programs are for administrative objectives, not criminal prosecution.

From the perspective of public personnel systems it is important to consider whether suspicionless testing is cost effective. The fact that a practice such as drug testing is constitutional does not mean it is desirable. One study found extremely low "hit rates," with positives in the range of only 0–1.7 percent in a variety of federal agencies (Thompson, Riccucci, and Ban, 1990). Unfortunately, it is difficult to interpret data of this kind. Are drug tests unnecessary because the overwhelming number of employees do not use illegal substances? Or do the tests effectively deter illegal drug use?

LIBERTY

The broad issue of public employees' constitutional liberty has also been the subject of significant litigation. This area of constitutional law is called "substantive due process." It focuses on the meaning of the word "liberty" in the Fifth and Fourteenth Amendments, which respectively prohibit the federal government and states (and their political subunits) from depriving anyone within their jurisdictions of life, liberty, or property without due process of law. Liberty clearly includes protection against unreasonable searches and seizures, free exercise of religion, such rights as freedom of speech and assembly, and other parts of the Bill of Rights. However, it also includes some personal freedoms, including the right to travel, which are not mentioned in the Constitution.

Problems arise in this area because governments often try to control their employees' behavior for a variety of work-related, morality, and public policy reasons. For instance, in the 1960s, Senator Sam Ervin found that public employees had been requested "to lobby in local city councils for fair housing ordinances, to go out and make speeches on any number of subjects, to supply flower and grass seed for beautification projects, and to paint other people's houses" (United States Senate 1967:9). More commonly they are pressured to take part in blood, United Way, or similar campaigns. Such conditions are likely to be constitutional unless they invade fundamental rights or are only tenuously connected to the interests of the governmental employer (see *United States v. National Treasury Employees Union,* 1995). The most important areas of liberty addressed by the Supreme Court have been public employees' reproductive decisions, grooming preferences, and residency.

Cleveland Board of Education v. LaFleur (1974) focused on the constitutionality of mandatory, unpaid maternity leaves for public school teachers. However, the Supreme Court's ruling that the leaves in question were unconstitutionally restrictive was broad enough to provide constitutional protection to public employees' choices regarding reproduction. The Court stated that ". . . it had long recognized that freedom of personal choice in matters of marriage and family life is one of the liberties protected by the Due Process Clause of the Fourteenth Amendment" and that "there is a right 'to be free from unwarranted governmental intrusion into matters so fundamentally affecting a person as the decision whether to bear or beget a child'" (639).

In the Court's view, the liberty to bear children must remain free of undue or purposeless governmental interference. Choices with regard to grooming and residence have been given lesser protection. In *Kelley v. Johnson* (1976) the Court found no constitutional barrier to grooming regulations applying to male police officers. Although a lower court held that "choice of personal appearance is an ingredient of an individual's personal liberty" (241), the Supreme Court placed the burden of persuasion on the employee challenging the regulation to "demonstrate that there is *no* rational connection between the regulation . . . and the promotion of safety of persons and property" (247; emphasis added). The challengers were unable to do this despite the fact that the government's rationale was exceedingly weak. It claimed that the grooming standards would make the police—who were in uniforms—more readily identifiable to the public and that they would promote esprit de corps—despite the police union's opposition to them.

Finally, in *McCarthy v. Philadelphia Civil Service Commission* (1976), the Court upheld the constitutionality of residency requirements for firefighters. It did so without much discussion and in the face of McCarthy's rather compelling concern for the well-being of his family. However, the decision remains good law and, consequently, public employees can be required to live within the jurisdictions in which they work.

EQUAL PROTECTION

Contemporary equal protection analysis under the Fourteenth and Fifth Amendments is of critical importance to public personnel management because it controls the constitutionality of affirmative action and procedures that have a disparate impact on different social groups. It also regulates overt discrimination against individuals based on race, ethnicity, citizenship, gender, age, and additional factors. Equal protection has a clear, if complex, logical structure.

The threshold question is whether a law, policy, decision, or practice classifies individuals according to some characteristic such as race, gender, wealth, residency, or education. Such classifications can be implicit. They need not be overt. However, in the absence of a classification there will be no violation of equal protection.

The importance of finding a classification was brought out in *Washington v. Davis* (1976). The Supreme Court made it clear that public personnel practices that are neutral on their face but bear more harshly on one racial group than another, as has often been the case with merit examinations, will not be unconstitutional simply because they have a disparate impact. To violate equal protection, they must manifest a discriminatory purpose of some kind. The Court emphasized that such a purpose need not be "express or appear on the face of the statute" and that it could be "inferred from the totality of the relevant facts" (*Washington v. Davis*, 1976:241–242). The existence of a classification will often indicate a discriminatory purpose because its intent is to treat people differently based on race, gender, wealth, or some other basis.

Suspect Classifications

Once it is determined that there is a classification, a three-tier structure comes into play. Classifications based on race or ethnicity are considered "suspect" because, historically, such measures have been used to disadvantage members of minority groups.

It is very difficult to justify suspect classifications. The courts subject them to "strict scrutiny," which means that the government will bear a heavy burden of persuasion and be given little deference. These classifications will be constitutional only if they serve a compelling governmental interest and are "narrowly tailored."

To date, workforce diversity has not been considered a compelling governmental interest by the Supreme Court. Affirmative action for members of minority groups may be viable if its purpose is to remedy past, proven discrimination against racial and/or ethnic groups. The leading case in this area is *United States v. Paradise* (1987), in which a federal judge imposed hiring and promotion quotas for African Americans in the Alabama Department of Public Safety. The case so divided the Supreme Court that it was unable to form a majority opinion. Nevertheless, most of the justices agreed that the remedy was a constitutional means to overcoming decades of discrimination and resistance to equal protection in the Alabama state patrol.

A majority also agreed that the relief was adequately narrowly tailored. In the public personnel context, narrow tailoring requires that five conditions be met:

1. Less drastic and equally efficacious remedies, such as fines, are impractical or unavailable.

2. There must be a fixed stopping point at which use of the classification ends. This can be based on time, e.g., 3–5 years, or successful remediation of the previous violations of equal protection, such as minorities having gained 25 percent of the positions in the governmental workforce involved.

3. The quotas, goals, or targets must be proportionate to the racial and/or ethnic composition of the relevant population base. For example a 25 percent quota for African Americans would be disproportionate in Vermont, but not in Alabama.

4. Waivers must be available so that if the agency is unable to find qualified candidates, then it will not be forced to hire or promote incompetents, on the one hand, or become significantly understaffed, on the other.

5. The approach cannot place a harsh burden on "innocent third parties." Firing or fur-loughing nonminorities to free up positions for minorities would be such a burden (see *Wygant v. Jackson Board of Education,* 1986).

It is important to note that racial and ethnic classifications will be considered suspect even if their purpose is to enhance minority employment opportunities. At various times since the Supreme Court began dealing with affirmative action in the 1970s, efforts have been made to distinguish between classifications which create "invidious discrimination" and those that are "benign" in the sense that their pur-pose is to promote the employment interests of minorities and women. In the 1995 case of *Adarand Constructors v. Pena,* a 5–4 majority of the Supreme Court sought to lay to rest the contention that benign racial or ethnic classifications pose little threat to equal protection because they lack a discriminatory purpose. The Court held that ". . . all racial classifications, imposed by whatever federal, state, or local gov-ernmental actor, must be analyzed by a reviewing court under strict scrutiny" (227). In the majority's view, requiring such scrutiny is the only way to ensure that there is no intent to discriminate, or if there is one, it is somehow justified by a compelling governmental interest and is narrowly tailored. In a concurring opin-ion, Justice Clarence Thomas took pains to explain that, in his view, the entire distinction between invidious and benign was untenable and irrelevant: ". . . government-sponsored racial discrimination based on benign prejudice is just as noxious as discrimination inspired by malicious prejudice. In each instance, it is racial discrimination, plain and simple" (241).

Nonsuspect Classification

Classifications based on residency, wealth, age, and similar factors are non-suspect. Public policies use such classifications for a variety of reasons—eligibility for benefits of some kind, voting, granting drivers' licenses, and so forth. They are subject to ordinary scrutiny, which is also called the "rational basis" test. The bur-den of persuasion is generally on the challenger to show that such classifications are not rationally related to the achievement of a legitimate governmental purpose. The courts typically pay a good deal of deference to the judgment of the govern-mental employer in such cases. For instance, the Supreme Court held that a state could require police to retire at age 50, even though many officers would be phys-ically and mentally fit to continue in their jobs (*Massachusetts Board of Retirement v. Murgia,* 1976).

Quasi-Suspect Classifications

Classifications based on gender are "quasi-suspect" and subject to interme-diate scrutiny. The burden is likely to be on the government to show that the clas-sification is substantially related to the achievement of important governmental ob-jectives. Originally gender-based classifications were considered nonsuspect. As the society and judiciary became more conscious of the discriminatory effects of efforts to "protect" women from long working hours, physically demanding jobs, and so on, these classifications were raised to an intermediate level. In the future, they may be treated similarly to suspect classifications as the government may be called upon to provide an "exceedingly persuasive justification" for them (*United States v. Virginia,* 1996:533).

Intermediate scrutiny poses a challenge to practices based on traditional thinking about "male" and "female" jobs, workplace behavior, physical strength, and other capacities. Practices based on past models of sex roles may be vulnerable to constitutional challenge. Although it is currently easier in a technical sense to justify affirmative action for women than for racial or ethnic minorities, personnelists should be alert to the likelihood that the courts will find such programs unconstitutional in the absence of a very strong governmental interest.

PROCEDURAL DUE PROCESS

The Fifth and Fourteenth Amendments also guarantee individuals a fair procedure when they are being deprived of life, liberty, or property by the federal or state and local governments. The extent of procedural due process to be afforded in administrative matters depends on a balancing of three factors: 1) the individual's interests, 2) the risk that the procedures used, if any, will result in an erroneous decision, and the probable value of additional procedures in reducing the likelihood of error, and 3) the government's interests, including administrative burdens and financial costs, in using the procedures in place. Full-fledged adjudicatory hearings, with the right to confrontation, cross-examination, and legal representation will be required when the individual's interest is great enough to command a very low error rate. Where the individual's interest is minimal, nothing more than notice of the decisionmaker's rationale and opportunity to respond may be required. In public employment, the balancing takes place within the framework of the public service model.

In *Board of Regents v. Roth* (1972), the Supreme Court identified four individual interests which would give public employees a right to a hearing in dismissal actions: (1) where the dismissal was in retaliation for the exercise of constitutionally protected rights, such as freedom of speech; (2) "where a person's good name, reputation, honor or integrity is at stake because of what the government is doing to him . . ." (573); (3) where the dismissal diminishes a public employee's future employability; and (4) where the employee has a property right or property interest in the position, such as tenure or a contract.

The public service model is important in determining both the timing of the hearing and its extensiveness. In *Cleveland Board of Education v. Loudermill* (1985), the Supreme Court held that a security guard who apparently lied on his application was entitled to notice of the charges against him, an explanation of the employer's evidence, and an opportunity to respond prior to being terminated. The Court noted that Loundermill had a property right in his job by virtue of being a "classified civil servant." The pretermination requirement is as an "initial check against mistaken decisions—essentially, a determination of whether there are reasonable grounds to believe that the charges against the employee are true and support the proposed action" (545–546). This serves the interests of the employee, but also those of the public and the government in not incurring additional personnel costs through unnecessary turnover and the possibility of subsequent litigation. A more elaborate post-termination hearing was available to Loudermill under Ohio's civil service law.

The balance changes when suspensions are involved. In *Gilbert v. Homar* (1997), the Supreme Court reasoned that no due process was required prior to suspending a law enforcement officer who had been charged with a felony. Here, the governmental and public interests in an effective workforce outweighed those of the employee. As the Court explained, "So long as a suspended employee receives a sufficiently prompt post-suspension hearing, the lost income is relatively insubstantial, and fringe benefits such as health and life insurance are often not affected at all" (932). The Court also noted that the government has reasonable grounds for the suspension of an employee who is formally charged with criminal behavior.

An adverse action triggering procedural due process protections may be based on a mix of factors, some of which involve constitutional rights and others which do not. For instance, an employee like McPherson may be incompetent as well as engaged in offensive speech. In such a case, the employer will have the opportunity to demonstrate "by a preponderance of the evidence that it would have reached the same decision . . . even in the absence of the protected conduct" (*Mount Healthy School District Board of Education v. Doyle*, 1977:287).

Because procedural due process analysis considers the probability that the government is acting in error, the public employer will often investigate an employee before taking disciplinary action. Employees who lie or make misleading statements to investigators in an effort to defend themselves may be disciplined for their falsehoods. In *Lachance v. Erickson* (1998), the Supreme Court held that such behavior is not protected by the due process clause. Where an investigation may lead to criminal charges, the employee has a right to remain silent under the Fifth Amendment. However, the due process right to be heard does not protect an employee from sanctions for disingenuousness.

As in other areas, the public service model's balancing approach in procedural due process cases may not afford sufficiently specific guidance to personnelists and other public employees. For instance, how "prompt" does a prompt post-suspension hearing have to be? The best way to keep track of such questions and answers is to follow the case law in one's jurisdiction, including rulings by the federal district courts and circuit courts of appeals.

LIABILITY

It is important to emphasize that for the public personnel manager, knowledge of the constitutional rights of public employees is anything but academic. As a result of several Supreme Court decisions over the past three decades, such knowledge has become a positive job requirement. Today, a public personnel manager in a state or local government may well be *personally* liable for compensatory and even punitive damages for infringing on "clearly established . . . constitutional rights of which a reasonable person would have known" (*Harlow v. Fitzgerald*, 1982:818; *Smith v. Wade*, 1983; *Hafer v. Melo*, 1991). Personnelists at the national level generally have greater protection from personal liability. However, their actions and policies may be reversed by the Merit Systems Protection Board, which serves as a check on unconstitutional treatment of federal employees (*Bush v. Lucas*, 1983).

Local governments and agencies can also be held liable for money damages when their policies are closely connected to violations of individuals' constitutional rights (*Monell v. New York City Department of Social Services*, 1978; *Pembaur v. Cincinnati*, 1986). A personnelist charged with implementing an unconstitutional law or policy has a constitutional right to disobey in order not to infringe on others' protected rights (*Harley v. Schuylkill County*, 1979).

In addition to the constitutional concerns noted in this chapter, each state has a constitutional law of its own which bears on public personnel matters. Where a state's protection of rights such as privacy or substantive due process exceeds that of the national Constitution, state and local personnelists must meet the higher standard. Gaining reasonable knowledge of the constitutional law that governs one's actions is the best way to avoid violating rights. Public personnelists do not need to be lawyers; they do need to recognize when decisions, actions, procedures, or policies may be vulnerable to constitutional attack. That much is doable, but what are its implications for promoting contemporary state-of-the-art strategic personnel management?

IMPLICATIONS FOR MODERN HUMAN RESOURCE MANAGEMENT

In recent years, the old model of public personnel administration which focused on developing, implementing, and enforcing personnel rules has been expanded to include aligning an organization's personnel practices with its strategic planning activities. This newer approach, called "strategic human resource management," requires personnelists to become partners with managers and employees. In the process, personnelists take on diverse roles that increase their exposure to organization-wide, as well as employee specific, personnel issues. Knowledge of constitutional law can enable them to be proactive in building constitutional protections into organizational practices and cultures. The objective would be to maximize the organization's objectives within the framework of what is permissible under the Constitution.

Bringing constitutional law into public personnel policy fits nicely with the personnelists' three new roles in strategic human resource management: (1) strategic partner; (2) employee champion; and (3) change agent (Ulrich 1997). As a strategic partner, personnelists work with management to "identify human resource systems that make strategy happen" (Ulrich 1997:26). This includes using recruitment, compensation, training, downsizing, or other personnel systems to achieve organizational goals. Knowledge of equal protection analysis is often critical in these areas, as for example when an organization wants to promote social diversity in its workforce. As employee champions, personnelists try to increase employee loyalty by helping managers listen and respond to employees' concerns. Here, personnelists can enhance communication by explaining the parameters of First Amendment rights. They can also build in procedural due process to protect employees against unfair (and unconstitutional) reprisals. As change agents, personnelists must balance the competing forces of innovation and stability, as well as delegation and control, to help managers and employees deal with changes in the work environment. In this area, the public service model can serve as a useful guide.

A constantly changing workplace is currently the norm for many government agencies. The push to "reinvent" the public sector in order to improve program results generally serves two components of the public service model—the governmental and public interests. However, the interests and rights of employees may receive limited attention. The tools of reinvention—downsizing, re-engineering, information technology, and outsourcing—can increase the immediacy of the Constitution to public administration.

For instance, downsizing and re-engineering can bump up against procedural due process and equal protection rights. Where civil service status or other property interests in employment are involved, dismissals cannot constitutionally be arbitrary, capricious, or discriminatory. If individual employees are picked as targets for reductions in force, they will almost certainly have substantial due process rights. Depending on the circumstances, and especially where agencies have been under court order to increase diversity (as in the *United States v. Paradise* case mentioned earlier), downsizing that has a harmful impact on the employment interests of minorities or women will be subject to challenge under equal protection. Information technology, such as e-mail, voice mail, and database systems, pose obvious threats to employees' Fourth Amendment privacy rights.

Outsourcing presents a special set of constitutional issues when it involves a public function (such as incarceration) or so enmeshes the government and a private organization that it is impossible to tell where one begins and the other ends (e.g., public-private partnerships). In those circumstances, the private organization and its employees may well become liable for violating individuals' constitutional rights. A private prison guard has the same constitutional obligations to the prisoners as does one who is publicly employed. However, the private guard faces a tougher liability standard. Unlike a public employee, he or she will be liable for the violation of constitutional rights regardless of whether they were clearly established or a reasonable person would have known of them (*Richardson v. McKnight*, 1997). As change agents, public personnelists could bring this constitutional dimension to bear on organizational decisions concerning outsourcing. Are the private organizations likely to be involved able to protect constitutional rights? Could they withstand liability suits? Would it be better public policy to keep the function within the government agency in order to make sure that the employees are properly trained with respect to their constitutional responsibilities?

When public personnelists are allowed to expand their roles and operate strategically, they work closer with managers on getting results as well as on day-to-day personnel concerns. They can project or see the impact of different organizational decisions on personnel issues and practices. A proactive role in alerting decisionmakers to constitutional issues will not only protect rights, which is one of the Constitution's main purposes, but also reduce susceptibility to law suits.

The expansion of personnelists' roles to include strategic partner, employee champion, and change agent makes the job of personnelists more challenging because they have greater interaction with managers and employees on several levels. But incorporating a constitutional dimension into strategic human resource management will give managers better and more consistent information and skills to protect employees' rights as well as to achieve organizational goals within the framework of our democratic-constitutional government.

REFERENCES

Abood v. Detroit Board of Education. 1977. 431 U.S. 209.

Adarand Constructors v. Pena. 1995. 515 U.S. 200.

AFSCME v. Woodward. 1969. 406 F.2d 137.

Board of Regents v. Roth. 1972. 408 U.S. 564.

Branti v. Finkel. 1980. 445 U.S. 507.

Broaderick v. Oklahoma. 1973. 413 U.S. 601.

Bush v. Lucas. 1983. 462 U.S. 367.

Chicago Teachers Union v. Hudson. 1986. 475 U.S. 292.

Civil Service Commission v. National Association of Letter Carriers. 1973. 413 U.S. 548.

Cleveland Board of Education v. LaFleur. 1974. 414 U.S. 632.

Cleveland Board of Education v. Loudermill. 1985. 470 U.S. 532.

Elfrbandt v. Russell. 1966. 384 U.S. 11.

Elrod v. Burns. 1976. 427 U.S. 347.

Fowler v. New York. 1989. 704 F. Supp. 1264.

Gilbert v. Homar. 1997. 520 U.S. 924.

Glover v. Eastern Nebraska Community Office of Retardation. 1989. 867 F.2d 461.

Hafer v. Melo. 1991. 502 U.S. 21.

Harley v. Schuylkill County. 1979. 476 F. Supp. 191.

Harlow v. Fitzgerald. 1982. 457 U.S. 800.

Harvard Law Review. 1984. Developments in the Law—Public Employment. 97:1611–1800.

Kelley v. Johnson. 1976. 425 U.S. 238.

Lachance v. Erickson. 1998. 522 U.S. 262.

Massachusetts Board of Retirement v. Murgia. 1976. 427 U.S. 304.

McAuliffe v. New Bedford. 1892. 155 Mass. 216.

McCarthy v. Philadelphia Civil Service Commission. 1976. 424 U.S. 645.

Monell v. New York City Department of Social Services. 1978. 436 U.S. 658.

Mount Healthy School District Board of Education v. Doyle. 1977. 429 U.S. 274.

National Treasury Employees Union v. Von Raab. 1989. 489 U.S. 656.

O'Connor v. Ortega. 1987. 480 U.S. 709.

Pembaur v. Cincinnati. 1986. 475 U.S. 469.

Pickering v. Board of Education. 1968. 391 U.S. 563.

Rankin v. McPherson. 1987. 483 U.S. 378.

Richardson v. McKnight. 1997. 521 U.S. 399.

ROSENBLOOM, DAVID H. 1971. *Federal Service and the Constitution.* Ithaca, N.Y.: Cornell University Press.

Rutan v. Republican Party of Illinois. 1990. 497 U.S. 62.

Shelton v. Tucker. 1960. 364 U.S. 479.

Smith v. Wade. 1983. 461 U.S. 30.

THOMPSON, FRANK, NORMA RICCUCCI, and CAROLYN BAN. 1990. Drug Testing in the Federal Workplace. Conference paper, American Political Science Association, 1990.

ULRICH, DAVID. 1997. *Human Resource Champions: The Next Agenda for Adding Value and Delivering Results.* Boston, Mass.: Harvard Business School Press.

United Public Workers v. Mitchell. 1947. 330 U.S. 75.

United States Senate 1967. *Protecting Privacy and the Rights of Federal Employees.* S. Rept. 519. 90th Cong., 1st sess. August 21.

United States v. National Treasury Employees Union. 1995. 513 U.S. 454.

United States v. Paradise. 1987. 480 U.S. 149.

United States v. Virginia. 1996. 518 U.S. 515.

Washington v. Davis. 1976. 426 U.S. 229.

Waters v. Churchill. 1994. 511 U.S. 661.

Wygant v. Jackson Board of Education. 1986. 476 U.S. 267.

4

Personnel Management in the Local Government Setting

ALAN L. SALTZSTEIN
California State University-Fullerton

The public administration profession assumes that personnel management is similar at all levels of government. We rarely differentiate "local" government personnel administration from personnel administration elsewhere. Yet there are basic differences between levels of government in the American system. This chapter argues that the local government setting has a profound effect on the practice of public personnel administration. The important features of American local government that influence personnel practice are these:

1. The legal position of local government is a weak one, requiring a great deal of dependence on state, and to some extent federal, policies. Thus, local officials' power is limited by court rulings and legislation more frequently than occurs at other levels.

2. Local governments are embedded in a network of vertical and horizontal government relations. Other jurisdictions can make demands on them. Needed funds must be obtained from other governments. Actions of local governments, thus, are closely intertwined with those of other governments. Personnel managers, therefore, have less autonomy than is likely at other levels of government.

3. The political traditions and practices of local governments differ from those at other levels. Stereotypical replicas of both the machine and reform traditions are present. Strong executives are common and electoral mechanisms are weak. The private sector often has a more significant political influence on local government than on state or national governments.

4. Local governments' actions, and by extension personnel policies, are related to variations in the social, economic, and political characteristics of the community.

5. The organizational setting of local government is typically characterized by diverse subunits, strong professional and employee organizations, and active clientele pressures. Central management often is relatively weak compared to management in some of the functional units. Personnel managers, therefore, face well-organized and often powerful adversaries.

The local government context, then, frames the character of personnel practice. Local government personnel specialists must understand the setting to carry out their mission effectively.

CONSTITUTIONAL LAW AND PRACTICE
LIMIT LOCAL GOVERNMENT POWERS

A sovereign government is one that possesses the power to make its own decisions, free from the legal influence or control of other governments. No governments are wholly sovereign. Legal traditions, economic and military realities, and the beliefs and practices of the citizens limit the authority of all governments. American cities, however, possess less sovereignty than most. No specific rights are granted to them in the federal Constitution. The Constitution makes no mention of local governments. The legal assumption then is that cities fall under the jurisdiction of the states.

In practice, states often grant some degree of autonomy to cities through charters and legislation. Even in the most independent of cities, however, state and federal judges remain frequent arbiters of city actions. In extreme cases, judges and state officials have taken over the reigns of government directly. A vivid example of such authority occurred in the Boston school system in 1974 when a federal judge assumed authority over the administration of the system in order to implement a busing order (Lukas, 1985). Another occurred in Orange County, California, in 1995 when State officials dislodged the elected Board of Supervisors following a drain of financial resources that resulted in bankruptcy. These actions can occur because the U.S. Supreme Court has tended to interpret the powers of local governments narrowly, generally following what is referred to as "Dillon's Rule," named after an important judicial ruling by an Iowa judge in 1911:

> It is a general and undisputed proposition of laws that a municipal corporation possess and can exercise the following powers and no others; First those granted in express words; second those necessary or fairly interpreted in or incidental to the powers expressly granted and third, those essential to the accomplishment of declared objectives and purposes of the corporation, not simply convenient but indispensable (Dillon: 1872 in Frug, 1980:1154)

While courts may have the right to control local governments, their actions have often expanded local sovereignty, drawing inspiration from American and continental political thought and the traditions of local self-government in Great Britain and colonial North America. Thus, court decisions have not consistently limited the powers of local governments nor always sided with federal authorities. State-granted city charters, for example, have legal standing. Unquestionably, however, the U.S. Supreme Court has assumed jurisdiction when conflicting interpretations of legislative intent or governmental practice have been raised. The decisions of state and federal courts, therefore, are important to personnel policy makers.

The recent history of the Fair Labor Standards Act as applied to local governments demonstrates the ability of the courts and Congress to alter local government personnel practices. The Act mandates, among other things, minimum-wage and maximum-hour provisions for employees. In 1974 the Act was amended to include state and local government employees for the first time. Cities in particular felt the application of these laws interfered with their ability to control personnel policies and budgets. Fire departments, in which overnight shifts are included in a 60-hour work week, would experience large increases in personnel costs if all hours above 40 required overtime pay.

The Supreme Court in *National League of Cities et al. v. W. J. Usery,* Secretary of Labor (1976) sided with the subgovernments, arguing that the Act interfered with the ability of states and cities to perform their duties as prescribed by the Tenth Amendment, which reserves to the states all powers not explicitly granted to the national government in the Constitution. As stated by Justice Rehnquist, "If Congress may withdraw from the States the authority to make fundamental employment decisions upon which their systems for performance of these functions must rest, we think there will be little left of the States' separate and fundamental existence." Thus, the Amendment was ruled unconstitutional where applied to traditional local governmental functions such as fire protection, public works, parks and recreation, and police.

In 1985, however, in the case of *Garcia v. San Antonio Metropolitan Transit Authority,* the Court overturned the *Usery* decision, arguing that the constitutional authority to "regulate commerce within foreign nations and among the several states and with Indian Tribes" (Article I, Section 8) gives Congress the right to regulate wages and hours. Analysts argued that the costs of compliance would be considerable, particularly for police and fire departments (Howard, 1985:739). The Court, however, based its decision on the legal inferiority of local governments in relation to states and the federal government.

Congress and the President responded to the concerns of cities and the Fair Labor Standards Act was amended in 1985. The amendments restored some of the autonomy local personnel officials had assumed prior to *Garcia*. States and localities were given a reasonable time to comply with the decision, and modifications were made in the need to enforce overtime provisions (Puls, 1986:85).

As the Court has shifted in a more conservative direction in the 1980s, proponents of the rights of cities have found signs that rulings might lead to a return to the *Usery* position. A 1993 case, *Moreau v. Klevenhagen,* indicates a tilt in that direction (Haas, 1991). The Court ruled that local governments have leeway under the Fair Labor Standards Act to give employees compensatory time rather than overtime payments when no collective bargaining agreement is present or when that agreement does not deal with the issue of compensatory time. *Christensen et al. v. Harris County et al.,* handed down by the court in the 2000 session, supported the policy of Harris County, Texas, which required employees to schedule time off in order to reduce the amount of accrued time. Thus with each court decision since the *Garcia* case, the Supreme Court has given local governments greater discretion interpreting rulings of the Fair Labor Standards Act. With each decision, local government personnel policy changes. Thus following the decisions of the judicial system has a pronounced effect on local government personnel policy.

THE FEDERAL SYSTEM LIMITS POLICY-MAKING AUTHORITY

Local governments exist within a complex setting of intergovernmental relations. Legal and political inferiority and fiscal dependence have made them subject to influence through federal grant programs and regulatory practices. Most local governments coexist with numerous other nearby governments and compete for more lucrative taxpayers. This competition dominates local government policy to a much greater extent than occurs at other levels of government. Thus personnel policy often has less emphasis in a local government setting. The private sector also exerts a significant influence on personnel policy. In many governments contracting for services is common and government agencies must compete with other governments and the private sector for employees. Personnel policy thus exists in an environment of numerous competing influences.

Federal and State Mandates

The inferior legal position of local governments subjects them to mandates from state and national legislation. These often take the form of requiring certain personnel. The inferior legal position of local governments subjects them often to direct control by state agencies and laws. "States can coerce their local governments into compliance with state policy objectives, and they do. This is perhaps most evident in states' long-standing propensity to mandate policy responsibilities to local governments often without providing the funds or taxing authority needed by local governments to carry out these newly assigned responsibilities" (Hanson, 1990:62).

Counties in California, for instance, must adhere to merit principles in personnel practices in the areas of health, welfare, and civil defense. Either the county personnel system must be accredited by the state or the state directly provides personnel services for the county, and therefore controls who is hired, fired, and promoted. State collective bargaining laws in California also apply to local governments obligating them to meet and confer with employees and bargain with regard to wages, hours, and working conditions (Koehler, 1983:137–140).

Relief from the financial impact of Federal mandates has followed from an important piece of legislation, The *Unfunded Mandates Reform Act of 1995*. This act gives members of Congress the right to raise a "point of order" any time there is a cost of at least $50 million to any congressional mandate imposed on state and local governments and requires consultation and cost-benefit analyses of any measure that significantly effects state and local governments (Kincaid, 1995). President Clinton significantly strengthened the act through an executive order in 1999, requiring significant consultation with state and local officials in any regulatory policy that affects state and local governments. These measures enhance the influence of state and local governments in intergovernmental policies, counteracting, to some extent, the legally inferior position.

Goals of Local Governments in the Federal System

City officials' goals are influenced by the power, jurisdiction, and resources of other units of government. Peterson's influential book *City Limits* (1981) argues that the place of cities within the federal system forces public officials to pursue growth and development goals at the expense of other concerns. Peterson maintains that city politics can best be described as "limited politics" (1981:4). Policy choices are affected by the larger political economy of the nation. The fundamental difference between the federal and local governments is the need to compete with other cities for new resources. City income is acquired primarily from the sources of wealth within city borders. Failure to attract wealth directly affects the city government's ability to meet its financial needs. Thus, cities by nature compete with one another for industry, commercial centers, and wealthy residents. Policies that enhance city wealth, called "developmental" by Peterson, dominate the city agenda.

Cities implement "allocational" policies, those which have "neither much of a positive nor much of a negative effect on the local economy" (Peterson, 1981:44), only as needed to complement developmental policies. Personnel functions are considered allocational. They are funded only to the extent that good employee practices are needed to attract the proper personnel to aid development policies or enhance the image of the city. "Redistributive" policies, those that assist the lower class at the expense of the wealthy, are resisted by local government officials because they have no effect on economic growth. Human resource and welfare policies are redistributive.

Peterson's typology assumes that competition for resources dominates the policy-making process at the local level. Allocational and redistributive concerns have less of a role in policy making because city officials see resource acquisition as their primary goal. Federal officials, on the other hand, assume that the resource base of the national government is unaffected by their acts. Thus, they can concentrate on allocational and redistributive policies. States, Peterson argues, occupy a midpoint between city and federal levels in interest in developmental policies.

Critics maintain that Peterson exaggerates the role of resource acquisition and downplays political conflict in city policy making (Stone and Saunders, 1987:1-20). His typology may have more relevance in growing areas and newer communities dominated by business-oriented public entrepreneurs and managers rather than community or party-based politicians. Others maintain, however, that the tax revolt, years of hard financial times in many states, and the decline of federal funds have encouraged the search for new resources in most cities.

When Peterson's analysis describes the behavior of city officials, personnel policy becomes a less important area of concern than those actions directly related to economic development. The personnel administrator in this setting may have less influence on policy because, by definition, he or she is an advocate of policies tangential to the dominant goals of central management and elected officials.

Relations Between Local Governmental Units and With the Private Sector

Cities exist adjacent to other municipal governments, often within the same metropolitan area. Various local jurisdictions and often the state government share common labor markets and frequently compete for the location of prized resources. Professional associations and the media encourage flows of information across such competing jurisdictions. Osborne and Gaebler's influential book, *Reinventing Government,* argues that this competition leads many cities to develop creative, cost-conscious solutions to public problems. Contracting with the private sector and other jurisdictions, automation, and the application of new methods and approaches, they suggest, are common solutions to a competitive environment and they lead to better government (1992).

Viewing local governments as competitors requires a different kind of personnel system. If the contracting of city services is an option, city personnel positions lack the security assumed under a civil service system. Employees will have less loyalty to the organization and more interest in gaining skills that will enhance their employability both within and without the organization.

Competition for valuable employees may affect salary structures. Wealthier cities, for instance, frequently try to lure skilled police officers from other cities by offering better salaries and benefits. Likewise, employee organizations and unions compare salaries with other jurisdictions and the private sector in an effort to improve compensation for their members. Thus, the measures of comparison for local government wages and salaries are often more tangible than in state or federal government. The presence of such competition may act to control personnel costs (Schneider, 1989).

With greater flexibility in service-delivery options, the ability of cities to contract or expand certain kinds of services increases. Thus, if city officials perceive that police services should be increased and human services decreased, the contracting option provides them with greater flexibility in doing so. Job security, frequently considered a trait of public employment, is less likely.

Those occupations lacking in prestige or demand may suffer in comparison to jobs that city officials perceive to be more in demand. Thus public safety salaries may increase while those of recreation and human services decrease. Perhaps this explains the frequency with which comparable worth becomes an issue in local government? Personnel resources may migrate to the more prestigious and competitive occupations. This may cause those occupations where the market is less competitive and prestigious to suffer lower compensation levels.

The backbone of the traditional civil service system is a series of rules designed to treat all employees similarly. Common salary structures, position classification based on duties, and job security enforced by a civil service commission assume that a similar set of rules governs all employees. A competitive system challenges this point of view. Employee conditions are likely to be different if the services are contracted. Salaries may be based on what market conditions or the needs of the organization dictate. In these ways, the local government setting tends to encourage differential treatment of employees.

POLITICAL TRADITIONS AND PRACTICES OF LOCAL GOVERNMENT AFFECT PERSONNEL POLICY

Much of the political history of American local governments is focused on two models of political organization: the "machine" or "boss system," said to describe most large cities around the turn of the century, and the "reform" model, based on principles of the Progressive Movement of the early twentieth century. While neither exists in its pure form today, the operations of most cities bear a strong resemblance to one or the other. Certain personnel policies are central to both types; thus, competing models of personnel management are present. The writings of Osborne and Gaebler (1992) and other accounts of recent changes in city government suggest that a third model, which contains some characteristics of both, may be emerging.

The Urban Machine as a Personnel System

The goal of the urban machine is to coordinate diverse and distinct subcommunities and provide a limited amount of central direction to city policy. This model assumes cohesive, culturally distinct neighborhoods with community organizations designed to promote the interests of the group. The "boss" coordinates the separate communities and relies on community members to acquire votes. In return, loyalists receive material inducements, one of the most important of which is jobs.

The machine as a personnel system is based on community identification and political loyalty, and often contains strong ethnic and racial components. Municipal employees work to serve the interests of the boss and provide a conduit of support to their ethnic or racial community. Personal loyalty and knowledge of the voting district or ward are the primary requisites for employment. Employees are expected to reflect the values of the community and to be sensitive to the community's needs. As Hahn points out, "The skills rewarded by the machine seemed to place greater emphasis upon sensitivity to the concerns of others and the capacity to establish rapport than upon technical expertise or accomplishments." Personnel decisions reflect a Jacksonian belief that all are intrinsically capable of serving in government positions (Hahn, 1977:41–42). Where the trappings of a civil service system exist, the rules are likely to be violated when they do not serve the interests of the machine (Tolchin and Tolchin, 1972:40).

The Personnel System of the Reform City

The reform model is premised on eliminating the political influence of the urban machine and creating a system where professional expertise and a broader view of the public interest dominate. Reform systems seek to eliminate partisan political control and the power of subcommunities. Personnel systems try to recruit and promote professionally trained employees and insulate them from political pressures. Employee selection, promotion, and removal in reformed systems are related to the ability to perform prescribed tasks. A politically neutral civil service commission or a professional city manager governs personnel matters. Ability to perform tasks associated with the particular position rather than political sensitivity, loyalty, or membership in a certain racial or ethnic group is the basis of all aspects of the personnel decision process. Elaborate rules and regulations designed to protect employees from political interference and promote professional competence are important components of this personnel system.

The Practice in Local Governments

National and state personnel systems tend to blend both of these traditions. At the federal level, an expanding layer of political appointees exits alongside a much larger number of civil servants who are insulated from political pressures. The Senior Executive Service (SES), as mandated in the Civil Service Reform Act of 1978, is an attempt to implement some of the positive features of both systems. The Act created a cadre of officials recruited primarily from the civil service and who retain some of their civil service rights. Their tenure in a high-level position, however, is at the discretion of a political appointee.

Local systems tend to approximate one model or the other. Most council-manager cities, for example, contain very few if any political appointees. Changes of elected officials in council-manager cities seldom result in other personnel changes. City employees are recruited through neutral testing procedures and afforded civil service protection. The selection of a city manager is considered the major personnel decision of a reform city council, but even in that decision the new manager is generally recruited outside of the city and is selected based on his or her professional qualifications.

The boss system has declined in importance as reform structures gained popularity, and the federal government assumed provision of many social services. A series of Supreme Court decisions focused on machine practices in Illinois but set precedents nationally. In *Elrod v. Burns* (1976), the court held that patronage appointments were limited to policy-making positions. *Rutan v. Republican Party of Illinois* (1990) extended protection to promotions, transfers, recalls, and hiring decisions.

Yet vestiges of machine government and patronage remain in local government. Hartman (1999) points out that "Recent efforts notwithstanding, it seems improbable that the courts will be able to root out patronage practices from political organizations. They have, however, curbed the blatant excesses" (61). Shafritz et al. (1986:47) argue in fact that the most striking difference between personnel management among different jurisdictions is that " . . . the merit system and the commission form of administering it have been far less successful in state and local governments than at the federal level." Confirmation of the continued existence of patronage personnel systems is found in two recent studies of large cities. Perry, Wise, and Martin examined hiring policies in Indianapolis and Marion County. They found that a patronage-based system in hiring and promotion policies and that firing and discipline were controlled by the mayor and appointed department heads (1994:44–46). Stein examined personnel policy making in St. Louis where the mayor was much more influential in personnel policy than was the civil service commission. At the county level she found that "(T)heir 800 odd employees receive their jobs because they are recommended by ward committeemen and committeewomen. Many of these offices have no classification system or even job descriptions and none are bound by city hiring rules" (1994:60). Thus, one should expect patronage-oriented personnel systems to continue in cities with well-defined ethnic communities.

Whom employees report to also varies in local governments. In council-manager systems, the city manager is the chief administrative officer; the personnel officer and all employees therefore report to him or her. In other cities the elected mayor, the city council, or appointed city commissions exercise authority over employees. City charter revision in mayor-council cities often revolves around the relative influence of mayor, council, and commissions. The recent revision of the Los Angeles city charter, for instance, gave the mayor for the first time the right to hire and fire department heads. Organized employees lobbied the charter commissions for the structural changes thought to be most supportive of employee influence.

Personnel officers in each system are expected to perform quite different tasks. The machine personnel officer must be close to the political leaders and sensitive to the sources of support for the system. He or she will act on an understanding of political influence patterns in communities. The reform personnel officer will be more insulated from politics and upper-level decision making. He or she must be skilled in techniques that differentiate the technical skills ascribed to particular positions. The personnel manager will also be expected to encourage skill acquisition and enforce civil service rules and regulations. The position requires both professional knowledge of human resource management techniques and general administrative abilities.

Electoral Mechanisms and Executive Leadership

In reform-dominated cities, electoral mechanisms are weaker than in state and national governments. Voter turnout is generally lower in cities; a turnout of 20 percent is considered high for small-city elections. The composition of the local electorate is also different. With lower turnout, poor and working-class voters tend to make up proportionally less of the voting public. Machine and partisan cities generally have much higher voting totals; cities with reform charactersitics generally exhibit lower voting turnout (Bridges, 1997:128–129; Heilig and Mundt, 1984; Karnig and Walter, 1985). The weak electoral system is usually indicative of a low degree of public interest in city politics, and managers are the logical ones to fill that void.

Studies of city managers' roles in personnel matters suggest that they are able to exercise much influence (Svara, 1985, 1999; Nalbandian, 1990). Thompson, for example, found that the Oakland city manager exerted considerable leverage over personnel decisions. "Unlike the President of the United States," he concluded, "the city manager has few worries about bureaucrats mobilizing outside constituents or legislative committees to resist the allocation of [personnel] slots." (1975:34).

Bosses, on the other hand, are strengthened by high turnouts. The boss's power and the machine thrive on strong ties to large groups of voters. A high turnout provides the means to extract resources from the private sector and from other levels of government; it is an indicator that the system can mobilize large numbers of people in support or opposition to policies. Personnel decisions are one of the main resources available to the boss as rewards for turnout. Thus, high voter turnout provides the boss greater influence over personnel decisions.

Recent events suggest that some convergence of the two traditions in cities may be occurring. Some reform cities are changing their electoral systems to select council members by districts rather than at large; the pay and privileges for council members and mayors have increased; and some managers have sensed greater politicization of their councils. Likewise, the *Rutan* (1980) decision and pressures exerted by the federal government through the Intergovernmental Personnel Act have led to a decrease in patronage appointments in machine cities.

TOWARD A THIRD MODEL

Two diverse models of personnel systems continue to describe local government personnel management. Personnel tasks vary depending upon which model dominates the political system. Since both models are embedded in the local government context, personnel officials in different settings are governed by different goals and values; they are often faced with conflicting value premises. Their tasks and purposes depend in part on the relative influence of the two traditions. Many must balance a professional commitment to selection, neutrality, and fairness with the political need to assist elected leadership.

The approach suggested by Osborne and Gaebler (1992) represents a third model. They advocate that budgetary decisions be tied to policy outcomes and that managers be given the flexibility to use various organizational arrangements to achieve those goals. These options include contracting of services, empowering communities to assist in service delivery, and tying compensation to meeting objectives. The personnel system suggested requires managerial flexibility in hiring, promotion, and termination; evaluation tied to policy outputs; elimination of tenure; and performance-based pay. Civil service systems are subject to a particularly strong attack. "Like the steam engine," they state, "civil service was a valuable breakthrough in its day. But that day has passed. We obviously need protection against patronage hiring and firing, but it is time to listen to our public entrepreneurs and replace a civil service system designed for nineteenth century with a personnel system designed for the twenty-first" (130).

This model presents a challenge to both traditions. It accepts the machine's flexibility in the use of personnel, and adopts the reform model's emphasis on political insulation, fairness, and neutrality. More faith in public managers as policy makers and implementers is assumed than in either of the traditional approaches by giving them greater authority over personnel resources.

THE DIVERSITY OF LOCAL GOVERNMENTS AFFECTS PERSONNEL PRACTICE

Local government settings are characterized by diverse social and economic environments, elected and appointed decision makers with considerable influence over policy, and varying organizational structures, rules, and regulations. Studies of local government policy making find that each of these concerns influences policy. Variables such as population, size, density, and ethnicity are related to government budget totals and various policies (Browning et al., 1984; Hawkins, 1971; Hahn and Levine, 1984:14). Attitudes of city council members and mayors have also been correlated with policy outputs (Eberts and Kelley, 1985; Eulau and Prewitt, 1973; Clark and Ferguson, 1983), as have governmental structure, partisan organization, and bureaucratic rules and routines (Welch and Bledsoe, 1988; Lyons and Jewell, 1988; Zax, 1990; Morgan and Pelissero, 1980; Lineberry and Fowler, 1967; Jones et al., 1984). Not surprisingly, personnel policy appears to be influenced by factors associated with the local setting.

Variations in Attitudes Toward Personnel Policy

Surveys of local government officials have discovered differing attitudes toward affirmative action and labor management relations (De la Garza, Graves and Setzler 1999; Slack, 1987a; Slack and Sigelman, 1987; Davis and West, 1984; A. Saltzstein, 1974; Saltzstein and Bott, 1983). Some are supportive of affirmative action, others are quite hostile. Two explanations for these variations are brought forth. Some find that city managers, department heads, and personnel directors favor affirmative action and the organization of employees in theory but are much less supportive of particular practices. Slack and Sigelman (1987:681), for instance, find that city managers concede a need for affirmative action yet "most do not look favorably upon specific practices to implement it." Others argue that officials voice strong support for the principle of merit employment and perceive certain affirmative action and labor relations measures as hostile to a merit system (Davis and West, 1984; Saltzstein, 1974). Support for affirmative action in cities may result from entrenched bureaucratic forces supportive of it and strong minority pressures (de la Garza et al., 1999:11).

Political Factors Affect Hiring Policies

Several studies find relationships between the hiring of females and minorities in city government and the presence of women and minority officeholders. Eisinger (1982), for example, found the size of the black population and the presence of a black mayor to be related positively to black employment.

Mladenka (1989) found similar links between black city employment and the size of the black workforce and argued that black representation on the city council is an important intervening variable. Browning et al. (1984) related incorporation of minorities into the decision-making process to minority employment. The presence of a female mayor is related positively to female employment (G. H. Saltzstein, 1986b). However, there is apparently little relationship between female representation on the city council and female employment (Welch, 1978). Mladenka (1989) and Wrinkle et al. (1992) discovered links between Hispanic council representation and the hiring of Hispanics.

Organizational and Structural Influences

Form of government appears to influence personnel policy. Stein (1986), for example, found that minorities were more likely to be hired in mayor-council cities and partisan election cities.

Specific personnel rules and regulations have also been linked to minority and female hiring. G. H. Saltzstein (1986a) linked personnel rules such as veterans' preference and the "rule of three" in hiring decisions to differences in female employment. Placing affirmative action matters in the office of the chief executive was also associated with increases in the hiring of females.

Personnel policy in local government, then, reflects the diversity of the setting. It is also influenced by the structures. Personnel administrators are actors in a setting where pressures from the environment impinge on their decisions.

THE ORGANIZATIONAL SETTING OF LOCAL GOVERNMENT ENCOURAGES DEPARTMENTAL AUTONOMY

Many local government services operate independently of central influence. The rise of employee organizations and unions representing employees departmentally rather than citywide has enhanced this separation of city and departmental policy making. Personnel administration in local government, therefore, often becomes segmented with different departments enforcing separate policies.

Several factors encourage this condition. First, local politics and interest-group activity frequently are based at the department level. Second, professional norms are influential in certain departments and encourage department-level decision making. Third, political and organizational activities of public employees have often been departmentally based.

Interest-Group Activity

Internal political issues in city government generally revolve around concerns of particular departments or subunits. Police issues are normally separated from those of health, parks, or welfare. Even interest in the overall economic health of the city becomes "economic development," and its implementation is detached from the policy processes of other departments. These connections may be reinforced by the city charter if oversight of the department is delegated to an appointed commission or the department head is insulated from the direct control of the mayor. Some have argued that interest group activity by those concerned with particular departments—aided by the functional specialists and policy makers who regularly deal with this policy area—dominates city decisions. Sayre and Kaufman (1960:711) found this situation particularly prevalent in New York City.

Functional specialized officials constitute the core groups for decisions in particular functional areas of governmental action. Each decision center is surrounded by satellite groups, especially concerned with its decisions. Usually the groups concerned with particular functions are uninterested in decisions in other unrelated functions. Many Los Angeles departments report to appointed city commissions rather than the city council. Commission members are appointed to terms longer than the city council's, and commission members are full time and handsomely paid. In some cases the commissions have sources of revenue that can be used independently of the city council. Employees are generally happy with the presence of a commission because it frequently means that advocates of the interest of the department are its leaders. Thus in discussions of charter reform recently, employee organizations generally came to the defense of the commission system and lobbied to limit the influence of the city council in the operations of their departments. Central governmental authority then in such a system may play a minor role in policy making. Personnel concerns become departmentally dominated;

department heads can frequently overrule or ignore commands from the central personnel office. Personnel officials may assign directly to departments and take orders from department heads rather than from the central personnel office.

Professionalism

Professional groups by definition seek to control entry, status, and discipline of members. In an organization dominated by career professionals, real personnel authority is officially or unofficially delegated from the central personnel office to the professionals themselves (Mosher, 1968:124). Large local governments contain departments with many of the traditionally powerful professionals such as doctors, lawyers, and engineers. Thus, health departments, city attorneys' offices, and public works and engineering departments delegate many personnel tasks to professional associations and teams of peers. Bar examinations and medical boards, for instance, serve as entry examinations in local governments instead of departmentally administered tests. Even the less professionally dominated areas such as police and fire often are influenced by peer personnel processes.

Employee Organizations and Unions

Public employee organizations and unions in cities tend to represent occupational units of the same kind in several cities and, therefore, they must deal with several organizations with diffent agendas. Different pay and benefit packages may result.

Frequently, union operations involve activity at the state level. Police and fire organizations in California, for example, have influenced state legislation protecting the working conditions, pensions, and tenure rights of local government employees throughout the state (Crouch, 1978:32–34). Initiatives and referenda have been used to raise the pay of police and fire employees alone. Collective bargaining rights have also been extended to some workers and not others through state legislation and referenda (Helburn and Barnum, 1978). Unions have been less successful in inducing members to support issues that benefit workers as a whole rather than only specific functional groups (Sears and Citrin, 1982:114).

Thus, local government personnel decisions are likely to be decentralized and strongly influenced by forces exterior to the central personnel staffs. Central personnel officers' positions are more involved in advising and coordinating than in implementing and directing personnel policy. The authority to make personnel decisions is strongly influenced by professional associations, diverse employee organizations and unions, and specific policy actors.

CONCLUSION: THE LOCAL GOVERNMENT SETTING ENCOURAGES A MORE POLITICAL PERSONNEL OFFICER

Government activities are strongly related to customs, traditions, and environment. Public administrators are advised to carefully coordinate their goals, values, and ambitions with those of the particular setting. Local governments contain an array of features that influences the personnel system so as to make its setting quite different from those at other levels.

Public personnel authorities have repeatedly urged an expanded role for the personnel function (Stahl, 1962:45; Shafritz et al., 1986:45). This chapter points out the difficulties in achieving this comprehensive role in a local government setting. Power and influence do not naturally accrue to the personnel department in local government. The personnel officer must be very sensitive to more dominant actors: city executives, department heads, and professional, employee, and community groups. A successful personnel officer in a local government setting must be a broker among various groups and interests. He or she must assume that the goals of the personnel profession will not always be accepted by policy makers.

A creative role for the personnel administrator is one that infuses the organization with the values of the personnel profession. In local government, personnel values are not by nature important ones; they must compete with other interests and values in the policy-making process, and their natural constituency may well be less powerful than others. Thus, the personnel officer must become an effective teacher and molder of ideas if professional personnel concerns are to influence policy.

REFERENCES

ADRIAN, CHARLES, R., and CHARLES PRESS. 1977. *Governing Urban America.* New York: McGraw-Hill Book Company.

BRIDGES, AMY. 1997. *Morning Glories: Municipal Reform in the Southwest.* Princeton, NJ: Princeton University Press.

BROWNING, RUFUS P., DALE ROGERS MARSHALL, and DAVID H. TABB. 1984. *Protest is Not Enough: The Struggle of Blacks and Hispanics for Equality in Urban Politics.* Berkeley: University of California Press.

Christensen et al. v. Harris County et al. 2000.

CLARK, TERRY NICHOLS, and LORNA CROWLEY FERGUSON. 1983. *City Money: Political Processes, Fiscal Strain and Retrenchment.* New York: Columbia University Press.

CROUCH, WINSTON. 1978. *Organized Civil Servants: Public Employer-Employee Relations in California.* Berkeley: University of California.

DAVIS, CHARLES E., and J. P. WEST. 1984. Implementing Public Programs: Equal Employment Opportunity, Affirmative Action and Administrative Policy Options. *Review of Public Personnel Administration* 4 (Summer):16–30.

DE LA GARZA, RODOLFO O., SCOTT GRAVES, and MARK H. SELTZER. 1999. Alive and Kicking: Municipal Affirmative Action Policy in Texas Cities, 1980s–1990s. *Policy Studies Journal* 27 (Spring):45–54.

EBERTS, PAUL R. and JANET M. KELLEY. 1985. How Mayors Get Things Done: Community Politics and Mayors' Initiatives. In Terry Nichols Clark, ed. *Research in Urban Policy.* J.A.I. Press. Greenwich, CT.

Elrod v. Burns. 1976. 427 U.S.

EULAU, HENIZ, and KENNETH PREWITT. 1973. *Labyrinths of Democracy: Adaptations, Linkages, Representation and Politics in Urban Politics.* Indianapolis: Bobbs-Merrill.

FRUG, GERALD E. 1980. The City as a Legal Concept. *Harvard Law Review* 6 (April) 1062–1154.

Garcia v. San Antonio Metropolitan Transit Authority. 1985. 469 U.S. 528.

HAAS, LAWRENCE J. 1991. States Bounce Back. *National Journal:* August 10.

HAHN, HARLAN. 1977. Alternative Paths to 'Professionalism': The Development of Municipal Personnel. In Charles H. Levine, ed. *Managing Human Resources: A Challenge to Urban Government.* Beverly Hills: Sage Publications, pp. 37–56.

——, and CHARLES H. LEVINE, EDS. 1984. *Readings in Urban Politics*. New York: Longman Press.

HANSON, RUSSELL L. 1990. Intergovernmental Relations. In Virginia Gray, Herbert Jacob, and Robert B. Abritton, eds. *Politics in the American States*. New York: Harper Collins.

HARTMAN, DAVID K. 1999. The Continuing Judicial Assault on Patronage. *Public Administration Review* 59 (January–February) 544–562.

HAWKINS, BRETT. 1971. *Politics and Urban Policies*. Indianapolis: Bobbs-Merrill.

HEILIG, PEGGY, and ROBERT J. MUNDT. 1984. *Your Voice in City Hall: The Politics and Procedures and Policies of District Representation*. Albany, NY: State University of New York Press.

HELBURN, I. B., and HAROLD T. BARNUM. 1978. Making Personnel Decisions by Public Referenda: Campaigns for Police and Fire Fighter Collective Bargaining in Texas. *Public Personnel Management* 7, 2 (March–April):119–126.

HOWARD, S. KENNETH. 1985. A Message from Garcia. *Public Administration Review* 45 (November, Special Issue):738–741.

JONES, BRYAN D., SAADIA R. GREENBERG, CLIFFORD KAUFMAN, and JOSEPH DREW. 1984. Service Delivery Rules and the Distribution of Local Government Services. In *Readings in Urban Politics*. New York: Longman Inc.: 224–248.

KARNIG, ALBERT, and B. OLIVER WILLIAMS. 1985. Municipal Voter Participation: Trends and Correlates. In Dennis R. Judd, ed. *Public Policy Across States and Communities*. Grenwich, CT: JAI Press.

KINCAID, JOHN. 1995. Intergovernmental Deregulation. *Public Administration Review* 55(September/October):495–498.

KOEHLER, CORTUS T. 1983. *Managing California Counties: Serving People, Solving Problems*. Sacramento: County Supervisors Association of California.

LINEBERRY, ROBERT L., and EDMUND P. FOWLER. 1967. Reformism and Public Policy in American Cities. *American Political Science Review* 61 (September): 701–716.

LUKAS, ANTHONY J. 1985. *Common Ground: A Turbulent Decade in the Lives of Three American Families*. New York: Alfred A. Knopf.

LYONS, W. E., and MALCOLM E. JEWELL. 1988. Minority Representation and the Drawing of City Council Districts. *Urban Affairs Quarterly* (March) 23:432–447.

MLADENKA, KENNETH N. 1989. Barriers to Hispanic Employment Success in 1200 Cities. *Social Science Quarterly* 20 (June):391–407.

——. 1980. The Urban Bureaucracy and the Chicago Political Machine: Who Gets What and the Limits to Political Control. *American Political Science Review* 74 (December):991–1006.

Moreau v. Klevenhagen. 1993. U.S. 91–1.

MORGAN, DAVID, and JOHN PELISSERO. 1980. Urban Policy: Does Political Structure Matter? *American Political Science Review* (December):999–1006.

MOSHER, FREDERICK C. 1968. *Democracy and the Public Service*. New York: Oxford University Press.

NALBANDIAN, JOHN. 1989. Tenets of Professionalism in Local Government. *Public Administration Review* 50 (November/December):654–662.

National League of Cities et al. v. W. J. Usery. 1976. Secretary Of Labor. 426 U.S. 833.

OSBORNE, DAVID, and TED GAEBLER. 1992. *Reinventing Government: How the Entrepreneurial Spirit Is Transforming the Public Sector from Schoolhouse to Statehouse, City Hall Pentagon*. Reading, MA: Addison-Wesley.

PERRY, JAMES, LOIS R. WISE, and MARGO MARTIN. 1994. Breaking the Civil Service Mold: The Case of Indianapolis. *Review of Public Personnel Administration* XIV (Spring): 40–54.

PETERSON, PAUL E. 1981. *City Limits*. Chicago: University of Chicago Press.

PULS, CYNTHIA M. 1986. The Fair Labor Standards Act: New Implications for Public Employees. In *Municipal Yearbook*. Washington, DC: International City Management Association.

Rutan v. Republican Party of Illinois. 1980. 455 U.S. 507.

SALTZSTEIN, ALAN. 1974. Organized Employees and the Roles of City Managers. *Midwest Review of Public Administration* 6 (November):13–25.

——, and VIRGINIA BOTT. 1983. Personnel Policy Making in Times of Crisis: California Public Personnel Directors Face the Aftermath of Proposition 13. *American Review of Public Personnel Administration* 16 (Summer-Fall):195–207.

SALTZSTEIN, G. H. 1986a. Female Mayors and Women in Municipal Jobs. *American Journal of Political Science* 30 (February):140–164.

——. 1986b. Institutional Barriers to Employment in Bureaucracy: The Residual Effects of Organizational Reform. *Administration and Society* 48 (May):77–90.

SAYRE, WALLACE S., and HERBERT KAUFMAN. 1960. *Governing New York City: Politics in the Metropolis.* New York: Russell.

SCHNEIDER, MARK. 1989. Inter-City Competition and the Size of the Local Public Sector. *Public Choice* 64 (February):167–177.

SEARS, DAVID O., and JACK CITRIN. 1982. *Tax Revolt: Something for Nothing in California.* Cambridge, MA: Harvard.

SHAFRITZ, JAY M., ALBERT HYDE, and DAVID ROSENBLOOM. 1986. Personnel Management. In *Government: Politics and Process,* 3d ed. New York: Marcel Dekker, Inc.

SLACK, JAMES D. 1987a. City Managers, Police Chiefs and Fire Chiefs in the South: Testing for Determinants and Impacts of Attitudes of Affirmative Action. *Review of Public Personnel Administration* 87 (Fall):11–32.

——. 1987b. Affirmative Action and City Managers: Attitude Toward Recruitment of Women. *Public Administration Review* 47 (March–April):199–206.

SLACK, JAMES D., and LEE SIGELMAN. 1987. City Managers and Affirmative Action: Testing a Model of Linkage. *Western Political Quarterly* 37 (December):673–684.

STAHL, O. GLENN. 1962. *Public Personnel Administration.* New York: Harper and Row.

STEIN, LANA. 1986. Representative Local Government: Minorities in the Municipal Work Force. *Journal of Politics* 48 (August):694–713.

——. 1994. Personnel Rules and Reform in an Unreformed Setting. *Review of Public Personnel Administration* XIV (Spring):55–63.

STONE, CLARENCE W., and HEYWOOD T. SAUNDERS. 1987. *The Politics of Urban Development.* Lawrence, KS: University of Kansas Press.

SVARA, JAMES H. Dichotomy and Duality: Reconceptualizing the Relationship Between Policy and Administration in Council Manager Cities. *Public Administration Review* 45 (January/February):221–232.

——. The Shifting Boundary Between Elected Officials and City Managers in Large Council-Manager Cities. *Public Administration Review* 59 (January/ February):44–53.

THOMPSON, FRANK J. 1975. *Personnel Policy in the City: The Politics of City Jobs in Oakland.* Berkeley: University of California.

TOLCHIN, MARTIN, and SUSAN TOLCHIN. 1972. *To the Victor . . . Political Patronage from Clubhouse to the Whitehouse.* New York: Vintage.

WELCH, SUSAN, and TIMOTHY BLEDSOE. 1988. *Urban Reform and Its Consequences.* Chicago: University of Chicago.

ZAX, JEFFREY S. 1990. Election Methods, Black and Hispanic City Council Membership. *Social Science Quarterly* (June) 71:339–355.`

5

The American Federal Bureaucracy
A Retrospective Look at Reinvention and Reform

PATRICIA WALLACE INGRAHAM
Syracuse University

In the United States and around the world, reform of public bureaucracy has been omnipresent in the last twenty years. The reasons for reform have been nearly as numerous as the settings in which the reforms have occurred. Size and cost of bureaucracy, lack of bureaucratic responsiveness to elected and appointed officials, and the failure of public bureaucracies to emphasize performance, to involve citizens, or to be fully accountable to multiple overseers were among the most common complaints (Peters and Savoie, 1998). The "Reinventing Government" movement in the United States and New Public Management reforms in Europe and elsewhere were responses to these perceived problems.

The reforms were remarkably similar across nations: privatization in those countries with a large nationalized presence, downsizing of the national bureaucracy, decentralization of decision making and service delivery whenever possible, new attention to the issues related to responsivenes of career civil servants to elected officials, and a strong emphasis on performance and productivity. The words of various national performance review reports in the United States summed up the objectives: smaller, better, faster, and cheaper government.

As contemporary as the solutions may seem, the problems they address are age old. Indeed, in the United States, Alexander Hamilton framed the fundamental issue: "The true test of a good government," he said, "is its aptitude and tendency to produce a good administration" (Federalist Papers # 68). As modern administrative states have developed, the power and presence of public bureaucracies have come to be a defining feature of government; ensuring that they are "good," however, is a modern conundrum (Skowronek, 1986). As a result, the issue that Hamilton so presciently summarized is a constantly underlying theme of reform.

How should necessary energy and vigor be maintained in public bureaucracy but arbitrary power and authority limited?

The problem is particularly troubling for public bureaucracies. Electoral processes can change—or remove—presidents, prime ministers, governors, and mayors. Even so, as the presidential election of 2000 demonstrated, the messages elections send are not always clear. Bureaucratic organizations are consciously isolated from elected officials and the change they represent by merit systems, by other laws, and by bureaucratic structures and are more removed from both popular sentiments and the changes they inspire (Ingraham, 1995). Many of the qualities that define public organizations—rules, regulations, and rigid structures—were created specifically to resist change, or to translate demands for change into predictable bureaucratic processes and procedures.

As the frequency and velocity of reform efforts have increased around the world, a set of reform dilemmas common to many national and subnational settings have emerged. Debates about centralization versus decentralization of control and authority have been one of the most consistently evident. In this context, many reform activities have fallen under decentralization's broad umbrella: decentralization of program delivery, devolution of authority and responsibility, restructuring of organizations and intergovernmental relations, and deregulation by central agencies and central controls have all been included (Peters and Savoie, 1998). Strongly centralized civil service systems, however, are a favorite target.

Early designers of civil service systems argued that centralized direction and standardized procedures were fundamentally important to the neutrality and fair treatment the new systems were intended to ensure. Quality and efficiency were also commonly linked to standardization and "fairness," or equal treatment. In many settings, merit systems came to be noted as much for the strongly centralizing and standardizing influences they exerted on public organizations as for the exclusion of patronage and promise of neutrality they were intended to create. Centralized recruiting and testing, standardized pay systems, and centrally enforced rules and regulations worked to create the same procedures for very different organizations and tasks. The National Weather Service and the Small Business Administration, for example, are subject to the same federal personnel rules. Under New York State law, so are cities as different as New York City and Buffalo. Even when substantive efforts to alter this centralizing influence have been made, as in the case of the Civil Service Reform Act of 1978, central control in the name of protecting merit has been difficult—and very slow—to change (Ban and Marzotto, 1984).

The reforms of the 1980s and 1990s wanted to change that pattern. Arguing that decentralization and devolution were more likely to lead to effective public services, these reforms were intended to replace strong centralization and standardization with new emphases on flexibility, discretion, and performance (Kettl, 1994). Key components of all major reforms included a movement away from the center (the national government and central agencies) to state and local governments, individual agencies, and both the private and not-for-profit sectors. In the 1990s, the move from standardization and from rigid personnel practices also included a new concern for the people—the very necessary "human capital" of public organizations (Ingraham, Selden, and Moynihan, 2000a). As processes are tailored more to specific organizations and their needs, missions, and problems, the value of the organization's employees as a resource to be developed has become a more frequent focus.

The newest reforms have also shifted the debate about public organizations and their authority in other ways. The reforms have introduced a focus on performance that has become increasingly significant in both individual and organizational terms. They have emphasized much more successfully than did past efforts the central role that citizens can play in assessing bureaucratic effectiveness and responsiveness. In the "old model," for example, citizens were considered somewhat trapped in their dealings with the bureaucracy. How many places were able to issue drivers licenses, for example? Only the Departments of Motor Vehicles—and you got the license on their terms. Now office times are different, locations are more diverse (in malls, for example), and sensitivities to waiting times, required documentation, and friendliness of service are much higher. Because the new reforms have linked decentralization and flexibility to performance and to improved communication with both elected officials and citizens, they have also had some success in reframing the debate about appropriate democratic controls on bureaucratic authority. Elected officials have a major role to play, but so do the citizens who receive the services. New ways of drawing citizens into the performance assessment process are being devised: on site performance ratings, satisfaction surveys, some benchmarking efforts, and other activities incorporating citizen perspectives. Measuring and rewarding good performance will always be difficult in public organizations. The increasing recognition, however, that excessive rules, regulations, and hierarchical controls do not contribute to either high performance or responsive organizations is an important step forward.

AFTER REFORM: FLEXIBILITY, PERFORMANCE, AND ACCOUNTABILITY

Performance is, in fact, a long-term part of the public personnel agenda, but in traditional civil service systems it was most often linked to standardization and regulation. In addition, much of the earliest discussion of performance focused on efficiency as defined by private sector assembly-line techniques. Hence, narrow and standardized job descriptions and requirements became the norm in civil service systems in the United States and elsewhere. Over time, the interactive effects of standardizing efficiency and enforcing merit through centralization and rigorous controls caused many public organizations to suffocate in processes and procedures, and performance became difficult to discern.

Flexibility and Decentralization

Reinventing government, at all levels of government, is a leading example of decentralization, deregulation, and flexibility in reform. Reinvention reforms took direct aim at excessive rules and regulations. "Better, faster, cheaper" government, or in Vice President Gore's terms, a "government that works better and costs less," was a consistently stated objective of reinvention. The organization created to carry reinvention forward in the federal government was the National Performance Review (NPR, 1994). Although reinvention had many objectives (some less clear than others), performance was generally to be improved through two major sets of activities: 1) increased flexibility and decentralization; and 2) renewed emphasis on rewarding and recognizing "good" performance.

The first, increased flexibility and decentralization, is the area in which NPR accomplishments are most notable. An early and very symbolic action was the elimination of the Federal Personnel Manual, a 10,000-page behemoth that had frustrated federal managers for decades. Another was the systematic disempowerment–some would call it dismantling–of the Office of Personnel Management (OPM), the central personnel agency created by the Civil Service Reform Act twenty years earlier. That agency, never central to reinvention or NPR activities decreased in both size and authority in the 1980s and 1990s. In fact, OPM is a leading example of the downsizing that has accompanied reinvention in the federal government, decreasing in total size by about one-half in the eight years of the Clinton Administration (National Performance Review, 1994).

It is important to note here that the objectives of decentralization and increased delegation sometimes conflicted with the governmentwide downsizing of the early and mid-1990s. Fewer personnel, decreased ability to hire for requisite new skills and expertise, and questions about future resources caused many agencies and programs to lose capacity and to "hunker down," rather than create the new ways of doing work that effective decentralization would have required. While this effort was one part of a broader cost cutting strategy, it had the unintended effect of limiting agency capacity at the time when delegated authorities and decentralization created the need for additional capacity to be present. Clearly the cross purposes at work in these cases did not contribute to overall effectiveness of reinvention reforms. Nor, for that matter, did the reforms succeed in lowering personnel costs, as they were partially intended to do. During the same period that total size of the federal civilian workforce was decreased by 12 percent governmentwide, the percentage of personnel costs as total costs actually increased slightly (Ingraham, Peters, and Moynihan, 2000).

The downsizing component of reform had another unintended consequence. Under the terms of the Federal Workforce Restructuring Act, early retirement buyouts were approved for some agencies. A number of employees at the mid to upper levels of managerial ranks took the options; with few exceptions, strategic workforce planning did not precede or accompany the buyout activities. Because new hiring activities were very limited or nonexistent in most agencies during the drawdown period, a demographic gap was created in many federal agencies. The best of the middle-aged group left, the youngest was not replenished, and large numbers of the older contingent that stayed will be eligible for retirement in the next ten years.

The impact of these demographic and experiential "blips" is substantial. The Department of Defense, the Veterans Benefits Agency, the Social Security Administration, and others face substantial recruiting and retention problems. In 1999, the National Academy of Public Administration (NAPA) reported " . . . many agencies find themselves without some of the critical skills needed to accomplish their missions" (National Academy of Public Administration, 1999:2). General Accounting Office data explain the continuing nature of the problems now confronted: "Just over 70 percent of the federal government's career senior executives will become eligible for retirement by the end of fiscal year 2005, though the actual retirement level is likely to be closer to 45 percent" (Ingraham, Selden, and Moynihan, 2000b:55).

It is also important to emphasize that many of the common sense flexibilities and delegations spurred by reinvention and other reform activities have had a positive impact. The vast majority of flexibilities requested and implemented in reinvention laboratory settings were changes to personnel processes and rules (Thompson, 1998). Many agencies discovered, when freed from the obvious burdens imposed by the Federal Personnel Manual, that in the past they had actually imposed constraints and unnecessary procedures on themselves. The more discretionary atmosphere created by reinvention and the experimentation it engendered permitted agencies such as the Department of Agriculture's APHIS and the Department of Veterans' Affairs Veterans' Benefit and Veterans' Health Administrations to create systems not only better fitted to their specific needs, but also better suited to the new performance demands they were confronting (Thompson, 1997; Government Performance Project, 1999, 2000).

Other efforts, while intended to be dramatic, were limited in their impact. Performance Based Organizations, for example, carried devolution of authority to extraordinary lengths in the American federal government. Modeled after the British Next Steps Agencies, PBOs were intended to accomplish two things: First, they were intended to clarify organizational purpose and mission and to make the organizational "bottom line" clear. Second, they were to provide the PBOs the discretion and authority they needed to accomplish missions and to direct resources in the most effective ways. Despite consistent efforts by the Clinton Administration to push PBO legislation forward, at the end of the Clinton term, Congress had approved only two PBOs. The Office of Student Financial Assistance in the Department of Education was approved in 1997; the Patent and Trademark Office in the Department of Commerce was approved in 1999. Implementation progress in both was very limited at the end of the Clinton presidency.

While there was little formal legislative activity specifically linked to the objectives of reinvention, legislation for other purposes turned out to be significant to reform. For example, in a 1996 effort to reshape a faltering Federal Aviation Administration, Congress removed the agency from virtually all of the provisions of Title V of the U.S. Code–the formal legislative base for most personnel law. Such flexibility and discretion could have been a dramatic step toward many of the objectives that reinvention espoused. By most accounts, however, the FAA did not use this newfound freedom aggressively; indeed, in 1999 they reported that they were just preparing to implement early changes (Government Performance Project, 1999).

Congress also gave the Internal Revenue Service special personnel flexibilities in broad legislation that restructured that agency in 1998. In the case of the IRS, flexibilities were related primarily to salary and hiring options. While some issues have been raised about the use of the flexibilities, the creation of a special IRS oversight board by Congress provided relatively close-up and consistent assessment of implementation. This oversight board also added a new twist to the usual decentralization scenario. IRS represents "directed decentralization" and flexibility, as well as a buffer between the Congress and the leaders of the agency as they proceed through implementation.

So what does this somewhat contradictory evidence about decentralization and delegation in the federal government add up to? This is a particularly relevant

question. Kettl and others argue that continuing reinvention is now almost inevitable in the United States; that is, the mandate for change is so strong that neither elected officials nor the career public service can safely ignore it (Kettl, 2000). Federal employees themselves report that, after downsizing and several years of reinvention, some change has occurred. They report that they are doing more work and that it is substantively different. There are several ways of interpreting this, however. The Merit Systems Protection Board (MSPB) reported in 1998, "From the perspective of these employees, downsizing and budget cuts, rather than improved operations, were the main purposes of government reinvention efforts." (Merit Systems Protection Board, 1998:21).

On the other hand, the same MSPB survey noted substantive differences between those employees whose organizations had made reinvention a priority activity and those that did not. Nearly 60 percent of employees whose organizations emphasized reinvention reported increases in productivity; compared to 32 percent in other organizations. Similarly, 60 percent of employees in organizations that were NPR-oriented reported being given additional flexibility; 38 percent of the employees in other organizations believed that they had not (MSPB, 1998:viii).

In its Annual Report and elsewhere, the National Performance Review has argued that the decentralization and deregulation components of reinvention have been successful at least partially because they have been incremental and are "ground up": they are owned by the agencies, rather than being legislatively or centrally imposed. Ban concludes that ". . . the effects have been mixed, with no success at passing legislation, but some significant administrative changes, and real reforms forced by the sharp downsizing of personnel staff" (Ban, 2000). She speculates that NPR may have forced decentralization so far that it is impossible for the pendulum to swing back to the more centralized old system. Perhaps. But the focus on performance in the current reform mix adds a complex and unpredictable dimension to predictive ability.

Performance

Performance based reforms in the United States have moved away from only a focus on efficiency to a broader emphasis on both organizational and individual effectiveness. Some reforms, such as performance incentives and bonuses, are based on private sector experience and on earlier legislation, such as the Civil Service Reform Act of 1978 (Ban, 2000). Other reforms, such as Performance Based Organizations, grew from policy diffusion from other nations (Ingraham and Moynihan, 2000). One of the most interesting, the Government Performance and Results Act, was a congressional initiative intended not only to clarify and measure the performance of federal agencies, but to use performance information in future budget decisions (Joyce, 1999). Each of these initiatives is worth discussing in a bit more detail because the lessons to be learned are somewhat disparate. Generally, however, performance reforms have, in Rainey and Kellough's terms, " . . . not worked out well" (Rainey and Kellough, 2000).

Individual or team based performance reforms fall into three broad categories: financial incentives, empowerment incentives, and task design incentives. The fit of these initiatives with the decentralization and regulation objectives of reinvention and similar reforms is clear.

In the United States and in other nations, it is fair to say that the least successful of the individual or team-based incentives were those involving monetary bonuses or awards. For a variety of reasons, ranging from motivation to culture, to lack of adequate resources, the failure rate of financial incentive reforms in public organizations has been very high (Perry and Wise, 1990; Ban, 1997; Rainey and Kellough, 2000).

Initially created by the CSRA, later abolished governmentwide, and still later adopted again on limited and experimental terms, merit pay and incentive bonuses are based on the premise of decentralized authority: individual managers must have the discretion and the authority to reward those who perform well and to discipline those who do not. In addition to other problems, well documented in the literature, performance pay also demonstrated a problem endemic to other decentralization efforts (Rainey and Kellough, 2000). The problem is that adequate and predictable resources, rather than the decreasing or erratic resources often found in public organizations, are critical to effective implementation. To the extent that rewards for performance are key to improved overall performance, this lesson is fundamental.

A variation on the theme of decentralized merit pay or performance incentives is provided by current experimentation with recruitment incentives and broad banding of classification schemes. Again initially created in the federal government by CSRA Title VII Demonstration Projects, such as China Lake, broad banding provides flexibility in both starting salaries and in individual movement through the promotion range. Although it is most often billed as a recruiting and retention tool for the organization, the roles it plays initially as a financial incentive and later as a performance incentive are also significant. Broad banding mandates substantial delegation or decentralization of authority, however, and in most cases in which it has been rigorously assessed, it has proven to increase personnel costs in its first years. This additional cost, rather than the predicted savings, has limited the expansion of broad banding (Rainey and Kellough, 2000; General Accounting Office, 1999).

Lack of comfort with additional managerial discretion and the difficulties encountered by previous financial incentive schemes, coupled with an increasing conviction that public employees are motivated by the desire to "do the right thing," have caused more emphasis to be placed on other—though still delegated and decentralized—performance management strategies (Perry and Wise, 1990). The early years of reinvention were built strongly on previous experience with Total Quality Management and similar activities, although often without tying individual or group empowerment to broader organizational mission and strategies (Thompson and Sanders, 1998). Vice President Gore's much heralded "Hammer Awards"—small hammer shaped lapel pins—were one example of the symbolic awards associated with individual and group empowerment; the hammers recognized teams that had hammered away unnecessary bureaucratic rules and processes.

Organizational performance and results, which while not standardized governmentwide do attempt to create organizationwide performance links, have now emerged as a central issue in the performance debate. The Government Performance and Results Act (GPRA) is a leading case. Designed to begin with a five year strategic planning and evaluation stage, demonstration projects in 35 High

Impact Agencies, and a formal performance plan and assessment from all federal agencies in 2000, GPRA focuses specifically on agency performance. Goals and targets included in the GPRA planning documents are intended to be specific, measurable, and easily communicated.

In conjunction with GPRA, the federal Office of Management and Budget was tasked with developing a *governmentwide* Performance Plan by 1998. The OMB document, unlike most of the agency plans that concentrate on measurable program-specific variables, focused on management and capacity issues across government. It is to be submitted to Congress in conjunction with the President's budget submission. In other words, the Governmentwide Performance Plan is intended to integrate management and budget decision-making processes in the Congress, or at least to provide a coherent framework for them. Improved *government* performance, based on improved agency performance, is the intended result. This, too, is a variation on the decentralization theme: performance itself, but not the processes leading to it, is mandated. Performance is viewed as a combination of disparate agency activities, performance factors, and plans, rather than a standardized set of measures and expectations.

That said, GPRA is a case of unusual congressional attention to performance. More commonly, the lack of legislative attention to performance and other reform legislation has been a very persistent fly in the ointment. It was the budget cut components of reinvention that captured congressional attention; with the exception of federal workforce restructuring and procurement reform legislation, broad reform proposals have received scant attention. Comprehensive civil service reform legislation was, for all practical purposes, not considered. Even the Government Performance and Results Act, Congress's own initiative, has received modest attention as its plans have been submitted. After the first performance reports were submitted in March 2000, there was agreement that congressional response was lukewarm and that the legislation was unlikely to fulfill its promise. Agencies, too, expressed lack of confidence in the system, arguing in some cases that GPRA processes and procedures were not related to the real performance management activities of the agency (GPP, 2000).

Accountability and Reform

Any reform in public organizations is ultimately about improved accountability to elected officials and to citizens. The reforms of the past decade are no different in that regard. They are also similar to past reforms in that they send conflicting messages about the new definitions of accountability (Rosenbloom, 1995). Deregulation and decentralization reforms, for example, are intended to create new and more responsive accountability responsibilities and to clarify accountability linkages. The decentralization reforms associated with reinvention, however, did not make at all clear what would replace the hierarchical accountability structures they attacked. In fact, in the absence of fundamental legislative reform to change the "rules of the game," the new mechanisms were often confusing "add-ons." Romzek describes the pattern: "new accountability mechanisms are not substituted for the accountability relationships which were in place at the time of the problem (which are . . . now perceived to be inadequate). Rather, they are simply added to the accountability relationships already in place. The resulting array of relationships provides numerous opportunities for holding public employees answerable for their performance" (Romzek, 2000:3).

The outcome of this "layering" is not only to create multiple mechanisms, but to create conflicts among them as well. The work of Thompson (1999) and others reveals the problems this caused for reinvention teams and leaders, whose efforts were frequently stopped or stymied by decision makers higher in the hierarchy. Further, research related to decision making in turbulent environments also demonstrates that hierarchy and long-established authority patterns will be the primary guide in determining responsibility or accountability in problem situations, whether or not decision making has been decentralized (Romzek and Ingraham, 2000).

New performance and reward structures are tangled in the same conundrum, but bear the additional burden of not violating concerns for equity and fairness in public organizations. Perceptions of what is "good" performance, for example, may vary widely. Kettl outlines the perspectives from which a single citizen or elected decision maker may view the same set of actions—as taxpayer, recipient of services, member of special interest group, etc. (Kettl, 1994). In this setting, decentralization and additional discretion may well mean expansion of these conflicting perspectives; this is particularly true with reinvention's emphasis on "customer satisfaction" (Kettl, 1994).

The IRS provided a nearly classic example of conflicting expectations and mechanisms for performance. Strongly under attack for poor performance, for failed technology, and for general inability to change, the IRS was instructed by Congress to utilize performance management measures more effectively. Specifically, IRS leaders were told that the organization should be more effective in collecting revenue and that those successful in such endeavors should be rewarded. They did and they were. In the process, however, some of the citizens from whom the additional revenue was being collected perceived that IRS authority was abusing them.

The equity concerns are also significant and surface on both an organizational and individual level. The issue of treating all employees fairly is always front and center in both design and implementation of performance reforms. One of the key impacts of decentralization and increased discretion was to loosen control on financial incentives and performance pay and to give managers more authority not only for reward, but also for discipline. In this case, the dilemma of ensuring that greater individual discretion complimented efforts to clarify and pursue organizational objectives was a continuing part of implementation concerns. Further, the closer partnerships with unions in many of the reformed organizations mandated that collective bargaining definitions of equity be merged with individual and organizational purpose.

As this discussion suggests, the issues addressed by federal reform efforts continue to be thorny and multifaceted. One of the drivers of constant reform efforts is lack of satisfaction with reforms that have preceded the current effort. The federal government has clearly made some progress in addressing problems of size, rigid hierarchy, and overall responsiveness of public organizations to performance concerns. In other areas—clarifying accountability structures and performance expectations, creating a new foundation for public management processes and changes in the future, and aligning individual and organizational performance incentives and measures—there is an unfortunately long way to go. How does this experience compare to that of other governments?

The Reform Experience in Other Settings

The federal government in the United States is surely not alone in its encounters with the dilemmas of reform. Early on, Herbert Kaufman described a nearly constant—and inevitable—cycle, or movement from centralization to decentralization and back again (Kaufman, 1956). Berry, Chakerian and Wechsler describe the reinvention reform experience in Florida as one whose scope was so vast and core purpose so murky that only limited reform components were amenable to implementation. Further, they note that critical political support is rarely maintained throughout key phases of implementation, ensuring that the activities and the issues will be revisited in the future (Berry, Chakerian, and Wechsler, 1999).

While it is true that human resource management reforms—particularly those related to decentralization and delegation of authority—have been problematic, the fundamental role that effective HRM plays in good government is increasingly clear. The comptroller general of the United States, David Walker, summarized: "There is still one critical missing link in current government reform efforts: the people dimension, what we . . . call human capital" (NAPA, 2000:1). This "missing link" has been identified in other settings and, indeed, has been the target of reform in many American states and several other nations.

In the states, for example, the traditional centralized civil service system structure is rapidly giving way to more decentralized operations. Some states, such as New York and Nevada, continue to operate with essentially rigid centralized authorities. Others, such as South Carolina and Texas, operate with a mostly decentralized personnel system. Over 90 percent of the states have decentralized hiring authority and nearly half have decentralized recruiting responsibilities (GPP, 2000).

Overall, the very strong trend in state governments is toward greater decentralization and deregulation of human resource management systems. Not only has hiring been decentralized, but the rigid "rule of three" has been all but abandoned (only three states continue to use it). Some states have moved to broad bands of qualified applicants and managers have the discretion to choose from within the band. Other states have moved to testing for core competencies rather than using centralized civil service exams, allowing for even greater flexibilities. A majority of states have moved to decrease the number of classifications in the system. Georgia, as noted earlier, abolished the state merit system altogether in 1996.

In another national setting, a dramatic approach to solving the problems of centralization and standardization is provided by New Zealand. Although the lessons from a small island nation are not easily transferred to other contexts, the New Zealand case does provide some of the most clear-cut evidence for the success of decentralization and deregulation reforms, if market indicators and reenergized governmental activities are the measure (Schick, 1998). In the New Zealand case, budgets, personnel authority, and performance management were decentralized and managed primarily through contracts with the chief executives of each agency. The size of the public service was dramatically reduced, as were personnel costs. Other nations, such as Canada, the United Kingdom, and Australia have also followed a decentralization/deregulation model of reform and have made civil service systems more flexible and nimble in the process.

CONCLUSION

The American federal government's experience with HRM and related reinvention reforms is really typical only of its own past reform experience. That experience reflects incremental, largely informal change; broad, somewhat unclear and sometimes conflicting objectives; and modest attention to careful implementation. The outcomes are difficult to assess. As Pollitt notes of management reform more generally, "The splendid coat of many colors envisaged by some reformers–slim, fast, effective, decentralized, open, trusted government–still lies more in the realms of hope and imagination than in demonstrated and warranted reality" (Pollitt, 2000:196).

There is still hope for human resource management reforms, however. The new recognition of human resources as critical to organizational success, as core parts of broader organizational capacity, and as resources to be carefully selected and developed necessarily moves away from old models of personnel management. Some states and some other national governments have already demonstrated that discretion and flexibility are not incompatible with accountability in public organizations. And as citizens and elected officials focus on better performance in public organizations, they must also be attentive to the public employees upon whom that performance depends.

REFERENCES

BAN, CAROLYN. 1997. Hiring in the public sector: 'Expediency management' or structural reform? In Carolyn Ban and Norma M. Riccuci (eds.), *Public Personnel Management*. New York: Longman.

BAN, CAROLYN. 2000. The National Performance Review as implicit evaluation of CSRA: Building on or overturning the legacy? In James P. Pfiffner and Douglas A. Brook (eds.), New York: Oxford University Press.

BAN, CAROLYN, and TONI MARZOTTO. 1984. Delegations of examining: Objectives and implementation. In Patricia W. Ingraham and Carolyn Ban, eds., *Legislating Bureaucratic Change: The Civil Service Reform Act of 1978*. Albany: State University of New York Press.

BERRY, FRANCES S., RICHARD CHAKERIAN, and BARTON WECHSLER. 1999. Reinventing Government: Lessons from a State Capital. In H. George Frederickson and Jocelyn M. Johnston, eds. *Public Management Reform and Innovation*. Tuscaloosa: University of Alabama Press, 329–355.

Federalist Papers #68. 1961. Edited by Clinton Rossiter. New York: Mentor, 414.

General Acounting Office. 1999. Human Capital: A Self-Assessment Checklist for Agency Leaders. Washington, DC: Government Printing Office.

Government Performance Project. 1999, 2000. http://www.maxwell.syr.edu/gpp/.

INGRAHAM, PATRICIA WALLACE. 1995. *The Foundation of Merit*. Baltimore: The Johns Hopkins University Press.

INGRAHAM, PATRICIA WALLACE, and DONALD P. MOYNIHAN. 2000. Criteria, components and characteristics: Preliminary lessons from high-performing states in managing for results. GPP working papers. Alan K. Campbell Institute of Public Affairs, Maxwell School, Syracuse University.

INGRAHAM, PATRICIA WALLACE, SALLY COLEMAN SELDEN, and DONALD P. MOYNIHAN. 2000a. People and Performance: Challenges for the Future Public Service. *Public Administration Review*, Jan/Feb.

INGRAHAM, PATRICIA WALLACE, B. GUY PETERS, and DONALD P. MOYNIHAN. 2000. Public employment and the future of the public service. In B. Guy Peters and Donald Savoi (eds.), *Governance in a Changing Environment.* Montreal: McGill University Press.

INGRAHAM, PATRICIA WALLACE, SALLY COLEMAN SELDEN, and DONALD P. MOYNIHAN. 2000b. People and performance: Challenges for the future public service—the report from the Wye River conference. *Public Administration Review,* Vol. 60, Number 1: pp. 54–60.

INGRAHAM, PATRICIA WALLACE, JAMES R. THOMPSON, and RONALD P. SANDERS (EDS.), 1998. *Transforming Government: Lessons from the Reinvention Laboratories.* San Francisco: Jossey-Bass Publishers.

Internal Revenue Service, IRS Restructuring and Reform Act of 1998, http://www.irs.gov/tax_regs/rra2-1102.html

JOYCE, PHILIP, and SUSAN SIEG. 1999. Using Performance Information for Budgeting: Clarifying the Framework and Investigating Recent State Experience. Paper presented at the CAP Symposium at George Washington University, Washington, DC: November.

KAUFMAN, HERBERT. 1956. Administrative decentralization and political power. *Public Administrative Review,* 1956. 29:3.

KETTL, DONALD F. 1994. *Reinventing Government? Appraising the National Performance Review.* Washington, DC: Brookings Institution.

KETTL, DONALD F. 2000. Reinventing Reinvention: Reforming the Federal Bureaucracy in the New Century. *Lafollette Policy Report,* Vol. II, No. 1, Spring.

Merit Systems Protection Board. 1998. The changing federal workplace. *Employee Perspectives* (March):12–28.

National Academy of Public Administration. 1994. Modernizing Federal Classification: Operational Broad-Banding Systems Alternatives. Washington: National Academy of Public Administration.

National Academy of Public Administration. 1999. Building the Workforce of the Future to Achieve Organizational Success. Washington: National Academy of Public Administration.

National Academy of Public Administration. 2000. Building Successful Organizations. Washington, DC: National Academy of Public Administration.

National Performance Review. 1994. www.npr.gov.

PETERS, B. GUY, and DONALD J. SAVOIE (EDS.), 1998. *Taking Stock: Assessing Public Sector Reforms.* Montreal: McGill-Queen's University Press, 1998.

PERRY, J. L., and L. R. WISE. 1990. The motivation bases of public service. *Public Administrative Review,* Vol. 50, No. 3: pp. 367–373.

PFIFFNER, JAMES P., and DOUGLAS A. BROOK (EDS.), 2000. *The Future of Merit: Twenty Years After the Civil Service Reform Act.* New York: Oxford University Press.

POLLITT, CHRISTOPHER. 2000. The Impacts of Public Management Reform. *Public Management,* June, Vol. 2:2:181–199.

RAINEY, HAL G., and ED KELLOUGH. 2000. Civil service reform and incentives in the public service. In James P. Pfiffner and Douglas A. Brook (eds.).

ROMZEK, BARBARA S. 2000. Accountability implications of Civil Service Reform. In Pfiffner and Brook (eds). *The Future of Merit: Twenty Years After the Civil Service Reform Act.* New York: Oxford University Press.

ROMZEK, BARBARA S., and PATRICIA WALLACE INGRAHAM. 2000. Cross pressures of accountability: Initiative, command, and failure in the Ron Brown plane crash. *Public Administration Review,* Vol. 60, Number 3: pp. 240–253.

ROSENBLOOM, DAVID. 1995. Introduction to the "Reinvention" Forum, *Public Administration Review* (55), Number 3, ii.

SCHICK, ALLEN. 1998. An Assessment of the New Zealand Reforms. The World Bank: Brussels.

SKOWRONEK, STEPHEN. *Building a New American State: the Expansion of National Administrative Capacities, 1877–1920.* 1982. Cambridge, Massachusetts: Cambridge University Press.

THOMPSON, JAMES R. 1997. Public Service Reforms: Issues of Accountability and Public Law (book review). *Journal of Public Administration Research and Theory,* April 1997 (7)2:333–336.

THOMPSON, JAMES R. 1998. Ferment on the front lines: Devising new modes of organizing. In Ingraham, Patricia Wallace, James R. Thompson and Ronald P. Sanders (eds.).

THOMPSON, JAMES R. 1999. Devising administrative reform that works: The example of the reinvention lab program. *Public Administrative Review,* Vol. 59, Number 4, pp. 283–92.

PETERS, B. GUY, and JON PIERRE. 2000. Citizens Versus the New Public Manager. The Problem of Mutual Empowerment. *Administration & Society.* Volume 32, Number 1, p. 9.

6

Deregulating the Public Personnel Function

Jerrell D. Coggburn
University of Texas at San Antonio

"Too often, personnel processes hinder, rather than help, public sector organizations to attract, motivate, and retain the talented people government needs to provide responsive services to our citizens." Robert Lavigna (1996:10)

INTRODUCTION

As the epigraph suggests, if one were to ask the typical public manager to itemize the most frustrating aspects of his or her job, there is little doubt that dealing with personnel regulations would make the list (see Ban, 1995; Elling, 1992; Ammons, 1992). The source of such frustration might range from having to select an employee from a narrow list of certified candidates (e.g., the so-called "rule of three," which limits the hiring discretion of agencies by requiring them to select from the applicants possessing the top three test scores) to negotiating the procedural labyrinth that often typifies employee termination. Whatever the specific source(s), the overriding point is that public managers often feel severely limited by the rules and regulations that constitute public personnel/human resource management systems. Facing these limitations, it is easy to see why traditional personnel processes would be described as a hindrance.

In some instances, the feeling of having one's hands tied has led public managers to undertake a variety of coping strategies. These efforts are employed in order to circumvent restrictive personnel regulations. Examples of such behavior might include hiring an employee on a temporary or provisional basis, which usually allows agency managers to hire more quickly than they could if they had to go through centralized, competitive exam processes, or "tailoring" a job description so that it precisely matches the knowledge, skills, and abilities (KSAs) possessed by an individual that a manager wants to hire (see Ospina 1992; Ban and Riccucci, 1997). When public managers make these or other questionable human resource management practices part of their managerial repertoire, they are said to be practicing "expediency management" (Ospina 1992), or to be "creatively coping" (Ban, 1995), or to be employing "underground merit" (Jorgensen, Fairless, and Patton, 1996). Whatever label one chooses to put on these behaviors, the underlying problem is the same: These practices detract from the efficiency and effectiveness of human resource management because "maneuvering to get around the rigidities of the personnel procedures eats up time and effort that might be more productively devoted to the core tasks of the agency" (Thompson, 1994:7).

Owing to the frustration of managers and to the obvious inadequacies (not to mention possible illegality) of these coping tactics, proponents of the concept of granting administrators greater flexibility over human resource management have identified another, more palatable approach: personnel deregulation. _Personnel deregulation,_ in essence, refers to the reduction and, where possible, elimination of rules and regulations that impede the effectiveness and efficiency of the personnel function (see DiIulio, 1994; DiIulio, Garvey, and Kettl, 1993). The rationale for making such changes is clearly captured by Paul A. Volcker and William F. Winter, the respective chairs of two recent administrative reform commissions:

> "Not even the most public spirited government workers can succeed if they are hemmed in on all sides by rules, regulations, and procedures that make it virtually impossible to perform well. The most talented, dedicated, well-compensated, well-trained, and well-led civil servants cannot serve the public well if they are subject to perverse personnel practices that punish innovation, promote mediocrity, and proscribe flexibility" (Volcker and Winter, 1994, XV).

And what specific personnel practices should be deregulated? The final report of the Winter Commission (1993; see pp. 24–34)–a commission created to find ways to improve state and local government public service–offers some specific recommendations:

- Decrease the reliance on written exams for hiring and promotions. Such exams are often out-of-date, biased, or invalid.
- Expand managerial discretion over staffing by allowing choice from more than the "rule of three."
- Reduce reliance on rules that give preference to certain groups (e.g., veterans' preference, seniority).
- Reduce the number of job classifications and pay bands to give agency managers greater flexibility in assigning and rewarding work.
- Drop or modify ineffective, paper-intensive pay-for-performance systems.
- Streamline the employee termination process so that poor performance problems can be resolved in a matter of days.
- Have central personnel offices serve as consultants and advisors to agencies rather than as procedural guardians.

In many instances, these deregulation themes are echoed in two reports issued by the National Performance Review: _From Red Tape to Results: Creating a Government that Works Better and Costs Less_ (NPR 1993a), and the accompanying _Reinventing Human Resource Management_ (NPR 1993b). _Reinventing Human Resource_

Management (NPR 1993b), for example, lists fourteen general recommendations and some forty-six specific actions that would "reinvent" federal human resource management. Examples of the deregulatory actions identified include:

- Phase out the entire *Federal Personnel Manual* and all agency implementing directives.
- Authorize agencies to establish their own recruitment and examining programs. Abolish central registers and standard application forms.
- Allow federal departments and agencies to determine that recruitment shortages exist and directly hire candidates without ranking.
- Provide agencies with the flexibility to establish broadbanding systems built upon the General Schedule framework.
- Reduce by half the time required to terminate federal managers and employees for cause. Make other improvements in the systems for dealing with poor performers.
- Deregulate training and make it more responsive to market sources.

Proponents of deregulation (hereafter referred to as deregulators), assert that measures like these can increase both the efficiency and effectiveness of public human resource management. Deregulated human resource management is more efficient, the argument goes, because decisions could be reached in less time, with less paperwork, and with fewer levels of clearance (see Ban, 1995). Similarly, the effectiveness of human resource management is increased by deregulation because it increases managers' discretion, thus enabling them to hire the best and brightest employees, to offer the incentives needed for employees (hence, agencies) to perform, and to remove employees who underperform. In an era that seems preoccupied with performance, it is hard to argue with the allure of such assertions.

This chapter deals with the topic of public personnel deregulation. It begins with a brief discussion of the pro-reform context in which deregulation has emerged. Next, the theoretical components of personnel deregulation are considered. The chapter then examines some empirical evidence that speaks to deregulation's prevalence in the personnel function at the various levels of government in the United States. Finally, a number of important issues associated with personnel deregulation are identified. How these various issues are addressed will go a long way toward determining the life expectancy of this latest brand of personnel reform.

THE CONTEXT OF PERSONNEL DEREGULATION

Understanding why personnel deregulation is receiving attention these days requires little more than taking stock of the reform climate surrounding government in recent years. The calls for personnel deregulation, like the more general calls to improve the performance of government, reflect "the culmination of decades of public dissatisfaction, professional discontent, and intellectual criticism" (Caiden, 1994:123). The discussion in the introduction to this chapter should provide a sense of the discontent felt by many public professionals who feel trapped by outmoded systems of human resource management. They simply feel that they do not have the latitude needed to effectively manage (e.g., recruit, reward, motivate) government's human resources in today's fast paced, high skilled, and technologically advanced environment. As for public dissatisfaction, one needs to look no further than to reports of the public's skepticism, criticism, suspicion, and lack of trust in government (e.g., Ruscio, 1996; Thompson and Radin, 1997). This complicates human resource management because qualified people are turned off to careers in government and because the financial resources needed to adequately fund the personnel function are made harder to come by. Finally, intellectual criticism has been levied by a number of scholars (e.g., Barzelay with Armajani, 1992; DiIulio, 1994; DiIulio, Garvey, and Kettl, 1993; Kettl, Ingraham, Sanders, and Horner, 1996; Wilson, 1989), administrative reform commissions (Volcker Commission, 1989; Winter Commission 1993), and the broader reinventing government movement (e.g., Osborne and Gaebler, 1992; National Performance Review, 1993b). In all of these cases, criticism is directed at the dysfunctional nature of regulatory overkill: the performance of agencies is hampered because managers do not have the discretion they need.

From these disparate sources emerges what appears to be a general consensus that government is not performing very well, and a that a key reason for this lack of performance lies with traditional modes of personnel management.

THEORETICAL FOUNDATIONS OF PERSONNEL DEREGULATION

Reduced to its simplest form, the theory of personnel deregulation asserts that removing excessive, restrictive procedural rules and regulations will enable agencies and their managers to generate more efficient, effective human resource management for government. Embedded within this theory, however, are a number of other theoretical positions that are worth identifying. More precisely, deregulation can be thought of as an administrative policy which incorporates a theory of the problem, a theory of desired outcomes, and a theory of intervention (see Weiss, 1999).

First, the theory of the problem is that human resource management in government is slow, rigid, ineffective, and inefficient (Jorgensen, Fairless, and Patton, 1996; DiIulio, Garvey, and Kettl, 1993). This state of affairs was brought about gradually as a result of the common practice of reacting to administrative problems by creating rules and procedures to prevent those problems from happening again (see Peters, 1996). Moreover, the central personnel offices responsible for enforcing these rules often place regulatory enforcement above the goal of meeting the human resource needs of government agencies (Barzelay with Armajani, 1992). Thus, deregulation holds the view that public employees are not the problem; rather, the problem lies in the overregulated, centrally enforced personnel systems in which they are forced to work.

Deregulation's theory of the desired outcomes is straightforward. It envisions efficient and effective human resource management that enables public managers and agencies to fulfill their missions. Managers would use their discretion to attract, select, retain, and motivate employees. Good work would be rewarded, while poor performance would be effectively addressed. Implicit here is an important assumption about the forces (i.e., public managers) that would bring about these desired outcomes. For example, removing regulatory constraints is desirable because public employees are "public regarding" (Dubnick, 1994; see also Peters, 1996). That is, public managers, freed from the binds of personnel regulation and centralized control, can be trusted to carry out the personnel function in a manner that meets their agencies' needs and promotes the public interest. Also implicit here is the idea that, when freed from regulation, managers will actually use their discretion.

Finally, deregulation's theory of intervention relates to effecting change from the problem to the desired outcomes. In other words, the intervention is what would move human resource management from a slow, bureaucratized state to the efficient, effective one described above. Here, the intervention favored is to remove the rules and regulations that impede performance.

While deregulation is seldom discussed in these theoretical terms, these various theories nevertheless combine to form the foundation on which the deregulation argument is built. To students and practitioners of public human resource management, it is important to recognize and evaluate the strength of these theoretical positions. Only through experience and analysis can the soundness of these theories be determined.

PERSONNEL DEREGULATION: AN IDEA WHOSE TIME HAS COME?

Given all of the talk about deregulation and all of the recommendations for its adoption, a natural question to ask is whether or not deregulation is having an impact on the personnel function. In other words, is there empirical evidence of personnel deregulation? The answer to this question is certainly "yes." In fact, examples of personnel deregulation can be found at the various levels of government in the United States.

First, at the federal level, the Office of Personnel Management (OPM) recently issued a report on personnel deregulation. The report, which is based on a survey of federal personnel directors, indicates that, "Overall, . . . OPM and [federal] agencies are reducing personnel rules and regulations at least to some extent . . ." (U.S. Office of Personnel Management [OPM] 1998:5). To be more specific, 87 percent of the respondents report that OPM has reduced personnel rules and regulations from "some extent" to "a very great extent," while 97 percent report that their own agencies have reduced their personnel rules and regulations from "some extent" to "a very great extent" (U.S. OPM 1998:5). Thus, the OPM study offers clear evidence of personnel deregulation at the federal level.

One can also get a sense of deregulation at the federal level from an examination of the fourth report of the National Performance Review, *The Best Kept Secrets in Government* (NPR, 1996). The report briefly highlights–in a tone that mocks the traditional personnel function–the accomplishments of the Clinton administration's efforts to reinvent federal human resource management. Deregulation-related changes mentioned include creating "common sense" job applications instead of using the "ridiculously long" SF-171 (the SF-171 was the standard application form that federal agencies were formerly required to use), and reducing red tape by "junking" most of the *Federal Personnel Manual (FPM)*(NPR, 1996:24). In short, these examples illustrate that personnel deregulation has occurred at the federal level under the guise of the Clinton administration's reinvention efforts.

Second, evidence of personnel deregulation can be found at the subnational level. On the local government level, for example, researchers have identified instances of personnel deregulation in places like Dallas and Baltimore (Hamman and Desai, 1995), Indianapolis (Perry, Wise, and Martin, 1994), and Philadelphia (Pierce, 1994). Similarly, state-level research shows that deregulation is a prominent theme of personnel reform initiatives in places like Florida (Pierce 1994; Wechsler 1993, 1994), New York (Ban and Riccucci, 1994), Wisconsin (Lavigna, 1996), and Georgia (Gossett, 1997; Facer, 1998). This is not to say that human resource management has been deregulated to the same extent in all of these places—indeed, social, political, and economic differences insure a measure of variability in deregulation from setting to setting—but, it does offer evidence that deregulation is occurring in cities and states.

Some of the most notable reforms at the state level have occurred in Georgia, South Carolina, and Wisconsin. Georgia, for example, has "gone to the edge" when it comes to personnel reform: the state eliminated civil service protections entirely for employees hired after July 1, 1996 (Barrett and Green, 1999). By significantly deregulating and devolving authority to line agencies, the state hoped to streamline many human resource practices, including employee discipline and termination. South Carolina's reforms seek to give managers more control over human resource management by, among other things, reducing the number of job classifications, giving managers more flexibility to award pay raises, and reorienting the state's Office of Human Resources from an agency of personnel specialists emphasizing regulatory control to one of human resource generalists emphasizing line agency service and consulting (Hays, 2000; Barrett and Green, 1999). For Wisconsin's part, the state has made great strides in streamlining employee selection by instituting walk-in testing for some positions, creating alternatives to written exams for professional positions, giving agencies the ability to quickly hire qualified candidates for "critical" areas (e.g., health, engineering), and eliminating limited certified lists (Lavigna, 1996; Barrett and Greene, 1999).

Table 6–1 offers some additional information on the extent of personnel deregulation in the states. The data represent the number of states whose personnel systems possess some of the forms of personnel deregulation mentioned in the introduction of this chapter. The data were gathered from a survey of top personnel officials in the states (Coggburn, 1999). As the table shows, some forms of deregulation have caught on more readily than others. For example, moving away from written exams (by giving agencies control over selection criteria) and increasing agency discretion by expanding the "rule of three" are quite common, while fewer states have dared to upset politically powerful veterans groups by removing veterans' preference. More generally, the data support the argument that personnel deregulation, at least in some manifestations, has taken place.

In light of this evidence, one can safely conclude that calls for personnel deregulation have fallen on receptive ears throughout government. Recognizing this, it is important to consider some of the major challenges associated with a deregulated personnel function. The next section considers some issues that will likely determine whether deregulation will become a permanent feature of the

TABLE 6–1   Number of States Exhibiting Forms of HRM Deregulation

Form of Deregulation	Number (Percent) Possessing
Eliminate restrictive selection criteria	30 (67%)
Line agencies develop selection criteria for hiring	32 (71%)
Streamline employee termination processes	14 (31%)
Eliminate veterans' preference for hiring	02 (04%)
Eliminate seniority-based "bumping rights"	13 (29%)
Eliminate the use of a standard state application form	09 (20%)
Implement broadbanding	17 (38%)

Source: Coggburn, 1999. Number of states responding = 45.

public human resource management landscape or if it will only be a short-lived experiment.

PROBLEMS AND PROSPECTS

Deregulation, like any other personnel reform, presents public managers and human resource managers with a variety of opportunities and challenges. The opportunities, as mentioned in the introduction of this chapter, center on giving managers the flexibility they need to make the personnel function more efficient and effective. In contrast, the focus of the following discussion is on several major issues and challenges surrounding personnel deregulation. While the list presented below is not exhaustive, it does contain some of the most serious and immediate challenges facing personnel deregulation.

Managerial Capacity and Incoherence

A primary issue that needs to be recognized concerns the new responsibilities deregulation confers upon human resource managers and line agency managers. While it may not be popular to think of the central personnel office as a convenience (deregulators argue the exact opposite), it is nonetheless true that having a central agency charged with the task of handling human resource issues relieves line agencies and agency managers of many personnel-related burdens. In a deregulated environment, however, these very responsibilities are shifted to agencies. What is more, the detailed guidelines that once delimited the personnel function are reduced, if not eliminated.

When and where such a shift of responsibility and reduction of detailed guidance occurs, it is crucial for both managers and human resource managers at the agency level to have the capacity to successfully take on their new roles. Do managers and human resource managers in line agencies possess the KSAs needed to perform their new tasks? This is a fundamentally important question, especially in light of the observation that many managers have advanced to their positions without adequate training in the area of personnel (see NAPA, 1983:39). A lack of such knowledge coupled with the reduction in detailed guidance raises the possibility that agency managers will be placed in positions of uncertainty when it comes to resolving human resource issues (Peters and Savoie, 1996).

In a similar vein, the roles and expectations of those working in central personnel offices must change in a deregulated environment. In particular, central personnel offices, once the guardians of personnel rules and regulations, will be called upon to serve as advisors or consultants to line agencies. Obviously, this represents a departure from their traditional regulatory enforcement focus. Will the employees of central personnel offices have the skills required to shift from a "policing" role to a consulting or advising role?

The answer to these questions are not all at once clear, but the sketchy evidence that does exist gives some reason for concern. Ban (1998), for example, reports on the findings of a 1993 Merit Systems Protection Board study (U.S. Merit Systems Protection Board [MSPB] 1993) of the federal personnel function. The MSPB report found that 56 percent of the managers and 46 percent of the personnelists surveyed indicated that either "to a large extent" or "to some extent" the difficulty of performing their personnel duties was increased because of personnelists' lack of skill (Ban, 1998:23). This same MSPB report shows that federal personnel managers candidly admit to a skill deficiency—57 percent responded that their knowledge and skill level allowed them to provide excellent service only "to a small extent" (Ban, 1998:23).

More recent evidence paints a strikingly similar picture. A 1999 MSPB report, for example, identifies a lack of knowledge on the part of agency managers and supervisors as a major obstacle for the federal government's deregulated and decentralized hiring activities (U.S. MSPB, 1999). Similarly, the OPM notes that a lack of knowledge regarding personnel deregulation has left federal managers, supervisors, and personnelists confused about what they can and cannot do (U.S. OPM, 1998). Given this, one can easily see why many federal managers and supervisors "feel that they need more training in personnel policy and issues to know how to most effectively use the [personnel] system" (U.S. OPM, 1998:11).

In short, doing away with centrally prescribed and enforced regulations may leave both managers and human resource managers in line agencies without the direction they need or, at least, have become accustomed to. This potential problem is exacerbated by the possibility that central personnel offices lack the capacity to advise line agencies properly. Together, this leaves open the possibility that human resource decisions will be made in an inconsistent, incoherent fashion across agencies. Avoiding this will require the successful adaptation to new responsibilities and the acquisition of the requisite KSAs by those working in central personnel offices and by managers and human resource managers working in line agencies.

Real Change or Chimera?

A second issue associated with personnel deregulation asks whether agency managers really want the flexibility and discretion that the deregulators suggest they are clamoring for. More specifically, the question is: If centrally imposed regulations and control are lifted, will that necessarily translate into the greater use of discretion by public managers?

The question may seem peculiar, but consider the case of the federal government following the demise of the OPM's *FPM* (mentioned above). This 10,000 plus page manual was, perhaps, the epitome of personnel overregulation and a prime target for the deregulation efforts of the NPR: the *FPM* was ceremoniously discarded in January 1994.

In the wake of the much ballyhooed elimination of the *FPM,* one would think that federal agencies and managers would be relieved by their newfound liberation. It might come as surprise to learn that in many instances just the opposite has proven to be true: federal agencies have ventured into the administrative trash heap, dusted off the discarded *FPM* and claimed it as their own (Peters, 1996:94). One can only speculate if this is occurring in other settings where deregulation has taken place, but the possibility remains real. Eliminating regulations at one level (the central personnel office) only to have them resurrected at another (line agencies) certainly does not constitute the type of deregulation envisioned by the deregulators.

Understanding why some managers are loathe to exercise the discretion deregulation provides may be understood by considering the nature of managers and public management. Some public managers, quite simply, may be more comfortable than others when it comes to exercising discretion (Ban, 1995). This recognizes that timid mangers find it more to their liking to "hide behind the rules" because of the security and certainty that rules entail (Facer, 1998; Peters, 1996). Such risk aversion is understandable when one considers the lack of incentives public managers have to take chances (e.g., the notorious inadequacies of pay-for-performance schemes; see Kearney and Hays, 1998) and the observation that a single administrative miscue can be fatal to a public administrator's standing or career (Romzek, 1998).

From this, it is clear that doing away with personnel rules and regulations does not necessarily mean that public managers will act in the ways envisioned by the deregulators. Therefore, the real issue may not be simply one of deregulating the personnel function, but one of providing managers the incentives to actually utilize the discretion that deregulation affords.

The Important Issue of Equity

A third issue facing deregulation is, perhaps, the most troubling. This is the issue of fairness or equity. Leaving aside the arguments about the slowness and rigidity of traditional personnel systems, there is little arguing that these systems have served to make human resource decisions more consistent, predictable, and equitable. What happens then when centrally prescribed regulations are dropped? Will public employees be treated fairly? Consistently?

The troubling nature of this issue has not been lost on the public administration community. Savoie and Peters (1996:287–288), for example, directly raise this issue in their worries about the "sameness of treatment" of public employees: "With the fall of centrally prescribed rules and regulations . . . , there will be less certainty and consequently less 'sameness' in how issues are resolved." Similarly, Kellough (1998) identifies the "equity problem" by arguing that current personnel reforms raise the potential for inequitable treatment of government employees and that mechanisms to prevent such treatment are not clearly established.

To be sure, the issue of equity is a real one, and failing to address it adequately may mean that deregulation runs into strong opposition. Public employees have come to expect equitable treatment (Peters and Savoie, 1996), and personnel rules and regulations offer a symbolically powerful assurance of equity. This is clearly evident in a study in which both public employees and human resource managers were found to view centrally prescribed personnel regulations as being key to insuring the fair treatment of employees (Elliott, 1985). Given this, one can anticipate that public employees will resist personnel changes (like deregulation) that might pose a threat to equity. In fact, this may be the main reason that public employee unions have opposed personnel deregulation in a number of settings (Ban and Riccucci, 1994; Wechsler, 1994; Coggburn, 1999). For deregulation to succeed, these fears will need to be allayed. How that can be accomplished, however, has not been fully established.

Corruption and Errors in a Deregulated Environment

Dealing with cases of personnel-related corruption and error represents a fourth problem for deregulation. First, there is little doubt that a deregulated personnel system is one that is more vulnerable to abuse and corruption than a regulated one (Thompson, 1994; Stein, 1994; Perry, Wise, and Martin, 1994; Ban, 1995). This presents a definite challenge given that the history of public personnel reform in the United States has been, for at least the last century, a history of battling partisan corruption and abuse. Opening the door to the possibility of corruption, as personnel deregulation does, would seem to fly in the face of an historic obsession with the "anticorruption project" (Anechiarico and Jacobs, 1996).

The same general problem applies to cases of honest, though equally intolerable, error on the part of public managers. If a public manager hires an incompetent person, inadvertently discriminates, or makes some other personnel gaffe, then there will no doubt be a reaction. The question centers on how strong that reaction will be. Is it realistic to expect politicians and the public to be tolerant of an occasional mistake made by a well-intentioned bureaucrat (see Kearney and Hays, 1998)?

The problem for personnel deregulation is rather obvious: in the face of documented abuse or an egregious error, pressure will be exerted on government officials to reinstate the central controls that will prevent such abuses or errors from occurring again. The potential for this reassertion of control has already been identified by those who warn of "reregulation" (Romzek, 1997, 1998; Peters, 1996). That this potential exists is understandable given the control-orientation of past reforms and the fact that deregulation is only in its infancy, relatively speaking. When problems surface, it could be all too easy to revert to the familiar rule-bound orientation. Whether the personnel function will be able to avoid such a regulatory boomerang is far from clear.

Trust and Accountability

Another telling indicator for the prospects of deregulation is trust. Simply stated, if administrators do not have the trust of elected officials (i.e., the president and congress at the federal level, governors and legislators at the state level, mayors and councils at the local level), and of the general public, then the prospects of loosening the controls over any function of administration—including personnel—would seem to be in serious doubt. In fact, it can be argued that deregulation and trust are inseparable—one cannot exist without the other (Dubnick, 1994:279; see also DiIulio, Garvey, and Kettl, 1993). Gaining the trust in administrators that deregulation requires will be no small task, as trusting government ". . . runs against the grain of a political culture built upon the suspicion of government" (Thompson, 1994).

Given that the public's trust of government may actually be declining (Ruscio, 1996) and, as shown above, that personnel deregulation is occurring (to varying degrees) throughout government, then deregulation may be steering public human resource management down a dangerous course. Speaking directly to this point, Romzek (1997, 1998) has warned that reforms like personnel deregulation may be moving public administration toward forms of accountability (e.g., reliance on the professional accountability of administrators as opposed to accountability ensured through hierarchical/bureaucratic rules) that the public is not ready for. Thus, it seems as if the deregulators are facing a two-edged sword: gaining trust in order to gain the flexibility and discretion needed to perform, while at the same time needing flexibility and discretion in order to achieve the results needed to gain trust.

The Danger of Throwing Out Useful Regulations

Throwing out needed/useful regulations in a rush to deregulate the personnel function represents yet another problem for personnel deregulation. The idea here is really quite simple: all personnel regulations are not bad, even if they impede managerial action. In other words, just because a particular rule complicates the personnel function does not necessarily mean that it should be eliminated. Such rules exist in the first place to meet legitimate purposes (e.g., ensuring merit, protecting public employees from political patronage) (see Lavigna, 1996). As Herbert Kaufman put it, "One person's 'red tape' may be another's treasured procedural safeguard" (1977:4; see also Peters and Savoie, 1996). The observation that not *all* rules are bad, but that deregulation is needed represents the "dilemma of deregulation" (Nathan, 1994:168).

This situation is one that is not lost on the deregulators. They readily acknowledge the need to identify the "essential" regulations (which should be kept) and the "marginal" ones (which could be eliminated) (Wilson, 1989:372). Unfortunately, firm guidance on making the distinction between these two types of regulation has not yet surfaced.

A good example of throwing out a useful requirement comes from the case of the SF–171. The SF–171 was the standard form used by job applicants to the federal government. Scrapping the long, detailed application was needed, according to the NPR (1996:24), because it sent a "welcome to the fun house" message which discouraged qualified applicants from applying. In its place, federal agencies were given the latitude to accept and review resumes so that applicants could apply "like regular people do for regular jobs" (NPR, 1996:24).

While doing away with SF–171 may sound like a good example of reinventing federal human resource management via deregulation, experience tells a different story. Roughly three-fifths (59 percent) of the respondents to a recent MSPB survey of federal managers indicated that "they would prefer a single prescribed form or format for job applications" (U.S. MSPB 1998:5). The reason? Managers are finding the process of reviewing applicants' resumes for the desired qualifications to be more difficult than reviewing the old SF–171s. This is because all applicants do not supply the same information, nor is the information that is supplied displayed in the same fashion from resume to resume (U.S. MSPB, 1998:4). Thus, those making human resource decisions have to sift through incomplete information, presented in an inconsistent format, to identify the best candidates (see also U.S. MSPB, 1999; U.S. OPM, 1998). It should come as no surprise that these decision makers reported concerns about the fairness and effectiveness of the non-SF–171 application review process: applicants often do not get as much credit as they deserve for their qualifications because they do not provide enough information on their resumes, so the "best" candidate may not be identified (U.S. MSPB, 1999:9).

While this is a rather simple illustration, it does point out that doing away with standard personnel requirements is not necessarily a sure road to greater administrative efficiency and effectiveness. Recognizing the difficulties that can accompany the elimination of useful rules and regulations, prudence may dictate following a deliberate, incremental approach to personnel deregulation (e.g., DiIulio, Kettl, and Garvey, 1993; Walters, 1992). Ban and Riccucci (1997, 201) state the challenge well: "we will always have to struggle to find the proper balance between the need for control to prevent abuses and the need to give managers enough discretion to do their jobs well."

The Politics of Deregulation

The final challenge to be considered here has the potential to be the most telling for the prospects of personnel deregulation. This challenge, in a word, is politics. Public human resource management and its deregulation (or any other reform for that matter) cannot be divorced from the political context of the public sector. In fact, it has become quite popular for elected officials to run for office on the promise of creating "better" government (see Rosenbloom, 1993; Arnold, 1995). Often, such promises focus directly on the civil service and the personnel function. Recent gubernatorial campaigns in places like Florida (see Wechsler, 1994, 1993) and Georgia (see Facer, 1998) exemplify this, as does the 1992 Clinton campaign for the presidency. Such campaigns tap into popular public sentiments by manipulating deregulation symbols like "red tape" and the "good people trapped in bad systems" argument. The underlying message is that government's performance is compromised by the existence of arcane personnel systems that prevent managers meeting their agencies' human resource needs. For now, at least, this is a politically popular position.

A prime example of the politics associated with personnel deregulation comes from the case of the *FPM*. Discarding the *FPM* presented an opportunity to capitalize on the symbolic appeal of battling red tape. This opportunity was not lost on the Clinton administration, which chose to make the *FPM*'s ride into the sunset a memorable one: "We actually hauled it out to a dumpster in a wheelbarrow" (NPR, 1996:24).

The important thing to remember is that deregulation, just like any other type of personnel reform, will produce effects—some anticipated and desirable, others unanticipated and undesirable. When the effects fall into the latter category, new symbols and political opportunities will be created. The image of the *FPM* being hauled out to the dumpster in a wheel barrow was certainly symbolically appealing and exploitable, but it would probably pale in comparison to the image of an unscrupulous administrator abusing his or her discretion over the personnel function to punish enemies, reward friends, systematically discriminate against women or minorities, or commit some other form of reckless behavior. One can easily imagine a political opportunist using such behavior to rail against the "ills" of deregulated personnel systems: "The government's personnel function is out of control. We need to eliminate the abuses that deregulation has encouraged!"

Avoiding such a fate for personnel deregulation will require the exertion of political will on the part of elected officials (Peters, 1996). When an error occurs or when corruption is uncovered, it will be incumbent upon politicians to resist the inevitable calls to reimpose controls over the personnel function. Of course, it is far from certain if such a requirement could ever be met. Simply put, politicians may not be able to resist the temptation to retaliate against administrative failings because "imposing rules and controls on bureaucracy is rarely bad electoral politics" (Peters, 1996:93; see also Kearney and Hays, 1998:45).

CONCLUSION: WHAT DOES THE FUTURE HOLD FOR DEREGULATION?

This chapter has considered the topic of deregulating the public personnel function. From an efficiency and effectiveness standpoint, there is no arguing that the case for deregulation is, at least on its face, a compelling one. Rules that serve no purpose other than impeding efficiency and effectiveness would seem to epitomize the often-cited charge that public personnel administration represents the "triumph of technique over purpose" (Sayre, 1948). In such cases, removing or modifying the suspect rules would seem to be a perfectly reasonable approach.

On the other hand, human resource management in the public sector is not merely about efficiency and effectiveness. Indeed, a variety of other values (e.g., merit, equity) are of no less importance. Hastily removing rules and regulations in the name of achieving more effective and efficient human resource management while downplaying the significance of other values and ignoring the seriousness of the challenges presented above may well signal a new triumph—one of ambition over purpose. The ultimate challenge, therefore, is to arrive at a place where public managers have the discretion they need to meet their agencies' human resource needs *and* where public employees are treated in an equitable, meritorious fashion. Finding this balance will be a task born of experimentation, modification, and, perhaps, luck.

REFERENCES

AMMONS, D. N. 1992. Productivity Barriers in the Public Service. In M. Holzer, ed., *Public Productivity Handbook*. New York: Marcel Dekker, Inc., pp. 117–136.

ANECHIARICO, F. and J. B. JACOBS. 1996. *The Pursuit of Absolute Integrity: How Corruption Control Makes Government Ineffective.* Chicago, IL: The University of Chicago Press.

ARNOLD, P. 1995. Reform's Changing Role. *Public Administration Review* vol. 55, no. 5 (Sept/Oct):407–417.

BAN, C. 1998. The Changing Role of the Personnel Office. In S. Condrey, ed., *Handbook of Human Resource Management in Government.* San Francisco, CA: Jossey-Bass Publishers.

——. 1995. *How Do Public Managers Manage?* San Francisco, CA: Jossey-Bass Publishers.

—— and N. M. RICCUCCI. 1997. Hiring in the Public Sector: 'Expediency Management' or Structural Reform. In C. Ban and N. M. Riccucci, eds., *Public Personnel Management: Current Reforms, Future Challenges.* New York: Longman, pp. 189–204.

——. 1994. New York State: Civil Service Reform in a Complex Political Environment. *Review of Public Personnel Administration* 14 (2):28–39.

BARRETT, K., and R. GREENE. 1999. Grading the States: A Management Report Card. *Governing* vol. 12, no. 5 (February).

BARZELAY, M., with B. ARMAJANI. 1992. *Breaking Through Bureaucracy.* Berkeley, CA: University of California Press.

CAIDEN, G. 1994. Administrative Reform–American Style. *Public Administration Review* vol. 54, no. 2 (March–April):123–128.

COGGBURN, J. D. 1999. In Search of Deregulation: Exploring Administrative Reform in the American States. Ph.D. dissertation, University of South Carolina.

DiIULIO, J. 1994. *Deregulating the Public Service: Can Government be Improved?* Washington, DC: The Brookings Institute.

——, G. GARVEY, and D. KETTL. 1993. *Improving Government Performance: An Owner's Manual.* Washington, DC: The Brookings Institute.

DUBNICK, M. J. 1994. A Coup Against King Bureaucracy? In J. DiIulio, ed., *Deregulating the Public Service.* Washington, DC: The Brookings Institute.

ELLING, R. C. 1992. *Public Management in the States: A Comparative Study of Administrative Performance and Politics.* Westport, CT: Praeger.

ELLIOT, R. 1985. Personnel Professional and State Employee Perceptions of Merit Systems Procedures. *Review of Public Personnel Administration,* vol. 5 (3):26–41.

FACER, R. L. 1998. Reinventing Public Administration: Reform in the Georgia Civil Service. *Public Administration Quarterly,* vol. 22 (1):58–73.

GOSSETT, C. 1997. Civil Service Reform: The Case of Georgia. Paper presented at the Annual Meeting of the Southern Political Science Association, November 1997.

HAMMAN, J. A., and U. DESAI. 1995. Current Issues and Challenges in Recruitment and Selection. In S. W. Hays and R. C. Kearney, eds., *Public Personnel Administration: Problems and Prospects,* 3rd ed. Englewood Cliffs, NJ: Prentice Hall.

HAYS, S. W. 2000. Changing Roles and Duties Within Government's Human Resources Profession: Contemporary Models and Challenges. In K. T. Liou, ed., *Handbook of Public Management Practice and Reform.* New York: Marcel Dekker.

JORGENSEN, L., K. FAIRLESS, and D. PATTON. 1996. Underground Merit Systems and the Balance Between Service and Compliance. *Review of Public Personnel Administration* vol. 16 (2):5–20.

KAUFMAN, H. 1977. *Red Tape: Its Origins, Uses, and Abuses.* Washington, DC: The Brookings Institute.

KEARNEY, R. C., and S. W. HAYS. 1998. "The New Public Management and Civil Service Systems in International Perspective." *Review of Public Personnel Administration* vol. 18 (4):38–54.

KELLOUGH, E. J. 1998. The Reinventing Government Movement: A Review and Critique. *Public Administration Quarterly* 22 (1):6–20.

KETTL, D., P. INGRAHAM, R. SANDERS, and C. HORNER. 1996. *Civil Service Reform: Building a Government That Works.* Washington, DC: The Brookings Institute.

LAVIGNA, R. 1996. "Creating a Responsive Personnel System." *PA Times* vol. 19, no. 11 (November 1, 1996):10, 14.

NATHAN, R. P. 1994. Deregulating State and Local Government: What Can Leaders Do? In J. DiIulio, ed., *Deregulating the Public Service.* Washington, DC: The Brookings Institute.

National Academy of Public Administration (NAPA). 1983. *Revitalizing Federal Management: Managers and Their Overburdened Systems.* Washington, DC: NAPA.

National Performance Review (NPR). 1996. *The Best Kept Secrets in Government: How the Clinton Administration is Reinventing the Way Washington Works.* Fourth report of the National Performance Review. New York: Random House.

———. 1993a. *From Red Tape to Results: Creating a Government that Works Better and Costs Less.* Report of the National Performance Review. Washington, DC: U.S. Government Printing Office.

———. 1993b. *Reinventing Human Resource Management.* Accompanying Report of the NPR. Washington, DC: U.S. Government Printing Office.

OSBORNE, D., and T. GAEBLER. 1992. *Reinventing Government: How the Entrepreneurial Spirit is Transforming the Public Sector.* New York: Plume.

OSPINA, S. J. 1992. Expediency Management in Public Service: A Dead-End Search for Managerial Discretion. *Review of Public Personnel Administration* vol. 12 (4):405–421.

PERRY, J., L. R. WISE, and M. MARTIN. 1994. Breaking the Civil Service Mold: The Case of Indianapolis. *Review of Public Personnel Administration* 14 (2):40–54.

PETERS, B. G. 1996. *The Future of Governing: Four Emerging Models.* Lawrence, KS: University of Kansas Press.

———. and D. J. SAVOIE. 1996. Managing Incoherence: The Coordination and Empowerment Conundrum. *Public Administration Review* vol. 56, no. 3 (May–June):281–290.

PIERCE, N. 1994. Is Deregulation Enough? Lessons From Philadelphia and Florida. In J. DiIulio, ed., *Deregulating the Public Service.* Washington, DC: The Brookings Institute.

ROMZEK, B. 1998. Where the Buck Stops: Accountability in Reformed Public Organizations. In J. Thompson and R. Sanders, eds., *Transforming Government: Lessons from the Reinvention Laboratories.* San Francisco, CA: Jossey-Bass.

———. 1997. Accountability Challenges of Deregulation. In C. Ban and N. M. Riccucci, eds., *Public Personnel Management: Current Reforms, Future Challenges.* New York: Longman, pp. 35–54.

ROSENBLOOM, D. 1993. Have an Administrative Rx? Don't Forget the Politics! *Public Administration Review* vol. 53, no. 6 (Nov–Dec):503–507.

RUSCIO, K. 1996. Trust, Democracy, and Public Management: A Theoretical Argument. *Journal of Public Administration Research and Theory* vol. 6, no. 3 (July):461–478.

SAYRE, W. A. 1948. The Triumph of Technique Over Purpose. *Public Administration Review* vol. 8 (Spring):134–137.

STEIN, L. 1994. Personnel Rules and Reform in an Unreformed Setting: St. Louis' Politicized Merit System. *Review of Public Personnel Administration* 14 (2):55–63.

THOMPSON, F. 1994. The Winter Commission Report: Is Deregulation the Answer for Public Personnel Management? *Review of Public Personnel Administration* 14 (2):5–9.

———, and B. RADIN. 1997. Reinventing Public Personnel Management: The Winter and Gore Initiatives. In C. Ban and N. M. Riccucci, eds., *Public Personnel Management: Current Reforms, Future Challenges.* New York: Longman, pp. 3–20.

U.S. Merit Systems Protection Board (MSPB). 1999. *The Role of Delegated Examining Units: Hiring New Employees in a Decentralized Civil Service.* Washington, DC: U.S. Government Printing Office.

———. 1998. SF-171: Not Gone, Not Forgotten. *Issues of Merit* (May):4–5.

———. 1993. *Federal Personnel Officers: Time for Change?* Washington, DC: U.S. Government Printing Office.

U.S. Office of Personnel Management (OPM). 1998. *Deregulation and Delegation of Human Resources Management Authority in the Federal Government.* MSE–98–3. Washington, DC: U.S. Government Printing Office.

Volcker Commission (National Commission on the Public Service). 1989. *Leadership for America: Rebuilding the Public Service.* Report of the National Commission on the Public Service. Washington, DC: National Commission on the Public Service.

VOLCKER, P. A., and W. F. WINTER. 1994. Introduction: Democracy and Public Service. In J. DiIulio, ed., *Deregulating the Public Service.* Washington, DC: The Brookings Institute.

WALTERS, J. 1992. How Not Reform Civil Service. *Governing* (November): 30–34.

WECHSLER, B. 1994. Reinventing Florida's Civil Service System: The Failure of Reform. *Review of Public Personnel Administration* 14 (2):64–76.

——. 1993. Florida's Civil Service Reform. *Spectrum* (Winter):45–51.

WEISS, J. 1999. Theoretical Foundations of Policy Intervention. In H. Frederickson and J. Johnston, eds., *Public Management Reform and Innovation: Research, Theory, and Application.* Tuscaloosa, AL: University of Alabama Press.

WILSON, J. Q. 1989. *Bureaucracy: What Government Agencies Do and Why They Do It.* New York: Basic Books.

Winter Commission (National Commission on State and Local Service). 1993. *Hard Truths/Tough Choices: An Agenda for State and Local Reform.* The First Report of the National Commission on State and Local Service. Albany, NY: Rockefeller Institute.

Section Two

The Techniques

One of the first thoughts that comes to mind when personnel techniques are mentioned is Wallace Sayre's classic observation that personnel administration represents the "triumph of technique over purpose." This phrase refers to the past tendency of public personnel administration to give exclusive attention to the means of the personnel function, and in so doing, losing sight of the organizational and social goals entrusted to it. By focusing on control activities to the virtual exclusion of other considerations, personnelists became unresponsive to both organizational and extraorganizational interests. These perceptions (criticisms) were largely true for much of the twentieth century, and the revolution that is now taking place in all aspects of public sector HRM essentially represents the resulting backlash.

As one indication that the field's preoccupation with techniques has waned, the number of chapters in this book devoted to HRM techniques over the years has gradually decreased. Another unmistakable verity is that the tone and content of each discussion of a specific personnel technique is profoundly different from what might have been expected one or two decades ago. Gone is the emphasis on centralized and regularized responses to staffing dilemmas. Now, the focus is almost exclusively on flexibility, decentralization, and making the techniques responsive to the needs of line managers.

This fourth edition of the book contains six chapters on various personnel functions. Although the topics covered are fairly traditional, the content of each chapter is not. The fundamental reorientation of the HRM function that has been taking place in recent years is examined by Joan Pynes in her chapter on strategic

HRM. Her analysis of the strategic role of personnelists sets an appropriate tone for the chapters that follow. Gary Robert's discussion of recruitment and selection, for instance, highlights the proactive and aggressive posture that has arisen in response to attraction dilemmas within civil services across the country. The following selection should resonate with anyone who has ever worked in a highly articulated merit system. Katherine Naff's chapter on "Why Public Managers Hate Position Classification" contains an obvious message about the sea of change that is taking place within career management systems in the public service. In the following chapter, Jim Perry provides a thoroughly convincing attack on one of the icons of HRM reform, merit pay. As a supposedly key component of contemporary efforts to motivate and reward civil servants for the increased risks they endure, Perry's essay fires a warning shot across the bow of the reform armada.

Chapter 11 addresses what is often considered to be the most intractable problem within merit systems and performance appraisal. Daley's treatment of performance appraisal techniques provides insights into why the problem is so paramount, and he offers not-too-optimistic projections about what the future holds. The final chapter in this section addresses employee benefits, the area in which civil servants have traditionally enjoyed a major advantage over their counterparts in business and industry. Cayer summarizes the various alterations that are being made in benefit packages due to transformations in the labor force, and then assesses the likelihood that traditional retirement packages (such as defined benefit plans) will survive into the future.

7

Strategic Human Resource Management

JOAN E. PYNES
University of South Florida

Public administration must meet the challenge of changing social needs and priorities, new directions in public policy, demands for greater citizen involvement in the decision-making process, as well as pressures for increased accountability and productivity in government. Public agencies must be prepared to adapt quickly to changes in their external and internal environments. As a result of these challenges, strategic planning, reengineering, quality process management, organizational capability, team management, and culture change are terms being used with increasing frequency by public sector agencies (Behn, 1999; Cohen and Eimicke, 1998; Franklin, 1999). These initiatives require new human resource management strategies and practices.

In many public agencies, human resource management departments are thought to be concerned with only the tasks or functions of human resource management such as staffing, evaluation, training, and compensation. Or they are perceived as regulators and enforcers, concerned with compliance to rules and regulations. Very rarely are they perceived as partners willing and able to work with line managers and staff to make public agencies more effective. Human resource management departments need to expand their scope of activities beyond their typical tasks and emphasis on enforcing regulations and instead link their activities into the everyday work of managers and employees.

This chapter discusses the importance of strategic human resource management (SHRM). SHRM is the integrative framework that links human resource management activities with strategic organizational needs.

STRATEGIC HUMAN RESOURCE MANAGEMENT

Ulrich (1997) identifies four major human resource management roles: management of firm infrastructure, management of employee contribution, management of strategic human resources, and management of transformation and change.

The management of firm infrastructure refers to routine tasks such as recruitment and selection, administering employment benefits, making sure employees are paid on time, and handling grievances. These traditional activities are important administrative roles, but are not likely to enable organizations to meet future competitive pressures.

The management of employee contribution role refers to the communication responsibilities associated with listening and responding to employee concerns. In this role, human resource management professionals work to ensure that employees are engaged and committed to the organization. They do this by offering employees opportunities for personal and professional growth and by training line managers in how to achieve high employee morale. HRM professionals serve as employee champions by linking employee contributions to the organization's success.

The management of strategic human resources role refers to the implementation of human resource activities, policies, and practices to make the necessary ongoing changes to support or improve the organization's operational and strategic objectives. Typically, this role focuses on the implementation of new or revised human resource management practices or substantive and procedural changes in policies and practices. For example, human resource management strategies to support improved quality processes were introduced by the City of Hampton, Virginia. Hampton reengineered its recruiting and placement process so there would be same-day referral and next-day start for all high turnover positions. Every applicant has a brief conversation with a recruiter who explains what skills the city is seeking. The applicants then decide whether or not to complete an application. If the applicants are not qualified for the position, they receive information on how to get the skills or license necessary, and they are directed to other employment opportunities in the community (Green, 1999).

Under the management of transformation and change role, the human resource management department serves as a change agent. In this role, new human resource management practices and systems accompany new organizational structures and may also accompany organizational cultural transformation. This occurs when an agency decides to make a fundamental change in the nature of its human resource management practices, changes in its organizational structure, and changes in its organizational culture to support strategic change. It is this role that prepares public agencies for the future and challenges human resources management departments to rethink, redefine, and reevaluate their own roles.

For this to happen, HRM departments must become more knowledgeable about the operations and services of public agencies/departments. This increased knowledge should be used to determine the current and future gaps in competencies that exist in the organization. Working with department directors, the HRM professionals can determine how to develop these competencies or decide to seek expertise outside of the organization.

To identify any potential gaps in competencies, these questions should be asked:

- What capabilities currently exist within the department/agency?
- What capabilities will be required for the future success of the department/agency?
- How can we align capabilities with service strategies?
- How can we design human resource management practices to create the needed capabilities?
- How can we measure the accomplishment of the needed capabilities? (Ulrich, 1997:11)

Strategic Planning

Strategic planning is a process that enables public organizations to guide their future activities and the use of their available resources. It assists elected officials, citizens, business partners, and public administrators in determining organizational purposes and objectives. By participating in the strategic planning process, the external forces that affect the organization and the people in it are identified. These forces may include workforce patterns, economic conditions, competition, regulation, social values, and technological developments. After the external factors are assessed, the internal strengths and weaknesses of the organization's incumbents must be identified. Factors to include in an internal assessment are current workforce skills, retirement patterns, demographic profiles, and employee capabilities. This information can be used to forecast the organization's capabilities to confront its future opportunities and threats. The ultimate feasibility of strategic planning depends on the people who make it operational.

Human Resource Planning

Human resource planning is a critical component of SHRM. It is the process of analyzing and identifying the need for and availability of human resources to meet the organization's objectives. Forecasting is used to assess past trends, evaluate the present situation, and project future events. Forecasting and planning complement each other because forecasts identify expectations while plans establish concrete goals and objectives.

Forecasting has become increasingly important as a large segment of the public work force is inching toward retirement. Forty-two percent of the 15.7 million individuals working for state and local government in 1999 were between the ages of 45 and 64 years old. Two-fifths of state and local government employees will be eligible to retire in the next fifteen years (Ehrenhalt, 2000). A 1998 analysis of Minneapolis's workforce revealed that one-third of the city's employees would be eligible to retire within the next five years. As a result, departments were asked to identify what skills would be lost and also anticipate how work force needs in the future may change (Walters, 2000).

Agencies must consider how to allocate people to jobs over long periods. Attempts must be made to anticipate expansions or reductions in programs or other changes that may affect the organization. Based on these analyses, plans can be made for the recruitment and selection of new employees, the shifting of employees to different programs or units, or the retraining of incumbent employees.

Confronted with a shortage of workers with information technology skills, the State of Nebraska has developed a six-month, full-time training program for state employees. The program is a partnership with Southeast Community College and is designed to train employees in PC, server, network, and data communication skills. During training, the employees remain classified at their current levels and earn their regular pay and benefits. At the conclusion of the training program, the employees are moved into information technology positions and their position classification and pay are adjusted to reflect their new responsibilities (Schock, 1998–1999).

Forecasting human resource requirements involves determining the number and types of employees needed by skill level. First, agencies need to audit the skills of incumbent employees and determine their capabilities and weaknesses. Positions must also be audited. In most organizations there are likely to be jobs that are vulnerable, jobs that technology or reengineering are ready to replace. Job analyses must be conducted to provide information on existing jobs. The basic requirements of a job should be defined and converted to job specifications that specify the minimum knowledge, skills, abilities and other characteristics (KSAOCs) necessary for effective performance. The skill requirements of positions do change so any changes that occur must be monitored and reflected in the job specifications. It is not enough to monitor changes in positions. Organizations must also keep abreast of the skills that their employees possess. Human resource planning utilizes data inventories to integrate the planning and utilization functions of SHRM. Data inventories compile summary information, such as the characteristics of employees, the distribution of employees by position, employees' performance, and their career objectives. Specific data that are typically catalogued are age, education, career path, current work skills, work experience, aspirations, performance evaluations, years with the organization, and jobs for which one is qualified. Expected vacancies due to retirement, promotion, transfer, sick leave, relocation, or termination are also tracked. Using a computerized human resource information system (HRIS) to compile these data makes the retrieval of information readily available for forecasting work force needs.

When forecasting the availability of human resources, agencies need to consider both the internal and external supply of qualified candidates. The internal supply of candidates is influenced by training and development, and by transfer, promotion, and retirement policies. A succession analysis should be prepared that forecasts the supply of people for certain positions. Succession plans should be used to identify potential personnel changes, to select backup candidates, and to keep track of attrition. The external supply of candidates is also influenced by a variety of factors, including developments in technology, the actions of competing employers, geographic location, and government regulations. San Diego County, for example, examined succession planning for its executive positions. The county put together a talent bank listing incumbent employees' current skills and areas of expertise, job preferences, and possible new skills the employees may need in order to be promoted. Succession planning becomes more important as the labor supply tightens and the unemployment rates hit low levels.

SHRM attempts to match the available supply of labor with the forecasted demand in light of the strategic plan of the organization. If necessary skills do not exist in the present workforce employees will need to be trained in the new skills or external recruitment must be used to bring those skills to the organization. The employer must identify where employees with those skills are likely to be found and recruitment strategies must be developed.

The State of Pennsylvania studied the age patterns among its employees to see what skills the state will lose in the next five to ten years and then began targeting recruitment toward acquiring those skills. The state has gone on direct recruiting campaigns to hire employees with accounting, budgeting, personnel administration, and computer technology skills. Those candidates are then placed in special state-run classes designed to develop their expertise (Walters, 2000:38).

Implementing Strategic Human Resource Management

To implement a SHRM system, it is important for Human Resource Management Departments to expand their scope of activities beyond the traditional HRM tasks and functions and enter partnerships with managers and employees. Working together provides managers and employees a better understanding of HRM issues. Likewise, HRM staff become more informed about the needs of the employees and departments.

SHRM is a process that must be implemented throughout the organization. The goal is to make the SHRM process one that becomes the template for organizational change and innovation.

To facilitate the partnership, HRM Departments should establish a human resource planning task force composed of managers and/or staff from a variety of departments, and staff from the HRM department who are responsible for identifying the trends and challenges that will impact the agency. The task force should involve other employees seeking their input and observations. This can be done through the use of surveys, focus groups, agency publications, or a needs assessment instrument. After the task force receives information, it should prioritize the most critical issues. HRM staff should be directed to develop strategies, solutions, and alternatives to address the issues.

Questions that should be investigated and planned for include:

- Is the top administration committed to quality and excellence?
- Are changes necessary?
- How can we meet employees' perceptions and concerns?
- Which employees will be affected?
- What barriers might there be to successful implementation of SHRM?
- Once program cost estimates are developed, will dollars be provided for training and development?
- Who will be responsible for the implementation of SHRM?
- Who will evaluate and adjust the planning process?

Once these questions have been answered, authority and resources must be assigned to the person(s) responsible for the planning and implementation of

SHRM. Failing to put human and financial resources into SHRM will relegate it to just another fad. Organizational leaders must demonstrate their commitment to SHRM and champion it.

STRATEGIC HUMAN RESOURCE MANAGEMENT IN THE CITY OF CLEARWATER, FLORIDA

One public sector organization that has adopted strategic human resource management and is transforming its HRM capability is the City of Clearwater, Florida.

The City of Clearwater is located on the west coast of Florida. Its population has remained relatively constant for the last ten years between 101,000 and 103,000 residents. Clearwater's market consists of a large tourism-based economy, but it has been able to attract some high technology companies. The city has no open land, so its strategy has been to improve its infrastructure and aesthetics and try to attract companies to redevelop existing properties.

Clearwater provides a full range of municipal services: police and fire protection; city operated marina; a business airpark; convention center and exhibition hall; planning, zoning, subdivision and building code regulation and enforcement; park and recreation programs; a public library system with four branch locations; solid waste collection and recycling; water supply and distribution, wastewater treatment and disposal, reclaimed water treatment and distribution; and the operation of a city-wide parking system.

The phrase "One City, One Future" was developed in 1996 to emphasize the importance of the city's citizens, business partners, city employees, and tourists. "One City, One Future" is posted on all construction project billboards and in other locations throughout the city. The city's mission statement is the following: *The City of Clearwater government provides the municipal services and infrastructure necessary for a high quality of life for all citizens.*

The values that accompany the mission statement include:

Caring: We will act in ways which promote a thriving community and citizenry. We will demonstrate concern and respect for our citizens and our employees by being attentive to all sides of an issue. We will encourage teamwork, trust, respect, and open communication.

Well-run: We commit to efficient, effective, economical provision of services. We will plan and organize to accomplish these goals through innovation, excellent service, and removing barriers. We will seek and retain the best leaders. Our employees will be knowledgeable and customer service oriented.

Integrity: We will be honest, straightforward, and courageous in our actions. We will be fair, ethical, and consistent as we strive to attain our vision.

Outstanding quality: We will set and maintain high standards. We will provide extraordinary service and require excellence at every level.

Future oriented decision-making: We understand that the decisions we make today establish the infrastructure, quality of life, and the direction of our community for future generations. We will make informed decisions by considering the pros and cons, the ramifications, the costs, and the alternatives.

Strategic Priorities

One City, One Future

Infrastructure which sets Clearwater apart as a high value community within Tampa Bay.

Customer Focus

Delivering courteous, understanding, efficient service that exceeds our customers' expectations.

Prosperity

Clearwater is a place that provides the opportunity for everyone to share in an economy where wealth is created and jobs support families.

Quality of Place

An attractive, safe, distinctive community that supports a progressive environment for living, learning, working and playing.

Safe, Healthy, and Caring Community

A clean and responsive city that respects and values the diversity of its citizens and visitors, and provides a secure and comfortable environment that promotes community involvement in the achievement of common goals.

To guide the city in its planning processes for fiscal years 2000–2004, a plan called *Strategies for Success Blueprint* was developed. The *Strategies for Success Blueprint FY 2000–2004* provides a framework to influence the future direction of the city. It focuses on organizational improvement efforts, provides guidance for day to day decision making, provides a means for assessing the effectiveness of city programs, and provides the justification for resource allocation decisions. Five citywide strategic priorities resulted from the city's strategic planning process. They are: *One City. One Future; Customer Focus; Prosperity; Quality of Place; and Safe, Healthy, and Caring Community*.

Citizens, city council members, business partners, tourists, and City of Clearwater employees provided input that led to the development of the *Strategies for Success Blueprint FY 2000–2004*.

The *Strategies for Success Blueprint* led to the design and redesign of the city's business systems and processes. City administrators and department directors played a critical role in the strategic planning process and are responsible for developing initiatives and internal performance measures in support of the overall *Strategies for Success Blueprint*. This includes identifying benchmarks to measure the city's performance against; implementing action plans and monitoring their progress; tracking, measuring and evaluating programs and services; improving the city's services and becoming more efficient through the use of state-of-the-art technology and business practices.

Human Resource Strategic Plan

The City's Human Resource Management Department developed its own strategic business plan consistent with the City's strategic plan, in particular the five principal citywide strategic priorities of *One City. One Future; Customer Focus; Prosperity, Quality of Place; and Safe, Healthy, and Caring Community.*

The Human Resource Management Department's mission is *To help the City of Clearwater provide premier service to our customers by recruiting, selecting, training, developing, and retaining a diverse, highly qualified, satisfied, motivated, and productive workforce.*

Its core HR Values are to be *Strategic, Responsive, Professional, Flexible, and Caring;* and its HR Vision is to *deliver results that add value and help our customers achieve their goals.*

Included in the HR's strategic business plan are five specific goals that are linked with the five strategic priorities, key intended outcomes, and measurable objectives. The linkages are provided in the box that follows.

Goal #1   Create a high performance organizational climate that encourages superior customer service and continuous quality improvement through effective recruitment, selection, and retention programs, training and development initiatives and reward and recognition programs.

Strategic Linkages (3)
One City. One Future; Customer Focus; and Prosperity

Key Intended Outcomes
Improve customer satisfaction
Increase customer trust and confidence in government
Develop employees who have the skill and commitment to deliver quality service

HR Initiatives FY 2001–2002
Strategic Planning and Management System
HR Strategic Planning Board
HR Liaison Program
SAMP* Performance Management System
HRIS Strategic Implementation System
New Employee Mentoring Program
Employee and Team Reward and Recognition Program
Long-Range Training Assessment Plan
SAMP Incentive Pay System
SAMP Paid Time-Off System
Labor-Management Partnerships
Leadership Development and Succession Planning Program

Measurable Objectives
- Increase the percentage of employees who agree with this statement: "HR staff helps recruit and retain high quality employees."
- Increase the percentage of employees who agree with this statement: "HR staff provides quality and timely service."

---

*SAMP refers to Supervisory, Administrative, Managerial and Professional. Employees who are exempt from belonging in a union under Florida law, or in mid and upper management positions.

- Increase the percentage of employees who agree with this statement: "I am able to apply the skills and knowledge learned through city sponsored educational, training, and development programs to improve my personal and organizational effectiveness."
- Increase the percentage of employees who agree with this statement: "I am motivated by the City's reward and recognition programs."

Goal #2   Improve communication, interaction, and cooperation between HR and its customers.

Strategic Linkages (2)

Customer Focus; Safe, Healthy & Caring Community

Key Intended Outcomes

Improve customer satisfaction; Increase customer trust and confidence in government
Strive for overall effective communication
Initiate capital projects needed to improve the levels of service

HR Initiatives FY 2001–2002

HR Customer Communication Plan (newsletter, Internet, intranet)
Revise SAMP* Manuals
HR Policy Handbook

Measurable Objectives

- Increase the percentage of employees who agree with this statement: "HR seeks and listens to employee input on issues and policies affecting employees."
- Increase the percentage of employees who agree with this statement: "I am satisfied with HR communication and liaison services."

Goal #3   Help foster an organizational climate that makes the City a "premier place to work."

Strategic Linkage (1)

Quality of Place

Key Intended Outcome

City recognized as a preferred place to live, work, and play

HR Initiatives FY 2001–2002

Employee Salary & Benefits Survey
Revise Light Duty Program
Employee Benefit Analysis
Employee Wellness Program
Job Evaluation System

---

*SAMP refers to Supervisory, Administrative, Managerial and Professional. Employees who are exempt from belonging in a union under Florida law, or in mid and upper management positions.

Measurable Objectives

- Increase the percentage of employees who agree with this statement: "I enjoy working for the City of Clearwater."
- Increase the percentage of employees who agree with this statement: "I am proud to be a City employee and would recommend City employment to a friend."
- Increase the percentage of employees who agree with this statement: "The City cares about my well being."
- Increase the percentage of employees who agree with this statement: "I am satisfied with my salary/wage range."
- Increase the percentage of employees who agree with this statement: "I am satisfied with my benefits package."

Goal #4   Promote programs and activities that expose the City's workforce to community organizations.

Strategic Linkage (1)

Safe, Healthy, & Caring Community

Key Intended Outcome

Proactive in promoting community well being

HR Initiatives FY 2001–2002

City-Community Education, Training, and Development Partnership Programs

Measurable Objectives

- Increase the percentage of employees who participate in City-sponsored community programs and activities.
- Increase the percentage of employees who agree with this statement: "The City and community benefit from employees who participate in City-sponsored community programs ands activities."

Goal #5   Promote an organizational workforce that reflects the City's demographics.

Strategic Linkage (1)

Safe, Healthy, & Caring Community

Key Intended Outcome

City that values diversity

HR Initiatives FY 2001–2002

Support City Diversity Plan
ESL and Bilingual Language Training Programs

Measurable Objectives

- Increase the percentage of minorities/protected class members in the workforce to more closely reflect city demographics.
- Increase the percentage of bilingual employees.
- Increase the percentage of employees who agree with the statement: "The City promotes a work environment in which diversity is valued."

PROBLEMS AND IMPLICATIONS OF STRATEGIC HUMAN RESOURCE MANAGEMENT

If strategic human resources management makes such intuitive sense, then why aren't more public organizations engaging in it? Researchers have suggested that organizational leaders claim they want a greater integration of the human resource management function with organizational strategy but often do not understand what this entails. They are reluctant to give human resources management professionals the flexibility to initiate new programs or to suggest new organizational structures. This is especially true when organizational change issues confront imbedded standard operating procedures and organizational culture.

Another reason why SHRM is neglected is because very often human resource management professionals lack the capabilities and skills necessary to move human resource management to a more proactive role. HRM professionals may need to be trained in the skills that are necessary to align the organization's strategy with its core competencies. HRM professionals may need training in organizational redesign, job and service redesign, and performance measurement. Kansas is piloting a Human Resources Training Academy (HRTA) for state human resource managers. The program is designed to enhance their effectiveness as strategic planners and organizational leaders. Senior human resource managers from a variety of state agencies are participating in the project and are joined by subject matter experts from the public and private sectors. The intent of the program is to challenge the participants to "go beyond the daily nuts and bolts of personnel management and to recognize the pivotal role they play in carrying out their agency's mission" (Andrews and Molzhon, 1999:5). However, not all public organizations are willing to invest the time and dollars in training nor are they willing to support the efforts of their HRM professionals in the change process.

Organizational change also requires higher levels of coordination across functions and departments; and employees and management must be committed to continuous improvement. There must be greater interdeparmental cooperation. Trust and open communication across the organization will have to be developed. Organizations must encourage creativity and recognize such creativity through their reward systems. Change requires fairness, openness, and empowerment (Beer, 1997). Fairness, openness, and empowerment may be contrary to an organization's culture and may require several incremental steps.

Some employees may be reluctant to change. Over the years they may have required a certain degree of proficiency in the performance of their jobs. Changing their routines and standards of performance, being required to learn new skills, or working with unfamiliar persons may be unsettling. Employees unwilling or unable to make the transition may choose to resign or in some cases may attempt to sabotage new initiatives.

There are also financial costs associated with SHRM. If you refer to the City of Clearwater's HR initiatives for FY 2001–2002, many of them require that some monies be spent. The City contracted with outside consultants to work with it in developing its HR Communication Plan, Employee Wellness Program, Diversity Plan, and the Performance Management System. Consultants were also hired to conduct a job evaluation and pay study, and an employee benefits analysis and review. Some public organizations may be reluctant to spend additional resources on employees fearing a backlash from its elected officials and citizens.

Sometimes the political realities of public organizations undermine change. Very often elected officials and appointed officials have a short-term perspective about how they want agencies to operate. Changes in policies and procedures take time to implement and are often not immediately apparent. They may want a quick fix and not be patient enough for systemic changes to occur. Elected officials may also be predisposed to favor short-term budget considerations over long-term planning. In the public sector support for top administrators may change quickly and often capriciously. To transform an organization requires chief executive and top administrative support, managerial accountability, fundamental changes in HRM practices, employee involvement, and changes in corporate culture (Gilbert and Ivancevich, 2000).

SUMMARY AND CONCLUSIONS

The future viability of an organization and its human resource capabilities are interrelated and must be considered together. HRM must be vertically integrated with strategic planning and horizontally integrated with other human resource functions such as training and development, compensation and benefits, recruitment and selection, labor relations, and the evaluation of the human resource planning process, to allow for adjustments to be made to confront rapidly changing environmental conditions. SHRM guides management in identifying and implementing the appropriate human resource learning activities for resolving organizational problems or adapting to meet new opportunities.

SHRM determines the human resource needs of the agency and ensures that qualified personnel are recruited and developed to meet organizational needs. Should there be a shift in demand for services, agencies must know whether there are potential employees with the requisite skills available to provide these services and whether the agency's finances can afford the costs associated with additional compensation and benefits. Forecasting an agency's human resource supply reveals the characteristics of its internal supply of labor; it also helps to assess the productivity of incumbent employees, implement succession planning and salary planning, and identify areas where external recruitment and/or training and development are necessary.

Training and development are essential to the effective use of an organization's human resources and are an integral part of its human resource planning. Training is used to remedy immediate needs, while development is concerned with long-term objectives and the ability to cope with change. Training and development should be viewed as a continuous process. There will always be new employees, new positions, new problems, changes in technology, and changes in the external and internal environments which require a planned approach to training and development and its integration with other HRM functions. Training and development influence recruitment, selection, career planning, and the compatibility between agency goals and employee aspirations. Training and development programs must be integrated to complement the organization's mission and operations. Organizations should use employees wisely with respect to the strategic needs of the organization.

Turnover, including retirements, must be anticipated and planned for. HRM departments must track the skills of incumbent employees and keep skill inventories. Recruitment and training must be tied to the organization's mission. The availability and stability of financial support; the advancement of technological changes, legal regulations, and social and cultural changes; and the evolution of human resource requirements must be considered when developing strategic plans.

At one time organizations hired employees to fit the characteristics of a particular job. Now it is important for organizations to select employees who fit the characteristics not only of the position but also the organization. HRM professionals must serve as internal consultants working with managers to assess human resource needs. Together they must project the demand for services, develop new resources, and determine the appropriate reallocation of services. The SHRM process, once established, can anticipate and prepare for major changes affecting the workplace.

REFERENCES

ANDREWS, MARK, and CANDACE MOLZHON. 1999. Kansas Offers New Training Academy. *Newsletter of the National Association of State Personnel Executives,* Summer:5–6.

BEER, MICHAEL. 1997. The Transformation of the Human Resource Function: Resolving the Tension Between a Traditional Administrative and a New Strategic Role. *Human Resource Management* 36(1):49–56.

BEHN, ROBERT D. 1999. Do Goals Help Create Innovative Organizations? In H. George Frederickson & Jocelyn M. Johnson, eds. *Public Management Reform and Innovation: Research, Theory, and Application.* Tuscaloosa: University of Alabama Press.

COHEN, STEVEN, and WILLIAM EIMICKE. 1998. *Tools for Innovators: Creative Strategies for Managing Public Sector Organizations.* San Francisco: Jossey-Bass, Inc.

COLLINS, DALE R. 1997. Human Resource Assessment–The Link to Mission. *Public Personnel Management* 26(1):1–6.

EHRENHALT, SAMUEL M. 2000. Quoted in Jonathan Walters (2000), The Employee Exodus. *Governing* 12(6):36–38.

FRANKLIN, AIMEE. 1999. Managing for Results in Arizona: A Fifth-Year Report Card. *Public Productivity & Management Review* 23(2):194–209.

GILBERT, JACQUELINE, A., and JOHN M. IVANCEVICH. 2000. Valuing Diversity: A Tale of Two Organizations. *Academy of Management Executive* 14(1):93–105.

GREEN, THARON. 1999. City of Hampton's Innovative Recruiting Efforts. *IPMA News* November:19.

SCHOCK, STEVE. 1998–1999. Update on Nebraska's Information Technology Training Program. *Newsletter of the National Association of State Personnel Executives,* Winter:4.

ULRICH, DAVE. 1997. *Human Resource Champions.* Boston: Harvard Business School.

WALTERS, JONATHAN. 2000. The Employee Exodus. *Governing* 12(6):36–38.

8

Issues, Challenges, and Changes in Recruitment and Selection

GARY E. ROBERTS

University of Memphis

Effective employee recruitment and selection practices are an essential component of a high-performance human resource management system. Government faces a present and future crisis in attracting and retaining the high-caliber employees that are needed to provide efficient and effective public services. The dimensions of the staffing crisis include a diminished trust in government, a highly competitive labor market, an aging work force, increasing labor force diversity, uncompetitive wages and benefits, changing organizational structure, and technological innovation affecting job design. The competition for talented employees will be a defining characteristic of the twenty-first century (Ingraham, Selden, and Moynihan, 2000). A recent employer survey found that 52 percent of the respondents viewed employee recruitment and retention as the number one employment issue (*HR Focus,* 1999). Unfortunately, the staffing function is also the source of much organizational dissatisfaction. A recent employee survey discovered that the most highly rated personnel functions were benefits administration (79 percent excellent), pay administration (70 percent excellent), employee orientation (59 percent excellent), and career counseling (48 percent excellent); recruiting and selection were in last place (42 percent excellent) (Smith, 1999).

The purpose of this chapter is to provide the student with an overview of governmental recruitment and selection tools with an emphasis on "cutting-edge" techniques and practices. The chapter begins by discussing the broad political and economic factors that are shaping the demand and supply of labor followed by a discussion of specific recruitment and selection tools and techniques. The chapter concludes with a presentation of selected retention practices that are associated with effective employee staffing processes.

THE BROADER POLITICAL AND ECONOMIC LANDSCAPE OF GOVERNMENTAL RECRUITMENT AND SELECTION

The U.S. economy is in the midst of the longest expansion in economic history. The long-term sustainability of high economic growth, low unemployment and robust productivity increases is a matter of debate among economists, but clearly there are major structural changes in our economic system that alter the parameters of conventional economic theory. The advent of the information age and its computerized integration of product and service delivery processes changes the fundamental nature of work. Organizations of all sectors and levels are re-engineering their work processes to realize the benefits of computerization, decentralized organizational structures, and real-time customer-driven service delivery (Popovich, 1998).

LABOR MARKET CHANGES—LOW UNEMPLOYMENT

Total government employment was 20.6 million in April of 2000, 15.7 percent of the 131.1 million total labor force. There were 2.9 million federal employees, 4.7 million state employees and 13.0 million local government employees (U.S. DOL, 2000). State and local governments were the engines of governmental employment growth given the substantial declines in the federal workforce. The federal civilian labor force decreased by 11 percent (approximately 300,000 employees), reducing its total share of governmental employment from 22 percent in 1970 to 14 percent in 1998 while state and local government jobs increased by 1.5 million (*IPMA News*, 1998).

The unemployment rate as of April 2000 was 3.9 percent, the lowest total since 1970 (U.S. DOL, 2000). The unemployment rate for managers and professionals was even lower, at 1.7 percent (U.S. DOL, 2000). The clear message for public employers is that the supply of qualified labor is very scarce. Professionals and managers comprise a higher percentage of the governmental labor force than in the private sector, hence a shortage impacts government more severely in these high-demand areas (Belman and Heywood, 1996). A seller's market drives up costs, leading to escalating salaries and benefits that increase the gap between public and private sector salaries. The labor shortage is highest in the information technology (IT) job market, with 10 percent of all IT positions unfilled (*IPMA News*, 2000c). A recent employer survey found that 60 percent of the respondents reported difficulty in filling IT vacancies and 25 percent indicated reductions in organizational productivity due to the shortage of qualified employees (*IPMA News*, 2000c).

AGING LABORFORCE

The governmental labor force is considerably older than that in the private sector. Forty-four percent of governmental employees are 45 or older, versus 30 percent for private employers, and 27 percent of governmental employees are less than 30 years old versus 43 percent in the private sector (Smith, 2000). Thus, governmental organizations face the challenge of replacing a large percentage of the workforce in an extremely competitive labor market. For example, 70 percent of federal executives will be eligible for retirement by 2005, with early retirement estimates approaching 45 percent (Ingraham, Selden, and Moynihan, 2000). The replacement needs are exacerbated by low retention rates. One-third of the employees hired by the federal government in the early 90s had left the federal service by 1998, further accentuating hiring pressures (Ingraham, Selden, and Moynihan, 2000).

Compounding this dilemma is the fact that the overall labor force growth rate is slowing. The rate of increase was 14 percent between 1986 and 1996, compared to an estimated 11 percent growth rate between 1996 and 2006 (Smith, 2000). The reduced workforce growth rates are more pronounced for key age cohorts. The 25 to 34 age group, the prime entry-level cohort, will shrink by 3 million in conjunction with a 15 percent increase in demand (Smith, 2000). The 35 to 45 age group, the prime mid-level management developmental cohort, will also shrink by 15 percent while labor demand increases by 25 percent (Smith, 2000).

Although all sectors of public employment are affected, the shortages are especially acute in education, law enforcement, and the military. These are essential public service functions that play major roles in the quality of life. For example, in 2000, the Los Angeles Police Department (LAPD) was understaffed by 700 officers (Avue Technologies, 2000). To eliminate the shortfall, the LAPD needed to hire 100 officers per month, but they could only fill 20 vacancies given the competitive labor market and reduced interest in law enforcement (Avue Technologies, 2000). In 1999, the Army was 7,000 enlistees short of its 74,000 recruitment goal in spite of larger signing bonuses (Davis, 2000). In the education arena, the annual turnover rate of teachers is predicted to range from 6 to 8 percent, further exacerbating teacher shortages (Boe, Bobbitt, and Cook, 1997).

WORKFORCE DEMOGRAPHIC CHANGE

In addition to the graying of the labor force, the composition is changing. Minorities and women will continue to manifest a higher rate of labor force growth. This phenomenon will ultimately reduce the representation of whites from 75 percent in 1996 to 73 percent of the labor force in 2006 (Smith, 2000). Government is a model employer relative to labor force diversity, with a higher percentage of women and minority workers than the private sector (Smith, 2000). Another major source of labor force diversification is immigration. Two-thirds of the projected increase in the U.S. population between 2000 and 2050 will consist of immigrants thereby increasing public sector employment challenges related to applicants with language, education, and training barriers (U.S. DOL, 1999).

WAGES AND BENEFITS

Wage and benefit comparability is an important principle underlying the governmental staffing function. Unfortunately, governmental salaries are less competitive in many areas, especially in the managerial and executive sectors (Belman and Heywood, 1996). The traditional governmental psychological employment contract entailed the provision of secure and steady work, reasonable hours, satisfactory wages, attractive core benefits (health and pension), and the intrinsic satisfaction of serving the public in lieu of the private sector's higher compensation, rapid advancement opportunities, generous perks, and innovative work-life benefits (such as flexi-place and child care) (Roberts, 2000). This compact is being eroded by governmental reinvention efforts that attenuate job security and work stability in conjunction with an absence of work-life benefits (Kettl, 1998; Roberts, 2000). Employees become disenchanted when performance expectations and accountability standards are elevated absent a concommitment increase in supportive workplace practices.

Public sector compensation approaches are becoming more diversified, reflecting the changing nature of work (Risher and Fay, 1997). The emphasis on individual performance appraisal and merit pay is being supplemented or supplanted by group and organizational-based compensation systems such as gainsharing (U.S. DOL, 1996). Given higher rates of job mobility and nontraditional employment relationships (such as contract, temporary, and part-time employment), there is a need for enhanced benefits portability, especially for pensions and health care (Ingraham, Selden, and Moynihan, 2000). Pension and benefits portability reduces barriers to labor mobility thereby increasing the number and quality of applicants for governmental jobs.

PUBLIC CONFIDENCE IN GOVERNMENT

The overall level of public confidence in government and our societal institutions has declined to alarming levels (Ingraham, Selden, and Moynihan, 2000). A recent poll by the Council for Excellence in Government (1999) found that only 21 percent of those surveyed manifested a high degree of confidence in the federal government. The levels for state and local government were slightly higher (33 percent and 35 percent respectively), but remain far short of a strong endorsement of our governmental institutions (Council for Excellence in Government, 1999). This absence of confidence is reflected in polling data and is exacerbated by media and politician attacks on government and public employees (Ingraham, Selden, and Moynihan, 2000). As a result, the prestige and attractiveness of governmental service are reduced, thereby increasing recruitment and retention difficulties. For example, only 43 percent of 18 to 29 years olds say they would be very or fairly likely to consider a job in government (Council for Excellence in Government, 1999).

CHANGING ORGANIZATIONAL STRUCTURE

Another significant factor that influences public sector recruitment efforts is the rapid change in governmental organizational structure. The hierarchical bureaucratic organization is ill-equipped for the rapid adjustments needed to address our complex service delivery and policy problems (Gore, 1993). The work of Osborne and Gaebler (1992) heralded a major shift in governmental organizational philosophy and structure. Governmental reinvention focuses on creating horizontal, decentralized organizational structures that enhance bottom-line accountability through the development of clear goals, objectives, and performance standards (Popovich, 1998). From a performance management standpoint, this requires an emphasis on intrinsic motivational approaches that rely on empowered, multi-skilled, and entrepreneurial employees comfortable in increasingly team-based work environments (Popovich, 1998).

THE ROLE OF LABOR COSTS IN STAFFING ISSUES

A clear consensus is emerging that organizational success will depend upon cultivating a high-performance culture, strong political and agency leadership, partnering with unions, intergovernmental cooperation, and increased human capital investment (Ingraham, Selden, and Moynihan, 2000). The appropriate amount of human capital investment is a major labor market and larger public policy issue. Is labor a cost of production to be minimized, or a valued asset essential to the long-term success of the organization? Clearly public and nonprofit organizations are labor intensive, with a substantial percentage of expenditures devoted to wages and benefits (Lee and Johnson, 1998). As such, effective program management entails efficiently and effectively deploying labor resources with a concurrent investment in employee training.

The human capital perspective views employees as the essential ingredient to organizational success (Klingner and Nalbandian, 1998). The organization must systematically provide the essential knowledge, skills, and abilities for long-term employee effectiveness. A major tool in human capital investment is the use of individual employee development plans (IDPs) to ensure the rational allocation of scarce training dollars (Viscasillas, 1999). The human capital approach advocates an employee-employer training partnership in order to upgrade the job-related competencies and the critical thinking skills associated with information-age jobs (Ingraham, Selden, and Moynihan, 2000). It has been suggested that public organizations need to increase training expenditures to 3 percent of the personnel budget from its current 1 percent average (Popovich, 1998). This will facilitate more effective IDPs to ensure that workers receive the training and education needed to maintain present and future job competencies (Klingner and Nalbandian, 1998).

One of the most significant labor market changes is the ascension of the nontraditional labor force (Bond, Galinsky, and Swanberg, 1998). Employers are embracing a variety of labor-cost reduction strategies including outsourcing, the utilization of temporary, part-time or leased employees, and supplementing paid with volunteer labor. Approximately 30 percent of the labor force works in the nontraditional employment sector (Smith, 2000). The increased reliance on nontraditional employees poses complex program management, employee motivation, and social equity challenges.

STRATEGIC HUMAN RESOURCE MANAGEMENT

The final macro-level trend influencing public sector staffing is the employment of the strategic human resource management model (Popovich, 1998). The traditional civil service framework emphasizes centralized provision of personnel recruitment and staffing services to realize economies of scale as well as to ensure adherence to merit principles. One of the main goals of the reinvention movement is to reduce support service process control in budgeting, procurement, and human resources (Gore, 1993). Staffing functions are delegated to line agencies possessing the information, understanding, and expertise to adapt more rapidly to changing employment and skill needs. The role of the central personnel agency becomes that of a consultant providing specialized expertise and technical assistance in mission achievement. The delegation of HR authority aids line management by reducing system red tape, thereby increasing the speed, efficiency, and effectiveness of the staffing process.

Recent studies in the federal civil service demonstrated great variability in the scope and effectiveness of human resource function delegation (U.S. OPM, 1998a). A major critique of the implementation of human resource decentralization comes from line managers who perceive that the reforms merely shift the locus of regulation from a central personnel agency to a departmental personnel agency with no net increase in autonomy (U.S. OPM, 1998a). Other barriers include inflexible legislation, union resistance, budget restrictions, and an absence of communication and education (U. S. OPM, 1998a). Related is the critique that the decentralization of human resource functions, absent concommitment programmatic autonomy, fails to address the core needs of line management for decision-making autonomy.

RECRUITMENT PRACTICES—NEEDS ASSESSMENT

Recruitment is a key, but frequently neglected, staffing function. The goal is to attract a satisfactory pool of highly qualified applicants for the lowest cost. An effective staffing process begins with a specific needs assessment (Witkin and Altschuld, 1995). The focus is on identifying present and future staffing needs in terms of the aggregate number of replacement employees, replacement figures for specific job titles, the associated competencies required for effective job performance, and employee training and development requirements (Clardy, 1997). A systematic needs assessment includes updated job analyses for all positions, an analysis of performance appraisal evaluations to identify strengths and weaknesses of present employees, and data on aggregate and job-specific employment by race and gender to identify underutilization of minorities (Klingner and Nalbandian, 1998). A sophisticated utilization analysis also includes an adverse impact analysis on all selection processes to identify potential discrimination against women and minorities.

For example, the State of Nevada engages in a sophisticated succession planning process to proactively identify hiring and associated training requirements (Truax, 1999). A 360-degree feedback system assesses the effectiveness of selection and training processes from the perspective of the employee and management (Truax, 1999). The goal is to cultivate internal recruitment of current employees, capture the knowledge of senior personnel, ensure that jobs meet the needs of new employees for challenging, intrinsically motivating work, and engage in innovative recruitment strategies (Truax, 1999). Based upon the information, specific hiring goals that are linked to an appropriate recruitment strategy are set.

RECRUITMENT STRATEGIES

Recruitment strategies can be classified on a continuum from passive, midrange, to active as shown in Table 8–1 below. Each source manifests unique strengths and weaknesses as well as cost implications. Passive recruiting strategies once were the norm for most governmental organizations. Governments could afford to invest little systematic attention to recruitment because job openings were scarce and a rich, deep, and high-quality applicant pool existed. With the advent of a highly competitive labor market, the associated skills shortages and increased employee replacement costs necessitate the implementation of midrange and active recruitment strategies. Active strategies are more effective at attracting higher-qualified applicant pools, but with an increased investment of organizational resources (time and money). For example, on-campus recruiting generates more qualified applicants than newspaper recruiting, but at a much higher cost per applicant (Werbel and Landau, 1996).

CENTRALIZED VERSUS DECENTRALIZED RECRUITMENT, RESIDENCY REQUIREMENTS, AND VETERANS PREFERENCE

There are several other key policy and management issues surrounding the public sector recruitment process. First, should recruitment be centralized in the human resource department or delegated to the line department? The trend in government is to decentralize, but by no means is decentralized recruiting the norm. Decentralized recruitment policies can increase merit system violations (i.e., political hiring) and undesirable variability in staffing practices (i.e., differential screening standards). The strengths of centralized recruiting include the economies of scale and reduced administrative costs associated with eliminating administrative duplication and the enhanced process control promoting uniformity and merit system adherence. The associated weaknesses include red tape and the absence of line input into staffing decisions. Centralized recruiting is best suited for widely distributed jobs with generalized skill requirements such as clerical positions.

Other key recruitment issues unique to government include residency requirements and veterans preference. Residency requirements can reduce the pool of applicants, while veterans preference can attenuate the employment and advancement of women.

TABLE 8–1

Passive	Midrange	Active
Job posting	Newspapers	On-site recruiting (campus, job fairs, conferences, community centers, and groups)
Unsolicited inquiries: mail, phone, walk-ins	Professional association publications	
Word-of-mouth recruiting	Web-sites	Web recruiting
	Television, radio	Internships/co-ops
		Active referral programs
		Employment agencies

EVALUATION OF RECRUITING PROGRAM EFFECTIVENESS

A systematic recruitment program includes a comparative assessment of the efficiency and efficacy of the various recruitment sources in attracting candidates. This entails compiling an inventory of the methods used to attract candidates and such data as cost per applicant, cost per qualified applicant, cost per hire, and average time to fill a vacancy (Trice, 1999a). A comprehensive recruitment process evaluation also assesses user attitudes toward the recruitment function from the applicant and requesting agency perspective (Thornton, 1993). Applicant perceptions are especially important to the success of the staffing process and will be discussed in a subsequent section.

INTERNAL VERSUS EXTERNAL RECRUITMENT

A major issue in employee recruitment is internal versus external recruiting. Internal employee recruiting has several advantages including: 1) more detailed, valid knowledge of employee performance; 2) fewer employee adjustment costs (e.g., organizational culture, political landscape); 3) high motivational value for other employees, and; 4) a statement of confidence in the abilities of current employees. The advantages of external recruitment include the ability to cultivate organizational innovation and change and increased employee diversity. Internal recruitment can be especially useful in filling vacancies in areas of applicant scarcity, especially when combined with relevant training programs (Trice, 1998).

EFFECTIVE RECRUITING PRACTICES

The ultimate effectiveness of the staffing process is heavily influenced by the organization's quality-of-work-life. Employers that provide a safe, stable, stimulating, fairly compensated, and career-advancing work environment possess an inherent advantage in the recruiting wars. Satisfied employees are low-cost sources of favorable publicity and become de facto recruiters. Word-of-mouth and employee referral recruiting are very effective strategies, but with the potential weakness of a loss of employee diversity (Sullivan, 2000). Public sector employers should actively cultivate "brand-name" recognition as an employer of choice, not an employer of last resort, as a favorable image is an important factor in cultivating higher job-offer acceptance rates (Rynes, 1993).

An effective recruiting process should begin with an understanding of the needs and preferences of applicants. In other words, what is a desirable recruiting process from the candidate's perspective? According to Rynes (1993) it includes: 1) early exposure to the organization through a co-op or internship experience; 2) information on the employing organization; 3) clear, specific and balanced (strengths and weaknesses) information on job characteristics and requirements; 4) clear feedback on the applicant's hiring chances; 5) warm, enthusiastic, concerned, credible, high status, and informative recruiters; 6) meetings with future supervisors and peer employees; 7) a clear explanation of the selection tools and process; 8) clear and timely information on candidate progress and status; and 9) a prompt job offer with sufficient time to make a decision (Connerley and Rynes, 1997; Rynes, 1993).

The ideal applicant process, unfortunately, conflicts with certain organizational requirements. For example, providing early notification of a job offer can cause backup candidates to withdraw (Rynes, 1993). The reality of recruiting is that most recruiters receive minimal training (about 1.3 hours) and 95 percent of applicants report excessive delays (Rynes, 1993). The key is to view the applicant as a customer to ensure a favorable recruitment experience and promote applicant perceptions that effective recruiters are representative of the organization as a whole (Thornton, 1993). Providing the applicant with the opportunity to meet future supervisors and peers is desirable, but at the cost of interactions that may accentuate negative aspects of the job or organization (Rynes, 1993). To ensure a positive experience, the organization needs to measure applicant perceptions and train all employees that have applicant contact (Rynes, 1993).

INNOVATIVE RECRUITMENT PRACTICES—WAGES

There are myriad innovative recruitment practices in the public, private, and non-profit sectors. They can be subdivided into three areas: wages, benefits, and recruitment process innovations. The federal government faces especially acute problems in maintaining compensation comparability with the private sector because of its nationwide presence and high percentage of professional and managerial employees. In 1990 the Federal Pay Comparability Act was passed to address growing external pay inequity. The Act permitted federal agencies to pay recruitment and retention bonuses of up to 25 percent for hard-to-fill positions (U.S. OPM, 1999). Other innovations include flexible salary schedules permitting a starting salary above the minimum, permanent salary differentials for hard-to-fill positions, and pay advancement to ease employee relocation burdens (U.S. OPM, 2000a; U.S. OPM, 2000b). Other inducements include relocation assistance to reimburse moving expenses and housing allowances (U.S. OPM, 2000a; U.S. OPM, 1999; Trice, 1998).

INNOVATIVE RECRUITMENT PRACTICES—BENEFITS

In terms of employee benefits, most governments possess competitive traditional benefits packages (health, pension, life insurance, etc.). It is in the newer category of work-life (child and elder care, flexi-place, etc.) benefits that private sector organizations demonstrate leadership in accommodating employee needs relative to work, family and personal time (U.S. OPM, 2000a; Tratt, 2000; Roberts, 2000). For example, 60 percent of employees reported that the ability to balance work and family is of great importance in job choice (Tratt, 2000). Seventy percent of the employees at Fel-Pro manufacturing reported that the availability of work-life benefits was a major factor in employee retention while a study of Scott Paper employees found that work-life benefits increased productivity by 35 percent (Tratt, 2000). A Sears study found that for every 5 percent increase in employee satisfaction, customer satisfaction increased by 1.3 percent and sales by .05 percent (Tratt, 2000).

Hence the availability of work-life benefits can have a very significant impact on recruitment and retention. Recent studies indicate that the rate of adoption of most work-life benefits is significantly lower in state and local government, a major competitive disadvantage (Roberts, 2000). The barriers to providing work-life benefits in government include the cost, absence of expertise/knowledge, perceived absence of need, and perceived public resistance (Roberts, 2000). Proposed solutions include regional benefits consortiums and service regionalization efforts to reduce benefit costs, knowledge dissemination programs to increase awareness of work-life benefits programs, and technical assistance in developing benefits programs and conducting needs assessments, among others (Roberts, 2000).

A powerful recruitment incentive can be the provision of employee training. Employers that enhance the present and future human capital of their employees will realize a powerful advantage in the competition for talent (U.S. OPM, 1999; Bailey, 1998; Trice, 1998).

In addition to recruiting, marketing the quality-of-life both in the organization and the surrounding community can influence applicant decisions. For example, an urban local government can market the advantages of employment in the center city including the cultural and recreational attractions as well as the reduced commuting hassles afforded by public transportation (Joinson, 1999; Trice, 1998).

INNOVATIVE RECRUITMENT PRACTICES—PROCESS INNOVATIONS

Process innovations in recruiting possess four major goals: 1) to reduce applicant barriers (speed, time, energy, and documentation); 2) to increase the number and quality of candidates; 3) to improve administrative efficiency (i.e., cost, documentation); and 4) to make more timely hiring decisions. The innovations are too numerous to discuss in great detail, but are summarized in Table 8–2 below.

TABLE 8–2   Summary of Recruitment Innovations

Automated or call-in job analysis and job-orders (Greene, 1999)
One-stop employment shop (U.S. OPM, 2000b)
Continuous recruiting (Trice, 1999b; Smith, 2000)
Web recruiting (Trice, 1998c; Viscasillas, 1999)

Employee referral or recruitment bonus (U.S. OPM, 2000a; U.S. OPM, 1999)
Using current employees as recruiters (Smith, 2000)
Family-nights, bring a friend to work (Smith, 2000)
Recruitment videos (Smith, 2000)

Service learning efforts (co-ops, internships) (Trice, 1998)
Partnering with schools, innovative curriculums (Gunnels-Perry, 1999; Trice, 1998; *IPMA News,* 2000c)

Internal recruiting (Trice, 1998)
Internal recruiting focused on older employees (Sullivan and Duplaga, 1997)
Leasing or temporary employees (Smith, 2000)
Consortium recruiting (Smith, 2000)

Automated job analysis, classification, and job requisitioning systems increase the speed and accuracy of filling vacancies. Continuous recruitment, one-stop employment shops, Web-based recruiting, and resumé databases expand the time and geographical recruitment area. Service learning efforts and school partnerships can improve employer visibility, applicant organizational knowledge, and provide early recruiting opportunities. Employee referral and hiring bonuses can increase the number of high-quality applications, while using employees as recruiters enhances organizational credibility. Involving family and friends in organizational activities enhances brand-name recognition and employer reputation. Internal recruiting can be a valuable source of in-house talent for hard-to-fill vacancies. Forming a regional labor pool or consortium can be a very effective strategy for filling vacancies in areas of applicant scarcity. Utilizing temporary or contract employment is a rational strategy for accomplishing tasks that are limited in scope or duration.

EMPLOYEE SELECTION

The recruitment process is only half of the staffing challenge as the applicant must undergo screening and formal selection. The goal of the selection stage is to increase the reliability, validity, and acceptability/utility of hiring decisions. This requires a selection process free from contamination (measuring nonperformance factors), deficiency (failing to measure important aspects of the job), and adverse impact on protected groups (Latham and Finnegan, 1993).

As was the case with recruitment, it is useful for organizations to examine the selection process from the "customer" perspective. An effective applicant selection system entails: 1) detailed information on job and organizational characteristics; 2) information on career advancement opportunities; 3) participation by applicants in the development and administration of assessment devices; 4) a clear overview of the steps, objectives, and job relatedness/relevancy of each selection device; and 5) honest and considerate feedback on performance (Thornton, 1993). From an employer standpoint, several of these objectives conflict with organizational goals. Providing honest and considerate feedback can be risky in today's litigious environment and participation by applicants in designing and developing selection devices can be impractical. However, the face validity and perceived fairness of the selection process are important factors in employee job acceptance and can reduce the probability of adverse candidate reactions.

SELECTION INNOVATIONS

The development of an effective employee selection process is impeded by several common barriers including an absence of knowledge or familiarity with effective practices, legal liability concerns (e.g., employing discriminatory general intelligence tests), resource constraints (e.g., inability to afford assessment centers), absence of training and expertise, and a lack of confidence in the job-relatedness of the practice (Terpstra and Rozell, 1997). Clearly, an important role of selection research is to enhance the organizational knowledge of "best-practice" standards and tools.

POLICY-RELATED SELECTION REFORMS

The recent reforms of governmental selection practices centered on two areas: 1) addressing the regulatory or policy-related barriers, and 2) identifying and overcoming process-related problems. Below is a summary of recent governmental selection policy and process innovations.

Policy-Related Selection Innovations
- Delegation of examining and hiring authority to line agencies
- Expanding of candidate pool by abandoning the rule-of-three
- Accelerating (speed) hiring permitting provisional appointments
- Permitting employees to accept a second job in hard-to-fill areas
- Remote hiring
- Permitting hiring of retired employees
- Utilization of volunteers

Process Oriented Innovations
- Resumé screening
- Computerized job applications
- Remote screening and interviewing (video, phone, computer)
- Computerized testing
- Walk-in testing services
- Concurrent applicant processing (complete all screening tasks up-front)

The list of policy innovations is headed by the delegation of examining and hiring authority to line agencies. Clearly this approach manifests the greatest potential to enhance the influence of line personnel on hiring, but the overall effectiveness of delegation attempts is unclear (Kettl, 1998). Expansion of the candidate pool addresses the absence of flexibility associated with traditional civil service practices (e.g., civil service test scores or ratings of training and experience) that limit the final list of job candidates to the top three or five scorers. The trend reflects a recognition of the limits of traditional selection instruments such as civil service tests to provide a complete picture of candidate qualifications. For example, Maricopa County, Arizona, groups candidates according to ratings (exceptional, meets standards, and meets minimum standards) and submits the entire register for potential employment interviews (Trice, 1999c). The major drawback is the potential for abuse based upon nonperformance factors.

Accelerated hiring is critical for areas of labor shortage such as information technology and engineering, but possesses value for other selection areas as well. Cumbersome and time-consuming selection processes impose costs on highly qualified applicants given their multiplicity of options (Sullivan, 1999). Research indicates that a major factor in a candidate's job offer acceptance is the speed of the hiring process with early offers receiving more weight. From an aggregate standpoint, research demonstrates that faster hiring decisions manifest no adverse impact on selection validity (assuming the preexisting validity of selection devices) (Sullivan, 1999; Rynes, 1993). As a result, provisional same-day hiring is being implemented in several jurisdictions (Trice, 1999c). Wisconsin's Critical Recruitment Program allows state agencies to hire highly qualified applicants within 24 hours in areas of shortage and within 30 days in noncritical areas (Lavigna, 1996). The federal government permits expedited hiring of candidates with grade point average of 3.0 or better (U.S. Office of Personnel Management [OPM], 2000b). Even with accelerated hiring and recruitment incentives, the pool of qualified candidates is frequently insufficient. Thus, human resource policies and procedures need to permit temporary hiring as well as other innovative practices such as allowing existing employees in areas of labor scarcity to accept a second job (U.S. OPM, 2000a). Another strategy for increasing the applicant pool is remote hiring. For example, Lansing, Michigan, hired a Wastewater Treatment Officer from New Mexico without an in-person interview by utilizing interactive video technology (Treadway, 1999).

Given the difficulty in filling vacancies with traditional applicants, public sector organizations may be forced to utilize retired employees or volunteers for selected functions. Retirees can be reemployed part or full-time for limited durations, while volunteers are usually part-time. The integration of retired and volunteer employees will entail the development of specialized staffing procedures and supervisory performance management competencies, however (see Brudney, 1998).

PROCESS-RELATED SELECTION INNOVATIONS

Process-related innovations attempt to reduce applicant and agency administrative costs. The traditional employment application is a source of candidate frustration while imposing significant agency record-keeping burdens. Many governmental organizations utilize resumés to prescreen candidates, thereby reducing applicant burdens and administrative costs associated with entering and storing data on unqualified applicants (Trice, 1999b). If applications are required by law, a computerized job application process can reduce administrative costs (Trice, 1999b). Wisconsin has developed one-stop employment shops where a candidate meets with a counselor to determine the jobs that the candidate is qualified for, completes an application, and takes the relevant computerized tests (Lavigna, 1996). With computerization, the number of testing sites increases significantly. In combination with remote screening and interviewing practices, the cost-effective geographic recruitment area expands greatly (Treadway, 1999). Another key process innovation is up-front candidate processing. Hampton, Virginia, has reengineered its entire screening process by employing a team-based approach that invests in accelerated candidate processing by concurrently performing most administrative functions (Greene, 1999). The goal is to screen unqualified candidates early in the process and identify attractive candidates for fast-track hiring decisions (Greene, 1999).

WEB-BASED RECRUITING AND SELECTION

The future of recruitment and selection practices is connected to the technological innovations afforded by the computer, including web-based recruitment and selection. An integrated web-based staffing process facilitates strategic human resource management. The first element is a web-site that posts vacancies detailing information on job requirements as well as organizational and community information (*IPMA News*, 2000a). The second element is a resumé or on-line job application process for initial screening (Trice, 1999b). If the candidate meets the initial standards, follow-up testing or interviews are scheduled, with the option of remote testing or interviewing (Smith, 2000). The screening process should provide candidates with some feedback on their employment prospects so informed self-selection can take place (*IPMA News*, 2000a).

Web-based recruiting enables the organization to review candidate web-sites or actively recruit qualified nonapplicants by such tactics as employee referral or by scanning list-servers, news groups, professional organizations, and chat rooms (*IPMA News*, 2000a). A liability associated with web-based recruiting is the increase in the number of external and internal applicants (Avue Technologies, 2000). Web-based computer programs (rule-wizards) that electronically screen resumés and applications can reduce the number of applicants for detailed review (*IPMA News*, 2000a). The computerized application process enables candidates to be informed at each stage, reducing a potential source of dissatisfaction, and can be integrated with an automated applicant tracking system (*IPMA News*, 2000a; Smith, 2000). Ideally, the web-based recruiting system is networked with an overall human resource management information system that serves as the foundation for personnel-related activities such as the generation of individual employee development plans, training needs assessment, compensation, and other staffing.

SELECTION METHODS

There are four basic selection methods: 1) resumés and applications, 2) written tests, 3) work sampling/performance tests, and 4) interviews. Each manifests unique strengths and weaknesses. The focus of this section is to provide general information on the application and utility of the respective methods. The thrust is to provide suggestions on improving the validity and reliability of the selection process in a cost-effective and nondiscriminatory fashion. Keep in mind that every screening and selection device must be validated and is subject to the 80 percent rule associated with the calculation of adverse impact. Adverse impact occurs when the selection or success ratio of a protected class is less than 80 percent of that of the nonprotected class (usually white males). An adverse impact analysis should be conducted for all entry-level and promotional selection processes to identify barriers to the advancement of women and minorities.

RESUMÉS AND APPLICATIONS—RATINGS OF TRAINING AND EXPERIENCE

Resumés and applications can be used as a valid screening and selection device with proper development. The use of personal-history data to make employment decisions has a long tradition in personnel selection (Cascio, 1982). The advantage of these systems is that candidates are rated on what they have accomplished, not on potential, as past behavior is a strong predictor of future behavior. The developmental process associated with a rating of training and experience includes a comprehensive job analysis. The applicant's work experience is then scored using a standardized rating system. This method can be very effective in prescreening candidates into qualified and unqualified groups. The downside is that the method is susceptible to candidate manipulation, is quite time-consuming, and requires in-depth training and development to ensure reliability and validity (Tompkins, 1998). Candidates need to be informed that all information submitted on a resumé or application is subject to verification with penalties for false information (Trice, 1999b).

WRITTEN TESTS

Written tests are a staple, but controversial, selection tool. The standard general intelligence test (IQ test), first attacked for its non-job-relatedness and adverse impact in the seminal *Griggs v. Duke Power* case, is undergoing a revival in its use for managerial selection (Behling, 1998). One of the key managerial competencies is problem solving, which is clearly linked to general intelligence (Behling, 1998). Recent studies indicate that general intelligence tests are the best predictors for training success and future job performance (Behling, 1998). Personality tests are also receiving increased attention for their value-added selection benefits. The level of conscientiousness is the best psychological predictor of interpersonal skill competency (Behling, 1998). The level of applicant confidence in the testing process is a key factor in generating favorable applicant perceptions and avoiding appeals or lawsuits (Thornton, 1993). Testing practices that are job-related and content valid generate more favorable perceptions of peers, supervisors, and the overall organization, as well as higher organizational commitment (Thornton, 1993). To enhance applicant test-practice acceptance (face validity), job candidates should receive information on the job-relatedness and utility of selection practices, especially personality and intelligence tests.

WORK SAMPLING AND PERFORMANCE TESTS

Work sampling and performance tests directly measure applicant performance on actual or simulated job components (Tompkins, 1995). This method possesses high reliability and validity and has less adverse impact on minorities (Tompkins, 1995). The assessment center, a specialized work-sampling tool, has proven especially useful in managerial selection situations (Cascio, 1982). In an assessment center, the applicant completes a series of group and individual exercises (e.g., problem solving, in-basket, leaderless group discussion) that is scored by a panel of trained evaluators (assessors). The main drawback to work sampling and performance tests is the cost and effort in test development and administration.

SELECTION INTERVIEWS

The ubiquitous interview is a staple selection practice across all organizational sectors. A recent survey of managers found that 70 percent of the respondents believe that the interview is the most effective selection method (Oliver, 1998). The problem is that most interviews are unstructured and therefore have very low levels of reliability and validity due to a plethora of contamination sources (e.g., contrast effects, race and sex stereotypes). A structured behavioral and situational interview process, with proper training and development, can increase the validity and reliability of the interview significantly (Tompkins, 1995). A behavioral interview asks employees how they conducted themselves in a specific job-related situation, while a situationally-based interview question assesses how the applicant would manage a hypothetical job scenario. The key is to link all questions to an in-depth job analysis. A structured interview process employs a panel of trained and knowledgeable interviewers to ensure reliability and validity, a standardized scoring system with documentation, and a structured interview protocol (same questions in same order, no or limited follow-ups) (Bernotavicz and Locke, 2000). The main weakness of structured interviewing is the time and resources devoted to the development of the interview protocol and the administrative costs associated with the interviewing process.

A realistic job preview (RJP) can be a very useful tactic to enhance the interview's effectiveness. In a RJP, the applicant receives both positive and negative information on the position, reducing unrealistic expectations and resulting in self-selection. Research on the RJP indicates its use is associated with higher employee job performance, elevated job satisfaction, lower turnover, and higher organizational commitment (Phillips, 1998; Thornton, 1993). For example, a social worker could be shown a film depicting a typical work day thereby illustrating the challenging work environment associated with high case loads and difficult clients.

EFFECTIVE RETENTION PRACTICES—ORIENTATION SESSIONS

No discussion of recruitment and selection is complete without discussing employee retention initiatives. The most effective selection process is attenuated if there are high levels of turnover. Replacing the average managerial employee can exceed $10,000, not to mention the loss of institutional memory and productivity (Tratt, 2000). Effective employee orientation programs are critical components of a sophisticated retention program. Orientation programs are important instruments for bonding employees to the organization, facilitating the acculturation process, providing job structure, and reducing entry stress (*IPMA News,* 2000b; Wanous, 1993). For example, the orientation program at Corning Glass increased retention by 69 percent while reducing the time to reach full productivity by two months (*IPMA News,* 2000b). The keys to effective orientation programs include: 1) active participation by managers and line employees; 2) the identification and origin of stressors associated with workplace problems; 3) providing desirable role models; and, 4) offering specific guidance and practice on coping/problem solving strategies for overcoming job difficulties and stress (Wanous, 1993). Another useful strategy is to assign new employees a mentor to provide additional guidance and feedback (Smith, 2000).

MANAGING ORGANIZATIONAL CHANGE
IN RECRUITMENT AND SELECTION PRACTICES

Successful staffing innovation requires overcoming employee resistance and skepticism. This entails the employment of sophisticated change management techniques that involve employees. A strategic human resource management staffing system partners with line agencies in the delivery of staffing services. This entails consulting with line managers on innovations, the employment of customer service standards, as well as general staffing performance standards (Lavigna, 1996). For example, Wisconsin uses a stakeholder survey developed from a focus group to assess the performance of the central human resource department on such factors as staffing timeliness, adequacy of communication, civil service exam quality, overall candidate quality and responsiveness (Lavigna, 1996). Charlotte evaluates the effectiveness of staffing programs by assessing cost per hire, cost per applicant, and average time to fill a vacancy (Trice, 1999a).

SUMMARY AND CONCLUSION

Recruitment and selection are basic and essential human resource functions that are undergoing a metamorphosis in conjunction with the larger global political, technological, economic, and social changes affecting the organizational environment. The public service faces seven fundamental recruitment and selection challenges to its long-term stability and effectiveness:

1. An aging public sector work force in conjunction with fewer promotional opportunities and higher replacement costs
2. A highly competitive labor market leading to shortages in key professional and information technology occupations
3. An erosion of governmental pay equity and comparability
4. Private sector leadership in the provision of work-life benefits
5. The challenges of managing a highly diverse workforce
6. The integration of computer and web-based technologies
7. The ascension of the alternate workforce (temporary, part-time)
8. Preserving merit-based, nondiscriminatory selection in a decentralized human resources system

For governmental organizations to be successful, there must be an appropriate degree of flexibility afforded to HR systems in conjunction with bottom-line accountability based upon deploying a balanced set of performance and customer satisfaction measures (line management, employees, applicants, and the public). A second key factor is the infusion of sufficient fiscal resources to improve wage and benefit comparability including the provision of work-life benefits. A third key factor is to upgrade the prestige and status of the public service to overcome the negative governmental stereotypes. These beliefs are difficult to rebut given the deep-seated public skepticism toward government. One suggestion is to institute a systematic school-based campaign to educate our children at early ages on the importance of government and the intrinsic rewards associated with public service careers. The development of magnet, service learning, and internship programs can expose students to government service in a systematic fashion. A final factor is the continued investment in staffing technology to enhance the efficiency of the recruitment and selection process.

In summary, there are great challenges associated with the staffing process in the public sector, and the absence of sustained attention and resources will reduce the competence of the public service to the detriment of our overall quality of life. Providing the requisite level of human capital investment in our public servants will clearly benefit both present and future generations.

REFERENCES

Avue Technologies. 2000. Strategic Recruitment of Law Enforcement Officers. *IPMA News* May 2000:10.

BAILEY, GEORGE. 1998. Training as a Recruitment Tool. *HR Focus* 75(7):11–12.

BEHLING, ORLANDO. 1998. Employee Selection: Will Intelligence and Conscientiousness Do the Job? *The Academy of Management Executive* 12(1):77–86.

BELMAN, DALE, and JOHN S. HEYWOOD. 1996. The Structure of Compensation in the Public Sector. In *Public Sector Employment In a Time of Transition,* Dale Belman, Morley Gunderson, and Douglas Hyatt, eds. Madison, WI: Industrial Relations Research Association.

BERNOTAVICZ, FREDA and AMY LOCKE. 2000. Hiring Child Welfare Caseworkers Using a Competency-Based Approach. *Public Personnel Management* 29(1):22–42.

BOE, ERLING E., SHARON A. BOBBITT, and LYNNE H. COOK. 1997. Whither Didst Thou Go? Retention, Reassignment, Migration, and Attrition of Special and General Education Teachers from a National Perspective. *Journal of Special Education* 30(4):371–389.

BOND, JAMES T., ELLEN GALINSKY, and JENNIFER E. SWANBERG. 1998. *The 1997 National Study of the Changing Workforce.* New York: Families and Work Institute.

BRUDNEY, JEFFREY. 1998. Utilizing Volunteers in the Workplace. In *Handbook of Human Resource Management.* Stephen E. Condrey, ed. San Francisco: Jossey-Bass, 97–117.

CLARDY, ALAN. 1997. *Studying Your Workforce.* Thousand Oaks, CA: Sage.

CASCIO, WAYNE F. 1982. *Applied Psychology in Personnel Management,* 2nd Ed. Reston, VA: Reston Publishing Company.

DAVIS, THOMAS M. 2000. Operation Dire Straits; Here's Why the Military is Failing to Attract the Right Recruits. *Washington Post* January 16, 2000:Page B01.

CONNERLEY, MARY L., and SARAH L. RYNES. 1997. The Influence of Recruiter Characteristics and Organizational Recruitment Support on Perceived Recruiter Effectiveness: Views from Applicants and Recruiters. *Human Relations* 50(12):1563–1586.

Council for Excellence in Government. 1999. *America Unplugged: Citizens and Their Government.* Council for Excellence in Government, July 1999. Available at: <http://www.excelgov.org/publication/excel/default.ht>

GORE, ALBERT. 1993. *Creating a Government That Works Better and Costs Less.* Washington, DC: Government Printing Office.

GREENE, THARON. 1999. City of Hampton's Innovative Recruiting Efforts. *IPMA News* November 1999:19.

Griggs v. Duke Power Co., 1971. 401 U.S. 424 at 436.

GUNNELS-PERRY, SHERRYL. 1999. Public/Private Partnerships as Recruiting and Retention Strategies. *Employment Relations Today* 26(2):1–13.

HR Focus. 1999. Employee Recruitment and Retention No. 1 Issue. *HR Focus* 76(12):16.

IPMA News. 1998. State and Local Government Jobs Increase in the 1990s. *IPMA News* February 1998:9.

——. 1999. Employees Speak Out on Job Training. *IPMA News* March 1999:16.

——. 2000a. Expert Tips on Recruiting via the Internet. *IPMA News* April 2000:15–16.

——. 2000b. New Employee Orientation Programs Key to Starting Employees Off Right. *IPMA News* April 2000:12.

——. 2000c. Shortage of IT Service and Support Workers Costs America Billions Annually. *IPMA News* February 2000:16.

INGRAHAM, PATRICIA WALLACE, SALLY COLEMAN SELDEN, and DONALD. P. MOYNIHAN. 2000. People and Performance: Challenges for the Future. *Public Administration Review* 60(1):54–60.

JOINSON, CARLA. 1999. Suburbs vs. Cities. (Workplace Location Will Affect Productivity and Recruitment). *HR Magazine* 44(3):34–39.

KETTL, DONALD F. 1998. *Reinventing Government: A Fifth-Year Report Card.* Center for Public Management Report CPM 98-1. Washington, DC: The Brookings Institution.

KLINGNER, DONALD E., and JOHN NALBANDIAN. 1998. *Public Personnel Management. Contexts and Strategies,* 4th ed. Upper Saddle River, NJ: Prentice-Hall.

LATHAM, GARY P., and BARBARA J. FINNEGAN. 1993. Perceived Practicality of Unstructured, Patterned, and Situational Interviews. In *Personnel Selection and Assessment: Individual and Organizational Perspectives,* Heinz Schuler, James L. Farr, and Mike Smith, eds. Hillsdale, NJ: Lawrence Erlbaum Associates, Publishers, 41–56.

LAVIGNA, ROBERT J. 1996. Innovation in Recruiting and Hiring: Attracting the Best and Brightest to Wisconsin State Government. *Public Personnel Management* 25(4):423–437.

LEE, ROBERT D., and RONALD W. JOHNSON. 1998. *Public Budgeting Systems,* 6th ed. Gaithersburg, MD: Aspen.

OLIVER, JUDITH. 1998. The Science of Professional Interviewing. *Management Today* February: 80–81.

OSBORNE, DAVID, and TED GAEBLER (1992). *Reinventing Government.* Reading, MA: Addison-Wesley.

PHILLIPS, JEAN M. 1998. Effects of Realistic Job Previews on Multiple Organizational Outcomes: A Meta-Analysis. *Academy of Management Journal* 41(6):673–690.

POPOVICH, MARK G., ed. 1998. *Creating High-Performance Government Organizations.* San Francisco: Jossey-Bass Publishers.

RISHER, HOWARD, and CHARLES H. FAY. 1997. *New Strategies for Public Pay.* San Francisco: Jossey-Bass.

ROBERTS, GARY E. 2000. Municipal Government Benefits Practices and Personnel Outcomes: Results from a National Survey. Paper Presented at the American Society of Public Administration Annual Conference. San Diego California, April 4, 2000.

RYNES, SARA L. 1993. When Recruitment Fails to Attract: Individual Expectations Meet Organizational Realities in Recruitment. In *Personnel Selection and Assessment: Individual and Organizational Perspectives,* Heinz Schuler, James L. Farr, and Mike Smith. Hillsdale, NJ: Lawrence Erlbaum Associates, Publishers, 27–40.

SMITH, MAUREEN. 1999. Measuring Employee Satisfaction Through Surveys. *IPMA News* March 1999:15–16.

——. 2000. Innovative Personnel Recruitment. Changing Workforce Demographics. *IPMA News* March 2000:12–14.

SULLIVAN, JOHN. 1999. Gaining a Competitive Advantage Through Increasing "The Speed of Hire." *IPMA News* June 1999:14–15.

——. 2000. Employment Branding. *IPMA News* May 2000:11–13.

SULLIVAN, SHERRY E., and EDWARD A. DUPLAGA. 1997. Recruiting and Retaining Older Workers for the New Millennium. *Business Horizons* 40(Nov–Dec):65–69.

TERPSTRA, DAVID E., and ELIZABETH J. ROZELL. 1997. Why Some Potentially Effective Staffing Practices are Seldom Used. *Public Personnel Management* 26(4):483–495.

THORNTON, GEORGE C. III. 1993. The Effect of Selection Practices on Applicants' Perceptions of Organizational Characteristics. In *Personnel Selection and Assessment: Individual and Organizational Perspectives,* Heinz Schuler, James L. Farr and Mike Smith, eds. Hillsdale, NJ: Lawrence Erlbaum Associates, Publishers, 57–70.

TOMPKINS, JONATHAN. 1998. *Human Resource Management in Government.* New York: HarperCollins.

TRATT, NOAH. 2000. Winning the Employee Recruitment and Retention Challenge. *Compensation & Benefits Management* 16(2):50.

TREADWAY, BOB. 1999. The City of Ann Arbor Goes High-Tech In Recruitment Process. *IPMA News* July 1999:25.

TRICE, ELEANOR. 1998. High-Tech Recruiting. *IPMA News* February 1998:27.

——. 1999a. Cost-per-hire: A Worthwhile Calculation? *IPMA News* March 1999: 17.

——. 1999b. Timely Hiring Best Practices. Cater to Your Candidates and Toss the Applications. *IPMA News* June 1999:11–12.

——. 1999c. Timely Hiring: Make Your Agency a Best Practice. *IPMA News* June 1999:10–11.

TRUAX, JERRY R. 1999. Succession Planning at the Nevada Operations Office. *IPMA News* August 1999:19.

U.S. Department of Labor (U.S. DOL) (1996). Working Together for Public Service. U.S. Department of Labor. 1996.

U.S. Department of Labor. 1999. Futurework–Trends and Challenges for Work in the 21st Century. Available at: <http://www.dol.gov/asp/public/futurework/>

——. 2000. The Employment Situation: April 2000. Available at: <http://stats.bls.gov/newsrels.htm>

U.S. Office of Personnel Management (U.S. OPM). 1998a. *Deregulation and Delegation of Human Resources Management Authority in the Federal Government.* U.S. Office of Personnel Management-Office of Merit Systems Oversight and Effectiveness. Report No. MSE–98–3. July. Available at: <http://www.opm.gov/studies/index.htm>

——. 1999. *The 3Rs: Lessons Learned from Recruitment, Relocation, and Retention Incentives.* U.S. Office of Personnel Management-Office of Merit Systems Oversight and Effectiveness. Available at: <http://www.opm.gov/studies/99-3r's.pdf>

——. 2000a. Demonstration Project Factsheet. Available at: <http://www.opm.gov/demos/demofact.ht>

——. 2000b. *Human Resource Flexibilities and Authorities in the Federal U.S. Government.* Available at: <http://www.opm.gov/demos/webflexs.pdf>

VISCASILLAS, RAFAEL. 1999. Retaining Your Top Talent by Becoming the Employer of Choice. *IPMA News* March 1999:14.

WANOUS, JOHN P. 1993. Newcomer Orientation Programs That Facilitate Organizational Entry. In *Personnel Selection and Assessment: Individual and Organizational Perspectives,* Heinz Schuler, James L. Farr, and Mike Smith, eds. Hillsdale, NJ: Lawrence Erlbaum Associates, Publishers, 125–140.

WERBEL, JAMES D., and JACUELINE LANDAU. 1996. The effectiveness of Different Recruitment Sources: A Mediating Variable Analysis. *Journal of Applied Psychology* 26(15):1337–1350.

WITKIN, BELLE RUTH, and JAMES W. ALTSCHULD. 1995. *Planning and Conducting Needs Assessments: A Practical Guide.* Thousand Oaks, CA: Sage.

9

Why Public Managers Hate Position Classification

KATHERINE C. NAFF

San Francisco State University

Position classification is simply a means for organizing work into groups (or "classes") and levels (or pay grades) on the basis of duties and responsibilities. Classification systems were developed in direct response to the disorderly and erratic processes of hiring and paying public sector employees that existed up until the early 1900s. At that time, scientific management, as espoused by Frederick W. Taylor, seemed to provide just the antidote. He believed that it was possible to determine the single best way in which a worker could perform each task. People were just as interchangeable as parts in a machine.

This conception of the most efficient way to organize work was embraced by other management luminaries at the time such as Luther Gulick, who was often called the "Dean of American Public Administration." Gulick argued that the "Division of work and integrated organization are the bootstraps by which mankind lifts itself in the process of civilization" and requires the establishment of authority and a network of communication and control (Gulick 1937). Applied to personnel management, this scientific approach called for defining work in terms of the *positions* needed to carry it out, rather than the *people* doing the work. Such a system, i.e. position classification, could ensure uniformity and consistency across government.

Why, then, do public managers hate position classification? This chapter addresses this question. It does so first by describing the purpose and structure of position classification systems and the problems they present for public managers in today's work environment. It then assesses the various proposals to reform classification that many jurisdictions are considering and the prospects for such reform to occur.

ORIGINS OF POSITION CLASSIFICATION

Most position classification systems in the public sector were developed in the early part of the twentieth century as an integral part of the efficiency movement that was sweeping the country. Central to this effort was the work of Frederick Winslow Taylor, who pioneered what came to be called scientific management. Taylor was obsessed with the notion that work could be broken down into specific tasks which could be tested and timed to determine in what way and with what tools the worker could produce the highest output in the least amount of time. While the primary application he had in mind was manufacturing, he argued that the principle should be applied everywhere (Taylor, 1919).

As government began to expand in the early part of the twentieth century, it became clear that civil service systems required more structure to ensure, among other things, equal pay for equal work. The lack of structure was causing considerable inequities in pay as well as poor morale, high turnover, and inefficiency (Shafritz et al., 1992). Taylor's thinking, then, seemed apropos. With pressure from the unions, Congress passed the Classification Act of 1923, which instituted grade levels and assigned salaries to each grade (Johnson and Libecap, 1994). A central authority—the Personnel Classification Board—was established to oversee position classification. (That responsibility has since been transferred to the government's central personnel agency—the Office of Personnel Management). The basic structure established by that Act is still in force in the federal government, and also forms the basis for many classification systems in state and local government.

A central tenet of traditional position classification was that positions would be classified, not people. Instead of hiring people based on patronage, finding work for them to do and paying them whatever the manager chose to, positions would be established based on work needing to be done. Qualification requirements would be identified, and people would be recruited and evaluated on the basis of those requirements. Employees would be paid the salary that was preassigned to that job classification and grade level based on job duties and responsibilities. Everyone working in the same class and grade level across government would have the same qualifications, receive the same pay, and have substantially the same levels of work responsibility.

By mid-century, government, especially at the federal level, had become highly centralized. The white-collar workforce was the dominant part of the personnel system. The Classification Act of 1949 established the General Schedule (GS) system for white-collar work and defined eighteen grade levels (5 USC §5103). The law required what is now the Office of Personnel Management (OPM) to define federal occupations and their official titles, and describe the grades of various levels of work. Blue-collar jobs remained in a separate "Wage Grade" (or WG) system. Thirty years later, senior executives, who previously held jobs at grades 16 to 18, were reclassified in a separate system called the Senior Executive Service by the Civil Service Reform Act of 1978.

The classification system, by design, became one which minimalized managerial discretion, and therefore potential abuse, and promoted equal pay for equal work as the cornerstone. In that sense, it was an important adjunct to the development of a civil service system in which hiring and promotion are to be based strictly on merit, and fairness and equity are fundamental. Managers, on the other hand, were inclined to view it as an inflexible system that served only as a stumbling block in their way of getting the people they needed to accomplish their work. But before discussing the specific difficulties that position classification systems presented to managers, it is important to understand precisely how classification works.

HOW DOES POSITION CLASSIFICATION WORK?

In a position classification system, the basic unit of analysis is a job. The first step, then, is to undertake a job analysis. Job analysis is the means for collecting all the relevant information about work duties and activities so that a classification and grade level can be assigned. In carrying out a job analysis, the analyst will discern:

- All of the tasks that are performed, their difficulty, and their relative importance
- The knowledge, skills, and abilities (KSA's) required for effective performance of those tasks
- The level of responsibility exercised by an incumbent in the position and the degree of supervision required

This information is often acquired through questionnaires completed by employees in the job, interviews with those employees and their supervisors, activity logs maintained by the employee, and discussions with subject matter experts.

Once all the relevant information is in hand, the usual procedure is to write a position description so the job can be classified. The format of the position description depends on the type of classification standard that will be used (see Table 9.1) but it usually includes the position's duties and responsibilities, the scope of the job, and nature of supervision. The goal is to assign the job its proper place in the organizational structure. The table illustrates that structure in the federal government. Before discussing the logic of that structure, it is necessary to define the terms.

An occupation is a type of job. In most classification systems, it has a number (or series) and job title associated with it. So, for example, in the federal system, a mail and file clerk is an occupation or job title, and the number associated with it is GS–305. GS stands for the General Schedule, the classification system for white-collar jobs established by the 1949 Classification Act. Within an occupation or series, work can be performed at various levels, and these are known as grade levels. The Xs in the table represent the grade levels that are associated with each of the listed occupations. Each grade has a specific salary level assigned to it by law. Within each grade level, there are ten steps, or pay increments. The salaries shown in Table 9.1 reflect the minimum (step 1) salary paid for each GS grade level in the year 2000.

Each position, then, occupies a place within the overall structure. Horizontally, a position's place will reflect equivalence to other jobs that share characteristics such as the level of responsibility exercised and nature of supervision. For example, if the job is considered an entry-level, professional job, where the incumbent is performing routine work under close supervision, it would likely be classified at the GS-5 level. This would be the case if the job were criminal inves-

TABLE 9–1   Structure of the General Schedule Classification System in the Federal Government*

Grade	Salary at Step 1 for Each Grade*	Sample Occupations			
		Mail and File Clerk (GS 305)	Biological Technician (GS 404)	Accountant (GS 510)	Criminal Investigator (GS 1811)
1	$13,870	X	X	...	...
2	$15,594	X	X	...	...
3	$17,015	X	X	...	...
4	$19,100	X	X	...	...
5	$21,370	X	X	X	X
6	$23,820	X	X	...	...
7	$26,470	X	X	X	X
8	$29,315		X		...
9	$32,380		X	X	X
10	$35,658	...	X		X
11	$39,178	...	X	X	X
12	$46,955	...		X	X
13	$55,837	...	...	X	X
14	$65,983	...	...	X	X
15	$77,614	...	...	X	X

* Since 1991, these salaries have been adjusted based on salaries paid for equivalent work in the location where the incumbents work.
Source: U.S. OPM. 2000. The Federal General Schedule. Washington D.C.: Office of Personnel Management.

tigator, accountant, chemist, or any of many other occupations. The pay for an employee in a GS-5 position is set by law, and is basically the same whether that employee works in Alaska or Washington, D.C. and regardless of the occupation.[1] In this way, the government carries out its commitment to equal pay for substantially equal work.

Note that the beginning grade for some occupations, in this case as an accountant or criminal investigator, is GS-5, whereas for mail and file clerks, technicians and others, the entry-level grade is GS-1. This is because the duties, responsibilities and qualifications required for an entry level accountant or investigator are greater than those of an entry level clerk or technician. A mail clerk who is in a grade 5 job is performing work substantially equivalent to an accountant (or anyone else) in a GS-5 job.

Vertically, the job is placed within an occupational series, or job title. For example, there is a criminal investigator series, an accountant series, a personnel specialist series, an occupational therapist series. A GS-13 criminal investigator would perform virtually the same work duties if he or she were employed in the U.S.

[1] Since 1991, salaries for each grade level are adjusted based on the cost of employment in the locality in which the federal employee works, as stated in table footnote.

Customs Service, the FBI, or any other federal agency that employs criminal investigators. Theoretically, while each agency and its clients might be different, the investigator position might be viewed as an interchangeable part.

Once the position description has been compiled, the next task, then, is to decide which series is the appropriate one for the job. This may not be easy because there are many from which to choose. The federal government has over 450 occupational series. Some states have even more. For example, New Jersey has 4820 series that are unique to the state government, 3120 that are unique to its local governments, and 324 which state and local government share (New Jersey, 1998). This means that many of the occupations are very specific about the work to be performed by those classified in those occupations.

Take, for example, a newly created position at the Environmental Protection Agency that needs to be classified. One would have to decide if it requires "professional knowledge and competence in the broad, multidisciplinary field of environmental science, which encompasses chemistry, biology, toxicology, health, physics, safety, and related areas." If so, it might belong in the General Physical Science Series, GS–1301. On the other hand, if it primarily requires "professional knowledge and competence in one or more specialized disciplines of environmental science," it might be more appropriately classified in the Ecology Series, GS–0408 or the Chemistry Series, GS–1360. Or, if the position required "professional knowledge and competence in the conservation or management of soil, water, plant, animal, or related natural resources for particular purposes or uses," it might belong in the Rangeland Management Series, GS–0454, or Wildlife Biology Series, GS–0486.

One can imagine how difficult it might be to choose a series if the position involved duties that cross more than one. Selection of the correct series is important because it will govern the qualification requirements for the job, the salary that will be paid, and the position's potential for career advancement—all of which affect recruitment. Once the appropriate series is decided, the proper grade level must be assigned. Again, it may not be easy to differentiate among grade levels. The federal government has 15 pay grades, but some states have more. The State of Virginia has 23 and the State of Washington has 85.

According to federal classification standards for the Physical Science series, if the incumbent works under immediate supervision, "with little opportunity for the exercise of independent judgment," it should be graded at GS–5. If, on the other hand, the employee will "to a limited extent, exercise independent technical judgment," it would fit the guidelines for GS–7. If the job does involve the application of judgment, one has to decide whether that judgment is limited or whether there is "considerable latitude for the exercise of independent judgment." In the latter case, the job may be most appropriately classified as GS–9.

Similarly, the GS–5 standard states that the incumbents "receive assignments that consist of specific, well defined tasks," whereas at the GS–7 level they receive assignments in terms of general instruction, and at the GS–9 level they plan and carry out routine work. What happens if the manager thinks she wants a GS–7 physical scientist and hires someone at this grade who turns out to be a quick learner, capable of performing the work of a GS–9 physical scientist? She must either keep that employee in a position for which he is overqualified or ask the classifiers to reclassify the job at a higher level. That would require the classifier to engage in a time and paper-intensive fact-finding process to determine if the employee really is performing duties associated with the GS–9 level.

The determination as to the appropriate grade is made using the classification standard. Those standards can take a number of forms. The more traditional standard is a "narrative one" which describes the nature of the work and level of responsibility for each grade covered by the standard. In comparing the position description in hand to the narrative classification standard, the classifier must think about the whole job. Table 9–2 presents a narrative standard for a GS–7 physical scientist. This kind of language is also used to describe the other grade levels that are represented within this occupation. At each successive grade level, the standard grows longer and more complex.

Classification standards also become increasingly complex as work becomes more specialized. Indeed, by the 1960s it had become very difficult to compare highly specialized jobs to one another in a reliable way. But such comparison is required to maintain the principle that jobs of equal difficulty and responsibility should be classified at the same grade level.

In order to preserve this principle in light of the increasing specialization of jobs, traditional classification underwent an internal reform. A new system, called factor evaluation, emerged that decomposed jobs into factors to better enable jobs to be compared to one another. For example, in the Criminal Investigator series (GS–1811), grade level determinations are based on two factors: complexity of

---

TABLE **9–2**   **Classification Standard for GS–1300 Physical Scientist**

The Law

"Grade GS–7 includes . . . positions the duties of which are—

(B) Under immediate or general supervision, to perform somewhat difficult work requiring—

   (i) professional, scientific, or technical training; and

   (ii) to a limited extent, the exercise of independent technical judgment . . ."

The Standard

This is the grade for advanced trainee positions in physical science professions. At this level, trainees perform a variety of technical tasks, such as selecting samples, interpolating missing data, uncovering clear discrepancies, solving minor problems, and performing scientific analyses in support of projects assigned to higher level scientists.

Advanced trainees receive assignments in terms of general instructions regarding work to be accomplished, quality and quantity expected, limitations, and suggested approaches. They exercise judgment in locating and selecting the most appropriate guides and references to apply, make routine decisions, and refer situations requiring significant deviation to the supervisor or a higher graded specialist.

Illustration—GS–7:

Performs work within established methods and procedures. Performs preliminary analyses, makes computations and applies correction factors, and plots preliminary prediction values; prepares computer programs for processing data based on established programs and techniques; and performs higher level tasks as training assignments. Exercises judgment in selecting the appropriate methods and procedures to carry out the analyses and tests. Independently completes recurring assignments, but refers all deviations and problems not covered by instructions to the supervisor.

Source: U.S. OPM, <http://www.opm.gov/fedclass/html/gsclass.htm>

assignments and level of responsibility. The broader the scope, and the greater the difficulty and sensitivity of the work performed, the higher graded it should be. At the same time, the more independently of supervision one performs, the higher graded it would be.

Another element of the factor system is the point-factor evaluation system. In this system, specific factors are defined and then point values are assigned. The grade level of each job is determined from the sum of points. Table 9–3 presents the factors that are used in the FES system in federal employment.

Points are then assigned to each factor. For example, depending on the level of knowledge required for a secretarial position, the classifier would assign a min-

---

TABLE 9–3   Factor Evaluation System Factors
_____

Factor 1—Knowledge Required by the Position

Kind or nature of knowledge and skills needed
How the knowledge and skills are used in doing the work

Factor 2—Supervisory Controls

How the work is assigned
Employee's responsibility for carrying out the work
How the work is reviewed

Factor 3—Guidelines

Nature of guidelines for performing the work
Judgment needed to apply the guidelines or develop new guidelines

Factor 4—Complexity

Nature of the assignment
Difficulty in identifying what needs to be done
Difficulty and originality involved in performing the work

Factor 5—Scope and Effect

Purpose of the work
Impact of the work product or service

Factor 6—Personal Contacts*

People and conditions/setting under which contacts are made

Factor 7—Purpose of Contacts

Reasons for contacts in Factor 6

Factor 8—Physical Demands

Nature, frequency, and intensity of physical activity

Factor 9—Work Environment
_____

*Note: In some FES standards the point values for factors 6 and 7 are combined into a matrix chart. The levels of each factor are described separately.

Source: U.S. OPM, *The Classifier's Handbook,* July 1999. Washington, D.C.: Office of Personnel Management.

TABLE 9–4   Point Ranges for Secretary and Accountant Positions
and Point Conversion to GS-Grades

Factor	Secretary	Accountant	Point Range	GS Grade
1	200–950	750–1550	190–250	1
2	25–450	25–650	255–450	2
3	25–275	25–650	455–650	3
4	25–150	75–450	655–850	4
5	25–150	25–450	855–1100	5
6	10–110	30–330	1105–1350	6
7	20–50		1355–1600	7
8	5	5	1605–1850	8
9	5	5	1855–2100	9
Total	340–2145	940–4090	2105–2350	10
			2355–2750	11
			2755–3150	12
			3155–3600	13
			3605–4050	14
			4055–up	15

imum of 200 to a maximum of 450 points (see Table 9–4). The knowledge required for an accounting position could warrant the assignment of as few as 750 points or as many as 1550. Once the classifier has assigned point values for each factor, they are totaled. The total number of points is then converted to a GS grade level (see Table 9–4). For example, if the total is between 855 and 1100 points, the job is GS-5. This is the minimum grade level for an accountant. If the total is between 1355 and 1600, the grade is GS-7.

Out of this process also come benchmarks. Each new job to be classified can be compared to a previously classified one. For each factor, the new job will be found to be at a higher, equivalent, or lower level than the previous one. This is another means for ensuring internal equity and consistency.

The advantages of a position classification system such as that described here should be readily apparent. Forcing managers to categorize the positions they supervise by occupational series and grade means that employees in that position should be doing the work they were hired to do at the pay that an objective evaluation has determined. The system achieves internal equity by ensuring that employees doing equivalent work are paid the same across occupations, agencies, and geographic locations. It provides to the employee and manager a common understanding of what a job entails, what acceptable performance of that job requires, and the value of that job to government (i.e., the level of compensation) thereby forestalling much potential for misapprehension. Classifiers and many personnel specialists still see position classification as "the backbone of government's information system for managing jobs, people and pay" (Holley and O'Connell, 1997:96). But the question remains, why are managers unhappy?

WHY MANAGERS HATE POSITION CLASSIFICATION

There are many reasons that managers find position classification to be objectionable. This section discusses managerial opposition in depth. Table 9–5 provides a summary list of ten top objections.

It may be evident at this point that while a classification system strives to be objective, it is also fairly rigid. What happens if a manager wants to hire someone whose job would include elements from both the chemistry and ecological science series? The job has to be classified and advertised as one or the other. What happens if the level of responsibility would be greater than that suggested by the GS–7 description, but less than that described by the GS–9 classification standard? What happens if some of the duties are performed at the GS–7 level and others at the GS–9 level?

At the same time, public institutions, facing declining confidence in government and citizens' simultaneous demands for higher quality services and lower taxes, are seeking ways to become leaner, more decentralized, flexible and innovative (Osborne and Gaebler, 1992; Osborne and Plastrik, 1997; National Performance Review, 1993). Organizations in both sectors are learning that such changes in organizational structures should include, in many instances, replacing traditional hierarchical work structures with teams that oversee a "whole" part of the enterprise. This goes beyond using teams to solve organizational problems; rather the expectation is that organizations will establish a culture that supports teams as the central platform for accomplishing work (Mohrman, Cohen, and Mohrman, 1995; Boyett and Conn, 1991; Linden, 1994; Lawler, 1996; Hyde, 1997).

In a team environment, workers often perform a variety of functions with differing levels of responsibility. One could be performing scientific work on one project, managing the project on another, and perhaps developing a web site for one's program on another. The traditional classification system, which requires that people be assigned work consistent with the duties described in the classification standard, impedes rather than facilitates such mutability of job responsibilities. Moreover, traditional classification systems emphasize hierarchy at a time when the transition to team-based structures requires employees to see each other as co-

TABLE 9–5   Ten Reasons Managers Hate Position Classification

Position classification often:

1. Creates narrow, rigid boundaries between jobs
2. Locks employees into functional silos
3. Accentuates hierarchy
4. Demands centralization and uniformity
5. Limits ability to offer competitive salaries
6. Assumes individuals' contribution to their job is static and never grows
7. Encourages playing havoc with merit promotion process
8. Fails to keep up with changing technology
9. Impedes employee development
10. Creates conflict between managers and the classifiers who must "police" classification decisions

equals (Risher, 1999). They demand centralization and uniformity at a time when organizations need to tailor work structures to better meet the expectations of an increasingly sophisticated and demanding public.

It should be clear that this rigid system for setting pay that is tied to the classification system has its drawbacks as well. A manager may have jobs that are clearly entry-level. That means that the most that she can pay is the salary specified for GS–5 or GS–7 employees, which may be considerably less than an entry-level person in that job would earn outside government.

Moreover, if a manager has a valued employee whom he or she wishes to pay more, often the only way to do so is to promote the person into a higher grade level. This has resulted in the phenomenon known as "grade creep." Those who speak about grade creep are usually suggesting that higher grade levels are assigned to work that has not increased in difficulty or responsibility, simply as a means to retain workers and/or improve morale (Lewis, 1997). Of course, managers might see this differently. They might see increases in the quality of work, familiarity with organizational policies and customers' needs, and other knowledge acquired as invaluable "human capital" for which individuals should be compensated. It might also be the case that as a result of downsizing or contracting out, employees' duties and responsibilities have grown beyond the level specified by the standard for the grade they are occupying.

In other cases, promotion to a new grade level may require opening that position to competition. A costly recruitment and selection process may ensue when, in fact, all the agency wanted to do was promote the person already on board. In still other cases, the only way a promotion can occur is by moving the employee into a supervisory position, whether that person has the interest and skills to be an effective supervisor or not.

Yet another problem arises in a job that is being redefined because of changes in technology or other innovations. A classification standard written for a secretary's position ten years ago is not likely to reflect the duties associated with that job in the age of personal computers on every staff member's desk.

Any one of these scenarios can, and often has, created tension between managers and classifiers, whose job it is to ensure that jobs are correctly classified and assigned to the appropriate grade level. Managers may want to upgrade the position in order to raise its pay and retain a valued employee. Classifiers are responsible for ensuring that "grade creep" doesn't occur because it can undercut the system of equal pay for equal work and increase salary costs for the agency. Managers, then, view classifiers as the cops who won't cooperate in that venture, constricting their discretion in how to manage their workforce and get the job done.

The federal position classification system has also been criticized for limiting employee development. There is no incentive for developing an employee as long as the work is seen in terms of positions rather than employees. If an employee wants to develop new skills and move into a job with a greater level of responsibility, that often requires competing for promotion to a higher graded job (should one even be available) instead of having the latitude to grow in the job he or she has (Friel, 1999, Colvard, 2000).

There are probably other objections, beyond those discussed here, but the list of ten provide some of the major grounds for why managers dislike position classification so intensely.

WHAT CAN BE DONE?

Public sector entities have found a number of ways to try to diffuse the pressure created by a position classification system born in an earlier, and very different, moment in history.

Rank in Person

An alternative to the position classification system is a rank-in-person system. Many organizations, including the U.S. military and Foreign Service, operate such systems. As an individual gains more experience and demonstrates higher capabilities, that person is promoted. In this system people are paid according to the knowledge and experience they bring to the organization, rather than according to how their job is defined.

Positions are still defined, however, and assigned grade levels, but a person carries his/her own rank and can be assigned to a position with a higher or lower grade level (as long as the grade level is not too distant from that person's rank). This allows for more flexibility in assignments and presumes that employee development is fundamental. However, there is also an expectation that the individuals will continue to compete for a limited number of promotions. In that sense, rank in person also emphasizes hierarchy.

In a rank-in-position system, the expectation is that if Albert Einstein wants to work as a GS–3 mail clerk, he can. But he is only going to get paid according to the work he does as a GS–3 mail clerk. In the rank-in-person system, Einstein takes his grade with him; it is not determined by the job that he is in. While a rank-in-person system would appear to provide organizations with more flexibility in work assignments, it also requires a substantial investment in creating this career service.

Congress attempted to establish a rank-in-person system when it created the Senior Executive Service (SES) as part of the 1978 Civil Service Reform Act. Civil servants were admitted to this elite corps of executives based on their qualifications. Agencies could assign them to almost any SES position in the agency, regardless of its place in the organizational hierarchy. Members of the SES were expected to be generalists who could move among agencies and geographical locations as needed. In practice, little of this mobility has occurred. Perhaps this is one reason why state and local governments, and other federal agencies, are not embracing this approach as the means for reforming their classification systems.

Adding or Subtracting Classifications

OPM's response to changes in the nature of work is to simply add additional occupational titles. A good example is the field of information technology where the number of people performing many different kinds of work has ballooned in the last decade. Many of these employees are doing much different work than existed when the original position classifications for computer specialists and telecommunication specialists were written. Hence, OPM has replaced those two series classifications with eleven new ones.

From OPM's point of view, this is the way to provide additional flexibility to managers. They can choose the job classification that most fits the work they need done. However, it is not a solution for managers who want an individual to perform a variety of functions. Now managers must decide whether the person they need will be a systems administrator or a systems analyst; a communications services specialist or a network services specialist. Moreover, the positions computer scientist (GS-1550) and computer engineer (GS-0850) aren't even included among the eleven. This complaint was raised by the IT director at the Department of Housing and Urban Development who said that all ten members of her eleven-member team have some of skills from each of the eleven specialty titles. "What do I call these people?" she asked (Saldarini, 1999).

Many state governments have also increased the number of position classifications. In the case of Georgia, this occurred as a result of its Georgia Gain project, which eliminated its centralized merit system, providing each agency with the authority to develop its own rules for managing its human resources. As a result, the number of classifications rose from about 1500 in 1991 to more than 3700 today. Other states have also increased the number of classifications without necessarily making other reforms. Some state and local governments have taken the opposite approach, and that is to reduce the number of position classifications. The idea is that if several narrow occupational titles can be consolidated into one broader one, managers have more flexibility as to how the jobs of their subordinates are defined. This practice can also increase managers' flexibility in redefining employees' work when restructuring or downsizing takes place. In writing about Michigan, John Kost (1996) noted that when mainframes were replaced by client server technology in the state's Department of Transportation, the agency laid off the mainframe support technicians and then hired new server technicians. This could have been avoided had they had *one* technology support classification.

An example of a jurisdiction that has been subtracting classifications is the State of Washington. In that state, duties that had been performed by people classified as clerk 3, clerk typist 3, clerk stenographer 3, and office assistant were consolidated into one classification called "office assistant senior" who "performs a variety of clerical duties in support of office or unit operations." Other states that have been working to subtract classifications are Illinois, which reduced the number of classifications by 40 percent between 1991 and 1998, and South Carolina, which reduced them by 78 percent (Selden, 1998). New Jersey is now in the process of reducing its over 8000 state and local position titles to 1500 (New Jersey State Department of Personnel, 1998).

That adding or subtracting classifications is not the antidote to managers' frustrations with the classification system should be apparent when one notes that some states have done both. Between 1986 and 1991, Michigan increased the number of classifications from 1766 to 2700. By 1998, the number was back down to 1500. Similarly, the number of classifications in West Virginia rose from 950 to 2000, and then dropped again to 750 over the same twelve year period (Shafritz et al., forthcoming).

Neither adding nor subtracting classifications, then, seems to be a viable long-term solution to an overly rigid classification system that does not allow for the flexibility and teamwork required in today's environment. Adding classifications may offer managers more options for classifying jobs, but the definitions of those jobs will remain constrained and may even create more functional job silos. Even seemingly large reductions in the number of classifications still leave managers with little more flexibility than they had before. In New Jersey, they will still have to decide which *one* of the 1500 classifications describes their subordinates' work. Moreover, managers are still left with the problem of identifying the appropriate grade level. A more popular and arguably radical reform approach to both of these problems is broadbanding.

Broadbanding   Broadbanding can be seen as an extreme form of subtracting classifications. In this system, highly specific occupational series are replaced with much broader job titles, and broader pay ranges replace specific grade levels. In this way, an agency can move employees horizontally and vertically among a wider range of work assignments and without the need for a formal time-intensive promotion process. For many years the National Academy of Public Administration (NAPA) has been urging Congress to amend the Classification Act to allow for such an approach (NAPA, 1991, 1995a, 1995b).

Table 9–6 provides one example of a broadbanding system–there are many possible variations on the theme.

TABLE 9–6   Paths/Bands Graphic: Single Mission/Single Function Agency

GS	Agency Occupation	Degree Required	Admin. & Evaluation	Technical Support	Office Services
15	M X	M X			
14	M X	M X	M X		
13	F	F	M X		
12	F	F	F	M X	
11	F	F	F	M X	
10	D	F	F	M X	
9	D	D	D	F	M X
8	D	D	D	F	M X
7	D	D	D	F	F
6	D	D	D	F	F
5	D	D	D	F	F
4	T	T	T	D	D
3	T	T	T	D	D
2				T	D
1				T	T

M = Manager; X = Expert, Supervisor, Leader; F = Full Performance; D = Developmental; T = Trainee.
Source: National Academy for Public Administration, 1995a, p. 34.

In the system illustrated in Table 9–6, five career paths have replaced hundreds of occupational series. In this agency, these comprise an agency-specific path, one where jobs require specific degrees, and administrative/evaluative, technical support, and office support paths.

By "agency specific" NAPA means an occupation that is of central importance to a particular agency—e.g., scientists in a research lab or attorneys at the Department of Justice. Because it is so critical to the agency's mission, the agency may want to keep it distinct from the other work performed in the agency. That occupation is defined as its own career path, beginning with a trainee position (replacing GS 3–4) and topping out at either a manager or expert level (replacing GS 14–15). The divide between managers and experts is recognition that all scientists or attorneys may not want to become managers, but should have the latitude to advance based on their expertise.

In the hypothetical agency depicted in Table 9–6, there is another career path for positions for which a degree is required; e.g., accountant, engineer, librarian. There is also a career track for administration/evaluation positions. These include people who work in administration, budget, personnel, evaluation, and the like. These two career paths also allow advancement into high-level managerial or expert levels. Finally, there are two support career ladders—one for technical support (e.g., accounting technician, budget assistant) and one for office support (e.g., secretary, messenger). These career paths also lead to managerial or expert positions, but at lower pay levels than the other career paths.

Instead of fifteen grade levels, in this example there are four pay *bands:* trainee, developmental, full performance, and manager/expert. The GS column at the left indicates how these pay bands translate from the GS system in the federal government. Grades as defined in the GS system would ultimately disappear as an agency converts to a broadbanding system. These pay bands clearly allow much more flexibility with respect to the minimum and maximum amounts of pay employees can receive without actually being promoted into the next level. The bands do, however, retain the notion of internal equity in that one who is in a developmental job earns less than one who is in a full performance job, with greater duties and responsibilities. Similarly, one who is in a full performance office support job is paid at a lower level than a full-performance, agency-specific job, which carries greater duties and responsibilities. NAPA suggests that it should be up to individual agencies to decide how pay increases within bands will be awarded. For example, pay increases can be based on performance or employee development (as in a rank-in-person system).

This is just one example of a broadbanding system. The city of Charlotte, North Carolina, has six pay bands that each include specific occupations. Support/clerical and labor, for example, are only paid within the limits of the first pay band (Risher, 1999). Agencies or jurisdictions could decide on the number and composition of their own career paths and the number and width of pay bands, as is appropriate for their missions.

Broadbanding was originally tested in the federal government at a Naval research organization in San Diego, called China Lake. Most agreed it worked well, and the system was made permanent at that site through legislation in 1994 (Shay and Risher, 1994). James Colvard, former Deputy Director of OPM, praised the system for strengthening "the relationship between employees and managers by giving the manager more control over the employee's status and pay" (Colvard, 2000). Several other agencies have also made use of OPM's authority to sanction a limited number of demonstration projects that test changes in personnel laws to institute broadbanding.

There has been some concern, however that the added flexibility for pay setting would increase salary costs for agencies that adopt it. Diane Disney, head of civilian personnel policy for the Defense Department, put it this way, "All pay-banding systems have raised costs. On balance, people would rather get more money than less. The problem is not the classification system, but the inflated rating system" (Friel, 1999).

In the federal government, legislation is required to detach federal agencies from the classification structure written into the 1949 Classification Act. Although such legislation has been introduced in the past, so far Congress has been unwilling to dismantle that structure. Legislators have, however, been willing to grant exceptions for some agencies. For example, following a lot of negative publicity about the IRS's treatment of taxpayers, Congress passed the Internal Revenue Service Restructuring and Reform Act of 1998 (P.L. 105–206). One provision of that legislation (Section 9509) granted the IRS the opportunity to develop a broadbanding system.

One agency that has made significant changes in its organizational structure, without legislation, is the New York Regional Office (NYRO) of the Veterans Health Administration. The agency collapsed seventeen different specialist positions into three. Instead of many different specialists handling every veteran's claim, one small two-to-three person team "owns" the claim from start to finish (Alliance for Reinventing Government, undated). The NYRO also attempted to fashion the GS pay system into one that emphasizes learning new skills for promotion. For example, for a Case Technician to qualify for promotion into Case Manager position, an employee must master a list of skills designated as the "transition skill block."

State and local governments have adopted pay-banding as well. These include South Carolina, which has ten pay bands (see Table 9–7) and Wyoming, which replaced thirty-six pay grades with eleven bands. Washington created a series of four pay bands for its management ranks. The band that a manager is

TABLE 9–7   Pay Bands in the State of South Carolina

Band	Minimum	Midpoint	Maximum
1	$10,712	$16,321	$21,931
2	$14,428	$20,561	$26,694
3	$17,556	$25,019	$32,482
4	$21,359	$30,437	$39,516
5	$25,989	$37,036	$48,083
6	$31,625	$45,067	$58,509
7	$38,478	$54,832	$71,187
8	$46,817	$66,716	$86,616
9	$56,963	$81,175	$105,387
10	$69,309	$98,767	$128,226

placed in is a function of that nature of management, the decision-making environment and policy impact, and scope of management accountability and control assigned to the position.

Broadbanding, then, may be the most realistic alternative to a traditional position classification system in that it grants managers considerably more flexibility than they had in the past. However, depending on how it is set up, there are still limits, which managers may chafe against, as to how broadly career paths and pay bands are defined. Moreover, in some jurisdictions, including the federal government, such a change would require legislation and legislators have been loathe to loosen their hold on salary setting.

WILL MANAGERS ALWAYS HATE POSITION CLASSIFICATION?

In summary, managers' dissatisfaction with position classification is a result of a system that works as it was intended. In response to the inconsistent and unruly way in which federal employees were placed and compensated for their jobs in the early part of the nineteenth century, a uniform and highly defined structure was put in place. But the structure that curtailed abuse decades ago, constrains management flexibility today. The structure that ensured equal pay for equal work overlooks the value of employees' development in their jobs. The structure that protected employees from capricious assignments through narrow job classifications impedes mobility, job redesign, and the creation of work teams today.

Unfortunately for position classification, it is viewed as part of the problem, not part of the solution. Perhaps public managers might have had less enmity toward the classification system had classifiers raised a hue and cry about the need to reevaluate grade levels in light of the massive restructuring and downsizing that many federal agencies contended with during the Clinton administration's reinvention effort. After all, classifiers were always at the forefront decrying the abuses of "grade creep" when job responsibilities didn't appear to warrant the assigned (or desired) grade levels. But as the federal government downsized and the remaining number of employees were required to take on more responsibility with higher supervisor-to-subordinate ratios, and greater numbers of contracts to oversee, few position classification advocates were demanding that federal jobs be upgraded.

Making matters worse for classification is a major shift in the human resources environment. The strong economy and low unemployment rate of the late 1990s have led the Comptroller General and the Director of the Office of Personnel Management to express grave concerns about the federal government's ability to manage human capital in the twenty-first century or compete in the "war for talent" (Walker, 2000, La Chance, 2000). In their strategies for change, neither OPM nor GAO even discusses classification. Nor did a January 2000 study of private sector human capital principles mention classification (U.S. General Accounting Office, 2000). The solution would be to replace a system that views people as generic entities that merely carry out the duties assigned to their positions with one that sees employees as assets with intrinsic value, requiring continual investment. Position classification, unfortunately, just doesn't seem to get it.

REFERENCES

Alliance for Reinventing Government. Undated. NPR Reinvention Laboratory Information: Department of Veterans Affairs, Veterans Benefits Administration. Available at <http://www.alliance. napawash.org>

COLVARD, JAMES. 2000. Restore the Human Touch, *Government Executive* 32 (1):56–58.

FRIEL, BRIAN. 1999. Seeking Systematic Change., *Government Executive* 31 (9):26–29.

GULICK, LUTHER. 1937. Notes on the Theory of Organization. In *Papers on the Science of Administration,* Luther Gulick and Lyndall Urwick, eds. New York: Institute of Public Administration, 3–13.

HOLLEY, LYN M., and JAMES R. O'CONNELL. 1997. Job Classification: The Support System for Personnel Decision Making. In *New Strategies for Public Pay,* Howard Risher and Charles H. Fay, eds. San Francisco: Jossey Bass, 76–97.

JOHNSON, RONALD N., and GARY D. LIBECAP. 1994. *The Federal Civil Service System and the Problem of Bureaucracy.* Chicago: University of Chicago Press.

KOST, JOHN M. 1996. *New Approaches to Public Management: The Case of Michigan.* Washington, DC: The Brookings Institution.

LACHANCE, JANET. 2000. Statement before the Subcommittee on Oversight of Government Management, Restructuring, and the District of Columbia, Committee on Governmental Affairs, U.S. Senate. Available at <http://www.opm.gov/speeches/2000 (March 9)>

LEWIS, GREGORY B. 1997. Grade Creep in the Federal Service? *American Review of Public Administration* 27 (1):4–21.

National Academy for Public Administration. 1991. *Modernizing Federal Classification: An Opportunity for Excellence.* Washington, DC: National Academy for Public Administration.

National Academy for Public Administration. 1995a. *Modernizing Federal Classification: Operational Broadbanding Systems Alternatives.* Washington, DC: National Academy for Public Administration.

National Academy for Public Administration. 1995b. *Alternatives for Federal Agencies: Summary Report.* Washington, DC: National Academy for Public Administration.

New Jersey State Department of Personnel. 1998. Request for Proposal: Employee Classification and Compensation Project for New Jersey's Merit System. (September 9).

RISHER, HOWARD. 1999. Are Public Employers Ready for a "New Pay" Program? *Public Personnel Management* 28(3):323–343.

SALDARINI, KATY. 1999. Changes to IT Job Profiles Debated, *Government Executive.* Available at <http://www.govexec.com/dailyfed/1299/121799k1.htm>

SHAFRITZ, JAY M., et al. Forthcoming. *Personnel Management in Government,* 5th ed. New York: Marcel Dekker.

——. 1992. *Personnel Management in Government,* 4th ed. New York: Marcel Dekker.

TAYLOR, FREDERICK W. 1919. *The Principles of Scientific Management.* New York: Harper and Brothers Publishers.

U.S. General Accounting Office. 2000. *Human Capital: Key Principles from Nine Private Sector Organizations* (GAO/GGD-00-28) Jan. 21.

WALKER, DAVID M., 2000. Managing Human Capital in the Twenty-first Century. Testimony before the Subcommittee on Oversight of Government Management, Restructuring, and the District of Columbia, Committee on Governmental Affairs, U.S. Senate. Washington, DC: U.S. General Accounting Office GAO/T-GGD-00-77 March 9.

10

Compensation, Merit Pay, and Motivation

JAMES L. PERRY

Indiana University

Organization theorists have long recognized that people are the principal component of social organizations (Barnard, 1938; March and Simon, 1958). They are vital to organizations not merely for effective functioning but also for their very existence. Because people are so important, organizations seek to motivate three types of behavior as means to survive and prosper (Katz, 1964). First, people must be persuaded to join and to remain with the organization. Second, members must perform assigned roles in a dependable fashion at some minimum level of performance. Finally, people must act innovatively and spontaneously to achieve those organizational goals that require behaviors that exceed assigned roles.

Organizations encourage desired behaviors—that is, membership, reliable role behavior, and innovative and spontaneous activity—by giving rewards in return for value received (Katz, 1964). The types of rewards are as diverse as pay and fringe benefits, responsibility and autonomy, and social affiliations.

One of the most powerful organizational rewards is pay. Like other types of organizational rewards, financial compensation comes in a variety of forms. The most common form is cash compensation, but organizations also reward employees financially through retirement plans, health and life insurance, and other indirect compensation. Financial rewards are intended to encourage membership and performance-related behaviors. For example, financial rewards accrue to individuals by virtue of their membership in the organization and thus provide incentives for individuals to enter and remain in the organization. Katz (1964) terms such compensation *instrumental system rewards* because it accrues to all individuals in the system as an incentive for membership.

In contrast to instrumental system rewards, compensation may be allocated differentially according to performance, what Katz (1964) terms *instrumental rewards geared to performance.* Among the common labels for such rewards are performance-based pay, pay for performance, contingent pay, and merit pay. It is this form of compensation that is the focus of the chapter.

The chapter begins by discussing the theoretical rationale for financial rewards geared to performance and the design choices involved when creating such systems. It then reviews problems and pitfalls associated with pay-for-performance systems. The concluding section addresses the prospects for future application of such systems in the public sector.

THEORY AND DESIGN OF PAY FOR PERFORMANCE

Performance-based pay programs emanate from a widely accepted theory of individual motivation, Vroom's (1964) expectancy theory. The theory posits that individuals who expect to receive a valued reward for high performance are more likely to strive for that level of performance than if they received no payoff. Pay for performance is expected to increase effort, and therefore performance, by changing the probability that performance will lead to a salary increase or other compensation increment that is assumed to be valued by most employees. Thus, employees must value pay as a reward and expect that their effort gives them a high probability of attaining it for performance-based pay to be effective.

As already noted, the term performance-based pay is often used to refer to a variety of contingent pay schemes. For instance, salespeople who work exclusively on commission are subject to a pure incentive system. In government organizations, pay for performance usually places only a small portion of an employee's potential salary at risk. For example, under the Performance Management and Recognition System (PMRS), which covered federal managers from 1984 to 1993, merit pay was equivalent to the amount of money paid to nonmanagement employees for within-grade increases. In addition, bonuses of at least 2 percent were typical for managers who received outstanding performance reviews. Thus, the amount of a manager's pay that was contingent upon performance, the "merit" portion, was typically much less than 10 percent of total annual salary.

The design of pay-for-performance systems involves several strategic choices about the pay system and broader organizational issues. These strategic choices have been conceptualized by Lawler (1981, 1990), who distinguishes between structural and process issues.

Structural Issues

Structural issues involve decisions about the design of a pay-for-performance system that have significant consequences for the system's motivational potential. Lawler (1981) identifies six structural issues: (1) level of aggregation; (2) the number of different plans; (3) salary versus bonus; (4) size of payouts; (5) measures of performance; and (6) frequency of payout.

Level of Aggregation. When designing a pay-for-performance system, organizations need to decide at what level or levels of aggregation performance will be measured. The most common choice is at the individual level, but there are alternatives. Performance could also be measured at the program level, the installation level, or the agency or bureau level. For example, the federal government conducted a gain-sharing experiment at McClellan Air Force Base (Siegel, 1994) in Sacramento that used budget savings aggregated to the organization level as the measure of performance.

Number of Different Plans.   Many organizations require multiple pay-for-performance plans because of differences in employees' work or other important organizational circumstances. For instance, the federal government operates a distinct performance management system for senior executives. The most common basis for differentiating plans is level in the organizational hierarchy, but some plans are designed to recognize the special circumstances of different organizational subunits.

Salary versus Bonus.   Organizations must also choose whether increments are awarded to employees as permanent adjustments to base pay or as one-time bonuses. The traditional method in most government organizations has been to incorporate pay increments into base pay, but bonuses have become increasingly attractive to system designers. Among the reasons for this increased attractiveness is that larger shares of an employee's compensation are at risk and the increments awarded for performance are more clearly identifiable. Navy laboratories are presently experimenting with pay systems that combine both types of incentive pay.

Size of Payouts.   From the perspective of individual motivation, the size of the pay award is a critical consideration when designing plans. Small rewards that are perceived by employees as trivial are not likely to encourage high performance. Identifying how much is enough is, however, hardly an exact science. Lawler (1981) suggests that 3 percent is a good rule of thumb to assure that an individual is likely to "notice a difference."

Measures of Performance.   Two prominent strategic issues are associated with the choice of measures for a pay-for-performance plan: comprehensiveness of the criteria and objectivity of the measures. Under any system, financial rewards are a function of *measured* performance, rather than performance itself, and this makes the measurement system vital to the system's success. Because employees will give disproportionate attention to measured elements of performance, it is imperative that the criteria encompass all important elements of performance (Lawler, 1981). The measurement system must also be perceived as valid. These requirements typically necessitate a trade-off between objective measures, which are more likely to be perceived as fair by employees, and subjective measures, which are more likely to be perceived as valid by supervisors.

Frequency of Payout.   The frequency with which desirable behaviors are reinforced is another important motivational consideration. Unfortunately, decisions about frequency of payout are often based on administrative convenience. For example, most government organizations routinely provide merit increments or bonuses on an annual basis. Although annual payouts may be acceptable for many employees, the most appropriate payout period depends on the nature of job tasks and other situational factors.

Process Issues

Process issues involve the procedures for establishing, implementing, and administering a pay-for-performance system. Lawler (1981) identifies three process issues: participation in system design, participation in system administration, and communication of pay decisions. The last issue, whether performance-based pay decisions should be communicated openly, is not salient for most government organizations. Most government organizations operate in a "fishbowl" and, therefore, have little choice but to openly communicate pay decisions. Experience in the public sector suggests, however, that another process issue, obtaining legislative agreement with system objectives, is important.

Participation in System Design. Organizations can design pay-for-performance systems either collaboratively, working jointly with employees and their representatives, or authoritatively, exercising top management's prerogatives. Lawler (1981) argues that bottom-up, participative design strengthens pay-performance relationships. Employee involvement is likely to provide better information about which plan designs are most attractive to affected groups and assure employee ownership of the plan that is subsequently implemented.

Participation in System Administration. The extent of employee participation in system administration may vary widely, from employee control of compensation increases to limited oversight responsibility. Although Lawler (1981) reports many instances of employee participation in pay decisions in private organizations, similar practices in the public sector are relatively rare. One instance in which public employees play a significant role in controlling pay decisions involves Performance Review Boards (PRB) in the federal Senior Executive Service. Among responsibilities delegated to PRBs are recommending final appraisal ratings and bonuses for senior executives and nominating candidates for Meritorious and Distinguished Rank awards. Probably the most common form of participation in government agencies involves establishment of employee oversight boards. These boards are often responsible for reviewing performance appraisal standards and procedures, assessing equity across raters and pay pools, and recommending changes to the system.

Another aspect of system administration is due process. Whether or not a mechanism exists for employee participation, it is important for the long-run viability of pay-for-performance systems to provide clear and equitable channels for appeal of ratings and financial awards. Effective due process channels are essential because pay for performance is unworkable without the trust such channels encourage.

Obtaining Legislative Agreement with System Objectives. Even if top administrators and employees agree about the advantages and value of pay for performance, it is important that wide support be obtained from legislators. Such support needs to be predicated on a meeting of the minds between administrators and legislators not only about the instrumental value of the pay-for-performance system but also about its ongoing cost, the probable distribution of rewards, and risks attendant to such systems. Failure to obtain legislative agreement based upon full disclosure could potentially result in a host of legislative impediments to operation of the system, including underfunding of pay increments.

COMMON PROBLEMS

Many governments, foreign and domestic, have experimented with pay for performance during the last two decades (Griener et al., 1981; Ingraham, 1993; Kellough and Lu, 1993; Kellough and Selden, 1997; Marsden and Richardson, 1994; Perry and Frederickson, 1999). The results of these experiments have fallen short of expectations. Some scholars (Deci, 1975; Meyer, 1975; Pearce, 1987; Perry, 1986; Pfeffer, 1998) trace the shortcomings of pay for performance to inadequacies in its theoretical underpinnings. Deci (1975) conducted a series of laboratory studies on the effects of externally mediated rewards, such as pay, on subjects' intrinsic motivation. He concluded that contingent pay is undesirable because it reduces intrinsic motivation and leads individuals to develop strategies to achieve rewards with minimal effort. Meyer (1975) argued that most employees have a highly favorable self-mage but the feedback implicit in merit pay awards undercuts that self-image. The effect is to damage employee self-esteem, a factor important in individual and organizational productivity.

Few rigorous field studies have been conducted on the performance consequences of contingent pay in the public sector. In the most rigorous study, Pearce, Stevenson, and Perry (1985) tested the performance effects of the introduction of merit pay for federal managers. The performance measure included four indicators of the productivity of the offices for which these managers were responsible. Productivity measures were available two years before the commencement of merit pay and for the first two years that managers' merit increases were based on these performance measures. They found that office productivity gradually improved over the four-year period but that the merit pay intervention did not contribute to the trend. Thus, merit pay did not result in improved performance.

Several reviews (Hamner, 1975; Lawler, 1981; Milkovich and Wigdor, 1991; Perry, 1986; Pearce, 1987; Pfeffer, 1998) provide insights into the most common problems surrounding merit pay. The three most significant problems are invalid performance appraisals, dysfunctional competition, and lack of adequate financial rewards.

Invalid Performance Appraisals

Interviews with supervisors about performance appraisals reveal an interesting dilemma that is central to the success or failure of many pay-for-performance programs. Many supervisors admit that appraising subordinate performance is a time-consuming and sometimes unpleasant task. But they also acknowledge that they can easily distinguish their best from their poorest performers. The primary problem supervisors encounter is not *knowing* who are the best performers, but rather *measuring* and *documenting* performance differentials. Pay for performance often fails as a motivational program because performance cannot be accurately and completely measured. Of course, if employees have no confidence that good performance will result in a good rating, then contingent pay is not likely to influence their behavior.

Many government employees have complained that performance appraisals have become "objective" by quantifying trivial features of jobs, resulting in meaningless appraisals. For example, Pearce and Perry (1983) reported that, over time, federal managers perceived performance appraisals to be less helpful for improving job performance at the same time that they became more certain of the standards used to evaluate performance and it became easier to document performance differences. They concluded that managers had a clearer understanding of the criteria on which they were judged, but felt that the criteria were not promoting improved individual performance or agency effectiveness.

Because government organizations must live within budgetary limits, the amount of money paid out is usually controlled by holding down average employee performance ratings (see, for example, Perry, Hanzlik, and Pearce, 1982). But there is an inherent contradiction between objective performance appraisals and the manipulation of ratings to control the amount of money paid out. In fact, the manipulation of ratings only undercuts the validity of performance appraisals, making it even more difficult in future periods to get employees to respond to merit pay incentives.

Dysfunctional Competition

Although much has been written recently about the need for teamwork in effective organizations, contingent pay may discourage cooperation. Bass, Hurder, and Ellis (reported in Bass, 1965) found that individual monetary incentives resulted in increased performance by those engaged in a simple task but decreased performance on a more complex task. Similar results are reported by Konovsky and Podsakoff (1984), who found that contingent pay decreased performance on a task in which subjects' performances were interdependent.

Most pay-for-performance systems are designed to reward individual rather than group performance. Thus, pay-for-performance systems tend to separate employees into two classes, "stars" and "also-rans." Unfortunately, far more employees fall into the "also-ran" category—simply because of the need to limit the number of the employees rated outstanding. As a consequence, pay for performance may damage the self-esteem and loyalty of employees (Meyer, 1975; Pearce and Porter, 1986). The nature of pay-for-performance systems also tends to reduce the willingness of employees to work outside of their performance contract. If an employee spends time on activities that are not in the contract, he or she risks losing ground to others in the scramble for financial rewards.

Lack of Adequate Financial Rewards

Unlike private organizations that have some flexibility in the amount of funds allocated, government agencies must live within a fixed budget. The budget constraint has at least two consequences. The openness of budgetary processes, frequently accompanied by politicization of pay issues, results in underfunding of pay-for-performance programs. Under the circumstances, high performers have few chances for big rewards, and funds may be inadequate to recognize other deserving employees. The budget constraint heightens the demoralizing effect of comparative ratings. Simply improving one's own performance is not enough; one must increase one's relative ranking by displacing another. Because one employee's gain is another employee's loss, it becomes more difficult to create expectations that rewards will be contingent upon performance.

WHAT WORKS IN THE PUBLIC SECTOR

In comparison with the range of different types of systems in the private sector, the public sector's experience with performance-based pay has been quite limited. The most prominent types of pay-for-performance systems, salary plans that reward individual-level performance, have generally not fared well among managers (Perry, 1986, 1992). In October 1993, the federal government abandoned a governmentwide merit pay system for middle managers originally introduced as part of the Civil Service Reform Act of 1978. It opted instead to decentralize responsibility for performance management and give it to departments. At the same time, Congress threatened to eliminate all appropriations for contingent pay, creating doubt about the viability of such systems in the federal government. These events were the result of the failure of merit pay systems to achieve expected results, new thinking about motivation (Walton, 1986), and fiscal stress.

Reports about the results of pay-for-performance plans in state and local governments are no more encouraging than in the federal government. For instance, the National Commission on the State and Local Public Service proposed that

> . . . state and local governments reevaluate their pay-for-performance plans. Almost half of all states, and a majority of counties and cities, now have at least some of their employees in pay-for-performance plans. Unfortunately, many of those plans promise far more than they deliver. Some of the systems are unbelievably complicated and paper-intensive. Others are simply poorly administered. Still others are launched without adequate funding. . . . States and localities should be exceedingly cautious about overselling what are likely to be small performance bonuses allocated through a cumbersome and potentially political process. (1993:29–30)

Despite reported failures, several considerations argue against abandoning experimentation with pay-for-performance systems in government. One consideration is that the variety of plans tested has been quite limited and reported failures involve designs predicated almost exclusively on an individual level of aggregation. Government agencies need to experiment more widely with group and organizational plans. This view was echoed by the National Commission on the State and Local Public Service:

> . . . Team-based pay-for-performance systems—whether the team is several employees, a small unit, or an agency—send the right signal, that employees rise or fall on the basis of outcomes. Gainsharing is a viable step toward such a system. Under a gainsharing formula, workers on a given team split the savings from higher

productivity equally with taxpayers, whether through a one-time bonus or an innovative investment for the team's future productivity improvements. (1993:30)

A second reason for continued experimentation is that pay for performance symbolizes to the public and its representatives that government employees are receiving a fair return for their efforts. The notion of "each according to his or her efforts" is ingrained in the American political culture, and it is likely to be with us for the foreseeable future. If this assessment is accurate, and recent trends in education (Cooper, 2000) and state government (Kellough and Selden, 1997) suggest it is, then prospects for the future involve what forms pay for performance will take (Brostek, 2000). Thus, public administrators and scholars must turn their attention to maximizing the advantages and minimizing the disadvantages of pay for performance.

A final consideration is that some of the reported failures of pay for performance are traceable to correctable errors. In essence, some of the reported failures of pay for performance were predictable because the structure or administration of the system violated one or more principles of system design. Enough experience has been garnered with pay for performance in government to suggest the following guidelines for organizations contemplating such plans.

Pay for Performance Should Follow Other "Gateway" Changes

Many organizations look upon pay for performance as a quick and easy fix for serious performance problems. The reality is that pay for performance is likely to be of little benefit to organizations with serious performance problems and may actually be harmful. Pay-for-performance plans are best suited to organizations with supportive cultures (Gabris and Irhke, 2000; Golembiewski, 1986). The absence of an organizational culture that facilitates agreement about the pay-for-performance system and holds values compatible with it necessitates organizational change before any pay intervention. Golembiewski (1986:15) writes: "Appropriate-culture creation should be viewed as conceptually related to the development and application of formal systems like merit pay, and often as requiring prior attention." In essence, pay for performance should not be a leading or "gateway" change, one that precedes other major interventions, but a lagging change, one that follows and reinforces other, more consequential organizational changes.

Design Should Be Contingent upon the Situation

Structural considerations relevant to the design of pay-for-performance plans were reviewed earlier in the chapter. Although many design options exist, most government agencies employ the same system, that is, individual rewards involving annual salary adjustments based primarily upon subjective supervisory ratings. Many of these systems are probably ill suited to the circumstances in which they operate. Given the problems of measuring individual performance in many government jobs, and the potential for more accurate and objective performance measurement at a group or organization level, one would expect to find more group- or organization-level plans than presently exist.

Similar arguments might be constructed about the frequency of payout, bonuses versus salary, and objective versus subjective measures. The point is that pay-for-performance plans should be designed contingent upon situational factors, including a jurisdiction's fiscal realities. If a system is not contingently designed, then it runs a high probability of failure.

Employees Should Participate in Design and Administration

Although there is relatively little systematic evidence drawn from experiences in government (one exception is Cohen and Murnane, 1985), the logic for high degrees of employee participation in system design and administration is compelling. Probably the greatest benefit from employee participation is that it facilitates patterns of interaction that are conducive to the success of pay-for-performance plans (Golembiewski, 1986). Employees are likely to view plans in which they actively participate with higher trust and greater approval.

Implementation Should be Gradual, with Special Concern for Measurement

As noted earlier, one of the biggest problems with pay for performance involves inadequacies of performance measurement systems. Organizations too frequently initiate contingent pay plans without tested and validated measurement systems. This implementation strategy is especially risky in large public bureaucracies that lack a history of performance measurement and for which measurement problems might be acute.

If pay for performance is to receive a fair trial, then significant time and effort must be devoted to designing and testing the performance measurement system. An agency's rush to implement a plan without adequate attention to the measurement system and other factors affecting success is likely to be counterproductive. Furthermore, organizations prepared to make a genuine investment in performance improvement are likely to find favorable changes during the three to five years it may take to develop an acceptable measurement system because of the benefits of the measurement system alone (Latham and Locke, 1979). Gradual implementation of the measurement system also creates an opportunity for organizational members to develop agreement about the pay-for-performance plan.

Organizations Should Develop a Range of Meaningful Rewards

The complexity of motivational problems in most government organizations precludes reliance on a single, dominant motivational program. This generalization is magnified for motivational programs that rely on contingent pay because of public and political pressures for fiscal restraint. Organizations must therefore design flexible reward systems that recognize a range of contextual factors—the types of individuals attracted to the organization, the job itself, the work environment, and changes in the external environment—that influence motivation (Perry and Porter, 1982). In addition, managers must be prepared to use a variety of informal rewards—those not mandated by the organization—to influence subordinates' actions (Pearce, 1989).

CONCLUSION

This chapter has reviewed several key considerations related to development of pay-for-performance systems. An organization seeking to introduce a system confronts a number of strategic choices about the structure and process of pay-for-performance programs. Recognizing and carefully considering these strategic choices improves significantly the chances for a program's success.

Future attempts to implement pay for performance in government need to build from experience and follow lessons learned in both government and the private sector. Among the lessons are these:

1. Pay for performance should follow other "gateway" changes.
2. The design of pay-for-performance programs should be contingent on situational factors rather than a "one-best-way" orientation.
3. Plans should be implemented gradually, with special consideration given to performance measurement.
4. High degrees of employee participation should be built into system design and administration.
5. Organizations should develop a range of meaningful rewards in addition to contingent pay.

REFERENCES

BARNARD, C. I. 1938. *The Functions of the Executive*. Cambridge: Harvard University Press.

BASS, B. M. 1965. *Organizational Psychology*. Boston: Allyn & Bacon.

BROSTEK, M. 2000. *Using Incentives to Motivate and Reward High Performance*. Statement before the Subcommittee on Oversight of Government Management, Restructuring, and the District of Columbia, Committee on Governmental Affairs, U.S. Senate, May 2. Washington, DC: U.S. General Accounting Office.

COHEN, D. K., and R. J. MURNANE. 1985. The Merits of Merit Pay. *The Public Interest* 80 (Summer): 3–30.

COOPER, K. J. 2000. Performance Pay for Teachers Catches on. *The Washington Post*, February 26, A4.

DECI, E. L. 1975. *Intrinsic motivation*. New York: Plenum.

GABRIS, G. T., and D. M. IHRKE. 2000. Improving Employee Acceptance Toward Performance Appraisal and Merit Pay Systems: The Role of Leadership Credibility. *Review of Public Personnel Administration* 20 (Winter):41–53.

GOLEMBIEWSKI, R. T. 1986. OD Perspectives on High Performance: Some Good News and Some Bad News About Merit Pay. *Review of Public Personnel Administration* 7 (Fall):9–26.

GRIENER, J. M., H. P. HATRY, M. P. KOSS, A. P. MILLAR, and J. P. WOODWARD. 1981. *Productivity and Motivation*. Washington, DC: The Urban Institute Press.

HAMNER, W. C. 1975. How to Ruin Motivation with Pay. *Compensation Review* 7:17–27.

INGRAHAM, P. W. 1993. Of Pigs in Pokes and Policy Diffusion: Another Look at Pay for Performance. *Public Administration Review* 53 (July/August):348–356.

KATZ, D. 1964. The Motivational Basis of Organizational Behavior. *Behavioral Science* 9 (April):131–146.

KELLOUGH, J. E., and H. LU. 1993. The Paradox of Merit Pay in the Public Sector: Persistence of a Problematic Procedure. *Review of Public Personnel Administration* 13 (2):45–64.

KELLOUGH, J. E., and S. C. SELDEN. 1997. Pay-for-performance Systems in State Government. *Review of Public Personnel Administration* 17 (Winter):5–21.

KONOVSKY, M. A., and P. M. PODSAKOFF. 1984. Effects of Individual and Group Incentive System and Task Interdependence on Group Productivity. Paper presented at annual meeting, Academy of Management, Boston.

LATHAM, G. P., and E. A. LOCKE. 1979. Goal Setting–A Motivational Technique that Works. *Organizational Dynamics* 8 (Autumn):68–80.

LAWLER, E. E. III. 1981. *Pay and Organization Development.* Reading, MA: Addison-Wesley.

——. 1990. *Strategic Pay: Aligning Organizational Strategies and Pay Systems.* San Francisco: Jossey-Bass.

MARCH, J. G., and H. A. SIMON. 1958. *Organizations.* New York: John Wiley.

MARSDEN, D., and R. RICHARDSON. 1994. Performing for Pay? The Effects of "Merit Pay" on Motivation in a Public Service. *British Journal of Industrial Relations* 32 (June):243–261.

MEYER, H. H. 1975. The Pay for Performance Dilemma. *Organizational Dynamics* 3 (Winter):39–50.

MILKOVICH, G. T., and A. K. WIGDOR, eds. 1991. *Pay for Performance: Evaluating Performance Appraisal and Merit Pay.* Washington, DC: National Academy Press.

National Commission on the State and Local Public Service. 1993. *Hard Truths/Tough Choices: An Agenda for State and Local Reform.* Albany, NY: Nelson A. Rockefeller Institute for Government.

PEARCE, J. L. 1987. Why Merit Pay Doesn't Work: Implications from Organization Theory. In *New Perspectives on Compensation,* D. B. Balkin and L. R. Gomez-Meija, eds. Upper Saddle River, N.J.: Prentice Hall, 169–178.

——. 1989. Rewarding Performance. In *Handbook of Public Administration,* J. L. Perry and Associates. San Francisco: Jossey-Bass.

——, and J. L. PERRY. 1983. Federal Merit Pay: A Longitudinal Analysis. *Public Administration Review* 43 (July–August):315–325.

PEARCE, J. L., and L. W. PORTER. 1986. Employee Responses to Formal Performance Appraisal Feedback. *Journal of Applied Psychology* 71:211–218.

PEARCE, J. L., W. B. STEVENSON, and J. L. PERRY. 1985. Managerial Compensation Based on Organizational Performance: A Time-Series Analysis of the Impact of Merit Pay. *Academy of Management Journal* 28 (June):261–278.

PFEFFER, J. L. 1998. Six Dangerous Myths About Pay. *Harvard Business Review* 76(May–June):108–119.

——. 1986. Merit Pay in the Public Sector: The Case for a Failure of Theory. *Review of Public Personnel Administration* 7 (Fall):57–69.

——. 1992. The Merit Pay Reforms. In *The Promise and Paradox of Civil Service Reform,* ed. P. W. Ingraham and D. H. Rosenbloom. Pittsburgh: University Pittsburgh Press, 199–215.

——, C. HANZLIK, and J. L. PEARCE. 1982. Effectiveness of Merit-pay-pool Management. *Review of Public Personnel Administration* 2 (Summer):5–12.

PERRY, J. L., and D. G. FREDERICKSON. 1999. Hong Kong's Civil Service Reform: Lessons Learned from the American Experience. *Public Administration and Policy* 8 (2):57–70.

PERRY, J. L., and L. W. PORTER. 1982. Factors Affecting the Context for Motivation in Public Organizations. *Academy of Management Review* 7 (January):89–98.

SIEGEL, G. B. 1994. Three Federal Demonstration Projects: Using Monetary Performance Awards. *Public Personnel Management* 23 (Spring):153–165.

VROOM, V. H. 1964. *Work and Motivation.* New York: John Wiley.

WALTON, M. 1986. *The Deming Management Method.* New York: Perigree.

11

The Trials and Tribulations of Performance Appraisal

Problems and Prospects on Entering the Twenty-First Century

DENNIS DALEY
North Carolina State University

At the beginning of the twenty-first century performance appraisal is poised to undertake major advancements. Experimental trials of various versions such as 360-degree, pass/fail, and team appraisal build upon the developments during the twentieth century of objective systems. These trials will test our abilities to engage in a process of cognitive ergonomics that will transform our appraisal systems into truly usable instruments. Yet, these new approaches will face the same tribulations that past performance appraisal systems had to endure. Advancement is dependent on our abilities to constantly deal with the problems of training, measurement, and inconsistency.

Research on and the practice of performance appraisal during the twentieth century has resulted in the ability to create highly complex, yet objective instruments with which to assess employee performance. Whether we focus on results, behaviors, or competencies, the performance appraisal process can map the job terrain (Daley, 1992, Latham and Wexley, 1981, Milkovich and Wigdor, 1991, Mohrman, Resnick-West, and Lawler, 1989, Murphy and Cleveland, 1995).

Yet, problems persist. It is not the ability to accomplish the performance appraisal process that is in question but the willingness to do it. Performance appraisal does not occur in isolation; it is an integral part of an organization's performance management system. Success is dependent upon how well processes and people are melded together. In essence, our difficulties are ones of cognitive ergonomics. Adjusting the cognitive fit between processes and people is analogous to the efforts undertaken in the area of physical ergonomics. Improvements enhance productivity. Just as physical materials need to be designed to work in accord with the realities of the human body, administrative processes must incorporate the ways in which the human mind actually functions.

At the beginning of the twenty-first century we are exploring ways to refine performance appraisal processes to better suit our needs. Following an overview of the performance appraisal techniques used in the twentieth century, this chapter examines three techniques—360-degree appraisal, pass/fail appraisal, and team appraisal—which are currently undergoing trial for use in the twenty-first century. However, these prospects also face problems. The chapter concludes with an examination of the continuing tribulations—training, measurement, and inconsistency—that have previously limited efforts at successful performance management.

OVERVIEW OF PERFORMANCE APPRAISAL TECHNIQUES

Subjective Instruments

Essays, graphic rating scales, and check lists are three of the formats which are basically subjective appraisals. The accuracy of the assessments derived when each of these formats is employed may prove exceedingly high. However, this accuracy flows more from the interactive combination of organization and individual rater than from the merits of the specific instrument being employed.

The essay appraisal format is a tabula rasa. Supervisors have a blank space on which they are free to write. Essay appraisals (along with the more modern audio or video log equivalents) are descendant from the traditional duty or fitness report. Almost all appraisals, including today's objective techniques, include an essay component.

The subjective graphic rating scale is perhaps still the most pervasive form of performance appraisal (Landy and Farr, 1980:83; Murphy and Cleveland, 1995:434; Milkovich and Wigdor, 1991:55–56). A graphic rating scale consists of a set of items addressing personal traits (trustworthy, loyal, helpful, friendly, courteous, kind, obedient, etc.) and job activities (communication skills, sets realistic goals, keeps files and records up to date, adheres to policies and procedures, knowledge of job, etc.). Employee "performance" on these items is then rated using another set of adjective evaluations (poor, acceptable, fair, good, exceptional, etc.), which are invariably linked to a system of numeric scores. This enables the calculation of an average or overall, summary numeric evaluation or rating.

Checklist or forced-choice appraisals include sets of items which are linked to the performance of specific jobs; they also include items for which no established relationships have been previously documented (Landy and Farr, 1980: 85–86; Mohrman, Resnick-West, and Lawler, 1989:52–54). In conducting a checklist performance appraisal, supervisors are asked to pick from a series of lists of four items in each set which are deemed to be most like and least like an employee. These are then compared against a code sheet and only those which match validated relationships are tabulated into a final score.

Interpersonal Comparisons

Interpersonal comparisons, such as rankings or forced distributions, may be based on either subjective or objective criteria. However, even when initially based solely on objective, job-related evidence, they experience serious shortcomings. Central to all interpersonal appraisal systems is the comparison or assessment of the individual against other individuals rather than with the specific job to be done.

One method for interpersonal comparisons is that of ranking. This is approached in a wholistic manner wherein an organization's employees are graded from best to worse. This requires a complete knowledge and understanding of the entire organization—purpose and people. While perhaps feasible only in very small organizations, a number of gimmicks can be used in order to extend its application to larger units.

An alternative ranking process can be employed in which an organization's best and worst employee are designated. The process is then repeated ad finem with the remaining employees whereby the next best and next worst employees are so indicated. In the end this peeling of the onion produces a composite list which ranks employees from best to worst.

Forced distributions are another means for making interpersonal comparisons (Mohrman, Resnick-West, and Lawler, 1989:182–183). Grading on the curve is not a new notion and, unlike rankings, can easily be applied to large organizations. However, it is just as prone to error. Forced distributions assume that employee performance fits some external model or distribution, usually envisioned along the lines of something like a normally distributed, bell-shaped curve.

Objective Instruments

Behaviorally Anchored Rating Scales (BARS) and Management by Objectives (MBO) essentially involve the same components but approach them with a slightly different focus in mind. Hence, the objective components which are common in both approaches are introduced into the appraisal process in a somewhat different order.

Behaviorally anchored rating scales are extensions of the subjective graphic rating scale. They are a clear attempt to translate the graphic rating scale into an objective appraisal system. They address and correct for many of the subjective issues that cloud the validity and inhibit the use of graphic rating scales (Bernardin and Beatty, 1984; Landy and Farr, 1980:83–85; Latham and Wexley, 1981).

Both the BARS and MBO approaches emphasize detailed job analyses. Ideally, performance appraisal should be able to work off the same job analysis system used in the development of an organization's position descriptions and position classification system (and employed as a guide in the selection process and for designing training programs). Unfortunately, many organizations, especially among those in the public sector, employ different systems of job analysis when it comes to selecting people to perform a job and when it comes to assessing their performance on that job.

Management by Objectives (MBO) is more focused on results; however, it obviously can also be adapted to situations in which outputs or processes are more involved than outcomes. MBO originated as a means for managers to translate their strategic plans into implementable programs. It is a basic command and control management system for implementation and monitoring (Odiorne, 1971, 1987; Swiss, 1991:61–127).

TRIALS

While we can design successful performance appraisal instruments, their use on a day-to-day basis often leads to failure. Our complex appraisal systems often fail to accommodate the workworld in which real management occurs. Supervisors and employees balance a myriad of techniques and tasks every day. This is a world in which neither the time nor energy exists to concentrate on "high maintenance" systems. Hence, performance appraisal must evolve into a more user-friendly version.

Three different versions are undergoing trial at the beginning of the twenty-first century: 360-degree appraisal, pass/fail appraisal, and team appraisal. With a strong developmental focus, 360-degree appraisal calls upon the perspectives of supervisors, subordinates, peers, and even self-review to form a well-rounded, balanced view. Assuming that most employees are indeed performing well, pass/fail appraisal simplifies the appraisal process into a binary yes/no decision. This allows corrective attention to be focused on the few problems rather than wasted on the "busy work" of documenting the obvious. Finally, team appraisal introduces an appraisal approach that focuses on the work group itself. While organizations are composed of individuals, their work is accomplished through cooperative teams. Compatible with Total Quality Management (TQM) and gainsharing/goalsharing system, team appraisal assesses this cooperative effort.

360-Degree Appraisal and Development

The combination of information sources (especially supervisor, subordinate, peer, and even self-ratings) is the basis for 360-degree feedback (Murphy and Cleveland, 1995:144–146, Pollack and Pollack, 1996, Edwards and Ewen, 1996, DeLeon and Ewen, 1997, DeNisi and Kluger, 2000, Ghorpade, 2000). With its low hierarchy and professional staff, the modern organization is, on the one hand, forced to seek out nonsupervisory sources for appraisal and, on the other, is blessed with highly knowledgeable employees. Hence, 360-degree feedback promises to provide a more balanced form of appraisal. Of course, the 360-degree appraisal is designed to serve as a developmental instrument. When it is transformed into a judgmental appraisal, 360-degree appraisal loses its effectiveness (and often engenders employee distrust).

This technique is especially useful when employed for developmental purposes (Lepsinger and Lucia, 1997, DeNisi and Kluger, 2000, Ghorpade, 2000, Daley, forthcoming). However, it is somewhat problematic when incorporated in a judgmental system. Subordinates and peers are especially likely to be concerned with an appraisal that is used judgmentally. Such a transformation is viewed quite negatively and erodes employee loyalty. Depending on the purpose (e.g., pay increase, promotion, demotion, etc.), individual ratings may change in up to a third of the cases (Waldman, Atwater, and Antonioni, 1998).

As with any performance appraisal system, 360-degree appraisals must be focused on job-related components. The training for raters (and the possible affects of rater error) is much more important. Since 360-degree appraisal is a highly participative technique, its success or failure has greater symbolic significance and implications (Waldman, Atwater, and Antonioni, 1998).

Pass/Fail and Progressive Discipline

While performance appraisal is one of the most researched aspects of management, it is exceeded by the effort devoted to the staffing process. Recruitment, testing, and selection have been the subject of study and improvement for most of the past century (Gatewood and Feild, 1998). Because of the enormous strides made here, we can propose the introduction of pass/fail appraisal. Since no organization consciously hires people to fail, and our selection devices are indeed rather good, the "average" workforce is, all in all, rather exceptional. In addition, as is evident from basic motivational theories, people want their work to make a difference.

Given the presence of employees selected for success and willing to work, there is little need to actually separate them into various grades (or performance ratings). In fact, most performance appraisal systems report ratings with restricted ranges. Most employees fall into categories that can be designated as "stars" or "superstars," and even these distinctions often prove problematic. Very few employees fail. Hence, for most employees the performance appraisal system is meaningless.

The introduction of a pass/fail appraisal greatly simplifies the endeavor. The vast bulk of the workforce is in actuality exempt from the more burdensome aspects of the process (they pass). Supervisors are then free to devote their efforts not in meaningless documentation but in productive management. Special appraisal processes can be introduced to deal with very specific concerns—problem employees and promotions (Daley, forthcoming).

The need to establish job-related documentation for undertaking disciplinary action gives rise to its association with the performance appraisal process. Although focused on negative behaviors, discipline fits in with both judgmental and developmental approaches to performance appraisal. However, the ultimate consequences of disciplinary action are clearly judgmental in nature. The requirement to include suggested corrective action provides only a slight developmental cast to this process. A true developmental approach to appraisal would most likely prefer that disciplinary cases be dealt with separately.

Inasmuch as a pass/fail appraisal process readily distinguishes problem employees, it allows the supervisor or manager to interact with most employees on a purely developmental level. Thereby, the supervisor-employee relationship can be virtually freed of the judgmental specter. Such an interpersonal relationship would be conducive to fostering organizational trust and commitment.

A separate disciplinary reporting process can be established. This would be triggered at the occurrence of a critical incident (i.e., a specific and substantive rule infraction or performance failure). Only at this point would a file be "opened" and a record of the specific event be made. If no other events occur or successful corrective action is undertaken, the file can become "inactive" or "closed" (legally all records must be preserved to document organizational behavior).

Progressive discipline is applied to specific behaviors and is designed to correct them. When an employee who has been subjected to progressive discipline for one behavior exhibits a new disciplinary problem, it is necessary to begin the process anew. Each type of infraction is dealt with separately. To lump all disciplinary infractions together creates an "out to get me" impression among employees and negates any successful or good faith efforts.

Team Appraisal and Gainsharing

Performance appraisal of individuals can readily incorporate measures of team work and overall team results. Where productivity is derived from the interdependent work of a team, individual incentive pay can be detrimental and divisive. Where success is based on multiple efforts, substantial pay differentials among individuals may not appropriately reflect (and reward) actual accomplishments. Individuals whose efforts are slighted in such an accounting may also harbor ill will towards those unduly/unjustly compensated for the work of others. In such circumstances a team-based incentive system is more appropriate (Bloom, 1999).

Gainsharing, an instrument for implementing pay for performance, is a synthesis of participatory management and profit sharing (Greiner et al., 1981, Graham-Moore and Ross, 1990, Markowich, 1993, Sanders, 1997, Patton and Daley, 1998, Risher, 1999). With the advent of interest in both pay-for-performance and Total Quality Management (TQM), gainsharing programs have attracted the attention of public sector organizations. Gainsharing is a means for encouraging or motivating employees through extrinsic expectancy rewards, yet staying within a group or organizational framework. Hence, it combines TQM's emphasis on the advantages derived from team work (and away from the distractions of individual competition) with the motivational effect of a strong individual reward system (Swiss, 1992, Cohen and Brand, 1993, Durant and Wilson, 1993, Wilson and Durant, 1994).

TRIBULATIONS

As with any performance management system, performance appraisal is plagued by continuous problems focused on maintenance. Regardless of which techniques are employed, including those currently undergoing trial, they will ultimately fail if they do not receive constant attention. It is these tribulations that make the job of management so difficult and so necessary. All systems require that those using them be trained in their use. What we often overlook is that this training needs to be constantly refreshed. While we are sharpening the knife of performance appraisal, we must remember that it can be put to many uses. Finally, performance appraisal is the chief instrument linked to the larger, motivational scheme. Inasmuch as that arena, currently dominated by the concept of pay for performance, is inconsistent or unreliable, no appraisal instrument can be successful.

Training and Rater Error

Performance appraisal is highly dependent upon the skill of the appraiser. With any tool it is only as good as the individual wielding it. Hence, when things go wrong, it is often considered convenient to blame appraisal problems on rater error. While such a ploy shifts attention from the appraisal system itself, it does not shift responsibility from the organization. Even when problems are indeed due to rater error rather than to environmental or organizational factors, the organization is still responsible for the lack of training or monitoring that contributed to that error's commitment.

Rater errors have been extensively treated in the performance appraisal literature (Landy and Farr, 1980, 1983, Latham and Wexley, 1981:100–104, Murphy and Cleveland, 1995:275–285). Their elimination or alleviation is the focus of most of the efforts at performance appraisal training. In many cases these errors are corrected through the employment of objective appraisal instruments. In other instances more thorough supervisory training is recommended. Even though supervisors strive to objectively evaluate employees, rater errors prey on the weaknesses inherent in the process of how humans actually think.

Errors are committed whenever the responsibilities inherent in the job itself are substituted for a measure of the incumbent's job performance (Robbins, 1978). An important and demanding job often implies, and certainly requires, an individual of like stature. Given the effort put into selecting individuals with such capabilities and the basic vagueness or qualitative aspect entailed in most managerial jobs, this is an error easily introduced into the appraisal process.

Similarly, individuals working in a critical unit may benefit from the perceived centrality or significance of their part of the organization. In this case the importance of the unit to fulfilling the organization's mission is substituted for the job performance of the individual in that unit. In neither instance is the individual's job performance actually measured. Objective appraisals inasmuch as they are focused on job performance, especially in terms of results, are a good check on such errors.

Contrast errors arise through interpersonal comparisons. Individuals are not assessed on their job performance but on their performance compared to someone else's performance, or, as is more often the case, someone else's personal traits and characteristics. Personnel profiles tabulating the social and leadership traits, demographic characteristics, or social, ethnic and gender differences of successful employees are compiled. These are then used—often unintentionally, but also explicitly as in the case of interpersonal comparisons such as with forced distribution appraisals—as the norm against which others are compared (Wexley and Nemeroff, 1974, Pizam, 1975, Rand and Wexley, 1975, Bigoness, 1976, Mitchell and Liden, 1982, Mobley, 1982, DeNisi, Cafferty, and Meglino, 1984, Kraiger and Ford, 1985, Shore and Thorton, 1986).

These social differentiation or similar-to-me approaches suffer significant validity problems. While the individuals upon which they are based may be examples of successful employees, the characteristics and traits chosen for the profile may not in any way be related to that success. Concomitantly, even if those traits and characteristics are valid indicators, they may not be the only such indicators. Contrast error excludes people who may be successful or potentially successful from receiving a fair and accurate evaluation. Again the validation of criteria used in assessing job performance is essential.

Unidimensional errors abound. In these instances one item dominates the evaluation process to such an extent that other, critical factors are ignored. Unidimensional errors can stem from either substantive or mechanical concerns.

Such traits and characteristics as age, longevity, or loyalty can be the basis for an overall evaluation even when other factors are formally specified in the appraisal instrument. Admittedly, these are factors that in many instances are desirable. Age and seniority are viewed as indictors of experience (Prather, 1974, Robbins, 1978, Ferris, 1985). On the other hand, loyalty is the trait supervisors often value the most among employees.

The problem here occurs when these measures are used in conjunction with other, supposedly independent factors. The subjective, unidimensional response eliminates the sought after balance that the intentional introduction of the other factors was designed to achieve. Correlational studies often show this as a problem in the employment of basic graphic rating scales.

Similarly, the vividness of one event can overshadow all other incidents. A halo effect occurs when a good performance in one aspect of a job becomes the basis for overall assessment; a horns effect indicates that an incident perceived as negative was the basis of the evaluation (Odiorne, 1965, 1971, 1987, Murphy and Cleveland, 1995:277–281).

Unidimensional error also occurs with regard to appraisal mechanics. First impression or recency error is introduced when early or late events are given extraordinary weight in the evaluation. The first impression error leads later performance to be discounted. The recency error places emphasis upon the time period nearest the decision at the expense of earlier contributions. Critical incident files (wherein a supervisor notes "good" and "bad" performance as it occurs and places these reminders in a "tickler file" to use later in writing up the formal appraisal) are often a means of countering this cognitive limitation.

Supervisors may also exhibit a central tendency (i.e, awarding everyone middle-range or average ratings) or restricted range (i.e., extremely good and bad ratings are not awarded) problem in which all employees receive the same rating or very close and similar ratings. This problem often emerges when supervisors are required only to justify high and low ratings. It is also likely where supervisors fear that employees would resent an individual who received a higher rating or themselves lose motivation from a lower rating (Glueck, 1978, Bernardin and Beatty, 1984, Murphy and Cleveland, 1995:275–277).

Constant error also occurs when supervisors exhibit tendencies toward awarding consistently high or low ratings or are overly lenient or strict in their rating evaluations (Robbins, 1978). While such errors are often applied equally to all employees within the work unit, they make interunit comparisons inaccurate. This poses a special problem when employee appraisal are used in determining rewards such as merit pay raises. If one supervisor's rating of a "three" is equivalent to another's "four," the latter employee could well be rewarded and the former not rewarded for what is objectively the same level of performance.

Interpersonal biases introduce intentional distortions into the appraisal process. The extent to which a supervisor's own performance and career is dependent upon a subordinate's performance, the more likely it is that favorable ratings will be awarded. This interdependence creates a mutual need for maintaining a harmonious relationship (Brinkerhoff and Kanter, 1980, Larson, 1984, Tjosvold, 1985).

Squeaky wheels also benefit from interpersonal bias. They may receive higher ratings than they otherwise deserve in order to avoid any unpleasantness. However, employees deemed difficult as well as those who make use of the organization's grievance process are likely to receive more critical attention in future performance appraisals (Klaas and DeNisi, 1989).

Interpersonal biases are also often found as examples of abuse rather than of errors. They may entail worksite politics wherein ratings are adjusted in order to support or hinder an employee's opportunity for advancement and reward. Supervisors may be influenced by the desires of others—superiors, peers, or subordinates (Robinson, Fink, and Allen, 1996). Lower than deserved ratings can be awarded in an effort to selfishly retain a valued and productive employee. Lower than deserved ratings are also a means for taking-out someone seen as a potential competitor (Teel, 1986, Longenecker, Sims, and Gioia, 1987).

Similarly, appraisal ratings can be affected by factors entirely extraneous to the working relationship. External preferences vis-a-vis politics, religion, and sex may be furthered through the manipulation of the performance appraisal process. Avoiding such abuses is one of the purposes underlying the recommendations for continuously monitoring the appraisal process. Requirements for the automatic review of appraisal by upper-level officials and an appeals process are designed with the intention to deter abuse.

Training individuals in the use of these tools is just as important as the development of objective appraisal techniques. Supervisory training requires care. Supervisory training can encompass organizational and employee considerations as well as those related to the appraisal process itself. Performance appraisal is part of an overall performance management system. As such, its interaction with the other systemic aspects is just as important a part of its functioning as are the mechanics of the appraisal process itself.

Measurement and Goal Displacement

Much of what passes as measurement error (i.e., the inability of supervisors to accurately assess or evaluate individual performance) is in reality supervisory adjustments in response to organizational demands (Daley, 1992:119–121, Longenecker, Sims, and Gioia, 1987, Murphy and Cleveland, 1995, Bowman, 1999). While the impact of these adjustments may be deemed as negative, they are neither accidental nor totally within the control of the supervisor to correct. Goals may be unclear or misunderstood due to communication problems. A hidden agenda may use performance appraisals as means of controlling employees rather than for encouraging productivity. The expectations of what can be done may simply be unrealistic. Finally, results may be due to activity of groups rather than of individuals. The supervisors endeavor to coordinate workers and obtain productivity within this system. As such, the performance appraisal is part of the organization's overall management control system (Swiss, 1991, Longenecker and Nykodym, 1996).

Structural problems can also undermine the appraisal instruments themselves. The failure to develop objective appraisal systems can lead to inconsistent or unreliable appraisals. The failure to provide adequate supervisory training in the use of objective systems can also result in a loss of consistency and reliability.

An inability or neglect in goal setting produces similar faults in the appraisal process. Objective appraisal systems operate only if results can be compared against expectations. The failure to establish goals and objectives leaves the system with no expectations. Since managers and supervisors take an appraisal's specific purpose into consideration in making their evaluations, using the appraisal for another, unintended purpose only confounds the process.

The performance appraisal process can also be abused when the decision making causal process is inverted. Instead of serving as an aid in decisions regarding employee promotion, pay, dismissal, or development, the appraisals are abused in order to justify predetermined decisions.

On a somewhat more technical level, problems arise wherein employees aim to match their behavior to the criteria used in the evaluation. It is difficult to fault employees for doing what is asked of them; yet, for organizations sins of omission are just as deadly as the sins of commission. Ideally, the appraisal system is designed to objectively encompass all the needed tasks. However, in reality important tasks are often ignored or unforeseen. Appraisals may only detail tasks included in out-of-date position descriptions. Tasks that are not easily quantified or are indeed qualitative in nature may be downplayed in favor of those that provide for a more "precise, technical" look. Redesigning the appraisal process is both essential and helpful in such circumstances.

Many organizations accord little priority to the job of administration per se or to the exercise of personnel practices in particular. An organization which is serious about its performance appraisal process incorporates numerous training and support services into its process. The organization also clearly indicates to its supervisors and employees that the supervisors are themselves evaluated on their use of the appraisal system (Mohrman, Resnick-West, and Lawler, 1989:125–130, Daley, 1992:127–131, Longenecker and Nykodym, 1996).

Inconsistency and Nonpay for Performance

Pay-for-performance incentives take numerous forms. While mostly focused at providing individual incentives (merit pay, bonuses, and skill-based pay), they are readily adaptable to group situations (gainsharing and team/group incentives). While it can be argued that the public sector greatly benefits from emphasizing its intrinsic, public interest, or ethos aspects (Perry and Wise, 1990, Naff and Crum, 1999), extrinsic pay-for-performance schemes for enhancing productivity are quite appealing.

The added benefits that can be derived from pay for performance are predicated on the existence of an adequate base pay rate that rewards job performance (and is adjusted for inflation and other cost-of-living factors). Failure to maintain this foundation erodes organizational trust and undermines the effectiveness of pay-for-performance incentives (Carnevale, 1995).

Pay for performance is also predicated on rewarding employees for desired, productive performance. The pay-for-performance "reward" works because it reinforces desirable employee behaviors. Inasmuch as the organization fails to identify and reward the "correct" behaviors, its pay-for-performance scheme will be less than effective (Luthans and Stajkovic, 1999).

CONCLUSION

Performance appraisal research and practice during the twentieth century witnessed the development of appraisal instruments from simplistic and subjective adjective checklists into sophisticated devices that can be used to objectively measure the actual tasks that an individual performs. While objective performance appraisal instruments have been developed, training in their use has tended to lag. In addition, research on decision making has enlightened us on the processes by which the human mind actually functions.

The twenty-first century begins with efforts to synthesize the use of these objective instruments with the functioning of human reasoning. Experiments examining the prospects for such approaches as 360-degree, pass/fail, and team appraisal are underway. The problems of training, accurate measurement, and the human fallibility of rater errors persist. However, these problems no longer go unrecognized. Now, efforts are consciously being made to address them.

REFERENCES

BERNARDIN, H. JOHN, and RICHARD W. BEATTY. 1984. *Performance Appraisal: Assessing Human Behavior at Work*. Boston: Kent.

BIGONESS, WILLIAM J. 1976. Effects of Applicant's Sex, Race, and Performance on Employer's Performance Rating: Some Additional Findings. *Journal of Applied Psychology*, 61:80–84.

BLOOM, MATT. 1999. The Performance Effects of Pay Dispersion on Individuals and Organizations. *Academy of Management Journal* 42,1 (February):25–40.

BOWMAN, JAMES. 1999. Performance Appraisal: Verisimilitude Trumps Veracity. *Public Personnel Management* 28,4 (Winter):557–576.

BRINKERHOFF, D. W., and R. M. KANTER. 1980. Appraising the Performance of Performance Appraisal. *Sloan Management Review*, 21 (Spring):3–16.

CARNEVALE, DAVID G. 1995. *Trustworthy Government: Leadership and Management Strategies for Building Trust and High Performance*. San Francisco, CA: Jossey-Bass.

COHEN, STEVEN, and RONALD BRAND. 1993. *Total Quality Management in Government: A Practical Guide for the Real World*. San Francisco, CA: Jossey-Bass.

DALEY, DENNIS M. 1992. *Performance Appraisal in the Public Sector: Techniques and Applications*. Westport, CT: Quorum.

——. Forthcoming. Developmental Performance Appraisal: Feedback, Interview, and Disciplinary Techniques. In K. Tom Liou, ed., *Handbook of Public Management Practice and Reform*. New York: Marcel Dekker.

DELEON, LINDA, and ANN J. EWEN. 1997. Multi-Source Performance Appraisals: Employee Perceptions of Fairness. *Review of Public Personnel Administration* 17, 1 (Winter):22–36.

DENISI, ANGELO, THOMAS CAFFERTY, and BRUCE MEGLINO. 1984. A Cognitive View of the Performance Appraisal Process: A Model and Research Propositions. *Organizational Behavior and Human Performance*, 33:360–396.

DENISI, ANGELO, and AVRAHAM N. KLUGER. 2000. Feedback Effectiveness: Can 360-Degree Appraisals Be Improved? *Academy of Management Executive* 14,1 (February):129–139.

DURANT, ROBERT F., and LAURA A. WILSON. 1993. Public Management, TQM and Quality Improvement: Towards a Contingency Strategy. *American Review of Public Administration* 22,3:215–245.

EDWARDS, MARK, and ANN J. EWEN. 1996. *360-Degree Feedback: The Powerful New Model for Employee Assessment and Performance Improvement*. New York: AMACOM Books.

FERRIS, GEORGE. 1985. The Influence of Subordinate Age on Performance Ratings and Causal Attributions. *Personnel Psychology*, 38 (Autumn):545–547.

GATEWOOD, ROBERT D., and HUBERT FEILD. 1998. *Human Resource Selection*. Fort Worth, TX: Dryden Press.

GHORPADE, JAI. 2000. Managing Five Paradoxes of 360-Degree Feedback. *Academy of Management Executive* 14,1 (February):140–150.

GLUECK, WILLIAM. 1978. *Personnel: A Diagnostic Approach*. Dallas, TX: Business Publications.

GRAHAM-MOORE, BRIAN, and TIMOTHY L. ROSS. 1990. *Gainsharing: Plans for Improving Performance*. Washington, DC: Bureau of National Affairs.

GREINER, JOHN M., HARRY P. HATRY, MARGO P. KOSS, ANNIE P. MILLAR, and JANE P. WOODWARD. 1981. *Productivity and Motivation: A Review of State and Local Government Initiatives.* Washington, DC: Urban Institute.

KLAAS, BRIAN S., and ANGELO S. DENISI. 1989. Managerial Reactions to Employee Dissent: The Impact of Grievance Activity on Performance Ratings. *Academy of Management Journal,* 32,4 (December):705-717.

KRAIGER, KURT, and J. KEVIN FORD. 1985. A Meta Analysis of Ratee Effects in Performance Ratings. *Journal of Applied Psychology,* 70:56-65.

LANDY, FRANK J., and JAMES L. FARR. 1980. Performance Rating. *Psychological Bulletin,* 87:72-107.

———. 1983. *The Measurement of Work Performance: Methods, Theories and Applications.* New York: Academic Press.

LARSON, J. R. 1984. The Performance Feedback Process—A Preliminary Model. *Organizational Behavior and Human Performance:* 33, 11:42-76.

LATHAM, GARY P., and KENNETH WEXLEY. 1981. *Increasing Productivity Through Performance Appraisal.* Reading, MA: Addison-Wesley.

LEPSINGER, RICHARD, and ANNTOINETTE D. LUCIA. 1997. *The Art and Science of 360-Degree Feedback.* San Francisco: Pfeiffer.

LONGENECKER, CLINTON, HENRY SIMS, JR., and DENNIS GIOIA. 1987. Behind the Mask: The Politics of Employee Appraisal. *Academy of Management Executive,* 1,3:183-193.

LONGENECKER, CLINTON O., and NICK NYKODYM. 1996. Public Sector Performance Appraisal Effectiveness: A Case Study. *Public Personnel Management* 25,2 (Summer):151-164.

LUTHANS, FRED, and ALEXANDER D. STAJKOVIC. 1999. Reinforce for Performance: The Need to Go Beyond Pay and Even Rewards. *Academy of Management Executive* 13,2 (May):49-57.

MARKOWICH, MICHAEL M. 1993. Does Money Motivate? *HRFocus* (August):1, 6.

MILKOVICH, GEORGE T., and ALEXANDRA K. WIGDOR, eds. with Ranae F. Broderick and Anne S. Mavor. 1991. *Pay for Performance: Evaluating Performance Appraisal and Merit Pay.* Washington, DC: National Academy Press.

MITCHELL, TERENCE R., and R. C. LIDEN. 1982. The Effects of the Social Context on Performance Evaluations. *Organizational Behavior and Human Performance,* 29:241-256.

MOBLEY, W. H. 1982. Supervisor and Employee Race and Sex Effects on Performance Appraisal—A Field Study of Adverse Impact and Generalizability. *Academy of Management Journal,* 25,3:598-606.

MOHRMAN, ALLAN M., JR, SUSAN M. RESNICK-WEST, and EDWARD E. LAWLER III. 1989. *Designing Performance Appraisal Systems: Aligning Appraisals and Organizational Realities.* San Francisco, CA: Jossey-Bass.

MURPHY, KEVIN R., and JEANETTE N. CLEVELAND. 1995. *Understanding Performance Appraisal: Social, Organizational, and Goal-Based Perspectives.* Thousand Oaks, CA: Sage.

NAFF, KATHERINE C., and JOHN CRUM. 1999. Working for America: Does Public Service Motivation Make a Difference? *Review of Public Personnel Administration* 19,4 (Fall):5-16.

ODIORNE, GEORGE S. 1965. *Management by Objectives: A System of Managerial Leadership.* New York: Pitman.

———. 1971. *Personnel Administration by Objectives.* Homewood, IL: Richard Irwin.

———. 1987. *The Human Side of Management: Management by Integration and Self-Control.* Lexington, MA: Lexington Books.

PATTON, KEVIN R., and DENNIS M. DALEY. 1998. Gainsharing in Zebulon: What Do Workers Want? *Public Personnel Management* 27,1 (Spring):117-131.

PERRY, JAMES L., and LOIS R. WISE. 1990. The Motivational Bases of Public Service. *Public Administration Review* 50,3 (May/June): 367-373.

PIZAM, ABRAHAM. 1975. Social Differentiation—A New Psychological Barrier to Performance Appraisal. *Public Personnel Management,* 4:244-247.

POLLACK, DAVID M., and LESLIE J. POLLACK. 1996. Using 360-Degree Feedback in Performance Appraisal. *Public Personnel Management* 25,4 (Winter):507-528.

PRATHER, RICHARD. 1974. Extending the Life of Performance Appraisal Programs. *Personnel Journal,* (October):739-743.

RAND, T. M., and KENNETH WEXLEY. 1975. A Demonstration of the Byrne Similar to Hypothesis in Simulated Employment Interviews. *Psychological Reports,* 36:535–544.

RISHER, HOWARD. 1999. Are Public Employees Ready for a 'New Pay' Program? *Public Personnel Management* 28,3 (Fall):323–343.

ROBBINS, STEPHEN P. 1978. *Personnel: The Management of Human Resources.* Upper Saddle River, NJ: Prentice Hall.

ROBINSON, ROBERT K., ROSS L. FINK, and BILLIE MORGAN ALLEN. 1996. The Influence of Organizational Constituent Groups on Rater Attitudes Toward Performance Appraisal Compliance. *Public Personnel Management* 25,2 (Summer):141–150.

SANDERS, RONALD P. 1997. Gainsharing in Government: Group-Based Performance Pay for Public Employees. In *New Strategies for Public Pay,* Howard Risher and Charles Fay, eds. San Francisco, CA: Jossey-Bass, pp. 231–252.

SHORE, L. M., and G. C. THORTON. 1986. Effects of Gender on Self-Ratings and Supervisory Ratings. *Academy of Management Journal,* 29,1 (March):115–129.

SWISS, JAMES E. 1991. *Public Management Systems: Monitoring and Managing Government Performance.* Upper Saddle River, NJ: Prentice Hall.

——. 1992. Adapting Total Quality Management (TQM) to Government. *Public Administration Review* (July–August):356–359.

TEEL, K. S. 1986. Are Merit Raises Really Based on Merit. *Personnel Journal,* 65,3:88.

TJOSVOLD, DEAN. 1985. Power and Social Context in Superior-Subordinate Interaction. *Organizational Behavior,* 35,3:281–293.

WALDMAN, DAVID A., LEANNE E. ATWATER, and DAVID ANTONIONI. 1998. Has 360-Degree Feedback Gone Amok? *Academy of Management Executive* 12,2 (May):86–96.

WEXLEY, KENNETH, and W. F. NEMEROFF. 1974. Effects of Racial Prejudice, Race of Applicant, and Biographical Similarity on Interview Evaluation of Job Applicants. *Journal of Social and Behavioral Science,* 20:66–78.

WILSON, LAURA A., and ROBERT F. DURANT. 1994. Evaluating TQM: The Case for a Theory-Driven Approach. *Public Administration Review* 54,2 (March–April):137–146.

12

Public Employee Benefits and the Changing Nature of the Workforce

N. JOSEPH CAYER

Arizona State University

The work place reflects continuous change in society generally; thus, employers face constant change in the demographics of the workforce. Traditionally, employers structured work to suit their needs; now, they must structure it to reflect the needs of employees if they are to be competitive in the labor market. The components of benefits programs demonstrate this trend toward accommodating changes in the work setting.

Policies in place since the 1960s created a more diverse workforce in terms of ethnicity, race, and gender (McCabe and Stream, 2000). Employers adjusted policies and programs to accommodate the challenges accompanying the shifts. Now, dual-earner couples are common and employees are older and better educated. More people (the sandwich generation) face the challenge of rearing children while they also need to care for elderly relatives. Same sex couples also increasingly press their demands for equal treatment with their heterosexual colleagues. Employees tend to be more educated and their expectations in the work place are very different from the traditional workforce. All of these changes produce pressures for policies to address the complex demands on employees both at work and at home. Benefits programs must go beyond the traditional benefits (usually health care and retirement pensions) and include many other elements that accommodate changing demands on workers while also serving the needs of the employer if employers are to compete in the labor market (Bond, Galinsky, and Swanberg, 1998).

In addition to the demographic changes in the workforce, employers face dramatic changes in the way work is accomplished. Information technology permits and even demands new ways of structuring work, leading to different ways of relating to employees as well as new demands on the employees. Constantly changing technology also requires emphasis on training and development of employees. Remaining competitive in the labor market demands that employers be attractive to potential and current employees. Employees have many more options, and they rate benefits as very important in their decisions to take or stay with a job (Platt, 2000).

Traditionally, employers referred to benefits as fringe benefits. The contemporary approach recognizes benefits as part of a total compensation package and integrates benefits with direct compensation to place a monetary value on positions. Typically, employers offered no benefits at the beginning of the twentieth century, but over the years certain benefits came to be standard among larger employers and gradually more were added (Hostetler and Pynes, 1995; Levine, 1993–94). The public sector generally is credited with having a history of providing better benefits than the private sector, but the record is mixed. Public employers offer generous health care and retirement benefits, especially since historically, they paid the complete cost of the benefits while the private sector normally required employees to share in the cost. As health care costs have risen sharply, public employers also have moved to having employees pick up some of the premium cost. Retirement benefits also increasingly include some employee contribution (Handel, 1992). In adopting innovative approaches to benefits, the private sector often leads the way, but in some instances, such as domestic partnership, governments moved first to offer them. Benefits plans may be divided by whether they are required by government policy (mandated benefits) or are voluntary on the part of the employer (discretionary). We now examine each category of benefits as provided by public employers.

MANDATED BENEFITS

National government policy requires provision of some benefits, including social security, unemployment compensation, workers compensation, and medical leave. Public and private sector employers, alike, must provide these benefits. Most of these benefits arose from the New Deal programs of the 1930s which were stimulated by the Great Depression. Benefits were viewed as providing a basic level of security and often are called social insurance programs. The Family and Medical Leave Act of 1993 created the newest mandated benefit, family and medical leave.

The Social Security Act of 1935 created several programs to protect the income security of individuals. The most well-understood program is the Social Security retirement program, which pays retirement pensions to people who have paid into the program or to their survivors. The Social Security program also includes Disability and Medicare benefits. Disability benefits include monthly cash benefits for disabled workers and Medicare provides hospital and medical insurance for the aged, disabled, and those with certain diseases. National government policy now requires coverage of state and local government employees under Social Security and Medicare. State and local governments had the option of participating in Social Security and Medicare until 1986. A 1981 law requires that any employee hired or rehired after March 31, 1986 by state or local government must be covered under Medicare. In 1991, the law was changed to require that state and local employees not covered by a public retirement system be covered by Social Security and Medicare. These programs are paid for by a combination of employee and employer contributions.

The Social Security Act also created the unemployment compensation program which provides temporary income benefits to people who were laid off or who quit their jobs and actively seek employment. They receive a fixed income over a specified number of weeks while they look for work. Employer contributions and national government funding finance the program.

Worker's compensation pays employees a portion of their wages or salaries when they are unable to work because of work-related injuries. The program also pays for medical and rehabilitation benefits. Employer contributions pay for the programs.

The Family and Medical Leave Act of 1993 created the newest mandated benefit. The law requires all employers with more than fifty employees to allow employees to take up to twelve weeks of unpaid family and medical leave during any twelve month period. The leave is for the birth of a child, adoption of a child, foster care placement, care of a family member, or for one's own health care for a serious medical condition.

As mandated benefits are imposed on virtually all employers, they do not affect the attractiveness of one employer over another to prospective or current employees. Discretionary benefits, though, do differentiate employers from one another and can have an impact on the desirability of any given employer, especially in a period of low unemployment when employers have to compete for good workers.

DISCRETIONARY BENEFITS

Public employers recognize that to be competitive they need to offer many optional benefits in addition to the mandated benefits discussed above. Most public employers include health care, retirement, and vacation and sick leave as discretionary benefits. Because these benefits are common among private sector employers, public employers have little choice but to offer them in order to remain competitive. In addition to these staples, many employers offer such discretionary benefits as educational leave, tuition reimbursement, subsidization of dependent care, and many others. Changes in the work force and the needs of individuals to balance work and personal life demands create pressure on employers to provide a wide variety of benefits. As a result, the list of discretionary benefits keeps growing (Boyd and Dickerson, 1990; Ellis, 1993; Levine, 1993–94). Reflecting the efforts to help employees balance personal and work challenges, many employers call their discretionary benefits work-life or family friendly benefits programs.

While employers attempt to offer a balance of benefits to meet varying needs of the workers, they also face other pressures. Available resources affect the ability of employers to offer optional benefits. Given that public sector employers depend on taxpayers to pay for benefits, employers need to tread carefully. Similarly, they need to maintain acceptable service levels to satisfy citizens. These concerns constrain public sector employers in what they can offer employees.

Discretionary benefits cover many types of situations. Health care, retirement, and various types of leave represent the most common types of discretionary benefits. Additionally, many employers offer one or more other optional benefits such as work schedule flexibility, dependent care, domestic partner benefits, career development opportunities, employee assistance, financial planning, or other specific benefits.

Health Care

Health care coverage represents the most commonly provided discretionary employee benefit in the public sector. Surveys show consistently that 90 percent of state and local governments offer health care coverage and that the percentage of employees covered under health care plans is about the same (Employee Benefit Research Institute, 1995 and 2000; U.S. Bureau of the Census, 1994). All public employers who offer benefits offer medical coverage and increasingly they offer mental health and dental coverage. Hoping to contain health care coverage costs, many employers provide and encourage employees to participate in preventive health programs. They encourage their employees to practice good nutrition, live healthy lifestyles, and reduce stress in their lives. They also provide exercise programs and encourage regular physical exams so as to identify potential health problems and to take corrective action before problems become critical.

Traditionally, employers offered indemnity health care insurance in which the employee chooses providers and submits claims to the insurance company. The insurance normally pays the provider directly. The sharp increases in health care coverage costs during the 1980s and 1990s led employers to turn to alternative approaches, particularly managed care (Cayer, 1995; Handel, 1992; Streib, 1996). The managed care programs include health maintenance organizations (HMO) and preferred provider organizations (PPO). In these plans, the insurer contracts with physician groups (HMO) or individual doctors (PPO) who act as gatekeepers for services. They agree to provide services at a fixed cost for each type of service or treatment. The employee/patient usually has to pay a nominal fee (called a copayment) for each visit or service. Employees usually can choose among indemnity, HMO, and PPO plans. Since employers normally provide a specific dollar amount toward the benefit, the employee pays the difference in premium between the employer's share and the cost of the insurance. As the employee chooses a more expensive plan, the cost to the employee increases.

The constantly rising cost of health care insurance creates debate about public policy concerning health care. One dimension of the debate is whether employer provided health insurance should be regulated by public policy. In fact, there already are many public policies that do just that. For example, the Omnibus Budget Reconciliation Act of 1985 (COBRA) requires employers to provide employees who leave the organization opportunity to continue coverage under the employer plan for a minimum of eighteen and maximum of thirty-six months. The former employee pays both the employer and employee part of the premium. Federal policy also now requires some portability of programs as employees move from one employer to another. Coverage of preexisting conditions also is required. Another policy issue debated nationally concerns universal health care coverage. Universal coverage is likely to occur incrementally. For example many proposals in Congress and by candidates for office call for some type of universal coverage for children. It is likely that such coverage will be the first step in a gradual expansion of coverage. An element of the universal coverage debate is a proposal to require all employers to provide coverage. Of course, the effect would be relatively small on public sector employers since most now offer such coverage.

Related to health care benefits are disability benefits. Many employers offer disability benefits beyond what is required by worker's compensation. Generally, state and local employers pay for short-term disability plans and make long-term disability plans available paid for by the employee at a lower premium than if purchased individually (Finkle, 1997). Employers often also provide a life insurance policy equal to one year's salary for employees and employees may purchase additional coverage at their own expense.

Leave

State and local government employee benefits packages typically include many types of leave, including holiday, vacation, and sick leave. Public employers generally follow the lead of the national government on holidays, but variations include providing employees holidays for days important to the state or local government. Statehood day is a typical example of a variation from the national government pattern. In all, holidays account for ten-to-twelve leave days per year for employees.

Vacation leave is universal for public employers also. Typically, employees receive five or ten working days vacation per year, accrued as a given number of hours per pay period. As employees remain with the jurisdiction, the amount of vacation leave may increase gradually.

Sick leave represents another benefit which is almost universal with the public sector. The national government provides sick leave and 95 percent of state and local governments provide it (U.S. Bureau of the Census, 1994). As with vacation leave, employees typically earn a set number of hours sick leave per pay period. Various policies govern how it may be used, including if a doctor's note is required and what happens if sick leave is unused. Many jurisdictions pay for unused sick leave at some preestablished rate such as 50 percent at the end of each year. In other cases, it is forfeited if it goes over a certain number of hours. Some jurisdictions pay for it upon retirement or leaving the organization. Again, the rate varies by jurisdiction. Maternity leave is provided by about 60 percent of public employers and paternity leave by about 45 percent beyond the Family and Medical Leave Act requirements (U.S. Bureau of the Census, 1994).

Personal leave represents another type of leave. Many employers provide a day or two per year as personal leave. The employee's birthday often is given as a personal day. Employers require that the employee schedule such days in advance.

Yet another type of leave is bereavement leave which is time off to attend a funeral of an immediate family member. The definition of an immediate family member varies greatly with some spelling out specifically what relationships are covered and others providing flexibility, especially in cases where domestic partnership benefits exist.

The variation in leave policies and complexity in administering them often leads to concerns about equity and abuse of policies. For example, some people use every hour or day of sick leave as soon as it is accrued and others never use their sick leave. Those who do not use it often complain of having to pick up the slack for those who are out. Verifying that people are actually sick puts supervisors in awkward situations as well. As a result of these types of concerns, many employers, including nearly half of state and local government now have paid time off (PTO) leave policies (Smith, 1996). Under PTO (sometimes also called comprehensive leave), employers combine all types of leave into one block of time given to employees. As with many other types of leave, the employee accrues a set number of hours per pay period. Generally, employees are expected to schedule the time in advance, although, when used for illness, that may be difficult. Unused leave usually is paid out in cash at the end of the year or upon leaving the organization.

Retirement Pensions

Public retirement systems enroll more than 17 million employees in plans with more than a trillion dollars (Beam and McFadden, 1994; Khavari, 1998). Public pension systems have been viewed as particularly generous in the public sector and one of the attractions for potential employees. In the public sector, the employer traditionally paid all of the contribution to the system. Elected decision makers also often found retirement pensions a good way of buying employee and labor support. They could agree to increases in pension benefits rather than wage increases because the bill for pensions could be put off, usually until long after the elected official had moved on. As governments faced tight financial times, especially in the late 1970s into the mid-1990s, public retirement systems came under increasing scrutiny and reform.

Most operate under defined benefits plans in which the employee receives a fixed amount in a retirement pension for as long as he/she lives. Surviving spouses are guaranteed the same benefit. Most systems figure the benefit according to a formula factoring in the number of years employed and the age of the retiree. Typically, the governmental jurisdiction would budget for the retirement costs as they became due thus they were pay-as-you-go systems. The combination of generous retirement benefits and reduced revenues caused by the tax revolts of the 1970s created financial stress for many employers, especially local governments. Public pension trust funds became more popular as a way of setting aside money for public retirement systems. While states have been more likely to have such trust funds in the past, local governments often did not have them. In many states, local governments were permitted to join the state system or a separate retirement fund was set up for local governments and all local governments could join.

Reform in public retirement systems resulted in many state and local governments developing defined contribution plans. Defined contribution systems set aside money in an account identified with each employee. Typically, the employer and employee both contribute an amount to the account equal to some percentage of the employee's salary. Upon retirement, the employee receives a pension based on the amount contributed to the account over time and on the earnings of the account. Thus, each employee's pension will vary depending upon salary history and investment earnings. In some cases, public employers allow individual employees to invest their retirement funds through an approved financial planner. Generally, more individualized investment plans have recorded better earnings than traditional public pension funds which tend to be very conservative in investment strategy. Public retirement systems continue to experiment with different approaches to provide maximum flexibility to employees at the same time they need to contain costs and insure that employee interests are protected.

WORK-LIFE BENEFITS

Increasingly, employers recognize that the traditional benefits described above do not meet all the needs of contemporary employees. Consequently, many have redesigned benefits packages to focus on what they call work-life benefits (Bond, Galinsky, and Swanberg, 1998; Bureau of National Affairs, Inc., 1993–97; Rayman and Bailyn, 1998). With globalization, constant rapid technological change, and demographic changes, employees have different expectations. They demand more job flexibility, greater say in work decisions, and more consideration of their non-work responsibilities. To accommodate these and other expectations of workers, employers constantly change their approaches and work-life benefits packages reflect that change.

Work-life benefits, sometimes called family friendly or work-and-family benefits, attempt to provide employees the tools and opportunities to balance the conflicting demands of their work and non-work lives. Employers provide such benefits because they recognize that the stresses of life cannot be separated from the work situation. Employers hope that accommodating employee needs for dealing with normal life routines will permit them to focus on their work and thus be better contributors to the work organization.

Work-life benefits programs vary greatly because each work place and each set of employees have different needs. Employers package their benefits in different ways. Many of the benefits included in work-life benefits packages are offered by employers without being called work-life benefits; thus, there is much variation. In recent trends, employers bundle many specific benefits under the rubric of work-life benefits. Among benefits commonly found in work-life benefits packages are flexible work hours, dependent care, domestic partner benefits, professional development, employee assistance, legal assistance, financial planning, and others.

Flexible Work Hours

Many employers created flexible work schedules (often called Flextime) during the late 1960s and 1970s as a way of increasing employee productivity and commitment to the organization. While many of the experiments resulted in initial improvement in productivity, long-term effects were not always positive. In the 1980s and 1990s, flexible working hours emerged anew as a way of accommodating the changing demographics of the work force. Dual career couples, in particular, often found flexible hours attractive so that they could arrange for day care for children more easily or so that one of the parents could be available after children finished school. Many employees just prefer schedules other than the traditional 8-to-5, five day work week. Allowing employees to make their own schedules within limits often results in more positive outlooks by employees. Flexible schedules usually mean that employees work their normal number of hours but in different time blocks. They may start later in the day and then stay later or just the opposite. They may work 10 hour days for four days or 12 hour days for 3 days. Some even like split schedules where they work early in the morning and have the midday free and come back in the evening. Of course, employers need to have the work place staffed during certain hours; so, the flexibility needs to take into account the needs of the employer as well. As long as the work place is staffed during the needed hours, it should not matter who is there at any given time. Since employers recognize that the important issue is whether the work gets done, they increasingly embrace flexibility in individual work schedules.

Flexibility also may mean part-time employment and job sharing. Many employees do not want to work full-time and employers can find very talented people if they are willing to accommodate the desire to work less than full-time. In some cases, employees job share; two people work the same job but one is there certain hours and the other at other times. The employer gets the job filled and two people who desire part-time work are accommodated. One issue with part-time employees is how they fit in the traditional benefits packages including health care and retirement. Increasingly, employers find formulas to allow part-time employees to enjoy these and leave benefits.

Reflecting other changes in society, many employers allow flexibility in the place at which work is done. Telecommuting is an approach to allow people to work from home (Center for Personnel Research, 1998). Telecommuting is attractive to many people who can avoid the traffic jams associated with traveling to the central work site. It also can be very attractive to those who have children or elders at home or have some disability that makes travel difficult. Some people tout telecommuting as a way to help the environment and to conserve fuel as well, noting that it takes people off the road during traffic rush hours. Satellite work sites also help cut down on travel and represent another type of flexibility in work scheduling.

Dependent Care

Contemporary employees find dependent care to be a challenge and employers recognize that help with dependent care can be effective in attracting and retaining employees. Some employers began helping with child care, usually in the form of subsidies for child care expenses. Over time, on-site child care facilities emerged along with discounts for employees with some vendors. The City of Phoenix, Arizona, for example, recently opened a day care center for children of city employees. Other services offered by employers include counseling in the selection of nannies, before- and after-school programs, and help with homework.

Many employees have elderly relatives who need constant care and employers often offer support for elder care to help alleviate the problem. The variety of programs include subsidies for nursing care or home care professionals, and subsidizing long-term disability insurance for elders (Center for Personnel Research, 1997). Adult care facilities, modeled after child care programs, have emerged as well. Some of the most effective programs combine child and elder care in intergenerational facilities. Activities are planned to bring both groups together (Kirrane, 1994). Flexible spending accounts often are offered for employees to support all types of dependent care.

Domestic Partner Benefits

Many employers now offer domestic partner benefits even though they remain very controversial. Public employers always face the possibility of citizens taking action to reverse extension of benefits to domestic partners. The intensity of the debate over the issue reflects the divisiveness of it. Domestic partnership policies generally raise the issue of homosexuality and the positions of people on morality and religion. While many domestic partnership policies do not distinguish between heterosexual and homosexual domestic partners, some do limit them to same-sex couples. The rationale for limiting the policy to same-sex couples is that heterosexual couples have the option of marrying if they wish to receive benefits while same-sex couples do not have that option. Thus, to be fair to same-sex partners, some employers extend the benefits to them. Of course, this rationale does not quiet many opponents of the policy.

Domestic partnership policies mean extending to domestic partners the same benefits as are available to married couples (Center for Personnel Research, 1996a). On a practical side, many opponents suggest that extending domestic partners benefits will increase costs; although, there is no evidence to indicate that employers with such policies have witnessed increased cost. Another issue is the administration of such policies. The definition of a domestic partner is not clear and determining what constitutes such a partnership requires careful consideration. Similarly, determining dissolution of such a relationship is not easy as there is no "divorce" proceeding for it. While the number of employers granting domestic partner benefits constantly grows, they still are in the small minority.

Professional Development

Constant changes in technology and growth in knowledge require that employees receive training and development opportunities. Otherwise, their skills and knowledge become obsolete very quickly. Training and development opportunities benefit the employees as well as the employer. Employees develop their capacity and experience more opportunity for advancement in the organization and even outside. Employers see training and development as an important tool in keeping good employees with the organization and enhancing employee loyalty as the employees view the employer as being concerned about them.

Training and development programs vary, but typically large organizations have an internal training and development unit which provides a variety of training opportunities ranging from specific skills such as mastery of a computer software program or supervisory skills to management development programs to prepare individuals for promotion to upper management levels. Most employers also provide funding for employees to obtain training from external programs. They may include tuition support for attending college or attendance at workshops and institutes. Small employers typically send their employees to outside training programs or join consortia of small jurisdictions to be able to support training activities.

Employee Assistance

Increasingly, employers consider their employees as assets and recognize that those assets need to be protected. Stresses of everyday life create problems for employees and those problems often interfere with employees' abilities to concentrate on the job. Employee Assistance Plans (EAPs) offered by employers help employees deal with their stress and problems and free them to focus on their work. The International Personnel Management Association found that 75 percent of its institutional members offered EAPs (Center for Personnel Research, 1996a).

Employee Assistance Programs evolved from alcohol abuse programs that many employers developed to help people whose work was affected by alcohol abuse and addiction. Gradually the programs grew to deal with other types of substance abuse such as drug addiction. Over time, EAPs began to address virtually every personal problem employees have. Many plans remain limited in services they offer, but many offer help with problems ranging from family issues to substance abuse and legal and financial problems. Many programs also offer counseling concerning adjustment to the new community for new employees and their families and support for new employee spouses or partners in finding a job.

Often the EAP is integrated with other programs such as those to encourage a healthier life style. They offer stress reduction programs and programs to help people to quit smoking, for example. Stress is a significant cause of accidents and illness leading to added costs for the employer. By offering programs to reduce stress, employers can benefit in the form of lower costs in the long run. Similarly, employees who quit smoking, lose weight, or exercise regularly, generally are healthier and are likely to make less use of health care benefits, thus helping to reduce the cost of health care programs.

Financial counseling and planning are also increasingly common in employee benefits plans, often as part of EAPs. Employees often get themselves into financial difficulty and need someone to help identify ways of working their way out of the difficulty. EAPs also may help in planning for future financial security.

The variety of potential benefits offered by employers is limited only by the types of issues employees have. Employers face the challenge of addressing important issues while not being the parties responsible for everything employees want or need. Especially in the public sector, officials wonder aloud about why the employer should be providing insurance programs for legal problems or counseling on financial responsibility. Thus, employers have to walk a fine line between being supportive of employees and ensuring that programs are cost effective. It is difficult to establish the benefit to the employer of many of these programs and how the public is served by their existence.

Most EAPs offer some internal counseling, at least to diagnose the problem and to offer suggestions on remedies. In some cases, the program may offer extended counseling. More typically, however, the programs diagnose the problem and then refer the employee and/or family members to outside help. Normally, the employer contracts with an outside vendor for provision of the actual counseling or problem-solving activity. As people resolve their problems, they can focus on their work and can be more productive.

ADMINISTERING BENEFITS PLANS

The many changes in the demographics of the workforce and the need to compete for employees creates the need for continuous assessment of and adjustments to benefits plans. Employers commonly survey employees about their benefits and their satisfaction with them. They also spend more time than they used to in communicating with employees about their benefits. Commonly, employees receive an annual individualized statement about their benefits. The statement informs them of just what benefits they enjoy and also of the value of the benefits. The statement is important in letting employees know that the benefits are not cost free. By reporting on the value of benefits and what the employer and employee contribute to the plans, the report serves a very important function in helping employees understand how much goes into personnel costs beyond direct wages and salary. A side effect may be more carefully considered use of benefits by employees.

With the increasing variety of benefits offered and increasing costs of many of the benefits, overall benefits costs have risen greatly. From 1979 to 1999, the state and local government cost of benefits as a portion of employer personnel costs increased from 22 percent of total compensation to approximately 30 percent (Bureau of Labor Statistics, 1999; Gold and Ritchie, 1993). While rapidly rising costs of health care plans contributed most to the increased benefits costs, the addition of new benefits also contributes to rising expenditures. Health care plans grew from 20 percent of benefits costs in 1970 to 40 percent in 1997. Just from 1994 to 1997, employer cost for health care rose from $305 billion to $313 billion. While the rate of increase has declined, costs still are rising. Retirement costs rose as well. In 1980 for example, state and local government spent approximately $19 billion on retirement plans; they spent $62.8 billion in 1997 (Employee Benefit Research Institute, 1997). Costs for all other benefits rose as well, increasing by an average of 2.1 percent from 1990 to 1997 or from $75 billion in 1990 to $87 billion in 1997. While continuing to increase, the rate of increase for all benefits leveled off during the 1990s, from an average 8.0 percent growth during the 1980s to 4.2 percent in the 1990s.

As benefits costs continue to increase, employers search for ways to limit the increases. To be effective in limiting cost increases, employers need to know exactly what their costs are. Thus, increasingly, employers do audits of their benefits costs, evaluate the value to the employer and employee for the purpose of prioritizing, and then decide how to proceed (Cascio, 1999; Paolella, 1995). With tight budgets and citizen/taxpayer interest, public employers experience particular pressure to contain costs.

Many employers offer cafeteria benefits plans and/or flexible spending accounts. These approaches can help with cost containment to the extent that employees use only the benefits they want. In cafeteria plans, employees choose the benefits they want with the usual proviso that they are required to participate in the health care and retirement plans. For dual career couples, coverage under one of the couple's health care plans usually will satisfy the requirement. Beyond the health care or retirement benefit, cafeteria plans mean that the employee has a fixed dollar amount to spend on benefits and can use the money for whatever benefits he/she chooses. Flexible spending accounts permit the employee to set aside money for specific purposes such as medical care or child care. The advantage is that the money is set aside before taxes are imposed, thus lowering the amount of money on which taxes have to be paid. The downside is that if the money is not used for the specified purpose, it might be forfeited. Cafeteria and flexible spending accounts can help employers spend lower amounts for benefits overall.

Education of employees on their benefits and their use is another way employers hope to encourage more effective use of benefits and perhaps lower costs. For example, typically, a small portion of the employees use the most health care services. By targeting the heavy users, encouraging healthier life styles, and strategizing to use the health plan most effectively, it is possible to reduce costs. Encouraging employees to practice preventive measures also helps.

Alliances or consortia represent another approach to reducing benefits costs. Small employers, especially, often find that if they work together to work with vendors, they can realize economies of scale. A health care provider, for example, is likely to offer a lower per capita cost to a consortium of employers who have a combined total of 1000 employees than to a local government that has 100 employees. The larger pool gives the employers leverage with vendors.

Public employers increasingly ask their employees to share in the cost of benefits programs, especially in health care and retirement plans. Traditionally, public employers paid all the cost of employee health care and retirement programs. Now employers typically ask employees to pay part of the premium for health care and to contribute a portion of their pay to the retirement plan. In health care plans, employers also have moved away from offering only indemnity plans to offering HMOs and PPOs to employees. These options allow the employees to decide how much to spend for the kind of health care plan they want. HMO and PPO premiums are generally lower than premiums for indemnity plans. With the employer paying a fixed sum, the employee chooses whether to go with a more or less expensive plan with the resulting differences in benefits.

The demand for ever-different and enhanced benefits is unlikely to diminish. Employers will have to continue to evaluate their plans and to consider their competitive status in the labor market. For the human resource manager, the ever-changing workforce will continue to present challenges in benefits programs.

REFERENCES

BEAM, B. T., and J. J. MCFADDEN. 1994. *Employee Benefits,* 3rd ed. Chicago: Dearborn.

BOND, J. T., E. GALINSKY, and J. E. SWANBERG. 1998. *The 1997 National Study of the Changing Workforce.* New York: Families and Work Institute.

BOYD, K. J., and S. S. DICKERSON. 1990. *Local Government Personnel Compensation and Benefits.* Baseline Data Report, Vol. 22, No. 3 Washington, DC: International City Management Association.

Bureau of Labor Statistics, U.S. Department of Commerce, 1999. Employment cost trends. <*http://www/bls/gov/news.release/ecec.nws.htm*>

CASCIO, W. F. 1999. *Costing Human Resources: The Financial Impact of Behavior in Organizations.* Cincinnati, OH: South-Western College Publishing.

CAYER, N. J. 1995. Local Health Care Benefits. *The Municipal Yearbook.* Washington, DC: The International City/County Management Association.

Center for Personnel Research. 1996a. *Personnel Practices: Domestic Partners.* Alexandria, VA.: International Personnel Management Association.

Center for Personnel Research. 1996b. *Personnel Practices: Employee Assistance Programs (EAP).* Alexandria, VA.: International Personnel Management Association.

Center for Personnel Research. 1997. *Personnel Practices: Elderly Issues.* Alexandria, VA.: International Personnel Management Association.

Center for Personnel Research. 1998. *Personnel Practices: Telecommuting.* Alexandria, VA.: International Personnel Management Association.

ELLIS, W. H. 1993. Employee Benefits: Trends and Issues in the 1990s. *Compensation and Benefits Review* 25 (November-December):37–41.

Employee Benefit Research Institute. 1997. *EBRI Databook on Employee Benefits.* Washington, DC: Employee Benefit Research Institute.

FINKLE, A. L. 1997. Designing a Safety Net for Employees. *Public Personnel Management* 26 (Spring): 123–138.

GOLD, S. D., and S. RITCHIE. 1993. Compensation of State and Local Employees: Sorting Out the Issues. In *Revitalizing State and Local Public Service: Strengthening Performance, Accountability and Citizen Confidence,* F. J. Thompson, ed. San Francisco: Jossey-Bass, 163–196.

HANDEL, B. 1992. Financing Health Care Coverage in the Public Sector: Costs, Risks and Options. In *Public Employee Benefit Plans,* M. J. Brzezinski, ed. Brookfield, WI: International Federation of Employee Benefit Plans.

HOSTETLER, D., and PYNES, J. E. 1995. Domestic Partnership Benefits–Dispelling the Myth. *Review of Public Personnel Management* xv (Winter):41–59.

KHAVARI, I. 1998. Choices for a Secure Retirement. *American City and County* 113, No. 9 (August):41–47.

KIRRANE, D. E. 1994. Wanted: Flexible Work Arrangements. *Association Management* (November).

LEVINE, C. 1993-94. Employee Benefits: Growing in Diversity and Cost. *Occupational Outlook Quarterly* (Winter):39–42.

MCCABE, B. C., and C. STREAM. 2000. Diversity by the Numbers: Changes in State and Local Government Workforces 1980-1995. *Public Personnel Management* 1 (Spring):93–106.

PAOLELLA, M. A. 1995. *Auditing Health Care Benefits: How to Manage Costs and Minimize Risks.* New York: John Wiley & Sons, Inc.

PLATT, R. K. 2000. Value of Benefits Remains Constant. *Workspan* 43, No. 6 (June):34–39.

RAYMAN, P., and L. BAILYN, et al. 1998. *The Radcliffe-Fleet Project: Creating Work and Life Integration Solutions.* Cambridge, MA: Radcliffe Public Policy Institute.

SMITH, K. D. 1996. Comprehensive Leave: Pros and Cons. *IPMA News* (July):22–23.

STREIB, G. 1996. Speciality Health Care Services in Municipal Government. *Review of Public Personnel Administration* 16 (Spring):57–72.

U.S. Bureau of the Census. 1994. *Statistical Abstract of the United States, 1994.* Washington, DC: U.S. Government Printing Office.

Section Three

THE ISSUES

New personnel policy issues are constantly emerging as long-standing problem areas undergo metamorphosis. The traditional, technical concerns of the personnel manager remain important, but an increasing proportion of his or her time must be invested in policy concerns such as productivity improvements, managing diversity, accommodating the handicapped, and serving as a buffer between line managers and the legal and practical requirements of a complex workplace. Increasingly, the personnelist's role is that of a consultant who assists line managers with sticky human resource problems arising from the issue areas that are discussed in the following chapters.

The first two chapters in this section focus on a closely related topic, the push for *productivity* that also includes pressures to *outsource* many public services (including human resource management functions). Berman analyzes the productivity and privatization theme in Chapter 13, and Lawther fine-tunes the treatment with a more focused examination of the outsourcing phenomenon.

Although they deal with a variety of critical topics, the next five chapters all relate to the issue of workplace *diversity*. Kellough provides an overview of the age-old EEO/AA topic. Succeeding chapters embellish the treatment by addressing gender issues (Mary Guy), the changing nature of the workforce (Sonia Ospina and James O'Sullivan), sexual harassment (Sally Selden), and the Americans with Disabilities Act (Bonnie Mani). Together these chapters comprise a primer on pitfalls and challenges that might befall any manager, and offer advice on how to avoid the traps that have caught large numbers of civil servants over the years.

Chapter 20 is representative of one of the most significant changes that has occurred in public management in recent years, the advent of nonprofit management and voluntarism as issues of major concern. Jeff Brudney's treatment of the volunteer worker provides a provocative look at both myths and realities, and suggests a number of practical strategies that can help public executives make maximum use of "unpaid" labor. The final chapter in the section—Jon West's discussion of ethics—once again demonstrates that the human resource office often is given responsibility for overseeing the behavior of the civil service. Understanding the fact that public employees are held to a higher standard of conduct than are workers in the private sector is an essential part of the education process for prospective government managers.

13

Productivity and Privatization
The Human Resource Management Connection

EVAN BERMAN
University of Central Florida

Productivity improvement encompasses a broad range of strategies, such as strategic planning, customer service improvement, reengineering, information technology, employee empowerment, privatization, and the use of public-private partnerships. Productivity improvement helps governments to improve the cost-effectiveness of their services and increase responsiveness to citizen and client needs. For example, through information technology, governments can improve communication and interaction with citizens, such as when they are able to submit requests and retrieve data with increased speed and accuracy (Berman, 1998; Light, 1998; Osborne and Plastrick, 1997). These strategies can also be used to enhance the effectiveness of human resource management, such as by privatizing benefits management and using information technology for on-line recruitment or job evaluation.

What is the role of human resource management (HRM) in productivity improvement? Salaries often comprise a huge part of government budgets and so efforts to improve the productivity of employees and managers are important. Specifically, the introduction of new work processes often requires employee training, perhaps for improving customer service or using information technology in some new way. HRM also assists in implementing productivity improvement efforts by reassigning existing workers or hiring new ones when doing so becomes necessary. HRM further impacts productivity through the organizational culture that it helps shape through its policies.

Bringing productivity improvement into the role of human resource management is to underscore the potential strategic, value-added contribution of HRM to the organization. HRM can lead in helping organizations improve, and

HR managers who assist line department managers in their reform efforts often find a receptive ear: A survey of city managers finds that almost three-quarters (74.8 percent) agree with the statement that "implementing productivity improvement makes me more attractive to other employers" and 68.4 percent state that it has helped their career (Berman and West, 1999). Very few respondents believe that it has hurt their career, and those who emphasize pay-offs from productivity improvement strongly associate it with managerial professionalism. Emphasizing productivity improvement in human resource management stands in contrast to traditional HRM roles that highlight compliance efforts with rules and legal regulations. Modern human resource management emphasizes value added, and balances the need for compliance with the desire for increases in organizational performance.

The following sections discuss: (1) ways through which HRM affects productivity by shaping organizational culture; (2) contributions of human resource management to specific productivity improvement efforts such as customer service improvement and reengineering; and (3) the role of HRM in privatization, and the effects of recent efforts to downsize and privatize the human resource management function.[1]

HRM AND THE ORGANIZATIONAL CULTURE

It is readily observed that some organizations are more prone to improving themselves than others. Cities such as Scottsdale, Arizona, have won international recognition for their excellence, whereas many others have not. Some states such as Minnesota are often at the forefront of social policy, whereas other states are not. A factor that explains this phenomenon is organizational culture. In some organizations, top managers consistently and persistently seek out new opportunities to better serve their clients and citizens, and they get enthusiastic collaboration from supervisors and employees for their efforts. Being innovative is the norm; it is what is expected of all members. These organizations need not imitate the management reforms that are pursued elsewhere; they are just as likely to invent new practices themselves without even labeling them as "innovative." While we do not know how widespread these orientations are, it is readily observed that some cities are indeed consistently at the forefront of innovation. This stands in marked contrast to many other organizations in which the collective mindset favors the status quo and "not rocking the boat." Such values, when widespread, work against improvement. They are unlikely to spur "homegrown" improvement or support those adapted from elsewhere (Levin & Sanger, 1994; Frederickson, 1999).

The term "organizational culture" has been defined in many different ways, yet a consensus exists that organizational cultures involve *an enduring pattern of fun-*

---

[1] Productivity is defined as the effective and efficient use of resources to achieve outcomes (Berman, 1998). Public productivity involves both the effectiveness (goal-attainment) and efficiency (cost-effectiveness) of services. For example, many citizens care that emergency response services arrive on time (effectiveness), and they are somewhat less concerned about the cost of such timely arrival (efficiency). By contrast, many definitions of productivity in the private sector emphasize only efficiency, which is linked to profitability. The coverage of productivity topics in the public sector is decidedly broad, reflecting emphases on effectiveness as well as efficiency.

damental beliefs, norms, values and assumptions that is held by a group (e.g., Schein, 1985). When "making the customer your first priority" is a consistent value that is held by a majority of its members, this value is said to be part of the organizational culture. The organizational culture is the sum of the widely held beliefs, values, norms and assumptions of its members. Although different units within an agency often have different organizational cultures, all are affected by the tone, examples, and strategies of top management. For example, when putting the customer first is widely espoused in word and deed by top managers, and followed up through rewards and sanctions, this norm is likely to affect behavior of employees and managers at lower echelons. It is widely acknowledged that top management plays a very important role in shaping organizational culture.[2]

Although organizational cultures are as varied as the workplaces in which they occur, Bardwick (1995) provides a typology of typically prevalent cultures that are relevant to productivity improvement. She distinguishes cultures of fear, entitlement, and revitalization. In short, *cultures of fear* often cause their members to experience high levels of stress due to threats of maltreatment. Members emphasize winning and "coming out ahead" by any means, at any cost. Managers in these environments may thrive on keeping others off guard as a means of gaining advantage. Fear may be augmented when organizations experience periods of limited resource growth, hence reducing promotion opportunities. Then, members exhibit frustration and resentment over personnel decisions that reflect more politics than merit. *Cultures of entitlement* are typified by a "rights" mentality: people should be left alone as long as they abide by workplace rules and regulations and generally do what is asked of them (from nine to five, of course). Workers in such organizations often appear lethargic and complacent, as rewards and job security are automatic. In cultures of both entitlement and fear it is as if the culture shouts to its members: "Don't rock the boat!," or, "if you don't like the way things are, take a hike!" Such values work against efforts to improve organizations.

Cultures of revitalization, which are sometimes called cultures of excellence or earning, are characterized by values that emphasize the importance of attaining missions and supporting the efforts of workers, clients, and other stakeholders. In such organizations, employees and managers are empowered and energized by challenging and rewarding assignments. They are judged by their accomplishments, not by their loyalties. Risk taking is encouraged, and mistakes are tolerated in view of positive outcomes. In these cultures, managers push themselves and others to excel just beyond the possible and are prepared for playing hardball and coping with misfortune. They pay attention to details, encourage ideas from others, delegate responsibility but insist on accountability, and keep learning from others inside and outside the organization. Modern productivity improvement efforts often emphasize values that are consistent with cultures of revitalization. Van Wart

---

[2] It is not always easy to know what the organizational culture is in a workplace. Longtime members know that slogans such as "Customers first!" are just that when they are not followed by enduring actions that cause them to find widespread acceptance among most organizational members. New slogans quickly disappear when they do not become ingrained in the organizational consciousness that is organizational culture. Yet, organizations often do not advertise their organizational culture: A chief role of top managers is to explain to members, through persistent actions, what the organizational culture is. Newcomers are especially subject to confusion about the true nature of an organization's culture: they learn it slowly over time, usually from responses that they receive from their actions.

and Berman (1999) discuss how modern productivity values underscore the importance of effectiveness, dependability, responsiveness, consultation, openness, and shared responsibility.

It is easy to see how revitalized cultures pull forth productivity. Workers whose opinions are sought and evaluated against the mission, and who are provided with feedback, encouragement, and responsibility are more likely to suggest opportunities for improvement and to be receptive to the ideas of others in this regard. Imagine how employee attitudes and behaviors are affected by routinely observing how others receive positive consequences from their efforts to improve the organization. Such workers, and their supervisors, come to expect improvement initiatives from time to time and realize that they are held accountable, in part, by how well they contribute to the mission and promote excellence. Managers who are prepared to deal with setbacks are also more likely to succeed in overcoming temporary obstacles that improvement efforts often encounter (Kearney and Berman, 1999; West and Berman, 1997).

Consequences for HRM

The task of human resource management is to shape and sustain productive work cultures. Human resource management affects organizational culture through its policies and sanctions. Productive work settings are built on productive behaviors, and positive reinforcement can be used to strengthen productive behaviors. In the words of B. F. Skinner, "behavior is shaped and maintained by its consequences" (Skinner, 1971). Examples of HRM policies that managers can use to reinforce productive behaviors include promotion based on achievement rather than loyalty or time in grade, rewards premised on achievement, employee empowerment, skills training, and other policies and sanctions consistent with cultures of revitalization. Employees must perceive the organization's policies and sanctions as sufficiently consequential to support productive behaviors. The challenge facing human resource management is to ensure that organizations have a broad range of such policies and sanctions which support revitalization, and also to ensure that managers use them for this purpose.

What types of consequences are "effective"? Consequences are effective when they are immediate, certain, and substantial (Daniels, 1994). In this regard, some managers complain about the lack of financial rewards to shape behavior and that such rewards are seldom immediate. Even private sector organizations have many constraints on the amount and frequency of such inducements. Rather, managers must rely on other positive consequences such as taking notice and giving appreciation, providing training or travel support for conference attendance, giving a choice assignment or opportunity, providing additional administrative support, allowing an employee to work at home on Friday, providing job rotation for a month, making someone team leader for a week or month, giving a small cash award, or book, or movie certificate.

Perhaps the greatest challenge to ensuring positive cultures of revitalization lies in the lack of positive reinforcement. HRM policies and rewards are ineffective when they are not used. Managers may fail to acknowledge excellence, perhaps mistakingly thinking that compensation is a sufficient positive reward. In fact, because compensation is largely automatic, it should not be regarded as a consequence at all. At best, the fear of losing compensation provides minimal motivation to avoid sanctions, but not to excel. Managers may also neglect to encourage ways in which employees and organizations can mutually improve themselves. Human resource management can play an important role by ensuring that managers use policies and sanctions that strengthen productive work cultures.

While positive consequences reinforce behavior, negative consequences squelch it. Negative sanctions include negative performance appraisals (which often are infrequent and seldom immediate) and critical verbal feedback and reprimands. Fortunately, many managers have learned how to provide negative feedback in a cautious way, balancing criticism with opportunities for future betterment. Then, negative feedback may be the first step in the process of progressive discipline, the process whereby subsequent sanctions are consistently more severe, leading up to suspension and termination. Many workers will alter their behavior in order to avoid negative sanctions while, hopefully, embracing actions that are consistent with increased productivity.

In conclusion, HRM policies and sanctions are consequences that managers can use for shoring up the organizational culture, not merely for exercising managerial power and control. Clearly, the task of HRM goes beyond performance appraisal and protecting the organization against legal entanglements due to employee conduct. The challenge of human resource management is to ensure that managers have access to a broad range of consequences and that they use these tools for the purpose of creating a culture that promotes productivity.

HRM AND PRODUCTIVITY IMPROVEMENT EFFORTS

It is highly probable that the 1990s will be remembered as the decade in which Total Quality Management (TQM) was first introduced into governments and ingrained in the organizational cultures of many jurisdictions (Brudney et al., 1999; Gore, 1996; West, 1995). At present, the major elements of TQM continue to be further implemented and developed. TQM is a management philosophy that encompasses various productivity improvement strategies: customer orientation, empowerment, reengineering, and performance measurement with an orientation toward continuous improvement. Now, at the beginning of a new century, most jurisdictions have had exposure to several of these strategies, and many have made at least some of them part of their modus operandi.[3]

Customer-friendly services, increased timeliness, the lack of errors, fewer hassles are values that find wide, indeed, global appeal with citizens, program clients, and consumers. Empirical studies show that many factors drive public

---

[3] Quality concepts were first developed in the United States during World War II, for the production of wartime machinery such as airplanes, radios, and tanks. Such equipment required a higher standard of precision and reliability than that used in consumer goods. These superior techniques were largely abandoned by U.S. firms after the war in support of cheaper conventional methods, but Japanese firms readily adapted these techniques as they rebuilt their economy. U.S. firms rediscovered these techniques in the late 1970s when confronted with then-superior quality and costs of Japanese goods, especially automobiles and consumer electronics. Following the response by U.S. multinational firms, other large firms begun to use TQM in the 1980s, and the federal government joined in during the late 1980s. Other levels of governments followed in the 1990s.

sector use of TQM, especially public complaints, budget pressures, and the search for new directions (Berman and West, 1995). TQM aims to address these problems. Although early applications of TQM emphasized a radical and simultaneous introduction of various strategies, in recent years a cautious, but effective, approach has emerged which introduces these strategies in a piecemeal fashion, implementing one strategy at a time. During the late 1990s, it became quite common to observe public organizations implementing different TQM-based strategies. Many strategies begin as pilot projects in organizations, and are diffused as the organization and its top managers gain more confidence in them.

Human resource management furthers the use of TQM and other productivity improvement strategies. First, many strategies require new employee skills which, in turn, require worker training and which also prompt organizations to hire workers in these new areas. For example, large public organizations often hire workers with skills in strategic planning or survey research. Second, some efforts result in the reassignment of employees, due to the elimination of old duties. Reassignment involves numerous human resource management tasks, including performance evaluation as well as promoting early retirement and out-placement options. Third, managers must address employees who resist change, and may require training or support from HRM when dealing with this challenge. Sometimes, the introduction of productivity improvement strategies is an expeditious occasion for dealing with "problem" employees. Fourth, new emphasis on customer orientation may require the modification of current performance appraisal and evaluation criteria. Sixth, managers and supervisors need to increase their awareness of new efforts, and human resource management can shape the accep-tance of productivity improvement efforts through the organizational culture.

Customer Orientation

Many government services increased customer-orientation during the last decade. Admittedly, some agencies still have a long way to go toward client satisfaction, but many examples of customer improvement come to mind: quick refunds from the Internal Revenue Service (including convenient electronic filing and deposit of refunds), one-stop shopping for grant and permit applications, and on-line access to public data and records. Norms of customer satisfaction increase emphasis on mission-orientation and work against protecting turf and other bureaucratic games. Organizations have restructured their service delivery and now routinely monitor whether clients are treated in a courteous, prompt and effective way. The term "customer" includes employees in other offices, not only "external" clients such as citizens.

Getting employees to act in more customer-oriented ways attests to the power of emphasizing consequences. Many government departments have developed tough, negative consequences for inappropriate customer conduct (Van Wart and Berman, 1999). Employees who cause customer complaints are removed from direct interactions with customers and thereafter may find their career opportunities limited. Expectations for customer service are unambiguously defined (being courteous, getting back to clients within specified time frames, etc.). Using three-hundred sixty degree (360°) feedback is a human resource management strategy that furthers customer service improvement. This performance appraisal strategy includes feedback from clients used to reward and encourage improvements. Clients are surveyed and their comments become part of an employee's performance record. Unsolicited comments are also part of the record, such as service compliments and complaints.

Of interest also are positive consequences that are given to managers for improving customer service in their units. Many managers receive favorable appraisals when they reduce complaints. This causes them not only to "crack down" on inappropriate behavior, but also to invest in redesigning service delivery processes to increase timeliness and client convenience, thus reducing dissatisfaction. An example would be extended business hours.

Training supports customer service. For instance, it helps employees to respond to particularly difficult situations. While some training is generic (for example, how to deal with upset or irrational customers), other training is task-specific, such as helping employees to learn new customer inquiry response systems, or assisting employees in addressing infrequent, but difficult requests. One example of such training is that of human resource management staff providing prompt and courteous responses to employees' requests for changes in, or information about, health care or retirement benefits.

Reengineering

This productivity improvement effort takes a "ground zero" or blank slate approach to redesigning existing delivery processes for the purpose of increasing timeliness and customer satisfaction, and reducing error rates and costs. Managers ask: "What is the best way to deliver this service, ignoring any commitment to how it is currently done?" Typical drivers of reengineering efforts are frequent delays in service calls, errors in invoicing, or approval processes which result in high levels of client rancor. These outcomes are sometimes caused by ill-structured work processes, rather than incompetent workers. An example of reengineered work processes is a one-stop shopping center in which service personnel coordinate customer requests and provide clients with a uniform response. This increases customer satisfaction by eliminating the contradictory information customers sometimes receive from different offices. It also increases timeliness because service personnel are usually empowered to get quick responses from staff who can cut through red tape (Linden, 1994; Hyde, 1995).

Many reengineering efforts require adaptive learning by employees and managers. Reengineered services often arise from customer and employee suggestions. They typically are new and untried, and mistakes must be expected and viewed as an opportunity for getting it right. On-the-job training may be unavailable because jobs are wholly new to the organization. Human resource management aids the success of these efforts by promoting norms of learning: continuous improvement and positive reinforcement, rather than punishment. Openness to suggestions, recognition of accomplishment, and mission-orientation contribute to success. Reengineering is not only facilitated by cultures of revitalization, it is also an opportunity for strengthening these cultures.

Employees may fear that such efforts will affect their jobs, and an important human resource management function is therefore to address this anxiety. Typically, employees are assured that they will be reassigned to comparable jobs in the event that existing jobs are eliminated. However, in some instances managers use reengineering as an opportunity for eliminating unproductive workers. Then, employees are required to apply for positions, and those who are not accepted may be dismissed. The dismissal of such workers may enhance opportunity for productivity improvement, yet it also raises concerns which may affect the motivation of remaining workers.

Employee reassignment and change in working conditions can bring reengineering within the scope of labor-management negotiations. Ban (1995) notes that the National Performance Review included an emphasis on labor-management partnership, in which employees were given a voice in identifying better ways of serving customers. Similarly, in Seattle, each department established an umbrella Labor-Management Committee which chartered Employee Involvement Committees around activities that were ripe for improvement and reengineering (Lyons and Vivenzio, 1998). These committees were allowed to discuss all issues (including work and working conditions), except those involving wages and benefits. Within two years, thirty-six committees had been established which proposed and helped implement new productivity improvement efforts. Such partnerships are still regarded as experimental at this time.

Empowerment

Employee empowerment is the strategy of giving employees greater authority while holding them accountable for outcomes. Empowerment is a cornerstone of productivity improvement: it strengthens outcome-orientation and enables employees to better meet the needs of their clients. For example, in one-stop shopping, frontline staff are empowered to meet clients' needs. Empowered employees define their roles in terms of outcomes, not simply by whether they have followed rules and regulations. Empowerment may also improve the effectiveness of work teams, by giving both employees and the team more responsibility for outcomes.

Employee empowerment requires management training. Human resource managers regularly face the challenge of persuading middle managers that employee empowerment will not reduce the ability of middle managers to control employees' outcomes, for which managers are responsible. Empowerment training for managers involves learning alternative styles of leadership, improved communication skills, team building, motivation, change management, and stress reduction. Empowerment emphasizes participatory and facilitative leadership styles, rather than those that limit employee initiative (Bowman, 1994). Often, human resource managers work with senior managers to establish new standards for appraising middle managers.

Many employees also resist empowerment, because it provides them less shelter from capricious managers. Some resist because they feel that they are being asked to do more with no additional rewards; others may refuse to abandon old processes. Therefore, managers must explain to workers why they are asking them to do more and assume more responsibility. They must provide employees with adequate authority for dealing with various problems that may occur, address new criteria for evaluation, and help employees meet these criteria through feedback and training. Empowerment is often frustrated by inadequate forethought to the risks and challenges associated with it (Kirkman and Rosen, 2000; Plunket and Fournier, 1991).

Information Technology

Information technology is ubiquitous as a productivity improvement strategy. Although not developed as a quality improvement effort, many applications of information technology are based on the same principles: making services more customer-friendly, timely, and less prone to error. In addition, information technology is used to reduce service delivery costs. Examples of information technology include Internet-based customer transactions (e.g., license renewals), e-mail and teleconferencing, electronic dissemination of documents, improved handling of telephone inquiries, automated inventory control, automatic billing, and so on. Information technology applications are also found in human resource management, such as automated payroll and benefits management.

The challenges of information technology for human resource management are in many ways similar to those already mentioned: training, adaptive learning, and reassignment. Managers often underestimate the cost of training associated with the use of new systems or the amount of errors that often occur within the first few months. The introduction of new information technology upsets existing routines and is apt to generate significant employee and customer confusion. Training sometimes costs 10–20 percent of the total expenditures for new information technology systems, and the absence of training delays implementation of a new technology. Human resource managers must budget for adequate training, time, and staff to avoid or deal with the ensuing problems.

In recent years, some jurisdictions have reviewed their strategic management of information technology. Increasingly, jurisdictions are recruiting senior managers who can guide their organizations in the proper use of information technology through better policies and productivity applications. Many have hired Chief Information Officers. They also need individuals who can ensure coordination between information technology units and the rest of the organization, as well as educate top managers and others in recent uses and developments in information technology. In short, information technology is increasingly viewed as a resource function that requires organization.

Information technology has raised other issues for human resource management, specifically the need to ensure that employees and managers use it in productive ways. HR policies are necessary to ensure that workers respect confidential information. Many jurisdictions have developed policies about the personal use of computer. Some jurisdictions allow employees to use their office computers for limited personal use, though not for personal gain. In a few instances, workers have used their computers to access and distribute pornographic material obtained through the Internet. Such actions have spurred new policies that prohibit this (Menzel, 1998).

Finally, information technology also affects how HRM carries out some other roles. For example, information technology provides new opportunities for implementing the provisions of the Americans with Disabilities Act of 1990. Specifically, information technology helps organizations to accommodate persons with auditory impairments (making speech visible), and recent keyboard enhancement packages help persons deal with visual and physical impairments. Many of these computer adaptations are quite affordable but pose a new challenge for HRM professionals in their regulatory compliance roles (Mondak, 2000).

Strategic Planning

Strategic planning is the effort to develop new goals and missions for agencies, and reach consensus about them. Although agency missions are broadly set in legislation, many agencies have undertaken to analyze their present and future conditions to suggest new courses of action. Strategic planning is a participatory process that scans the external environment of agencies, takes into account internal strengths and weaknesses, and develops priorities that assist in allocating subsequent resources and efforts. Strategic planning is now routine in the public sector, and many public managers contribute to it. A variant of strategic planning is community-based strategic planning. This involves public agencies working with their stakeholders to formulate plans and strategies for dealing with community problems, requiring the efforts of numerous public and private organizations. These efforts are often embraced by elected officials, who welcome their constituencies' participation in shaping the roles of public agencies.

Strategic planning is increasingly applied to human resource management. Specifically, an enduring challenge for the public sector is to ensure adequate, qualified personnel. Many managers appear to believe that they will be able to count on adequate personnel, yet qualified employees are sometimes hard to secure. A need exists for more competitive compensation, making public sector employment attractive for recent graduates, ensuring a diverse workforce and giving adequate incentives to employees to upgrade their skills. Strategic planning for human resources can help address this problem. In some locales, this will help organizations to catch up with existing practices in other jurisdictions, such as flextime, providing access to day care, giving tuition reimbursement and paid leave for education, and mandatory supervisory training. Strategic planning for human resource management can also identify new productivity improvement needs, such as empowerment and reengineering, to create the structures in which the workforce can be more productive (National Academy of Public Administration [NAPA], 1998; Thompson, 1993).

HRM AND PRIVATIZATION

Privatization is the effort to reduce the role of the public sector in the economy; contracting for service delivery with private firms is one such strategy. Privatization of public services is a widely used strategy for reducing costs and is frequently used in municipal waste collection, janitorial services, park maintenance, fleet operations, security, snow removal, and employee training. Private firms often have lower costs than governments due to economies of scale that come from providing services to numerous organizations. They sometimes also have greater flexibility, which allows them to keep costs down. Even space and defense contractors have made the case that they can more efficiently manage operations than public agencies.

Privatization has an antigovernment bias and is controversial. During the early 1980s, privatization found great interest among conservative leaders who used it for reducing the role of government in society. Early efforts included airline and banking deregulation which led to uncontrolled risk-taking that eliminated many efficiency gains. Cutbacks on welfare spending also produced costly side effects, such as increases in homeless persons. However, contracting for service delivery yielded some mixed successes (Boyne, 1998; Hirsch and Osborne, 2000). In some instances, firms indeed are more efficient providers. Yet, some firms underbid in order to get public contracts, and then sharply raise prices in subsequent years, hence eliminating cost savings for citizens. This appears to be the case with cable TV rates in many jurisdictions. The quality of service may also suffer. For example, private trash collectors may be less responsive to citizens than municipal service crews, especially in small towns.

Despite these problems, contracting for service delivery remains popular. Some municipalities deal with the above problems by contracting no more than one-quarter of a service during a contract period. This allows agencies to re-bid in subsequent years and ensures competition for private providers. Private contracting has caused some agencies to improve their cost structures and also to reduce red tape (Enos, 1996; Cohen and Eimicke, 1999). Some agencies include performance standards in their contract which allow jurisdictions to terminate contracts or to penalize ineffective providers. They also allow jurisdictions to renegotiate terms and conditions without fear of lengthy litigation or service disruption, always credible threats by providers (McGillicuddy, 1996).

Despite widespread fear among employees, contracting does not always produce layoffs (Elam, 1997). Many employees are reassigned, and some staffing problems are handled through natural attrition. Yet, fear of demotion or job loss may spur employee litigation and grievances, and collective bargaining agreements may require governments to negotiate with unions when public service jobs are to be replaced by those of contractors, regardless of whether or not lay-offs occur. Penalties for violating the negotiation requirement typically include immediate reinstatement with back pay of employees who are affected. HR managers play an important role in negotiating with unions and thereby keeping privatization efforts moving forward. In some instances, they also negotiate with private firms to ensure continued employment and comparable benefits of public workers who are laid off (Becker and Silverstein, 1995).

Privatization has also been used to reduce the cost of some human resource management activities (Davidson, 1998). Many jurisdictions have contracted out their employee training, benefits administration, Employee Assistance Programs, temporary staffing, and payroll. Private firms are able to provide these routine services, but HR managers remain responsible for policy development and ensuring that services meet the needs of employees. For example, using outside consultants as trainers does not relieve the responsibility for identifying new training topics and thinking about improvement in delivery.

Privatization of human resource management can help overworked HR departments focus on strategic issues. As routine tasks are shed, human resource managers can focus on such activities as risk management, ensuring that potential employee problems are resolved before they result in litigation. HR managers may also address steps that are required to adapt the workplace to the twenty-first century, ensure a diverse and skilled workforce, and help other managers in their productivity improvement efforts.

CONCLUSION

All organizations must strive to improve their productivity. Human resource management supports productivity improvement in different ways. It shapes the organizational culture and supports efforts of managers to implement a broad range of productivity strategies. Human resource managers also provide training, rewards, sanctions, staffing, and reassignment assistance in efforts to improve productivity. As expectations for productivity improvement increase, so, too, does the demand for these HR activities. Managers who wish to place human resource management at the center of their agencies can do so by raising awareness about the organizational culture and rewards and sanctions, as important strategic concerns. They also work with managers to ensure a useful set of rewards and provide a range of training and other activities that support the efforts of managers. Through these activities, human resource managers increase the value of HRM to their organizations.

REFERENCES

BAN, C. 1995. Unions, Management and the NPR. In D. Kettl and J. DiIulio, eds. *Inside the Reinvention Machine: Appraising Governmental Reform.* Washington, DC: Brookings Institution, chapter 5.

BARDWICK, J. 1995. *Danger in the Comfort Zone.* New York: AMACOM.

BECKER, F., and G. SILVERSTEIN. 1995. Public Employee Job Security and Benefits: A Barrier to Privatization in Mental Health Services. *Public Productivity & Management Review* 19 (1):25–34.

BERMAN, E. 1998. *Productivity in Public and Nonprofit Organizations.* Thousand Oaks, CA: SAGE.

———, and J. WEST. 1999. Career Risk and Reward from Productivity. *Public Personnel Management* 28 (3):453–471.

———. 1995. Municipal Commitment to Total Quality Management. *Public Administration Review* 55 (1):57–66.

BOWMAN, J. 1994. At Last, an Alternative to Performance Appraisal: Total Quality Management. *Public Administration Review* 54 (2):129–136.

BOYNE, G. 1998. Bureaucratic Theory Meets Reality: Public Choice and Service Contracting in U.S. Local Government. *Public Administration Review* 58 (6):474–484.

BRUDNEY, J., T. HEBERT, and D. WRIGHT. 1999. Reinventing Government in the American States: Measuring and Explaining Administrative Reform. *Public Administration Review* 59 (1):19–30.

COHEN, S., and W. EIMICKE. 1999. Is Public Entrepreneurship Ethical? *Public Integrity* 1 (1):54–74.

DANIELS, A. 1994. *Bringing Out the Best in People.* New York: McGraw-Hill.

DAVIDSON, L. 1998. Cutting Away Non-Core HR. *Workforce* 77 (1):41–47.

ELAM, L. 1997. Reinventing Government Privatization-Style—Avoiding the Legal Pitfalls of Replacing Civil Servants with Contract Providers. *Public Personnel Management* 26 (1):15–34.

ENOS, G. 1996. Compete or Else. *Governing* 10 (2):40–41.

FREDERICKSON, H. 1999. Hijacking Public Administration. *PA Times* 22 (3):9.

GORE, A. 1996. *The Best Kept Secrets in Government.* New York: Random House.

HIRSCH, W., and E. OSBORNE. 2000. Privatization of Government Services: Pressure-group Resistance and Service Transparency. *Journal of Labor Research* 21 (2):315–327.

HYDE, A. 1995. A Primer on Process Reengineering. *Public Manager* 24 (10):55–68.

KEARNEY, R., and E. BERMAN. 1999. *Public Sector Performance.* Boulder, CO: Westview Press.

KIRKMAN, B., and B. ROSEN. 2000. Powering up Teams. *Organizational Dynamics* 28 (3):48–66.

LEVIN, M., and M. SANGER. 1994. *Making Government Work.* San Francisco, CA: Jossey-Bass Publishers.

LIGHT, P. 1998. *Sustaining Innovation: Creating Nonprofit and Government Organizations that Innovate Naturally.* San Francisco, CA: Jossey-Bass.

LINDEN, R. 1994. Reengineering to Capture the Customer's Voice: *Public Manager* 23 (2):47–50.

LYONS, L., and A. VIVENZIO. 1998. Employee Involvement in Seattle: Reengineering Government in a City Lacking a Financial Crisis. *Public Personnel Management* 27 (1):93–102.

MCGILLICUDDY. J. 1996. A Blueprint for Privatization and Competition. *Public Manager* 78 (10):8–13.

MENZEL, D. 1998. *www.ethics.gov:* Issues and Challenges Facing Public Managers. *Public Administration Review* 58 (5):445–452.

MONDAK, P. 2000. The Americans with Disabilities Act and Information Technology Access. *Focus on Autism and Other Developmental Disabilities* 15 (1):43–52.

National Academy of Public Administration. 1998. *Work/Life Programs: Helping Managers, Helping Employees.* Washington, DC: author.

OSBORNE, D., and P. PLASTRICK. 1997. *Banishing Bureaucracy.* Reading, MA: Addison-Wesley Publishing.

PLUNKET, L., and R. FOURNIER. 1991. *Participative Management: Implementing Empowerment.* San Francisco, CA: Jossey-Bass.

SCHEIN, E. 1985. *Organizational Culture and Leadership.* San Francisco, CA: Jossey-Bass.

SKINNER, B. F. 1971. *Contingency of Reinforcement.* East Norwalk, CT: Appleton.

THOMPSON, F., ed. 1993. *Revitalizing State and Local Public Service.* San Francisco, CA: Jossey-Bass.

VAN WART, M., and E. BERMAN. 1999. Contemporary Public Sector Values: Narrower Scope, Tougher Standards, and New Rules of the Game. *Public Productivity & Management Review* 22 (3):326–347.

WEST, J., and E. BERMAN. 1997. Administrative Creativity in Local Government. *Public Productivity & Management Review* 20 (4):446–458.

WEST, J. 1995. *Quality Management Today.* Washington, DC.: International City/County Management Association.

14

Privatizing Personnel
Outsourcing Public Sector Functions

WENDELL C. LAWTHER
University of Central Florida

Privatization or outsourcing of services formerly provided in-house has become a strategy used by an increasing number of local and state governments nationwide. A recent survey of municipal officials indicated that most officials privatized in order to lower service delivery costs and/or to improve service quality (Greene, 1996). Most of these officials are satisfied with the results of privatization efforts.

At the federal level, the issuance of the A-76 Circular by the Office of Management and Budget in 1967 directed all agencies to contract out or privatize all existing commercial activities that were not considered essential to government (Kettl, 1993). More recently, the National Performance Review, in its efforts to encourage reinvention and reengineering of government, spawned additional interest in privatization (Gore, 1993).

On a broader, international level, privatization is part of a worldwide revolution in public management, entitled the New Public Management (NPM). The NPM indicates that public managers should make service delivery decisions that are the most efficient and based upon the satisfaction of those who receive these services. Citizens are viewed as customers, and they must be given choices in the same way as they would in the market place. The competition inherent in privatization efforts, as private vendors—and often public employees—compete to win the contract to deliver a service, provides the best and most efficient services.

This commitment to increased customer service and employee productivity that accompanies privatization has provided new roles and challenges for the human resource (HR) manager. As government privatizes existing services, the HR manager is called upon to:

- assist in allaying employee and union concerns
- help with cost savings analyses
- participate in writing the privatization request for proposal
- train public employees who wish to compete
- help to limit the number of discharged employees
- interpret appropriate laws and personnel regulations as privatization occurs

In addition, the complementary trend to decentralize HR in many governments, as well as removal of many of the civil service rules and regulations, has increased the flexibility of governments to become more receptive to outsourcing HR functions. Demographic trends, such as the need to replace many of the baby boomers who will be retiring, also provide new challenges to the HR manager that could be faced most effectively by outsourcing.

This chapter analyzes three of the most significant challenges that privatization presents to the HR manager. First, when a jurisdiction is considering privatizing an already existing service, the public employees delivering the service become quite concerned about their future. Public union officials may voice concerns, as well, and may counter the privatization efforts. At a minimum, both the public employees and union officials need to be kept informed of all deliberations and involved in the decision-making process as much as possible. Otherwise, an effort to privatize that would save costs and/or improve service quality may be derailed.

Second, once the decision to privatize has been made, there are serious implications for the public employees presently providing the service. In some cases, employees have been simply laid off, with no consideration given to their future employment. In most cases, however, governments have shown concern for their employees in various ways. The HR manager can help to encourage and/or train them to create a bid in competition with private vendors. In the contract with the private vendor, public employees can be guaranteed the "right of first refusal" for jobs with that vendor. Often the HR manager can help find positions within other government agencies for employees who do not wish to work for the vendor or who are close to retirement. Finally, outplacement services are offered as well. The HR manager potentially can play a variety of roles in implementing the concern that city officials may have for their employees.

Third, HR managers are not only implementers of privatization; many HR functions and services are also the targets in both public and private sectors. For some services, such as employment assistance programs, there is a long-standing tradition of outsourcing to private and nonprofit firms. For others, such as flexible staffing and payroll, private firms are more likely to outsource these functions than their public sector counterparts.

THE ENVIRONMENT SURROUNDING PRIVATIZATION DECISIONS

When a city is deciding whether to privatize an already existing service, cost and service quality are usually the driving reasons. The perceived source of savings or of improved quality provides insights into the ease or difficulty facing the HR manager as he/she helps with the transition to private control. Cost savings come primarily from reduced labor costs. The private vendor can provide the same service with fewer full-time employees because of different work policies and assignments, the need for fewer levels of supervision, the greater use of part-time or temporary employees, and economies of scale.

Lower labor costs result from lower salaries and benefits. If city employees' salaries are above market rates because the compensation system has rewarded longevity, then private sector full-time replacements are likely to receive lower salaries. Public works department laborers, for example, that have been employed by a city for fifteen years are likely to receive salaries above those paid for similar work in the private sector.

Similarly, benefits such as medical and pension are likely to be greater for public employees than their private sector counterparts (Becker, Silverstein, and Chaykin, 1995). The reasons are several. If the city's workforce is much larger than that of the private vendor, then its health care coverage costs will be more. Typically, pension costs to the city and benefits to the public employee are also higher, especially given the nature of the service in the private sector. In a given labor market, for example, private janitorial firms may not offer pensions to employees (Hartmann and Denhardt, 1999). If the city privatizes these services, substantial savings are likely.

If improved service quality is a reason for privatization, then there is the perception that the private sector can do the job better. This may be because of work related policies and procedures that lead to increased productivity in the private sector, and/or because the public workers are perceived as not motivated to become more productive. It may be that HR policies unduly protect the incompetent or less than competent public employee. A public union may be perceived as protecting current employees to the extent that changes in work rules and policies that may lead to greater productivity are challenged.

THE DECISION TO PRIVATIZE

Once government officials decide to consider privatization, public employees begin to have concerns about their future. Rumors about what will happen are likely to circulate. Many may equate privatization with job loss, fearing that they will be fired or laid off. They also may be concerned that they will have to perform the same work in the future for a private vendor at a lower salary level. As a result, morale suffers and lower productivity is likely.

Union representatives also voice these concerns. Even before a decision to privatize is finalized, the union will approach government officials, including the HR manager. Opposition to privatization is highly likely, accompanied by threats of negative publicity in the local press. City officials, for example, may be accused of being "cold and heartless," of putting long-term city employees "out into the street." Citizens may be told that city employees whom they have known for many years will be replaced by nameless private sector employees who will not provide the same level of service.

The HR manager is likely to be an essential participant in resolving these issues. There are a great variety of strategies or approaches that can be taken to lessen concerns and resolve problems. These approaches may begin during the time period devoted to privatization consideration, and extend after the decision to privatize has been made.

To ensure fair treatment of public employees and lessen unfavorable publicity, public employees must be given the opportunity to ask questions and communicate concerns to city officials. These may occur at employee meetings, at public hearings that include citizenry, and by forming a committee comprised of key government officials including the HR manager, as well as employee representatives. The purpose of this committee is to review a potential privatization decision. Public employees and union members, if applicable, can participate in the requisite studies of costs and benefits that should be part of any privatization decision (Martin, 1999b; Denhardt et al., 1995; Becker, Silverstein, and Chaykin, 1995).

AFTER THE PRIVATIZATION DECISION

Once the decision to privatize has been made,[1] a variety of strategies are possible—all of which can be coordinated by the HR manager. These strategies can be discussed and planned in the preprivatization decision phase and implemented at various times during the privatization process.

One of the most immediate strategies is to involve representatives from management of the affected service in the creation of the Request for Proposal (RFP) that is issued to elicit bids from private vendors. The committee established to write the RFP can also rate or grade the responses.

The involvement of management is an important consideration, as at least one of this group is likely to serve as contract manager once the contract with the private vendor has been signed. The greater the commitment of the manager to the increased efficiency and quality of service that privatization can bring, the greater the benefits of privatization (O'Leary and Eggers, 1993).

LIMITING THE DISPLACEMENT OF PUBLIC WORKERS

Another approach is to limit the displacement of public workers as much as possible. Several strategies can achieve this goal. First, privatization of the existing service could be implemented in a piecemeal fashion, working within the natural rate of attrition. The former Assistant County Manager of Orange County (Florida) privatized janitorial services over a five-year period. As vacancies occurred among the public employees, the work assignments of remaining employees were shifted to allow the maintenance of individual buildings to be privatized. One by one, almost all of the county facilities and buildings were eventually privatized. (Denhardt et. al., 1995). As a result, there was little public outcry.

This strategy will work if the service can be segmented in such a way that public and private service providers do not have to interact. Solid waste collection could be privatized in a similar fashion, with different routes or areas of the city

---

[1] Elected officials are ultimately responsible for approving a decision to privatize. This may occur at the urging of a city manager, for example, and other administrators.

assigned to different providers (Flanagan and Perkins, 1995). In other cases, such as summer recreational services provided to the youth of a city, it would be far less awkward logistically to privatize all services at one time.

A second strategy is to place the affected public employees in vacancies that exist in other government departments. Unless there are relevant personnel regulations, such as bumping rights (discussed below), the HR manager will attempt do this informally for those employees who do not wish to work for the private vendor. City officials can be seen as benevolent, taking care of the loyal public employees. It allows those more senior employees who are vested in the pension system to retain those rights and not suffer reduced benefits by switching to the pension system of the private vendor. In addition, opposition from unions and the threat of lawsuits are erased (Ravitch and Lawther, 1999).

The success of this internal placement effort depends upon a number of factors. Ideally, with sufficient foresight and planning, vacancies in related departments that are not being privatized could be held open, anticipating that transfers from the privatized department will occur (Flanagan and Perkins, 1995). Otherwise, a successful "match" between the job skills of the transferred employee and the needs of the new position may be difficult. In this case, filling vacancies will work best if the job requirements for the new position do not require specialized training or experience. It is far easier to transfer a public employee who mowed grass for a city to the street cleaning crew than it would be to transfer a social services counselor to another position.

A third strategy is to offer early retirement incentives. These incentives may take several forms, such as adding years to the formula that determines retirement benefits, and cash payouts. This may be viewed as a "win-win" solution for both the government and the employee. The loss of morale that may accompany downsizing and privatization efforts will be avoided. The employee can retire years earlier than originally anticipated at a higher level of benefits. The government will accrue savings if the salaries of the affected public employees are above those that will be paid to private sector employees.

O'Leary and Eggers (1993) report that Governor William Weld of Massachusetts signed early retirement legislation in April 1992. Over 3,500 state employees took advantage of incentives, thereby saving Massachusetts an estimated $16 million for fiscal year 1993 and $29 million for fiscal year 1994. At the federal level, King (1997) reported that as part of the downsizing that accompanied the National Performance Review, about 128,000 employees made use of an early retirement program.

The potential downside of these efforts occurs if these incentives are offered to all government employees, for example, not only those in the privatized agencies. The government then may lose its most productive employees, who may be difficult to replace, as these employees view the incentives as an opportunity to begin a new career.

JOB SECURITY, WAGES, AND BENEFITS

Another strategy to limit worker displacement is to encourage the private vendor to hire the affected public employees. Language can be inserted into the RFP and the subsequent contract that affects job security, wages, and benefits for those public employees. Such language places minimum requirements or levels in each of these areas that must be met by the private vendor.

Government officials are often faced with making difficult choices between ensuring employment but at reduced wages and benefits for their former employees, and insisting on similar wages and benefits in a privatization contract that contains higher costs. For example, city officials could state that public employees be given "the right of first refusal" for all vacant private vendor positions created as a result of the privatization contract. This statement alone, without any mention of wages and benefits, provides minimal job security. The private vendor may hire these employees, paying them lower salaries and benefits, and fire them for low productivity at any time. Under some conditions, however, these public employees are likely to retain the same wages, if not the same level of benefits. If the public employees' wages are less than the market rate, the private vendor needs experienced personnel, or the private vendor does not wish to create negative publicity, then the public employees are likely to be recruited and hired at the same or even higher wages.

In the case of wages or salaries, the RFP could specify that all public employees who are hired by the private vendor shall not receive a reduction in salary. Such language reflects an extreme amount of concern for the well-being of the affected public employees. Vendors will be willing to abide by this standard if they anticipate delivering the service with fewer employees, by using more part-time or temporary employees, or if savings can accrue from the use of more productive equipment. Any such language, however, is likely to raise the bids made by private vendors if large numbers of public employees are affected.

The HR manager will likely provide relevant wage and benefit information that influences the choice of language that appears in the RFP. Since lower labor costs provide the greatest savings, there is clearly a trade-off between restricting the private vendor's discretion in these areas and the amount of dollar savings that the government will be able to claim after privatization.

PUBLIC-PRIVATE COMPETITION

In an increasing number of cities and states, public employees are given the chance to compete against private vendors. This strategy represents a change in philosophy. In contrast to a belief that "the private sector can do it better," public-private competition suggests that there is no preference. It asserts that public employees may be more productive than their private sector counterparts (Martin, 1999b).

If public employees are given the opportunity to bid against private vendors in response to an RFP, the HR manager must first determine if the affected group needs training as well as verbal encouragement. Training may be needed to help these employees put together a bid package (O'Leary and Eggers, 1993). Management and employees must revise work procedures and policies to achieve greater efficiencies. In Charlotte, North Carolina, for example, the city offers training to its employees concerning how to reengineer their jobs to make them more productive and competitive (Martin, 1999a).

Governments use a variety of models or processes to ensure valid public-private competition. Indianapolis relies upon significant involvement of city unions. Prior to creating RFPs that initiate competition, affected unions are consulted. If the decision to issue the RFP is made, the city makes sure affected employees have the analytical skills to compete effectively. Next, a union-management team reviews the bid document and determines the information needed to submit a response. The number of employees needed to provide the work is identified, along with the equipment, materials, and appropriate financial information. The resulting bid is submitted along with those from private vendors. Public and private bids are then opened together (GAO, 1997).

The role of the HR manager is crucial throughout the public-private competition process. In addition to providing training, the HR manager analyzes the impact on personnel rules and regulations concerning layoffs, bumping rights, etc. (Denhardt et al., 1995). This essential information is then provided to the public employee group preparing the bid.

TRANSITIONAL ISSUES: INTERPRETING LAWS, PERSONNEL REGULATIONS, AND UNION CONTRACTS

After the privatization contract has been signed, the HR manager assists in transitioning public employees. For those who do not wish to work for the private vendor, government personnel regulations (or those specified in union contracts) such as bumping rights and reduction in force (RIF) rules must be implemented. Those public employees who are hired by the private vendor must be formally terminated and, for example, paid for any accumulated vacation or sick leave they have accrued (see Ravitch and Lawther, 1999).

These transitional issues are likely to be raised before the privatization decision is made. Some employees will find other employment as privatization proceeds, choosing to leave the government and not consider employment with the private vendor. To the extent that financial costs are incurred, such as sick leave payouts, such calculations should have been made as part of the privatization decision. It is the responsibility of the HR manager to answer employee questions, monitor the potential application of all regulations for each affected employee, and apply the regulations once the transition phase begins.

If bumping rights exist, they usually allow a more senior employee who will be RIFed to "bump" a less senior employee from a position for which he/she meets minimum qualifications. Unless there are restrictions (e.g., bumping cannot occur outside an identified bargaining unit), the privatization of a service can have severe impacts on other governmental functions. As one person is bumped, he/she can in turn bump another less senior employee. Although not a frequent occurrence, it is possible for a mid-level manager to assume a clerical position. Depending on the size of the government and the number of employees privatized, it may take months to completely implement bumping rights.

RIF or lay off provisions are less complex, usually based on seniority. Since those hired by the private vendor will be formally RIFed, they must be given appropriate notice, and placed on any "call-back" lists. For a given period of time, such as one year after termination, the HR manager will have to notify all eligible employees of any future vacancies. The termination of any employee also requires conducting the usual associated activities such as exit interviews, termination from health plans, and the payout of any accumulated sick and/or vacation time.

THE ROLE OF THE HR MANAGER IN PRIVATIZATION: OVERALL ASSESSMENT

The success of any privatization effort depends upon many factors, several of which concern the public employees who are most affected. If there is a strong public employee union, many government officials, including the HR manager, have learned it is far more effective to include these unions in all decision making concerning privatization. Otherwise, efforts to contract out may be derailed by union opposition (Martin, 1999a).

Much also depends upon the organizational culture as it perceives increasing productivity and efficiency. If government officials have created this culture, thereby motivating and encouraging public employees, then these employees will be much more receptive to competing with private vendors. In this scenario, the HR manager plays an essential role in improving not only the performance of employees, but also in encouraging the perception that government employees can become more productive.

OUTSOURCING OF THE HUMAN RESOURCE FUNCTION

In a recent survey of U.S. businesses conducted by the American Management Association, over 94 percent of respondents stated that they had outsourced or privatized some aspect of their HR function. Especially in the area of compensation and benefits, an increasing number of companies had experienced outsourcing by the end of the 1990s. Globally, outsourcing of HR functions grew by 35 percent for the 12 months ending in June 1997 (Greer, Youngblood, and Gray, 1999).

In the private sector, the recent trends of downsizing, reengineering, and employee empowerment have led businesses to define core competencies that they can excel in, outsourcing all other functions, including much of the HR function (Marcella, 1995). As a result, there is better "response time" to the customer as the vendor has more highly specialized, up-to-date technology and information processing capabilities. Moreover, since technology is advancing quickly, outsourcing is an efficient way to keep up with the latest advances without having to periodically invest in upgraded software and hardware.

Especially for the small- to medium-sized businesses, advantages are numerous. Increasing complexity of laws and government regulations has made it much more cost effective to outsource HR functions rather than develop relevant expertise in-house. The growing use of Human Resource Information Systems (HRIS), coupled with the continuing shortage of Information Technology (IT) specialists, has also proved to be an incentive for outsourcing.

In the United States, the National Performance Review efforts have spawned a variety of outsourcing options at the federal level (National Academy of Public Administration, [NAPA], 1996). State and local governments in the United States have been less responsive to the contemporary outsourcing HR trend than private sector businesses. For some HR services, however, to provide needed expertise not found in-house and to solve short-term problems, outsourcing has occurred. Many governments contract with private vendors/consultants to perform salary surveys and recommend adjustments to salary structures and other aspects of compensation.

Outside consultants are also called upon to perform such diverse tasks as specialized recruitment and testing, counseling on a variety of HR problems, and training and employee development (Rainey, 1998).

For some HR functions, such as recruitment, many governments have historically not needed to exert much effort, as turnover has been low (Walters, 2000). To the extent that increased contracting has occurred for services for which governments do not have in-house expertise, the need for outsourcing the relevant HR function has been eliminated. Also, the increasing global competition faced by private businesses has not affected state and local HR functions to nearly the same degree.

Following are analyses of three HR functions that have been successfully outsourced in the private sector. In each case, there are signs of greater public sector usage. These include employee assistance programs (EAPs), flexible staffing alternatives, and the wide variety of services offered by Professional Employment Organizations (PEOs).

EMPLOYEE ASSISTANCE PROGRAMS

The purpose of the EAP is to identify and counsel "troubled" employees before their productivity begins to deteriorate. Evolved from the alcohol treatment programs of the 1940s, EAPs now help employees with a broad array of needs, including personal difficulties, marital conflict, and emotional problems.

The use of EAPs has become almost universal. A 1986 change in regulations requires federal agencies to offer EAPs. This regulation has been expanded to include state agencies as well as some subcontractors. In the private sector, Sous (1996) reports the results of a survey that found 76 percent of companies with more than 1,000 employees have an EAP. All recognize that the benefits in terms of lower absenteeism and increased productivity far outweigh the costs.

In the past, many EAPs were handled in house. But several factors have contributed to their increased outsourcing. Costs are likely to be less. The increased recognition that usage depends greatly on confidentiality, however, is the most significant factor. The troubled employee may be hesitant to discuss problems with counselors who are employed by the same organization, fearing that reports of these problems may find their way into personnel records. If the EAP is outsourced, the employee talks with counselors in a setting removed from the workplace. Quarterly reports provide the employer with utilization percentage, not identifying specific users.

FLEXIBLE STAFFING

The greater emphasis on efficiency sparked by reengineering efforts has led both private and public organizations to make greater usage of flexible staffing alternatives. These organizations obtain needed skills and handle workforce changes by using supplemental employees that are not their own. In a 1997 survey of more than 500 private companies, over 72 percent use regular, part-time workers, while

38 percent use short-term hires (Houseman, 1997). Similarly, Sumser (1998) reports 100 percent of twenty federal, state, and local agencies have used temporary workers.

For those agencies that have varying or seasonal workloads, flexible staffing is an ideal solution. No longer would the city have to find work during summer months for those workers who drive snowplows in the winter. When unexpected workload arises, temporary workers can help meet the demand. Employment costs are less, largely because of lower (or nonexistent) pension and health care contributions. Plus, since these workers are not full-time, record and paperwork requirements are minimal and firing the unproductive employee is not a problem (Houseman and Polivka, 1999).

PROFESSIONAL EMPLOYER ORGANIZATIONS

The PEO can provide a variety of services associated with employee leasing, including payroll, employment tax administration, and cafeteria benefits. For small businesses, these services have become increasingly attractive. Although company employees become members of the PEO, they are considered "co-employees," as hiring and firing decisions remain with the contracting company. The employee can benefit as well, with a greater variety of cafeteria plan benefit alternatives to choose from than would be available from the small business. Savings in worker's compensation premiums are also likely, since the PEO has a larger employee base. In addition, a full-service PEO can provide a vast array of duties associated with keeping employee records, sending out notices of hire, and even creating employee handbooks (O'Conner, 1998).

Iowa is one of the few public sector examples of PEO usage. Because of downsizing, Iowa has hired increasing numbers of independent contractors. These are largely self-employed consultants, who are often hired to work in federally funded programs for usually longer than six months. They are not considered full-time state employees, nor do they work for temporary employment agencies. Iowa has contracted with a PEO to provide a full range of HR services for these employees (Davis, 1999).

OUTSOURCING HUMAN RESOURCES: WHAT SHOULD REMAIN?

Private businesses are always looking for the competitive edge. For them, outsourcing HR reduces costs, increases innovation, and leads to greater employee productivity. A 1997 survey of HR trends, based upon responses from more than 1700 employers, reported that more than 50 percent expect to outsource more HR functions within the next three years (Maurer and Mobley, 1998). Similar pressures in the public sector have led to increased outsourcing as well.

For both sectors, however, there are core HR competencies that should remain as part of the HR department or office. Although labor experts may be hired as consultants during the collective bargaining process, everyday labor relations issues, including the grievance process, must be handled by a company or government representative. In this manner, clarity of views and the consistent application of policies can be maintained. Employee trust is less likely to diminish.

Similarly, performance appraisal cannot be contracted out to those unfamiliar with the everyday performance of employees. Consultants can help to establish pay for performance systems, for example, but their consistent application is an essential part of the long-term employee-employer relationship (Greer, Youngblood and Gray, 1999).

CONCLUSION

Privatization/outsourcing efforts will likely increase in the future. The benefits for government are too great for policy makers to ignore. A 1996 survey of over 200 state and local officials, for example, reported that 83 percent of all policy officials and 77 percent of all agency executives indicated that outsourcing has led to improved customer service. In addition to cost savings, outsourcing provides access to new technology and skills that otherwise would be difficult to obtain. Over 66 percent of the respondents felt that information technology services would be outsourced within the next few years (Davies, 1996).

At the same time, public-private competition is increasing. Governments are more than willing to encourage public employees to reengineer existing work processes and staffing levels to obtain greater efficiencies and increased customer service (Sclar, 2000). Increasing privatization may have the effect of helping to dispel the perception that government employees are nonproductive. This trend complements the efforts of the National Performance Review at the federal level and similar activities found at state and local levels.

The success of privatization efforts will rely to a large extent on how well government can act as a "buyer" of services from the private sector (Kettl, 1993). As most of these relationships are governed by contracts, governments must give increasing attention to contract management. The greater the complexity of the privatized service, and the more uncertainty there is about how to best perform the service, the more time and effort the government needs to invest in contract management. Too often this essential function is ignored or understaffed. As a result, vendor performance problems may be overlooked until they become extremely difficult to solve. Governments run the risk of becoming "captured" by the vendor when it becomes time to renew the contract, as competition may have disappeared. The cost savings and increased customer satisfaction may not continue indefinitely unless government exercises sound contract monitoring and management practices.

Much of successful privatization falls on the shoulders of the HR manager. Not only will he/she participate in privatization process leading to the initial contract, but increased responsibility for contract management is also likely to occur. If the operation of a prison is privatized, for example, it may be the responsibility of the HR manager to determine if private prison staff has undergone the training as required by the contract. If the turnover among private employees reaches unacceptable levels, the HR manager may negotiate changes in private sector management policies that will lower turnover. When problems occur, the HR manager may become an essential part of the negotiation process that leads to solutions. More recent analysis of privatization efforts indicates that the most significant contributing factor to achieving high service quality is whether it is delivered by the public or private sector (Hodge, 2000; Sclar, 2000). Efficiency and good management practices are judged to be the primary determinant. Although governments throughout the world will continue to engage in privatization, in some instances services may be taken back from private vendors. With the increased emphasis on employee empowerment that is part of the New Public Management trend, innovative ways to reorganize, deliver, and even finance services may become more common. The role played by the HR manager must remain flexible and adaptable to ensure continued effectiveness and accountability.

REFERENCES

BECKER, F., G. SILVERSTEIN, and L. CHAYKIN. 1995. Public Employee Job Security and Benefits: A Barrier to Privatization of Mental Health Services. *Public Productivity and Management Review* 19 (1):25–33.

DAVIES, T. 1996. Survey In On Outsourcing. *Government Technology* 9 (14):1, 50.

DAVIS, C. P. 1999. The State of Iowa and PEO Services. *The Public Manager* 28 (4):42–44.

DENHARDT, K., J. RAFFEL, E. JACOBSON, M. MANLOVE, D. AUGER, and J. LEWIS. 1995. *Employee Issues in Privatization.* MIS Report 27 (10):1–12.

FLANAGAN, J., and S. PERKINS. 1995. Public-Private Competition in the City of Phoenix, Arizona. *Government Finance Review* 11 (3):7–12.

GAO Report/GGD-97-48. 1997. *Privatization: Lessons Learned by State and Local Governments.* Report to the Chairman, House Republican Task Force on Privatization 3/14/97:1–31.

GORE, A. 1993. *Creating a Government That Works Better and Costs Less.* Washington, DC: The Review.

GREER, C. R., S. A. YOUNGBLOOD, and D. A. GRAY. 1999. Human Resource Management Outsourcing: The Make or Buy Decision. *Academy of Management Executive* 13(3):85–97.

GREENE, J. D. 1996. How Much Privatization? A Research Note Examining the Use of Privatization by Cities in 1982 and 1992. *Policy Studies Journal* 24 (4):632–639.

HARTMANN, J., and K. DENHARDT. 1998. The Human Side of Privatization. In *Managing Local Government: Cases in Decision Making* 2nd ed. J. Banovetz, ed. Washington, DC: International City Management Association.

HODGE, G. A. 2000. *Privatization: An International Review of Performance.* Boulder, CO: Westview Press.

HOUSEMAN, S. N. 1997. *New Institute Survey on Flexible Staffing Arrangements.* Kalamazoo, MI: W. E. Upjohn Institute for Employment Research.

——, and A. E. POLIVKA. 1999. *The Implications of Flexible Staffing Arrangements for Job Stability.* Kalamazoo, MI: W. E. Upjohn Institute for Employment Research, Working Paper No. 99–056.

JOHNSON, R. A., and N. WALZER. 1996. *Competition for City Services: Has the Time Arrived? Privatization in Illinois Municipalities.* Springfield, IL: Illinois Office of the Comptroller.

KETTL, D. F. 1993. *Sharing Power: Public Governance and Private Markets.* Washington, DC: The Brookings Institution.

KING, J. B. 1997. The Government of the Future: A Personnel Perspective. *The Public Manager* 26 (2):21–22.

LAVERY, K. 1999. *Smart Contracting for Local Government Services: Processes and Experiences.* Westport, CT: Greenwood Publishing Group, Inc.

LAWTHER, W. C. 1999. The Role of Public Employees in the Privatization Process. *Review of Public Personnel Administration* 19 (1):28–40.

——, K. DENHARDT, A. JUDD, J. JURIE, and E. ROSELL. 1993. *Privatization of Toll Collection: Feasibility Study*. Orlando, FL: The University of Central Florida.

MARCELLA, A. 1995. *Outsourcing, Downsizing and Reengineering*. Chicago, IL: Institute of Internal Auditors.

MARTIN, L. L. 1999a. Public-Private Competition: A Public Employee Alternative to Privatization. *Review of Public Personnel Administration* 19 (1):59–70.

——. 1999b. Determining a Level Playing Field for Public-Private Competition. Arlington, VA: *The PricewaterhouseCoopers Endowment for the Business of Government*.

MAURER, R., and N. MOBLEY. 1998. Outsourcing: Is It the HR Department of the Future? *HR Focus* 75 (11):9–11.

National Academy of Public Administration. 1996. *Improving the Efficiency and Effectiveness of Human Resource Services*. Washington, DC: Author.

O'CONNOR, T. 1998. Outsourcing Saves Money on Human Resource Tasks. *Denver Business Journal*, November 11. <http://www.bizjounrals.com/denver/stories/1998/11/09/smallb4.html>

O'LEARY, J., and W. D. EGGERS. 1993. *Privatization and Public Employees: Guidelines for Fair Treatment*. Los Angeles, CA: The Reason Foundation.

RAINEY, G. W. 1998. Choosing and Using Human Resource Consultants: Focusing on Local Government. In *Handbook of Human Resource Management in Government*, S. E. Condrey, ed. San Francisco, CA: Jossey-Bass Publishers: 474–496.

RAVITCH, F. S., and W. C. LAWTHER. 1999. Privatization and Public Employee Pension Rights. *Review of Public Personnel Administration* 19 (1):41–58.

SCLAR, E. D. 2000. *You Don't Always Get What You Pay For: The Economics of Privatization*. Ithaca, N.Y.: Cornell University Press.

SOUS, C. 1996. EAPS Gaining Ground in Effort to Reduce Workplace Costs. *San Antonio Business Journal* 10 (41):16.

SUMSER, R. 1998. New Options, New Talent. *The Public Manager* 27 (3):37–40.

WALTERS, J. 2000. Older Than Ever. *Governing* 13 (6):36–39.

15

Equal Employment Opportunity and Affirmative Action in the Public Sector

J. EDWARD KELLOUGH

University of Georgia

It is widely known that discrimination directed against racial, ethnic, and other minorities, and women has a long and distressing history. This chapter is about the ways in which government in the United States has responded to historic patterns of discrimination in the public employment process. Obviously, there are many reasons why government should be involved in combating such behavior. Fundamental notions of merit and justice, for example, require that the public service be free from prejudice. As Hays (1998) notes in a broad discussion of civil service selection procedures, "public jobs are public resources, to which everyone has a potential claim." It follows, then, that the process by which those resources are distributed must not be closed to selected groups of people because of factors such as gender, race, or ethnicity. In addition, it is clear that government should, through its own employment practices, provide an appropriate example for nongovernmental organizations (Krislov, 1967). If government cannot protect women and minorities from discrimination within the ranks of its own workforce, how can we expect it to effectively counter discrimination in private employment and other areas? Government efforts to open the public employment process to underrepresented groups are desirable also because it is becoming increasingly clear that a government bureaucracy reflective of the public it serves, in terms of such characteristics as race and ethnicity, helps to ensure that minority interests are appropriately considered in the policy formulation and implementation process. There is a growing body of research to demonstrate that a more representative public bureaucracy promotes greater government responsiveness to a variety of public interests (Meier, 1993, Meier and Stewart, 1992, Selden, 1997, and Selden, Brudney, and Kellough, 1998).

EARLY ACTION IN RESPONSE TO DISCRIMINATION

Despite the strong arguments for equal employment opportunity, and notwithstanding constitutional guarantees of equal protection of the law and merit system rules designed to ensure that applicants for public employment would be judged only on the basis of their abilities, discrimination in the public sector was common and openly practiced well into the twentieth century. Rosenbloom (1977) notes, for example, that during the administration of William Howard Taft, a policy of segregation of whites and African Americans was initiated within the Census Bureau, and African American appointments were reduced in areas of the country such as the South where whites objected to their employment. Under the subsequent administration of Woodrow Wilson, other discriminatory practices were encouraged or condoned, such as the segregation of offices, rest rooms, and lunchrooms. It was also under Wilson that a photograph was for the first time required to accompany applications for federal employment. Although that requirement was eventually dropped, at the time it was apparent that "the color of one's skin had become a test of fitness for federal employees" (Rosenbloom, 1977:54).

It was not until the 1940s that the most egregious discriminatory practices were first confronted by the federal government, and then, meaningful action was taken only after early civil rights leaders threatened a mass rally in the nation's capital to protest discrimination by the government and defense industry contractors. The Roosevelt administration was decidedly cool to the idea of such a public expression of African American sentiment. The Administration feared that a massive protest rally in Washington D.C., designed to call attention to racism within the United States, would divide the country along racial lines just as we were being forced to contemplate the possibility of being drawn into a war against Germany and its racist ideology. There was speculation that the march would turn violent, that social unrest would spread across the country, and that military discipline would be disrupted.

Nevertheless, efforts by Roosevelt to dissuade leaders of the March on Washington movement failed until the president agreed to establish, through issuance of a new executive order (No. 8802), an administrative organization with authority to investigate allegations of discrimination by defense contractors and federal agencies. This organization, known as the Fair Employment Practices Committee (FEPC), was the first federal government agency designed to protect minority interests since the period of reconstruction following the Civil War (Reed, 1991:15). Roosevelt's order creating the FEPC, issued on June 25, 1941, led to the anticipated protest march being canceled only days before it was scheduled to occur. The order rested on the president's ability to act independently of Congress to set the terms and conditions of executive agency contracts and to regulate the federal personnel system under existing civil service law. At this point in American history and politics, there was no chance that a substantive antidiscrimination program would come from Congress since numerous key leadership positions in that institution were filled by conservative southern Democrats favoring segregation. Consequently, reliance on executive authority was essential if a policy of nondiscrimination was to be pursued. To avoid the need to ask Congress for funding to support the FEPC, money for the Committee's operation came from a presidential discretionary fund appropriated for the operation of agencies within the Executive Office of the President.

The FEPC soon established itself as a serious force in the struggle against discrimination. The Committee held highly publicized hearings to investigate alleged discriminatory practices and began a process of directing public attention to the plight of minorities in important segments of the labor market. But as might be expected, this work generated substantial opposition, especially among influential southern Democrats whose support Roosevelt needed on a number of other issues, and as a result, the Committee placed the president in a somewhat difficult position politically. Congress eventually refused to appropriate money for operation of the Committee and on June 28, 1946, the FEPC filed its final report and officially went out of business. During the years of its operation, however, the Committee achieved considerable success in documenting discriminatory practices by a number of defense contractors and federal agencies.

In the years immediately following abolition of the FEPC, there was no administrative agency to implement a policy of nondiscrimination in the federal civil service. President Truman urged Congress to act, but when it became clear that congressional action would not be forthcoming, he found it necessary to respond by issuing yet another executive order (No. 9980) creating a Fair Employment Board (FEB) within the Civil Service Commission. The responsibilities of the FEB, which was established in 1948, were limited to the investigation of complaints of discrimination arising from within federal government agencies. It could hold hearings and make recommendations, but it could not force agencies to comply with its opinions. In 1955 Eisenhower abolished the FEB and established, again by executive order, a new committee independent of the Civil Service Commission.

Eisenhower's new organization was known as the President's Committee on Government Employment Policy (PCGEP). The PCGEP was set up as an agency-funded entity so that direct appropriations from Congress for its operation were not needed. The Committee continued the work of investigating complaints of discriminatory practices within federal agencies—complaints that had been undertaken earlier by the FEPC and the FEB, but, as was the case with its predecessors, it could not compel agencies to change employment decisions, even if it found convincing evidence of discrimination. The effectiveness of the program rested to a considerable extent, therefore, on the persuasive abilities of Committee members.

A MORE AFFIRMATIVE APPROACH

During the Truman Administration, staff members from the FEB realized that a policy resting primarily on the investigation of complaints might not be the most effective means of confronting discrimination. It was suspected that the extent of discriminatory practices was much broader than what was suggested by the number of formal complaints filed. Many minority group members, it was found, were hesitant to register complaints because they feared retaliation or retribution if they spoke out. As a result, the FEB initiated a very limited and experimental program of "constructive action" to counter discrimination. This program, which Rosenbloom (1977: p. 64) describes as somewhat "ill-defined and ineffective" consisted of "conferences with fair employment officers and outside organizations, periodic surveys and appraisals, and the adoption of some new recruitment techniques, better training programs, and steps toward further integration" (Rosenbloom, 1977: p. 64). Eisenhower's committee maintained this program, although it apparently did little to emphasize the approach. Dramatic change was to occur, however, when John F. Kennedy entered the presidency.

At the very beginning of the Kennedy Administration, the president fundamentally reorganized the federal antidiscrimination effort. Executive Order 10925, issued on March 6, 1961, consolidated programs regarding government contract compliance and the federal civil service under a newly established authority known as the President's Committee on Equal Employment Opportunity (PCEEO). The committees that had operated during the Eisenhower years were dissolved. The PCEEO received and investigated complaints as the earlier committees had done, but Kennedy's order required substantially more than what had been mandated earlier. The new order required that the positive program of recruitment and outreach to the minority community, begun under Truman, be a primary and integral part of the federal effort. Under Kennedy, this approach became known as "affirmative action."

Kennedy's program placed a substantial new burden or obligation on federal agencies. Earlier efforts were focused primarily on prohibiting federal employers from engaging in discriminatory behavior. That is, agencies were directed, for the most part, *not to do* certain things. They were not to disadvantage minority job applicants or employees because of race or ethnicity. Kennedy maintained these requirements, but in addition, he stressed that federal organizations were *to do* other things, that is, they were to undertake and emphasize certain actions such as minority recruitment and the provision of training to promote greater equality of opportunity. The difference between the two approaches is that which exists between a negative prohibition on the one hand and an affirmative requirement on the other. The PCEEO under the direction of Vice President Johnson, who Kennedy selected as chairman of the Committee, was very aggressive in pursuing this strategy, but all of the Committee's work was grounded firmly on the principle of nondiscrimination. Affirmative action in the form of minority recruitment and outreach certainly did not mean that agencies stopped recruiting nonminorities, and since training and upward mobility programs were made available to all lower-level employees regardless of race, ethnicity, or sex, such efforts served to reinforce a doctrine of equal opportunity.

Following Johnson's rise to the presidency in 1963, a number of additional significant developments occurred regarding the structure and operation of the federal program. First, Congress finally acted to prohibit discrimination by private employers and organizations receiving federal assistance through passage of the Civil Rights Act of 1964. That legislation marked a fundamental shift in government's approach to the problem of discrimination, but significantly, its provisions did not initially apply to the federal civil service. Also, there was no requirement under the law that employers engage in affirmative action. Consequently, the PCEEO, which was continuing its program of requiring affirmative action by federal contractors, came under strenuous attack by certain members of Congress who argued that the Committee's work was no longer needed since the Civil Rights Act had established the Equal Employment Opportunity Commission (EEOC) to implement a policy of nondiscrimination, and contractors would fall under the jurisdiction of the EEOC (Graham, 1990). In order to save the federal affirmative action program, President Johnson, through Executive Order 11246 of 1965, transferred authority for the nondiscrimination effort within the federal civil service to the Civil Service Commission and gave the Department of Labor authority with respect to federal contractors. In 1967, through Executive Order 11375, Johnson added language prohibiting discrimination on the basis of sex to the existing affirmative action programs.

Progress in the employment of minority group members was slow throughout the remainder of the 1960s, however, and the social unrest characteristic of much of that decade helped to persuade many people that additional action to strengthen the campaign against discrimination was needed. Urban rioting in the largely black ghettos in many metropolitan areas had risen to unprecedented levels. In the African American community there was a growing sense of black nationalism and a feeling that we should move from simple equality of opportunity to equality of results. In this context, and in the face of unrepentant discrimination against minorities in the private sector construction trades, the Department of Labor in 1967 through its Office of Federal Contract Compliance Programs began a program in the city of Philadelphia requiring that federal construction contractors establish goals for minority employment as a condition of receiving federal contract dollars (Graham, 1990). The Nixon Administration subsequently strengthened this program, which became known as the "Philadelphia Plan," and eventually required this type of action by all major federal contractors. This approach to affirmative action placed an increased positive burden on employers by forcing them to establish realistic objectives for minority employment and plan for their accomplishment. In 1971, this type of affirmative action was endorsed by the chairman of the U.S. Civil Service Commission, Robert Hampton, who issued a memorandum on May 10 of that year authorizing federal agencies to establish numerical goals and timetables for minority employment (Rosenbloom, 1977: pp. 107–110). Under this approach, numerical goals were targets for the representation of women and minorities in an organization. Timetables were dates or time frames within which specified goals were planned to be accomplished. Although goals and timetables required no organization to accept individuals who did not possess necessary qualifications, they did allow for the consideration of race, ethnicity, and gender in selection or placement decisions.

The policy decision to authorize goals and timetables marked a dramatic shift in the nature of the federal equal employment opportunity (EEO) program. An employment goal, if it is meaningful, may imply that a limited preference will be extended to minority group members or women when they possess requisite qualifications. That is to say, an employer who has established a goal for increasing the employment of minorities or women, who then subsequently locates qualified minority or female job applicants, will likely prefer those individuals over equally qualified nonminorities or men. To do otherwise would suggest that the goal is essentially meaningless. This indicates, however, that the use of goals and timetables may transcend a strict or literal interpretation of nondiscrimination in that selection policies may not be purely neutral. This approach to affirmative action, which eventually came into wide use, was authorized, however, only when minority group members or women were significantly underrepresented in an organization. Nevertheless, affirmative action in this form spawned substantial controversy and judicial activity. In fact, so much attention has been focused on numerical strategies for affirmative action in public employment and elsewhere that goals and timetables, and the limited preferences they can imply, now form the dominant paradigm of affirmative action policy in the minds of many people.

With the establishment of affirmative action in the form of goals and timetables, the federal government's EEO program rested on several distinct elements. The earliest initiatives, begun under Roosevelt, consisted of executive orders prohibiting discrimination and procedures for the investigation of complaints. The first affirmative action programs emerged later under Kennedy in the form of recruitment efforts, training programs, and other positive measures designed to promote the employment of minorities and women. Eventually, goals and timetables were authorized which implied limited preferences for minority group members and women under certain circumstances. Table 15–1 illustrates these components of the program. In general, it should be clear that by the early 1970s, affirmative action could take many specific forms, and implications for the principle of nondiscrimination were different for different approaches. In all cases, however, affirmative action involved, and still involves, efforts to promote the employment of members of groups that have historically suffered discriminatory treatment.

As the nation was dealing with the social tumult of the 1960s, other actions occurred with respect to equal employment opportunity. One of the more important was passage of the Age Discrimination in Employment Act (ADEA) of 1967. Congress had considered prohibiting discrimination on the basis of age earlier when it debated and passed Title VII of the Civil Rights Act of 1964, but it was decided that legislative action on that issue should wait until after the Department of Labor had investigated the problem and issued a report. The ADEA, which was passed three years later, prohibits employment discrimination against persons aged 40 years or older. When it was first enacted, protection was extended only through age 65, but through subsequent amendments, that restriction was eliminated. Most significantly for our purposes, the law was also amended in 1974 to cover all state, local, and federal government organizations.

TABLE 15–1   Affirmative Action and Equal Opportunity

Individual-Based "Reactive" Policies	Group-Based "Proactive" Policies (Affirmative Action)	
1. Executive orders and other laws prohibiting discrimination 2. Procedures for the investigation of complaints	3. Early approaches to affirmative action consisting primarily of: —Upward mobility training programs —Recruitment and outreach efforts	4. Numerically based approaches to affirmative action —Numerical goals and timetables
	Equal opportunity programs based on a literal interpretation of nondiscrimination	Programs that transcend equality of opportunity and nondiscrimination in a strict sense by granting preferences under some circumstances

Another major development in the growth of EEO law and affirmative action was the decision by the U.S. Supreme Court in 1971 in *Griggs v. Duke Power Company* (401 U.S. 425). In that case, the Court unanimously ruled that Title VII of the 1964 Civil Rights Act proscribed not only intentional discrimination but also actions that were "fair in form, but discriminatory in operation." This ruling meant that an employer, whose actions might not be intentionally discriminatory, could still be in violation of Title VII if its employment practices screened out a disproportionate number of minorities or women, and those practices could not be shown to serve a legitimate business necessity. An examination for employee selection, for example, could not be used if it eliminated disproportionate numbers of minority applicants, and there was no evidence that it was a valid measure of ability to perform on the job.

This concept of unintentional discrimination eventually became known as disparate impact, and the idea was elaborated by the court through subsequent decisions. It is contrasted with disparate treatment which is the term used to describe purposeful or intentional discrimination. In a disparate impact case, according to guidelines originally laid out by the court, a minority plaintiff, for example, would first bear the burden of demonstrating through the use of appropriate statistics that an employer's practices had resulted in a substantial disparity between minority and nonminority selection or promotion rates. At that point, the burden would shift to the employer to demonstrate that the practices that produced the disparity served a legitimate business purpose. If the employer was successful in demonstrating that point, then no violation of Title VII would have occurred, unless the plaintiff could demonstrate that there were other, less discriminatory, practices that would serve the identified business interest equally well.

In 1989, this application of the burden of proof in disparate impact cases was overturned by a more conservative Supreme Court in the controversial decision in *Wards Cove Packing Company v. Atonio* (490 U.S. 642). In that decision, the Court ruled that the burden would remain on plaintiffs throughout the process, and that plaintiffs would need to show that employers selected challenged employment practices because of their discriminatory effect. Thus the concept of disparate impact was substantially undermined. Congress responded to this and other Court decisions from the 1989 term with the Civil Rights Act of 1991 which, among other things, amended Title VII to specifically incorporate the standards associated with disparate impact analysis as they had been originally articulated in *Griggs*. The implications of the Griggs case and the concept of disparate impact have been substantial. Except for the period between the *Wards Cove* decision and passage of the Civil Rights Act of 1991, employers have had a strong incentive to engage in employment practices, including affirmative action in its various forms, to help ensure that minorities and women are not denied opportunity. In other words, one way for an employer to be shielded from claims of discrimination under disparate impact theory would be to make certain that its work force is sufficiently integrated to make any claim of statistical disparity along racial, ethnic, or gender lines impossible.

The incentive for affirmative action provided by disparate impact theory was made applicable to the public sector with passage of another important piece of federal legislation, the Equal Employment Opportunity Act of 1972, which brought all state, local, and federal government entities under coverage of Title VII of the Civil Rights Act of 1964. This legislation gave the EEOC direct responsibility for monitoring state and local employment practices. Under EEOC guidelines, state and local governments were required to collect and report data on minority and female employment, and by the mid-1970s goals and timetables and the preferences they imply were well established as a part of the affirmative action process at these levels of government. Regarding the federal government, the 1972 law reaffirmed the program implemented by the Civil Service Commission, but a reorganization order by President Carter that coincided with the 1978 Civil Service Reform Act transferred authority for supervision of federal EEO and affirmative action practices to the EEOC (Kellough and Rosenbloom, 1992). In issuing guidelines for the federal program, the EEOC initially placed great emphasis on numerical goals and timetables in agency affirmative action plans, but during the Reagan years (1981–1988), the agency backed away from that approach. EEOC regulations issued in 1987 permitted but did not require agencies to develop numerical goals for minority and female employment in instances when those groups were underrepresented.

In the 1970s, the federal government also began to address the problem of discrimination against the disabled. The Rehabilitation Act of 1973, for example, prohibited discrimination against "otherwise qualified handicapped individuals" by any organization receiving federal financial assistance or by federal contractors or agencies. The purpose of the law was to ensure that no qualified individual who also happened to have a disability would be subject to discrimination under any program or activity supported by the federal government. The provision that recipients of federal funding be barred from discrimination essentially meant that all state and local governments would be covered by the law. Provisions prohibiting discrimination by federal contractors and federal agencies also required "affirmative action" by those organizations, which has involved recruitment, outreach, and training.

In 1990, Congress addressed the problem of discrimination against the disabled once more through the Americans with Disabilities Act (ADA). This new law was based on principles established by the Rehabilitation Act of 1973 and the regulations that had been issued to implement that earlier legislation (Kellough, 2000). The ADA is comprehensive in that it extends prohibitions on discrimination against the disabled to private employers without federal contracts, but it also applies directly to state and local governments, although affirmative action is not mandated. Federal agencies are not covered by the ADA, however, because it was reasoned that they are sufficiently governed by the Rehabilitation Act and its affirmative action requirements. (The ADA receives more detailed treatment in Chapter Nineteen of this book.)

THE AFFIRMATIVE ACTION CONTROVERSY

As previously noted, affirmative action policies, especially those involving preferences for minorities and women, have engendered significant debate. The dispute over affirmative action is best understood, however, when we realize that such policies are intended to have the effect of redistributing opportunity from those who have been historically advantaged to groups that have suffered disadvantages because of race, ethnicity, gender, or other traits or circumstances (Edley, 1996). In the context of government affirmative action, this redistribution of opportunity involves highly valued jobs. Thus, the stakes are high, and the outcomes can be extremely important for people on both sides of the issue. Employment, after all, provides the means by which most individuals support themselves and their families financially. Beyond that, employment can be an avenue to self-fulfillment, a way of defining who we are and what we do. We should expect, therefore, that policies operating to alter the distribution of employment opportunities will very likely be opposed by some individuals for ideological or perhaps more self-serving reasons.

We should also realize that affirmative action, which involves the use of limited preferences, is more vulnerable to criticism than other approaches such as recruitment or outreach. This is true simply because the existence of preferences appears to contradict the concept of equality of opportunity. It is difficult for anyone to oppose efforts based firmly on the principle of nondiscrimination, such as broader recruitment or upward mobility programs, but numerical approaches including goals and timetables are more easily opposed by those who argue that a strict interpretation of equal opportunity should prevail. From the view point of those opposed to affirmative action, preferences amount to reverse discrimination; numerical goals, often referred to as "quotas," have the effect, it is argued, of illegitimately discriminating against nonminority males and sometimes nonminority women.

The key question is whether the racial, ethnic, and gender distinctions drawn by affirmative action goals and the accompanying preferences can be justified. Those who equate affirmative action with reverse discrimination argue that such distinctions cannot be defended. They suggest that selection decisions should be based solely on individual merit without consideration of factors such as race, ethnicity, or gender.

However, others remind us that precise measures of individual merit or qualifications are often beyond our reach. They argue that limited advantages for women and minorities in such personnel actions as selection, promotion, assignment, and transfers should be allowed to make up for past or current discrimination. Usually, this view rests on an idea known as compensatory justice, which is the notion that groups, such as minorities or women, who have suffered discrimination and have been denied opportunity as a result, should be given certain advantages to compensate for that injustice. Proponents of affirmative action draw a distinction between discrimination motivated by racial or gender animus, on one hand, and limited minority or female preferences, on the other, that are sometimes present in affirmative action programs intended to assist those who have historically been the victims of racism, ethnocentrism, or sexist attitudes.

Opponents of affirmative action counter that while the compensatory argument may hold for identifiable victims of discrimination it should not be applied across-the-board to groups, since some group members may not have suffered discriminatory treatment. But it can be very difficult or impossible to determine whether any particular individual has or has not been victimized by discrimination. It should also be remembered that affirmative action is not intended to benefit particular individuals, but rather, it is a means of requiring employers or other institutions to ensure that their employment processes give consideration to all qualified people. Additionally, arguments for race-, ethnic-, and gender-conscious affirmative action are not limited to remedial justifications alone. Such programs are also often defended in more utilitarian terms in that they work to integrate society more rapidly, reduce income inequalities, further distributive justice, and promote efficiency by ensuring that the talents of all individuals are used (Taylor, 1991).

The emergence of a Republican majority in Congress in 1994, as well as conservative gains in state legislatures across the nation at that time, helped to push the issue of preferential affirmative action to a prominent position on the public agenda. In 1995, the Republican leadership in Congress advocated efforts to eliminate the use of affirmative action (Holmes, 1995). In response, the Clinton Administration conducted a complete review of federal affirmative action programs and concluded that such approaches should be continued (Stephanopoulos and Edley, 1995). Considerable debate over the issue has also taken place at the state level, with California figuring prominently in the struggle. A Republican governor of California, Pete Wilson, campaigned vigorously against affirmative action on his way to reelection to a second term in 1994, and in 1995 the Regents of the University System of California voted to prohibit the consideration of race or gender as a factor in decisions regarding admissions to state universities. More significant, however, was passage of Proposition 209 by California voters in November 1996. Proposition 209 was a ballot initiative that amended the state constitution to prohibit the use of preferences based on race, ethnicity, or gender associated with affirmative action by the state and local government jurisdictions within the state. The success of Proposition 209 indicated that citizen initiatives could be effective tools against affirmative action, and a similar initiative was undertaken in the state of Washington. The Washington initiative (I-200) appeared on the ballot in November 1998, and passed with the support of 58 percent of the voters, making Washington the second state to prohibit racial, ethnic, or gender preferences in state employment, contracting, or higher education.

It is interesting to note that debate on affirmative action has taken place in the absence of definitive answers to questions about the impact of the policy. Has affirmative action been successful? Much of the difficulty we face in trying to answer that question stems from our inability to demonstrate conclusively that affirmative action is the cause of observed growth in the employment of minorities and women. In general, trends in minority and female employment in government have been upward, but it is difficult to separate the impact of affirmative action from that of innumerable other forces that could be driving such change. It is true, nevertheless, that significant increases in the employment of minorities and women in the federal civil service did occur following the initiation of affirmative action in the 1960s, and it seems likely that at least part of those increases could be due to the affirmative action program. Furthermore, an analysis of federal employment during the 1970s finds limited evidence that agencies that developed numerical goals and timetables for the selection of minorities and women made greater progress in the employment of those groups than agencies that failed to develop preferential affirmative action policies (Kellough, 1989).

THE SUPREME COURT AND PREFERENTIAL AFFIRMATIVE ACTION: EXAMINING THE LIMITS OF LEGAL PERMISSIBILITY

From a legal perspective, preferential affirmative action arises in three ways. It may be the result of (1) a court order, (2) a consent decree sanctioned by a court to settle litigation, or (3) a voluntary decision by an organization. Affirmative action required by court order is authorized by the 1964 Civil Rights Act based upon a finding of discrimination by a court. Standards for the review of court ordered preferential affirmative action are articulated by the Supreme Court in *Firefighters Local v. Stotts,* 467 U.S. 561 (1984) and *United States v. Paradise,* 480 U.S. 149 (1987). Guidelines for permissible preferential affirmative action embodied in consent decrees are quite similar to those for voluntary affirmative action and are established in *Firefighters v. City of Cleveland,* 478 U.S. 501 (1986). Voluntary affirmative action, consisting of race- or gender-conscious practices established by an organization without external persuasion or compulsion arising out of litigation, would include preferential programs such as numerical goals and timetables set by a government agency for the employment of specified numbers of minorities or women (Selig, 1987). Because most affirmative action is "voluntary," in the sense that the term is used here, a closer look at the legal parameters of such action is warranted.

In general, preferential affirmative action programs voluntarily adopted by government organizations are limited by the prohibitions on discrimination contained in the Civil Rights Act of 1964 (as amended) and constitutional guarantees of equal protection of the law. Section 703 of Title VII of the 1964 Civil Rights Act defines as unlawful any employment practice that discriminates against any individual on account of race, color, religion, sex, or national origin. Thus, race- or gender-conscious affirmative action implemented by public institutions must be reconciled with those Title VII prohibitions on discrimination. Likewise, the equal protection clause of the Fourteenth Amendment forbids states to deny to any person within their jurisdictions the "equal protection of the laws," and distinctions established by states and their local subdivisions on the basis of race and gender incorporated into affirmative action plans must therefore be reconciled with that equal protection guarantee. Because the Fourteenth Amendment applies only to actions of the states, however, its restrictions do not limit the federal government, but the due process clause of the Fifth Amendment, which applies to the federal action, has been interpreted by the Supreme Court as requiring equal protection of the laws (*Bolling v. Sharpe* 347 U.S. 497), and thus constitutional constraints are also imposed on federal affirmative action.

Statutory limitations on affirmative action established by Title VII have been interpreted by the Supreme Court in two important cases (Kellough, 1991). The first was *United Steelworkers of America v. Weber* (443 U.S. 193, 1979). At issue was the legality of a plan negotiated as part of a collective bargaining agreement between Kaiser Aluminum and Chemical Corporation and the United Steelworkers of America, which reserved for African Americans 50 percent of the openings in an in-plant craft training program until the black proportion of craft workers in the plant approximated the proportion of blacks in the local labor force. The Supreme Court upheld the legality of the affirmative action plan arguing that although

Title VII, as indicated in section 703(j), cannot be interpreted as requiring preferential treatment to overcome a racial imbalance, it does not preclude voluntary efforts to overcome such an imbalance. In view of the legislative history and purposes of Title VII, the Court held that the prohibition on discrimination could not be read literally to proscribe all race-conscious affirmative action plans. Writing for a majority of the Court, Justice Brennan noted that if Congress had meant to prohibit all race-conscious affirmative action it easily could have done so "by providing that Title VII would not require or *permit* racially preferential integration efforts" (*Steelworkers v. Weber,* p. 205, emphasis in original).

Because *Weber* addressed the legality of voluntary affirmative action by a private employer, the question remained as to whether its outcome would guide the statutory review of similar programs undertaken by a public employer. This question was addressed in 1987 in *Johnson v. Transportation Agency, Santa Clara County, California* (480 U.S. 616). The Court applied the criteria outlined in *Weber* to a voluntary race- and gender-conscious affirmative action plan adopted by the Transportation Agency which provided that, in making employment decisions within traditionally segregated job classifications where women or minorities were significantly underrepresented, the Agency could consider the sex or race of a job candidate along with the individual's qualifications. No specific number of positions was set aside for minorities or women, but the eventual objective was to have minorities and women employed in positions roughly in proportion to their representation in the relevant local labor force. Following the *Weber* precedent, the Court upheld the agency's affirmative action plan and with the announcement of the *Johnson* decision, a relatively clear set of standards emerged for judging the statutory legality of voluntary race- or gender-conscious affirmative action programs by government employers. When challenged under Title VII, such programs must be designed to address a manifest racial or gender imbalance in traditionally segregated job categories. Further, when considering whether a manifest racial or gender imbalance exists, the employer must consider the proportion of minorities or women in traditionally segregated positions relative to their proportions with the requisite qualifications in the local labor force. Affirmative action must also be constructed as a temporary strategy, and race or gender may be only one of several factors included in the decision process.

Constitutional restrictions on voluntary affirmative action by government organizations evolved through a series of cases in the 1980s and 1990s and are considerably more rigorous than the constraints imposed by the Court in *Weber* and *Johnson*. Consequently, these restrictions establish the effective operational limits for governmental affirmative action. As was noted earlier, the issue turns on judicial interpretation of the concept of equal protection of the laws. In most instances, the courts apply one of two analytical standards when deciding whether government actions that create classifications among people violate the equal protection components of the Fifth or Fourteenth Amendments. The first standard simply requires that a reasonable or rational relationship exist between the distinctions imposed and a legitimate governmental end. Under this standard, individuals challenging governmental policies bear the burden of showing that classifications or distinctions drawn by government between people are unreasonable. In practice few laws reviewed under this standard of scrutiny are found in violation of equal protection (Grossman and Wells, 1988).

But when government classifications limit fundamental freedoms or rights or force distinctions based on race or national origin, the second major standard requiring a heightened level of scrutiny commonly known as strict scrutiny has usually been applied. Under the application of strict scrutiny, the government must defend the validity of its actions by demonstrating that they serve a compelling governmental interest and are narrowly tailored in that there are no less-intrusive or less-drastic alternatives available to meet the government's end. This is the standard by which affirmative action by government is judged. In 1986, in *Wygant v. Jackson Board of Education* (476 U.S. 267), a plurality of the Supreme Court endorsed the principle that strict scrutiny should be the basis for review of affirmative action by state or local government, and later, in 1989, in *City of Richmond v. Croson* (488 U.S. 469) a majority endorsed the application of strict scrutiny to review affirmative action by subnational governments.

Strict scrutiny also became the appropriate level of review for federal government affirmative action programs as the result of the Supreme Court's ruling in 1995 in *Adarand v. Pena* (515 U.S. 200). Following that decision, any racial classifications incorporated into voluntary affirmative action programs by state, local, or federal employers must be shown to serve a compelling governmental interest in order to achieve Constitutional legitimacy. Exactly what type of interest will be sufficiently compelling to permit such action is unclear, but it is likely that the correction of past discrimination by the government employer involved may be one such interest. Once a compelling governmental interest is identified, the method used to achieve that interest must be narrowly tailored. This means that affirmative action should not impose any undue burden on innocent third parties, that is, the government must use the least intrusive means available to achieve its end. Affirmative action that compromises a bona fide seniority system during times of layoffs, for example, will not withstand constitutional scrutiny if it places an undue burden on nonminorities. Affirmative action in the form of hiring or promotion goals and timetables may be less intrusive than a program that violates seniority rights (see *Wygant*), and given evidence of past discrimination by government, such an approach would presumably be acceptable, although there is no way to know with certainty how the Court will respond to such a case.

EQUAL EMPLOYMENT OPPORTUNITY
AND AFFIRMATIVE ACTION IN THE FUTURE

Will affirmative action survive long into the twenty-first century? If the employment of minorities and women continues to increase in areas where they are currently underrepresented, it will eventually become difficult to sustain political support for preferential forms of the policy. Ultimately, then, such practices may come to an end. But, of course, the debate will focus, and to a considerable extent has already focused, on the question of how much progress for minorities and women is sufficient. At this time, women and minorities remain underrepresented in higher-level positions in most government agencies, so we can expect that the issue will remain on the agenda for some time to come, provided there is no further action by the Supreme Court to tighten current Constitutional limitations imposed on preferential programs. Such a ruling by the Court could come, however, in the form of a very restrictive interpretation of the circumstances that would comprise a government interest sufficiently compelling to enable preferential affirmative action to survive strict scrutiny. Of course, preferential affirmative action by the federal government could be curtailed also through Congressional action, and states may move to prohibit such policies, as has already been done in California and Washington.

An extremely restrictive court ruling on affirmative action has already emerged at the circuit court level. The Fifth Circuit Court of Appeals ruled in 1996 that the circumstances that would permit the use of race as a factor in state university admissions were exceedingly narrow (*Hopwood v. State of Texas*, 78 F. 3d 932). The Supreme Court later refused to take this case under review, thus allowing the decision to stand, although the high Court did not officially endorse the circuit court opinion. Similar cases are currently progressing through the judicial process, and if an appropriate case does eventually make it to the Supreme Court, given the current composition of that body, affirmative action that involves goals and limited preferences could be in jeopardy.

What will be left of affirmative action if goals and preferential policies are eliminated? In that situation, future programs might resemble affirmative action typical of the early 1960s, based largely on minority outreach or recruitment efforts. Employers, for example, could still work to attract minorities or women into their pool of applicants, but actual selection decisions would be required to be free from the consideration of race or sex. Whether such policies will be effective in overcoming discrimination against women and minority group members is open to question. One factor that may work to the advantage of minorities, however, is the ever-increasing racial and ethnic diversity in the United States. As minorities become a larger segment of the population nationally, many organizations may find increased advantages in drawing on the talents and abilities of all people, regardless or racial or ethnic background. The manner in which this factor will ultimately operate, and the effectiveness of future efforts to combat discrimination, will be revealed in the coming years.

With respect to federal law and the regulation of state and local equal employment opportunity programs, there have recently been some very significant rulings by the Supreme Court. This development began in 1996, in *Seminole Tribe v. Florida* (517 U.S. 44) where the Court ruled that Congress does not have power under Article I of the constitution to abrogate a state's sovereign immunity in federal court. In other words, state governments cannot be sued in federal court for a failure to implement provisions of federal law enacted pursuant to the authority of Congress contained in Article I. The Supreme Court's decision in this case rests on a rather expansive interpretation of the Eleventh Amendment to the constitution, and it could have grave implications for state employees seeking relief from alleged state violations of a wide variety of federal statutes that presumably would include the Civil Rights Act of 1991 and the Equal Employment Opportunity Act of 1972 which establish and outline state and local government responsibilities under Title VII of the Civil Rights Act of 1964. Indeed, at the time of this writing, the Court is considering a challenge to the Americans with Disabilities Act. In effect, these laws (and others) may apply to the states, but state employees may not have the ability to sue the state to seek enforcement unless, of course, the state waves its right to immunity. In 1999 in a similar case (*Alden et al. v. Maine*, 119 S.

Ct. 2240) the Court ruled that Congress also lacks the power to abrogate a state's sovereign immunity in state court. This ruling, which is based on the same reasoning as Seminole, has the effect of preventing state employees from suing a nonconsenting state in its own courts to force compliance with federal law. Finally, in what to date is the most significant development along these lines, the Court ruled on January 11, 2000, in *Kimel v. Florida Board of Regents* (No. 98-791) that the application of provisions of the Age Discrimination in Employment Act of 1967, which would allow state or local government employees to sue their employers under the law, also represented an unconstitutional abrogation of state sovereign immunity by Congress, acting under authority of the Fourteenth Amendment. While practical implications of these decisions are not yet entirely clear, they raise fundamental questions about the effectiveness of federal statutory law as a mechanism to combat discriminatory behavior by state governments, and it may well be that state law itself will become the primary check against discriminatory behavior by state and local government institutions in the future.

REFERENCES

EDLEY, CHRISTOPHER, JR. 1996. *Not All Black and White: Affirmative Action, Race, and American Values.* New York: Hill and Wang.

GARFINKEL, HERBERT. 1959. *When Negros March: The March on Washington Movement and the Organizational Politics for FEPC.* Glencoe, Illinois: Free Press.

GRAHAM, HUGH DAVIS. 1990. *The Civil Rights Era: Origins and Development of National Policy, 1960–1972.* New York: Oxford University Press.

GROSSMAN, J. B., and R. WELLS. 1988. *Constitutional Law and Judicial Policy Making.* New York: Longman.

HAYS, STEVEN. 1998. Staffing the Bureaucracy: Employee Recruitment and Selection. In *Handbook of Human Resource Management in Government,* Stephen E. Condrey, ed. San Francisco: Jossey-Bass, pp. 298–321.

HOLMES, S. A. 1995. Programs Based on Sex and Race Are Under Attack: Dole Seeks Elimination *New York Times* (March 16, 1995):p. 1A.

KELLOUGH, J. EDWARD. 1989. *Federal Equal Employment Opportunity Policy and Numerical Goals and Timetables: An Impact Assessment.* New York: Praeger.

KELLOUGH, J. EDWARD. 1991. "The Supreme Court, Affirmative Action, and Public Management: Where Do We Stand Today?" *The American Review of Public Administration,* Vol. 21, No. 3 (September):255–269.

KELLOUGH, J. EDWARD. 2000. The Americans with Disabilities Act: A Note on Personnel Policy Impacts in State Government, *Public Personnel Management* Vol. 29, No. 2 (Summer):211–224.

KELLOUGH, J. EDWARD, and DAVID H. ROSENBLOOM. 1992. Representative Bureaucracy and the EEOC: Did Civil Service Reform Make a Difference? In *The Promise and Paradox of Civil Service Reform,* Patricia W. Ingraham and David H. Rosenbloom, eds. Pittsburgh: University of Pittsburgh Press, pp. 245–266.

KRISLOV, SAMUEL. 1967. *The Negro in Federal Employment: The Quest for Equal Opportunity.* New York: Praeger.

MEIER, KENNETH J. 1993. Representative Bureaucracy: A Theoretical and Empirical Exposition. In *Research in Public Administration,* James L. Perry, ed. New Greenwich, Connecticut: JAI Press, pp. 1–35.

MEIER, KENNETH J., and JOSEPH STEWART, JR. 1992. The Impact of Representative Bureaucracies: Educational Systems and Public Policies, *The American Review of Public Administration.* Vol. 22, No. 3 (September):157–171.

MORGAN, RUTH P. 1970. *The President and Civil Rights: Policy-Making by Executive Order.* New York: St. Martin's Press.

REED, MERL E. 1991. *Seedtime for the Modern Civil Rights Movement: The President's Committee on Fair Employment Practice, 1941–1946.* Baton Rouge: Louisiana State University Press.

ROSENBLOOM, DAVID H. 1977. *Federal Equal Employment Opportunity: Politics and Public Personnel Administration.* New York: Praeger.

SELDEN, SALLY COLEMAN. 1997. *The Promise of Representative Bureaucracy: Diversity and Responsiveness in a Government Agency.* Armonk, New York: M. E. Sharpe.

SELDEN, SALLY COLEMAN, JEFFERY L. BRUDNEY, and J. EDWARD KELLOUGH. 1998. Bureaucracy as a Representative Institution: Toward a Reconciliation of Bureaucratic Government and Democratic Theory. *American Journal of Political Science* Vol. 42, No. 3 (July):717–744.

SELIG, JOEL L. 1987. Affirmative Action in Employment: The Legacy of a Supreme Court Majority. *Indiana Law Journal* Vol. 63:301–368.

STEPHANOPOULOS, GEORGE, and CHRISTOPHER EDLEY, JR. 1995. *Affirmative Action Review: Report to the President.* Washington DC: U.S. Government Printing Office.

TAYLOR, BRON RAYMOND. 1991. *Affirmative Action at Work: Law, Politics, and Ethics.* Pittsburgh: University of Pittsburgh Press.

16

Sexual Harassment in the Workplace

SALLY COLEMAN SELDEN

Lynchburg College

Over the past decade, the number of sexual harassment lawsuits has increased, the media attention to these incidents has heightened, and the employer and employee costs associated with sexual harassment have mounted. In the 1990s, the public witnessed a number of sexual harassment scandals, including the nomination of Clarence Thomas to the Supreme Court, Paula Jones's allegations against President Clinton, and sexual misconduct at the Navy Tailhook Convention and the Army's Aberdeen training school. Despite growing attention to the issue, the Supreme Court remained relatively quiet on the subject, ruling on just two cases prior to 1998. In 1998, twelve years after ruling on its first sexual harassment case, the Supreme Court addressed four cases that clarified, at least to some extent, the parameters of sexual harassment.

The story of General Kennedy, the Army's highest ranking woman, raises questions of the pervasiveness of sexual harassment and how it should be handled organizationally. In early 2000, General Kennedy reported that General Smith, recently appointed as Deputy Inspector General of the Army, grabbed and attempted to kiss her in 1996. At the time, she elected not to report the incident. Kennedy finally went public because Smith's new position would put him in charge of investigating wrongdoing by Army officials, including accusations of sexual harassment (Meyers, 2000). The case prompted other female military officers to reveal their stories of sexual harassment (Becker, 2000). Also in 1999, two high-profile cases against the University of North Carolina's soccer coach and Syracuse University's tennis coach raised concerns about the increase in sexual harassment incidents in women's sports (Finn, 1999).

Sexual harassment in the workplace and in educational institutions is not a new issue, but its heightened visibility has forced human resource managers to review organizational policies and dissemination strategies. While most employers have a sexual harassment policy, many do not publicize it or train their employees adequately. The National Collegiate Athletic Association (NCAA), for example, does not have a sexual harassment policy—a problem it openly acknowledges (Finn, 1999).

The direct and indirect costs of sexual harassment are numerous. From an employee's perspective, working in a hostile environment caused by sexual harassment results in mental and emotional stress. Sometimes employees take leave without pay or resign from their jobs because of the stressful work environment. Other times, employees are demoted or overlooked for promotion. Still others lose their jobs after being harassed. Sexual harassment imposes costs not only on employees, but also on the organization as a whole. For example, between 1992 and 1994, the U.S. Merit Systems Protections Board (1995:23) estimated that sexual harassment cost the federal government approximately $327 million because of turnover, use of sick leave, and lost individual and group productivity. In 1999, the Ford Motor Company reached a settlement with the Equal Employment Opportunity Commission (EEOC), paying almost $8 million in damages to women employees who alleged sexual and racial harassment. Moreover, Ford estimated that it would cost nearly $10 million to train all of its employees properly about forms of discrimination on the job. Recently, a jury awarded $80.7 million to a former United Parcel Service (UPS) manager who alleged that the organization retaliated against her after she accused a driver of inappropriate behavior (ChicagoLegal-Net.com, 2000). As suggested above, however, the true cost of sexual harassment exceeds the direct damages from litigation paid by an employer.

The purpose of this chapter is to introduce the concept of sexual harassment and discuss the current policy environment. First, the chapter briefly describes the origins of the concept. Then, it provides statistics about the prevalence of sexual harassment in the workplace. Third, the chapter discusses the policy arena, including pertinent legislation, relevant Supreme Court decisions, and administrative regulations governing sexual harassment. Finally, broad guidelines for designing an organizational sexual harassment policy are outlined.

EVOLUTION OF SEXUAL HARASSMENT AS A CONSTRUCT

The women's movement in the late 1960s and early 1970s was critical in calling attention to sexual harassment in the workplace. In 1966, the National Organization for Women (NOW) formed to exert pressure on the Equal Employment Opportunity Commission (EEOC) to enforce Title VII's prohibition against sex discrimination in employment (De Hart, 1991). Members of NOW were effective in their lobbying efforts to expand affirmative action guidelines to include women, and in challenging systems of sex segregation in different organizations (De Hart, 1991). By the mid-1970s, many feminists focused on women's sexual exploitation in the workplace. In 1975, Working Women United (WWU), a group formed in Ithaca, New York, defined the term "sexual harassment" as "the treatment of women workers as sexual objects" (Farley, 1980; Schultz, 1998). One of the earliest publications to use the term sexual harassment was Carroll Brodsky's book, *The Harassed Worker*. As opposed to the early feminist movement, Brodsky defined sexual harassment in nonsexual terms: "Harassment behavior involves repeated and persistent attempts to torment, wear down, frustrate or get a reaction from another. It is treatment that persistently provokes, pressures, frightens, intimidates, or otherwise discomforts another person" (Brodsky, 1976:2). Brodsky (1976) also contended that harassment could be both vertical (top-down—supervisor to subordinate—and bottom up—subordinate to supervisor) and horizontal (peer to peer).

In 1980, the EEOC issued formal guidelines defining sexual harassment for all employers. According to the U.S. EEOC (1997), sexual harassment includes "unwelcome sexual advances, requests for sexual favors, and other verbal or physical conduct of a sexual nature . . . when submission to or rejection of this conduct explicitly or implicitly affects an individual's employment, unreasonably interferes with an individual's work performance or creates an intimidating, hostile or offensive work environment." In the workplace, two types of sexual harassment are legally recognized 1) quid pro quo and 2) hostile work environment. Quid pro quo harassment is defined as a situation where a person demands or requests sexual favors from an employee in return for employment benefits, such as a promotion or salary increase, or as a condition of employment. When an employee refuses to succumb to sexual advances, the harasser denies the employee tangible economic or job benefits. Hostile working environment harassment occurs when behaviors create an offensive or hostile work climate, such as touching, sexual remarks, and overtures. For both types of harassment, the victim, as well as the harasser, may be of either gender, and the victim does not necessarily have to be of the opposite gender of the harasser. As Brodsky argued earlier, harassment can occur both vertically and horizontally. The harasser can be a supervisor, a peer, or a subordinate in the organization, as well as a nonemployee, including for example, a client or a contractor of the organization.

CURRENT ENVIRONMENT: THE GAP BETWEEN INCIDENTS AND REPORTING OF SEXUAL HARASSMENT

Sexual harassment is a growing area of concern for all organizations and their employees. In 1992, a Washington Post-ABC poll showed that 85 percent of persons surveyed believed sexual harassment was a problem in the workplace. Moreover, sexual harassment filings with the EEOC and the Fair Employment Practices agencies (FEPA) have been increasing (see Table 16–1). Between 1992 and 1999, the number of charges filed with the EEOC under Title VII grew 44.5 percent from 10,532 to 15,222. During this period, the percentage of complaints filed by men increased from 9.1 percent to 12.1 percent. The trend in federal government agencies is also upward with the number of sexual harassment issues alleged increasing by 83 percent between 1982 and 1998 (see Table 16–2).

Studies have shown that many women and men experience harassment and that some harassment occurs repeatedly and for long periods of time (U.S. General Accounting Office [GAO], 1995a and 1995b). However, many individuals who are sexually harassed elect not to report the incident or to use an employer's sexual harassment policy (Reese and Lindenberg, 1997). Because of this tendency,

TABLE 16–1   Sexual Harassment Charges Filed with EEOC and FEPA
Under Title VII FY 1992–FY 1999

Fiscal Year	Number of Charges Filed	Percentage Filed by Men
1992	10,532	9.1%
1993	11,908	9.1
1994	14,420	9.9
1995	15,549	9.9
1996	15,342	10.0
1997	15,889	11.6
1998	15,618	12.9
1999	15,222	12.1

Source: U.S. EEOC, 2000.

the number of formal complaints filed may underestimate the pervasiveness of sexual harassment in an organization. For example, a 1995 U.S. General Accounting Office study reported that of the 32 percent of National Institute of Health employees who were sexually harassed, 96 percent did not elect to report the situation. An alternative mechanism to determine the scope of the problem is to ask employees directly whether they have been sexually harassed. Using this approach, Gutek (1985) found that approximately 50 percent of the civilian women and 37 percent of the civilian men surveyed had been victims of sexual harassment. None of the women who experienced harassment sought legal recourse, however, and only 22 percent even told another person about the incident. In 1991, *The New York Times* reported that, in a poll taken with CBS, 38 percent of women indicated they had experienced unwanted sexual attention from their supervisor.

The prevalence of sexual harassment in the federal government looks similar. The U.S. Merit Systems Protection Board surveyed employees about their experiences with sexual harassment in 1980, 1987, and 1994. Forty-four percent of women and nineteen percent of men responding to the 1994 survey indicated that they had been sexually harassed (U.S. Merit Systems Protection Board [MSPB], 1995:15). Between 1980 and 1987, these percentages increased slightly both for women and men. In 1994, the Departments of State and Veteran's Affairs reported

TABLE 16–2   Sexual Harassment Charges Filed By Federal Agencies
FY 1982–FY 1998

Fiscal Year	Sexual Harassment Complaints Filed
1982	890
1988	315
1989	488
1995	1,478
1996	1,473
1997	1,507
1998	1,629

Source: U.S. EEOC, 1982, 1989, 1998.

the highest incidence of sexual harassment among men, whereas, women experienced more harassment in the Departments of Transportation, State, and Navy than in other federal agencies.

Although survey data provide a more complete picture of the pervasiveness of sexual harassment in the workplace, the data must be interpreted with caution. For example, reviewing surveys of uniformed Army personnel over time suggests that the percentage of soldiers experiencing sexual harassment is declining (Walters, 1997). However, upon closer inspection, we find that the survey results are difficult to interpret. Women soldiers polled in 1995 responded differently to three sets of questions regarding harassment. One survey asked if the person had been sexually harassed, with 25 percent indicating they had. The second instrument asked if the person had experienced one of ten types of harassing behavior; 61 percent responded affirmatively. The third survey queried whether the person had experienced one of twenty-four types of harassing behavior, and about 82 percent answered yes.

While the evidence suggests that sexual harassment is an enduring and pervasive workplace concern, it is difficult to ascertain the exact magnitude of the problem because individuals define and experience sexual harassment differently and often elect not to share their experience with the organization formally. In order to understand the gap between incidents of sexual harassment and reporting of those situations, Reese and Lindenberg (1997) examined two public sector organizations. They found that between 21 and 25 percent of their sample had been sexually harassed, but only 8 percent had reported an incidence of sexual harassment. According to the survey findings, 75 percent of respondents were aware of the organization's sexual harassment policy. However, some employees opted not to report the incident because they feared negative personal consequences. Other employees (45 percent) preferred to handle the situation informally.

THE PUBLIC POLICY ARENA OF SEXUAL HARASSMENT

Relevant Legislation

Sexual harassment is a complicated area of employment law, partly because employers must comply with both state and federal laws, which have been interpreted differently by the courts. Before turning to a discussion of the judicial decisions that provide broader policy direction to the interpretation of federal law, this section briefly reviews laws that govern sexual harassment cases and workplace policies in both the public and private sector. Practitioners should note that when state sexual harassment laws offer greater employee protection, they take precedence over federal guidance. Illinois, for example, was the first state to ban sexual harassment of state employees. Considerable variation exists among states with respect to the legal doctrine governing sexual harassment. Some states, such as New Jersey, Pennsylvania, Rhode Island, and Wisconsin, have antisexual harassment laws. These antisexual harassment laws employ EEOC's definition of sexual harassment, but they vary in terms of policy requirements and punishments. For example, in Rhode Island, employers with fifty or more employees are required to adopt and distribute a workplace policy and statement against sexual harassment.

Wisconsin's law requires the Board of Regents to include sexual assault and sexual harassment in its orientation program for newly entering college students.

At the federal level, three laws are of particular significance to employers: Title VII of the Civil Rights Act of 1964, Title IX of the Education Amendments of 1972, and the Civil Rights Act of 1991. Title VII prohibits employment discrimination based on race, sex, national origin, or religion. It applies to public, nonprofit, and private organizations, with one exception (see Lee and Greenlaw, 1995 for a discussion of how the law pertaining to a hostile environment varies among employers). Military personnel are not covered by Title VII, although Department of Defense civilian employees are (Lee and Greenlaw, 1997). Over time, Title VII prohibition against sex discrimination has been interpreted to include sexual harassment. In 1976, for example, a federal district court found that firing an employee for refusing the sexual advances of a supervisor was illegal under Title VII (*Williams v. Saxbe*, 1976). In 1980, the EEOC issued regulations that defined sexual harassment as a form of sex discrimination prohibited by the Civil Rights Act of 1964. These EEOC regulations were validated by the 1986 Supreme Court case of *Meritor Savings Bank, FSB v. Vinson* (1986).

Title IX of the Education Amendments of 1972 prohibits sex discrimination in schools and school programs that receive federal funding. The law applies to elementary, secondary, and postsecondary schools and is enforced by the Office for Civil Rights of the Department of Education. When sex discrimination has occurred, schools, colleges, and universities are given an opportunity to correct the problem. If an appropriate action is not taken by the educational institution, federal funding may be revoked.

Lastly, the Civil Rights Act (CRA) of 1991 includes provisions that expand a victim's right to sue and collect compensatory (punitive) damages for sexual discrimination or harassment. Prior to this legislation, plaintiffs could only collect back pay and attorneys' fees. In an organization with more than 200 employees, for example, a victim of sexual harassment may recover a combined award of compensatory and punitive damages up to $300,000. Moreover, and arguably, the most significant provision of the 1991 CRA grants sexual harassment plaintiffs the right to jury trials.

Supreme Court Decisions

Defining Sexual Harassment under Title VII of the Civil Rights Act of 1964. The courts have identified two basic types of sexual harassment that are actionable under Title VII—quid pro quo and the hostile work environment. Much of the case law defining the parameters of sexual harassment emerged first from lower courts. For example, the 1981 judicial decision *Bundy v. Jackson* was critical in forming today's legal definition of sexual harassment. Sandra Bundy worked for the District of Columbia's Department of Corrections where she was sexually propositioned by at least three of her supervisors. After rejecting their sexual advances, Bundy's employment status was not changed; that is, she suffered no tangible job consequence. The court ruled that "Bundy proved that she was the victim of a practice of sexual harassment and a discriminatory work environment permitted by her employer. Her rights under Title VII were therefore violated." The sexually stereotyped insults and demeaning propositions to which Bundy was subjected caused her undue anxiety and created an "offensive or hostile" work environment.

Thus, a two-dimensional approach to sexual harassment claims emerged. Sexual harassment claims could be classified as quid pro quo within the realm of a hostile work environment.

Five years after the *Bundy* case, the Supreme Court issued its first landmark decision regarding sexual harassment—*Meritor Savings Bank, FSB v. Vinson* (1986). The Court affirmed the distinction that emerged from *Bundy v. Jackson* (1981), holding that two types of harassment are actionable under Title VII: harassment that involves the conditioning of employment benefits on sexual favors (quid pro quo) and those where a hostile environment is created. Mechelle Vinson testified that Sidney Taylor, her supervisor and a vice president of Meritor Savings Bank, repeatedly demanded sexual favors from her, usually at the bank both during and after work hours. Vinson indicated that she and Taylor had sex between 40 and 50 times, that Taylor had fondled her in front of other employees, and that Taylor had forcibly raped her on several occasions. Finding for Vinson, the Court ruled that noneconomic injury was a form of sex discrimination covered by Title VII, but the Court did not address employer liability with the same clarity. The Court strongly agreed with the EEOC that Congress wanted the courts to apply agency principles—defining a supervisor as an agent of his employer and imputing responsibility to the employer when a supervisor exercises authority delegated to him by his employer—to guide decisions on employer liability. Nevertheless, the Court remanded the case to lower courts to determine the conditions under which employers are held responsible. The Supreme Court disagreed with the Court of Appeals decision "that employers are always automatically liable for sexual harassment by their supervisors. . . . For the same reason, absence of notice to an employer does not necessarily insulate that employer from liability." While the *Meritor* decision offered clarity to the legal definition of sexual harassment, it left considerable uncertainty around what forms of behaviors constitute harassment, especially those that create a hostile environment, and the extent of employer liability or responsibility for such an environment (Lee and Greenlaw, 1995).

By the early 1990s, lower court rulings varied tremendously concerning the severity and pervasiveness of behaviors required to create a hostile work environment (Lee and Greenlaw, 1995). In 1993, the Supreme Court addressed this issue in its decision, *Harris v. Forklift Systems, Inc.* The Court ruled that victims need not show that they suffered serious psychological injury as a result of the harassment in order to prevail in court. The Court affirmed the standard stated in *Meritor Savings Bank v. Vinson*—"Title VII is violated when the workplace is permeated with discriminatory behavior that is sufficiently severe or pervasive to create a discriminatorily hostile or abusive working environment" as determined or perceived by a "reasonable" person. While the Court did not elaborate on the definition of a "reasonable" person, the EEOC has stated that "the reasonable person standard should consider the victim's perspective and not stereotyped notions of acceptable behavior" (U.S. EEOC, 1994). The issue is whether a "reasonable" person in the "victim's circumstances would have found the alleged behavior to be hostile or abusive" (U.S. EEOC, 1994).

In this case, Charles Hardy, the president of the company, had referred to Harris, the plaintiff, as a "dumb ass woman," made unwanted sexual innuendoes to her, and asked her (and other female employees) to get coins from his front pants pocket. Harris complained to Hardy about his conduct, who promptly apologized and promised to cease. Within a month, Hardy resumed his behavior, leading Harris to quit and subsequently file suit against Forklift Systems, Inc. The company argued that because Teresa Harris had not demonstrated any obvious psychological harm as a result of Hardy's actions, Title VII was not violated. Finding for the plaintiff, the Court unanimously ruled that Title VII "comes into play before the harassing conduct leads to a nervous breakdown. A discriminatorily abusive work environment, even one that does not seriously affect employees' psychological well being, can and often will detract from employees' job performance, discourage employees from remaining on the job, or keep them from advancing their careers."

Prior to 1998, the Supreme Court had not heard an harassment case involving persons of the same sex. The Court ruled in *Oncale v. Sundowner Offshore Services, Inc.* (1998) that "nothing in Title VII necessarily bars a claim of discrimination . . . merely because the plaintiff and the defendants . . . are of the same sex." In this case, Joseph Oncale worked on an eight-man crew aboard an oil platform in the Gulf of Mexico. Oncale contended that his male supervisors and coworkers abused and sexually taunted him, pushing a bar of soap into his anus and threatening homosexual rape. Although he complained to his employer, the company did not respond, so Oncale quit. The Court judged that Title VII's prohibition against discrimination "because of sex protects men as well as women." This decision provides numerous employees, previously overlooked, protection against sex discrimination under Title VII. The Court, however, noted that Title VII "does not prohibit all verbal or physical harassment in the workplace" but makes actionable only conduct "so objectively offensive as to alter the 'conditions' of the victim's employment." Thus, "ordinary socializing in the workplace—such as male-on-male horseplay or intersexual flirtation" is not illegal. The Court noted that "common sense, and an appropriate sensitivity to social context, will enable courts and juries to distinguish between simple teasing or roughhousing among members of the same sex, and conduct which a reasonable person in the plaintiff's position would find severely hostile or abusive." The Court, however, gave little guidance for determining when conduct crosses the line to sex-based discrimination, leaving lower courts to work out what proof is required to establish that same-gender harassment is because of sex (Carleton and Carleton, 2000). As a result, the Court's broad, conduct-based analysis might be interpreted by lower courts in ways that allow standards to vary depending upon the work environment.

Defining Employer Liability for Sexual Harassment under Title VII of the Civil Rights Act of 1964.

Courts have addressed the conditions under which an employer is held liable or responsible for sexual harassment. In 1998, the Supreme Court ruled on two such cases, one involving a public employer and one involving a private employer.

In *Faragher v. Boca Raton* (1998), the Court determined that public employers can be held liable for harassment under Title VII even if the employee has not explicitly alerted the employer about the sexual harassment. However, the employer may raise an affirmative defense to liability or damages depending on the situation. While attending college, Beth Ann Faragher worked as a lifeguard for the City of Boca Raton, Florida. During her five-year employment, her immediate supervisors repeatedly subjected Faragher and other women lifeguards to "uninvited and offensive touching." Faragher also testified that her supervisors made lewd remarks and spoke of women in offensive terms. For example, one of her supervisors told her "date me or clean toilets for a year." The City of Boca Raton asserted that because the harassment was not reported to higher authorities and occurred in a remote location, it should not be held liable. While the city had a sexual harassment policy, it had not widely disseminated the policy. The Court held that this failure defeated any invocation of an affirmative defense to liability. Clarifying conditions of an employer's vicarious liability, the Court adopted the following stance:

> An employer is subject to vicarious liability to an . . . employee for an actionable hostile environment created by a supervisor. . . . When no tangible employment action is taken, a defending employer may raise an affirmative defense to liability or damages. . . . The defense comprises two necessary elements: (a) that the employer exercised reasonable care to prevent and correct promptly any sexually harassing behavior, and (b) that the plaintiff employee unreasonably failed to take advantage of any preventive or corrective opportunities provided by the employer or to avoid harm otherwise.

The Court confirmed that no affirmative defense is available when an employee is terminated, demoted, or undesirably reassigned.

In a separate but related decision about employer liability, *Burlington Industries v. Ellerth* (1998), Kimberly Ellerth's second-level supervisor, Ted Slowik, repeatedly threatened her job unless she succumbed to his advances. She never registered a formal complaint nor was her job ever jeopardized, but after fifteen months as a salesperson for Burlington Industries she resigned because of the constant harassment. Burlington Industries argued that it should not be held liable because Ellerth had suffered no job consequence and had even been promoted; moreover, she had failed to use the company's sexual harassment complaint procedure.

The Court stated that Congress gave an explicit instruction to the courts to interpret Title VII based on agency principles, by defining the term "employer" to include its "agents." Building on this rationale and consistent with its decision in *Meritor,* the Court confirmed in Ellerth that the employer is strictly liable under the quid pro quo theory for a supervisor's harassing or discriminatory actions that lead to significant changes in a person's employment status. Moreover, consistent with its ruling in *Faragher,* the Court judged that an employer could be held liable in situations where a supervisor causes a hostile work environment, even when the employee suffers no tangible job consequence, and the employer was unaware of the offensive conduct. That is, the employer may be liable where a supervisor causes a hostile work environment by his or her severe or pervasive inappropriate conduct, subject to an affirmative defense. Based on this case and *Faragher,* employers, both public and private, are best protected by developing and disseminating an antiharassment policy. However, if an employee has reason to fear retaliation for coming forward and using the policy, the employer is not able to use policy as an affirmative defense. The burden of proof for any affirmative defense rests on the employer.

Defining Employer Liability for Sexual Harassment Under Title IX of the Education Amendments of 1972.

In the late 1990s, the Supreme Court ruled on two cases involving liability for sexual harassment in educational institutions. The first dealt with student-teacher harassment and the second with student-student harassment.

The 1998 Supreme Court case, *Gebser v. Lago Vista Independent School District,* concerned harassment of a student by a teacher. The Court ruled in a 5–4 decision that school districts were only liable for student harassment by teachers if school officials knew of the problem and refused to intervene. In this case, when the school district discovered a teacher, Frank Waldrop, having sex with a student, he was arrested and promptly fired. Prior to this incident, a group of parents had complained to the school about sexual comments Waldrop made in class, but these concerns had not been reported to the superintendent. Also, the school district had not promulgated or distributed a formal antisexual harassment policy or procedure for lodging such a complaint. The Court, however, viewed Title IX as a contractual framework, distinguishing it from "Title VII, which is framed in terms not of a condition but of an outright prohibition." The Court was unwilling to subject schools to liability absent a clear directive from Congress. The Court voiced concern that the award of damages might unfairly exceed the amount of federal funding actually received by the school. The Court held that a school is liable for teacher-student sexual harassment only when someone with authority to take corrective action has received actual notice of the harassment and has exhibited "deliberate indifference." In a strong dissent, Justice Stevens warned that the rule crafted by the Court might create a disincentive for schools to take steps to discover harassment and avoid liability through an "ostrich" defense.

In 1999, the Supreme Court tackled the question of a school district's liability for harassment of a student by another student in *Davis v. Monroe*. LaShonda Davis was in the fifth grade when she first complained to her teachers that a student sitting next to her was sexually harassing her. Over a five month period, the harassment took various forms, including offensive language, fondling, and sexual abuse. The student and her mother reported the encounters on numerous occasions both to her teachers and to the school principal. The school did not provide any protections to Davis other than, after three months, changing her seat. After the school refused to take action, the child's mother reported the situation to the Sheriff's department. The harassing student was charged with and subsequently pleaded guilty to sexual battery. The Davis family filed against the school district because it took no disciplinary action to protect the victim. The Court found that the child was the victim of repeated acts of harassment and that the misconduct was severe, pervasive, and objectively offensive. Applying the standard set out in *Gebser,* the Court ruled that public schools can be sued and forced to pay damages for failing to stop sexual harassment by students but only where the school district is cognizant of the incident and is "deliberately indifferent." In addition, the harassment must be deemed so severe that it deprives the victim of access to educational opportunities or benefits provided by the school district.

Thus the Supreme Court has provided guidance to employers about the parameters of sexual harassment and the conditions under which employers can be held responsible. The Court has made a clear distinction about employer liability, depending upon whether a case falls under Title VII of the Civil Rights Acts of 1964 or under Title IX of the Education Amendments of 1972. Lee and Greenlaw (1997:133) project that the recent "rulings will lead to greater litigation in the realm of sexual harassment and may emphasize the need for some action by Congress and/or the Equal Employment Opportunity Commission."

The EEOC: Providing Guidance and Enforcing the Law

The Equal Employment Opportunity Commission is the agency responsible for publishing regulations governing sexual harassment in the workplace and providing policy and enforcement guidance to help employers interpret and apply EEOC regulations, federal law, and judicial decisions governing sexual harassment (U.S. EEOC, 1990; 1999). Annually, the EEOC publishes its regulations about sexual harassment in Title 29 of the Code of Federal Regulations (CFR). The EEOC also produces policy guidelines to help employers interpret and understand judicial rulings. Recent policy guidance provided by the EEOC, for example, deals with the issue of employer liability in light of the *Burlington Industries* and *Faragher* Supreme Court decisions. In addition to formulating regulations and policy guidance, the EEOC can be involved in the investigation and prosecution of sexual harassment claims. Despite its multiple roles, the EEOC has continually reiterated that all employers need a written, antidiscrimination (including sexual harassment) policy.

FORMULATING A WORKPLACE POLICY

Employers are liable for sexual harassment in their workplace that they are aware of, unless they take prompt and effective actions to remedy the situation. Even if employers are unaware of the harassment, they are still potentially responsible. Employers may limit their liability in hostile work environment cases by taking appropriate actions and providing avenues to employees to raise harassment complaints. According to the EEOC (1999:9), "it is necessary for employers to establish, publicize, and enforce anti-harassment policies and complaint procedures." Such policies must be in writing and disseminated widely to employees. At a minimum, a sexual harassment policy must address three objectives. First, the policy's goal must be to prevent incidents of sexual harassment in the workplace. Second, the policy must encourage employees to report incidents as soon as possible so that the employer can correct the problem. Finally, the policy must be consistent with the applicable legislative and case law.

In light of these objectives and as suggested by the above mentioned EEOC regulations and guide posts, an antidiscrimination policy should do the following:

1. Clearly define behaviors that constitute harassment.
2. Declare that behaviors defined as harassment will not be tolerated and are prohibited in the workplace.
3. Assure that employees who make complaints of harassment or provide information related to such complaints will be protected against retaliation.
4. Establish a formal complaint procedure within the organization that mandates a prompt, thorough, and impartial investigation of every complaint.
5. Provide for prompt corrective action, including appropriate disciplinary action if unlawful harassment has occurred.
6. Assure that the employer will protect the confidentiality of harassment complaints to the extent possible.
7. Include training and education to sensitize all employees to harassment issues and the organization's policy.

An employer's policy should prohibit harassment by all persons in and associated with the organization, including supervisors, co-workers, and nonemployees. Moreover, the policy should encourage employees to report harassment *before* it becomes severe or pervasive so as to prevent its escalation to a level that violates federal law (U.S. EEOC, 1999).

A successful prevention program requires that employers communicate their policies to employees in as many ways as possible, starting with a training and education program. The policy should also be included in the staff handbook, posted in the organization in places staff gather and obtain news, and communicated orally during employee orientation. Moreover, the policy should be redistributed at least annually to employees and managers and also whenever it is updated.

An important ingredient of a successful sexual harassment program is the human resources (HR) department. The HR department plays a critical leadership role in the development, interpretation, and communication of an organization's sexual harassment policy. Typically, HR professionals are responsible for translating legal doctrine, including recent judicial rulings, into workplace policy and training employees about sexual harassment. HR staff schedules meetings with employees to discuss sexual harassment, conveys management's disapproval of sexual harassment, and informs employees of their rights and the methods for lodging complaints of harassment. HR professionals serve as important resources for managers and supervisors who need to be able to respond to situations involving sexual harassment quickly and effectively. In addition, HR departments are involved in the receipt and resolution of sexual harassment complaints.

CONCLUSION

Sexual harassment is an issue that confronts managers in all organizations and is costly to all parties involved. Although employers cannot completely eradicate the risk of sexual harassment incidents, they can significantly limit their liability by properly designing and implementing a sexual harassment policy. The role of the human resource professional is critical to the successful implementation of a sexual harassment policy and complaint procedure. The human resource professional needs to understand the issue's significance, the hidden and direct costs of sexual harassment, the legal and regulatory policy environment governing sexual harassment claims, as well as the employer's preventive policy and investigative procedures.

REFERENCES

BECKER, ELIZABETH. 2000. "Women in Military Say Silence on Harassment Protects Careers." *New York Times* A1 (May 12).

BRODSKY, CARROLL M. 1976. *The Harassed Worker*. Lexington, MA: Lexington Books.

Bundy v. Jackson 1981. 641 F.2d. 934 (D.C. Cir. 1981).

Burlington Industries v. Ellerth. 1998. 118 S. Ct. 2257.

CARLETON, FRANCIS, and JENNIFER CARLETON. 2000. Oncale and its Aftermath: The Damage Done? Paper presented at the Midwest Political Science Association Annual Meeting, April 27–30, 2000.

ChicagoLegalNet.com. 2000. Sexual Harassment Update. <www.chicagolegalnet.com/sh003.htm> Printed 5/13/00.

Davis v. Monroe. 1999. 119 S. Ct.

DE HART, JANE SHERRON. 1991. The New Feminism and the Dynamics of Social Change. In *Women's America: Refocusing the Past,* 3rd edition, Linda K. Kerber and Jane Sherron De Hart, eds. New York: Oxford University Press.

Faragher v. City of Boca Raton. 1998. 118 S. Ct. 2275.

FARLEY, LIN. 1980. *Sexual Shakedown: The Sexual Harassment of Women on the Job.* New York: Warner Books.

FINN, ROBIN. 1999. Out of Bounds: Growth in Women's Sports Stirs Harassment Issue. *New York Times* Section 1, 1 (March 7).

Garber v. Saxon Business Products, Inc. 1977. 552 F. 2d 1032 (4th Cir. 1977).

Gebser v. Lago Vista Independent School District. 1998. 118 S.Ct. 1989.

GUTEK, BARBARA A. 1985. *Sex and the Workplace.* San Francisco, CA: Jossey-Bass.

Harris v. Forklift Systems, Inc. 1993. 114 S.Ct. 367.

LEE, ROBERT D. JR. and PAUL S. GREENLAW. 1995. "The Legal Evolution of Sexual Harassment." *Public Administration Review* 55, 357-364.

——. 1997. "A Legal Perspective on Sexual Harassment." In Carolyn Ban and Norma M. Riccucci, eds., *Public Personnel Management: Current Concerns, Future Challenges,* 3rd edition. New York, Longman Press.

Meritor Savings Bank, FSB v. Vinson. 1986. 106 S.Ct. 2399.

MEYERS, STEVEN LEE. 2000. General in Harassment Case Faces an Accusation Herself. *New York Times* (April 8).

Oncale v. Sundowner Offshore Services, Inc. 1998. 118 S.Ct. 998.

REESE, LAURA A., and KAREN E. LINDENBERG. 1997. "Victimhood" and the Implementation of Sexual Harassment Policy. *Review of Public Personnel Administration* Winter:37–57.

SCHULTZ, VICKI. 1998. Reconceptualizing Sexual Harassment. *Yale Law Journal* 107:1683–1805.

U.S. Equal Employment Opportunity Commission. 1999. *Enforcement Guidance: Vicarious Employer Liability for Unlawful Harassment by Supervisors.* <http://www.eeoc.gov/docs/harassment.html> Printed 1/17/00.

——. 1994. *Enforcement Guidance on Harris v. Forklift Sys., Inc.* <http://www.eeoc.gov/docs/harris.html> Printed 9/21/00.

——. 1997. *Facts about Sexual Harassment.* <http://www.eeoc.gov/facts/fs-sex.html> Printed 2/15/00.

——. 1998. *Federal Sector Report on EEO Complaint Processing and Appeals: Fiscal Year 1998.* Washington, DC: GPO.

——. 1990. *Policy Guidance on Current Issues of Sexual Harassment.* <http://www.eeoc.gov/docs/currentissues.html> Printed 1/17/00.

——. 1982. *Report on Pre-complaint Processing: FY 82.* Washington, DC: GPO.

——. 1989. *Report on Pre-complaint Counseling and Complaint Processing by Federal Agencies for Fiscal Year 1989.* Washington, DC: GPO.

——. 2000. *Sexual Harassment Charges EEOC & FEPAs Combined: FY 1992–FY 1999.* <http://www.eeoc.gov/stats/harass.html> Printed 5/8/00.

U.S. General Accounting Office. 1995a. *Equal Opportunity: DOD Studies on Discrimination in the Military.* GAO/NSAID-95-103. Washington, DC: GAO.

——. 1995b. *Equal Opportunity: NIH's Handling of Alleged Sexual Harassment and Sex Discrimination Matters.* GAO/GGD-95-195. Washington, DC: GAO.

U.S. Merit Systems Protection Board. 1995. *Sexual Harassment in the Federal Workplace: Trends, Progress, Continuing Challenges.* Washington, DC: U.S. Government Printing Office.

WALTERS, NOLAN. 1997. Public Given Distorted Image of Sexual Harassment in Military. *The Houston Chronicle* A, 20 (October 17).

Williams v. Saxbe. 1976. 413 F. Supp. 654 (D.D.c. 1976).

17

Working Together
Meeting the Challenges of Workforce Diversity

SONIA OSPINA AND JAMES F. O'SULLIVAN

New York University

INTRODUCTION

If you walked into a public office in the 1950s, you would probably see a workforce segregated by race and gender, if diversity existed at all. Managerial jobs would be held by white men, clerical staff with strictly limited duties would be women, and if any persons of color were in evidence they would likely be limited to men in manual or janitorial jobs. Today, in most organizations one expects to see a different picture, with a mixed group of employees working at all levels and decision-making capacities throughout the organization.

As the workforce in organizations has moved from homogeneous to mixed groups of individuals, employees now interact with co-workers, clients, supervisors or employees of different ethnicities and cultures, as part of daily work life. For some individuals, this may by itself be a novelty and a learning experience. In the same way, managers face a new set of challenges and functions as organizations have become more diverse. They must figure out how to adjust organizational structures and cultures to capitalize on this diversity, thus ensuring both quality of work life and organizational effectiveness.

For both program and human resource (HR) managers, meeting the imperative of diversity takes time, effort, and commitment. Yet it must be done, in order to meet legal, demographic, social, ethical, and strategic requirements and expectations from all the stakeholders of a public agency—clients, managers, staff, elected officials, taxpayers, and suppliers. Traditional affirmative action and equal employment opportunity efforts remain important but are not sufficient to manage today's diverse workforce effectively, if organizations wish to remain competitive both in the public (U.S. Merit Systems Protection Board [MSPB], 1993) and private sectors (Jackson and Schuller, 2000).

As organizations become more demographically diverse in response to external and internal pressures, managers must monitor the extent to which their practices reflect these changes. They must adjust the workplace accordingly, so that the organization's primary resource—its people—feel welcome and valued as individuals and as organizational citizens. Furthermore, in public bureaucracies the diversity agenda also responds to the mandate of constituting a governmental workforce that adequately reflects the diversity of the population it serves (Pynes, 1997).

Today, state of the art management literature in both public and private sectors views workforce diversity not as a problem to be managed away but as an opportunity to enhance personal and organizational effectiveness (Gentile, 1996). Diversity management is, nevertheless, a challenge, and cannot happen without organizational leadership, vision, and commitment. All members of the organization must *choose* to meet the challenge and all managers—senior, departmental, and HR—must assume the responsibility. A partnership between HR and line managers can contribute greatly to achieve diversity success.

In this chapter we provide an overview of the problems and prospects of addressing the diversity challenge and discuss the meanings of diversity and different approaches to creating diversity in public organizations. To do so, the chapter is structured in four sections. After providing an example of a diversity initiative in the public sector, we introduce and define the concept of workforce diversity, and describe the various approaches used to address it as an organizational and managerial challenge. In the next section we discuss the factors and conditions required to maximize the advantages of a diverse workforce and present guiding frameworks for managers. Finally, we explore the idea of a partnership between HR and program managers, and some implications for managing a diverse workforce in public organizations.

A PUBLIC SECTOR INITIATIVE: SAN DIEGO'S DIVERSITY COMMITMENT

The City of San Diego's "Diversity Commitment" illustrates the complexity of diversity efforts, as well as the range of stakeholders and strategies involved and potential benefits of its thoughtful implementation (Dobbs, 1996). This initiative was triggered by a request from the city manager for a training program on diversity. The director of the city's Office of Organizational Effectiveness studied initiatives in the public and private sectors and decided to recommend instead an organizationwide culture change.

To pursue this agenda, a Diversity Team of four persons was formed as a steering committee, but members from all levels of the organization were invited to participate. Short- and long-term strategies were developed based on a detailed diagnosis, which included employee focus groups and action planning. Designed as a comprehensive initiative, the Commitment intends to create an environment in which differences are valued and all employees participate in team service delivery.

Interventions in the San Diego initiative included short-term strategies such as: creating multicultural and bi-gender interview panels to increase representation in the promotion and selection processes; introducing diversity modules in supervisory and management training programs; and forming task forces to address the priorities identified by employees for career development, communication, and promotions. For the long term, San Diego is implementing changes in policies and procedures and a broad employee communications effort. This includes monthly meetings of the Diversity Team with employee associations, unions, informal city employee groups, and representatives of police and fire department HR divisions, and a forum with managerial and union participation to discuss and resolve diversity issues as they arise.

The San Diego Commitment illustrates some of the best practices in public and private sector diversity efforts. Note the variety of stakeholders involved in this effort—it's a partnership! The Diversity Commitment effort is the shared responsibility of all the management of the City of San Diego as an organization (HR managers, program managers, and top managers). And the specification of long- and short-term goals suggests that San Diego's managers expect diversity to be an ongoing, evolving process.

However, while the San Diego example highlights only the positive side of the story, the literature suggests that there are also obstacles and challenges in diversity-related change processes (Jackson and Associates, 1992; Ospina, 1996a). Designing and implementing a diversity initiative is a complex managerial agenda that demands sensitivity and skills from the manager, as well as thoughtful and careful preparation for its success throughout the organization. The issues and dimensions to be considered include, among others, clarifying what diversity means, distinguishing among various approaches to diversity, understanding what makes a workplace diverse, deciding how to choose the right strategies and steps to pursue this goal and determining who will be accountable for the effort. In the following sections of this chapter we will address these issues one at a time.

It may be too early to assess the impact of the San Diego effort. However, lessons from the literature suggest that managers in this City can expect to reap many benefits if they continue their diversity commitment. Indeed, much has been written about the benefits associated with implementing a successful diversity agenda. Applying them to the public sector, Ospina (1996a) summarized the most cited benefits of increased workforce diversity and classified them according to the types of gains, considering ethical, legal, public policy, HR management, and organizational benefits.

The ethical benefits are that diversity promotes fairness and justice in the workplace, and it helps create economic opportunity and reduce social inequality. Among the legal and public policy benefits are greater compliance with HR legal requirements, increased representation and responsiveness in the bureaucracy, and increased grassroots support for agency programs and policies. Among the identified HRM benefits are increased competitiveness in recruitment and selection by enhancing the agency's reputation and ability to attract and keep the best employees, and promoting creative and innovative approaches to work. Organizational benefits include increased internal capabilities due to greater organizational flexibility and ability to address change and greater fluidity in organizational design, decreased discrimination litigation, and increased organizational legitimacy due to enhanced reputation and higher effectiveness.

San Diego's initiative illustrates only one of many possible strategies to address the diversity challenge in a particular organization. However, there is no one best way to do so. For example, Baytos (1995) provides an inventory of approximately 275 activities related to diversity. These programs include "pure" diversity initiatives as well as mixed affirmative action and work and family activities, designed to operate in conjunction with broader diversity efforts. All together, they represent efforts that influence almost every aspect of the employment relationship. The number and the variety of these strategies, and the originality of San Diego's initiative, point to two important considerations: first, pursuing diversity requires creativity in design and implementation; second, diversity has become an integral aspect of effective management in contemporary organizations.

DEFINING DIVERSITY: AN ORGANIZATIONAL AND MANAGERIAL CHALLENGE

At the most general level, Gentile (1996) suggests that in the United States diversity has become a code word to discuss issues related to the impact of various types of difference on individual's and groups' life experiences. Diversity can therefore be studied at a societal level or within particular institutions. When considering diversity in organizations, Gentile includes three categories of organizational diversity: structural diversity (differences based on organizational functions—administrative vs. operational employees, for example), business diversity (different markets, products, and services), and workforce diversity.

Workforce diversity refers to the variety of identities of the employees in the organization, such as their gender, race, ethnicity, religion, sexual orientation, physical ability, age, family status, economic, educational, and geographic background and status. It can also encompass behavioral diversity such as differences in learning, communication, and work styles among individual employees (Loden and Rosener, 1991).

Workforce diversity may be characterized in different ways, as well. Occupational diversity encompasses the range of occupations employed to fulfill the mission (e.g., engineers vs. nurses). Professional diversity focuses on the range of training and professional degrees an organization requires from its members. And social diversity refers to variations in the characteristics that identify a person with a given "cultural" community or group identity.

In this chapter we focus specifically on diversity related to group identities because, from an HRM perspective, this type of workforce diversity offers the hardest challenges to managers. The infinite combinations of these primary and secondary social attributes produce the particular "social types" that make up an organization's workforce (Ospina, 1996a), and the particular challenges of diversity. Social diversity involves both self-definition and attributes perceived by others (Cox, 1993; Zuckerman and Simons, 1996). Each employee of an organization fits into several potential diversity categories. Parts of peoples' identities occur simultaneously, so that a "typical" black employee may be a member of a certain religion, could be gay or straight, or may have a disability not readily apparent to the naked eye.

Finally, diversity management cannot promise—nor should it—that public agency clients will only be served by employees who "look" like them. That would mean a return to segregation. Instead, in a diverse setting most clients will see people who look like them serving in all capacities in the agency's work. Achieving this requires a conscious strategy to develop a balanced approach to manage workforce diversity in public agencies.

WORKFORCE DIVERSITY EFFORTS: NARROW, BROAD, AND BALANCED APPROACHES

The following examples of diversity statements show how one public service and one nonprofit organization choose to define and approach the diversity challenge:

> "Harvard Pilgrim Healthcare is committed to increasing the diversity of staff at all levels while paying special attention to improving the representation of women and minorities in key positions to creating an inclusive, respectful and equitable environment; to serving our diverse members with culturally sensitive services; and to changing the organizational culture through leadership, policies and practices" (Society for Human Resources Management [SHRM] Home Page, 2000).

> "The Postal Service requires new thinking and new structures that regard Diversity Development as fundamental to business success to achieve our corporate strategic goals. Diversity is that which makes each of us unique. It can be our birthplace, education, age, gender, neighborhood, race, social circle, economic status, values, skills, appearance, lifestyle, etc. Valuing diversity is accepting and appreciating people's uniqueness. Developing diversity involves building tools and nurturing a culture that fully utilizes uniqueness and talent to support the organization's goals" (U.S. Postal Service, 1999).

These statements illustrate subtle differences in the approach each organization takes to achieve diversity. The differences refer to how broad or narrow each approach is, a choice that managers must make when planning a diversity effort. The practice-based literature on diversity management emphasizes a broad definition of diversity, such as the ones proposed by the U.S. Postal Service above. In this view, differences in personality, work style, and visible manifestations of diversity are considered critical resources as organizations move toward more flexible, team-based arrangements for service provision.

In contrast, as illustrated by the Harvard Pilgrim HealthCare approach, the research-based diversity literature pays particular attention to what the law calls "protected classes," that is, women, racial and ethnic minorities, persons with disabilities (and in some jurisdictions, but not all, gay, lesbian, bisexual and transgendered individuals). There is a reason behind this focus. Pynes (1997) argues that emphasis on a "narrow" focus may stem from the historical need to create incentives via legislation, executive orders, and administrative rulings, to combat past and current discrimination against these groups. Indeed, without these incentives, organizations would be less diverse today.

Both approaches to diversity have advantages and disadvantages that need to be considered when making organizational choices around diversity efforts. The broad approach places diversity within a context that expands beyond compliance to the law, thus linking the mandate of managing diversity to the strategic concerns of the organization. The danger, however, in the broad approach is that managers can easily ignore the patterns of organizational inequality to which certain groups have been subjected by ignoring institutionalized discrimination. In this case, managing diversity can become just a "nice" public relations program rather than a sustained effort to ensure organizational equality and fairness in the work place. The narrow approach has the advantage of directly calling attention to the existing patterns of inequality to explicitly identify and interrupt practices that reproduce such disparities.

The management literature seems to favor a broad definition over a narrow one. In this view, the ultimate goal of diversity is an organization that serves its stakeholders creatively and effectively because it draws on many talents in its work. Moreover, with too narrow a focus, those threatened by the diversity efforts may try to minimize them by associating them with low quality, rather than with better outcomes. Adapting policies and procedures to a broad definition of diversity may thus help the organization avoid the resistance that diversity efforts sometimes inspire.

Thomas (1991) argues that both approaches to diversity are necessary: without rigorous "narrow" efforts to recruit and promote persons not part of the dominant social groups, no "new faces" will enter the organization or managerial ranks. But without a "broad" organizational adjustment to make the organization a welcoming place to the new faces, those persons will soon leave the organization for more rewarding professional and personal opportunities. When that happens, the organization loses the experience of that employee and incurs the costs of recruiting and training a replacement.

FROM EEO/AA TO VALUING, MANAGING, AND MAXIMIZING DIVERSITY

In its most simplistic form—and in an approach originally adopted in the wake of the Civil Rights Act of 1964 and the Equal Employment Opportunity Act of 1972—diversity in the workplace was measured by counting the number of employees that fit into each of the desired "social categories" and creating "quotas" where there were gaps. Perceptions that people were hired and promoted based on their social characteristics rather than on job-related skills led to a backlash to outright quotas. This has influenced popular conceptions of diversity management, which is frequently confused with affirmative action. While the latter is an important effort in and of itself, it should not be equated with the former.

Despite the presentation in the literature of logical steps leading to a more diverse work place, the transition is not always smooth. Few diversity efforts in the beginning happened spontaneously, and some were a response to demands from different groups that produced changes in legislation. For example, women, people of color, individuals with disabilities, older employees, and gays and lesbians have traditionally been the target of discrimination. Some identity groups have started to challenge their previously marginalized status and to demand equal treatment in the workplace (Cozzetto et al., 1996; Crampton et al., 1996; Lewis, 1997).

Since the mid-1960s, three distinct phases of diversity management have evolved. In theory, the phases take place sequentially, but in practice many organizations implement aspects of all three phases simultaneously. First, affirmative action and equal opportunity employment policies created legal obligations based on numerical measures to increase the representation of minorities and women in many areas of employment and, in general, to reduce discriminatory practices. Later, to try to change the workplace culture once persons from different backgrounds were in the organization, many workplaces instituted awareness courses and celebrations of diverse characteristics (i.e., "Black History Month") in a strategy broadly known as Valuing Diversity. These activities were often isolated from organizational strategy or job needs, however.

Finally, a new type of effort, known as "managing diversity," has developed in response to the earlier phases not being fully effective. It connects work changes and different methods of accomplishing organizational goals to workforce diversity. Thomas (1991) defines it as "a comprehensive managerial approach aimed at creating an organizational environment that works naturally—without special effort, consideration, or programs—for all employees, regardless of how different they might be. This approach helps managers inspire employees to give their best to an organization" (p. 24). While respecting legal requirements, this approach to diversity is not implemented just for compliance or to avoid lawsuits. Instead, diversity is maximized when managers see its strategic connection to business and when employees who are part of a diverse workforce are viewed and treated as individuals with unique contributions to organizational goals.

CREATING AN ENVIRONMENT WHERE DIVERSITY CAN THRIVE

Today, the state of the art in both public and private management views workforce diversity as an imperative for organizational effectiveness and a requirement to gain competitive advantage. Indeed, managerial understanding of the diversity challenge is rooted less on a moral mandate toward equity and justice and more on environmental pressures that managers must address when creating and implementing organizational strategy.

Efforts pursued by the California Franchise Tax Board (FTB) illustrate how environmental forces can motivate an organization's managers to pursue workforce diversity (Barzelay and Moukheibir, 1993). In the early 1990s, FTB, California's main revenue agency, started a corporate strategy to deal with the challenges of recruiting, training, and retaining the employees needed to fulfill its mission. Among these pressures, FTB's leaders identified: a) the changing demographics of a shrinking labor force in the state of California; b) rapid changes in the technology to achieve FTB's core tasks, which required more frequent retraining of existing employees; and c) an increasing sense that the agency's workforce represented a broad range of ethnic, cultural, occupational, and educational backgrounds with very different needs, values, and skills.

After surveying employees and identifying best practices by benchmarking with several large private employers, FTB management designed a four-part strategy for diversity. The strategy included: 1) implementing flexible, on-site, training programs appropriate to every level of the organization; 2) working with local schools, junior colleges, and universities to help design educational strategies and to build bridges between these institutions and employment opportunities at FTB; 3) increasing the agency's visibility among professionals in key fields; and 4) creating a comprehensive, organizationwide employee support and development system offering employee assistance in critical areas identified by employees themselves, such as child care, financial planning, substance abuse, commuting to work, and preventive health care. With these strategies, FTB sought to build an organization in which all felt welcome and able to thrive and advance.

The specific demographic and diversity changes that exert pressures on an agency's management may vary, but they affect all public organizations. In FTB's case, as in many other public agencies, the demand for public services was increasing and managers knew they could not compete with the salaries private sector employers offered the professionals needed to do the job. As for most organizations, when the workforce became diverse, strategies for training and compensation had to incorporate new options, and thus become diverse, also.

MOTIVATIONS TO ADDRESS THE DIVERSITY CHALLENGE

Among the motivations that move managers to think about and address diversity, the following are particularly pertinent to public agencies: legal and regulatory pressures, changes in labor market demographics, and a diversifying client base. In addition, external social pressure may be a critical motivator in some cases. For example, community, religious, and/or political groups and coalitions may object to particular products, services, or ways in which these are offered to particular populations and clients, or may apply pressure for greater representation of particular groups in the organization's workforce.

Similarly, internal employee pressures may generate interest in diversity efforts. For example, employees may defend their rights or respond to perceptions of unfairness, discrimination, or harassment by filing complaints and/or engaging in behaviors such as turnover, absenteeism, conflict, lower productivity, and even sabotage. They may also request new policies and procedures that respond to their particular needs, such as flexible schedule and benefit policies. Finally, individual leaders and managers who view diversity as an important organizational issue may become personally committed to championing efforts to ensure fairness and employee well-being in the work place (Gentile, 1996).

These pressures, argues Gentile, can trigger managerial responses that range from reluctant compliance (following the letter of the law without addressing the real issues), to creative strategies that address diversity as a whole rather than considering issues in isolation. The literature indicates that managers in high-performance organizations do not necessarily wait until these pressures affect them directly. Instead, taking a strategic approach, they anticipate the changes and address the issues that will help the organization position itself within its competitive environment in a proactive rather than in a reactive way.

As organizations become more diverse and are affected by broader societal changes toward more participatory and inclusive forms of governance, traditional organizational structures, systems, and cultures will have to be transformed accordingly. Employees also need to be able to work in diverse teams, but they (and managers) may not have the skills to do so. In this context, a diversity effort becomes a strategic managerial tool and diversity success becomes a desirable outcome.

TOWARD DIVERSITY SUCCESS: CONFRONTING
THE REALITIES AND PURSUING A VISION

The lack of diversity affects organizational performance. There are also costs of ignoring diversity issues in the workforce or of merely assuming a window-dressing response to the mentioned pressures for inclusiveness. Consider the following diversity-related incidents:

> Example 1. A Midwestern state's Department of Health and Welfare is responsible for all statewide health programs and its welfare program. Its affirmative action plan documents a demographic composition of 750 employees that matches well the population of the Midwest state where the agency is located, with African Americans representing the largest minority group. But the agency has had three lawsuits claiming discrimination and wrongful discharge in the last five years. Employees complain that groups are slotted into certain jobs, and that the agency had a hostile environment to racial minorities. Some African Americans have reported instances of name-calling, racial jokes and minor damage to cars. They mentioned that the few Hispanics seem to be promoted faster, and that all Asian Americans are in well paying information systems positions. The Native Americans, on the other hand, who are employed in clerical, janitorial, or driver positions, have not complained, but there is an unusually high turnover in these positions (Powell, 1994).
>
> Example 2. A Nassau County, N.Y. correction officer was awarded over $1.5 million by a federal jury in July 2000 after suing for suffering antigay harassment. The man said he was subject to three years of assaults, taunts, and insults, and posting of offensive materials in his locker and in public areas where both inmates and fellow staff members could see them. He finally left the force after his supervisors refused several requests to curtail the harassment. Although there are no federal, state, or county laws prohibiting harassment based on sexual orientation, the man's lawyers successfully sued under the federal Constitution's Fourteenth Amendment for equal protection under the law. It was the second time in a year Nassau County municipal officials were assessed monetary damages for allowing antigay harassment against an employee (LeDuff, 2000).

These cases illustrate fairly common incidents. Similar examples still abound in public and private workplaces. They reflect undesirable organizational consequences of discrimination or patterns of social exclusion in society as they have been translated into the world of work. They also illustrate the potential impact of diversity-related incidents as they affect, in the first case, entire groups of employees, and in the second case, a single employee. Finally, they show the difficult work environments that managers and organizations face and the danger of ignoring diversity-related situations as they get expressed at work. To say the least, the uncomfortable environment created by poorly handled diversity conflicts affects both managers and employees across an organization.

The extent to which the described situations developed, and their outcomes, depended greatly on factors such as the degree of sensitivity of the managers involved, the willingness of the affected employees to voice their concern (and the ways in which they did so), the lack of an articulated diversity approach or strategy in the organization, and the extent to which HR and program managers worked together to address the issues once they surfaced. Leaving the issues unresolved was not an option—faced with employees demanding recognition, the organizational climate would only deteriorate and legal liabilities might ensue (and did in the New York example).

The organizational costs of not attending to workforce diversity challenges are both material and symbolic. Indeed, equity and fairness issues are not disconnected from the organization's bottom line nor from employees' responses to the experience of work (Ospina, 1996b). Unresolved diversity problems can result in consequences such as: diverting scarce financial and human resources to deal with litigation or to pay punitive damages; losing good employees and having to defray additional expenses to identify and recruit their replacements; managing conflict among diverse groups or dealing with resultant low employee morale; and creating a reputation that the organization is not a good place to work.

Organizations vary according to the degree to which they reflect these broader exclusionary patterns and the traditional employment practices, that produce them. These variations are evidenced in the differences in demographic composition, that is, how homogeneous or how mixed the workforce is, as well as in the way that the organization's culture, structures, policies, systems, human resource practices, and overall HR philosophy fit the requirements of its diverse employees. Only by knowing where an organization *is* in terms of its diversity can its managers develop strategies to move forward toward diversity success.

THE "DIVERSITY CONTINUUM": ORGANIZATIONAL TYPES AND DIVERSITY PHILOSOPHIES

Diversity scholars have developed helpful typologies that allow an observer to assess an organization's closeness or its distance from achieving diversity success. Cox (1993) and Minors (1996) classify organizations according to the degree to which they use exclusionary practices. They identify three organizational types that are part of what Minors calls a "continuum of growth" from discrimination to nondiscrimination.

The first is the "monolithic organization," where most employees are similar in terms of their primary and secondary characteristics and where the culture and systems value and reward only those who conform to the characteristics of the dominant group. In these organizations the dominant group's standards are universally applied, and informal communications, networks, and key decision-making bodies are closed to nondominant employees (Loden and Rosener, 1991).

Typically, monolithic organizations will be characterized by a series of undesirable organizational features which prevent deserving employees from moving laterally to better positions or upward to positions of prestige and responsibility.

The reproduction of sexist, ageist, homophobic, and other stereotyped attitudes and behaviors may also result in hostile work environments for those who do not happen to be part of the dominant group. A good illustration of this practice is presented in Example 2, where the New York correction officer was penalized for not complying with the dominant heterosexual lifestyle.

In the middle of the continuum, nondiscriminatory organizations have begun to work on the agenda of inclusiveness. But because they do not challenge or change structures, systems, and modes of delivery, these organizations hold the same underlying assumptions as the discriminatory ones, with similar consequences, despite their good intentions. Cox calls this type "the plural organization." It has a mixed group of employees but the systems and culture are still highly influenced by the values of one dominant group. A good illustration is Example 1, in which the Department of Health and Welfare employees don't feel treated on equal terms.

The third organizational type is the multicultural or antidiscriminatory organization, in which the systems and culture foster, value, and reward differences as potential organizational assets and where the demographic composition reflects such philosophy and practices. In this organizational type, managers have an explicit philosophy and practice social inclusion. They make efforts to redress power inequities, work actively to eliminate all forms of oppression, and are responsive to the various constituencies they serve as well as reflecting them in their workforce.

In Minors's words, an organization in the antidiscriminatory stage "reflects the contributions and interests of various groups in its mission and operations. Members of the larger community participate at all levels and help make decisions that shape the organization and influence its direction. . . . Its members support efforts to eliminate all forms of social oppression and to enhance the work of all." These organizations "are equitable, responsive and accessible at all levels" (p. 204).

The third organizational type in both Minors's and Cox's schemes allows us to imagine what diversity success would look like. Minors also helps us consider the importance of addressing diversity issues with respect to organizational stakeholders other than employees, thus maximizing the knowledge, skills, and talents of staff, volunteers, and community members.

Efforts to move from discriminatory to nondiscriminatory practices vary depending on the underlying diversity philosophy of the managers involved. According to Thomas and Ely (1996) some efforts are based in a philosophy that aims to achieve proportional representation, but also expects all employees to assimilate to the dominant culture. Deviations from the norm are viewed at a minimum as a nuisance. Other efforts acknowledge diversity inasmuch as it helps target minority consumer groups. In this approach, diverse employees are not allowed to integrate their unique features into the larger organization but instead are often pigeonholed and valued only because they interact with customers of similar backgrounds.

Finally, in some organizations employees are not pegged to market niches; they are encouraged to use their diverse backgrounds to enhance productivity, to create new opportunities, and to develop new systems and strategies. Furthermore, managers are open to innovation, creativity, and diversity in perspectives to problem solving and decision making. This description represents the ultimate vision for those who want to pursue the diversity challenge. It represents the desired diversity philosophy, one that would be typical of antidiscriminatory, multicultural organizations.

Being consistent with this philosophy is not an easy task. Despite the best intentions, if not handled well, diversity efforts may in fact, backfire. Because more diversity may increase the potential for ambiguity and complexity in an organization, it may also enhance the risk for confusion, miscommunication, and conflict (Adler, 1988). These consequences must be managed too. Consider the following example: In the local branch of a governmental organization that has implemented a solid diversity initiative for several years, a group of gay employees posted information on a bulletin board regarding a gay pride festival. Management received several calls from individuals who felt that the posting was inappropriate. Instead of brainstorming for solutions with employees, or providing sensitivity training about sexual orientation, management simply removed the posting. A few weeks later, a Christian prayer group held a vigil in the cafeteria. Some Jewish employees felt that the vigil should be addressed in the same manner as the gay pride posting. Conflict between identity groups escalated until the branch received direct command from headquarters to re-post the gay pride information.

The HR Department then decided that identity groups would have to obtain approval before posting any information or conducting any celebrations. However, there was no attempt to use conflict resolution to promote integration and inclusiveness among employees, who remained pigeonholed to their own identity groups (Chu et al., 1999). In this case, while resolving the conflict, managers lost an opportunity to move toward a true multicultural environment.

Addressing the diversity challenge successfully requires not only implementing the right programs, but also managing the consequences that follow in ways consistent with the desired diversity philosophy. Moreover, if there are stages in the "diversity continuum" it may be helpful to define the challenge of diversity as an evolutionary process highly sensitive to circumstances and context.

TOWARD A DEVELOPMENTAL AND CONTINGENT APPROACH TO DIVERSITY

Organizing a set of diversity initiatives by itself is not a guarantee for diversity success. According to Dass and Parker (1999) organizational efforts to address diversity may be episodic, freestanding, or systemic. There are many diversity initiatives that are put into place in an isolated and disjointed (episodic) manner, usually not integrated into core organizational activities, and often appearing in response to a single threat or incident. In other cases, freestanding diversity efforts offer formalized and regular activities that are still not integrated to the organization's core and often do not form a set of coherent strategies. In contrast, some diversity efforts are linked to existing systems and core organizational activities to form a coherent whole. In these efforts, responsibility for diversity is assigned to both line and HR managers.

How can managers make sure that their efforts are proactive, systemic and strategic enough to generate the desired impact? In the same way that each organization must determine the overall strategy to accomplish its mission, it must also determine and tailor its diversity agenda accordingly. The mandate of diversity is contingent on the organization's overall strategy, and also on its demographic profile, which must be understood and documented through careful study. Only then can managers decide the type of diversity strategies to put into place.

Organizations cannot skip steps. First, there must be agreement among the leadership about the desire to move forward toward "diversity success." Once this happens, programs and strategies must be based on a diagnosis of the organization's stage in the "diversity continuum" (between discriminatory and nondiscriminatory, from monolithic to multicultural). Championing and implementing a diversity vision will require a well thought-out plan and specific managerial strategies that respect the developmental nature of the change process. For example, an organization that has a homogeneous workforce cannot manage diversity, it must first pursue strategies to become diverse (Ospina, 1996a).

Using Cox's classification, Ospina proposes a framework that builds on this developmental and contingent nature of the diversity challenge. She describes the type of efforts that are most likely to succeed at each level, as managers try to move the organization from exclusion to diversity. Along this progressive movement, Ospina proposes to differentiate among four consecutive managerial tasks: *considering, pursuing, managing, and maximizing* diversity, depending on the organization's place in the diversity continuum.

When *considering* diversity, organizational stakeholders get involved in tasks that help them become aware of the benefits of increased diversity (and recognize the monolithic nature of the organization). Examples of strategies to consider diversity include: performing a diversity audit, conducting exit interviews or promoting core groups of managers to meet regularly to discuss diversity.

When *pursuing* diversity, managers look for strategies to create a diverse workforce (and try to move from the monolithic to the plural stage). Strategies to pursue diversity include: conducting periodic voluntary employee surveys to identify barriers, creating task forces to propose innovative plans to attract diverse employees, focusing on EEO techniques, and doing cultural assessments, etc.

When *managing* diversity, leaders find ways to support the now diverse workforce (making the organization more pluralistic). Strategies to manage diversity include: promoting networks, support groups, and internal advocacy groups; doing compensation equity analysis, creating mentoring programs, and designing career-development programs as well as job rotation programs to open up opportunities; and using conflict resolution techniques whenever diversity-related issues emerge.

And finally, when *maximizing* diversity, managers use the workforce strategically to add value to the organization's strategic goals by supporting the unique contributions each organizational member brings, independent of their background (striving to become a multicultural organization). Examples of maximizing diversity include: creating diverse teams throughout the organization, including diversity in managers' performance evaluations, goals, ratings, and promotion decisions; adding new benefits and new choices within the existing ones to encompass a broader range of employee benefit options; developing managerial succession plans; and continuously introducing new policies as new issues are identified.

These stages are not mutually exclusive, but instead, the lower-level ones continue to be developed when the organization moves to higher stages in the diversity growth continuum. For example, as managers try to maximize and manage diversity, they must also continue to consider the need for future diversity and pursue what will become the next generations of employees.

A final managerial consideration is: Where should diversity initiatives be placed in an organization and who should administer them? This issue has generated considerable debate among practitioners and scholars (Baytos, 1995; Jackson and Schuller, 2000). Some argue that a program to promote organizational diversity that is embedded in the human resource department is at risk of being marginalized or becoming a simple bureaucratic hoop that department managers feel they must pass through without really being a part of it. Others argue, however, that if the diversity initiatives of an organization are not centrally organized, the activities pertaining to diversity will get lost in the shuffle as line managers deal with the demands of production.

The solution to this dilemma lies, again, in considering the developmental and contingent nature of the process to achieve diversity success. Depending on the organization's attainment of diversity to date, its diversity initiatives may be organized in a separate function, when much remains to be done, and become more integrated as the organization becomes more sophisticated and sensitive to diversity. In the first case, for example, an organizational unit, task force or manager will be charged with championing the diversity mandate. In the second case, diversity efforts are incorporated in all units, and indicators of diversity success become part of the managerial performance appraisal. Ideally, the diversity challenge is woven into the organization's strategic goals, systems and functions, and overall management decisions, and becomes embedded in all practices and routines of the organization. This state is typical of a multicultural organization.

DIVERSITY AND THE PERSONNEL FUNCTION: A NEEDED PARTNERSHIP TO CREATE, MANAGE, AND MAXIMIZE A DIVERSE WORKFORCE

The recognition of the strategic importance of diversity to recruiting and managing employees while serving an expanding base of clients leads to the necessity of personnel and line managers working together on all aspects of diversity. It also leads to the need to adopt a broader definition of diversity, including a recognition that each employee of an organization fits into several potential diversity categories, without ignoring the importance of continuing to "protect" the most vulnerable categories to avoid backlash.

Managing workforce diversity represents an important HRM responsibility that is shared by both personnel specialists and program managers (Jackson and Schuler, 2000). The latter are responsible for embracing the diversity philosophy and effectively developing and implementing organization policy. Personnel managers, in turn, are responsible for the design and maintenance of HRM systems that will support the successful execution of policies and programs that sustain the philosophy. Personnel and program managers, therefore, work in partnership to ensure that the diversity challenge is woven into the organizational strategic goals, its systems and functions, and the overall management decisions, thus becoming embedded in all practices and routines, rather than being conceived as isolated programs.

The core HR functions—recruitment, hiring, staffing, compensation, performance management, training and development, labor relations, occupational safety and health and workforce planning—must be executed in a way that ties together the organization's needs for excellence and the requirements for diversity. In addition to applying these activities to individuals and groups, the human resource manager concerned with recruiting, managing, and retaining a diverse workforce will also need to actively train managers and supervisors in managing the diversity challenge itself. Training can help managers and their employees in several ways. For example, Valuing Diversity and cultural awareness workshops can help prevent overt and subtle intolerant attitudes; training in sexual harassment and other forms of discrimination avoidance can limit exposure to lawsuits and prevent valued employees from feeling that they must leave; and enhanced sensitivity can help managers identify needs such as skills-training for employees, avoiding ageism, or reducing homophobia.

The challenges of creating, managing, and maximizing diversity, however, span the entire organization. Diversity responsibility may cycle between personnel and program managers: personnel managers adjust policies and set expectations and program managers implement new procedures to nurture them. The partnership fails if either side falters in their role or if one fails to see the importance of the other. For example, while personnel managers must consider legal restraints, program managers and personnelists together need to consider options for reducing barriers to entry and advancement within an organization to truly achieve diversity. Consider the case of persons for whom dyslexia or learning disabilities create obstacles to attain a job in which they can perform well, or persons for whom English is not their first language. Special accommodations such as providing extra time to complete entry exams might be possible to ensure equal opportunity and a broader range of candidates in the competition for desired jobs. Challenging a traditional view, this approach invites employers to consider disabled employees as individuals offering "a non-standard bundle of abilities . . . and skills" rather than considering them less able employees (Veiga et al., 1999:p. 86).

Indeed, managers and personnel professionals must work together on the accommodations required—by law or by choice—to fulfill commitments to diversity. Accommodations for religion and disability must often be implemented, for example, but such actions need not cost the organization too greatly. A study published in 2000 showed that the average firm in the New York City area spent less than $300 per employee to meet disability access standards, including equipment purchases and training needs (Koss-Felder, 2000).

Program managers and personnel professionals may actively collaborate in innovative recruitment, as well. They must make efforts to search for alternative sources of recruitment to increase the pool of candidates. For example, one such source has been developed by the American College of Healthcare Executives, through a job bank for prospective candidates in their World Wide Web site. With the explicit intent of reaching out to minority prospects for health care management positions, lists of potential employers, mentors, and other discussion groups and networking possibilities have broadened access to a wide number of people. Over 500 job candidates and 200 potential mentors signed up to the site in its first few months of operation (see www.diversityconnection.com for information) (Moore, 1999).

In setting compensation, employers that offer "cafeteria" plans allow employees to choose the benefits that favor them personally. For example, older workers, and some lesbian and gay employees, may not find health insurance for dependents as attractive as other options, and lower-skilled workers may prefer to use flex time and educational benefits to obtain the training they need to advance. Working together to explore what is the appropriate combination for each organization is a joint task for program and personnel managers.

In several ways human resource professionals can lead the partnership: They have knowledge of the benchmarks for obtaining diversity in a particular sector, knowledge of consultants, training needs, and a mandate to provide organizational perspective. For program managers, additional "people" skills are needed to manage a diverse workforce, in contrast to those needed to manage the daily functions of their department. Managing a diverse workforce effectively requires creating a nurturing environment that builds upon individual strengths and on respect for people's uniqueness. Managers must learn to build, maintain, and manage relationships based on true empathy, understanding, and genuineness. The skills to accomplish this—difficult to learn and often time-consuming to implement—must be exercised while maintaining a focus on excellence of product and service, attaining the organization's goals, and dealing with stakeholder demands and changes in the environment.

CONCLUSION

Whether managers choose to implement a narrow or a broad approach to diversity, in the most effective organizations program managers and human resource managers have a common desire to make workforce diversity become "normal." In these organizations, understanding and valuing differences and promoting employee development are critical human resource management goals, and diversity is a strategic imperative for all managers. Ultimately, the diversity partnership must bring together human resource specialists and program managers to ensure that their efforts coincide in creating a workplace in which:

- The workforce adequately mirrors the demographic composition of the larger community the agency serves.

- All employees feel they are treated as unique individuals whose identities and abilities are not only respected but also appreciated for their contributions to the organization.

- The right policies, systems, and processes exist to ensure the agency's ability to attract, retain, and develop employees with diverse backgrounds and qualifications that help them maximize the organization's mission.

- Traditional segregation among job classifications, such as women in clerical positions and people of color in maintenance positions, no longer exists.

While this vision of "diversity success" is optimistic, it is needed to drive existing efforts and to motivate organizations to move forward in the right direction (Baytos, 1995). But at the same time, each organization's diversity challenge is unique. Labor force and other environmental pressures affect agencies differently;

organizations' workforces have become more diverse at different paces and to different degrees; each organization's structure and culture has adapted to the broader societal changes at its own pace and with its own idiosyncrasies. Strategies must therefore be carefully crafted to fit each organizational type in general, and the specific characteristics of each agency and its environment.

REFERENCES

ADLER, NANCY. 1988. *International Dimensions of Organizational Behavior*. Boston, MA: PWS-Kent Pu. Co. pp. 93–221.

BAYTOS, LAWRENCE. 1995. *Designing and Implementing Successful Diversity Programs*. Co-published with the Society for Human Resource Management. Upper Saddle River, NJ: Prentice Hall.

CHU, SUNYU, JUANITA ERB, JACOB KURIAKOSE, and NATALIE RICHARDSON. 1999. *Team Project Report on Cultural Diversity*. Managing Public Services Organization. New York, NY: Robert F. Wagner Graduate School of Public Service.

COX, TAYLOR, JR. 1993. *Cultural Diversity in Organizations: Theory, Research and Practice*. San Francisco: Berrett-Koehler.

COZZETTO, DON A., THEODORE B. PEDELISKI, and TERENCE J. TIPPLE. 1996. *Public Personnel Administration: Confronting the Challenges of Change*. Upper Saddle River, NJ: Prentice Hall.

CRAMPTON, SUZANN, JOHN HODGE, and JITENDRA MISHRA. 1996. Transition–Ready or Not: The Aging of America's Workforce. *Public Personnel Management* Vol. 25, No. 2 (Summer 1996).

DASS, PARSHOTAM, and BARBARA PARKER. 1999. Strategies for Managing Human Resource Diversity: from Resistance to Learning. *Academy of Management Executive* Vol. 13, No. 2:68–80.

DOBBS, MATTI. 1996. Managing Diversity: Lessons from the Private Sector. *Public Personnel Management*, Vol. 25, No. 3:351–367.

GENTILE, MARY. 1996. *Managerial Excellence Through Diversity*. Prospect Hills, IL: Waveland Press.

JACKSON, SUSAN and Associates. 1992. *Diversity in the Workplace: Human Resources Initiatives*. New York: The Guilford Press.

JACKSON, SUSAN, and RANDALL SCHULER. 2000. *Managing Human Resources, a Partnership Perspective*. South West College Publishing.

KOSS-FEDER, LAURA. 2000. Technology helps companies comply with Disabilities Act. *Crain's* June 19–25:34.

LEDUFF, CHARLIE. 2000. Former Nassau Jail Guard Wins $1.5 Million Gay Bias Award. *The New York Times*, July 20.

LEWIS, GREGORY B. 1997. Lifting the Ban on Gays in the Civil Service: Federal Policy Toward Gay and Lesbian Employees since the Cold War. *Public Administration Review* Sept/Oct 1997, Vol. 57, No. 5:387–395.

LODEN, MARYLIN, and JUDITH B. ROSENER. 1991. *Workforce America: Managing Employee Diversity as a Vital Resource*. Homewood, IL: Business One Irwin.

MINORS, ARNOLD. 1996. From Uni-Versity to Poly-Versity: Organizations in Transition to Anti-Racism. In *Perspectives on Racism and the Human Services Sector: A Case for Change*, Carl James, ed. Toronto: University of Toronto Press, pp. 196–208.

MOORE, DUNCAN J., JR. 1999. Tapping Hidden Resources. *Modern Healthcare*, December 13:30–36.

OSPINA, SONIA. 1996a. Realizing the Promise of Diversity. In *Handbook of Public Administration*, James Perry, ed. San Francisco: Jossey Bass, pp. 441–459.

OSPINA, SONIA. 1996b. *Illusions of Opportunity: Employee Expectations and Workplace Inequality*. Ithaca: Cornell University Press.

POWELL, GARY. 1994. *Gender and Diversity in the Workplace. Learning Activities and Exercises*. Thousand Oaks: Sage Publications.

PYNES, JOAN. 1997. *Human Resources Management for Public and Nonprofit Organizations*. San Francisco: Jossey-Bass.

Society for Human Resources Management (SHRM) Home Page. 2000. Workplace Diversity Initiative: <wysiwyg://17//http:/www.shrm.org/diversity/launch2/htm>.

THOMAS, D., and ROBIN ELY. 1996. Making Differences Matter. A New Paradigm for Managing Diversity. *Harvard Business Review* Cambridge, pp. 79–90.

THOMAS, R. ROOSEVELT, JR. 1991. Managing Diversity: A Strategic Opportunity. *The Municipal Year-Book.* Washington, DC: International City Management Association, pp. 24–28.

U.S. Postal Service. 1999. *Diversity Business Plan.* Washington, DC: U.S. Postal Service.

U.S. Merit Systems Protection Board (MSPB). 1993. *The Changing Face of the Federal Workforce. A Symposium on Diversity.* Washington, DC: U.S. Government Printing Office.

VEIGA, JOHN, KARLA FOX, JOHN YANOUZAS, and KIM EDDLESTON. 1999. Toward Greater Understanding in the Workplace. *Academy of Management Executive* Vol. 13, No. 2:81–87.

ZUCKERMAN, AMY J., and GEORGE F. SIMONS. 1996. *Sexual Orientation in the Workplace.* Thousand Oaks, CA: Sage Publications.

18

The Difference That Gender Makes[1]

MARY E. GUY

Florida State University

Your gender drives most of what you do and how you do it. It shapes your mannerisms, communication styles, career choices, friendship networks, and life course. It influences the amount of autonomy and discretion you will have on the job, your salary, the height at which your career ceiling will be fixed, and your retirement income. How can gender make so much difference? This chapter explains the effect of gender in the workplace and how the human resource function factors into the equation.

In the job market, women and men start out fairly even in their late teens and early twenties—but their paths soon diverge. By the time workers are in their thirties, women's wages level dramatically while men's continue to rise until they reach their mid-fifties, after which men's earnings decline and converge with women's once again. As their careers unfold, men can expect to move higher up the career ladder, to hold jobs that afford more discretion and autonomy, and to enjoy higher career earnings. The U.S. Department of Labor reports that in 1999 women working full-time, year-round averaged 76.5 cents for each dollar that men earned (U.S. DOL, 2000a).

Why is this the case? Two reasons account for most of the difference: First, many human resource practices that are taken for granted were designed decades ago for married men whose wives did not work out of the home. Second, labor economics mirror cultural values and, in American society, men's work is ascribed more value than women's.

---

[1] The author wishes to acknowledge the assistance of Karen Fowles in the preparation of this chapter.

WORKPLACES DESIGNED FOR MEN BUT INHABITED BY WOMEN

From a human resource perspective, the core of the problem is that women are not men. How could a fact so obvious be a problem? The policies that govern the workplace were designed during the industrial revolution when men were the primary out-of-home workers. The standard full-time workweek was arbitrarily defined as 40 hours and benefits packages, designed for men to support their families, were attached to full-time jobs to aid in recruitment and retention. With wives to run errands, pick children up after school, shop for groceries and household items, and handle miscellaneous tasks, men were free to pursue their careers and have leisure time after work and on weekends. Concerns about workers' family obligations were afterthoughts.

The demographics of the workforce have changed faster than the human resource practices that govern classification, compensation, and benefits. As social and economic conditions evolved, women entered the workforce and remained even after they married and had children. The proportion of married-couple families with children under 18 in which both parents work grows each year. In 1999 almost two/thirds (64 percent) of married-couple families with children under age 18 had both parents employed (Bureau of Labor Statistics, 2000). Additionally, increasing numbers of women are heads of households.

Women comprise about 44 percent of all workers in local, state, and federal government (U.S. Equal Employment Opportunity Commission, 1997). This proportion has been on a steady increase since data have been collected and closely tracks the proportion of women in the total civilian workforce as shown in Table 18–1.

Though the aggregate data in Table 18–1 show steady increases in the proportion of women in the workforce, the numbers obscure the dramatic changes taking place throughout a woman's life span. Table 18–2 presents labor force participation rates by gender and age. It shows that for the past four decades there have been steady increases in the participation rate of women through their peak earnings years, ages 20 through 64. Contrary to the rising pattern for women, the table shows that men's participation rate has decreased slightly across all age groups.

Why is Table 18–2 important? It says that women and men enter the workforce in roughly equal numbers during their teen years. During the childrearing years, women increasingly enter the workforce and stay. For example, in 1950, only 34 percent of women ages 25 to 34 were in the workforce. By 1990, 74

TABLE 18–1   Women as Percentage of All Workers

	1960	1965	1970	1975	1980	1985	1990	1995	1997
% in workforce	33.3	34.8	37.7	39.6	42.4	44.1	45.4	46.1	46.2
% of all full-timers	no data	no data	32.8	34.4	37.4	39.2	40.1	41.1	41.6
% of all part-timers	no data	no data	65.1	76.7	67.3	67.6	66.2	68.0	68.0

Data Source: U.S. Department of Labor, 1998.

TABLE 18–2　Labor Force Participation Rate by Gender and Age

	1950 Women/Men	1960 Women/Men	1970 Women/Men	1980 Women/Men	1990 Women/Men
16–19	41%/63%	39%/56%	44%/56%	53%/61%	52%/56%
20–24	46%/88%	46%/88%	58%/83%	69%/86%	72%/84%
25–34	34%/96%	36%/98%	45%/96%	66%/95%	74%/94%
35–44	39%/98%	43%/98%	51%/97%	66%/96%	77%/94%
45–54	38%/96%	50%/96%	54%/94%	60%/91%	71%/91%
55–64	27%/87%	37%/87%	43%/83%	41%/72%	45%/68%
65 and older	10%/46%	11%/33%	10%/27%	8%/19%	9%/16%

Data Source: U.S. Department of Labor, 1998.

percent were in the workforce. It is this huge increase that drove Congress to pass the Family and Medical Leave Act and President Clinton to sign it shortly after his inauguration in 1993. This increase is also driving reconsideration of how, where, and in what time frame, work gets done. The proliferation of telecommuting, flextime, and contingent workers is due in large part to the numbers of women who enter the workforce and now remain there throughout their childrearing years. Doing double duty—at work and at home—necessitates changes in the traditional 8 A.M. to 5 P.M. format.

GENDERED JOBS/GENDERED WAGES

The workplace is a microcosm of cultural values and biases. Despite the fact that women are almost half the workforce, remnants of human resource practices of a bygone era remain. Classification and compensation schemes reward "men's" jobs with higher wages, more autonomy, and more discretion, while "women's" jobs are accorded lower pay, less autonomy, and less discretion. A look at the past helps to explain this.

History of Women in Civil Service

The first jobs held by women in the federal government were as post-mistresses in small towns or as "female clerks" within agencies such as the Treasury Department (Van Riper, 1958). It was routinely assumed that women should be paid less than men since the latter were supporting their families, and it was considered morally questionable for a woman to work outside the home. When the first legislation passed in 1864 to address women's salaries, it set the salary of female clerks at $600 a year, about half that of men for similar work, and it was considered positive social policy for preserving the traditional family unit (Van Riper, 1958).

A more substantial rise in the number of women in the civil service occurred after the passage of the Pendleton Act in 1883, which established merit system employment based on competitive exams, tenure and political neutrality (Van Riper,

1958). Invention of the typewriter allowed employers to standardize clerical duties and the job of typist was developed. Though the job classification was not designed to provide opportunities for promotion, the work was an improvement over the manufacturing jobs women had occupied in the past, and by 1904 women in federal civil service accounted for 7.5 percent of the total service (Goldin, 1990; Van Riper, 1958).

With the outbreak of World War I, government relied on an influx of women workers. During that time, women received the majority of new appointments and ultimately made up more than 20 percent of civil service employees. The growing strength of women's political activism, coupled with the rapid increase of women college graduates, prompted the Civil Service Commission to act when the Department of Labor's Women's Bureau issued a report in 1919 indicating that women were denied access to 60 percent of civil service exams. In response, later that year the Civil Service Commission opened all tests to both women and men (Van Riper, 1958). This victory was followed by the Classification Act of 1923, which required that men and women federal employees receive equal salaries for doing the same work.

On the heels of the suffrage movement, an era that produced unparalleled gains for women's political equality, women attended college at the same rate as men until about 1930. From then until the 1960s, though, social forces discouraged women from venturing outside the home except during the labor shortages of World War II or in cases of dire financial straits (Woloch, 1994). Despite the bubble of educated women, the workplace relegated women to second class status. Ginzberg (1966) surveyed women who had earned graduate degrees during the 1920s and quotes a respondent who had earned a Ph.D. in economics and worked for a leading oil company. She reported that the company "would not allow women economists to make formal reports to directors. All had to be relayed through a man" (p. 104). Though such blatant discrimination is rarely found today, remnants of these practices remain threaded through human resource practice, especially when one looks at the number of executive posts that have never, in the history of the agency, been held by women.

Today it is common to find agencies whose lowest paid workers are predominantly women and whose highest paid workers are predominantly men. It is common to find that men hold most of the jobs that provide autonomy and administrative discretion and most of the women hold jobs that are routine, dead-end, and supportive in nature. For example, a 1999 survey conducted in the State of Florida found that out of sixty county manager/administrator positions in the State, only one is held by a woman. Of the fourteen largest cities with managers, only one is a woman, and in only seven out of twenty-seven state agencies do women comprise more than 40 percent of senior management posts (Economic-Entrepreneurial Task Force, 2000).

Education

One explanation for why women lag behind men in earnings and promotions is that women workers do not have as much education as men. Although this was the case in the past, it no longer is. The past forty years have seen women achieving bachelor's and master's degrees in increasing numbers. As of 1985, the

Table 18–3   Percentage of College Degrees Awarded to Women

	1960	1965	1970	1975	1980	1985	1990	1995	1997
Bachelor's	35.3	42.8	43.1	45.3	49.0	50.5	53.2	52.6	55.4
Master's	31.6	32.9	39.7	44.8	49.2	50.1	52.6	55.1	52.7

Data Source: U.S. Department of Labor, 1998.

number of degrees awarded to women matched those awarded to men. Table 18–3 shows that since that time, women have surpassed men in graduate education. If there is one thing we know about higher education, it is that it instills in college graduates a desire for autonomy and discretion on the job—two attributes that are missing in most "women's jobs." It should come as no surprise that work conditions that used to be shrugged off as inescapable now are challenged by young women who expect nothing less than equal opportunity across the board. For this reason we can predict a growing number of legal challenges to the wage gap and other work conditions that provide less opportunity for women.

Pay Gap

Despite women's rising level of education and increasing work experience, weekly wage data show that women earn less than men in 99 percent of all occupations. Women in executive, administrative, and managerial occupations earned wages that were 69.7 percent of men's pay, while women in the professions averaged 75 percent of men's weekly wages. "Even among medicine and health managers, 76.8 percent of whom were women, women earned 74 percent of what men earned (U.S. Department of Labor, 1998:p. 30).

The Women's Bureau of the U.S. Department of Labor conducted a national survey to ask working women about their jobs. In *Worth More Than We Earn: Fair Pay for Working Women,* the Labor Department (2000b) reports that "Improving pay scales" was a top priority. Moreover, nearly 60 percent of American women who work year round and full-time earn less than $25,000 per year. Over half of all women work in traditionally female jobs, such as clerical worker, nurse, child care worker, cook, cleaner, and librarian. Women of color are crowded into the very lowest paying of these jobs.

Almost forty years after the Equal Pay Act, pay inequity remains a serious problem. The reason it persists is because women occupy jobs that are different from those that men occupy. To quote the U.S. Department of Labor (2000b:p. 2): "Traditional "women's work" (education, food service, health care, to name a few) has been undervalued in part because people thought of it as an extension of women's family and household responsibilities, and therefore not appearing to require any special or additional skills."

Job Segregation

Cultural biases about the proper roles for women and men are manifested in the phenomenon known as *job segregation.* Just as housing segregation contributes to the homogeneity of neighborhoods, job segregation contributes to the homogeneity of workers in particular jobs. Relatively few job categories are occupied in even numbers by women and men. This is true around the world (Department of Economic and Social Affairs, 1999). As evidence of the undesirability of "women's" work, women are more likely to work in "men's" jobs than men are to work in "women's" jobs. Women's jobs include a narrower range of occupations than men's. They dominate in clerical and secretarial jobs and low-end service occupations; as professionals, they are most likely to be teachers or nurses.

A corollary to job segregation is that jobs identified as "women's" automatically pay less. On average, jobs for which men are thought more capable pay about 24 percent more than jobs for which women are thought more capable (Guy and Killingsworth, in press). Close to three-fourths of all paraprofessionals are women and almost ninety percent of support jobs are held by women. Though these jobs require skills of a level comparable to the skills required of craft workers, an occupational category that is ninety percent male, they are compensated at lower rates because they are "women's work" (U.S. Equal Employment Opportunity Commission, 1997).

Job segregation occurs in two dimensions: horizontal and vertical. Horizontal segregation refers to the distribution of men and women across occupations, such as women as secretaries and men as truck drivers. Vertical segregation refers to the distribution of men and women in the job hierarchy in terms of status within an occupation, such as women as nurses and men as physicians, women as staff assistants and men as directors.

Of the twenty leading occupations for women in the United States in 1998, they held only 29.8 percent of the managerial and administrative posts. Women who landed the top posts earned only 66.9 percent of what men in the same positions earned (U.S. Department of Labor, 1998). In federal employment, women hold about 41 percent of the GS 9 through 12 jobs and about 19 percent of the GS 13 through 15 jobs (Naff and Thomas, 1994). In the United States, it was legal to advertise jobs as being open to either women or men until 1969. Newspaper "help wanted" ads would specify that "women need not apply" for men's jobs and vice versa. Though EEOC guidelines issued in 1969 put an end to publicly announcing which gender would fill the job, there are informal expectations among hiring authorities as well as job applicants. This holds true for administrative posts as well as lower-level jobs.

Though it exists around the globe, segregation varies according to culture. For example, horizontal segregation is lowest in the Asia-Pacific region and highest in the Middle East; vertical segregation is higher in Asia and the Pacific than in other parts of the world (Department of Economic and Social Affairs, 1999). Vertical segregation is perpetuated by preconceived notions about masculinity and femininity. Leadership is often equated with masculinity and followership is often equated with femininity. Likewise, communication styles that are congratulated in men—directness, forthrightness, assertiveness—are often criticized when practiced by women. Even behaviorally anchored performance evaluations, which attempt to be free of bias, fall victim to gender stereotyping and the halo effect.

Because job segregation is embedded in cultural and economic notions of women's versus men's roles, it is invisible to those who elect not to see. Pay scales that value traditional "men's" jobs as opposed to "women's" jobs are rooted in history. Reproductive safety is interpreted in ways that impose special burdens on women. Family obligations fall heaviest on the shoulders of women and squeeze them between job and family. Traditional views of parental obligations, which place the primary burden on mothers, cause employers to be wary of placing women with children in top posts. As icing on the cake, sexual harassment in the workplace serves to exploit the power imbalance that women face and causes many victims, most of whom are women, to forfeit seniority and move from job to job in order to escape their harassers (see Chapter Sixteen).

Part-Time Work

Because of the cultural burdens of caregiving, women work a double shift, on call at both the office and home. To help them cope with double demands on their time, many women elect to work part-time jobs so that they can "manage" both shifts. Part-time jobs are usually reserved for less complex tasks for which workers can be easily hired and trained.

The definition of full-time versus part-time is important for its economic consequences. Unlike their full-time compatriots, part-timers are usually ineligible for benefits, such as paid vacation, personal days, and sick leave, as well as health, disability, and life insurance, and retirement benefits. This arbitrary custom has a disparate impact on women, who hold 68 percent of all part-time jobs (U.S. Department of Labor, Bureau of Labor Statistics, 1996). And, once retired, this means that those who worked part-time receive lower Social Security payments for the rest of their lives and have no employer-sponsored pension.

The U.S. Department of Labor (1999, 1996) reports that part-time workers earn 56¢ for every $1.00 that full-time workers earn, and this figure does not take into account the wage gap for women, whose average wages are lower than men's. Because women hold 68 percent of all part-time jobs, the wage disparity has a double whammy. Women earn less per hour than they would if employed full-time *and* they lack benefits. A woman who cobbles a series of part-time jobs together during the childrearing years will face retirement with significantly lower earnings and no retirement nest-egg.

Employers, on the other hand, benefit from employing part-timers. On an hourly basis it costs about one-third as much to compensate a part-time worker as it does to compensate a full-time employee. The hourly wage is less and there are no insurance, paid leave, or retirement obligations (U.S. Bureau of the Census, 1997). Part-time work does a halfway job of allowing workers to balance family demands with work responsibilities. It affords personal time for the worker but extracts a high price in terms of economic benefits.

Contingent Workers

From an employer's standpoint, contingent workers offer many of the same advantages as part-timers. They can hire workers when they need them and dismiss them when the project is finished. The disadvantage for workers is that benefit packages favor permanent full-timers. One can predict that women will hold the majority of contingent jobs, just as they hold the majority of part-time positions. To retain the personal time advantage that part-time workers enjoy but provide incentives to remain on the job, benefits need to be prorated for part-time or temporary work.

Although a contingent workforce provides flexibility it has a downside. If workers cannot be expected to remain at a job for long, employers will be reluctant to invest in them. This starts a vicious cycle for women—they obtain a short-term job but do not receive training that will allow them to advance. Thus, they bounce from one dead-end job to another, never able to improve their lot. Women workers are disproportionately disadvantaged by such trends because a greater proportion of them work in contingent jobs with higher turnover, and employers mistakenly believe that women are more likely to leave their jobs to meet caregiving responsibilities. In fact, when women and men hold equivalent jobs with equivalent benefits, women are no more likely than men to leave for another job.

For women in bottom-end jobs, it becomes a self-fulfilling prophecy: with no incentives, such as benefits, to make it worth their time to stay, they shop for jobs elsewhere. It is necessary for employers to raise productivity by investing in workers rather than relying on cost cutting to increase competitiveness. It is also important to promote equal access to training and retraining among women and men.

Prospects

Employers will be faced with fewer and fewer applicants for predominantly female jobs unless they change their wage-setting practices to make sure they are paying equal wages for work that is of equivalent value. Job evaluation studies are a useful tool for comparing all positions within a jurisdiction, despite job dissimilarity. These studies measure several factors including the skill, effort, responsibility, and working conditions of each job. They can head off expensive litigation by identifying and correcting wage practices that fail to reward work of equal value with equal pay.

In the absence of corrective action, employers can expect more union organizing. In 1998, union workers averaged $17.76 per hour while nonunion workers averaged $15.10 an hour (U.S. DOL, 1999). This means that nonunion workers, women and men combined, earn 85¢ for every $1.00 that union workers earn (U.S. DOL, 1999). As unions seek new members, the wage gap between women and men is a persuasive lever for union organizers in women-dominated fields such as healthcare, social services, education, and clerical work. More progress toward fair pay has been made in the public sector than in business, partly because the wages and job descriptions of government employees are public information.

Class action lawsuits are another means women are increasingly using to gain equity. Laws that require equal pay for equal work have been on the books for decades but they have been honored in the breach more often than not. The following discussion enumerates the major laws affecting women in the workplace.

PLENTY OF LAWS, TOO LITTLE ENFORCEMENT

What are the prospects for tailoring the workplace to fit the lifestyles of both women and men? Since 1963, a number of laws have been passed by Congress that should serve as levers to level the playing field and provide opportunities for women that match those available to men (see Table 18–4). Demands for these laws resulted from discrimination in a variety of forms: unfair salary disparities,

TABLE 18–4   Laws Designed to Equalize Opportunities for Women

Classification Act of 1923	Requires that men and women federal employees receive equal salaries for doing the same work.
Equal Pay Act of 1963, an amendment to the Fair Labor Standards Act of 1938	Requires that employers pay equal wages for work that is substantially equal unless the employer can show that a difference in wages is attributable to a factor other than gender.
Civil Rights Act of 1964, Title VII	Employers may not refuse to hire nor discharge any person on the basis of sex. Neither may they discriminate with respect to compensation, terms, conditions, or privileges of employment.
Executive Order 11375, 1967	Extended the protections to women that were afforded to minorities in Executive Order 11246; requires nondiscrimination and positive action by federal contractors on behalf of women.
Equal Employment Opportunity Act of 1972, an amendment to the Civil Rights Act of 1964	Strengthened the EEOC and gave it the ability to go to court for direct enforcement action.
EEOC Guidelines re: sex discrimination, 1969, 1972	Barred hiring based on stereotyped characterization of the sexes, classifying jobs as men's or women's, and advertising under male and female listings.
Pregnancy Discrimination Act of 1978	Prohibits employment discrimination on account of pregnancy.
Civil Rights Act of 1991	Sets standards for employers when they attempt to justify discriminatory actions or policies based on business necessity, shifts the burden of proof to the employer after the plaintiff has established a *prima facie* case, and provides the right to a jury trial, compensatory and punitive damages.
Family and Medical Leave Act of 1993	Employees are entitled to 12 weeks of unpaid leave during any 12-month period for the recent birth or adoption of a child; to care for an ill child, spouse, or parent; or for the employee's own health condition that precludes working.

denial of promotion opportunities, penalties for pregnancy, childbearing and childrearing, and sexual harassment. These problems have arisen because workplace policies have treated all employees as if they were men and have penalized women for their nonmale characteristics, including childbearing, childrearing, and gendered roles.

In combination with one another, these laws should pry open the doors of economic parity. Despite more than forty years of laws, though, conditions persist. Why? *The laws are only as strong as the will to enforce them.* Many employers wait for disgruntled employees to threaten legal action before correcting illegal pay scales and hiring practices.

BALANCING FAMILY AND WORK

Dual benefits accrue when employers become family friendly. Not only do mothers benefit, but fathers also enjoy the advantage of being able to tailor their work

TABLE 18–5   Percentage of Married Women with Children in the Labor Force

1960	1965	1970	1975	1980	1985	1990	1995	1997
27.6	32.2	39.7	44.9	54.1	60.8	66.3	70.2	71.1

Data Source: U.S. Department of Labor, 1998.

life to their family life rather than vice versa. Expanded leave arrangements, dependent care, choice of benefits, telecommuting, and flextime advantage both genders. Slowly but surely, employers are adjusting their practices to accommodate employees who must balance family obligations with work demands. The explosion of information technology has made the task easier.

Table 18–5 demonstrates the rapid growth of the number of mothers who are in the workforce. Currently at over 70 percent, the increase shows no sign of stopping. This high proportion of mothers in the workforce means that the pressure on employers to innovate will continue.

Flexible Schedules

We are seeing greater flexibility, with greater choices for where work is conducted and when the workday begins and ends. The Internet has made telecommuting from home a reasonable alternative for many knowledge workers. Just as the linear logic of the assembly line is giving way to the chaos of the Internet, the quantum physics notion of being two places at once is manifesting itself in workers who work for employers but out of their own home.

The proportion of full-time workers on flexible schedules has risen sharply in the past decade (Bureau of Labor Statistics, 1998) . In 1991, 15.1 percent of full-time workers were on flexible schedules; by 1997, 27.6 percent were. Private firms are more likely than government agencies to allow flexibility: in 1997, 28.8 percent of private sector workers had flexible schedules while only 21.7 percent of government workers did. Flexible work schedules are not distributed evenly across all levels of government. Federal employment offers the highest amount: 34.5 percent of federal workers enjoy flextime; 29.4 percent of state workers have it, and 13.1 percent of local government workers have it.

Expanded Concepts of Paid Leave

For full-time workers, an increasing array of leave benefits has developed to accommodate employee needs. The old standbys of sick leave and vacation leave have given way to personal leave, leave for family sickness, family leave for childbirth and adoptions, unpaid sabbaticals, and more. An expanded concept of sick leave is also on the horizon. On June 10, 2000, President Clinton announced family sick leave for federal employees. In the past, federal employees were allowed to use up to thirteen days of sick leave each year for family care purposes. Now, employees may use up to twelve weeks of sick leave each year to care for a family member with a serious health condition. The definition of family includes an employee's spouse and parents-in-law; children and their spouses; parents; siblings and their spouses; and "any individual related by blood or affinity whose close association with the employee is the equivalent of a family relationship" (*Federal Times,* 2000:p. 10).

Benefits

Benefits packages are being reworked to compensate for the fact that workers from dual career households require options rather than take-it-or-leave-it benefits. For example, if a husband works for an agency that offers good family health insurance and the wife also works for an employer that provides good family health insurance, there is no need for both to subscribe. The worker who opts not to subscribe to an offered benefit has nothing to substitute for it and foregoes the benefit. A cafeteria plan, on the other hand, provides each worker with a choice of benefits. Benefits are offered for selection as if on a buffet line. Workers are allotted a set number of dollars worth of benefits. It is up to them to select the combination of benefits within the prescribed dollar amount that best suits their needs. This is more equitable than the traditional practice of employees opting either in or out of specific benefits with nothing to substitute for the benefits declined. Included in the new buffet of benefits are funds to cover child care and elder care costs, medical expense accounts, pension alternatives, and insurance for legal services.

Child Care

Child care is a concern from both the benefits standpoint and the classification and compensation side of the coin. As a benefit for parents, it is a valuable component of a compensation package. For public entities that provide day-care services, training and compensation of child care workers is an emerging concern. The wages of child care workers are notoriously low. As a result, turnover among workers is high, which jeopardizes quality and raises operational costs. Many states impose minimum training and education requirements for child care workers and this will grow as quality problems catch the public eye (Kimmel, 2000).

An added dimension to child care is the time that mothers take off from work immediately following childbirth. A recent study in the State of Minnesota reveals that new mothers with paid maternity leave take approximately four more weeks off than new mothers whose leave is unpaid. This is a substantial difference and suggests that the mere availability of unpaid maternal leave works better in theory than in practice for women who are economically vulnerable (McGovern, Dowd, Gjerdingen et al., 2000). Many women have no choice but to forego maternity leave if it means foregoing income.

Eldercare

By the year 2030, the percentage of the population age 65 and older will rise to 20 percent of the total U.S. population (Weinberg, 2000). Eldercare is becoming a major concern for working adults and for women in particular. (A poignant reflection of the squeeze many women feel while caring for elderly parents and struggling to maintain their careers and personal lives is reflected in the book

A Good Enough Daughter: A Memoir by Alix Kates Shulman). At their peak earnings years, women find themselves pulled away from their jobs to care for frail parents and in-laws. The more that employers can do to accommodate the time and energy demands of eldercare, the less likely it is that they will endure productivity slumps or, worse, lose valuable employees.

Work/Life Specialists

Leave policies, innovations in benefits packages, and accommodating child and eldercare concerns come under the heading of work/life issues. Work/life professionals are specialists within human resource management who focus on workplace innovations that ease the tensions between family obligations of workers and the employer's concern for productivity. Those who study productivity and are sympathetic to the cross-cutting pressures of family and work argue that work/life innovations reduce stress and absenteeism. It is up to work/life specialists to assess the effectiveness of innovations and determine which have the greatest impact on retention and productivity. The impact of work/life programs and policies needs to be measured for the same purpose as other aspects of an organization's activities. Human resources is an integral dimension to every organization and the ongoing evaluation of its processes and practices will help employers stay abreast of changing needs.

Employee benefits, altered work arrangements, and a process for introducing and monitoring family-friendly human resource practices, are innovations that are employed in dots and dashes around the country. The prospect for full scale accommodation to the difference that gender makes—and the time frame for reaching it—is far into the future.

PROSPECTS FOR THE FUTURE

This chapter has touched on a number of issues that differentiate men from women in the workplace. The pay gap, segregation into less desirable jobs, and forfeiture of benefits in part-time work, all disadvantage women. Despite a variety of federal laws and the fact that more women achieve college degrees than men, the workplace is not a level playing field. On the other hand, the chapter also touches on human resource practices that advantage both women and men. The expanding concept of paid leave and accommodation to family responsibilities frees men to play a more active role in the family than their fathers could. In order to have enduring change, alterations in the standard way of doing things must advantage both women and men. Otherwise, a backlash occurs and men will close ranks to take away women's gains that they believe imperil their own. The national effort to do away with affirmative action provides a case in point.

The Anti-Affirmative Action Trend

Though affirmative action has not closed the pay gap, it has opened doors for women. First, it raised people's consciousness about fairness and giving women a chance in jobs that had formerly shut them out. Now it is not unusual to find women working on public works crews, heading agencies, and having line authority where they used to occupy only staff positions. The anti-affirmative action trend across the country puts many of these gains at risk. The door slammed shut to women once before—in the 1930s. If history is a predictor, this means that social forces will try to close the door again. In the absence of a conscientious effort to desegregate jobs, there is no indication that women's recent progress will continue without steady pushing, most likely through a proliferation of class action lawsuits to enforce the laws that are on the books.

Workplace Changes

Public sector employment is expected to increase from 19.8 million jobs in 1998 to 21.7 million jobs in 2008. While the federal sector will contract—losing about 136,000 jobs—state and local governments will grow by an estimated 2 million jobs in this ten year span, especially in education (Thomson, 1999). This spells opportunity, but what will it look like? What shape would a gender neutral work environment take? A gender neutral workplace would mean that people no longer take note when a woman is appointed to head an agency.

At this point, it still makes headlines when a woman is named to the top job. Deil Wright and his colleagues have tracked the rate at which women have been appointed to head agencies across the states (Bowling and Wright, 1998; Wright, 1999). They find that there has been a steady increase in the proportion of agencies headed by women. In 1964, only 2 percent of agencies were headed by women. By 1998, 22 percent of agencies were headed by women. The greatest inroads have been in the newest agencies, such as Elder Affairs, Victims Advocacy, and agencies that focus on arts, history, and cultural events.

The more powerful an agency is in terms of its level of administrative discretion and resource allocation functions, the more likely it is to be headed by a man. The State of Florida provides a case in point: The Department of Elder Affairs has the highest representation of women (67 percent) on its senior management team; the Citrus Commission, which has four senior management posts, relies exclusively on males to lead the agency. This commission also has the highest salary average for any state agency: $145,692. Outside of local and state government, women in Florida have made the greatest inroads in nonprofit hospitals, landing 32 percent of executive posts (Economic-Entrepreneurial Task Force, 2000).

Rethinking Women's Versus Men's Jobs

Job segregation has been a fact of the workplace since people started working for employers. Yet, it is not enough to shake one's head and lament. Gender relations play an important role in the division of labor and the distribution of work and income. By implication, economic behavior is gendered. Traditional macroeconomic analysis ends up being gender-ignorant rather than gender-neutral because it assumes the legal and institutional structure of the economy as a given. To fall back on the *status quo* and argue that the market dictates jobs and salaries is to fall back on history and let things continue as they always have. That is not good enough for racial equality, and it should not be good enough for gender equality.

REFERENCES

BOWLING, CYNTHIA J., and DEIL S WRIGHT. 1998. Change and Continuity in State Administration: Administrative Leadership Across Four Decades. *Public Administration Review* 58(5):429–444.

Bureau of Labor Statistics. 2000 (June 15). Employment Characteristics of Families Summary. USDL 00-172. <http://stats.bls.gov:80/news.release/famee.nr0.htm>. Accessed July 6, 2000.

Bureau of Labor Statistics. 1998 (March 26). Workers on Flexible and Shift Schedules in 1997 Summary. USDL 98-119 <http://stats.bls.gov/news.release/flex.nws.htm>. Accessed 7/8/2000.

Department of Economic and Social Affairs, Division for the Advancement of Women. 1999. *1999 World Survey on the Role of Women in Development.* New York: United Nations, Publication E.99. IV.8.

Economic-Entrepreneurial Task Force. 2000 (March). *Women Opening Windows in Florida's Glass Ceiling.* Available from Florida Women's Consortium, Inc. and Florida WWINS, Inc., 2721 Neuchatel Drive, Tallahassee, FL 32303.

Federal Times. 2000. Sick Leave for Family Care. (June 26):10.

GINZBERG, ELI. 1966. *Life Styles of Educated Women.* New York: Columbia University Press.

GOLDIN, CLAUDIA. 1990. *Understanding the Gender Gap: An Economic History of American Women.* Oxford: Oxford University Press.

GUY, MARY E., and JENNIFER A. KILLINGSWORTH. in press. Framing Gender, Framing Work: The Disparate Impact of Traditional HRM Practices. In Ali Farazmand, ed. *Building Human Capital for the New Century.* Westport, CT: Greenwood Publishing Group, Inc.

KIMMEL, JEAN. 2000. Employment-Related Child Care Issues: What We Know and What We Do Not. *Employment Research* 7(1): 5–6. Available from W. E. Upjohn Institute, 300 S. Westnedge Avenue, Kalamazoo, MI 49007-4686. <www.upjohninst.org>.

MCGOVERN, PATRICIA, BRYAN DOWN, DWENDA GJERDINGEN, IRA MOSCOVICE, LAURA KOCHEVAR, and SARAH MURPHY. 2000. The Determinants of Time Off Work After Childbirth. *Journal of Health Politics, Policy and Law* 25(3):527–564.

NAFF, KATHY C., and S. THOMAS. 1994. The Glass Ceiling Revisited: Determinants of Federal Job Advancement. *Policy Studies Review* 13(3/4):49–272.

SHULMAN, ALIX KATES. 1999. *A Good Enough Daughter: A Memoir.* New York: Schocken.

THOMSON, ALLISON. 1999. (November). Industry Output and Employment Projections to 2008. *Monthly Labor Review* (November):33–50.

U.S. Bureau of the Census. 1997. Labor Force Employment and Earnings, Table 676, In Statistical Abstracts of the United States. 1997. http://www.census.gov/prod/3/97pubs/97statab/labor.pdf Accessed 7/8/2000.

U.S. Department of Labor. 2000a. Household Data Annual Averages. <http://ftp.bls.gov/pub/special.requests/lf/AAT39.TXT>. Accessed 7/8/2000.

U.S. Department of Labor. 2000b. *Worth More Than We Earn: Fair Pay for Working Women.* <http://www.dol.gov/dol/wb/public/programs/fpcworth.htm>. Accessed 6/12/2000.

U.S. Department of Labor, Bureau of Labor Statistics. 1999 (December). National Compensation Survey: Occupational Wages in the United States, 1998. Washington, DC: Author. Summary 99-12.

U.S. Department of Labor (Women's Bureau). 1998 (June 10). *Equal Pay: A Thirty-Five Year Perspective.* Washington, DC: U.S. Department of Labor. Available <http://www.dol.gov/dol/wb/>. Accessed 6/12/2000.

U.S. Department of Labor, Bureau of Labor Statistics. 1996. A Different Look at Part-time Employment. *Issues in Labor Statistics,* 96–99.

U.S. Equal Employment Opportunity Commission. 1997. *Indicators of Equal Employment Opportunity—Status and Trends.* Washington, DC: Author, p. A6.

VAN RIPER, P. 1958. *History of the United States Civil Service.* Evanston, IL: Row, Peterson and Company.

WEINBERG, JOANNA K. 2000. The Past, Present, and Future of Long-Term Care—A Women's Issue? *Journal of Health Politics, Policy and Law* 25(3):566–582.

WOLOCH, NANCY. 1994. *Women and the American Experience,* 2nd ed. New York: McGraw Hill.

WRIGHT, DEIL S. 1999 (December). Summary of ASAP Results. Available from author c/o American State Administrators Project (ASAP), Odum Institute for Research in Social Science, The University of North Carolina, Chapel Hill, NC 27599-3355.

19

Disabled or Not Disabled

How Does the Americans With Disabilities Act Affect Employment Policies?

BONNIE G. MANI

East Carolina University

INTRODUCTION

According to the U.S. Department of Education (1998), 32.1 million working-age Americans have a disability. Nearly 15 million (8.7 percent) of these people have severe disabilities (see Table 19–1). Presently 75 percent of individuals with disabilities are unemployed (National Council on Disability, 1999) and those who do work are likely to be paid less than employees with no disabilities (Johnson and Baldwin, 1993). The median monthly earnings of men with severe disabilities is $1,262 while their counterparts without disabilities earn nearly $2,200 per month. Disabled women's disadvantages are even greater. The median monthly earnings of women with severe disabilities is $1,000, while their counterparts without disabilities make nearly $1,500 for the same period (refer to Table 19–1).

In 1999, the Social Security Administration and the National Council on Disability's (NCD's) *Summary of Data on Young People with Disabilities* (1999) made it clear that young Americans with disabilities had significantly greater disadvantages than their peers. Compared to households that do *not* include a youth with a disability, households that do are nearly twice as likely to have a head of household with less than a high school education, are nearly twice as likely to have household income less than $12,500 per year, and are nearly three times as likely to have household income less than $25,000 per year (see Table 19–1). If disabled Americans have limited access to education and employment, then their prospects for overcoming these disadvantages are poor.

The Americans with Disabilities Act (ADA) was passed by Congress in 1990. The goal of the law is to eliminate discrimination against people with

TABLE 19–1   Demographics of Americans with Disabilities

Total population	
With a disability	20.0%
With a severe disability	10.0%
Working age population (ages 15 to 64)	
With a disability	32.1 million
With a severe disability	14.9 million
Population 15 to 21 years of age (25.1 million people)	
With a disability	12.1%
With a severe disability	3.2%
Head of household with less than a high school education	
Households including youth with a disability	41.0%
Households in general population with youths age 12 to 17	22.0%
Household income less than $12,500	
Households including youth with a disability	35.0%
Households in general population with youths age 12 to 17	18.0%
Household income less than $25,000	
Households including youth with a disability	68.0%
Households in general population with youths age 12 to 17	18.0%

Median monthly earnings	Men	Women
Severe disability	$1,262	$1,000
Nonsevere disability	$1,857	$1,200
No disability	$2,190	$1,470

Source: National Institute on Disability and Rehabilitation Research (NIDRR) at the Department of Education (DOED) *Chartbook on Work and Disability in the United States in 1998;* and, the NIDRR and Social Security Administration *The Summary of Data on Young People with Disabilities in 1999.* Data are drawn from National Health Interview Survey, National Center for Education Statistics, Current Population Survey, and Survey of Income and Program Participation.

disabilities. To comply with the Act, to take full advantage of available human resources, and to avoid costly litigation employers need to know the provisions of this law. Thus this chapter discusses federal, state, and local statutes and will present the most recent case law. Specific disabilities, such as human immunodeficiency virus (HIV) and acquired immunodeficiency syndrome (AIDS), alcohol and drug abuse, and mental health and emotional problems are discussed to a more limited extent.

DISABILITY POLICIES

Before July 26, 1992—the effective date of the Americans with Disabilities Act (ADA) of 1990—many people with disabilities experienced discrimination in employment but had no legal recourse. In the workplace, the disabled faced intentional exclusions as a result of qualification standards and criteria and structural barriers. As a result these employees had limited access to services, programs, activities, benefits, jobs, and other opportunities. In general, the 1990 law prohibits discrimination against qualified individuals with disabilities. Employers must make reasonable accommodations so that qualified disabled employees can fulfill their job responsibilities. The law applies to "job application procedures, the hiring, advancement, or discharge of employees, employee compensation, job training, and other terms, conditions, and privileges of employment" (U.S. Congress, ADA, Publ L.101–336, 1990).

The Americans with Disabilities Act was not Congress's first policy affecting employment rights of the disabled. The Rehabilitation Act of 1973 prohibited employment discrimination in hiring, placement, and advancement decisions in the federal government and allowed remedies and attorney's fees when the law was violated (Pub.L. 93–112). The Rehabilitation Act was amended after the broader ADA was passed. Now, the law prohibits employment discrimination against qualified employees with disabilities by any employer with fifteen or more employees.

All of the states have addressed the need to protect employees and prospective employees. Most of the states (thirty-nine of them) have adopted the definition of disability given in the federal law. Others developed statutes that give more or less protection, based on broader or narrower definitions of disabilities. For example, some states specifically protect those with the human immunodeficiency virus (HIV) or related conditions like the acquired immunodeficiency syndrome (AIDS). As written, North Carolina's statute would allow some forms of discrimination but the ADA overrides the state's law. Many local governments—especially those communities with large numbers of citizens with HIV/AIDS like New York, Los Angeles, and San Francisco—also protect those with HIV (Gostin, Feldblum, and Webber, 1999).

DEFINITIONS

Many disputes to date have revolved around questions of coverage. The ADA gives a three-pronged definition of disability:

- An individual with physical or mental impairment that substantially limits one or more of the major life activities of such individual
- A record of such an impairment
- Being regarded as having such an impairment

The law does not specifically define "physical or mental impairment." However, the EEOC regulations for implementation states that the definition given in the Rehabilitation Act of 1973 will apply in ADA cases. According to the 1973 law, a physical or mental impairment is "any physiological disorder or condition, cosmetic disfigurement, or anatomical loss affecting one or more of several body systems, or any mental or psychological disorder" (U.S. Equal Employment Opportunity Commission [EEOC], 1996). For example, a physiological disorder might affect neurological, musculoskeletal, respiratory, cardiovascular, digestive, and endocrine systems. Mental or psychological disorders could include mental retardation, organic brain syndrome, emotional or mental illness, and specific learning disabilities (U.S. EEOC, 1996).

If employees start a rumor that a coworker is HIV positive when he is not, then is the victim of the gossip covered by the Americans with Disabilities Act? Yes, an employee who is *regarded* as having an impairment is covered by the ADA. An employee or applicant who is HIV positive but asymptomatic is also covered (*Bragdon v. Abbott*, 1998). Can an employee who has a heart condition and has recovered from a heart attack claim discrimination under the ADA when she is fired? Yes, an employee who is perceived to be disabled by the employer, whose condition no longer substantially limits one or more life activities, is covered by the Act (*Haiman v. Village of Fox Lake, Illinois*, 1999). Can an individual who is totally disabled according to the Social Security Administration's definition of a disability claim that an employer discriminated on the basis of a disability, if he is not hired? Yes, an individual might meet one set of standards for total disability, but still be qualified for a job according to the ADA's definition (*Cleveland v. Policy Management Systems Corporation*, 1999). Is a visually impaired job applicant covered by the ADA? Although uncorrected vision might be impaired, one's major life activities would not be limited if vision is corrected with lenses. Thus twin sisters who applied for positions as airline pilots were not covered by the ADA (*Sutton v. United Air Lines, Inc.*, 1999).

Congress did not specifically define the term "the major life activities of an individual." However, the Equal Employment Opportunity Commission (EEOC)—the federal agency with primary responsibility for implementation of the law—has given some guidelines. The EEOC refers to breathing, walking, standing, talking, learning, seeing, hearing, or other activities that the average person can perform with little or no problem, as major life activities. The EEOC warns prospective employers that interview questions about these activities could violate the ADA because they would very likely yield information about disabilities. The questions can be asked if and only if they specifically relate to the applicant's ability to perform the job (U.S. EEOC, 1995).

The extent to which a major life activity is "substantially limited" must be determined on a case-by-case basis. One might have an impairment but not be disabled because the impairment presents no restriction on major life activities. To decide whether an impairment is a disability covered by the ADA, the court would ask how long the individual has been impaired, how severe the impairment is, and whether the problem is recurrent. Temporary impairments that will heal with treatment, such as a broken leg or a sprained wrist, would not substantially limit a major life activity. Physical and personality characteristics, and cultural and economic disadvantages are not impairments. To define this concept within the context of the workplace, "substantially limited" means that an individual is "significantly restricted in the ability to perform either a class of jobs or a broad range of jobs in various classes as compared to the average person having comparable training, skills, and abilities" (Naeve and Servino, 1998).

Is a diabetic who is treated with insulin considered "substantially limited" and disabled? Initially, the EEOC said that an insulin dependent diabetic is disabled and covered by the ADA. The First, Third, Seventh, Eighth, Ninth, and Eleventh Circuit courts agreed. However, the Fifth, Sixth, and Tenth Circuit courts **did** consider medications and other assistive devices when deciding whether an impairment substantially limits a major life activity. In these three circuits, if diabetes was treated the condition would not be considered "substantially limiting," and the diabetic would not be covered by the ADA (O'Neill, 1998). These inconsistencies were resolved by the Supreme Court. After the Court issued decisions in *Sutton v. United Air Lines, Inc.* (1999) and *Murphy v. United Parcel Service, Inc.* (1999), the EEOC revised its interpretive guidelines. Mitigating measures such as medications or assistive devices that eliminate or reduce the effects of an impairment **must** be considered in disability determinations.

An "employer," according to the ADA, is "a person engaged in an industry affecting commerce who has . . . employees for each working day in each of twenty or more calendar weeks in the current or preceding calendar year." As of July 26, 1992, employers with twenty-five or more employees were affected by the ADA. In 1994 smaller companies—those with fifteen or more employees—were phased in. An "employee" is any individual employed by an employer.

To reduce the likelihood that employers would discriminate during the hiring process, the ADA outlines procedures for screening job applicants. According to the Act, employers cannot ask questions that would elicit information about physical or mental impairments before a job offer is made. Neither can prospective employers require medical examinations. Before the job offer, employers may ask applicants whether they would be able to meet the requirements of the job *with or without* accommodation. Applicants can answer questions phrased this way without revealing whether or not they are disabled.

Thus before a job is offered employers may require physical agility tests or physical fitness tests designed to measure whether an applicant could meet job requirements. However, the employer could not measure physiological or biological responses to exercise—heart rate or blood pressure—because these measurements would be considered medical examinations. Before a job is offered, an employer may ask applicants to take psychological tests that are related to job requirements, as long as the tests do not identify mental disorders or impairments. For example, an employer may ask an applicant for a salesperson position to complete an instrument that measures extroversion, but not an instrument that measures excessive anxiety, depression, or certain compulsive disorders. Instruments that assess mental impairments and disorders in the American Psychological Association's *Diagnostic and Statistical Manual of Mental Disorders (DSM)* are medical examinations. Extroversion would not be among these but anxiety, depression, and certain compulsive disorders would be. Vision tests that assess an applicant's ability to read material that they would have to read on the job or to distinguish between objects they would see on the job are not medical tests. But an examination by an optometrist or an ophthalmologist is a medical examination. The ADA permits tests to identify illegal drug users. These are not considered medical tests under the ADA. However, tests to measure alcohol consumption would not be permitted because these are medical tests, and the ADA makes no exception for them (U.S. EEOC, 1995).

After an employer has evaluated an applicant's qualifications and other nonmedical information and made an authentic conditional job offer, questions about disabilities and medical examinations are permitted. If the employer finds that the applicant has a disability that prevents the applicant from performing the duties of the job with reasonable accommodations, then the employer may withdraw the conditional job offer for legitimate, job-related reasons (U.S. EEOC, 1995). With this sequence of events, it would be clear that the applicant was rejected based on information obtained in the medical examination.

Employers must protect all medical information obtained during the hiring process. However, there may be legitimate reasons to share the information with first aid personnel, a new employee's supervisor or manager, workers' compensation state offices or insurance carriers, or government officials investigating compliance with the ADA. These reasons are excluded from the confidentiality requirements of the Act (U.S. EEOC, 1995).

Suppose a prospective employer makes a conditional job offer, then learns that an applicant is impaired and withdraws it. There are two significant issues: whether the applicant is otherwise qualified and whether the employer could provide a reasonable accommodation that would enable the applicant to perform the job. First, the ADA defines a qualified individual with a disability as someone who could perform the essential functions of the job with or without accommodations. Employers' job advertisements and job descriptions written before a job is advertised are evidence of employers' perceptions of essential functions. Second, according to the ADA reasonable accommodations may include job restructuring, part-time work schedules, reassignments to vacant positions, acquisition of equipment or devices, or changes in existing facilities so that employees with disabilities have access. Accommodations might include qualified readers for the blind, interpreters for the hearing impaired, job restructuring, or adjustments in policies related to administration of examinations.

As the law was originally written, employers were required to provide accommodations to disabled workers unless the costs would threaten the existence of the business (Tucker and Goldstein, 1991). The law that was passed was more ambiguous and vague, saying that employers must make accommodations unless doing so would provide an "undue hardship." There are four criteria used to analyze the degree of hardship for an employer.

- Nature and cost of accommodation needed
- The financial resources of the facility and the impact that accommodations would have on operations. Also, the number of employees and the effect that providing the accommodations would have on expenses and resources
- Overall financial resources of the employer, employment agency, labor organization, or joint labor-management committee (the covered entity); the overall size of the business; and the number, type, and location of facilities
- The composition, structure, and functions of the workforce; geographic autonomy of units; and, relationship between the facility where the employee would work and the covered entity (ADA 42 USC 12111 § 101)

So, for instance, it would be very difficult for a university campus that is part of a state system to prove that providing accommodations would present an undue hardship when resources could be augmented by the legislature. On the other hand, a small private company might be unable to accommodate a hearing impaired employee who would need an interpreter and special equipment to perform the essential functions of a job.

Certainly, an employer would not want to spend time or money accommodating an employee when it is not necessary. For example, one employee claimed the need for a modified work schedule so that he could report to work much later than the employer let other employees report. His employer claimed that existing work schedule options were a reasonable accommodation and fired him when he repeatedly reported late for work. In this case, questions remained about whether the employee's chronic tardiness was related to his arthritis and whether the employer's accommodations were reasonable (*Michael Ward v. Massachusetts Health Research Institute, Inc.,* 2000, remanded for trial). The point is that failing to accommodate a disabled employee can lead to costly litigation. Moreover, employers who lose talented disabled employees pay other costs that are more difficult to quantify—like knowledge, skills, and abilities that may be hard to find in others.

Ideally, employers will make wise hiring decisions and minimize some of these costs. But care must be taken to avoid discrimination against the disabled as a way of avoiding costs of accommodations. Employers may ask applicants about their attendance records in prior jobs, since there may be many reasons for absenteeism. However the interviewer must avoid any questions that might require the applicant to reveal any information about impairments or disabilities. For example, questions about an applicant's workers' compensation history would certainly reveal information about medical conditions. These questions can only be asked after a real, conditional offer of employment has been made.

Suppose a recruiter must decide whether to withdraw a conditional job offer extended to an individual after finding that the individual is disabled. First, the recruiter needs to determine whether the applicant would be able to perform essential job functions. Then there is a need to determine whether the accommodations that the applicant would require are reasonable. The ADA does **not** eliminate the need for the applicant to perform essential job functions. Often problems arise when employers are trying to determine exactly which job functions are essential. The job description written before the recruiting process began and the job advertisement will give some guidance. However, these may include duties that are not truly *essential.* In these situations employers should consider restructuring the job to remove nonessential duties. Duties that appear in another employee's job description that the disabled employee can perform could be replaced with the duties that the disabled employee cannot perform. Whether this is a reasonable accommodation would be decided on a case-by-case basis. The most important point here is that the ADA does not lower performance standards and requirements for disabled employees.

For example, in one organization a professional employee who was responsible for information systems developed chronic back pain and, as a result, was unable to lift computers. Prior to submitting medical documentation and requesting reasonable accommodation, the employee had been moving equipment to new office space and setting it up for end users. His expertise included knowledge of information systems, and he was able to properly install hardware and software and assist end users (Personnel Law Update, 2000). If the employer has other employees whose job descriptions require them to move furniture (likely a lower-paid employee), then the requirement to move computer equipment could be reassigned to them. This accommodation would allow the higher-paid employee to spend more time performing duties which require higher-level knowledge, skills, and abilities (KSAs). The modifications to the second employee's job description would be minor and the KSAs required would be commensurate with his/her current job requirements. The employer would need to fully explore the impact of such accommodations on each employee's workload, the organization's ability to meet established deadlines, and customers' needs.

As previously stated, whether the accommodations the applicant needs are reasonable would be determined on a case-by-case basis. The choice of accommodations should be made by both the employer and the employee. There should be an informal, interactive process to define the limitations of the disability and the accommodation options. For example, Patrick Jackan held a Safety and Health Inspector (SHI) position that required driving, climbing ladders, and crawling through small spaces. He passed the physical examination and his performance was satisfactory for the first year. Then he underwent spinal surgery. After he recuperated his doctors cleared him for work at a desk job because he could no longer lift or crawl. He asked to be transferred to the job he held before he was transferred to the SHI position but his request was denied. One year later he was fired. The Second Circuit Court of Appeals dismissed his ADA claim. The Court agreed with the employer who said that civil service rules prohibited his transfer because preferred lists or reemployment rosters were used to fill the job that he wanted. There were no suitable vacancies. According to the Second Circuit, an employee who requests a transfer must show that a vacancy exists, and then the burden shifts to the employer to accommodate the request or prove that the request would pose an undue hardship (*Patrick C. Jackan v. New York State Department of Labor,* 2000).

Suppose the employer and disabled employee identify a reasonable accommodation. The employee can reject the accommodation. But the consequence of that rejection—if the employee is then unable to perform the essential functions of the job he or she holds—is that the employee will no longer be considered a qualified employee with a disability. So if there is an adverse personnel action—such as a reprimand, suspension, or firing—then the employee cannot claim discrimination under the ADA (29 C.F.R. § 1630.9:pp. 342–343).

Rulings on whether employees who are regarded as disabled have rights to accommodations have varied in the federal courts. Recall that the third prong of the ADA definition of an individual with a disability includes those who are regarded as disabled. Bonnie Cook's case serves as an example. In 1999, when Bonnie Cook reapplied for a job she held twice before and voluntarily left twice, she was not rehired. The Rhode Island hospital that refused to hire her predicted that she would not be able to perform the duties of the job because she was morbidly obese, even though the prehire physical revealed that she was physically able to perform the duties of the job for which she applied. The hospital claimed that she would be unable quickly to evacuate patients in an emergency and that she was more susceptible to infections than those who are not obese. The hospital claimed that if she was hired, Cook would be more likely to be absent and more likely to file workers' compensation claims than other employees. The EEOC supported her claim that she was covered by the ADA because she was regarded as disabled by her prospective employer. The First Circuit Court of Appeals ruled in Cook's favor (*Cook v. State of Rhode Island, Department of Mental Health, Retardation, and Hospitals,* 1992). If she had been hired, would she have been entitled to reasonable accommodation? Although she was perceived to be disabled, she claimed she was not. What accommodation could an employee who is **not** disabled request? In a similar case, Carolyn Haiman recovered from a heart attack and asked her employer if she could work part-time at home. The employer denied her request. The fact that the employer sent her home the day of her heart attack because she was experiencing chest pains, considered with the employer's comments about sick employees causing increases in health insurance costs, led the federal district court to rule that she was regarded as disabled and that she had a right to sue under the ADA (*Haiman v. Village of Fox Lake, Illinois*, 1999).

Cook's and Haiman's cases are examples of **discrimination** based on **prejudice.** The terms are different. Prejudice is "an adverse or hostile attitude toward a person who belongs to a group, simply because he belongs to that group and is, therefore, presumed to have objectionable properties ascribed to that group" (Allport, 1954). Prejudice may cause discrimination, that is, decisions about employment or wages that are not based on productivity (Phelps, 1972). By this definition, an employer who pays a disabled employee a lower wage because he or she is less productive than a nondisabled employee has not discriminated. However, if the employer fails to offer reasonable accommodations that would enable the disabled worker to match the nondisabled worker's productivity, then the employer has violated the law—unless the accommodations would result in undue hardship for the employer (Johnson and Lambrinos, 1983).

Fears and stereotypes lead some people to perceive that others are disabled when there is no real impairment. The law gives some specific examples of such conditions and states that these are not covered by the ADA. For example, homosexuality and bisexuality, compulsive gambling, pyromania, and kleptomania, conditions resulting from the use of illegal drugs, and transvestism, and other sexual behavior disorders are among the conditions that are not considered disabilities according to the ADA. If individuals with these conditions experience discrimination they cannot file charges under the ADA.

Also, fears and stereotypes lead people to discriminate against others who truly are disabled. Donald Perkl, a mentally retarded janitor working for Chuck E. Cheese's, was fired and his supervisor was criticized for hiring one of "those people" even though Perkl was fully qualified for his job and he received satisfactory performance ratings during his three weeks of employment. A jury awarded him $13,070,000 in punitive and compensatory damages. Although the award had to be reduced because the maximum allowable award is $300,000, the jury sent a strong message to corporations that discriminate against the disabled (*Perkl v. CEC Entertainment, Inc.*, 2000).

Employers and coworkers tend to fear and prejudge employees who have contracted the HIV virus. Prior to *Bragdon v. Abbott* (1998), many believed that the ADA did not cover those with asymptomatic HIV. This was not an employment case, but the decision that Bragdon was disabled and covered by the ADA has clear implications for employers. Bragdon told her dentist, Dr. Abbott, that she was HIV positive. He, therefore, refused to fill her cavity in his office. She filed suit and the Court ruled that she was indeed disabled according to the Americans with Disabilities Act. One of her major life activities, reproduction, was substantially limited because she was HIV positive. In an employment setting, Bragdon would be covered by each of the three prongs of the ADA definition of individuals with disabilities. First, the Supreme Court specified that Bragdon was substantially limited in a major life function. Also, those with HIV are more vulnerable to certain infections which are only *intermittent* physical impairments. An employee who learns that he or she is HIV positive will go through emotional adjustments such as depression which, as a mental impairment, is covered by the ADA. Second, there would be a record of such an impairment, even after the HIV employee recovers from opportunistic infections or depression. Third, even though they are asymptomatic, HIV-positive employees may be regarded as being disabled. Thus public misconceptions about the disease may lead to prejudice and disparate treatment—similar to Bragdon's treatment by her dentist (*Bragdon v. Abbott*, 1998; Slack, 1997).

HIV/AIDS, ALCOHOLISM, AND MENTAL ILLNESS: COSTS AND STRATEGIES

James Slack (1997) gives public sector organizations several specific recommendations for dealing with **HIV/AIDS** employees and the Americans with Disabilities Act. First, analyze the agency's capacity to offer these employees' reasonable accommodations. For example, analyze job descriptions and identify the essential functions of each job. Then consider job restructuring so that the infected employee will be able to remain in a job as long as he or she is able to perform essential functions. The employer could also allow time during the day for stress relieving breaks or walks outside. The daily costs of short, intermittent breaks would be lower than the cost of a day of sick leave. Infected employees will want to conserve sick leave for later stages of the disease, so flexitime options in the earlier stages would be helpful. However, bear in mind that agencies may use discretion with flexitime options and sick leave decisions. The ADA does not require agencies to grant unlimited amounts of leave or to make extensive changes in flexitime policies offered to all employees (*Michael Ward v. Massachusetts Health Research Institute, Inc.*, 2000). Be certain that HIV employees have healthy food choices and rest rooms with hot water (many healthy employees also might appreciate these) so the HIV employee will be less susceptible to infections that are spread among coworkers. Prepare to comply with law's requirement for protecting employees' rights to confidentiality of medical information. Finally, provide employee assistance program (EAP) services. But be aware that asking employees about their problems and referring them to employee assistance programs are indications that the employer regards the employee as disabled, and this could come back to haunt (*Holihan v. Lucky Stores, Inc.*, 1997).

HIV and AIDS are costly both to the individual who is infected and to the agency. For the *employee* with HIV/AIDS the total cost of treatment from onset of the disease until death is $119,274 (U.S. Department of Health and Human Services, 1998; stated in 1992 dollars). DeSario, Faerman, and Slack (1994) estimate the cost for a *self-insured workplace* to be $270,000 over the course of twelve years, and for a *workplace with a group insurance plan* to be $135,000 over the same period of time (per employee with HIV/AIDS). These figures may seem high, but the costs of litigation associated with noncompliance with the ADA would be much higher. For example, the ADA would be violated if an agency failed to hire an asymptomatic HIV-positive individual because they were HIV positive, when the applicant could perform the essential functions of the job. Thus it is important to develop policies and to train anyone who plays a role in the hiring process. The

U.S. Department of Health and Human Services (HHS), Centers for Disease Control and Prevention (CDC) can help agencies develop workplace policies and training programs. In addition, the CDC provides catalogues of materials, answers to frequently asked questions, and information about health insurance options and costs (U.S. Department of Health and Human Services Centers for Disease Control and Prevention [CDC], 1998). Agencies' policies would have to comply with state statutes and, as previously mentioned, these differ.

The Centers for Disease Control suggest that workplace policies give managers guidelines for reasonable accommodation, assistance available to them and their employees, and the importance of confidentiality. These policies also should express a commitment to:

• Comply with federal, state, and local laws.
• Respect the rights of those with life-threatening illnesses.
• Communicate to employees that there is no scientific and epidemiological evidence to indicate that the virus can be transmitted through ordinary workplace interactions.
• Teach employees strategies for reducing the risk of contracting the virus in their own lives.
• Protect confidential medical information.
• Eliminate any HIV screening in preemployment or physical examinations.
• Implement infection control procedures in occupational settings where there may be a potential risk of exposure to the virus.

Another costly problem for agencies is **alcoholism**. Alcoholism conforms to the ADA definition of a disability: ". . . a physical . . . impairment that substantially limits one or more of the major life activities of such individual" (ADA, 1990). The disease costs $107 billion per year in productivity losses alone. When the costs of health care expenditures, crime, social welfare administration, motor vehicle crashes, and fire destruction are added, total costs reach $148 billion per year (Harwood, Fountain, Livermore, 1998; stated in 1992 dollars). Alcoholism is a factor in 47 percent of industrial accidents and the average cost of one on-the-job injury is $16,800. The absenteeism rate of alcoholic employees is four times the rate of other employees (Mani, 1998b). About one of every twenty workers—5.39 percent of all full- and part-time employees—are alcohol dependent (U.S. Department of Health and Human Services Substance Abuse and Mental Health Services Administration [SAMHSA], 1999). Ten to 15 million Americans have major problems with alcohol, as do 35 million family members, friends, and co-workers of alcoholics (Mani, 1998a).

After the National Institute of Alcoholism and Alcohol Abuse was formed in 1971, the federal government began distributing funds for occupational alcohol programs. Grants were given to states to hire consultants and to help public and private employers establish programs. At the same time, federal agencies were required to establish programs to help alcoholic employees. There are no consistent, formal policies requiring local governments to establish similar programs. Nevertheless, between 1950 and 1994 the overall number of employee assistance programs—broader services for alcoholics and employees with various other problems—increased from 50 to over 10,000 (Mani, 1998b).

Many agencies that treat alcoholics as disabled individuals and deal with alcoholics in a humane manner reap financial benefits. For example, agencies that pay the $12 to $20 average costs per employee for employee assistance services can expect to realize $5 to $16 in benefits for each dollar invested (Mani, 1998a). The fact that benefits could exceed such great costs supports the underlying premises of the ADA—rehabilitation and employment of the disabled is not only humane, it is cost-beneficial.

An employer that complies with the ADA unknowingly might hire a recovered alcoholic. During the pre-offer stage, employers may ask about drinking habits generally, but may not ask any question that might elicit information about alcoholism specifically. The interviewer may ask applicants whether they drink alcohol or if they have been arrested for driving while intoxicated, but may not ask how much applicants drink or whether they have participated in an alcohol rehabilitation program. There is no statutory exception for tests to measure alcohol consumption—these are medical tests and are not permitted during the pre-offer stage, even though there is a statutory exception for medical tests to identify illegal drug users (U.S. EEOC, 1995). After a conditional job offer is made, employers may ask disability related questions and may require a medical examination if those questions and the examination apply to all job applicants in that job category. If a disability is discovered, the offer may be withdrawn **only** if that disability is job related and based on a business necessity. That is, the employer must prove that the applicant could not, with reasonable accommodations, perform the essential functions of the job (Naeve and Servino, 1998).

As a final example, consider **emotional and mental health** problems. Fifty-six percent of companies surveyed in 1990 reported that mental health and emotional problems were "fairly pervasive" in their companies. Thirty-six percent of them reported that stress, anxiety, and depression greatly affected employees' ability to function on the job. According to the Substance Abuse and Mental Health Services Administration (SAMHSA), 6 percent of full-time employees and 8 percent of part-time employees reported a major depressive episode in the year of the survey—one of four mental health diagnoses examined. In addition 1 to 3 percent of employees reported diagnoses in each of three other categories—general anxiety, agoraphobia, and panic attacks (SAMHSA, 1999). The absenteeism rate of employees with emotional problems is five times the rate of the average employee—about 16 days of work per year per employee (Mani, 1998b; Mani, 1998c). Mental illness cost the United States over $200 billion in 1994 (SAMHSA, 2000). Absenteeism, death, lost productivity, health care, crime and incarceration, social welfare administration, family care giving, accidents, and expenses associated with property destruction contribute to the total costs. Although the costs of such disabilities are great, the benefits of rehabilitation outweigh the costs by 6 to 1. Many of the EAPs that were originally developed to reduce costs by helping alcoholic employees have expanded. In recent years these programs also have provided services to employees with emotional problems, as previously stated (Mani, 1998b; Mani, 1998c; SAMHSA, 2000).

Although illnesses such as alcoholism, depression, paranoia, or posttraumatic stress syndrome are covered by the Americans with Disabilities Act, the courts have made several decisions that favored *employers* of individuals with these impairments. For example, employers may discipline or terminate disabled employees for threatening behavior or misconduct, as long as the personnel action imposed is the same action that would be imposed upon an employee who is not disabled. That is, it is no greater. In one case, a federal court of appeals upheld the termination of an employee who threatened to kill her supervisor. In another case, the court upheld the termination of a police officer who physically assaulted two people, one of whom was a fellow police officer (Bernert, 1998). These decisions were supported by the Act. First, the Act defines a direct threat as "a significant risk to the health or safety of others that cannot be eliminated by reasonable accommodation" (42 USC 12111, § 101). Second, the Act allows employers to set qualifications standards which state that employees "shall not pose a direct threat to the health or safety of other individuals in the workplace" (42 USC 12113, § 103).

COMPLIANCE

The Equal Employment Opportunity Commission (EEOC), the Attorney General, and the Office of Federal Contract Compliance Programs are empowered to enforce the Act. The EEOC received a $279 million appropriation in 1999—the full amount recommended by the Clinton administration.

The remedies for noncompliance cases are the same as the remedies for noncompliance with the Civil Rights Act of 1964: reasonable attorneys' fees, back pay and front pay, injunctive relief, and equitable relief. In come cases, violators may also be required to pay compensatory and punitive damages under the Civil Rights Act of 1991. For example, the jury award in the Chuck E. Cheese case was reduced to the maximum allowed under the ADA—$300,000 in punitive and compensatory damages. The EEOC reported that the total monetary benefits awarded between July 26, 1992, and September 30, 1999 exceeded $261 million (see Table 19-2).

Nearly 126,000 ADA charges of discrimination were filed between the effective date of the law and the end of fiscal year 1999 (see Table 19-2). The EEOC implemented a Comprehensive Enforcement Program (CEP) in 1999, making it easier to file lawsuits affecting large groups rather than individuals, and easier to file lawsuits addressing systemic problems or discriminatory policies. As a result, the inventory of unresolved cases was significantly reduced from over 52,000 in 1998 to less than 40,300 in 1999. But the significance of unresolved cases is apparent in Table 19-2. In seven years since the ADA was enacted, 129,140 charges have been resolved. If 40,300 cases are unresolved in one year, these cases will be carried in the next year's inventory. This is a burgeoning problem. To address this problem, the agency also issued new regulations to improve internal procedures. The new regulations eliminated unnecessary layers of review, changed the data collection process, addressed perceptions of unfairness, and utilized alternative dispute resolution at all points in the process (NCD, 2000).

Note the disposition of cases (see Table 19-2). No reasonable cause was found in over half of the cases. Reasonable cause was found in only 4.4 percent of all cases. Settlements were reached in nearly 5 percent of the cases, and monetary benefits, excluding those obtained through litigation, exceed $260 million—a relatively large amount considering these data. Obviously, it pays to comply.

TABLE 19–2   Charges filed under the Americans with Disabilities Act of 1990: 1992, 1999, and Cumulative Totals for 7/26/92 through 9/30/99

	1992	1999	Cumulative Totals 07/26/1992 through 09/30/1999
Charges received	1,048	17,007	125,946
Charges resolved[a]	88	22,152	129,140

Type of Resolution as a Percentage of All Charges Resolved During Time Period

	1992	1999	07/26/1992 through 09/30/1999
Settlements	12.5% (*n* = 11)	6.5% (*n* = 1,433)	4.9% (*n* = 6,334)
Withdrawals with benefits	8.0% (*n* = 7)	3.9% (*n* = 867)	5.2% (*n* = 6,668)
Administrative closures	70.5% (*n* = 62)	24.5% (*n* = 5,434)	33.1% (*n* = 42,729)
No reasonable cause	8.0% (*n* = 7)	57.6% (*n* = 12,753)	52.4% (*n* = 67,717)
Reasonable cause	1.1% (*n* = 1)	7.5% (*n* = 1,665)	4.4% (*n* = 5,692)
Totals[b]	100.1% 88	100.0% 22,152	100.0% 129,140
Monetary benefits (millions)[c]	$0.2	$49.9	$261.2

[a] Charges resolved each year may exceed charged received each year because workload is drawn from a combination of charges pending, new receipts, and charges transferred from Fair Employment Practice Agencies, rather than from new charges only.
[b] Totals may not equal 100% due to rounding.
[c] Monetary benefits shown on table do not include monetary benefits obtained through litigation.
Source of data: Office of Research, Information, and Planning, Equal Employment Opportunity Commission (EEOC), January, 2000. Charge Data System <http://www.eeoc.gov/stats/ada-charges.html>.

CONCLUSIONS

Before the Americans with Disabilities Act, disabled employees were an untapped source of skilled workers. Now human resource managers must be disability blind as they make personnel decisions, and they must be disability conscious as they accommodate employees' needs. With the proper balance some of the problems facing human resource managers in the new millennium will be ameliorated.

REFERENCES

ALLPORT, G. (1954). *The Nature of Prejudice*. Garden City, NY: Doubleday.

BERNERT, KATHRYN A. 1998. "Disability Decisions Tend to Favor Employers." In the Council on Education in Management's *National Personnel Law Update*, June 1998:3.

Bragdon v. Abbott. 1998. Supreme Court Docket Number 97–156 (appealed from the U.S. Court of Appeals, 1st Circuit), decided June 25.

Cleveland v. Policy Management Systems Corporation. 1999. Supreme Court Docket Number 97–1008 (appealed from the U.S. Court of Appeals, 5th Circuit), decided May 24.

CODY, KAREN J. 1998. Turnover Climbed to an Eight Year High in 1997, BNA Survey Finds. <http://www.bnatax.com/press/release6.htm>. March 27.

Cook v. State of Rhode Island, Department of Mental Health, Retardation and Hospitals. 1993. 10 F. d 17 (First Circuit, 1993).

DESARIO, JACK P., SUE R. FAERMAN, and JAMES D. SLACK. 1994. *Local Government Information and Training Needs in the 21st Century*. Westport, CT: Quorum Books.

FOX, CHARLES, and NAN DAUGHERTY. 1995. ADA Critics Should Focus on Intent, Not Implementation. *PA Times* 18(6):10.

GOSTIN, LAWRENCE O., CHAI FELDBLUM, and DAVID W. WEBBER. 1999. Disability Discrimination in America: HIV/AIDS and Other Health Conditions. *The Journal of the American Medical Association* 281:745–752.

Haiman v. Village of Fox Lake, Illinois. 1999. No. 98C0158 WL 476973 (N.D. Ill.).

HARWOOD, HENRICK, DOUGLAS FOUNTAIN, and GINA LIVERMORE. 1998. *The Economic Costs of Alcohol and Drug Abuse in the United States 1992*. Rockville, MD: U.S. Department of Health and Human Services.

Holihan v. Lucky Stores, Inc. 1996. No. 95-55409, (9th Circuit Court of Appeals).

Patrick C. Jackan v. New York State Department of Labor. 2000. Docket No. 98–9589 (Second Circuit), March 3.

JOHNSON, WILLIAM G., and MARJORIE BALDWIN. 1993. The Americans with Disabilities Act: Will It Make a Difference? *Policy Studies Journal* 21(4):775–788.

JOHNSON, W. G., and J. LAMBRINOS. 1983. Employment Discrimination against the Handicapped. *Society* 20(3):47–50.

Kepner-Tregoe, Inc. 1999. Avoiding the Brain Drain: What Companies Are Doing to Lock In Their Talent. Kepner-Tregoe, Inc., Business Issues Research Group: Research Monograph One, January 1999.

MANI, BONNIE G. 1998a. Alcoholism. *International Encyclopedia of Public Policy and Administration*, Vol. 1. Boulder, CO: Westview Press, pp. 101–103.

MANI, BONNIE G. 1998b. Employee Assistance Programs. *International Encyclopedia of Public Policy and Administration*, Vol. 2. Boulder, CO: Westview Press, pp. 753–756.

MANI, BONNIE G. 1998c. Stress. *International Encyclopedia of Public Policy and Administration*, Vol. 4. Boulder, CO: Westview Press, pp. 2178–2180.

Michael Ward v. Massachusetts Health Research Institute, Inc. 2000. Docket No. 99-1651 (First Circuit), April 12, 2000.

Murphy v. United Parcel Service, Inc. 1999. Supreme Court Docket Number 97-1992 (appealed from the U.S. Court of Appeals, 10th circuit), decided June 22.

NAEVE, ROBERT A., and MARK D. SERVINO. 1998. ADA and the Non-Disabled Employee: Why Regarding an Employee as Disabled Can Cost You Millions. In *Personnel Law Update*. Walnut Creek, CA: Council on Education in Management.

National Council on Disability. 2000. National Disability Policy: A Progress Report. <http://www.ncd.gov/newsroom/publications/policy98-99.html> (May 28).

O'NEILL, MAUREEN. 1998. Corrective or Mitigating Measures Under the ADA. In The Council on Education in Management's *National Personnel Law Update*, May 1998:4.

Perkl (Donald) v. CEC Entertainment, Inc., d/b/a Chuck E. Cheese's. 2000. U.S. District Court for the Western District of Wisconsin, 98–C–698–X, March.

Personnel Law Update. 2000. This dilemma was presented by a participant in a seminar conducted by the Council on Education in Management. Greensboro, North Carolina, September 26 to 27, 2000.

PHELPS, E. S. 1972. The Statistical Theory of Racism and Sexism. *American Economic Review* 62:659–661.

SLACK, JAMES D. 1997. AIDS and Disability Policy: How Can the Public Sector Prepare Itself? In *Public Personnel Management: Current Concerns, Future Challenges,* 2nd ed. Carolyn Ban and Norma M. Riccucci, eds. White Plains, NY: Longman Publishers USA.

STOUT, JOANNA L. 2000. Recruitment in the Public Sector: An Analysis of the Current Needs of Public Sector Recruitment Efforts and the Impact of Enhanced Recruitment Programs on Turnover. Unpublished Master of Public Administration Professional Paper. Greenville, NC: East Carolina University.

Sutton V. United Air Lines, Inc. 1999. Supreme Court Docket Number 97–1943 (appealed from the U.S. Court of Appeals, 10th Circuit), decided June 22.

TUCKER, B. P., and B. GOLDSTEIN. 1991. Legal Rights of Persons with Disabilities. Hursham, PA: LRP Publications.

U.S. Congress. 1990. *Americans with Disabilities Act of 1990.* Pub. L. 101–336, 101st Congress, 2nd session, 1990.

U.S. Congress. 1973. *The Rehabilitation Act of 1973.* Pub. L. 93–112, 93rd Congress, 1st session, 1973.

U.S. Department of Education, National Institute on Disability and Rehabilitation Research (NIDRR). Chartbook on Work and Disability in the United States in 1998. Cited by the National Council on Disability, National Disability Policy: A Progress Report. <http://www.ncd.gov/newsroom/publications/policy98-99.html.>

U.S. Department of Education, National Institute on Disability and Rehabilitation Research (NIDRR) and the Social Security Administration. The Summary of Data on Young People with Disabilities. Cited by the National Council on Disability, National Disability Policy: A Progress Report. <http://www.ncd.gov/newsroom/publications/policy98-99.html.>

U.S. Department of Health and Human Services, Centers for Disease Control and Prevention 1998. *Business Responds to AIDS: Manager's Kit.*

U.S. Department of Health and Human Services Substance Abuse and Mental Health Services Administration. 1999. Substance Use and Mental Health Characteristics by Employment Status. Rockville, MD: Substance Abuse and Mental Health Services Administration (SAMHSA).

U.S. Department of Health and Human Services Substance Abuse and Mental Health Services Administration (SAMHSA). 2000. Mental Illness—Costs by Disorder. <http://www.samhsa.gov/OAS/srcbk/costs-05.htm>. (9/12/2000).

U.S. Equal Employment Opportunity Commission. 1995. ADA Enforcement Guidance: Preemployment Disability-Related Questions and Medical Examinations. Washington, DC: ADA Division, Office of Legal Counsel, October 10, 1995.

U.S. Equal Employment Opportunity Commission. 1996. Regulations to Implement the Equal Employment Provisions of the Americans with Disabilities Act. 29 C.F.R. § 1630.2(H)(1) & (2).

U.S. Equal Employment Opportunity Commission. 1999. Regulations to Implement the Equal Employment Provisions of the Americans with Disabilities Act. 29 C.F.R. § 1630.9.

U.S. Equal Employment Opportunity Commission. 2000. Americans with Disabilities Act (ADA) of 1990 Charges FY 1992–FY 1999. <http://www.eeoc.gov/stats/ada-charges.html>.

Wolf, James. 1995. ADA "Hyperpluralism" Hinders the Democratic Process. *PA Times* 18(6):10.

20

Supplementing Common Myths With Uncommon Management

The Effective Involvement of Volunteers in Delivering Public Services

JEFFREY L. BRUDNEY
University of Georgia

Volunteer service has long held the imagination of elected leaders, public and non-profit organization officials, and the general public in the United States. A series of biennial national surveys conducted by the Gallup Organization concerning Americans' philanthropic behavior beginning in the 1980s and extending through the 1990s document an impressive record of volunteering. According to the most recent Gallup survey completed in 1999 of a representative sample of 2,553 adults 18 years of age and older, an estimated 55.5 percent of Americans volunteered in 1998, giving a total of 19.9 billion hours, valued at $225.9 billion (Independent Sector, 1999). This level of participation was the highest ever registered—an increase of 13.7 percent over the last survey in 1996—but by no means an anomaly. The rate of volunteering in the United States, as ascertained by survey research, has hovered around half the population since the inception of the series. The roots of this tradition extend as far back as the 1830s, if not before, when the prescient French visitor, Alexis de Tocqueville, characterized the young republic as a nation of "joiners" of causes, endeavors, and associations of seemingly endless variety.

Over the past forty years, presidents of both political parties have celebrated and expanded this venerable tradition. The Peace Corps originated in the Kennedy administration; the VISTA program (Volunteers in Service to America) or the "domestic peace corps" under President Johnson; and the ACTION agency, intended to consolidate federal volunteer programs, under President Nixon. President Carter is the most famous volunteer to the Habitat for Humanity organization, as well as the father of the Atlanta Project, a massive grass-roots effort to revitalize that city. In his two terms in office, President Reagan frequently extolled the virtues of volunteering. His successor, George Bush, promoted "Points of Light," a vision that survives his presidential administration in a foundation that bears that name. President Bush also created a White House Office of National Service, the first office ever established in the White House devoted to promoting volunteerism (Brudney, 2000:44). President Clinton, too, endorsed volunteer service. On September 21, 1993, he signed into law the National and Community Service Trust Act, which authorized the AmeriCorps program. President George W. Bush has also sought to extend volunteer efforts.

The historical roots of volunteerism in the United States and the high-level political support accorded to this activity are not the sole reasons that students of public personnel administration need to develop an appreciation and understanding of volunteer involvement. More often than they might expect, students who choose a career in government may find themselves working with volunteers, either directly or indirectly, to accomplish the public's business. Volunteers are prevalent in the delivery of many government services, for example, health care, education, social services, recreation, environmental preservation, fire protection, public safety, and culture and the arts. Although the statistics elude precise calculation, governments in the United States are responsible for at least 20 to 30 percent of all volunteer activity, programs, and support services. In addition, government agencies are very frequently interconnected with nonprofit organizations—the chief employers of volunteer labor—in complex, service-delivery networks. As Lester M. Salamon (1999, 55) observes, "a complex 'mixed economy' of welfare exists in the United States, with nonprofit, for-profit and government institutions all deeply involved, sometimes on their own, but increasingly in collaboration with each other." Thus, even if their agency does not use volunteers directly, public personnel administrators may well find that their job requires them to work with nonprofit organizations that do, and to handle all attendant personnel matters.

Despite the high profile of volunteerism, the everyday issues and challenges of involving nonpaid workers in the delivery of public services have had comparatively little exposure. This topic is not a standard feature in the formal education of administrators employed in either the public or the nonprofit sector (Brudney and Stringer, 1998). As a result, several myths have arisen regarding volunteer involvement. Like most myths, the ones in this domain have a germ of reality, but they have been exaggerated to the point that they are no longer useful and, in fact, impede successful management of a vital human resource. Accordingly, this chapter critically examines—and debunks—five primary myths regarding the participation of service volunteers in public and nonprofit organizations.

THE VOLUNTEER AVAILABILITY MYTH: *IF YOU BUILD IT, THEY WILL COME*

This reassuring adage may well apply to and gratify the ownership of professional sports franchises, who typically find that adoring fans will seek out the action on their own and support the team, even when the franchise relocates to a new city. Unfortunately, public and nonprofit organizations that rely on volunteers for their important work encounter a much different reality. The only situations for which any evidence exists that large numbers of volunteers will come forward spontaneously to lend their time and talents are natural and man-made emergencies, crises, or disasters. Evidently, the glare of publicity and the manifest needs of the victims are overpowering lures to many volunteers. These situations are transient, however, and do not produce lasting assistance from volunteers. As emergencies fade from view or are tamed, the energy, zeal, and helping instinct of citizens recede with them.

The purposes and circumstances for which leaders of government and nonprofit agencies seek volunteers are far different. Most often, they want volunteer participation to assist their organizations with the ordinary, nonspectacular, though no less essential, tasks of providing services to clients. Normally, these activities must be performed on a continuous rather than episodic basis (as in emergencies), and they occur well outside the public (and media) eye. Providing emergency medical services, counseling youthful offenders, visiting the home-bound elderly, officiating and coaching in youth leagues, offering adult literacy classes, preparing meals at a homeless shelter, and helping citizens to fill out income tax forms are examples of the tasks that government and nonprofit organizations routinely need and ask volunteers to perform. (For listings of many other ways in which governments involve volunteer workers, see Volunteer Programs in Cities and Counties, 1999; Manchester and Bogart, 1988:73–82, 139–216).

Recruitment is a key managerial function in volunteer programs. But if as documented above, half or more of the population volunteers—defined as "not just belonging to a service organization, but actually working in some way to help others for no monetary pay" (Hodgkinson and Weitzman, 1996, E-192)—how great an obstacle can recruitment pose? The answer is that attracting citizens for volunteer roles may well be the single most difficult task confronting the use of this service option. Surveys of those whose job it is to manage volunteers bear out this contention (Brudney, 1993; Duncombe, 1985). In some service domains such as fire protection, potential volunteers have proven sufficiently scarce or resistant to calls for assistance that it can actually prove cost-effective to hire paid personnel instead (Brudney and Duncombe, 1992).

The source of the recruitment problem is two-fold. First, from the perspective of organizations that seek volunteers, survey estimates of the gross rate of volunteering are markedly inflated. The percentages derived from national surveys (such as those undertaken by the Gallup Organization described above) encompass all acts of volunteering, both formal (to an organization) and informal (outside of organizational auspices), regular (on a continuous basis) or sporadic (one-time only or episodic), to all types of institutions (secular or religious), over a calendar year (irrespective of the number of times and the amount of time the individual volunteers during this period). By this inclusive definition, a person who volunteers two hours every week to the humane society and a person who volunteers one time over a 12-month period to help a friend move are equally counted as "volunteers." Correcting for these factors, Brudney (1990a) estimates that the effective pool of volunteers available to government agencies is probably only about one-third the size suggested by most survey research.

The second source of the recruitment problem is that although the volunteer population remains substantial after these corrections, it is highly prized by huge numbers of government departments as well as nonprofit organizations, and even an increasing number of for-profit businesses. To borrow an apt analogy from the world of paid work, the interest of several potential "employers" in this labor drives up its "price," making it more valuable in the marketplace for volunteers.

To intensify the recruitment problem still further, nonprofit organizations and governmental agencies need volunteers not only to assist in their day-to-day operations but also to serve in a policy-making or governance capacity. Almost all nonprofit organizations and many public agencies have governing boards, commissions, review panels, advisory committees, and the like that must be staffed by citizen volunteers. The involvement of volunteers in policy making is crucial not only to ensure citizen input and representation to the organization but also to provide long-term guidance, strategic direction, and community legitimacy (Carver, 1997).

As a result of these factors, organizations must compete for the services of volunteers. Fortunately, a variety of sound methods can assist them in recruitment battles:

- Job design strategies that focus on meeting volunteers' needs and motivations through the content and variety, as well as progression in responsibility, of the tasks and positions made available
- Human capital strategies, which enable participants to acquire contacts, training, and references on the volunteer job that increase their market value for paid employment
- Organizational change and development strategies that center on building an agency culture receptive to volunteers
- Facilitation strategies, such as extending the opportunity to volunteer beyond traditional work-hours (evening and weekends), or reimbursing all out-of-pocket expenses incurred by volunteers (for example, mileage, parking, meals, and child-care)
- Flexibility strategies, such as establishing volunteer jobs that can be performed outside the agency (for example, in the home or automobile), or tasks and assignments that are conducive to group-based volunteering (for example, by the family, religious congregation, or work department or organization)
- Outreach strategies, which include publicizing the volunteer program at the workplace, school, church, synagogue, neighborhood group, civic and other associations, and so forth
- Policy strategies, such as service on agency boards, commissions, panels, and committees, which afford volunteers the opportunity to take an active role in organizational governance
- Ceremonial strategies, which allow volunteers the chance to affiliate with important groups and organizations, meet elected officials or other dignitaries, and receive public recognition for service

If administrators in public and nonprofit organizations build worthwhile programs—*and* develop and implement coherent strategies for recruitment—then, indeed, volunteers are likely to come.

THE VOLUNTEER (NON)MANAGEMENT MYTH:
YOU CAN'T FIRE (OR DISCIPLINE) A VOLUNTEER

This chestnut has long been a favorite of administrators and employees who reject volunteer involvement reflexively. The myth holds that volunteers cannot be managed, presumably because without the leverage of pay or compensation to keep them in line, nonpaid workers cannot be controlled.

The grain of truth sustaining this myth is that it is more difficult to manage a nonpaid than a paid workforce. Volunteers are less dependent on the organization than are paid staff, both because they do not have to take their livelihood from it, and they almost always enjoy many more options (organizations) who are willing to "employ" them, that is, to engage their services (since they are offered to the agency at very low cost). This greater dependence of paid personnel on the organization generally translates into increased compliance among this group with traditional means of agency control, such as rules, procedures, directives, and hierarchical superiors, as well as heightened sensitivity to the threat (and imposition) of disciplinary action. It is also true that despite the manifest need for them, governing boards, commissions, panels, and committees staffed by citizen volunteers can sometimes be ill-informed, impatient, intrusive, and even inept.

Yet, as scholars and practitioners have discovered, pay is not the only tool of the manager; moreover, for some purposes, such as motivating employees to better performance, its potency is subject to considerable dispute (for example, Rainey, 1997). Some experts hold the organization, rather than members of its governing board, responsible for any lapses in governance and policy making (for example, Carver, 1997); a small army of organizational consultants insists that appropriate board training and development can address such maladies (Brudney and Murray, 1998). In the field of volunteer administration, textbooks (for example, McCurley and Lynch, 1996; Ellis, 1996; Fisher and Cole, 1993) suggest a variety of useful techniques that can be instituted for managing nonpaid workers:

- Concise organizational mission statements, to emphasize and elucidate the vital and complementary roles of volunteers and paid staff in achieving agency goals
- Job descriptions for volunteer positions, to elucidate the duties and responsibilities of nonpaid jobs and attendant lines of supervision
- Screening devices, such as interviews and application forms, to make sure that prospective volunteers have appropriate background and interest in the agency positions available
- Orientation sessions, to acquaint volunteers with the mission and goals of the agency, its norms and values, and work environment and procedures, and to allow citizens a chance to reevaluate their decision to donate time
- Policy manuals, to elaborate further the expectations of the agency regarding the behavior and performance of volunteers, as well as the attendant privileges, rights, and protections enjoyed by nonpaid staff
- Training classes and other learning opportunities, to build competence and confidence on the part of volunteers
- Nonpaid "career ladders," to build volunteer commitment and motivation through jobs that offer increased responsibility

- Evaluation procedures, to ascertain the level and quality of volunteer performance; identify and remedy any problems, whether emanating from the organization or the volunteer; and renegotiate volunteer roles as circumstances warrant
- Recognition techniques and ceremonies, to celebrate and honor meritorious achievement, lengthy service, or special commitment on the part of volunteers

Even with these mechanisms in place, however, it can prove necessary, albeit dispiriting, for the volunteer administrator to fire or otherwise discipline a volunteer (most managers of employees do not relish this prospect either). Still, the alternative—countenancing the transgression, thus, sending the wrong message to employees, other volunteers, and agency clients that the staff (nonpaid or paid) are free from organizational direction and oversight—is much worse. One purpose of the policy manual for volunteers highlighted above is to explain these (and other important) provisions of the workplace. Eminent management authority Peter F. Drucker (1990:183) counsels that in cases of egregious misconduct, volunteers "must be asked to leave."

Should a problem arise with a volunteer worker, a responsible course for the manager to follow is:

- Ascertain the facts: If the problem concerns an employee-volunteer relationship, for example, do not assume that the volunteer is at fault. Investigate the complaint.
- Be firm: If the investigation warrants, point out the seriousness of the problem to the volunteer. Make sure that she or he understands the seriousness of the breach, and the consequences of further violation.
- Follow through: If the problem persists, apply sanctions consistent with agency policy.

In order to motivate and guide work behaviors toward agency goals, the management of volunteers does call for the application of complimentary techniques to the hierarchical control procedures commonly used in business firms. For example, managers who strive to build a climate of trust, cooperation, teamwork, challenge, growth, achievement, and commitment among volunteers are more likely to be rewarded with successful performance (see Brudney, 1990b; Walter, 1987). Interestingly enough, in their influential study, *In Search of Excellence*, Thomas J. Peters and Richard H. Waterman (1982) find that "America's best-run companies" use this approach for managing paid employees—with enviable bottom-line results. Perhaps in this domain, the field of volunteer administration has important insights to offer the world of paid personnel administration. Albert C. Smith and F. B. Green (1993) make this connection explicit: Their article recommends "Managing Employees as if They Were Volunteers."

THE VOLUNTEER COST-SAVINGS MYTH: *THINK OF ALL THE MONEY WE'LL SAVE*

In the movement to involve volunteers in the delivery of public services, no motive is mentioned more often, or given greater credibility, than the cost-savings that will presumably follow. Implicitly or explicitly, most discussions of volunteers in service to government or nonprofit organizations allude to this possibility, or even certainty. Yet, more often than not, the potential for volunteer assistance to generate savings has been assumed, rather than demonstrated. Since volunteer labor is donated or "free," how could the conclusion be otherwise?

At least two factors jeopardize this presumption, however. The first might be evident from the earlier discussions of recruitment and managerial issues: organizations must invest resources in the volunteer program and its effective management. The use of volunteers imposes costs, including those incurred for the following program elements:

- A paid volunteer coordinator
- Liability insurance protection for nonpaid workers
- Reimbursement of the work-related expenses of volunteers
- Volunteer recruitment, screening, orientation, training, placement, and evaluation activities
- Training for employees in working with volunteers
- Policy manuals and other informational materials
- Office space, furnishings, utilities, equipment, supplies, postage, and so forth

Other program elements (and costs) might well be appended to this list, including volunteer recognition awards and events, a volunteer newsletter, and identification badges and uniforms as needed.

Even if volunteers were a truly free resource, a second factor would dispute the presumption of cost-savings to be realized by public and nonprofit organizations from citizen involvement in the delivery of services. Stated simply, introducing volunteers will not save any money unless cutbacks are exacted elsewhere in agency budgets. Given the substantial difference in labor costs between volunteers and employees, some government officials (and members of the general public) have no doubt eyed paid positions as the target for budget reductions, with the idea that volunteers might step into them. No matter how attractive this policy might seem from a fiscal perspective, it is most ill-advised, for several reasons.

First, public law and contracts with employee unions prohibit many government organizations from substituting volunteers for paid staff. Second, the effects on employees of such labor substitution (or its anticipation) are highly demoralizing. The apprehensions and antagonisms that arise impair the ability of both paid staff and volunteers to perform their jobs and distract attention and resources from organizational missions. Third, a strong ethic pervades the field of volunteerism that volunteers should not be utilized to the detriment of paid staff. In its Code of Ethics and Standards, the Association for Volunteer Administration subscribes to the principle that volunteer administration exists "to enhance and extend the work of professional and other employed persons in certain service fields," not to displace them (quoted in Fisher and Cole, 1993:177). Fourth, the technical nature of the services provided by many government and nonprofit agencies, and the qualifications personnel must have to participate in various aspects of the service process, impose a final constraint on the potential for labor substitution.

While achieving cost-savings is a legitimate priority in both the nonprofit and public sectors, the legal, ethical, and practical dilemmas raised by possible displacement of paid staff for volunteers offer convincing evidence that the strategy would undermine the very effectiveness of volunteer participation (for a complete discussion of these issues, see Brudney, 1990b:32–36). Even when agency officials have effected cutbacks, and subsequently endeavored to recruit volunteers to bolster performance (in opposition to such prescriptions), assertive leadership, rather than volunteers *per se,* is the source of whatever budgetary savings may have been realized. For volunteers to "save money," budget cuts had to be enacted through some other means.

Nevertheless, the involvement of volunteers does offer important economic and productivity benefits to government and nonprofit organizations. First and foremost, volunteers can help these entities to increase cost-effectiveness—that is, to hold costs down in achieving a given level of service, or to boost service quality or amount for a fixed level of expenditure. The reason is not hard to find. From an economic perspective, the definitive characteristic of the approach is that it spares the expense of compensating monetarily citizens whose donations of time and talents can dramatically expand organizational capability. Since pay and fringe benefits account for a significant proportion of agency budgets, a volunteer program holds the promise of a healthy economic return to sponsoring organizations. In area after area of activity—law enforcement, parks and recreation, libraries, human services, recreation, programs for the elderly, education, culture and the arts, and so forth—volunteers have greatly assisted organizations in extending the reach and scope of services at minimal cost. The typical experience of most agencies that enlist volunteers is that the amount of funding necessary to support them is relatively insignificant—especially when compared to the number of hours donated, the market price for this labor, and the activities that would otherwise not be performed. Funding for the volunteer program can finance services valued at several multiples of actual dollar outlays. For example, the National Park Service boasts some 77,000 volunteers and estimates that it derives $32 worth of service for each dollar invested in recruiting and training.

Second, in addition to raising the level of organizational productivity directly through donating their time and talents, volunteers can also increase the productivity of paid staff members. By assuming a portion of agency work responsibilities, volunteers relieve pressures on beleaguered employees. When volunteer involvement allows these staff to devote greater care and attention to the tasks for which professional training and expertise qualify them, and less to mundane duties that would otherwise occupy their time, human resources are allocated more efficiently, with consequent improvements in agency performance. In law enforcement, for example, police officers typically work in criminal investigation and apprehension, while citizen volunteers (and neighborhood groups) assist them with routine surveillance and reporting. Conversely, volunteers might assume technical duties, such as legal, computer, accounting, or strategic planning, in an agency in which employees lack these skills or requisite experience.

Third, volunteers contribute to the resource base necessary for innovation in government and nonprofit organizations. By allocating the labor and skills of its volunteers to a new project, an agency can experiment quickly and inexpensively with a policy initiative, without first having to obtain start-up funding for a demonstration or pilot program. The speed and dispatch with which a volunteer effort can be up and operating are inspiring. For instance, within a few short weeks of a court order in Alabama amending traditional practices for training election poll workers, volunteers were in the field carrying out the judicial mandate (Montjoy and Brudney, 1991). Such an option is not "free," of course, but it does allow an organization to test promising changes and alternatives in policies, procedures, or services without great delay or generous funding. Particularly in a climate of fiscal austerity, the resource flexibility presented by a volunteer program should not be overlooked.

One further economic benefit merits consideration. Although experts caution that volunteering should not be treated as a credentialing process for paid employment, trained volunteers are an attractive and convenient source of proven recruits for regular positions. The federal government as well as several state and local personnel systems accept relevant volunteer work as experience for paid jobs.

As these points illustrate, a more accurate and persuasive frame than cost-savings for interpreting the economic value of volunteer involvement is the gains in productive capability the approach offers to public and nonprofit organizations. As the director of the department of human resources in a Florida county commented (Lotz, 1982:10):

> During the last fiscal year, volunteers provided over $930,000 worth of services. True, we didn't save that amount in taxes, but financially strapped programs used volunteers creatively to enhance objectives and to get more bang for the buck.

THE VOLUNTEER LIABILITY MYTH: *BUT WE CAN'T AFFORD THE RISK*

More than a few agency leaders have seized on liability issues as a reason for not introducing volunteer workers into their organizations. Because volunteers can put themselves, clients, and the organization at risk—and the organization is responsible for the actions of its employees and volunteers (Vargo, 1995b:329)—these matters deserve attention at the highest levels. Yet, anxiety should not preclude action: Well-developed procedures exist for dealing with the risks occasioned by volunteer involvement. Moreover, a comprehensive plan for risk management carries many organizational benefits, to include encouraging safe actions, protecting agency assets, conserving assets, increasing employee loyalty and productivity, and reducing insurance costs (Vargo, 1995b:322).

Because the risk management plan requires considerable research and preparation and can affect many areas of organizational operations, a good practice is to form a management committee representing the various departments to design and implement it. Developing a risk management plan for volunteers comprises four steps (Kahn, 1993:912–913).

The first step consists of identifying and evaluating potential risks that may be encountered in the volunteer program. The risk management committee should examine the activities of each volunteer position and enumerate the ways that the volunteer could cause injury to others, and the ways in which the volunteer could be personally injured. The committee should prioritize the risks by evaluating which can be expected to occur most often, which might cause greatest damage or harm, and which are most likely to result in liability for the organization.

The second step in the risk management process consists of devising strategies for reducing, or possibly avoiding, the risks identified. The risk management committee may conclude that in certain areas the risks are too great and recommend that agency leadership make a policy decision to terminate these activities (consider, for example, a sterile needle exchange program for drug users). In other areas, however, the committee may determine that the organization can and should continue the activity but must impose safeguards to limit risk to an acceptable level. Well-designed policies in the context of risk management not only limit the probability that accidents will occur but also help ensure that volunteer jobs are staffed and functions are performed as effectively as possible (Kahn, 1993:912–913). In short, they are good volunteer administration practice.

The third step in the risk management process is implementation and periodic re-assessment of the plan. Because agencies, services, activities, personnel, and information all change with the passage of time—possibly raising new or unforeseen hazards and risks as well as offering novel solutions to address existing or emerging problems—periodic reevaluation of the risk management plan is highly recommended. Even when the organization has invested substantial time, effort, and care in formulating and implementing a risk management plan, accidents involving volunteers (or employees or clients) as well as lawsuits can still occur. These occasions afford an opportunity to reevaluate the risk management plan to see what changes might be warranted to prevent re-occurrence in the future. They also point up the need to provide liability insurance protection for volunteer workers.

The risk management plan incorporates a sensible series of steps to identify, evaluate, and limit the risks and hazards associated with volunteer service in the organization. It is a complement, not a substitute, for insurance coverage for volunteers. It cannot eliminate risk altogether, but it does offer a realistic approach to the problem. For those risks it has judged reasonable and necessary for the effective performance of the agency, leadership needs to make certain that the agency's liability insurance coverage embraces volunteers as well as employees. The purchase of insurance protection is the last technique used in developing the risk management plan; all other methods should be evaluated and considered prior to seeking liability insurance (Vargo, 1995b:327).

To determine the type and amount of liability coverage an agency may require for its volunteer workers, organizational leadership will need to consult an industry professional. Myths to the contrary, well-established practices for risk management exist for volunteers, and liability insurance coverage as part of the risk management plan is available (Vargo, 1995a, 1995b; Ellis, 1996:146–150; McCurley and Lynch, 1996:143–148: Graff, 1995:130–135).

THE VOLUNTEER ADVERSARY MYTH:
HOW CAN WE BE FRIENDS?

One impediment to the involvement of volunteers known for exasperating program leadership and citizen participants alike is the often indifferent or antagonistic reception by paid staff (for example, Graff, 1984; Wilson, 1981). When paid workers must share the work place and environment with nonpaid counterparts, especially in a climate of fiscal austerity, they may come to view volunteers as competitors—for organizational resources, clients, and positions—rather than as collaborators in attaining agency goals. While discord may be understandable, it is enervating, and must be alleviated. Part of the answer to this problem is adoption of the managerial methods discussed above for governing the volunteer program and clarifying its purpose and parameters, for both employees and volunteers. Part of the answer, too, lies in airing the myth that volunteers are the adversary of paid staff.

To begin, volunteers are no more enamored with the prospect of replacing paid personnel than are volunteer administrators (see above) or the employees whose jobs might be at stake. Volunteers have always embraced the moral tenet that they not fill the positions of paid staff members (Manser, 1987:848). For the vast majority of citizens, volunteering is not motivated by a desire to cut back or limit agency spending. National surveys conducted by the Gallup Organization indicate that just 2 to 5 percent of volunteers donate their time with the intent to "help keep taxes down" (Gallup, 1986:37–41). Moreover, in communities that have enacted limitations on the taxing authority of local governments, volunteers are actually less likely to be involved in delivering services than they are in other cities (Ferris, 1988).

Not only does the volunteer community reject the idea of labor substitution as a goal for involvement, but also volunteer activity appears to breed respect and approbation, rather than complaints or ridicule, for the public sector. Despite the oft-noted apprehension of employees regarding their participation, volunteers make effective advocates of agency interests who help to further organizational missions, achieve increased appropriations, and, thereby, preserve government budgets and paid positions (for example, Marando, 1986). No evidence exists that volunteers are motivated by a desire to cut agency budgets or paid staff. On the contrary, they are much more likely to press for increases in the policy domains where they have chosen to give their time and attention. Typically, they focus on these domains precisely because they believe that more resources ought to be allocated to them. Much as people vote for preferred candidates at the ballot box, volunteers "vote" for favored policy or service arenas through donating their time to specific organizations and/or becoming program advocates.

As residents and members of the community, volunteers can aid an organization in promoting good public relations, including creating awareness of the constraints that frequently plague employees in pursuing agency missions. They can also engage in crucial support activities with external constituencies normally precluded to government employees, such as fund-raising and lobbying. Partly as a result of the independence and credibility that the public attributes to them, volunteers have earned the distinction of premier fund-raisers. They are just as adept at mobilizing popular support and petitioning centers of power. Lobbying campaigns by volunteers helped to shield the California public library system from the depredations of Proposition 13 (Walter, 1987) and the U.S. Small Business Administration from repeated attacks by President Reagan and his appointees (Brudney, 1990b).

Volunteers are not interested in replacing paid staff members. Instead, they choose to lend their support to agency missions and, in general, become effective proponents of these goals. Additional ways in which volunteers assist employees include:

- Sparing employees from mundane duties that nevertheless must be performed, and affording them greater latitude to focus on the tasks for which they have professional training or expertise.
- Giving employees access to specialized skills and abilities that they do not currently possess and that can assist them on the job.
- Presenting employees with the opportunity to gain valuable experience as managers and supervisors.
- Offering empathy and emotional support to employees, who may labor in psychologically draining and volatile service environments, such as those related to AIDS, homelessness, child welfare, and substance abuse.
- Providing employees with constructive feedback and advice, not generated through normal channels, that may be a source of productive innovation and change.
- Increasing the ability of employees to learn first-hand about community needs, conditions, and expectations, and evaluations of agency services.

In sum, volunteers offer advantages to paid staff members, in addition to those reaped by their organizations. In an era in which many political leaders, as well as a large segment of the population, have embraced initiatives to "privatize" government operations, public employees should realize the allies they have in volunteers.

CONCLUSION

Directly or indirectly, students and administrators in the public personnel field are likely to encounter volunteer workers on the job. Volunteers already assist myriad organizations at all levels of government, and their use is accelerating. In addition, through contracting and participation in complex service-deliver networks, nonprofit organizations provide a huge and growing proportion of all publicly financed human and social services. They rely heavily on volunteers to do so.

This chapter has elaborated five key issues concerning the involvement of volunteers in service delivery in public and nonprofit organizations. The discussion was intended to expose and dispel popular myths regarding volunteers that can impair the constructive utilization of this vital human resource. First, while a substantial proportion of Americans volunteer, they are not poised to come to the aid of any particular agency; they must be recruited to service in a sharply competitive market for their time and talents. Second, although volunteers pose a genuine challenge for effective management, a set of useful techniques has been developed and refined for this purpose. Third, volunteer involvement may not directly yield monetary savings to stressed agency budgets, but this option can assist officials in maintaining, or even enhancing, service quality and amount and making the most cost-effective use of all organizational resources. Fourth, introducing volunteers may entail the risk of liability and exposure to sponsoring organizations, but risk management procedures can accommodate the risk and yield stronger overall management as well. Finally, despite the difficulties that have sometimes marred their successful participation, volunteers are not adversaries of employees. Volunteers can and do assist paid staff, their agencies—and perhaps most important of all–the clients and constituencies who are the chief beneficiaries of their services.

REFERENCES

BRUDNEY, J. L. 2000. "Points of Light: Building Social Capital?" In *Social Structures, Social Capital, and Personal Freedom*, Dale McConkey and Peter A. Lawler, eds. Westport, CT: Praeger Publishers, pp. 43–59.

——. 1993. Volunteer Involvement in the Delivery of Public Services: Advantages and Disadvantages. *Public Productivity and Management Review* 16 (3):283–297.

——. 1990a. The Availability of Volunteers: Implications for Local Governments. *Administration and Society* 21 (February):413–424.

——. 1990b. *Fostering Volunteer Programs in the Public Sector: Planning, Initiating, and Managing Voluntary Activities*. San Francisco, CA: Jossey-Bass.

——, and W. D. DUNCOMBE. 1992. An Economic Evaluation of Paid, Volunteer, and Mixed Staffing Options for Public Services. *Public Administration Review* 52 (September–October):474–481.

BRUDNEY, J. L., and V. MURRAY. 1998. Do Intentional Efforts to Improve Boards Really Work? The Views of Nonprofit CEOs. *Nonprofit Management and Leadership* 8 (Summer):333–348.

BRUDNEY, J. L., and G. E. STRINGER. 1998. Higher Education in Volunteer Administration: Exploring–and Critiquing–the State of the Art. In *Nonprofit Management Education: U.S. and World Perspectives*, Michael O'Neill and Kathleen Fletcher, eds. Westport, CT: Greenwood/Praeger, pp. 95–109.

CARVER, J. 1997. *Boards That Make a Difference: A New Design for Leadership in Nonprofit and Public Organizations*, 2nd ed. San Francisco, CA: Jossey-Bass.

DRUCKER, P. F. 1990. *Managing the Non-Profit Organization: Practices and Principles*. New York: Harper-Collins.

DUNCOMBE, S. 1985. Volunteers in City Government: Advantages, Disadvantages and Uses. *National Civic Review* 74 (9):356–364.

ELLIS, S. J. 1996. *From the Top Down: The Executive Role in Volunteer Program Success*. Revised Edition. Philadelphia, PA: Energize.

FERRIS, J. M. 1988. The Use of Volunteers in Public Service Production: Some Demand and Supply Considerations. *Social Science Quarterly* 69 (1):3–23.

FISHER, J. C., and K. M. COLE. 1993. *Leadership and Management of Volunteer Programs: A Guide for Volunteer Administrators*. San Francisco: Jossey-Bass.

Gallup, Inc. 1986. *Americans Volunteer, 1985*. Princeton, NJ: Gallup Organization.

GRAFF, L. L. 1995. Polices for Volunteer Programs. In *The Volunteer Management Handbook*, T. D. Connors, ed. New York: John Wiley, pp. 125–155.

——. 1984. Considering the Many Facets of Volunteer/Union Relations. *Voluntary Action Leadership* 1984 (Summer):16–20.

HAEUSER, A. A., and F. S. SCHWARTZ. 1984. Developing Social Work Skills for Work with Volunteers. In *Voluntarism and Social Work Practice: A Growing Collaboration*, F. S. Schwartz, ed. Lanham, MD: University Press of America, pp. 23–34.

HODGKINSON, V. A., and M. S. WEITZMAN, 1996. *Giving and Volunteering in the United States: Findings from a National Survey*. Washington, DC: Independent Sector.

Independent Sector. 1999. *Giving and Volunteering in the United States, 1999: Findings from a National Survey*. Available at <http://www.indepsec.org/GandV/s_keyf.htm>. Accessed May 15, 2000.

KAHN, J. D. 1993. Legal Issues in the Involvement of Volunteers. In *The Nonprofit Management Handbook: Operating Policies and Procedures*, T. D. Connors, ed. New York: John Wiley, pp. 907–919.

LOTZ, A. R. 1982. Alternatives in Health and Human Services. *Public Management* 64 (10):10–12.

MANCHESTER, L. D., and G. S. BOGART. 1988. *Contracting and Volunteerism in Local Government: A Self-Help Guide*. Washington, DC: International City Management Association.

MANSER, G. 1987. Volunteers. In *Encyclopedia of Social Work, Volume 2*, A. Minahan, ed. Silver Spring, MD: National Association of Social Workers, pp. 842–851.

MARANDO, V. L. 1986. Local Service Delivery: Volunteers and Recreation Councils. *Journal of Volunteer Administration* 4 (4):16–24.

MCCURLEY, S., and R. LYNCH. 1996. *Volunteer Management: Mobilizing all the Resources in the Community.* Downers Grove, IL.

MONTJOY, R. S., and J. L. BRUDNEY, 1991. Volunteers in the Delivery of Public Services: Hidden Costs . . . and Benefits. *American Review of Public Administration* 21 (December):327–344.

RAINEY, H. G. 1997. *Understanding and Managing Public Organizations,* 2nd ed. San Francisco, CA: Jossey-Bass.

SALAMON, L. M. 1999. *America's Nonprofit Sector: A Primer.* 2nd ed. New York: Foundation Center.

SMITH, A. C., and F. B. GREEN. 1993. Managing Employees as If They Were Volunteers. *SAM Advanced Management Journal* 58 (3):42–46.

VARGO, KATHARINE S. 1995a. Board Member Liability and Responsibility. In *The Volunteer Management Handbook,* T. D. Connors, ed. New York: John Wiley, pp. 309–321.

——. 1995b. Risk Management Strategies. In *The Volunteer Management Handbook,* T. D. Connors, ed. New York: John Wiley, pp. 322–338.

Volunteer Programs in Cities and Counties. 1999. *International City/County Management Association Service Report* 31 (8) August.

WALTER, V. 1987. Volunteers and Bureaucrats: Clarifying Roles and Creating Meaning. *Journal of Voluntary Action Research* 16 (3):22–32.

WILSON, M. 1981. Reversing the Resistance of Staff to Volunteers. *Voluntary Action Leadership* Spring: 21.

21

Ethics and Human Resource Management

JONATHAN P. WEST

University of Miami

Ethics is a widely debated topic in government and public administration. There has been increasing attention devoted to unethical behavior in government at all levels. Newspapers, magazines, television, and the Internet have exposed instances of scandals, fraud, waste, abuse, and corruption. In response to these problems, public sector organizations have undertaken efforts to foster integrity and increase commitment to ethical behavior. The institutionalization of ethics is a major challenge for public institutions. Human resource managers are in a position to help meet this challenge. Their role and activities provide opportunities to build a commitment to integrity and to convince those in the organization that ethics does matter.

Recently HR managers have assumed a leadership role in identifying the need for ethics programs and implementing them. A national survey of 500 members of the Ethics Officers Association reported that ethics officers (members of senior management responsible for implementing and maintaining ethics programs) interacted most frequently at work with HR managers, equaled only by legal officers, and that they were among the most supportive of ethics promotion efforts (Driscoll and Hoffman, 1998). Ethics officers themselves often come from an HR background, many inquiries addressed to ethics "hotlines" are personnel-oriented, and HR managers often provide a sounding board for ethics/compliance officers. Petrick (1992) reports that focus groups among HR managers also indicate a willingness to make the HR department the responsible unit for ethics-related workplace matters. Indeed, this is already happening in the corporate world: a national survey found eight in ten HR professionals claimed that they were responsible for ethical leadership in their organizations, and even higher percentages (95 percent) said "HR staff should be responsible for ethical leadership" (*SHRM/CCH Survey*, 1991:p. 4). While HR is increasingly assuming ethics-related responsibilities, and organizations are continuously developing ethics standards, more recent surveys of business indicate the need to go further in integrating ethical standards into daily operations (Anonymous, 1998). It is likely that similar trends and needs exist in the public sector.

This chapter briefly reviews the responses that organizations are taking to the ethics challenge and some of the strategies that have been employed to build integrity in the public sector. The particular ethical challenges facing the human resource manager are reviewed by briefly examining specific components of public human resource systems and processes that are vital in building and maintaining an ethical organization. Leverage points for strategic responses to these ethical challenges by the HR professional are considered. Throughout the chapter the problems and prospects for public integrity and human resource management are discussed.

GENERAL ORGANIZATIONAL RESPONSES

Responses to the ethics challenge have been multifaceted, but typically they have taken two complementary tracks: legal and behavioral. Legal action seeks to curb wrongdoing; training activities seek to promote ethical behavior by raising the ethical consciousness of employees. Among the ethical concerns addressed by the legal response are prohibitions of unethical activities (e.g., sexual harassment, discrimination) and mandates regarding such matters as financial disclosure and post-service employment (Berman, West, and Bonczek, 1998). Legal responses have their limitations; they are quite narrow in scope, and they may help in defining the black and white areas of permissible and impermissible behaviors; but they provide insufficient guidance in dealing with the gray areas. As a private sector ethics officer noted using a different color-coding scheme: "It's easy to tell what's red and what's green most of the time, but it's that yellow light where you really have to make those tough decisions" (cited in Driscoll and Hoffman, 1998). Furthermore, an action may be legal, but unethical (e.g., intentionally breaking promises, violating confidences, or scapegoating personal failures) (Brumback, 1998). Another shortcoming of the legal response is that aggressive prosecution can heighten public awareness of ethical wrongdoing that can negatively influence public trust in government.

The behavioral response emphasizes training and information dissemination to help managers and employees recognize and cope with ethical problems and conflicts. Such guidance seeks to better inform ethical decision making, to minimize ethical missteps by altering attitudes and promoting ethical awareness, and to provide resources for consultation to aid in thinking through tough ethical issues. Mission, vision, values, and pledge statements have been adopted by some jurisdictions; ethics codes and standards of conduct are used as well. These topics are typically reviewed in training sessions. Increasingly, however, training has gone beyond this, using case studies, role plays, scenarios, games, and other techniques to more closely approximate the "real world" conditions confronting managers and employees and to foster ethical responsibility. A set of carefully designed training materials that incorporates these latter approaches are available and customized for the public sector (e.g., Kazman and Bonczek, 1999).

SPECIFIC ORGANIZATION RESPONSES AND STRATEGIES

Code-Based Strategies

Organizational strategies can be further examined by distinguishing between code-based strategies and approaches that stress principles and relationships. Code-based strategies can be categorized as aspirational, prohibitive, and hybrid. The aspirational codes go beyond the letter of the law and are characterized by norms of desired behavior, with provisions ranging from general to specific statements. For example, such a code might contain provisions stressing trust, responsibility, integrity, and public service. The prohibitive codes, by contrast, focus on illegal and ethical conduct, hearings, investigations, and sanctions for violations. For example, a prohibitive code might contain reference to conflict of interest, use of public office for personal gain, and gifts. Finally, the hybrid codes contain a blend of both aspirational and prohibitive provisions. Such codes might simultaneously encourage desired behaviors (e.g., fair treatment) and prohibit undesirable behaviors (e.g., disclosure of confidential information). While codes alone are insufficient as a strategy for institutionalizing ethics, they can help alert individuals and groups to the ethical values of their organization (Bell, 1997). Such jurisdiction-specific codes are not the only source of code-related guidance. Public sector professional associations (e.g., ASPA, ICMA) have their own codes, as do professional associations of human resource managers (IPMA, SHRM).

Principle and Relationship Strategies

Ethical principles and stakeholder relationships can be emphasized as another strategic option for managing ethics. Principled approaches to ethical decision making can be categorized as deductive, inductive, or a combination of the two. Use of the deductive approach entails a top-down process where decision makers are guided by abstract ethical principles (e.g., honesty, loyalty, justice) when confronting situations involving moral choice. For example, an official may weigh whether the principle of justice or mercy is the best guide to action in a particular discipline case. By contrast, use of the inductive approach is a bottom-up process that focuses on the stakeholders who are most affected by the decision and the relationships among them. For example, use of this approach may lead to consideration of a decision maker's duty and responsibility to key stakeholders without necessarily relying on abstract ethical principles as a guide. Obviously, a training session could be designed which would combine both of these approaches. For example, it may combine an examination of general principles (e.g., liberty, rights, justice) as abstract guides with case studies or role plays to provide context and consideration of the situationally specific stakeholder relationships that may affect or be affected by various decision options (Bell, 1997; Svara, 1997; Garofalo and Geuras, 1999). The literature contains numerous examples of efforts that use each of these three approaches to ethical training. Table 21–1 provides a list of ethical principles and the guiding questions posed by each.

TABLE 21-1   Ethical Principles and Guiding Questions

Consequences	*What course of action will do the most good and the least harm?*
Utilitarian ethic	What course of action brings the greatest good for the greatest number of people?
Proportionality ethic	What are the good and bad results of this decision and do the good outweigh the bad?
Theory of justice	Does this action apply impartially to each employee and organizational unit?
Golden rule	If I were in the position of another person affected by my decision, would my actions be considered fair by that person?
Reversibility rule	Would I be willing to change places with the person affected by my contemplated action?
Protect health, safety, and welfare	What course of action will best protect the health, safety, and welfare of others?
Integrity	*What plan can I live with, which is consistent with the basic values and commitments in my organization?*
Virtuous character	Would this action be undertaken by someone of exemplary or virtuous character?
Disclosure rule	What course of action would I be comfortable with if it was examined by my friends, family and associates?
Professional ethic	Can my action be explained before a committee of peers?
Intuition ethic	Which course of action feels right to me?
Rights	*Which alternative best serves others' rights, including stakeholders' rights?*
Principle of equal freedom	Will my contemplated action restrict others from actions that they have a legitimate right to undertake?
Rights ethics	Will my action deprive any person affected by it of a right that must be respected?
Practicality	*Which course of action is feasible in the world as it is?*
Conventionalist ethic	What action will further my self-interest without violating the law?
Darwinian ethic	What course of action will enable me to succeed and survive in this organization?
Organizational vs. personal ethic	Is this action consistent with both organizational ethics and personal ethics and do organizational considerations override personal ones?
Organizational loyalty	What are the organizational goals and what can I do that is good for the organization?

A jurisdiction's decision to pursue a law-based or behavior-oriented approach to institutionalizing ethics or a code-based or principle-oriented strategy should be preceded by examining the organization's values, visualizing the ethical environment, and surveying the ethical climate. There are various conceptual aids and methods to make such assessments. Three specific alternatives are considered here: clarification of basic values, the structure of the ethical environment, and an ethics climate survey.

Values Clarification

As mentioned previously, some jurisdictions have adopted mission, vision, values, or pledge statements. Such statements are relevant because they often contain content regarding managing the public service. Important public service values include such things as valuing employee talents, promoting fairness, developing teamwork, ensuring high quality service, and maintaining ethical principles. These values coincide with values of professional human resource management—efficiency, economy, fairness, and high performance—and are useful guides to behavior. However, organizations and individuals differ in the extent of value consciousness. Van Wart (1998) identifies three levels of individual and organizational values consciousness: unconsciousness, elementary consciousness, and advanced consciousness. Those at Level 1 (values unconsciousness) are neither aware of nor understand organizational values, policies, purposes or processes and may well act inappropriately or illegally. Those at Level 2 (elementary values consciousness) do understand the values, mission, laws, and procedures, and they comply to stay within legal bounds and avoid acting inappropriately. Organizational members at Level 3 (advanced values consciousness) are fully aware of the unit's values, purposes, and vision, and their actions are likely to mirror the ideals associated with the principles of public service—maintaining productive work environments, serving the customer, and so forth.

Managerial efforts to build an ethical workplace can be aided by consideration of the level of value consciousness existing in their unit. For example, educational strategies are needed if employees lack awareness of agency values, missions, and purposes. Human resource managers operating in a Level 1 environment cannot tolerate employee ignorance of sexual harassment laws, affirmative action requirements, and negotiated grievance procedures or actions which fail to show concern for others or contribute to unfair treatment. HR professionals who see their job as insuring compliance with laws, rules, and procedures (Level 2) will be focused primarily on detecting and correcting illegal or unethical behavior. In a Level 3 environment a more expansive role is available to human resource managers because employees fully appreciate organizational values, missions, and purposes and see human resources as crucial to the improved performance of government service (Berman et al., 2000).

Ethical Environment

Related to the need for values clarification is the need to better understand and visualize the organization's ethical environment. Driscoll and Hoffman (1997) suggest a useful framework for such visualization—a four-part pyramid. At the base is ethical awareness, in the middle is ethical reasoning, at the top is ethical action, and at the peak is ethical leadership. Beginning at the bottom, human resource managers can test for ethical awareness on the part of managers and employees: Can those in the organization detect ethical problems in the workplace or are they so preoccupied with their own daily work assignments that they have ethical blinders on? Hypothetical scenarios in training sessions can help to determine the presence or absence of moral vision. Moving up the pyramid to ethical reasoning, the HR professional will be interested in whether, once detected, the ethical problem can be reasoned through to solution by managers and employees. If all issues are framed in legal terms, without regard for ethical implications, then attention to moral reasoning instruction is called for. Nearing the top of the pyramid, ethical action is required. It is one thing to identify an ethical problem and reason through the solution, but then consistently failing to use such insight as a guide to ethical action is a crucial impediment to the institutionalization of ethics and requires strategic intervention. Finally, at the peak of the pyramid is ethical leadership. Here moral leadership can be found by those located at all levels of the organization that benefit by having an ethical compass to guide their actions. The challenge to HR managers working in such an environment is to maintain and expand the capacity for moral leadership.

Ethical Climate Survey

Human resource managers may have an intuitive grasp of whether they are operating in a Level 1, 2, or 3 environment using Van Wart's schema, or at one of the four levels in Driscoll and Hoffman's pyramid typology. Nonetheless, more systematic approaches have been suggested to assess the ethical climate of public sector organizations. Van Wart (1998) suggests the use of an ethics assessment and Kazman and Bonczek (1999) have designed an ethics climate survey. In both instances, the objectives are to better understand the organization's values and perceptions of right and wrong as well as the differences between stated values and actual ethical performance. Specific survey items and instructions are provided to aid managers in diagnosing the nature of the ethics climate of their organization. To be most effective assessments should rely on data from controls, documents, and stated policies as well as perceptions, beliefs, attitudes, and behaviors regarding ethics, operations and support. Results from such surveys can better inform the strategic responses of public managers generally, and human resource managers specifically.

In addition to the above mentioned responses to institutionalizing ethics there are other organizational variables that need to be examined. Up to now we have considered strategies available to those operating in the broader organizational environment. Next we shift and narrow the focus to those factors that relate more closely to the responsibilities of the human resource manager. These factors are especially important because both explicit and implicit aspects of ethics programs are subject to the influence of HR managers. Explicit factors are specifically created programs designed to promote ethics (e.g., employee orientation and training programs); implicit aspects are inherent in the culture, systems, and processes of the organization (e.g., incentive systems and performance evaluation). Both factors are vital in creating and maintaining an ethical organization. The analysis that follows considers the HR systems and processes that reinforce this effort.

HUMAN RESOURCE IMPLEMENTATION STRATEGIES

Hiring

Ethical considerations are important in the recruitment and selection process. Subtle and not so subtle messages about organizational ethics are communicated in job announcements, screening procedures, and communications with applicants. At each stage of this process the mission, vision, and values of the organization can be emphasized and reinforced. For example, job announcements might highlight "ethical sensitivity" or "meeting customer needs" as a crucial qualification. Similarly, the selection interview presents an opportunity for employers to discuss organizational values and clearly communicate the importance of ethics to job prospects, including examples of acceptable and unacceptable conduct. Interview questions could include situation-specific questions (e.g., "What would you do if your spouse and children had colds and would be alone at home if you left for work?") with responses scored high ("I'd go to work, a cold is not serious") or low ("I'd remain home") (cited in Brumback, 1998). Interviewees can probe the employer's ethical stance by raising questions about things it mentions in its Values Creed or Code of Conduct book. More general questions might give clues as well: "What is the profile of a successful person in your jurisdiction?" "Are there any unusual demands in this job that I should be aware of?" Some jurisdictions require a signed pledge from new hires to adhere to ethical principles. Integrity tests, prohibited in certain states and legal in others, are used to assess applicant attitudes on wrongdoing in the workplace or to identify the propensity for irresponsible behavior. However, caution should be used in employing such screening devices due to increasing legal complexities and litigious job applicants. Employers can also demonstrate their commitment to values like fairness and respect in their courteous acknowledgment of receipt of job applications and tactful letters of rejection (Gibelman, 1996).

Orientation

New employee orientation sessions afford an opportunity to increase ethical awareness by explicit discussion of the goals and values of the organization as well as the policies and procedures managers and employees are expected to use as guides to behavior and decision making. Among the topics that might be included in new employee orientation are clear statements by top officials of expectations regarding ethical behavior of all employees, and review of relevant laws, ethics codes, rules/regulations, and procedures and the penalties for noncompliance. Other key topics could involve discussion of management's philosophy regarding the organization's mission, values, rules, and the processes for enforcement, safeguards against unfairness, and channels for appeal. More specific orientation subjects might include discussion of: behaviors promoting organizational values (e.g., promise keeping, honest dealings) and unethical practices (e.g., conflict of interest, use of public resources for private gain). Also, consideration of frequently encountered dilemmas (e.g., outside employment, gifts) and resources available to aid ethical decision making (e.g., ombudspersons, ethics officers or committees, ethics hotlines, ethics newsletters) is useful.

Compensation

"Equal pay for equal work" was a reform-theme in the late 1800s and has been a core value espoused by merit system advocates since that time. However, implementing this principle has proven difficult, and complaints about pay inequities abound. Monetary incentives to do things right and to do the right thing are absent if organizations are rewarding unproductive and unethical behavior or failing to reward productive and ethical behavior. When pay is not linked to performance, but based more on the personal views and prejudices of managers, the potential increases for misuse of discretion and unfairness to employees. Failing to reward top performers and moral exemplars for their efforts sends a powerful message. Often the reward system communicates to employees the "real story" regarding the employer's commitment to ethical behavior.

Training

HR managers who decide to deliver ethics training have various tools and resources available. Numerous books or manuals serve as useful training materials (e.g., Bell, 1997; Local Government Training Institute, 1995-1998; Lewis, 1991; and Wright and Cooper, 1992) as do resources available from professional associations (e.g., Kazman and Bonczek, 1999; Berman, West and Bonczek, 1998; Kellar, 1988; American Society for Public Administration [ASPA], 1990, International Personnel Management Association [IPMA], 1999). Recently the American Society for Public Administration joined with the International City/County Management Association, and the Council of State Governments to co-sponsor the quarterly journal *Public Integrity*, published by Westview Press. These resource materials contain case studies, commentaries, scenarios, role plays, self-assessment instruments, field reports, individual and group exercises, profiles of moral exemplars, analytic frameworks, sample ethics codes, and essays that help reinforce public service values like fairness, honesty, integrity, and belief in democratic processes.

The objectives of ethics training are multiple as well as varied. Training may be designed to: increase ethical awareness; insure familiarity with key legal, code and policy requirements; explain and discuss ethical standards and expectations; foster insight from situationally specific examples; provide tools and frameworks for resolving ethical conflicts; stimulate ethical reflection; and support practical ways to approach ethical decision making. Such training is needed not just for newly hired employees, but for all employees who periodically need a "booster shot" to inoculate against wrongdoing (West et al., 1998).

Ethics instruction takes many forms. Ponemon (1996) offers a concise summary of twelve key features or ingredients of successful ethics training programs: live instruction, small class sizes, a decision-based focus, the use of a professional trainer, a powerful message from the manager, realistic case materials, significant group interaction, at least four hours of training, comprehensive involvement of employees, separate courses for compliance areas, follow-up communications, and new-employee programs. The potential benefits resulting from ethics training include increased legal protection, improved ethical climate, and enhanced trust linked to more open communication channels. It also helps to assess multiple ethical perspectives, clarify values, and guide ethical action.

Performance Appraisal

Merit is the stated basis for appraising employee performance in public personnel systems. When questionable appraisal practices occur, it undermines merit principles and systems (Bowman, 1999). The gap between theory and practice can be reduced, according to Bowman, when top officials model appropriate behavior, sound policies and procedures are supported by managers and employees, appropriate tools are selected, raters are trained, and continuous, positive or corrective feedback is provided. Performance appraisals can also more explicitly include ethics as a dimension of evaluation. For example, Brumback (1991) suggests that administrators' performance be evaluated on the general conduct and ethics factor together with the more customary managerial or professional/technical factors. Building an ethically sound government requires that managers and employees recognize that ethical concerns are inherent in their job responsibilities. Using ethics as a criterion in evaluations, addressing ethical violations consistently and fairly, and publicly acknowledging examples of positive ethical conduct can demonstrate a unit's commitment to ethical behavior. Relevant questions to consider are: Is the employee performing in compliance with relevant laws, rules, and regulations? Does he/she set a positive example in circumstances where discretion is exercised? Does he/she demonstrate commitment to the organization's mission, goals, and values? Are self-appraisals truthful? Considering answers to these questions brings ethics into the performance appraisal process. However, a caution should be noted: The existing appraisal process itself might inadequately address ethical issues. For example, does the system provide a clear avenue of recourse for an employee who doesn't concur with a job evaluation and fails to resolve the issue with a manager?

Adverse Actions

Fairness and due process considerations are crucial in discipline or employee discharge cases. Nonprobationary public sector employees have traditionally enjoyed job protection and appeals procedures designed to shield workers from arbitrary or capricious punishment and/or wrongful discharge. While there has been some movement in the direction of employment-at-will (e.g., State of Georgia), civil service procedures typically create a "property interest" or expectation of continued employment assuming satisfactory performance for such employees. Where these protections exist, employees will be terminated only for cause (Kellough, 1999). Managers need to be aware of legal strictures and to be guided by ethical principles of fairness, rights, and proportionality in taking adverse actions against employees.

Diversity

Public sector ethics codes often have equal opportunity or nondiscrimination clauses. For example, the International City/County Management Association code stresses merit-based personnel actions based on fairness and impartiality. ICMA's implementing guidelines go further and support equal employment opportunities for all persons, prohibit discrimination against those in protected categories, and promote affirmative action programs. Similarly, the American Society for Public Administration's code, in the section on Serve the Public Interest, states, "Oppose all forms of discrimination, and harassment, and promote affirmative action." The International Personnel Management Association's Statement of

Principles and Values contains similar language (see Table 22–1). As "keepers of the policies," HR managers clearly need to be vigilant in ensuring a workplace free of discrimination where personnel actions are merit based, fair, and impartial. While reasonable people can disagree on the contentious issue of affirmative action (e.g., Wardlaw, 2000), it continues to be supported in ethics codes of visible national and international professional associations.

Union-Management Relations

Historically, union-management relations in the United States have been characterized as adversarial. Increasing fiscal pressures have led many government and union leaders to change the way they look at union-management relations. Competing models emphasizing partnership and cooperation have been proposed and tried in selected jurisdictions (IPMA, 1998). Briggs and Siegele (1994) have proposed that government employers and their unions jointly commit to ethical conduct by formalizing an ethics standards clause in collective negotiation agreements. They further suggest that joint labor-management committees be formed to seek ethical solutions to grievances.

The ethics standards clause is not without precedent: it was negotiated in a private sector contract between management and the United Auto Workers at Chrysler's New Castle, Indiana, plant. The preamble to that agreement pledges to move from the adversarial to the cooperative model of labor relations and acknowledges that "equity, fair play, and trust . . ." will be the " . . . cornerstones of such a relationship with the dignity and the respect of each individual paramount to all else" (p. 184). The adversarial model of union-management relations is based on conflicting interests and is not likely to change in the near term. Nonetheless, public sector efforts to create labor-management partnerships based on common interests are promising, and an ethics standards clause is one way to emphasize the value to be derived from fair play and trust between parties.

HRIS

Human resource information systems contain personal data about each employee. The creation and use of such data should be guided by both legal and ethical considerations. Privacy-related issues such as the types of information placed on the system (e.g., pay and health information) and determinations of who has access to such data will confront HR managers. Under the fifth and fourteenth amendments to the U.S. Constitution, an individual's rights to life, liberty, and property cannot be denied without due process of law. Applying these statements to HRIS raises issues of property and liberty interests in HR records management. Those controlling personnel records need to be aware of privacy concerns, and to determine what is and what is not confidential, what may or may not stigmatize an employee, and what information deserves restricted access (Hubbard, Forcht, and Thomas, 1998). Along with legal concerns, moral rights of employees–to fair treatment, respect, and privacy–should be respected (Velasquez, 1998). These legal and moral issues should be kept in mind when employers are responding to requests for job references.

Health, Safety and Accessibility Issues

Government agencies face ethical challenges in keeping the workplace healthy, safe, and accessible. Fiscal constraints have prompted cost cutting which, in some cases, has resulted in compromised health and safety conditions in the government workplace (e.g., accidents, contaminated food, fires resulting from outdated electrical wiring). Deregulation and privatization may increase the potential risks to health and safety where proper safeguards, monitoring mechanisms, information disclosure, and sanctions are inadequate. Health and safety issues can be partially addressed through orientation and training programs, well-conceived contingency plans, and emergency response capabilities. Accessibility issues have emerged in response to the Americans with Disabilities Act and its requirements for reasonable accommodations. Richter and Richter's (1999) analysis of health, safety, and accessibility in international travel demonstrates that providing access to transportation, accommodations and attractions to the handicapped raises several " . . . ethical questions of fairness and distributive justice, of utilitarian or Rawlsian notions of decision making" (p. 605). These authors admonish public administrators, and we might add HR managers, to acknowledge and confront the ethical issues surrounding health, safety, and accessibility, many of which are neglected in academic training programs.

Productivity and Quality

The twin pressures to improve government performance while simultaneously cutting costs have intensified in the past decade. Calls for diffusing the quality paradigm to the public sector have continued along with admonitions to reengineer, reinvent, and reorganize to improve government service delivery. Francis Burke (1999) refers to the "three Es" of efficiency, effectiveness, and economy as vital and enduring values with deep historical roots and contemporary applications in our culture; Paul Light's (1998) analysis of reform tides highlights the importance of these values to the heritage of the public service. Burke outlines a new "three E" paradigm—empathy, evaluation, and ethics—that builds upon the earlier values and provides management tools for the future. She sees benefits in stronger networking (empathy), enhanced accountability (evaluation), and strengthened leadership (ethics). Both sets of "three E" values serve as powerful guides to behavior. Empirical research findings in the 1990s have confirmed a link between ethics and organizational performance (see e.g., Menzel and Carson, 1999 for a thorough literature review; also Berman and West, 1997, 1998). HR managers would do well to follow Burke's advice to employ the tools of efficiency, effectiveness, and economy together with those of empathy, evaluation, and ethics. Such leadership by HR managers can help to enhance the integrity as well as the productivity of the organization.

Privatization

Ethical issues surrounding the move to privatization have been addressed repeatedly in the public administration literature (e.g., Timmons, 1990; Frederickson,

1999; Kettl, 1993; and Kobrak, 1998). Timmons notes five adverse impacts that privatization can have on career employees: "career disruption and dislocation; morale and productivity; relocation and reciprocity; erosion of civil service and merit systems; and undermining of trust and credibility" (p. 106). He suggests that employers have an ethical obligation to provide workers with retraining, reciprocity provisions, and advance notice. The other three authors cited above, but writing separately, point to additional adverse consequences of privatization and contracting out for services: kickbacks, skimming, fraud, cozy politics (contractors winning or keeping a contract via politics), conflicts of interest, and monitoring problems. HR managers may support or oppose efforts to privatize, but two crucial parts of their role are to serve as advocates for the public sector employee and for the public interest. As advocates, they should exercise due diligence, insisting that the pros and cons of privatization initiatives are carefully considered and that harm done to public employees and/or the public interest is avoided or minimized.

ETHICS AND HUMAN RESOURCE SUBSYSTEMS

Ethics in HRM can be further examined by tying the earlier discussion of Van Wart's (1998) three-level typology of work cultures to the above analysis of HR subsystems. Combining selection, socialization, and performance into one subsystem and appraisal, rewards, and development into a second subsystem simplifies the analysis. First, managing the "joining up process" would be handled differently in a Level 1 environment than it would be in a Level 2 or 3 culture. Absent basic consciousness of values and acceptable ethical conduct by employees, managers in a Level 1 environment often rely on fear, threats, and punishment to ensure ethical conduct or use educational initiatives to raise consciousness. By contrast, at Level-2 efforts are centered on getting employees to conform to work processes and comply with required standards. At Level 3, employees' and managers' ethical sense is well honed and the reasoning behind such standards is well understood; therefore emphasis can be placed on democratic participation and shared responsibility for setting moral standards.

The second subsystem—appraisal, rewards, and development—can be analyzed in the same manner. Responses are nonexistent, selective, or reactive in a Level-1 culture: unethical or exemplary conduct is disregarded or punishment/praise is slow in coming. Empowerment or intrinsic motivation initiatives are absent as are various forms of career guidance (feedback, organizational development efforts). This subsystem takes on different characteristics in a Level-2 environment: policies to appraise, reward, and develop employees are emphasized, implemented, and monitored. Legal compliance and conformity to established standards is sought and praised as commendable ethical behavior. Finally, at Level 3, ethical behavior is factored into individual and group appraisal and rewarded. Career development initiatives are inclusive, fair, and go beyond legal requirements. Sanctions are applied to wrongdoers and rewards are given to moral exemplars. Intrinsic motivation is evident, performance feedback is continuous, and employees are empowered (Petrick and Quinn, 1997; Berman, et al., 2000).

It is incumbent upon HR managers to assist their units to develop from Level-1 to Level-2 or, ideally, Level-3 consciousness. Accomplishing this objective heightens ethical awareness, minimizes ethical wrongdoing, and establishes a positive climate for professional development. Assuming a leadership role on ethical matters will help public organizations move up the four-level pyramid described by Driscoll and Hoffman (1997) as well. Regardless of whether HR units are designated with a formal leadership role as the organizational locus of ethics management activities, HR managers can informally exercise ethical leadership by effectively managing the subsystems directly under their control.

SUMMARY AND CONCLUSION

Building public organizations of integrity is the business of all public servants. Top-level officials have a plethora of explicit or implicit strategies to choose from in "managing ethics." Human resource managers have special opportunities and obligations to ensure that priority is given to ethics. As Thompson (1992) observes, "Because other issues are more important than ethics, ethics are more important than any issue" (p. 255). Those with human resource responsibilities must recognize the relative importance of government ethics as a precondition for good government. Ethical leadership is required to signal that adherence to ethics standards is expected and that avoiding the appearance of impropriety is also important. The personnel system contains numerous leverage points where ethical leadership can be exercised.

The prospects for achieving and maintaining organizational integrity are enhanced when top officials model exemplary moral leadership, adopt an organizational credo that promotes aspirational values, conduct an ethics audit, and develop and enforce an ethics code. Using ethics as a criterion in hiring and promotion, factoring ethics into performance appraisal, and including ethics in management and employee-training programs further increases the prospects of institutionalizing ethical behavior. In addition, orientation programs highlighting ethical concerns, pay policies that reward productive and ethical behavior, and fairness in handling discipline and adverse actions enhance the ethical climate.

Prospects for institutionalizing integrity also increase as HR professionals seek ethical resolution to employee grievances; keep the workplace healthy, safe and accessible; and act as strong advocates for employee and public interests in privatization initiatives. Continuing efforts to ensure a diverse workforce, protect the legitimate privacy interests of employee records, and improve quality service delivery help to create the ethical environment. In short, building organizational integrity and advancing a strong sense of public service ethics is one of the major human resource challenges in the twenty-first century. Leadership by those with human resource responsibilities is critical to meeting this challenge.

REFERENCES

American Society for Public Administration. 1990. *Combating Corruption/Encouraging Ethics*. Washington, DC: ASPA.

Anonymous. 1991. Survey Reinforces Need to Develop Workplace Ethics Guidelines. *HR Magazine* 43 (11):118.

BELL, A. FLEMING. 1997. *Ethics, Conflicts, and Offices: A Guide for Local Officials.* Chapel Hill, NC: Institute of Government.

BERMAN, EVAN M., and JONATHAN P. WEST. 1998. Responsible Risk Taking. *Public Administration Review* 58 (4):346–352.

——. 1997. Managing Ethics to Improve Performance and Build Trust. *Public Integrity Annual* 2:23–32.

—— and Stephen J. Bonczek. 1998. *The Ethics Edge.* Washington, DC: ICMA.

BERMAN, EVAN M., JAMES S. BOWMAN, JONATHAN P. WEST, and MONTGOMERY VAN WART. 2000. *Human Resource Management in Public Service.* Thousand Oaks, CA: Sage.

BOWMAN, JAMES S. 1995. Ethics and Quality: A "Right-Good" Combination. In *Quality Management Today: What Local Governments Need to Know,* J. P. West, ed. Washington, DC: ICMA:64–69.

BOWMAN, JAMES S. 1999. Performance Appraisal: Verisimilitude Trumps Veracity. *Public Personnel Management* 28 (4):557–576.

BRIGGS, STEVEN, and MILTON H. SIEGELE. 1994. The Ethical Standards Clause: A Lesson From the Private Sector for the Public Sector. *Journal of Collective Negotiations in the Public Sector* 23 (3):181–186.

BRUMBACK, GARY B. 1991. Institutionalizing Ethics in Government. *Public Personnel Management* 20 (3):353–363.

BRUMBACK, GARY B. 1998. Getting the Right People Ethically. *Public Personnel Management* 25 (3):267–277.

BURKE, FRANCIS. 1999. Ethical Decision-Making: Global Concerns, Frameworks and Approaches. *Public Personnel Management* 28 (4):529–540.

DRISCOLL, DAWN-MARIE, and W. MICHAEL HOFFMAN. 1997. Spot the Red Flags in Your Organization. *Workforce* 76 (6):1325–1326.

DRISCOLL, DAWN-MARIE, and W. MICHAEL HOFFMAN. 1998. HR Plays a Central Role in Ethics Programs. *Workforce* 77 (4):121–123.

FREDERICKSON, H. GEORGE. 1999. Public Ethics and the New Managerialism. *Public Integrity* 1 (3):265–278.

GAROFALO, CHARLES, and DEAN GEURAS. 1999. *Ethics in the Public Service.* Washington, DC: Georgetown University Press.

GIBELMAN, MARGARET. 1996. Managerial Manners—Notably Lacking in Personal Recruiting. *Administration in Social Work* 20 (1):59–72.

HUBBARD, JOAN C., KAREN A. FORCHT, and DAPHYNE S. THOMAS. 1998. Human Resource Information Systems: An Overview of Current Ethical and Legal Issues. *Journal of Business Ethics* 17 (12):1319–1323.

International Personnel Management Association. 1999. *Public Personnel Management* 28 (4) (Ethics Special Issue).

International Personnel Management Association (IPMA). 1998. *Public Personnel Management* 27 (1) (Special Issue—Labor-Management Cooperation).

KAZMAN, JANE G., and STEPHEN J. BONCZEK. 1999. *Ethics in Action.* Washington, DC: ICMA.

KELLAR, ELIZABETH. 1988. *Ethical Insight, Ethical Action.* Washington, DC: ICMA.

KELLOUGH, J. EDWARD. 1999. Reinventing Public Personnel Management: Ethical Implications for Managers and Public Personnel Systems. *Public Personnel Management* 28 (4):655–671.

KETTL, DONALD. 1993. *Sharing Power: Public Governance and Private Markets.* Washington, DC: Brookings.

KOBRAK, PETER. 1998. Privatization and Cozy Politics. In *The Ethics Edge,* E. Berman, J. West, and S. Bonczek, eds. Washington, DC: ICMA:178–193.

LEWIS, CAROL. 1991. *The Ethics Challenge.* San Francisco: Jossey-Bass.

LIGHT, PAUL. 1998. *Tides of Reform.* Washington, DC: Brookings.

Local Government Training Institute. 1994–1998. *Ethics, Honesty, and Fairness in the Public Service.* Tacoma, WA: LGI.

MENZEL, DONALD C., and KATHLEEN J. CARSON. 1999. A Review and Assessment of Empirical Research on Public Administration Ethics: Implications for Scholars and Managers. *Public Integrity* 1 (3):239–264.

PETRICK, JOSEPH A. 1992. Organizational Ethics Development and the Human Resource Professional. *Personnel Administrator* (Summer):71–76.

PETRICK, JOSEPH A., and J. F. QUINN. 1997. *Management Ethics: Integrity at Work.* Thousand Oaks, CA: Sage.

PONEMON, LARRY. 1996. Key Features of an Effective Ethics Training Program. *Management Accounting* (October):66–67.

RICHTER, LINDA K., and WILLIAM L. RICHTER. 1999. Ethics Challenges: Health, Safety and Accessibility in International Travel and Tourism. *Public Personnel Management* 28 (4):505–615.

SHRM/CCH Survey. 1991. Part 11. Chicago, IL: Commerce Clearing House, Inc.:1–12.

SVARA, JAMES H. 1997. The Ethical Triangle: Synthesizing the Bases of Administrative Ethics. *Public Integrity Annual* 2. Lexington, KY: Council of State Governments:33–42.

THOMPSON, DENNIS. 1992. Paradoxes of Government Ethics. *Public Administration Review* 53 (2):254–259.

TIMMINS, WILLIAM M. 1990. *A Casebook of Public Ethics and Issues.* Pacific Grove, CA: Brooks Cole.

VAN WART, MONTGOMERY. 1998. *Changing Public Sector Values.* New York: Garland.

VELASQUEZ, MANUEL G. 1998. *Business Ethics: Concepts and Cases.* Upper Saddle River, NJ: Prentice Hall.

WARDLAW, J. LEW. 2000. Strong Disagreement with ASPA Code of Ethics. *PA Times* 23 (5):10.

WEST, JONATHAN P., EVAN BERMAN, STEPHEN BONCZEK, and ELIZABETH KELLAR. 1998. Frontiers of Ethics Training. *Public Management* 80 (6):4–9.

WRIGHT, N. DALE and TERRY COOPER. 1992. *Exemplary Public Administrators.* San Francisco: Jossey-Bass.

Section Four

REFORM AND THE FUTURE

As should be evident by now, any discussion of public sector personnel management inherently involves *reform*. The question as to whether or not reform will take place has long since faded into irrelevancy. Reform is here to stay, and the basic outline of what to expect is fairly obvious. The chapters in this section provide both summaries of these developments, and projections as to the ultimate consequences that can be expected.

The first chapter discusses how public sector unions have fared, and are likely to be further affected by contemporary pressures for reinvention and corresponding attacks on merit systems. Kearney offers a balanced assessment of these trends, suggesting that reinvetion represents both a threat and an opportunity to employee unions and the public managers who must deal with them. The final three selections look at the reform trends in a broader perspective. Drawing on the Georgia reform experience, Hal Rainey provides a fascinating discussion of how fundamental alterations in HRM can produce both positive and negative—both intended and unintended—effects. A more upbeat note is sounded in Robert Lavigna's chronicle of HRM Best Practices in state and local governments. As one of the nation's foremost HRM reformers, and the leading figure in the International Personnel Management Association's (IPMA) effort to catalogue promising reforms, Lavigna draws on his long experience to provide a sampling of the changes that are possible in public personnel systems, provided that they are properly led. The final chapter in the volume poses the pregnant question, "Where Do We Go

From Here?" Lloyd Nigro's essay weaves together many of the themes that are addressed earlier in the book, workplace diversity, reinvention, decentralization, and arrives at the conclusion that "grand scheme" reforms may subside at least long enough for the profession to take stock of what has been accomplished–and at what cost–thus far. He makes a most compelling point that, regardless of the specific direction of continued change, public personnel managers will and *must* play critical roles in the unfolding reform drama.

22

Problems and Prospects for Public Employee Unions and Public Managers

RICHARD C. KEARNEY

East Carolina University

A variety of negative forces has rocked unions during the past decades, provoking a national debate on the chances for their very survival as organizations. In 1956, one out of three private sector, nonagricultural workers claimed union membership. According to recent figures from the U.S. Bureau of Labor Statistics (2000), fewer than one in ten such workers belongs to a union today. Unions in government are experiencing their own set of challenges and some of the same debilitating forces that have been buffeting industrial unions. So far, however, public employee unions have not started down the road to decline and possible disappearance that their private sector counterparts stepped on years ago.

Union growth and development in the public sector lagged behind that in the private sector by about thirty years before blossoming in the late 1960s. Organizing success was attributable to legal actions by the federal and state governments that enabled collective bargaining, burgeoning growth in public employment, social change and turmoil that characterized the 1960s and 1970s, and, ironically, the notable accomplishments of private sector unions in winning wage and benefit increases and improvements in working conditions for their members (Kearney, 2001: Chapter 1). Public sector union membership peaked in the late 1970s at some 45 percent of the total government workforce, declined slightly in the 1980s, and has held fairly steady since then at about 37 percent. By level of government, 34 percent of federal workers, 38 percent of state employees, and 44 percent of local government employees belonged to unions in 2000 (U.S. Bureau of Labor Statistics, 2001) (see Figure 22–1). Membership levels vary substantially by function and unit of government and by region of the country. For instance, unions are strongest in the Northeast and industrial Midwest and weakest in the Sunbelt.

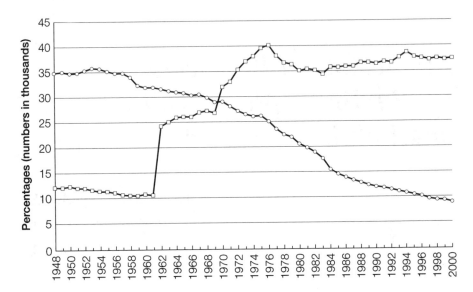

FIGURE 22-1   Public vs. Private Union Membership (1948–2000)
Data Source: US. Bureau of Labor Statistics, 2000

To some, government unions represent irritating and unproductive anachronisms that should be resisted and repressed. To others, they provide a voice for fairness and democracy in the workplace. Notwithstanding one's personal point of view, for many public managers unions are a reality and a significant force to be contended with in day-to-day management activities. This chapter considers the current conditions and challenges for unions in government and the problems they present for public managers. An assumption is made that public employee unions will remain a permanent fixture in nearly half of all public jurisdictions for the foreseeable future. If unions and managers are to conduct the people's business efficiently and effectively in this era of reinventing government and whatever lies beyond, they must work cooperatively through processes such as participative decision making.

THE LEGAL AND POLITICAL SETTING

Private sector labor relations and collective bargaining take place under the terms of the National Labor Relations Act (Wagner Act) of 1935, as amended by the Taft-Hartley and Landrum-Griffin acts. The National Labor Relations Act (NLRA) does not apply to the public sector. However, its basic assumptions and procedures were embodied in Title VII of the federal Civil Service Reform Act of 1978 (CSRA) and in most state collective bargaining statutes. One major exception is the right to strike, which is prohibited for all federal employees and for most but not all state and local employees. The CSRA provides bargaining rights for the vast majority of federal civilian employees, but (for a second major exception) excludes collective bargaining over wages and benefits for most federal workers, whose compensation is determined by the president and Congress. Thirty-six states grant some or all of their local government employees bargaining rights through statute or gubernatorial executive order, and 31 offer collective bargaining rights to state workers. Bargaining is not authorized at any level in eight states (Kearney, 2001:61–64).

Naturally, union density is much greater in states that are bargaining-friendly. Whether one favors the theory that strong and comprehensive bargaining laws produce high levels of union membership (Freeman and Vallella, 1988), or the competing notion that high levels of unionization impel such laws (Burton and Thomason, 1988), there is a strong, positive association between the legal environment and membership. For instance, 75 percent of state workers are covered by collective bargaining contracts in union-friendly Connecticut, compared to less than 8 percent in anti-union South Carolina. Around 60 percent of federal employees are represented in bargaining units, but because of the narrow scope of bargaining and restrictions on union security provisions that encourage free riding, only around one-third of federal employees belong to a union and pay dues. The U.S. Postal Service and a handful of other federal entities enjoy individual statutory or administrative bargaining rights that permit negotiation of wages and benefits, and thereby encourage higher numbers of paying members.

The politics of public employee unions and collective bargaining differs substantially from those prevalent in the private sector. For a variety of reasons, public officials and managers have been significantly less resistant to unions and more tolerant of challenges to their authority than their private sector counterparts. In permissive bargaining environments, public managers and elected officials have little to gain and much to lose from taking on public employee unions. Public employee votes and union campaign assistance are valued commodities for political candidates. For their part, managers are public employees, too, and many of them are loathe to sacrifice valuable time and resources in confrontations with unions. There is mutuality and symbiosis of interests among elected officials and appointed and career employees of all political persuasions (Spero and Capozzola, 1973). Moreover, the incentive structure for public managers differs from that of corporate managers when dealing with unions. Corporate negotiators and human resource managers are held directly responsible for bargaining outcomes and contract administration; and if they perform poorly, they stand to lose their jobs. In large government jurisdictions, collective negotiations and certain aspects of contract administration may be contracted out to law firms; in small and medium-sized units of government, management bargaining team members are likely to be on loan from their full-time positions and unlikely to suffer personally or lose their jobs as a result of an unfavorable settlement. Similarly, civil service provisions protect most public managers from adverse actions resulting from errors in administering a negotiated contract.

PROBLEMS FOR PUBLIC EMPLOYEE UNIONS

To fully understand the current context of public sector labor relations, it is important to consider labor relations in the corporate sector. The longstanding and consistent decline in union membership and influence in the private sector is of serious concern to unions in government. The reasons for the fading fortunes of private sector unions have been widely debated and discussed. Membership losses are attributed to far-reaching economic changes in the United States and abroad that have pushed jobs from high-wage, unionized regions of the country into low-wage states hostile to organized labor. Globalization of production and labor, along with the massive shift of jobs and wealth into information technology, have altered forever the traditional organization of work that favored industrial unions. Union proponents and sympathizers also lay blame on a legal environment that constrains organizing and tolerates management bias against labor unions and actions intended to "bust" them. Others suggest that old-style, corrupt, or self-serving union leaders have failed to steer their organizations effectively in a new economic climate, faltered badly at organizing members of the new labor force, and proved to be poor cultivators of public opinion. Appeals by union leaders to Congress generally have fallen on deaf ears, leaving labor "neck deep in its own failures and betrayals, corruptions, and bad faith" (Fraser, 1998). The election of John J. Sweeney as president has revitalized and reenergized the AFL-CIO and produced some remarkable union victories at the bargaining table and in organizing employees in the health care and other sectors, but overall membership figures continue to languish.

Like their counterparts in business, unions in government confront serious challenges. They have not yet been able to rise above a plateau in membership growth reached in the early 1980s. Recently, they have also encountered a disturbing number of public and legislative attacks, widespread calls for privatization of public services, citizen resistance to taxes and fees, negative public opinion, hostile reports in the media, and legislative rollbacks of longstanding collective bargaining provisions. For purposes of discussion, the critical challenges facing public employee unions may be categorized as fiscal, structural, policy, and strategic.

1. Fiscal Challenges

Since the mid-1970s, governments at all levels have experienced several long periods of fiscal retrenchment. Growth in government employment and payrolls was even modest during the 1990s, despite unprecedented national economic prosperity. The federal government's attack on the budget deficit succeeded to a certain extent at the expense of public employees. The size of the federal workforce was substantially reduced. Devolution of financial and programmatic responsibilities has pressured government at all levels to contain operating budgets, the largest proportion of which consist of personnel costs. Meanwhile, of course, service demands have not diminished and persistent policy problems such as public education, illegal drugs, corrections and criminal justice, environmental protection, and rising health care costs compete for a share of the public purse. Hiking taxes or adopting new fees is anathema to most elected officials and very difficult in the context of taxation and expenditure limitations and widespread antitax sentiment.

The repercussions for public employee unions have been disturbing. Compensation gains for public workers have been moderate, barely keeping up with increases in the cost of living. Public employment has grown very marginally in most functions and units of government, and, as noted, declined significantly in the federal sector (by approximately 300,000 jobs during the 1990s). In conjunction with the contracting out of public services to private and nonprofit providers, this has limited opportunities for union membership gains and corresponding growth in union financial resources and bargaining power. Job security, once a certainty for public employees, has become little more than a fond memory in some jurisdictions. Ironically, while public workers may perceive a compelling need for union representation as a consequence of these trends and developments, unions appear to be less capable of delivering membership benefits.

2. Structural Challenges

The global forces reshaping corporations and the way they do business are buffeting public organizations as well (Perry, 1994). Among those that are impacting public employee unions are technological change, the magnetic attraction of market-based approaches to service delivery, and the changing demographics of the labor force.

The primary threat of technological change is job displacement. The personal computer has reduced the ranks of clerical employees, the scanner has replaced data-entry employees, and automated garbage trucks have lessened the demand for sanitation workers. Many other examples of labor-saving technology are under experimentation or on the drawing board.

The movement to transfer government functions and activities to the private and nonprofit sectors is propelled by the conventional wisdom that the private sector can deliver services more cheaply than government. The effects of privatization are subtle, in that they depress employee and union demands for pay and benefit increases. And the effects are also explicit when jobs are transferred to a nonpublic provider. To date, privatization's bark has been worse than its bite, but several states are actively considering turning over such labor-intensive services as public assistance program administration and public education to market-based organizations, placing at risk hundreds of thousands of government jobs.

Demographic changes affect the nature and composition of the work force, which is increasingly female, older, Hispanic, African American, Asian, and immigrant. Dramatic changes in the culture of work have important implications for unions, which are challenged with attracting, organizing, and representing these new members of the work force. To succeed, unions must convince workers that they can effectively represent their interests and serve their needs. So far, public sector unions such as the American Federation of State, County, and Municipal Employees (AFSCME) and the Service Employees International Union (SEIU) have a record superior to that of their private sector counterparts (AFSCME is essentially an all-public union whereas SEIU organizes workers in all sectors, but has a majority of its membership in government and nonprofit organizations). Research indicates that members of the new work force have a strong affinity for unions, and most would join if given an opportunity (Leigh and Hills, 1987).

3. Public Policy Challenges

The most salient policy factor for public employee unions in any given jurisdiction is their legal status. The favorable legal environment of a comprehensive bargaining state is associated with strong membership figures and economically and politically powerful unions. Once granted, bargaining rights are extremely difficult to take away. To date, no comprehensive bargaining rights have been retracted by any state legislature. The obverse is that the legal status quo is very difficult to modify when it comes to expanding bargaining rights as well. For public employee unions to recruit substantial numbers of new members, additional states and localities must adopt permissive collective bargaining laws. Yet such actions must be considered highly unlikely in the present political context. Incremental extensions of bargaining rights in states that already permit bargaining in a limited number of functions are certainly within the realm of possibility, but not likely in most jurisdictions.

Without recruiting new members, unions in the public sector risk stepping into the miasma of stagnation and eventual decline that has afflicted their private sector counterparts for the past several decades. Meanwhile, efforts to privatize public services through downsizing, rightsizing, reinventing, or any other moniker casts a shadow that makes unions throughout government very uncomfortable and understandably defensive. Federal employee unions alone lost at least 165,000 members to reforms associated with the National Performance Review (Downsizing Hits Unions, 1997). Persistent pressures to contain labor costs and the size of government through market-based approaches could increase the toll on state and local unions in the future.

4. Strategic Challenges

The fiscal, structural, and policy problems confronting public employee unions present daunting strategic choices. *How* can unions effectively address the threats of tax resistance, globalization, and privatization? Clearly, politics at multiple levels is the most promising venue for exerting union influence on policy makers. Historically, organized labor has worked within the Democratic Party to seek political influence. Increasingly, however, public employee unions are learning to work both sides of the partisan table, developing symbiotic relationships with candidates and elected and appointed officials of all political persuasions, and stressing mutual interests such as improved pay and benefits and greater efficiency in service provision. Nonetheless, elected and appointed officials in some jurisdictions have assumed a more aggressive posture regarding public employee unions. Public opinion in favor of unions and organized labor is still fairly positive in terms of general approval levels and views of what unions do for their members, but little confidence is expressed in union leadership (Center for Survey Research, 2000).

Compared to their private sector counterparts, public employee unions have generally demonstrated a remarkable degree of adaptability to a difficult and constantly changing economic and political environment. They have successfully organized large numbers of women and people of color in a wide variety of employment settings, leveraging employee dissatisfaction into membership growth (Johnston, 1994). They have sought to win improvements in pay, benefits, and working conditions for custodial, nursing home, and health care workers, and have attacked gender-related pay inequities in state and local employment. Union leaders, including Al Shanker and Sandra Feldman (American Federation of Teachers), Robert Chase (National Education Association), Gerald McEntee (AFSCME), and John Sweeney (SEIU) have coached their respective organizations to adapt strategically to profound changes and threats in their organizational environments.

Challenges, of course, also present opportunities. The chances of securing significant pay increases for bargaining unit members may be slim, given the present political and economic constraints, but nonmonetary benefits and working conditions remain fair game. Telecommuting policy, for instance, is becoming an increasingly common bargaining topic, as powerful, portable computers and information technology move the virtual office from concept to reality. Equipment needs, ergonomic furnishings, and health and safety considerations are appropriate bargaining issues. Reinventing government proposals pose challenges to unions, but by involving themselves in the design, development, and execution of reinvention initiatives (as opposed to knee-jerk opposition to them), unions can demonstrate their ability to participate in productivity gains and compete with the private sector (Gerhart, 1994:125–129).

Finally, several potentially rich organizing opportunities are available for public employee unions to mine. Low-wage workers toiling in dangerous, tedious, or unhealthy working conditions have always been receptive to unions. There are many of them who remain unorganized in government, including case workers, custodial workers, and health care employees. Opportunities exist for unions to link the interests of low-wage employees to social causes such as comparable worth for women, social justice for minorities and immigrants, and quality, affordable health care for all (see Johnston, 1994). Unions, in other words, can show that they exist to enhance the interests of many—not just dues-paying members (Sulzner, 1997:166).

PROBLEMS FOR PUBLIC MANAGERS

Unions are a permanent part of the economic, political, and personnel landscape in a large proportion of government jurisdictions. In many units of government in which union recognition and collective bargaining are not legally permitted, they take place anyway (Brown and Rhodes, 1991; Swanson, 1993). And even where recognition and bargaining do not occur, employee organizations are on the scene as interest groups and political actors. For the foreseeable future, public employers and managers must deal with unions across the bargaining table, in grievance hearings, in the halls of state capitols and local council chambers, and on picket lines.

It is important to understand that public employee unions did not suddenly emerge through some form of organizational immaculate conception; there was a demonstrated need for them. Federal, state, and local employee organizations have earned a measure of management respect for their members along with generous increases in wages and benefits and markedly improved working conditions. Unions provide psychological and social benefits along with material ones. Collective representation of employees' needs and interests by unions can also benefit employers through improved communications and, in some instances, productivity gains (Freeman and Medoff, 1984).

But there is no contesting the fact that unions pose special problems for public managers. It would be the rare manager indeed who would purport to *prefer* managing in a union environment. Unions significantly affect the organizational environment, decision making, intraorganizational and interorganizational politics, and the settlement of labor-management disputes. Their presence makes a public manager's job more challenging and difficult.

When unions first penetrated many units of government in the 1960s and 1970s, they were greeted with little sympathy or support in most quarters. The very idea of a union negotiating wages, benefits, and terms and conditions of employment for public employees was anathema to political conservatives, who argued that it was a violation of sovereignty. According to the sovereignty argument, in a representative democracy the people are sovereign and their will is served by elected representatives. Collective bargaining violates sovereignty because *appointed* officials (human resource managers, city managers, budget directors, and the like) negotiate terms and conditions of employment with union representatives, who are neither elected by the voting public nor appointed by political officeholders. This represents an illegal delegation of the people's sovereign power that coincidentally has significant implications for taxing and spending decisions.

The strike issue was another major reason for opposition to unions in government. Under the National Labor Relations Act of 1935, private sector unions have virtually unrestricted rights to engage in work stoppages over recognition issues, unsatisfactory contract negotiations, or other matters. But the CSRA and most state and local bargaining laws prohibit strikes under the assumption that they undermine government authority, violate the people's will, distort the bargaining process, and diminish democratic decision making (Wellington and Winter, 1971:25). According to this perspective, a community can be held hostage by striking workers in the essential services of law enforcement, corrections, fire protection, sanitation, and health care because no alternative service providers are available.

Employee strikes can threaten the public health and safety, and they certainly inconvenience service recipients. During the 1960s and 1970s strikes were so frequent and serious as to cause genuine alarm and fear in some jurisdictions. The trend today, however, is to recognize the failure of strike prohibitions to prevent work stoppages, and to grant public employees a legal, although restricted, right to strike in nonessential services. The alternative is to rely on the proven dispute resolution procedures of mediation, fact finding, and arbitration. As of 2000, ten states had legislation permitting at least some of their employees to strike (VT, PA, HI, AK, MT, OR, MN, WI, OH, and IL) and in an additional four states (CA, CO, ID, LA) public employee strike rights had been established through state supreme court rulings (see Kearney, 2001:235–237).

Moreover, public managers who once considered a strike a catastrophic event have become more adept at preventing, planning for, and if necessary, coping with work stoppages. Strike threats do not spawn the same fear and loathing they once did. As Bernstein (1985) observed:

> Public management came of age in the 1970s. . . . Public sector negotiators have learned well from the private sector that there are 10,000 ways to say "no" to a union's demands. . . . And they have learned the ultimate lesson from private sector management: Never blink an eye at a union's strike threats; talk softly and carry a big strike contingency plan.

As a consequence of this aggressive management attitude, bolstered by growing public opposition to striking workers and an increased citizen willingness to support government officials who take a hard-line stance in union negotiations, the incidence of strikes in government has declined greatly since the late 1970s. In some instances, strike threats are perceived as empty gestures. In other cases, however, they are realized. Every September, teachers refuse to report for classroom duty in Pennsylvania and other states until contract issues are settled. Transportation workers have shut down transit systems in San Francisco, New York City, and other cities. Even university faculty occasionally walk out of the classroom and off the job.

Public managers in nonunion work places can issue instructions and orders to subordinates, and, however arbitrary, they are likely to be obeyed with few questions asked. Where negotiated contracts govern organizational decision making, however, an entirely different response is likely. A management decision or order that is perceived by a member of the bargaining unit to be arbitrary, unfair, or in violation of contract language will be complied with in the immediate sense, but it is very likely to trigger a formal grievance (the union slogan is "obey now, grieve later"). Whether by intent, accident, or ignorance, managers can ill afford to violate contract language. Grievance procedures are time consuming, taking managers away from other pressing concerns. They can be highly frustrating, particularly when the grievant wins. And, when they are filed in large numbers in relatively short periods of time, they can poison the work environment. During the Vietnam War some abusive or seriously unpopular officers were "fragged" with anonymous grenades tossed into their tents at night. A nonviolent work place version of fragging occurs when arbitrary and unpopular managers find their union employees "working to the rule" (refusing to do anything not explicitly provided for in their contract) or generating tens or even hundreds of grievances against them. Unions can, in short, make a supervisor's life miserable.

To be successful, the public manager in a bargaining setting must be cognizant of the language of the contract in its smallest detail and consistently avoid violating its terms. He or she must also strive to be even-handed in treatment of employees, and never to play favorites. When a manager wants to take an action that is not covered in the contract or that has consequences for members of the bargaining unit, the union steward or other union leaders should be consulted beforehand.

Another problem for managers in a union environment is how to motivate employees. Contracts typically provide for across-the-board raises over the life of the contract (usually two or three years). Merit pay is rare, and when included in a contract, usually very modest in amount. The manager finds it very difficult if not impossible to provide material rewards to top workers. The annual performance appraisal may become a meaningless exercise, with consequences only for those whose performance is deemed to be unsatisfactory. Therefore, the manager must seek other, nonmaterial ways to reward subordinates that do not violate the contract. Promotions, position reclassification, and job enrichment are among the many possibilities.

Union-management relationships have stabilized and matured greatly in most bargaining jurisdictions since the tumultuous early years. Mutual expectations about what a final contract will look like are often communicated indirectly but accurately through informal methods and off-the-record discussions between negotiators, and, after the requisite posturing, formalized later at the bargaining table. Where expectations are not met, or where other factors are important—such as face-saving or the union negotiator's inability to "sell" a contract to the members of the bargaining unit—third-party dispute resolution measures are available and widely used.

But generally speaking, labor-management relations are not in a state of good repair. The conventional adversarial relationship that has guided interactions between unions and management since organized labor's inception in the United States is increasingly inappropriate and dysfunctional for coping effectively with the challenges confronting government today. Adversariness often translates into tedious bickering over relatively insignificant issues and waste of the employer's time and the taxpayer's money. Managers feel like their hands are tied by inefficient work rules embedded in contracts (e.g., bumping rights, ponderous position classification plans) and outdated compensation practices (e.g., seniority pay, excessive sick leave and vacation leave). Members of bargaining units feel frustrated and unappreciated, and union leaders feel threatened by demands for change in work rules and employment practices. They want to be treated as intelligent adults who know their jobs best and who are willing to contribute their part to create a high performance work place.

There is a compelling need to reinvent labor-management relations. As John Sturdivant, president of the American Federation of Government Employees, observed, "There will be no reinventing government . . . only bureaucratic tinkering around the margins—without fundamental changes in the union's role in the workplace" (Sturdivant, as quoted in Walters, 1993). What will a reinvented labor-management relationship look like? The best bet is for a more collaborative relationship that involves extensive employee participation in organizational decision making at all levels.

PROSPECTS FOR REINVENTING PUBLIC SECTOR LABOR-MANAGEMENT RELATIONS

The dominant change model proposed for a "new" labor-management relationship is referred to here as participative decision making (PDM). Its contemporary roots are in quality circles, total quality management, labor-management committees, employee involvement programs, quality of work life programs, and interest-based (win-win) bargaining. All of these approaches involve regularly scheduled meetings of labor and management representatives to discuss, analyze, and resolve problems arising in the work place. They may address problems defined under the terms of a bargaining contract or those arising outside the purview of the contract. In one form or another, these approaches recognize all employees as stakeholders in the operations of their organization, and they assume that employees at all levels should be involved in making decisions about how the organization structures and delivers services. Employee involvement should be meaningful, with employee views and decisions receiving serious consideration by management.

PDM initiatives and programs are widespread in the private sector, with an estimated 50 percent of large firms having adopted them in some form (Delaney, 1996:47). PDM's application in firms, however, is restricted by the language of the

NLRA, as interpreted by the National Labor Relations Board and federal courts. Specifically, if labor-management committees or similar mechanisms are created and dominated by the employer, they are illegal. If such programs are established and operated with a substantial amount of employee independence from management, they are permissible. The implication is that the only legal PDM approaches in the private sector are those involving strong employee decision-making authority or those established and implemented with union participation (Delaney, 1996).

Formal legal barriers to PDM in the public sector are minimal, with the exception of federal employment. Civil Service Reform Act provisions that restrict the scope of bargaining are not facilitative of PDM, but federal unions and management have found ways to dance nimbly around certain restrictions. The principal constraint on adoption of participative approaches in state and local government is NLRA-type language in labor relations statutes along with the heavy, traditional weight of adversary interactions, which discourages managers and members of the bargaining unit from embarking together on collaborative ventures. Published research on the PDM experience in government is sparse, but there are indications that it is becoming increasingly popular.

Participative approaches offer many possible advantages. The literature on PDM in the private sector indicates positive impacts on individual worker productivity, job satisfaction, personal growth and development, and willingness to change (Kearney and Hays, 1994). Such individual benefits are believed to contribute directly and indirectly to desired organizational outcomes. For instance, if PDM enhances employee satisfaction and commitment to the job, it may encourage less turnover, fewer absences and sick days, lower accident rates, and stronger commitment to the organization as well (Schwochau et al., 1997:381; Verma and McKersie, 1987). Other purported benefits of PDM include improved technical skills, improved adaptation to change, and fewer formal grievances (Mohrman and Lawler, 1988:47; Gabris and Kenneth, 1986). PDM may also improve organizational performance by facilitating early detection of work problems (Levine, 1995), and may even stimulate individual self-sufficiency and responsibility (Delaney, 1996:46).

Examples of successful partnering are accumulating at all levels of government. In Illinois, state agencies and AFSCME have employed joint labor-management committees and quality involvement committees to address employee health and safety, expedited grievance procedures, and drug testing, among other issues (Ball, 1996:26). San Francisco's sanitation district was suffering low employee morale, lack of trust, and a negative union-management climate, but a comprehensive change effort opened up communication channels between union and management representatives, facilitated less conflictual contract negotiations, and achieved improvements in operations and problem solving (Berzon, Drake, and Hayashi, 1999). Interesting cooperative programs have emerged in the public schools. For instance, site-based management, in which teachers and administrators jointly determine rules, procedures, and operating policy for a school district through collaborative approaches linked to collective bargaining has been reported in various jurisdictions (Rubin and Rubin, 1997). In the federal sector, cooperative ventures have enjoyed some degree of success in the Internal Revenue Service, the Postal Service, and other agencies. The IRS relationship with its major organization, the National Treasury Employees Union, is notable for its level and scope of activities. Partnership experiments have been conducted in such areas as EEO, grievance procedures, unfair labor practices, an incentive pay system, and quality improvement (Ferris and Cooper, 1994).

Public sector labor relations are ripe for new, cooperative approaches. Relationships between labor and management remain testy in many settings, but generally more harmonious than those prevailing in the private sector. The fierce battles that were joined in many government jurisdictions in the 1960s and 1970s have moderated in most cases, and been replaced by more stable and mature roles and expectations. PDM has a certain appeal to public service professionals at all levels who are concerned with searching out and attending to the public interest. Program success and eventual productivity gains can produce compensation enhancements for all public employees and special recognition for managers, while helping hold at bay the common enemies of bureaucrat bashers, spoils politicians, and hostile public opinion (Kearney, 2001:340).

PDM is not appropriate for all organizations or all labor-management relationships. To succeed, it cannot be imposed from the top by a change-minded elected official or agency head. What successful PDM does require is a foundation of trust and mutual respect among managers and workers, a strong level of commitment by key parties to make the program work over the long haul, win-win expectations, and a workable mechanism for bringing PDM to fruition.

To build a foundation of trust and respect requires union leaders to overcome their natural suspicion that PDM is yet another means for manipulating workers and their unions and that it is likely to weaken collective bargaining, grievance systems, and employee commitment to the union. Mid-level managers may also experience doubt and suspicion, feeling threatened by a potential loss of authority, or even their jobs, if PDM programs are implemented (Lawler and Mohrman, 1985). As a general principle, trust and respect must be constructed from the ground up. Setbacks and failures must be expected. For example, the U.S. Postal Service's history of confrontational labor relations, autocratic management style, rigid work rules, and tough working conditions has created a setting predisposed against meaningful PDM (U.S. General Accounting Office, 1994). Workplace conflict, low morale, and divisions in the internal ranks of both management and unions in Miami, Florida have derailed labor-management partnerships (Bryson et al., 1999). Nonetheless, some jurisdictions have reported victories in converting hostile relationships into productive collaborations between union and management representatives (Berzon et al., 1999).

Long-term commitment to make a PDM innovation work is needed on the part of all involved. Significant levels of time, attention, and resources must be invested in the program if it is to succeed over the long haul. Mid-level managers and union leaders shoulder the heaviest burden, but sustained commitment to work cooperatively with former adversaries must be evidenced by all key employees. Top-level organizational officials must exercise strong and vocal leadership and make available necessary financial and human resources for training, oversight, and implementation. Unfortunately, top-level support is always problematic following elections, when newly elected officials and their appointees routinely jettison the programs adopted by their predecessors.

Win-win expectations mean, of course, that both the union and management must have a reasonable belief that they will derive benefits from cooperating to solve organizational problems and conflicts. If PDM is to have longevity in the organization, such expectations must at least occasionally be realized. Win-win negotiations, also known as "interest-based" or "principled" bargaining, has earned growing support as a set of assumptions and techniques for ensuring that each party exits the negotiating table, labor-management committee, or other encounter feeling that it "won" something of value (Fisher and Ury, 1981). Successful win-win experiences are accumulating at all levels of government, addressing problems ranging from grievance prevention and resolution to incentive pay systems and gain-sharing arrangements (Ferris and Cooper, 1994; Brainerd, 1998).

Finally, PDM requires an appropriate and workable technique for effective implementation. Many tools are available to structure participative interactions. Health and safety committees and quality of work life programs were among the earliest to be used, and continue to be viable in various units of government. Total quality management (TQM), an innovation widely adopted during the early 1990s, also survives in some form in many state and local governments. TQM involves a participative strategy that focuses on continuously improving services, preventing errors, and satisfying customers. Employees and their unions are systematically involved and empowered to engage as partners in organizational decision making (Verma and Cutcher-Gershenfeld, 1996:223). Gain-sharing is another PDM possibility. Here, a portion of dollars saved from adopting work rule changes, process improvements, and other efficiencies is distributed to members of the bargaining unit (Walters, 1994). The most popular participation strategy is found in various permutations of an old technique, the labor-management committee. These committees operate at all levels of government to bring together management and union representatives to tackle problems and resolve issues away from the bargaining table. The labor-management committee approach was mandated in the form of partnership councils in federal agencies by President Clinton's Executive Order 12871.

Although it remains the best hope for moderating nonproductive adversarial relationships and improving the environment for public service in union environments, labor-management cooperation confronts significant obstacles. The legal framework and conventional operating procedures and assumptions of traditional collective bargaining continue to embrace an adversarial mentality. Decades of ugly organizing and bargaining encounters cannot be overcome overnight. Distrust and suspicion persist among union and management representatives in most jurisdictions. Management's innate discomfort with organized labor is amplified by the nagging fear of losing authority and control over subordinates. Union leaders, many of whom earned their reputations by aggressively fighting management, worry that participative management proposals are Trojan horses that will release demands to cut jobs, dilute union power, impose concessions and givebacks, and ultimately displace unions as the collective voice of workers (Kearney, 2001:343).

LABOR-MANAGEMENT RELATIONS IN THE 2000'S: CONCLUSION

Despite the near death experience afflicting unions in the private sector, unions in government remain vital and significant factors in a large proportion of labor-management environments. They confront fiscal, structural, policy, and strategic challenges, but generally speaking they are holding their own in terms of membership and political and economic power. Public employee unions must, however, seriously consider reinventing themselves if they are to remain relevant for the increasingly diverse public workforce. Traditional adversarial bargaining has its place, as do negotiated grievance procedures, but there are indications that zero-sum relationships are becoming antiquated and dysfunctional for both unions and management. If unions are to do well what they do best—collectively express the voices and interests of those whom they represent—unions must identify the needs of the changing workforce. If the best way to meet member needs is through cooperation with management through PDM and related approaches, then unions need to take that path.

For its part, public management is tasked with finding ways to identify, organize, and provide public services as effectively and efficiently as possible. Where unions are part of the management equation, they must also be part of the solution. Respect for the right of unions to participate in a serious and meaningful way in matters affecting or potentially affecting members of the bargaining unit is critically important.

It is a truism that change is a constant in public administration. It should become increasingly evident that coping effectively with the dramatically changing workplace of the future is a responsibility that must be widely shared by management and unions. Innovation and experimentation in labor relations participative decision structures and processes promise improvements in service delivery, while at the same time offering enhanced dignity, morale, and quality of work life for public employees at all levels.

REFERENCES

BALL, CAROLYN. 1996. Is Labor-Management Cooperation Possible in the Public Sector Without a Change in the Law? *Journal of Collective Negotiations* 25 (1):23–30.

BERNSTEIN, J. 1985. The Evolution of the Use of Management Consultants in Labor Relations: A Labor Perspective. *Labor Law Journal* May:292–299.

BERZON, JUDITH R., DRAKE, DAVID, and HAYASHI, STEPHEN T. 1999. Reinventing Local Government Together. The National Academy of Public Administration. <www.alliance.napawash.org>.

BRAINERD, RICHARD. 1998. Interest Based Bargaining: Labor and Management Working Together in Ramsey County, Minnesota. *Public Personnel Management* 27 Spring:51–68.

BROWN, ROGER G., and RHODES, T. L. 1991. Public Employee Bargaining Under Prohibitive Legislation: Some Unanticipated Consequences. *Journal of Collective Negotiations* 20 (1):23–30.

BRYSON, WILLIAM, et al. 1999. The Miami Story: The Pros and Cons of the Comparative Process. National Academy of Public Administration. <www.alliance.napawash.org>.

BURTON, JOHN F., and THOMASON, TERRY. 1988. The Extent of Collective Bargaining in the Public Sector. In *Public-Sector Bargaining*, Benjamin Aaron, Joyce M. Najita, and James L. Stern, eds. Washington, DC: Bureau of National Affairs:1–51.

Center for Survey Research. 2000. *Archives*. Storrs, CT: University of Connecticut.

DELANEY, JOHN T. 1996. Workplace Compensation: Current Problems, New Techniques. *Journal of Labor Research* IX Summer:45–61.

Downsizing Hits Unions. 1997. *Government Executive* August:19.

FERRIS, FRANK, and COOPER, RICHARD. 1994. Two Views of One Agency: The IRS and NTEU: National Treasury Employees Union. *The Public Manager* 23:27–31.

FISHER, ROGER, and URY, WILLIAM. 1981. *Getting to Yes.* New York: Penguin Books.

FRASER, STEVE. 1998. Is Democracy Good for Unions? *Dissent* 45 Summer:33–39.

FREEMAN, RICHARD B., and MEDOFF, JAMES L. 1984. *What Do Unions Do?* New York: Basic Books.

FREEMAN, RICHARD B., and VALLELLA, R. G. 1988. The Effects of Public Sector Labor Laws on Labor Market Institutions and Outcomes. In *When Public Sector Workers Unionize,* Richard B. Freeman and Casey Ichniowski, eds. Chicago: University of Chicago Press:81–106.

GABRIS, GERALD T., and KENNETH, M. 1986. Personnel Reforms and Formal Participation Structures: The Case of Biloxi Merit Councils. *Review of Public Personnel Administration* 7 Summer:99–114.

GERHART, PAUL F. 1994. Maintenance of Union-Management Relationships. In *Handbook of Public Sector Labor Relations,* Jack Rabin. New York: Marcel Dekker:97–132.

JOHNSTON, PAUL. 1994. *Success While Others Fail: Social Movement Unionism and the Public Workplace.* Ithaca, NY: ILR Press.

KEARNEY, RICHARD C. 2001. *Labor Relations in the Public Sector.* 3rd edition. New York: Marcel Dekker Publishing Co.

KEARNEY, RICHARD C., and HAYS, STEVEN W. 1994. Labor-Management Relations and Participative Decision Making: Toward a New Paradigm. *Public Administration Review* 54 (1):44–51.

LAWLER, EDWARD E. III, and SUSAN A. MOHRMAN. 1985. Quality Circles After the Fed. *Harvard Business Review* 85 Jan-Feb:65–71.

LEIGH, DUANE E., and STEVEN M. HILLS. 1987. Male-Female Differences in the Potential for Human Growth Outside Traditionally Unionized Industries. *Journal of Labor Research* 8 Spring:131–141.

LEVINE, DAVID L. 1995. *Reinventing the Workplace: How Businesses and Employees Can Both Win.* Washington, DC: Brookings Institution.

MOHRMAN, SUSAN A., and EDWARD E. LAWLER. III. 1988. Participative Management Behavior and Management Change. *Journal of Organizational Change Management* 1 (1):45–59.

PERRY, JAMES L. 1994. Revitalizing Employee Ties with Public Organizations. In *New Paradigms for Government: Issues for the Changing Public Service,* James L. Perry, ed. San Francisco: Jossey-Bass.

RUBIN, BARRY M., and RICHARD S. RUBIN. 1997. A Heuristic Model of Collaboration within Labor-Management Relations. *Journal of Collective Negotiations* 26 (3):185–202.

SCHWOCHAU, SUSAN, et al. 1997. Employee Participation and Assessment of Support for Organizational Policy Change. *Journal of Labor Research* XVIII Summer:379–401.

SPERO, STERLING D., and JOHN M. CAPOZZOLA. 1973. *The Unions and the Cities.* New York: Dunellen.

SULZNER, GEORGE T. 1997. New Roles, New Strategies: Reinventing the Public Union. In *Public Personnel Management: Current Concerns, Future Challenges* 2nd ed., Carolyn Ban and Norma Riccucci, eds. New York: Longman:157–172.

SWANSON, CHERYL. 1993. Defining a Political Instrumentality Model in a Non-Bargaining Environment. *Review of Public Personnel Administration* 13 Summer:85–93.

U.S. General Accounting Office. 1994. *U.S. Postal Service: Labor-Management Problems Persist on the Workroom Floor.* Washington, DC: Government Printing Office. GAO/GGO 94-201 A.

U.S. Bureau of Labor Statistics. 2001. Union Members Summary. <www.bls.gov/news.release/union>.

VERMA, ANIL, and CUTCHER-GERSHFELD, JOEL. 1996. Workplace Innovations and Systems of Change. In *Public Sector Employment in a Time of Transition,* Dale Belman, Morley Gunderson, and Douglas Hyatt, eds. Madison, WI: IRRA Press:201–242.

VERMA, ANIL, and MCKERSIE, ROBERT B. 1987. Employee Involvement: The Implication of Noninvolvement by Unions. *Industrial and Labor Relations Review* 40 July:556–568.

WALTERS, JONATHAN. 1994. The Tradeoff Between Benefits and Pay. *Governing* 7 December:55–56.

WALTERS, JONATHAN. 1993. The Chastening of the Public Employees. *Governing* 6 January:26–30.

WELLINGTON, HARRY H., and RALPH K. WINTER, JR. 1971. *The Unions and the Cities.* Washington, DC: The Brookings Institution.

23

Facing Fundamental Challenges in Reforming Public Personnel Administration

HAL G. RAINEY
The University of Georgia

A Dilbert cartoon begins with a staff member briefing the boss. She reminds the boss that he is scheduled to fire an employee named Ted at 10 A.M., and she says that she will begin organizing Ted's farewell party. The boss, always depicted in Dilbert cartoons as insensitive and incompetent, says that he can think of a more efficient way of handling both matters. The final frame in the cartoon shows Dilbert and his co-workers decked out in party hats, with Dilbert asking, "What happens after we all yell, 'Surprise'?"

A surprise farewell party, ordered by the boss as a way of firing somebody more efficiently—why is this amusing? Probably because holding a party to surprise someone with the news that she or he is fired is so outrageous that it becomes funny.

While it will insult some high ranking public officials, academic experts, consultants, journalists, and managers in government, one can argue that they come a lot closer to playing the role of the boss in this cartoon than to other roles in it. Providing supervisors with more authority to fire employees served as a central theme in the Civil Service Reform Act of 1978, and in recent, widely noted reforms in the state of Georgia that eliminated merit system protections for newly hired employees (Kellough and Nigro, 2000; Nigro and Kellough, 2000). Another very prominent theme in public management reform around the world in recent decades has been the drive to provide managers with more authority to control their subordinates' pay, through systems that tie employees' pay increases to their superiors' ratings of their performance. The widespread persistence in pursuing such reforms, even in the face of discouraging results, has been striking (Kellough and Lu, 1993; Ingraham, 1993). These reforms have been well intentioned and have pursued some valuable objectives. They have, among other objectives sought to provide public managers with flexibility they say they need. They have been part of an elaborate array of issues and actions in reforms of governmental human resource management. They have, nevertheless, tended to emphasize enhancing a superior's control over subordinates.

The important role of these provisions in civil service reforms is striking because of their inconsistency with contemporary thinking among management experts about how organizations need to manage people. Across this century, management theory and practice have evolved away from hierarchical direction and control of people working in organizations, toward a greater emphasis on self-direction and individual development. Currently, writers on management emphasize empowerment, trust, flexibility, decentralization, reduction of bureaucracy, teamwork, individual learning and development, and similar practices. They justify these approaches not simply as bright ideas they have developed, but as practices of the most successful organizations.

Experts on management and organizations have been arguing for decades that most organizations operate in increasingly complex, rapidly changing environments, with increasingly complex tasks carried out by highly skilled people (among many examples, see Daft, 2001; Perry and Mesch, 1997). They point out that the evolution has come about because traditional hierarchical organizations are too slow and inflexible and have too many constraints on the people who must use their knowledge to do the work. Organizations have to find more flexible and adaptive ways of stimulating and coordinating individual and team efforts without excessive bureaucratic hindrances. Actually, these ideas and practices have often been used and proposed in government (e.g., Carnevale, 1998; Ban, 1995; Ingraham, Selden, and Moynihan, 2000; Rainey and Steinbauer, 1999).

Nevertheless, some of the most prominent reforms actually put into effect by legislative action or chief executive directives in the public sector have emphasized such measures as making it easier to fire government employees and trying to tie their pay more closely to supervisors' evaluations of their performance. These priorities have tended to crowd out others of the sort mentioned above.

With other values and ideas competing for attention, why have such control-oriented priorities often taken center stage in major civil service reform initiatives? This chapter considers the emphasis on them as a reflection of fundamental challenges for management in government, in general, and for management of human resources and human resource reforms more specifically. These challenges include the necessity to operate human resource systems under the supervision of governmental authorities such as legislatures and elected officials, and hence to attain political support for major investments and initiatives in human resource management (Carnevale, 1998). Reformers must obtain political support in a context of skepticism and constant criticism of government, where beliefs about bad performance of government prevail. These beliefs, or *myths,* include the widespread conviction that government performs poorly, the widely accepted view that the performance problems arise from excessive protection against firing and inadequate linkage of pay to performance, and the need for other controls over indolent government employees. The chapter discusses the nature of these myths, their influence and their dubious accuracy, and the challenges of dealing with them when one proposes reforms of the public service more in line with contemporary thinking about effective management. Such reforms would include an enhanced image of the public service, investments in better management of it, investments in leadership development, increased salaries for top officials in the public service, and improved designs for incentives in addition to pay and discipline, such as interesting work.

THE NATURE AND IMPORTANCE OF THE CHALLENGES

Reforms that would pursue priorities such as those just mentioned will confront fundamental challenges that we all need to consider, whether or not all of us support such reforms. Many discussions and some initiatives in governmental personnel administration do emphasize some of the more contemporary themes mentioned above, but this raises the dilemma of how we build political support for such ideas and practices. One can discern in some of the reform initiatives an apparent lip service to the contemporary themes that wanes as the reforms ultimately go forward. One can see, too, instances where reformers' sincere and sophisticated intentions are pared away as legislation moves along. Ink's (1998a) description of the historic Civil Service Reform Act of 1978 (CSRA) provides a very significant example of this dynamic. According to Ink, those originally involved in designing the reforms sought to enhance training, quality of working life, pilot testing and evaluation of new human resource procedures, and other enlightened measures. While the CSRA enacted valuable changes to the federal civil service system, its influence has fallen well short of these plans of the original designers of the reform. Apparently, the reformers could not protect the original conception of the reforms, amid the complex process of implementation and against the political climate of skepticism and criticism of the public service.

Apparently, political leaders have found the more control-oriented and punitive reforms attractive because they appeal to voters. In turn, they apparently appeal to voters because they respond to beliefs embedded in the culture about the need to control bureaucrats, and respond to mythical beliefs about the poor performance of government and the reasons for it. As Kearney and Hays (1998) contend, some reform proposals reflect this context by attacking aspects of the civil service that have served this and other nations well. This attractiveness then raises difficult questions about how to attain the necessary support for the more contemporary themes, and for establishing the conditions required to implement them. For example, in a political system where we need to control a large, diverse, unwieldy, and potentially dangerous government through public criticism and political oversight, how do we build conditions of trust and empowerment for the employees of that government? Where people hate to pay taxes, how do we convince them of the value of investing in leadership and individual development?

We need to consider these questions and issues now, because government faces increasing challenges in the current context of rapidly changing, more complex, and technologically sophisticated environments and tasks. The workforce is evolving toward higher general skill levels, with jobs requiring lower skill levels declining as a proportion of available jobs, and with increasing competition among organizations for the people with the higher-level skills (Ingraham, Selden, and

Moynihan, 2000). Seventy per cent of the senior agency executives in the federal government (that is, members of the Senior Executive Service) are eligible for retirement by 2005 (Littman, 2000). Their replacements must be found under current conditions where salaries for executives and professionals in the private sector now vastly exceed those of comparable positions in government. Government now has to compete for highly skilled workers and for executive and professional talent, with intense competition not just in salary offers, but also in working conditions and opportunities.

PRIVATE SECTOR RESPONSES TO THE CHALLENGES

To consider the challenges that such competition imposes, we can look at the competition, in a sense. We can look at what leading corporations do to attract and develop talent. In recent years, many people interested in management in government have sought to identify "best practices" in the private sector, to use in government (Hays, 2000). If we look at human resource management policies in major corporations these days, we often find them quite different from the emphases in the government human resource management reforms described earlier.

Representatives of IBM Corporation, for example, report that their recruiting of employees heavily emphasizes quality of life and quality of work-life issues. The IBM website for potential job applicants addresses questions about the importance of the company's mission, whether the impact of a person's work will endure, whether people matter, whether a person will "make a difference," and how the company will support an employee's work-life balance (IBM, 2000). Obviously, IBM must compete financially, but these quality of life and work-life issues figure importantly in the job choices of highly skilled people.

Another example comes from accounts of the retirement of the CEO of General Electric, Jack Welch (Murray, 2000). In 2000, Welch, one of the world's most prominent and respected corporate executives, prepared for his retirement. Asked whether GE could continue the enormous success it had achieved under his leadership after he departed, Welch said he felt that it could. In justifying his confidence, he referred primarily to the corporation's well-developed processes of leadership development. GE invests heavily in training and development of leaders, including such steps as careful circulation among assignments and extensive leadership training at the corporation's education center, where Welch himself has frequently taught some of the leadership development courses (American Productivity and Quality Center, 1998:1). Welch emphasizes "social architecture" as one of the main strengths of the company, and that in turn supports his characterization of GE as a "business laboratory" infused with "intellectual capacity," "learning," and "sharing" (Murray, 2000).

It would be naïve to think of large corporations as warm, fuzzy places where nurturance, intellectual contemplation, and mutual support pervade the culture. Welch earned the nickname "Neutron Jack" at one point because of his penchant, like a neutron bomb, for eliminating all the people in an office area without destroying the building. Clearly these large corporations want profits and must compete hard for them, and the internal environments must certainly have strong elements of ambition and competitiveness. Yet this makes the emphasis on learning, quality of work life, and individual development all the more striking in contrast to some of the emphases in recent civil service reforms.

These emphases by hard-driving corporations drive us back to the issue of how one develops widespread support for such priorities in government, and why they have tended to get pushed out of major civil service reforms. As noted, government agencies and reform processes do indeed follow many sophisticated and very current human resource practices (e.g., Blunt, 2000), and government employees and agencies often perform very well in general. Reform movements and initiatives, like the recent Reinventing Government movement and the related National Performance Review undertaken by the Clinton administration, have sought to disseminate many sophisticated practices. These efforts, however, often have involved relatively heroic, isolated efforts by leaders in the public sector determined to do good things in spite of many obstacles. In some cases, as well, they tend to represent rather piecemeal efforts in relation to the government as a whole. Often they buy into the beliefs—or myths—that government has failed and is failing. Hence they convey a negative message, in spite of the ironic tendency to call for correcting these failures by adopting practices that government leaders and organizations already follow (Osborne and Gaebler, 1992). As a more concrete example of this point, there are a lot of very good leadership development activities in government—but consider the likely reactions by public watchdog groups, legislators, and political candidates to a comprehensive program of leadership development in government, on a par with the GE program in expense, time, and other resources devoted to it. Even to propose such a program would invoke complaints and editorials about wasting the taxpayers' money on boondoggles and frills.

As suggested by this example, the fundamental challenge might be posed as follows: How do we build popular and political support for sophisticated human resource management policies in government, involving such programs as well-developed (and expensive) leadership development processes and programs to enhance the quality of work life for employees? Facing this challenge requires consideration of some very basic conditions and characteristics of the political system of the United States.

FUNDAMENTAL CHOICES FOR A NATION

Nations face basic choices about the design of their political and economic institutions, and these choices determine crucial aspects of the context of administration in general, and human resource administration more specifically. Inevitably, some functions fall to government to perform, and many of these functions do not admit to control by economic market mechanisms such as prices, profits, and sales (Lindblom, 1977; Dahl and Lindblom, 1953). They require political direction and oversight, and these controls follow patterns influenced by the history, culture, and political institutions of the nation. One important aspect of these processes involves the ongoing controversies over the roles of governmental and nongovernmental organizations and institutions, and the division of responsibilities among them.

Among many examples of the influences of this context is the greater freedom that private business firms have in setting personnel policies such as the compensation of high-level executives. In sharp contrast, pay levels in governmental human resource systems require authorization by oversight officials, who in turn tend to need public and political support for their decisions about these matters. This leads to sharply lower pay for high-level government officials, as compared to counterparts in the private sector. Actually, "counterparts" for public officials become the beginning professionals in the private sector. In a public service advertisement, ExxonMobil Corporation (2000) recently pointed out that state government judges make less than attorneys just out of law school, who are taking entry-level positions in major law firms.

As the example of pay levels illustrates, political control of governmental administrative systems also reflects characteristics of American culture, including the basic values and beliefs we hold about government. The United States was virtually founded on resistance to strong government, and one of the ironies of American life involves the coexistence of a strong popular support for one of the most orderly and effective governments in human history, coupled with a strong tradition of excoriating that same government. Criticizing government now represents a sizeable industry in the United States, including arrays of people and organizations that make their living in substantial part by scrutinizing government. In addition, in the United States there has always been a strong element of belief in the superiority of business over government, or at least the sanctity and importance of a private enterprise system relatively free of governmental direction and control.

These patterns of belief in turn relate to other beliefs and values that influence public personnel administration. For example, as a nation we adhere to the general idea that public service should not be for personal financial profit and for the pursuit of personal economic gain. We find it acceptable for private business investors and executives, and private professionals such as doctors and attorneys, to make in salary many times what our president, governors, U. S. Senators, members of Congress, justices, and governmental agency executives make. If one takes the amount paid in total annual compensation to about a dozen of the most highly paid executives in any of the top Fortune 500 firms, one could pay the president of the United States, both houses of Congress, all the federal judges, and all the top federal agency executives, for the amount paid to executives in that one firm.

CONTROL THROUGH POLITICS RATHER THAN MARKETS

These differences between government and business mean that, to oversimplify quite a bit, we must critique government, complain about it, and make political authorities control it. Initiatives and actions in government require political support. While political and public relations pressures have immensely important impacts on business firms all the time, the firms are still subject to controls by markets. Government activities usually face less of such market-based controls. If we want to make government perform well and stop it from performing badly, we have to have critics who will attack the wrongs in government and seek political support for righting them. If we want to manage government well, and reform and improve that management, we have to rely on political processes.

This requirement leads to a dilemma. We have to have criticism and political pressure on government, and on the administrative systems within government.

These criticisms and pressures draw on cultural beliefs about the poor performance of government, and extend them. They tend to build a climate of harsh criticism of government administrative systems, as well as webs of controls and constraints on those systems. As noted earlier, this climate often runs counter to the themes in contemporary practice and thought on how to get the most out of organizations and the people in them. So, we have an inherent need to criticize governmental systems and to subject them to strong oversight and control, but these processes tend to aggravate the performance problems about which we are concerned, or at least to fail to take the most effective approach to dealing with them. We often end up treating government agencies and employees as if they are villains, while hoping that they will behave like angels.

THE MYTHS OF POORLY-PERFORMING GOVERNMENT

This dilemma, of needing to attack and control government, while wanting government to behave nobly, draws on the myth that government generally performs poorly. That myth and various versions and parts of it drive many reforms aimed at correcting this alleged bad performance, including reforms of civil service personnel systems. These reforms often fail to conform to what contemporary management thought would say is needed to support good performance, so we need to examine these myths. Also, it is obviously controversial to assert that government does not perform badly—that this is a myth—since many people make all or part of their living by claiming that it does, and a lot of people agree with them.

Before taking on some of the myths about government performance, we need to consider the nature of myths themselves. Myths do not have to be entirely true or untrue. A myth can simply be a set of beliefs that fulfill some function, such as what Hargrove and Glidewell (1990) refer to as a government agency's myth— a set of shared beliefs and values concerning what a government agency does and is supposed to do, and what differences it makes for society. Another way of making this point is to use Greek mythology as an example. While most of us would consider the gods in this system of myths to be imaginary figures, these deities can express certain types of meaning and truth for all of us. They can carry an allegorical truth, for example, in which they represent human conditions and characteristics in a very meaningful way.

In the *Iliad,* for example, we learn that a Trojan prince had visited the home of a Greek nobleman, where he and this nobleman's wife fell in love and ran off to Troy with all her riches. This caused trouble. In the war that followed, Athena, goddess of wisdom, favored the Greeks, while Aphrodite, goddess of love, favored the Trojans. As we all know, love did not conquer all in this case, and in fact when the Greeks got through with Troy it took centuries for anyone to even find the place! While we may not believe that the two goddesses existed then or now, this oversimplified version of the great epic poem shows that it expressed a great deal of truth. It illustrated that if love overtakes two people such that the man steals another man's wife and her possessions, and the woman runs away from her husband with her possessions, this may be defensible and even something they cannot help doing. It is definitely not an exercise in wisdom, however, and the two should expect trouble. In the great poem, the two goddesses play important roles in the dramatization of the ancient contest between certain versions of human love and human wisdom.

Similarly, the myth of bad government performance may not be entirely true, but it may have some truth to it and it may serve valuable purposes. If we believe in a free enterprise system and limited government, and need to defend people against the excesses and bad things that government can do, we may need to keep reminding ourselves of these points through stories that illustrate them. People who oppose excessive government and prefer private enterprise and individual freedom can make a strong case that they need to keep hammering on this theme of bad government in order to control government's bad tendencies. From this perspective, scathing criticisms of government bureaucrats and bureaucracy, cartoons and jokes about them, constant calls for lower taxes and less government, incessant criticisms of governmental gaffes and goofs, and a never-ending series of calls for governmental reforms, all serve an indispensable purpose. One can claim that these aspects of American culture serve the purposes of other ceremonies and symbols, like pledging allegiance to the flag, honoring war heroes and patriots, and singing the National Anthem. Any intelligent person knows that some war heroes have been vicious sociopaths, and that patriotic embracement of the flag, as the saying goes, has sometimes been the last refuge of scoundrels. Some music critics insist that the national anthem is a musical disaster. Still, we cherish the ceremonies, symbols, and songs because of the good things they mean, not the bad. Similarly, the attacks on government may often be unfair and destructive, but people continue them in part because of their convictions that such criticisms have indispensable value.

Myths, then, have value, but they also raise problems because of their half-truthful or partially truthful nature, and their dubious implications for human action and decision. We may believe that wisdom should hold sway over physically oriented romantic love, but that does not necessarily mean that we should make sacrifices before statues of Athena in our living rooms. Part of the problem in figuring out the implications of the myth comes from assessing just how untrue it is, and in what way.

HOW MYTHICAL IS THE MYTH?

Regarding the myth of bad government, we have to face the question of whether the myth is really untrue, since it is so widely shared. In recent years, many people have pointed to the sharp declines in confidence in government, as measured by public opinion surveys. A privatization movement in the United States and around the world draws on the assumption that the private sector can perform better than government. How true are these beliefs and assumptions? We need to pursue this question; because confronting it becomes part of the process of espousing fundamental changes in the way the nation views its civil service.

How true? Not very, according to some strong evidence. We may distrust government for good reasons, and we may want to limit government for good reasons. There is plenty of evidence, however, that government and its agencies and programs often perform very well by reasonable standards, often as well as the private sector or even better (Rainey and Steinbauer, 1999). Part of the problem is that no one can really say whether or not business performs better than government, or whether government performs less well than it should, because those questions are actually quite complex and hard to answer.

Surveys of satisfaction with customer service now show that business firms do somewhat better than government agencies on such measures (CustomerService.Gov, 2000). This means that these government agencies did about as well as the business firms even though the survey included organizations such as the naturally unpopular Internal Revenue Service and regulatory agencies such as the Occupational Safety and Health Administration in the mix of government agencies. The highest-scoring organization was a federal agency, and many federal agencies had scores exceeding those of many business firms.

Proponents of the privatization and contracting out of government services point to evidence that the private sector regularly performs the privatized tasks more efficiently (Savas, 2000). More careful studies find the evidence mixed, however, and emphasize the problems with bringing in the private sector (Hodge, 1996; Lowery, 1998; Sclar, 2000). Studies of productivity have found evidence that government agencies compare well with private firms (Downs and Larkey, 1986).

One can also point to many examples of government agency performance that appears quite good by any reasonable standard. The Desert Storm operations of the U.S. military during the Gulf War had plenty of shortcomings, but also represented something of a miracle of military success with minimal casualties. The Social Security Administration delivers the basic social security program with a very high level of operating efficiency (Eisner, 1998), and a very effective general performance at processing social security claims and related client needs. The Social Security Administration also placed number 1 in a national survey of customer satisfaction with telephone customer service systems, with a higher rating than business firms with excellent reputations for customer service that were also covered by the survey (Gore, 1995). From all this evidence and these examples, the upshot is that no one ever produces convincing proof that government agencies inherently and typically show performance inferior to private firms (Simon, 1998).

Within the broad question of whether government performs poorly arise more specific questions about why it does, if it does. Observers and experts offer many interpretations of government performance problems, such as too much red tape, too much political intervention, too much change at the top due to elections, too little of the profit motive, and others. Many of these explanations prove very hard to substantiate, however. For example, one of the most pervasive and widely repeated assertions holds that government employees have elaborate protections against being fired and disciplined (e.g., Savas and Ginsburg, 1973; U.S. Office of Personnel Management, 1999). With these protections, the story goes, government employees do not have to work hard and work well, so some of them do not. Government thus performs poorly, according to this view, because too many bad or poorly performing employees remain in government. As mentioned earlier, this depiction of a major government problem played an important role in the Civil Service Reform Act of 1978, with its emphasis on streamlining procedures for dismissal and discipline. Similarly, under the widely noted reforms in Georgia in the 1990s, newly hired employees no longer receive merit system protections (Kellough and Nigro, 2000).

Surprisingly, in relation to the importance that reformers have attached to these supposed conditions in the public sector, one encounters serious difficulties in proving that the problem even exists, much less serves as a cause of poor performance. A recent study by the U.S. Office of Personnel Management (1999) found no evidence that the federal government discharges employees less frequently than private sector organizations do. Part of the problem arises because organizations, especially business firms, do not keep good records of why people leave. In both business and government, people who have done something wrong or who have performed poorly often leave voluntarily after a warning or counseling session that convinces them of the wisdom of departing. The evidence that one can pull together, however, indicates departure rates in the federal government similar to those in the private sector.

In addition to the systematic studies, one can examine the examples of good performance in public agencies where these protections exist. In the military operations mentioned above, and the Social Security Administration, people cannot be more easily fired than in any other federal agency. One regularly encounters the observation that the higher education system in the United States is the best in the world. This system includes public and private institutions, of course, but a system of faculty tenure has for a long time protected many faculty members from firing except for serious misbehaviors. For many years, this tenure system has been subject to complaints and stereotyping of the sort directed at civil service systems. Somehow having tenure did not deter from a lifetime of productive research a large number Nobel Laureates who held tenure at universities, nor did it more generally deter the professorate from contributing to the development of a great university system. One can conclude that the inability to fire people provides a pretty weak basis for analyses of performance problems in government, and hardly deserves the major status that reformers have conferred upon it. The more general conclusion, however, is that reforms have tended to be too narrow and unsophisticated, and not representative of contemporary management thought, and not well conceived as responses to the challenges facing government and other organizations.

PROPOSALS FOR MORE EFFECTIVE INCENTIVE SYSTEMS IN GOVERNMENT

Even if we discount some of the beliefs that have driven major civil service reforms as mythical or at least poorly founded, we still face fundamental challenges in advancing proposals that will support the priorities characterized earlier as representing contemporary management thought. We can begin to confront these challenges by considering difficulties with some of these proposals, and some suggestions for contending with those difficulties.

A Better Public Discourse on the Public Service and Improvements in Its Image

What if one were to propose that we need a more sophisticated public discussion of the civil service and its role? (U.S. General Accounting Office [GAO], 1988). What if we further propose that this improved discourse should lead to an enhanced public image of the civil service that would confer greater prestige and respect on its members, and that in turn would strengthen the political support for the sorts of human resource practices described earlier—i.e., the ones considered most effective for well-performing contemporary organizations? (e.g., Hays, 2000). This proposal is hardly original. It would involve increased investments in the sorts of efforts already undertaken or underway by such organizations as the Volker Commission, the Partnership for Trust in Government, the National Association of Schools of Public Affairs and Administration (NASPAA), and the American Society for Public Administration. These organizations have called for a more sophisticated general discourse about the public service, in which participants in it, such as journalists, political candidates, and others, would countenance the need for an effective public service. The organizations just listed, and others, have sometimes sought to promote the sorts of effective human resource management practices described above. They have more generally sought to publicize good news about the performance of people in public service, and to encourage the media and political leaders to do so.

The suggestion that people should publicize good work by public servants and public agencies, however, raises some dilemmas. Of course we do not want government employees spending a lot of tax money to promote and publicize their own efforts. This could create incentives for public employees to propagandize for themselves at the taxpayers' expense, thus enhancing a monopolistic position they sometimes have. We would also encounter cries of outrage from the critics of government and the civil service, who would flatly reject the assumption that a more sophisticated discourse about the civil service would be more favorable and supportive. Some critics would almost certainly claim that more public attention to the civil service would heighten public outrage over bungling and self-serving behaviors. They will argue that the public discussion of the civil service should concentrate not on respecting and enhancing it, but on defending the public against both its excesses and its inadequacies, against its entrenched bureaucratic base, and against the misuse of its monopolistic powers.

Similarly, encouraging the news media to publicize effective performance of public servants poses various problems. We need the press to remain aggressive in pursuit of governmental misconduct and incompetence. Would we propose that such criticisms be muddled and softened with mealy-mouthed disclaimers in which an investigative reporter or editorialist pauses to express recognition that there are actually many good public servants out there? Still another dilemma arises for the media representatives who have to try to attract the attention of readers, listeners, and viewers who show a low interest in objective information about the effective performance of government and public servants. Television networks frequently run investigative reporting series that clearly reflect their assumption that to compete for an audience they have to dramatize and even exaggerate the supposed wrongdoings they scrutinize. These series also tend to reflect the basic assumption that television watchers have little taste for careful, informative material that conveys good news about the work of government and public servants.

However, these dilemmas suggest not less, but *more* effort to drive into public discourse the issue of the need for an effective civil service and for sophisticated dialogue and action for maintaining one. The history of government and public affairs in the United States is a history of vociferous and spirited debate among parties with divergent views and interests. The drumfire of criticism of government justifies the efforts of those who defend the public service, since they hardly seem ready to dominate the nation with their perspectives. The mythical nature of the negative views of government, described earlier, and the stereotypical nature of the criticisms, justify the effort to force the public, including various spokespersons and supposed experts, to confront the challenge of developing to a realistic view of the public service. Increased determination of those interested in the public service, not to selfishly propagandize for government and government employees, but to steadily present this challenge in a variety of ways, in a variety of places, can have a lot more impact than we may at first assume.

This movement can go forward in both large and small ways. On a larger and more aggregated scale, the activities by associations and commissions such as those mentioned above should continue and expand to other organizations. At a more personal and individual level, more people can follow the example of an MPA student whose letter to the editor of a local newspaper was published on the day that this is being written. An editorialist had attacked government and government programs as useless, and the student in his letter described numerous examples of government programs that virtually all Americans value, support, and benefit from.

Political Leaders as Leaders of the Public Service

Consider this proposal: We need a corresponding change in the role of elected political leaders and politically appointed executives, to conceive their roles as leaders and stewards of the civil service rather than as mere critics and cutback managers. Political leaders should embrace more seriously their role in supporting agencies in achieving their missions, and their responsibilities to act as real leaders who avoid intrusive interventions in agencies and micro management.

Political leaders confront dilemmas similar to those facing decision makers in the news media. They can get little political credit and support for promoting "good government" examples and initiatives. Kettl (2000) points out that after seven years of effort that Vice President Gore and others in the Clinton administration devoted to the National Performance Review and National Partnership for Reinventing Government initiatives, a public opinion survey found that only about half of the respondents had even heard the term "reinventing government." Kettl further notes that although the administration claimed to have reduced federal employment by 351,000 employees (that is, to have eliminated one out of every seven workers) about two-thirds of the respondents to the survey did not believe such a reduction had taken place. Significantly, in the campaign for the presidency between Vice President Gore and Governor Bush, Mr. Gore hardly mentioned the NPR efforts and reforms. This situation provided an ominous echo of Kettl's (1989) description of the Carter administration's work on the Civil Service Reform Act of 1978. He describes how the Carter administration promoted this reform as a good government initiative, but found that the press so quickly concentrated on the parts of the reform concerned with firing bad employees that the administration shifted much of its emphasis in promoting the reforms to that issue. These examples emphasize the problems that political candidates and leaders have in trying to gain some political benefit from reforms aimed at improving governmental management and personnel management and the attractiveness to the press and the public of the negative myths about government.

Political candidates and officials also have incentives to attack the civil service. Elected officials need to control the government agencies and programs, and the "bureaucrats" that run them, and attacking, criticizing, and investigating provides one means of trying to exert control. They can gain political support by intervening with government agencies on behalf of constituents who have appeals and complaints. Elected officials, having been duly elected, often have the right to feel frustrated at their limited control over civil servants and government agencies.

For a lot of reasons, then, political leaders have little incentive to adopt the sort of constructive, positive leadership role towards the civil service that one might propose, but again, that provides all the more reason to call for it and to consider how to achieve it. Herein lies the justification for the point that we can express simply: we need more effectively to press into public discussion the point that elected officials and other high-level leaders in the United States should embrace their responsibility to serve as leaders of the civil service, responsible for its nurturance and development, rather than as carping critics, control-obsessed tyrants, or neglectful political opportunists. The associational and individual actions described above can, along with other objectives, seek to provide recognition and rewards for those political officials who already take seriously their leadership roles—because there certainly are some—and for those who come to do so.

Increase Support for Leadership and Management in Government

For a long time, experts, associations, and commissions have lamented the inadequate investment in developing and supporting leadership and management in the government. Some expert observers have pointed to weak development of the concept and role of leaders and managers in government (Golembiewski, 1985). For example, this problem shows up in managerial assignments that still involve nonmanagerial duties, such that they assume the status of "worker-manager" or "pseudo-supervisor" (Ban, 1995). Other observers note the weak incentives and weak tendencies for higher-level executives to devote attention to the development and nurturance of the agencies they lead, especially in such matters as leadership development. Still others have pointed out that there has been too little central and institutional support for leadership development and for dealing with managerial challenges and issues. They complain, for example, that the Office of Management and Budget at the federal level, and similar offices at other levels of government, concentrate on budgeting, with insufficient attention to the leadership and human resources issues in management (e.g., Benda and Levine, 1986; Ink, 1998b; Yao, 2000). For years, still others have pointed out that federal agencies spend much less on leadership development than the most successful and profitable private firms (Malek, 1974). All these criticisms and concerns, however, have not driven large-scale reforms, in the form of legislation or other major official actions, away from the concentration on pay-for-performance and streamlining disciplinary procedure described in earlier sections.

One can certainly understand why infusing administrative leadership and management into the public debate, and gaining more support and resources from them, raise daunting challenges. As noted earlier, observers have repeatedly pointed out that political leaders get little credit for such efforts. Opponents can easily attack investments in leadership, management, and investments in purportedly improved and sophisticated human resource practices as frills that simply run up the burden on the taxpayers without clear benefit. Again, however, one can point to the actions of the profit-oriented and successful private firms profiled earlier, as justification for continuing to emphasize the need to follow their lead.

Actually, one has cause for cautious optimism due to the steady stream of developments in effective and innovative governmental management described earlier. These developments include many that address management and leadership, and effective human resource practices. For example, at the recommendation of the National Performance Review, the President's Management Council (PMC) was established. The PMC is chaired by the deputy director for management of OMB, and consists of the Chief Operating Officers of major agencies and the heads of such oversight and central administrative agencies as the Office of Personnel Management. The PMC has operated without much public attention, as the first-ever council of deputy secretaries focusing on governmentwide management issues. An entity such as the PMC can provide one of many activities and stimuli supporting the sorts of comprehensive, contemporary, and sophisticated human resource management policies currently needed in government.

As another example of causes for optimism, the Presidential Transition Act of 2000 was signed into law (Klein, 2001). Executive transitions in government provide an example of a major leadership and management responsibility that has received far too little attention in research and practice (Schiro, 2000). The Act provides resources and requirements that will support more effective transitions of presidential administrations. Other activities are also concentrating on improvements in the transition process (Schiro, 2000). While transitions may have indirect implications for human resource management, attention to transitions represents attention to core leadership and management issues in government. This builds a context of serious attention to leadership responsibilities for developing and nurturing the organizations and people that make government work.

Increased Investment in Leadership Development

The PMC, the Presidential Transition Act, and other examples and developments that support the importance of effectively leading and managing the public service, should support the proposal to invest more aggressively in the development of leaders of and in the public service. Given the importance attributed to leadership in excellent agencies, and the common observations about the weaknesses of leadership development in government, we should sharply increase investments in leadership development to a level approximating that of major private firms.

One must avoid unfair implications about leaders and agencies in government or supporting government that already devote attention to leadership development and personal development (among many examples, see U.S. Office of Personnel Management, 1998; U.S. Internal Revenue Service, 2000; Littman, 2000). The point here is to emphasize the need for more support for such efforts, more validation of their legitimacy, and more attention to their proper design and implementation. Of course no one wants to see the taxpayers' money devoted to "leadership development" in the form of sporadic exercises in psychobabble by lightweight consultants, and of course such programs will have to display sufficient quality to withstand the attacks of critics who will undoubtedly condemn them as frills. The examples of effective programs already underway in the private sector and in government, as well, provide a basis for effective responses to such challenges.

Increased Salaries and Other Incentives for Governmental Agency Executives

In part because it provides an interesting illustration of the challenges of human resource management in government, and the pressures, myths, and cultural context discussed earlier, one finds it hard to resist proposing a sharp increase in the salaries of leaders in government. In the early 1990s, opponents, including such activists as Ralph Nader, mounted a major public outcry against a proposed increase in pay for the top federal officials. This opposition unfolded amid the interesting irony that the officials testifying before Congress in favor of the increase included top officials of the Reagan administration, an administration that had advanced a core philosophy advocating the reduction in size, scope, and power of the federal government.

The conservative officials who favored the increase expressed concern over the problem that executive compensation levels are vastly higher in the private sector than in government. The difference in pay levels makes it increasingly difficult for those officials, managers, and professionals who have a choice between the sectors to give up the much higher levels of resources in the private sector, even though many talented people would be willing to work in the public service for substantially less than they make in the private settings.

Consider the following proposal: the pay of all high-level executives and officials in the federal government, including the president, justices, the Congress, and top agency executives, should be increased to at least one third of the average annual salaries of the top executives in the top 100 firms in the Fortune 500. With stock options and performance bonuses, the industry executives' compensation would still vastly exceed those of public sector counterparts. This step would also reflect acceptance of the essential nature of an effective public service. Again, if we really want to run government like an effective business, the implications are obvious.

CONCLUSION

We need more careful and comprehensive consideration of reform in government. Many of the reforms making their way through the legislative process in recent decades will not accomplish the objectives their proponents seek. Reforms associated with pay-for-performance systems and with easing the removal of government employees and weakening their legal protections have shown little ability to induce higher levels of performance in government organizations. Indeed, such measures have the potential to damage productivity and morale by creating perceptions of inequity in the way individual employees are treated. The nation needs a broader concept of reform in the public service, based on a more sophisticated assessment of the critical role public servants fill in our society. Reforms also need a more sophisticated grounding in contemporary management thought that recognizes the value of such priorities as leadership and employee development and managerial training. Political leaders and opinion leaders in public discourse need to embrace their responsibilities for providing constructive oversight and support for such developments.

REFERENCES

American Productivity and Quality Center. 1998. Leadership Development: Building Executive Talent. Houston, Texas: American Productivity and Quality Center.

BAN, C. 1995. *How Do Public Managers Manage?* San Francisco: Jossey-Bass.

BENDA, PETER M., and CHARLES H. LEVINE. 1986. The "M" in OMB: Issues of Structure and Strategy. A paper presented at the annual meeting of the American Political Science Association, Washington, DC.

BLUNT, RAY. 2000. *Leaders Growing Leaders: Preparing the Next Generation of Public Service Executives*. Arlington, VA: PricewaterhouseCoopers Endowment for the Business of Government.

CARNEVALE, DAVID G. 1998. The High Performance Organization in Government: Strategic Thinking and Human Resource Management, In *Strategic Human Resource Management in Government*, Stephen E. Condrey, ed. San Francisco: Jossey-Bass.

CLINTON, WILLIAM, and AL GORE. 1995. *Putting Customers First: Standards for Serving the American People*. Washington, DC: U.S. Government Printing Office.

CustomerService.Gov. 2000. <www.customersurvey.gov>.

DAFT, RICHARD L. 2001. *Organization Theory and Design*, 7th ed. Cincinnati, OH: Southwestern College Publishing.

DAHL, ROBERT A., and CHARLES E. LINDBLOM. 1953. *Politics, Economics, and Welfare*. New York: Harper & Row.

DOWNS, GEORGE W., and PATRICK LARKEY. 1986. *The Search for Government Efficiency: From Hubris to Helplessness*. New York: Random House.

EISNER, ROBERT. 1998. Cut Social Security? No, Expand It. *Wall Street Journal* Dec.16:22.

ExxonMobil Corporation. 2000. The Third Branch. *The New York Times* October 19:A31.

FIGURA, SUSANNAH ZAK. 2000a. The Human Touch. *Government Executive*. August 20. <www.govexec.com>.

FIGURA, SUSANNAH ZAK. 2000b. Human Capital: The Missing Link. *Government Executive*. March 1. <www.govexec.com>.

GOLEMBIEWSKI, ROBERT T. 1985. *Humanizing Public Organizations*. Mt. Airy, MD: Lomond.

GORE, AL. 1995. *Common Sense Government: Works Better and Costs Less*. Third Report of the National Performance Review. Washington, DC: U.S. Government Printing Office.

GORE, AL. 1993. *From Red Tape to Results: Creating a Government That Works Better and Costs Less*. Report of the National Performance Review. Washington, DC: U.S. Government Printing Office.

HARGROVE, ERWIN C., and JOHN C. GLIDEWELL. 1990. *Impossible Jobs in Public Management*. Lawrence, KS: University Press of Kansas.

HAYS, STEVEN W. 2000. *Best Practices in Human Resource Management*. Washington, D.C.: Annie E. Casey Foundation.

HODGE, GRAEME ARTHUR. 1996. *Contracting Out Government Services: A Review of International Evidence*. Clayton, Victoria, Australia: Montech, 1996.

IBM. 2000. <www.ibm.com/employment>.

INGRAHAM, PATRICIA W. *Of Pigs in Pokes and Policy Diffusion: Another Look at Pay-for-Performance*. Public Administration Review, 1993, 53:348–356.

INGRAHAM, PATRICIA W., SALLY COLEMAN SELDEN, and DONALD P. MOYNIHAN. 2000. Public Service—the Report from the Wye River Conference. *Public Administration Review* 60 (1):54–61.

INK, DWIGHT. 1998a. What Was Behind the 1978 Civil Service Reform? A paper presented at the conference on The Future of Merit: Twenty Years after the Civil Service Reform Act. The Woodrow Wilson Center, Washington, D.C.

INK, DWIGHT. 1998b. Testimony before the House Subcommittee on Management, Information, and Technology, May 12, 1998.

KEARNEY, RICHARD C., and STEVEN W HAYS. 1998. Reinventing Government, The New Public Management, and Civil Service Systems. *Review of Public Personnel Administration* XVIII (4):38–54.

KELLOUGH, J. EDWARD, and LLOYD G. NIGRO. 2000. Report on the Findings of a Survey of Georgia State Employees about GeorgiaGain and Act 816 for Georgia Merit System. Grant report submitted to Georgia Merit System, 12 September.

KELLOUGH, J. EDWARD, and HAORAN LU. 1993. The Paradox of Merit Pay in the Public Sector: Persistence of a Problematic Concept. *Review of Public Personnel Administration* XIII:45–64.

KETTL, DONALD F. 2000. Reinventing Government: Reforming the Federal Bureaucracy in the New Century. *LaFollette Policy Report* 11 (1):8–10.

KETTL, D. F. 1989. The Image of the Public Service in the Media. In *Leadership for America,* The Volcker Commission. Lexington, Mass.: Heath, pp. 95–112.

KLEIN, COURTNEY. 2001. Transition Dialogues: Management Matters. *PA Times* 24 (1):1.

LINDBLOM, C. E. 1977. *Politics and Markets.* New York: Basic Books.

LITTMAN, IAN (Ed.) 2000. *The Business of Government.* Arlington, VA: PricewaterhouseCoopers Endowment for the Business of Government.

LOWERY, DAVID. 1998. Consumer Sovereignty and Quasi-Market Failure. *Journal of Public Administration Research and Theory* 8(2):137–172.

MALEK, FREDERIC V. 1974. The Development of Public Executives—Neglect and Reform. *Public Administration Review* 34 (3):230–233.

MARKOWITZ, DEBRA L. 1995. The Demise of At-Will Employment and the Public Employee Conundrum. *The Urban Lawyer.* 27 (2):305–331.

MCGREGOR, EUGENE B. 1991. *Strategic Management of Human Knowledge, Skills, and Abilities.* San Francisco: Jossey-Bass.

MURRAY, MATT. 2000. Can the House That Jack Built Stand When He Goes? Sure, Welch Says. *Wall Street Journal Interactive Edition.* April 13. <www.interactive.wsj.com/archive>.

NIGRO, LLOYD G., and J. EDWARD KELLOUGH. 2000. Civil Service Reform in Georgia: Going to the Edge? Unpublished Manuscript, Department of Public Administration and Urban Affairs, Georgia State University.

OSBORNE, DAVID, and TED GAEBLER. 1992. *Reinventing Government.* Reading, MA: Addison-Wesley.

PERRY, JAMES L., and DEBRA MESCH. 1997. Strategic Human Resource Management. In *Public Personnel Management: Current Concerns, Future Challenges* 2nd ed., Carolyn Ban and Norma Riccucci, eds. New York: Longman, pp. 21–34.

PERRY, JAMES L. 1994. Revitalizing Employee Ties With Public Organizations. In *New Paradigms for Government: Issues for the Changing Public Service,* Patricia Ingraham and Barbara Romzek, eds. San Francisco, CA: Jossey-Bass, pp. 191–214.

PETERS, B. GUY., and DONALD SAVOIE. 1994. Civil Service Reform: Misdiagnosing the Patient. *Public Administration Review* 54(5):418–425.

RAINEY, HAL G., and PAULA STEINBAUER. 1999. Galloping Elephants: Developing Elements of a Theory of Effective Government Organizations. *Journal of Public Administration Research and Theory* 9 (1):1–32.

RAINEY, HAL G., and BARTON WECHSLER, Executive Transition in Government. *Public Productivity Review* Vol. XII, No. 1 (Fall, 1988):43–44.

SAVAS, EMANUEL S. 2000. *Privatization and Public-Private Partnerships.* New York: Chatham House.

SAVAS, EMANUEL S., and SIGMUND G. GINSBURG. 1973. The Civil Service: A Meritless System? *The Public Interest* 32 (Summer):72–84.

SCHIRO, JAMES J., ed. 2000. *Memos to the President: Management Advice for the Nation's Top CEO's.* New York: John Wiley & Sons.

SCLAR, ELLIOT D. 2000. *You Don't Always Get What You Pay For: The Economics of Privatization*. Ithaca, NY: Cornell University Press.

SIMON, H. A. 1998. Why Public Administration? *Journal of Public Administration Research and Theory* 8 (1):1–12.

U.S. General Accounting Office. 1998. *The Public Service*. Washington, DC: U.S. General Accounting Office, November, GAO/OCG-89-2TR.

U.S. Internal Revenue Service. 2000. Leadership Competency Model. Washington, DC: U.S. Internal Revenue Service.

U.S. Office of Personnel Management. 1999. *Poor Performers in Government: A Quest for the True Story*. Washington, DC: U.S. Office of Personnel Management, Office of Merit Systems Oversight and Effectiveness.

U.S. Office of Personnel Management. 1998. Senior Executive Service Executive Core Qualifications. SES–98–02A. Washington, DC: U.S. Office of Personnel Management.

Volcker Commission. 1989. *Leadership for America: Rebuilding the Public Service*. Lexington, MA: Heath.

YAO, MARGARET L. 2000. *The President's Management Council: An Important Management Innovation*. Arlington, VA: PricewaterhouseCoopers Endowment for the Business of Government.

24

Reforming Public Sector Human Resource Management
Best Practices From the Practitioner's View

ROBERT LAVIGNA
State of Wisconsin

REFORM IN THE PUBLIC SECTOR: THE CHALLENGE

Across the nation, all levels of government are being called on to improve service and responsiveness. These calls for reform, often called reengineering or reinventing government, address virtually every aspect of public sector structure and operations, including size, organization, cost, responsiveness, quality, timeliness, service, budgeting and procurement practices, and regulatory activities. The *National Performance Review* report glibly summed up this demand for reform by concluding that government should ". . . work better and cost less." Inevitably, discussions about government reform focus on personnel and human resource management (HRM). There seems to be almost unanimous agreement that public sector HRM systems are not working—that personnel is inflexible, inefficient, and unresponsive (Gore, 1993).

Demands for more efficient government are justified and perhaps even overdue, and reform is clearly possible, especially in HRM. However, to be successful, reform cannot be based solely on the need for efficiency—reformers must also pay attention to the powerful forces that influence government, and influence the people who manage government.

Calls for reform often seem to be based on the premise that government institutions are rational organizations with clear goals and objectives, efficiency being chief among them. In fact, managing government requires constantly balancing complex and conflicting goals and influences, some of which are decidedly not rational. In this environment, *managing* government is tough enough; *reforming* government is an even tougher challenge.

The conflicting goals of government, as well as the diverse and often opposing constituencies governmental institutions must balance, often prevent the public sector from operating efficiently. For example, is it efficient to conduct lengthy public hearings before making critical decisions, or to require time-consuming rule-making processes to implement important policies, or to reward an agency's cost-efficiency by taking away unspent funds, or to require time-consuming bidding before buying an item that can be purchased faster and maybe even cheaper over the counter?

Similar examples of apparent inefficiencies abound in public sector personnel. Is it rational to give employees job security that prevents managers from firing poor performers, or to appoint chief executives who have little relevant experience and who may serve for only a year or two, or to recruit widely and solicit applications for months when the hiring manager already knows whom he or she will hire?

These practices may not be efficient, but they exist for valid reasons. Public hearings, lengthy rule-making processes, budget and purchasing controls, employment safeguards, political appointments, and open competition for jobs exist to meet legitimate goals and stakeholder interests. These often-inefficient practices were conceived to provide public access, hold government accountable for spending tax dollars carefully, ensure fairness and merit, and maintain the balance of power in our pluralist political system.

Moreover, government also serves a demanding and diverse group of stakeholders—elected chief executives and their political appointees; state legislatures and local government councils; the courts; oversight agencies (e.g., budget, personnel, auditing); the media; clients who demand services; employees; unions; lobby groups; and the public. Each of these constituent groups has a different view of what government's role should be overall and what individual agencies' goals and priorities should be in particular. Inevitably, some stakeholders will be dissatisfied with the results of government's attempt to manage the difficult balancing act of resolving conflicting demands.

The public sector must also be productive while operating under often intense public scrutiny. While public hearings and "freedom of information" requirements provide necessary access to decision making, these processes often interfere with timeliness, efficiency, and productivity.

Finally, public sector managers cannot rely on market influences to stimulate, measure, and reward efficiency. Many government managers would welcome the chance to be judged by clear and objective measures such as revenue, profit, and market share. Instead, they must constantly try to develop indirect measures of success.

In this complicated environment, government organizations trying to improve efficiency face unique and difficult challenges. Even when government managers want to streamline operations—". . . work better and cost less"—it is not as easy as it sounds. Reform efforts that do not recognize that government must respond to a wide range of influences are doomed to failure.

The question therefore is how to resolve the inevitable conflict between rational management that emphasizes efficiency, productivity, and speed and political public management that emphasizes consensus, compromise, and openness. Does this conflict mean that government can't be reformed? Of course not—it just makes changing government more complicated.

REINVENTING GOVERNMENT HUMAN RESOURCE
MANAGEMENT (HRM) SYSTEMS

At every level of government, personnel/HRM systems are being criticized as in-flexible, unresponsive, slow, rule-bound, and user-*un*friendly. Civil service systems are criticized for not meeting the needs of their customers—both the customers within the organization that personnel exists to support and the citizens govern-ment exists to serve. Too often, HRM processes are viewed as hindering, rather than helping, public sector organizations attract, motivate, and retain the talented people government must have to provide responsive service to its citizens (Na-tional Commission on the State and Local Public Service, 1993).

While almost everyone seems to agree that personnel/HRM systems must become more responsive and flexible, turning this rhetoric into reality is a tough challenge in the complex environment of government.

For example, one "common-sense" approach to personnel reform is to make it easier to fire, demote, or transfer employees. The current process can indeed be lengthy and frustrating—why can't an incompetent bureaucrat simply be fired?

One answer is because firing "at will" conflicts with one of the fundamental reasons civil service/merit systems were created—to prevent patronage and other abuses. While firing processes can indeed be inefficient, they also prevent em-ployees from being removed for the wrong reasons. The U.S. Supreme Court has even ruled that public sector employees have property rights to their jobs and can-not be fired without due process. This philosophy is profoundly different from the private sector's "employment at will" approach, which is itself being eroded.

It is also important to understand that public sector employees are fired for cause, proving that the system *can* work. Further, removing poor performers in the private sector isn't always easy either, especially in large companies with labor unions. Bureaucracy is certainly not unique to government.

HR reformers must also recognize that much of the so-called "red-tape" cre-ated by the Congress, state legislatures, city councils, etc., was not created arbi-trarily. These laws and rules were designed to base personnel decisions on merit, protect employee rights, provide the public with access, and limit political influ-ence. Although the corruption and abuse that created the need for civil service sys-tems may no longer be as widespread as it was when these systems were devised, this doesn't mean these systems should be scrapped. Consider what the chairman of the House Post Office and Civil Service Committee said about civil service re-form: "I'm not interested in a reform that makes it easy for an agency manager to hire his neighbor's son or daughter over a more qualified applicant. Simply giving greater discretion to managers is a recipe for bringing back the spoils system" (Hill and Johnson, 1998). In other words, there are two sides to the reform coin—what is reform to one person may appear to be a license for abuse to another.

Appeals for more flexibility in hiring and firing can conflict with other pres-sures for merit-based hiring, affirmative action, veterans' preference, due process, or whistle-blower protection. For example, the public sector has historically em-ployed a higher percentage of women and minorities than the private sector, in part because of affirmative action requirements that can be inefficient but have nonetheless helped many public sector organizations achieve diversity.

Personnel reformers must also consider the many constituencies government serves—managers; employees; unions; veterans, minorities, and women's groups;

Congress, state legislatures and local government councils; personnel appeals commissions and boards; the courts; job applicants; the public; and so on.

In addition, government personnel processes are designed to be open and accessible, not just efficient. The spoils systems that civil service replaced often operated efficiently, but no one wants to bring patronage back.

Best Practices in HR Reform

Despite these daunting challenges, there is evidence that public sector personnel systems can indeed become more efficient, effective, and responsive. There is broad consensus across the nation that government personnel systems must be overhauled. For example, the National Commission on the State and Local Public Service (1993) called for an end to "civil service paralysis." Some specific suggestions were:

- Decentralize personnel processes to give greater authority to operating units and managers.
- Eliminate outdated and restrictive rules.
- Simplify job classification, compensation, and performance management systems to give managers more flexibility to assign, motivate, and reward employees.
- Make hiring easier and faster.
- Make firing truly poor employees easier.
- Provide more and better employee training.

Some jurisdictions are successfully putting these ideas into practice by creating more flexible personnel systems. Several national projects are identifying these "best practices." These projects include the benchmarking/best-practices initiative of the International Personnel Management Association (IPMA) and the National Association of State Personnel Executives (NASPE), as well as innovation-awards programs separately administered by both organizations (IPMA 1998; NASPE 1997). These benchmarking and awards programs have highlighted innovative practices in federal, state, and local government that show that public sector organizations are reforming their HRM systems. In key areas—including recruiting and hiring, classification and compensation, diversity, training, and labor relations—the public sector is successfully adopting new and more effective approaches.

Recruiting and Hiring Talent

To meet the challenge of recruiting talent in the most competitive labor market in recent history, public sector organizations are creating more responsive, timely, and user-friendly hiring processes that still preserve fundamental merit principles. Traditionally, public sector hiring practices have focused on the testing process, to identify the best-qualified candidates. The assumption has been that enough qualified applicants would take civil service exams to create a pool of qualified candidates for each vacancy.

It is indisputable that written civil service exams used by many jurisdictions are valid and reliable and therefore work well to identify the best-qualified candidates. However, as the labor market has become extraordinarily tight across the nation, public sector organizations are realizing that a valid and reliable testing instrument will not guarantee a good hire, particularly if many qualified applicants refuse to participate in what can be a lengthy and frustrating process. Moreover, after decades of "government bashing," the public sector is no longer the career of choice for most job seekers. As a result, it has been said that too often the civil service exam process identifies not "the best and the brightest," but "the best of the desperate."

Government is rising to the challenge of competing in a labor market that has become a seller's market for talent. Jurisdictions have amended civil service laws, expanded recruiting activities, developed more competitive alternatives to traditional written exams, and applied technology to the hiring process.

Some jurisdictions have successfully amended civil service laws to make hiring processes more flexible. Wisconsin state government, for example, repealed the "rule of five" that limited hiring managers to interviewing only the top few qualified candidates. Wisconsin's former law was so restrictive that if two candidates were ranked fifth with identical civil service scores, to the one one-hundredth of a point, both candidates could not be interviewed—the central personnel department was forced to break the tie somehow. As in most jurisdictions with rigid laws like this, the rule of five slowed down hiring (because all applicants had to be numerically ranked), limited supervisors' hiring choices, and frustrated and even drove away applicants.

In 1997, however, the Wisconsin governor signed amendments that repealed the rule of five, replacing it with a more flexible provision that eliminated all arbitrary restrictions on the number of qualified candidates who can be interviewed. Now, the central personnel department works with individual operating agencies to determine how many qualified candidates to refer to hiring managers. The result is a more timely and flexible process that gives larger numbers of candidates realistic job opportunities. Lists of qualified candidates are routinely produced as soon as the application period ends. In some cases, hiring agencies can now make immediate job offers to well-qualified candidates, a practice that was impossible under the old law (IPMA News, 1999).

Local governments have also moved away from rigid limits on the number of qualified candidates who can be referred to hiring managers. For example, the Shreveport, Louisiana, Personnel Department provides hiring managers with all candidates with the top three civil service scores. While this may seem restrictive, managers almost always receive many more than three names because all candidates with the highest three scores (including ties) are forwarded.

Other jurisdictions such as Maricopa County, Arizona, and the South Florida Water District have even more flexible practices. In these jurisdictions, there are no restrictions on the number of qualified candidates hiring managers can interview. If a hiring manager chooses to, he or she can interview all candidates who qualify.

Of course, no hiring system can be effective unless qualified applicants apply. For that reason, many government agencies are aggressively expanding recruiting, which in the past was often viewed as primarily a private sector activity. Some in government even believed that recruiting violated merit principles because recruited applicants received more assistance and encouragement than other applicants. The realities of today's labor market are changing these attitudes. Government organizations are now hiring full-time recruiters, expanding marketing efforts, and even going head-to-head with private sector employers. The Metropolitan Council in the Twin Cites of Minneapolis and St. Paul is a good example. The Council, which has over 3,800 employees, now has a full-time recruiter who focuses heavily on recruiting candidates for hard-to-fill positions in information technology and other technical fields. Rather than apologizing for recruiting for a government agency, the Council's recruiter emphasizes the advantages of public service. Marketing itself as a stable, family-friendly, long-term employer enabled the Metropolitan Council to fill all vacancies in information systems (IS) positions, even at the height of the Y2K "crisis" (IPMA News, 2000).

The South Florida Water District routinely recruits on college campuses, going head-to-head with private sector firms. In order to compete more effectively, the District involves hiring managers in on-campus recruiting and gives them the ability to make immediate job offers to exceptionally well-qualified candidates. This approach has made the District much more competitive for college graduates in professional and technical positions. Maricopa County also recruits aggressively and has developed a system to automatically fax job ads each week to local community and other organizations that have been sources of recruits in the past.

Of course, even the best recruiting will not work unless the hiring process itself is effective, efficient, and user-friendly. That is one reason why public sector organizations are relying less and less on traditional civil service written exams, and more and more on alternative assessment approaches. For example, the 2000 IPMA/NASPE benchmarking survey of over 180 public sector jurisdictions showed that less than one-half rely on written job knowledge exams as one of their three most often-used assessment approaches (IPMA News 2000).

Alternative assessment approaches include training and experience evaluations known as achievement history questionnaires, in which candidates submit narrative information relating their backgrounds to required skills and experiences. Another approach is the skills inventory, where candidates report their training, education, and/or experience in key skill areas, often using a checklist format. Maricopa County, for example, makes extensive use of skills checklists, where applicants check the descriptions that best reflect their skill/experience levels. Candidates are then added to databases and referred to hiring managers based on each job's particular needs. Wisconsin uses the same approach for occupations with easily identifiable skill requirements such as IS jobs.

Government organizations are also relying more heavily on requiring candidates to submit résumés as their application materials, again in part to compete with the private sector. San Jose, California, for instance, frequently requires candidates to submit résumés and cover letters. Candidates are then evaluated and grouped into "bands" (e.g., "best qualified," "qualified") based on analyses of their cover letter and résumé information.

Of course, many public sector organizations still rely on written exams. However, some of these organizations are creating more timely and efficient systems to administer and score them. For example, Baton Rouge, Louisiana, offers continual "walk-in" testing for jobs that require multiple-choice exams. This approach has eliminated delays resulting from requiring candidates to mail applications and then schedule testing sessions. Now, candidates can test at any time, and lists of qualified candidates (registers) are created or updated each week.

Maricopa County has also adopted walk-in testing and has taken this approach a step further by immediately scanning and scoring all written exams. Test takers receive immediate results and are continually added to employment registers. In conjunction with more efficient and user-friendly methods like these, public sector organizations are using shorter application periods to speed the hiring process. In the past, in an effort to ensure that the public was given the widest possible access to government job opportunities, jurisdictions often used application periods of up to two months. While this does provide wide access for potential applicants, this practice can also slow down the hiring process. Well-qualified candidates with job options may accept other jobs by the time the application period ends. In response, government agencies have begun to use shorter application periods, often complemented by aggressive recruiting.

For example, Maricopa County often uses a five-day application period and then provides hiring managers with lists of qualified candidates within five days. Of course, the Maricopa Personnel Department recruits aggressively during the one-week application period. Shreveport, Louisiana, also has a five-day recruiting period that enables the city Personnel Department to provide hiring managers with lists of qualified candidates within five days. Shreveport announces vacancies each Monday on its web site and automatically faxes or emails vacancy announcements to over 120 recruiting sources, including colleges, community-based organizations, and even churches (NASPE, 1997).

On the other end of the spectrum are organizations that recruit for hard-to-fill and high-volume vacancies by allowing candidates to apply at any time, without any deadlines. This continuous application approach allows these jurisdictions to recruit and accept applications without the restrictions of deadlines. For example, Wisconsin accepts applications continuously for hard-to-fill jobs in fields such as information technology, health care, and accounting/auditing. Candidates are entered into applicant databases and referred to hiring managers when there are vacancies. Similarly, Fairfax County, Virginia, uses open continuous recruiting for many positions. Candidates apply, are entered into a database, and are then eligible for hiring consideration for six months (Hill and Johnson, 1998).

Another hiring innovation that combines several new approaches is on-site interviewing and immediate job offers. To meet tough labor market competition, some public sector agencies are conducting immediate interviews at job fairs and on college campuses. Candidates are quickly screened to determine if they are qualified and then the qualified applicants are interviewed by line managers. These managers have the authority to make immediate job offers. Usually, these job offers are contingent on reference or other background checks.

The South Florida Water Management District, for example, arranges for teams of personnel staff and line managers to travel together to job fairs and college campuses. The personnel staff accept résumés, review them immediately, and decide which candidates are qualified. The qualified applicants are then interviewed by the hiring managers, who have the authority to negotiate salaries and make contingent job offers. These offers are contingent on successful completion of the remainder of the hiring process, including employment verifications, reference checks, drug screening, etc. This approach has made the District a much more competitive employer for technical staff such as IS professionals, attorneys, environmental scientists, geographers, chemists, and construction inspectors.

About 80 percent of the District's 1,700 employees work in technical fields like these.

Wisconsin has adopted a similar approach for hard-to-fill positions in fields such as IS and accounting. Like the South Florida Water Management District, Wisconsin personnel staff and line managers attend job fairs together. The personnel staff administer a short self-assessment questionnaire to interested candidates to determine their eligibility. The questionnaire is developed beforehand in cooperation with the hiring managers. Eligible candidates are then interviewed by hiring managers, who can make immediate, contingent job offers. More often, the best-qualified candidates are immediately scheduled for a more detailed follow-up interview in the offices of the hiring agency. Oregon uses a similar approach for IS candidates at job fairs. Oregon personnel staff immediately schedule candidates for interviews, which are conducted within one week of the job fair (Lavigna, 2001).

In addition to these new assessment approaches, public sector organizations are using technology to help recruit qualified applicants in a more timely and efficient way. The South Florida Water Management District, for example, allows candidates to submit applications through the Internet. Candidates who do not have Internet access can submit paper applications, which the District then immediately scans into its on-line database. Hiring agencies directly access this data base, enter their requirements, and receive lists of candidates who meet their specifications.

Wisconsin has adopted a similar approach for IS jobs. Candidates complete an on-line skills inventory and are immediately added to the applicant database. Hiring managers then access the database on-line, specify their skill requirements, and receive lists of qualified candidates. In the future, Wisconsin plans to expand this system to other job classifications.

Fairfax County has automated its hiring process by creating a computerized résumé bank. Candidates submit their résumés, which are then scanned into a computerized database that county personnel staff use to provide hiring agencies with candidate lists. In addition, Fairfax allows candidates to apply by telephone or through the county's web site. If an applicant has already submitted a résumé, he or she can apply for any other county job by simply calling the county's interactive voice response system or accessing the web site and identifying the other position(s) they wish to apply for.

Creating Flexible Classification and Compensation Systems

Many public sector organizations are reforming their practices in another key HR area—classification and compensation. Compensation, in particular, is one area where government has lagged behind other employers, in part because many public sector organizations must negotiate compensation changes with labor unions. Recently, however, governments have begun to dramatically change classification and compensation systems, in some cases in cooperation with unions.

In classification, perhaps the most significant reform has been aggressive efforts to reduce the number of classifications to decrease system complexity and increase flexibility. South Carolina's Office of Human Resources, for example, conducted a comprehensive review of its classification system, which consisted of over 2,500 different job classifications and 50 separate salary ranges. The review showed that employees were confused by this complex system and did not understand the frequently minor distinctions between job classifications. In addition, the small (4 percent) difference between salary ranges was too small to recognize legitimate differences between the values of different jobs.

The Office of Human Resources responded by reducing the number of job classifications from 2,500 to 500, and the number of pay ranges from 50 to 10 wider pay bands. As a result, job classification is now much simpler and the broader pay ranges provide operating agencies with much greater flexibility to manage employee compensation (NASPE, 1999).

Other jurisdictions are also reducing the number of job classifications. New York State, the oldest and one of the largest state civil service systems (with over 170,000 employees), eliminated over 2,000 job classifications. This change enabled the state to update its job specifications and reduce a backlog of over 600 civil service exams. At the other end of the size spectrum is the town of Blacksburg, Virginia, that has only a few hundred employees. Blacksburg transitioned from a complex system that had 80 job classifications and 15 pay grades to a system with 50 classifications and just 4 broader pay bands. The new system gives Blacksburg's managers far greater flexibility to adjust employee compensation to meet market conditions, thus improving the town's ability to recruit and retain employees.

Other jurisdictions have also changed their compensation approaches to improve their ability to recruit, retain and reward employees. New approaches include awarding hiring bonuses for hard-to-fill positions (state of Minnesota), giving bonuses to employees who refer candidates who are hired (Minnesota and the Metropolitan Council of the Twin Cities), and awarding bonuses and pay raises to employees who acquire new skills or take on special projects (Kansas and South Carolina).

This trend toward more flexible compensation systems has moved to the federal government, which has traditionally used a rigid grade and step compensation system, in which pay raises were determined almost exclusively by tenure and seniority. The Federal Aviation Administration (FAA), for example, has redesigned its compensation system, in cooperation with its unions. Now, instead of granting pay increases to employees solely on tenure, FAA bases pay and pay raises on skill, knowledge, ability, and performance. The new compensation system also provides the flexibility to establish separate compensation systems to meet business needs (e.g., creating a separate system for executives).

Kansas has gone beyond many other public sector organizations by implementing an "employee contracting program" for IS staff. Employees with critical IS skills can sign a three-year contract in which they forfeit civil service status. In exchange, the employees receive salary increases of up to 15 percent and additional training. This program has helped keep turnover in IS positions below the overall turnover rate in Kansas state government.

As mentioned above, another compensation approach gaining popularity is "broadbanding" of pay ranges. Broadbanding means reducing the number of pay ranges and expanding the width of these ranges (now called "bands"). Along with this structural change, broadbanding typically gives hiring managers more flexibility to set starting salaries and award pay raises and bonuses. For example, Wisconsin's broadband system (which covers over 6,000 professional employees) allows hiring managers to negotiate starting salary anywhere within the pay range. Before broadbanding, the starting salary was limited to the minimum of the pay range. In addition, managers can award yearly pay increases or bonuses of up to 10 percent of annual salary for a variety of reasons, including matching a competitor's salary offer. The broadband system, which was first applied to IS staff and has now been expanded to other professionals, has helped reduce both vacancies and turnover. The Wisconsin broadband system was also initially implemented through negotiation with a labor union. This is significant because unions have traditionally resisted systems that provide managers with this kind of pay flexibility (Lavigna, 2001).

Achieving Work Force Diversity

Historically, the public sector has been a leader in creating and maintaining workforce diversity. The IPMA and NASPE best practice leaders demonstrate some of the approaches government agencies have taken to achieve diversity.

In Washington, for example, diversity activities are directed by the governor's office through the governor's Affirmative Action Committee which was established by Executive Order. The committee provides statewide policy guidance, approves agency affirmative action plans, monitors progress by individual agencies, and shares successes with all agencies. To support the committee, the Washington Department of Personnel has aggressively expanded diversify recruiting, in part by developing a comprehensive directory of recruiting sources and distributing the directory to all state agencies.

Washington also continually evaluates barriers to diversity by reviewing exit interviews completed by protected class members to identify any patterns that may reveal barriers to diversity. Minimum job qualifications are also continually analyzed to ensure they are not creating barriers for protected groups. Finally, managers' individual performance standards include measures of their efforts to diversify their staffs.

Oklahoma also has a strong commitment to diversity that is also driven by support from the governor's office as well as state law. Oklahoma has a statutory Affirmative Action Review Council that advises the state's personnel director on diversity standards and approaches. The council includes two members appointed by the governor, two appointed by the speaker of the House of Representatives, and two appointed by the president of the Senate. Also by state law, any agency that does not make progress toward achieving diversity must take corrective action including participating in special recruiting programs, developing diversity training, or even submitting all hiring and promotion recommendations to the central personnel department for approval. The law even empowers the state personnel director to take over the personnel functions of agencies that fail to show progress toward achieving a diverse workforce.

In many jurisdictions, a key to achieving diversity is conducting "utilization analyses" to identify the occupational groups where minorities and females are underrepresented. Utilization analyses compare on-board representation of these groups to labor market availability, often by specific job classification. Wisconsin and the city of St. Petersburg, Florida, for example, base their diversity recruiting strategies on these utilization analyses. The Wisconsin Department of Employment

Relations has a full-time affirmative action recruiter who works closely with colleges and community-based organizations to attract minority applicants, particularly for job classifications where women and/or minorities are underrepresented (i.e., where on-board representation is less than the overall labor market availability for these groups).

St. Petersburg has an even more aggressive diversity strategy. When the city's utilization analysis reveals underrepresentation, the city's affirmative action plan requires a "1 for 1" hiring policy—at least one member of a protected class must be hired or promoted each time a nonprotected class member is hired or promoted. The city complements this aggressive diversity policy by requiring all top managers to attend diversity training and by providing diversity instruction as part of orientation for new employees.

These approaches are succeeding in diversifying the workforces of these jurisdictions. The state government workforces in Oklahoma and Wisconsin, for example, now have higher percentages of women and minorities than the percentages of these groups in both states' overall labor forces. Washington has also achieved parity for minorities in state government, based in large part on a 35 percent increase in minority state employees from 1987 to 1998. In St. Petersburg, minority and female representation has increased in nearly every job category including protective services, professionals, and senior managers.

Improving Skills Through Training

Too often in the public sector, employee training does not receive enough resources or attention and is one of the first activities to be cut back during all-too-frequent budget crises. While this is also true in the private sector, it is a particular problem in government where public and legislative pressure to reduce spending often leads to budget reductions. Of course, cutting training budgets is shortsighted because the primary resources of government are the skills and abilities of public employees.

To enhance these skills and abilities, some public organizations are expanding training efforts. Oklahoma, for example, has identified the basic competencies required for each managerial level in state government and has based its training curriculum on these competencies. Oklahoma defines competencies as "human qualities or characteristics associated with effective performance of a task." In 1998, for example, the state estimated that its competencies-based training approach returned over $1 million in savings and cost reductions.

Other public jurisdictions are also developing new approaches to evaluate training effectiveness and results, a key step in obtaining resources to maintain and expand training. The New Jersey Personnel Department, for example, has established a Human Resource Development Institute to provide training to state agencies and local governments. In addition to providing direct training, the Institute offers distance learning through teleconferencing, and self-paced learning through CD ROM and the Internet. The Institute evaluates training effectiveness several ways. Participants' immediate reactions to training are evaluated through surveys that are entered into a central database, which is used to evaluate statewide training effectiveness. In addition, the Institute uses pre- and post-tests to evaluate what participants learn.

Phoenix has a more aggressive training evaluation strategy that attempts to link employee training to citizen satisfaction with services. Phoenix evaluates the effectiveness of the city's more than 150 courses four ways:

- Participant evaluations at the end of each class
- Employee focus sessions that assess how training is being used on the job and how training can be improved
- Statistically reliable surveys that, among other things, ask employees to evaluate whether they have received the training they need for their jobs
- Statistically reliable surveys of citizens' opinions of city government, including satisfaction with city government services

Although the citizen surveys are not a direct measure of training effectiveness, city leaders believe that citizen satisfaction with city government is a reflection, in part, of how well city employees are trained.

Enhancing Labor-Management Cooperation

Labor-management relations is a critical human resource function in almost every organization. In government, cooperation between organized labor and management is critical because, unlike the private sector, union membership continues to increase. Specifically, by 2000, union membership in the public sector had grown to over 38 percent of all employees, while union membership in the private sector had declined to only 9 percent. Therefore, in order to be effective, government must establish and maintain cooperative relationships with unions. In some public sector jurisdictions, labor and management have recognized this imperative and are working to improve cooperation. Even in jurisdictions that do not have unions, management has recognized the need to establish cooperative partnerships with employees.

One approach to improve labor-management cooperation is to reform the employee grievance process in order to make it less adversarial and more timely. For example, Ohio, in cooperation with the Ohio Civil Service Employees Association, has successfully implemented a "nontraditional arbitration" program to handle employee grievances. In this process, both parties submit information to an independent arbitrator who quickly reaches a binding decision. Arbitrators can hear up to forty cases in a single day. This process is faster, more informal, and less adversarial than the traditional multistep grievance process. The union and employees support the expedited process because it is fast and efficient and produces timely decisions supported by clear rationales. The Ohio Human Resources Division estimates that the expedited grievance process saves the state more than 4,000 work hours each year.

In South Carolina, state government has also implemented alternative dispute resolution techniques to reform the employee grievance process. The Office of Human Resources uses mediators at the beginning of the grievance process instead of holding a formal arbitration conference or grievance hearing. This change has replaced the costly and lengthy grievance process with a nonconfrontational forum for problem solving. In the first year of the new process, over

72 percent of mediations produced a signed agreement that avoided a formal grievance hearing (Lavigna, 2001).

In Wisconsin, a key element of the strategy to reform the state's HRM system is the cooperative relationship state government has forged with labor unions, particularly the 27,000 member Wisconsin State Employees Union (WSEU). In 1991, Wisconsin became the first state to use a cooperative approach–"consensus bargaining"–to reach agreement with a large union. The consensus approach, which emphasizes cooperation and problem solving instead of confrontation, is based on the principle that labor and management have complementary, and not competing, interests.

A fundamental distinction in consensus bargaining is the difference between "positions" and "interests." A position–each side's solution to a problem–has traditionally been the starting point for bargaining. An interest, on the other hand, is a basic need or concern. Because consensus bargaining focuses on interests and not positions, bargainers attempt to identify the best approaches to meet both parties' needs without dealing with predetermined, hard-and-fast positions.

Since the first time Wisconsin used consensus bargaining in 1991, the state and the WSEU have reached agreement on six biennial contracts using this approach. State and union representatives agree that the problem-solving approach has created more cooperative labor-management relations. For example, 83 percent of union members ratified the first consensus agreement in 1991. Union members have ratified subsequent agreements with similar majorities. Before consensus bargaining, union rank-and-file often approved agreements by slim majorities even after lengthy negotiations.

Consensus bargaining has also saved time. In 1991, the state and the union reached agreement in a then-record four and one-half months. More recently, negotiations were completed even faster–in only two months.

The consensus process has been particularly effective in shaping contract language on issues other than compensation. For example, one contract change enables employees with attendance problems to use leave instead of being suspended without pay. The employee continues to work but gives up an equal amount of leave time, thus avoiding a loss of pay. Other creative provisions that have been negotiated through consensus include:

- A provision allowing workers who transfer to new jobs in state government to return to their former jobs within a few days if the new position is not working out
- A "catastrophic leave" program that allows employees to donate unused vacation or personal leave to co-workers who have health problems that could lead to loss of income
- Joint labor-management committees to review issues such as union access to new technology

In addition, hundreds of grievances have been resolved at the bargaining table. During negotiations for one contract, for example, over 400 grievances were resolved during bargaining (Lavigna, 2001).

A recent labor-management project called "working together" identified and replicated "best practices" in labor-management cooperation across Wisconsin's state government. These best practices included allowing labor representatives to participate in hiring decisions, designing more positive ways to discipline employees, involving employees in developing fairer work schedules for around-the-clock operations, reducing excessive absenteeism and sick leave use, creating self-directed work teams, and improving labor-management communication.

HOW CAN LASTING HUMAN RESOURCE REFORM BE ACHIEVED?

There is great momentum across the nation for innovation and change in government human resource systems. As described in this chapter, some public sector organizations are making progress in creating more timely, responsive, and flexible systems. In hiring, these organizations are amending civil service laws to make them more flexible, expanding recruiting, developing more user-friendly alternatives to written civil service exams, and using technology to improve system access and efficiency. In classification and compensation, public sector agencies are reducing classification system complexity and adopting more flexible, performance-based pay systems. Government organizations are diversifying their workforces by expanding recruiting, systematically evaluating barriers to diversity, and making managers accountable for diversity. In training, some government organizations are expanding training programs, linking training to key employee competencies, and adopting new approaches to evaluate training effectiveness and results. Finally, public sector jurisdictions are working with labor unions to reduce conflict and increase cooperation.

Despite these notable advances, and many others not discussed here, large-scale personnel reform is too often still a goal rather than a reality. To move from rhetoric to reality, personnel departments must embrace change, without reacting defensively, without hiding behind rules and procedures ("we've always done it that way"), or trying to protect their turf.

Lasting HR reform will not be achieved solely in the name of efficiency, because government is not exclusively in the efficiency business. Some reformers believe that efficiency can be achieved by eliminating civil service systems. To the contrary, it is not necessary to "repeal" merit systems to improve public sector HRM performance. Instead, in the best case, public sector human resource practices that have outlived their usefulness must be improved. These practices—including arbitrary limits on the number of qualified candidates who can be interviewed, written exams for all jobs, pay solely for longevity, and endless grievance procedures—can be reformed without eliminating merit systems entirely.

As more and more government jurisdictions are demonstrating, it *is* possible to create lasting HRM reform that improves service and responsiveness but still retains the fundamental principles and best features of civil service, such as merit hiring and removal for just cause. The challenge for personnel reform is to change *responsively*, but also *responsibly*. To do this, government must involve its many customers and stakeholders in the change process, always striving to reconcile the often conflicting demands of these stakeholders. If these demands are ignored, reinvention efforts will fail. Reforming government is far too important to let that happen.

REFERENCES

GORE, A. 1993. *Creating a Government that Works Better and Costs Less.* Report of the National Performance Review. Washington, DC: U.S. Government Printing Office.

HILL, DANIEL, and GILBERT JOHNSON. 1998. Information Technology (IT) Recruitment and Retention Best Practices, Human Resource Benchmarking Project, International Personnel Management Association. Alexandria, VA, 22 pp.

International Personnel Management Association. 1998. IPMA/NASPE Pilot Human Resource Benchmarking Summary Report. Alexandria, VA, 31 pp.

IPMA News. 1999. 1999 Agency Awards for Excellence, August:5–6.

IPMA News. 2000. 2000 Agency Awards for Excellence, August:5–7.

LAVIGNA, ROBERT J. 2001. *Best Practices in Public Sector Human Resources: Wisconsin State Government.* Arlington, VA: International Personnel Management Association.

National Association of State Personnel Executives. 1997. 1997 Eugene H. Rooney, Jr. Awards. Lexington, KY, 57 pp.

National Association of State Personnel Executives. 1998. 1998 Eugene H. Rooney, Jr. Awards. Lexington, KY, 54 pp.

National Association of State Personnel Executives web site. 1999 Rooney Award Winners, 2000 Rooney Award Winners <http://www.naspe.net/Rooney%20Awards/2001%20Rooney%20Winners.htm>.

The National Commission on the State and Local Public Service. 1993. *Hard Truths/Tough Choices: An Agenda for State and Local Reform.* Albany, NY: The Nelson A. Rockefeller Institute of Government.

25

The Reform Agenda
Where Do We Go From Here?

LLOYD NIGRO

Georgia State University

There are, of course, many possible future *agendas,* so generalizations are very likely to be at least somewhat off the mark for any given moment or place. On all levels of government, civil service reform is *local* with regard to purposes and methods. The reasons for civil service reforms, however, do fall into two categories: (1) those undertaken largely for political or power-related purposes, and (2) those designed to make technical improvements that enhance performance and efficiency on one or more levels of organizational activity (Facer, 1998).

In the political category are found reforms designed largely to alter power relationships among clusters of interests, including bureaucratic, legislative, and executive players. It is not unusual for these kinds of reforms to be "sold" to policy makers, organized interests, and the public as needed to force improvements in bureaucratic efficiency, but they are really about who will have the power and authority to control the allocation of material and human resources in this arena (Thompson and Ingraham, 1996). President Carter's reorganization of federal personnel administration under the 1978 Civil Service Reform Act (CSRA), which created an Office of Personnel Management (OPM) and Senior Executive Service (SES), both under the direct administrative control of the president, is a classic example. Although its architects did not protest when the mass media described it in these terms, the CSRA had very little to do with making it easier for federal managers to get rid of "non-performers." It did have a great deal to do with enhancing the White House's policy control over the federal bureaucracy (Ingraham and Ban 1984).

The technical-efficiency category, in contrast, is made up of reforms largely devoted to making operational improvements in human resource methods, procedures, and techniques. They may have high internal visibility and tangible consequences for those involved, but they are typically uninteresting to politicians and the general public. They deal with technical issues related to system performance that are interesting to human resource professionals, like classification and pay structures, performance evaluation technologies and processes, training curricula, career development and planning, and recruitment and selection methods.

There are significant, sometimes unanticipated, overlaps and interactions between the two sets. Reform packages will almost certainly contain elements of both. A good example is pay-for-performance, which offers a reform of compensation and performance management systems *and,* as James Perry (1991) points out, a "message from politicians and the public that the governed are in control and things are as they should be." Political reforms involving the transfer of authority over the personnel system from a commission to the executive hierarchy may make it easier to achieve long-needed technical changes on the agency level, such as extensive delegations of authority to tailor job designs, pay ranges, and selection procedures to fit agency needs. Technical reforms, such as broadbanding classification structures, may have some of their intended effects on recruitment, retention, and management flexibility. They may also have cost-raising and other budgetary outcomes that provoke coalitions of stakeholders to pursue legislative agendas involving the imposition of reforms like privatization and downsizing on the bureaucracy. They can also generate strenuous opposition from groups of public employees who see themselves as disadvantaged by a technical reform, mobilize their allies, work to change the outcome by using their electoral clout with elected representatives and, in so doing, create highly charged political issues. At this point, human resource specialists arguing the technical virtues or vices of whatever is at issue are missing the point, and they are more often than not ignored.

Keeping all of the above in mind, there are themes that may be found in the civil service reform initiatives of the past quarter century, many of which have been discussed in other chapters, and they offer clues about where, at least in the relatively short term, the "tides of reform" are likely to take us (Light, 1997). They have labels like decentralization, deregulation, flexibility, privatization, reinvention, reengineering, empowerment, and managerialism (Durst, and Newell, 1999). Recently, a distinguished student and practitioner of public administration, Harlan Cleveland, added another—uncentralization (Cleveland, 2000). In a variety of forms and emphases, all of these and other purported remedies for the ills of bureaucracy have been prescribed and applied to the public service at a breakneck pace and, more often than not, without pause to see if they show much sign of really achieving their declared purposes, be they political, technical, or some combination of the two (Fox, 1996).

Indeed, the past few years of civil service reform in the United States have at times resembled more a stampede than the orderly working out of an agenda. It is, in other words, always possible that a provocation or "vision" will put a reform herd into motion, and where it will go is anybody's guess. Assuming that there are no major stampedes, the following is a not entirely unlikely scenario for the coming decade or two. It is based on three interrelated questions:

- Will there be a winding down of interest in launching new "grand reforms," combined with an effort to fine tune and evaluate those that have taken place?
- Will making difficult choices about the future of the employment relationship in government be on the agenda?
- Is there now an open window of opportunity for extensive reforms in the area of human resource planning and development?

For all three, the answer is "probably."

THE FUTURE OF GRAND REFORM

The era of unrestrained enthusiasm for comprehensive "big ticket" or grand reform has probably run its course. Quite a few public employees, if asked about a reform experience like pay-for-performance, might say that while it sounded good in theory, mostly it did not work in practice, leaving in its wake a less satisfying, threatening, workplace. The anticipated cost savings, promised enhancements in bureaucratic performance and efficiency, and predicted improvements in citizen confidence in government simply have not materialized. In part, these results flow inevitably from the chronic "overselling" of large scale reforms that has to be done in order to mobilize the required political support. Reforms of all kinds, in other words, may become fads. It has been relatively easy to convince the public that government bureaucracies and those who work in them are almost by definition incompetent, inefficient, and unresponsive. Americans have always been more than willing to believe these things. The bureaucrat-bashing rhetoric of today's reformers is as uncomplicated (some might say superficial) as that of a century ago: the entrenched protectionist personnel system must be swept aside and replaced with one that demands and rewards performance, surely and swiftly punishes nonperformers, assures responsiveness to executive leadership and public opinion, and lets managers manage.

Governors like Georgia's Zell Miller, who was successful in pushing dramatic changes in his state's civil service law through the legislature on a very fast track, enthusiastically endorsed the idea that traditional merit systems, with all their rules and procedures, had reached the point where they were the embodiment of what one writer (Howard, 1994) called "the death of common sense." He was not unusual; elected executives all over the country have argued that it has become virtually impossible under existing merit systems to get rid of the incompetent, lazy, unresponsive bureaucrats who flourish under the protection of an entangling web of antiquated rules and procedures. Like many such reforms, the Georgia reform, the centerpiece of which was a phasing out of the state's classified civil service and its replacement with an "at will" workforce, was sold as *the way* to get performance and accountability (Walters, 1997).

The experience has been that "grand reforms" of this kind consistently have failed to achieve their ambitious goals or to keep the sweeping promises their advocates made in the process of selling them to legislators, elected executives, voters, and public employees. While big reforms like the federal government's CSRA get a lot of attention, critics note that opportunities for real and sustainable small-scale or incremental improvements have typically been neglected and received little administrative or political support. Small successes are rarely held up by policy makers, academic researchers, or the media as evidence that reform can work under certain circumstances. The bottom line, as Downs and Larkey (1986) have pointed out, has been widespread disappointment and cynicism about *all* government reform initiatives, big and small, in government (Downs and Larkey, 1986). For example, the now twenty-five-year experience with merit pay, pay-for-performance, and other efforts to manage performance in government using variable increases to base pay or one-time bonuses seems to be fast approaching the cynicism stage for many states and localities. It got there some time ago in the federal service. One frustrated administrator with experience in a state where major policy-level reforms have been effectively blocked was reported to have said in so many words that the existing system needed to be destroyed, since it could not be reformed (Ban and Riccucci 1994).

In addition to the likely failure of "grand" reforms to keep their promises in the long run, they often have very punishing effects on public employees. The reality or prospect of being none-too-gently "de-privileged" or stripped of traditional merit system protections, downsized, or privatized, has energized many public employees and their unions to varying degrees of resistance using a variety of political, legal, and bureaucratic means. In some states, like Georgia, whatever resistance to civil service reform existed at the time was blown away, but this has not been the case in other places, like Florida and New York (Weschler 1993, 1994; Ban and Riccucci 1994). In combination, spreading awareness among policy makers and human resources professionals that many of the grand reforms implemented during the last quarter of the twentieth century did not deliver what they promised, stiffening opposition from public employees and their allies, and pressures created by emerging—and imposing—technological, economic, and social challenges may divert reform into new channels.

None of this is to suggest that a counter-reformation is going to happen in the foreseeable future. Civil service reform, like all significant reform in democratic governments, will continue to be a political business. The old-style regulatory, centralized, and rules-oriented merit systems will be discarded and replaced with ones that better address new and pressing political realities, organizational needs, and public expectations. While practice has often lagged behind theory, many of the diagnoses and recommendations of the Winter and Volcker Commissions, The National Performance Review, the National Academy of Public Administration, and others have had a major and long term impact on public policy makers' thinking about the mission, goals, and organization of the human resource or personnel function in government (Ban 1998). Today's state of the art is very different from what it was in 1950, but there is little of note on the current agenda that represents a radical departure from themes rooted in the last half of the twentieth century.

In part, therefore, where we go from here is almost certainly into a period of consolidation and refinement of reforms (grand and otherwise) that have already been put into effect. "Making it work" will be a big item on the agenda. The human resources function enters the new century still focused on realizing an ambitious agenda: decentralization and deregulation, flexibility and responsiveness, and a collection of reengineering and quality-oriented policies and practices designed to support the effort to build high performance governments and service delivery networks. The standards used to judge the performance of human re- source systems will stress contributions to organizational performance and pro- gram success, not merely faithful adherence to civil service rules and procedures. These goals and criteria are now conventional, largely unchallenged, elements of state-of-the-art human resources policy and management.

One important adjustment to be hoped for is more critical scrutiny of the (at times) seemingly almost sacrosanct proposition that privatization and de-privileging are necessary, if not sufficient, means to efficiency and responsiveness in modern governments. A much broader willingness among elected policy makers and their appointees to sponsor objective evaluations of the effects of limited experiments with alternative means of achieving the ends of reform should be very helpful to those trying to figure out what really works. There are, however, few signs that this kind of sea change is underway.

There also will be efforts to test limits. Georgia's Civil Service Reform Act (Act 816) could offer a preview of things to come (State of Georgia, 1996a). On January 10, 1996, Governor Miller delivered a State of the State Address in which he announced his plan to revise a merit system that had been established in 1943 to "create a professional workforce that was free of political cronyism" (State of Georgia, 1996b). In the Governor's words, reform was needed because:

> Folks, the truth of the matter is that a solution in 1943 is a problem in 1996. The problem is governmental paralysis, because, despite its name, our present Merit Sys- tem is not about merit. It offers no reward to good workers. It only provides cover for bad workers (State of Georgia, 1996b:6–7).

The result was decentralizing-deregulating legislation that in one important respect went beyond anything attempted by other states or the federal government because it made *all* state hires after July 1, 1996 so-called at will positions, not sub- ject to the rules and regulations of the State Personnel Board (Nigro 1997). In the words of *Governing,* a magazine directed at state and local government administra- tors: "While other states have been reforming their civil service laws, Georgia went to the edge. . . ." (Governing, 1999, 39). By 2010 or so, most of Georgia's state employees will be in the unclassified service, occupying positions that at least in theory do not afford any of the procedural property rights accorded tenured civil servants. They will also be working in a personnel system that has been so extensively decentralized that it is actually *several* departmental systems operating within very broadly defined and highly flexible state policies and procedures.

While at this writing no other states have gone so far as to put their classi- fied civil services on a legislated road to oblivion, political pressures for extending reform in this direction are still potent (Selden, 1999). The Georgia at will model could spread to other states. It may be particularly attractive to limited government and tax cutting interests, business leaders, and entrepreneurs, all groups that are influential in the policy debates over how effectively to reform government per- sonnel policy and administration. After all, it is said, workers in private settings do not enjoy "property rights" in their jobs or due process protections, implied or oth- erwise. Why should government employees enjoy these protections, especially since they are an open invitation to sloth and indifference to public opinion?

THE FUTURE OF THE EMPLOYMENT RELATIONSHIP

Governments will continue to experience fiscal stresses and related political pressures to jettison any commitment to the idea they should try to be "model employers." In brief, being a model employer means offering all employees wages and benefits that permit at least a decent standard of living; maintaining humane and safe working conditions; assuring that all productive workers enjoy a reasonable degree of job security and fairness of treatment; and to the degree possible, creating broad opportunities for career progress and development within the organization. Government, in other words, should assume an ethical obligation to maintain the highest possible standards in these areas of the employment relationship and, hopefully, in so doing, to encourage all other employers to do the same. Under no conditions, accordingly, should public employers try to find the bottom of the compensation and working conditions barrel as a part of their strategies to improve productivity, control costs, and be more "businesslike."

Optimizing performance, maximizing cost-savings, and extending management control are high priority values in government, and they all underscore the advantages offered by human resource strategies designed to promote targeted investments in *essential,* not *all,* workers. On the one hand, logic dictates that those workers providing critical knowledge, skills, and abilities should be recruited, retained, and developed as organizational "assets" or "capital." On the other, workers who are not essential in the sense that they are relatively easy to find, attract, and replace are best treated as "costs" to be minimized.

In effect, and somewhat ironically, this point of view says that governments' practices should be reformed in important respects to mirror those of the private sector. As the costs associated with building the cadre of essential personnel required to meet escalating demands on organizations increase steadily, controlling and lowering labor costs in other areas has become a prime objective for many public as well as private employers. Two conventional ways of trying to achieve this objective through changing the employment relationship have been privatization or contracting-out and widespread use of temporary and part-time workers.

Privatization comes in several forms, including transferring public functions to the private sector and contracting of services traditionally performed by public employees. Contracting, the prevalent form of privatization in the United States, inevitably changes the employment relationship. In practice, it may signal the end of any expectation of mutual obligations or commitments beyond those specified in written contracts. Contracting can be a threat, if not a reality. Employees and their unions are told that unless productivity goes up or labor costs go down, and management gets more flexibility to manage performance, they will be subjected to a reduction in force (RIF) and replacement by contract workers who are not unionized, will be paid less, and enjoy fewer if any benefits. Often contracting does have these results, often to an extent that has meaningful political consequences. Recently, for example, the City and County of Los Angeles, Baltimore, Boston, Chicago, Milwaukee, and Portland, Oregon, enacted laws requiring their bottom line oriented contractors to offer "living wages" and health care benefits to workers. (Los Angeles Times, 1999; Haberman, 1999).

There is a growing reliance on temporary and part-time employees in government. All of the signs are that this trend toward using disposable and interchangeable workers will accelerate. In an effort to keep personnel budgets down, to preserve flexibility, to evade unions, and to provide services that are demanded by the public while deflecting changes of bureaucratic bloat, governments on all levels are entering into service contracts with private firms that use large numbers of temporary workers. Temporary workers are employees supplied to clients by these firms. Although the client supervises the temporary worker, he or she is on the payroll of the help supply firm. The temporary help sector of the labor market has grown rapidly since 1989 (by about 43 percent). By the mid-1990s, there were over 1 million "temps." About half are in white-collar jobs, while the rest work in blue-collar and service positions (Bureau of Labor Statistics, 1999a). In 1999, there were 25 million part-time workers in the United States, with about 19 million of these comprising a relatively stable pool available to employers. This is a significant proportion of the entire labor force of about 130 million.

If benefits are an indicator, part-time and temporary workers are not "essential." In comparison to full-time employees, they receive fewer, less generous, benefits. Contractors' ability to provide services at lower costs than public agencies often can be explained by their not having to spend a great deal on employee benefits. Many temporary help supply firms claim that they offer benefits, such as paid holidays, paid vacations, and health insurance. Health insurance is available to about half of all temporary employees, and paid holidays and vacations are available to about three-quarters. However, the Bureau of Labor Statistics (BLS) notes that in reality:

> [F]ew temporary workers actually receive these benefits, either because they fail to meet the minimum qualification requirements or, as in the case of insurance plans, they elect not to participate. In firms employing most of the temporary workers, less than one-half of the workers—often less than one-tenth—qualified for holiday and vacation benefits. Similarly, most firms reported that less than 10 percent of their temporary workers participated in a company-sponsored health insurance program. (Bureau of Labor Statistics, 1999a:3)

In comparison to those working in the private sector, most *full-time employees* of state and local governments enjoy a substantial advantage across *all* categories of benefits. In certain respects, however, those who work part-time for private establishments do somewhat better. *Part-time* public employees are *less* likely to have some benefits than their private sector counterparts. For example, 40 percent of all part-time workers in the private sector receive paid holidays in comparison to 30 percent in state and local governments. Paid vacations for part-time personnel also are more common in the private sector. For all other kinds of benefits, state and local part-time workers do substantially better than their counterparts (Bureau of Labor Statistics 1999b). From a purely bottom-line point of view, the benefits of public employees are expensive and, therefore targets of cost-cutters. To the degree that government contracting out brings more private sector part-time workers into the labor force engaged in delivering public services, pressures to reduce the benefits of part-timers employed by public agencies may build. Another result may be a steady decline in the number of part-time workers in civil service on all levels, as governments seek to exploit the advantages of lower labor costs through contracting. Seeking the bottom of this barrel seems not to be out of the question for many public employers.

The policy issues confronting public employers regarding the future of the employment relationship are complex and politically explosive. The outlines of what may become a contentious policy debate are fairly clear. Should public agencies follow the lead of the private sector and concentrate on developing competitive pay, generous benefits, and good working conditions for a relatively small "core" of highly skilled workers deemed essential? Should they turn away from the traditional employment relationships in favor of a reliance on large numbers of temporary, part-time, and contract workers? Is it government's obligation to establish a higher than ordinary standard, to set a positive example for the rest of society in areas such as equal opportunity, pay equity, employee rights and legal protections, meaningful jobs for the disabled, and benefits? As choices are made about how to provide or arrange public services, how important should these values be in comparison to organizational efficiency, program cost-effectiveness, and management flexibility? The future of public service as a career and our expectations of government as an employer will in large measure be defined by the answers to these questions that emerge over the coming decade or two.

HUMAN RESOURCE PLANNING AND DEVELOPMENT

It is now a given that while governments in the United States may get smaller people-wise, they will not get easier in either a political or technical sense. A steadily growing proportion of government jobs requires highly trained, extensively educated, and experienced professionals who must be provided the policy support and material resources they need to continuously upgrade their abilities to keep pace with expanding and changing demands of their positions.

Public employers have a long history of failing to make sustained investments in training and development for most if not all categories of civilian workers. Legislative bodies have been notoriously reluctant to spend the money needed to provide anything but the most basic training, and agency training and development budgets traditionally are among the first to be cut or eliminated during periods of fiscal stress. Training and development initiatives designed to position public agencies to meet future needs for new or enhanced skills, knowledge, and abilities (SKAs) have been precarious affairs at best. This situation may be changing somewhat, at least potentially.

Centralized, regulatory merit systems did little to encourage much more than a static view of the "fit" between organizational needs and workforce qualifications. Personnel specialists were not asked to think along managerial lines or to worry much about future human resources needs. There were few incentives to do so. It was taken for granted that if the system was working as intended, those hired would have the skills, knowledge, and abilities needed to perform the jobs in question. The future would, so to speak, have to take care of itself. Position-based systems, to make matters worse, made formal career planning and development systems difficult to justify or establish because they did not assume that employees would be moving through a predictable series of different and increasingly more complex and challenging roles. Under these conditions, there is little incentive for employers to build the training and development infrastructures needed to support *careers,* as opposed to *positions.* Even if they did a good job of supporting position structures, the pace of change has long since reached the point where job analysis and classification plans are almost always out-of-date, and at best belatedly responsive to agencies' changing mandates, technological developments, and the shifting patterns of supply and demand in the labor market. Reforms that have undermined or replaced these traditional instruments of personnel administration, moved human resources from a regulatory to a service function, empowered management and decentralized authority, and focused human resource thinking on efforts to support organizational goals and objectives may encourage new human resource planning and development reforms.

In combination, the heavily managerial orientation of the latest wave of civil service reforms, a related willingness to give human resource specialists a mainstream role in the planning processes of agencies, and the challenges posed by a very competitive market for highly skilled workers have created conditions necessary to put human resource planning and development on the active reform agenda. They probably are not sufficient to realize actual and sustainable reform on a significant scale, because that will require successfully coupling investments in human resource planning and development to the political engine of reform. Making this connection requires that the following message be taken to heart in a political as well as technical sense: Neglecting to anticipate and respond to human resource needs is a very risky proposition in a climate of public opinion that demands high levels of productivity, performance, and responsiveness of public employees, executives, and elected representatives. The costs, political and otherwise, associated with not planning or making needed investments in development and then having to address serious (maybe disastrous) performance problems in a crisis mode could be very high. On a note of realism, it must be acknowledged that this is a lesson often learned and forgotten by citizens, administrators, and politicians alike.

If significant reform initiatives do take place in this area, they may be along Human Resource Development or HRD lines. HRD "is the integrated use of training and development, organization development, and career development to improve individual, group, and organizational effectiveness" (American Society for Training and Development, 1990:3-4). In brief, HRD encompasses three key areas of practice:

- *Training and Development,* which involves identifying and helping to develop in a planned manner "the key competencies that enable individuals to perform current or future jobs."

- *Career Development,* or coordinating individual career planning and organizational career management processes to "achieve an optimal match of individual and organizational needs."

- *Organization Development,* which concentrates on building effective and productive working relationships within and between work groups in organizations.

In many governments, the term "training program" is gradually being replaced with "human resource development program." What this means in practice remains to be seen, but the federal approach may suggest the outlines of future reform initiatives on the state and local levels. Federal agencies' HRD programs are now authorized to offer a wide variety of training and development opportunities, including programs designed to equip key employees with the skills and knowledge they will need to handle future job responsibilities. In addition, federal agencies now are required by law to have processes for identifying their performance improvement needs, and they must have human resource development programs designed to meet these needs in efficient and effective ways. These processes, according to OPM, should include identifying performance gaps that might be closed by training and development programs, regularly collecting and analyzing information needed to make effective decisions about organizational training needs, and involving workers on all levels in the planning and implementation of HRD activities (U.S. Office of Personnel Management, 1999).

CONCLUSION

Where do we go from here? First, the job of making reform work will require a human resource function that offers public agencies high levels of creativity, new skills, openness to change, and political awareness. The authors of grand reform seldom have long attention spans or, for that matter, tenures in office. Their interest in the details of implementation is notoriously low and short-lived. This reality leaves the career service to deal with the many devils in the details, to resolve inconsistencies and contradictions, and to build operating personnel systems that realize the central political values and broad technical purposes of reform (Hays and Whitney, 1997). Public administrators and managers, once they see that the reforms they supported are not self-implementing, will be asking for help from their human resource experts. Taking a "I told you so" posture and plotting a return to the "good old days" seems an unlikely formula for professional success or organizational relevance (Hays, 1999).

Second, addressing issues concerning the employment relationship surely will force human resource professionals to confront and to make difficult ethical and moral choices about the policy options they will support and seek to implement. It is to be hoped that the ethical content of decisions about pay and benefits, job security, and other facets of the employment relationship will be fully illuminated and carefully considered. In this regard, if they are prepared to engage the debate in ethical as well as instrumental terms, the voices of human resource professionals may be heard as these critical choices are made about the ways governments will relate to their employees. Being an influential player in this arena will require seeing professional ethics as more than a matter of memorizing codes of ethics and avoiding illegalities. Applying ethical reasoning skills to human resource questions will be critical (Van Wart, 1998).

Third, and finally, human resource professionals should get into the habit of scanning their horizons for emerging problems, challenges, contingencies, and opportunities. The potential of human resource planning and HRD as viable additions to the reform agenda flows from potentially huge problems governments will face trying to recruit and retain the high-skill professionals needed to support advanced technologies, new organizational forms, and evolving policy mandates. Anticipating organizational human resource needs and taking steps in advance to meet them will be major challenges that public employers can ill-afford not to meet squarely. Taking advantage of opportunities requires a finely tuned capacity to see in existing or emerging conditions improved chances for success in particular areas, like human resource planning and development (Swiercz, 1995; Templer and Cattaneo, 1995). Human resource executives who are capable of sustained leadership will be valuable commodities. Developing and supporting these leaders should be high on the agenda, since they will be asked to provide:

- The creativity and insight to identify new missions and programs for the human resource function

- The political skills needed to build strong external and internal constituencies for needed human resource reforms and changes to existing approaches

- The ability to accurately "read" their human resource organizations' internal and external environments for areas of vulnerability in policy and practice that need to be addressed and for opportunities for enhancements that may be exploited (Doig and Hargrove, 1990:7–8).

In the final analysis, all public administrators need to appreciate the increasingly critical role the human resource function plays—or can play—in organizational performance. It is now commonplace to say that human resource professionals should be full contributors to the strategic planning and other decision making processes of organizations. It has been, however, too common for civil service and personnel reforms to be designed with little or no effort to involve these professionals in meaningful ways. They are left to struggle with the unpleasant and frustrating consequences of efforts to impose changes that "sounded good at the time." Where we should go from here is toward making the human resource function a fully capable and effective contributor to the reform agenda.

REFERENCES

American Society for Training and Development. 1990. *An Introduction to Human Resource Development Careers,* 3rd ed. Alexandria, VA: American Society for Training and Development, September.

BAN, CAROLYN. 1998. Reinventing the Federal Service: Drivers of Change. *Public Administration Quarterly* 22 (1):21–34.

——, and Norma Riccucci. 1994. New York State: Civil Service Reform in a Complex Political Environment. *Review of Public Personnel Administration* 14 (2):28–39.

Bureau of Labor Statistics. 1999a. Employee Benefits Survey: Table 3, Percent of Employees Participating in Selected Employee Benefits Programs, Various Employment Groups, 1995–1997. Washington, DC: Department of Labor, 5 May.

——. 1999b. New Survey Reports on Wages and Benefits for Temporary Help Services Workers. Washington, DC: Department of Labor, 5 May.

CLEVELAND, HARLAN. 2000. The Future is Uncentralized. Paper presented at the National Conference of the American Society for Public Administration, 4 April.

DOIG, JAMESON, and ERWIN C. HARGROVE, eds. 1990. *Leadership and Innovation: Entrepreneurs in Government.* Baltimore: John Hopkins University Press.

DOWNS, GEORGE W., and PATRICK D. LARKEY. 1986. *The Search for Government Efficiency: From Hubris to Helplessness.* New York: Random House.

DURST, SAMANTHA L., and CHARLDEAN NEWELL. 1999. Better, Faster, Stronger: Government Reinvention in the 1990s. *American Review of Public Administration* 29 (1):61–76.

FACER, REX L. II. 1998. Reinventing Public Administration: Reform n the Georgia Civil Service. *Public Administration Quarterly* 22(1):58–73.

FOX, CHARLES J. 1996. Reinventing Government as Postmodern Symbolic Politics. *Public Administration Review* 56 (3):256–262.

Governing. 1999. Grading the States: A 50-State Report Card on Government Performance: Georgia. *Governing* 12(5):39.

HABERMAN, DOUGLAS. 1999. County OKs "Living Wage" on Contracts; 15,000 Workers Could See Raise in Pay. *The Daily News of Los Angeles.* Valley Edition, 16 June, N8.

HAYS, STEVEN W. 1999. Changing Patterns in Human Resource Practice: The Emerging Model? Paper presented at the Southeastern Conference on Public Administration, 8 October.

——, and Shawn Benzinger Whitney. 1997. Reinventing the Personnel Function: Lessons Learned From a Hope-Filled Beginning in One State. *American Review of Public Administration* 27 (4):324–342.

HOWARD, PHILLIP. 1994. *The Death of Common Sense: How Law is Suffocating America.* New York: Random House.

INGRAHAM, PATRICIA W., and CAROLYN BAN, eds. 1984. *Legislating Bureaucratic Change: The Civil Service Reform Act of 1978.* Albany: State University of New York Press.

LIGHT, PAUL C. 1997. The Tides of Reinvention. *Government Executive* 29 (1):23–24.

Los Angeles Times. 1999. Local Laws '99: A Guide to New Legislation in LA County. Home Edition, B2, 24 December.

NIGRO, LLOYD G. 1997. Public Law in the Changing Civil Service. In *Handbook of Public Law and Administration,* Philip J. Cooper and Chester A. Newland, eds. San Francisco, CA: Jossey-Bass, 344–355.

PERRY, JAMES L. 1991. Linking Pay to Performance: The Controversy Continues. In *Public Personnel Management: Current Concerns—Future Challenges,* Carolyn Ban and Norma Riccucci, eds. New York: Longman, 73–86.

SELDEN, SALLY K. 1999. Human Resource Practices in State Governments: Findings from a National Survey. Paper presented at the 60th National Conference of the American Society for Public Administration, 10–14 April.

State of Georgia. 1996a. Code Sections 45-20-1, 45-20-2, and 45-20-6 Amended. No. 816 (Senate Bill No. 635), *General Acts and Resolutions, Vol. 1,* 684–691.

——. 1996b. Remarks by Governor Zell Miller. *State of the State Address.* Atlanta, GA: Office of the Governor, January.

SWIERCZ, PAUL MICHAEL. 1995. Research Update: Strategic HRM. *Human Resource Planning* 18 (3):53–59.

TEMPLER, ANDREW J., and R. JULIAN CATTANEO. 1995. A Model of Human Resources Management Effectiveness. *Canadian Journal of Administrative Sciences* 12 (1):77–88.

THOMPSON, JAMES R., and PATRICIA W. INGRAHAM. 1996. The Reinvention Game. *Public Administration Review* 56 (3):291–298.

U.S. Office of Personnel Management. 1999. Government Overview of Training in the Federal Government with Questions and Answers. <http://www. opm.gov/hrd/lead/faq.htm> 23 April.

VAN WART, MONTGOMERY. 1998. *Changing Public Sector Values.* New York: Garland.

WALTERS, JONATHAN. 1997. Who Needs Civil Service? *Governing* 10 (11):17–21.

WECHSLER, BARTON. 1993. Florida's Civil Service Reform. *Spectrum: The Journal of State Government* 66 (1):45–51.

——. 1994. Reinventing Florida's Civil Service System: The Failure of Reform. *Review of Public Personnel Administration* 14 (2):64–76.

Index